GREAT BRITAIN
WITH BELFAST AND DUBLIN

researcher-writers
Asa Bush
Rachel Lipson
Benjamin Naddaff-Hafrey

staff writers
Meghan Houser
Dorothy McLeod
Simone Gonzalez
Alexandra Perloff-Giles
Qichen Zhang

research manager
Matthew Whitaker

editor
Meagan Michelson

managing editor
Daniel C. Barbero

CONTENTS

IRELAND

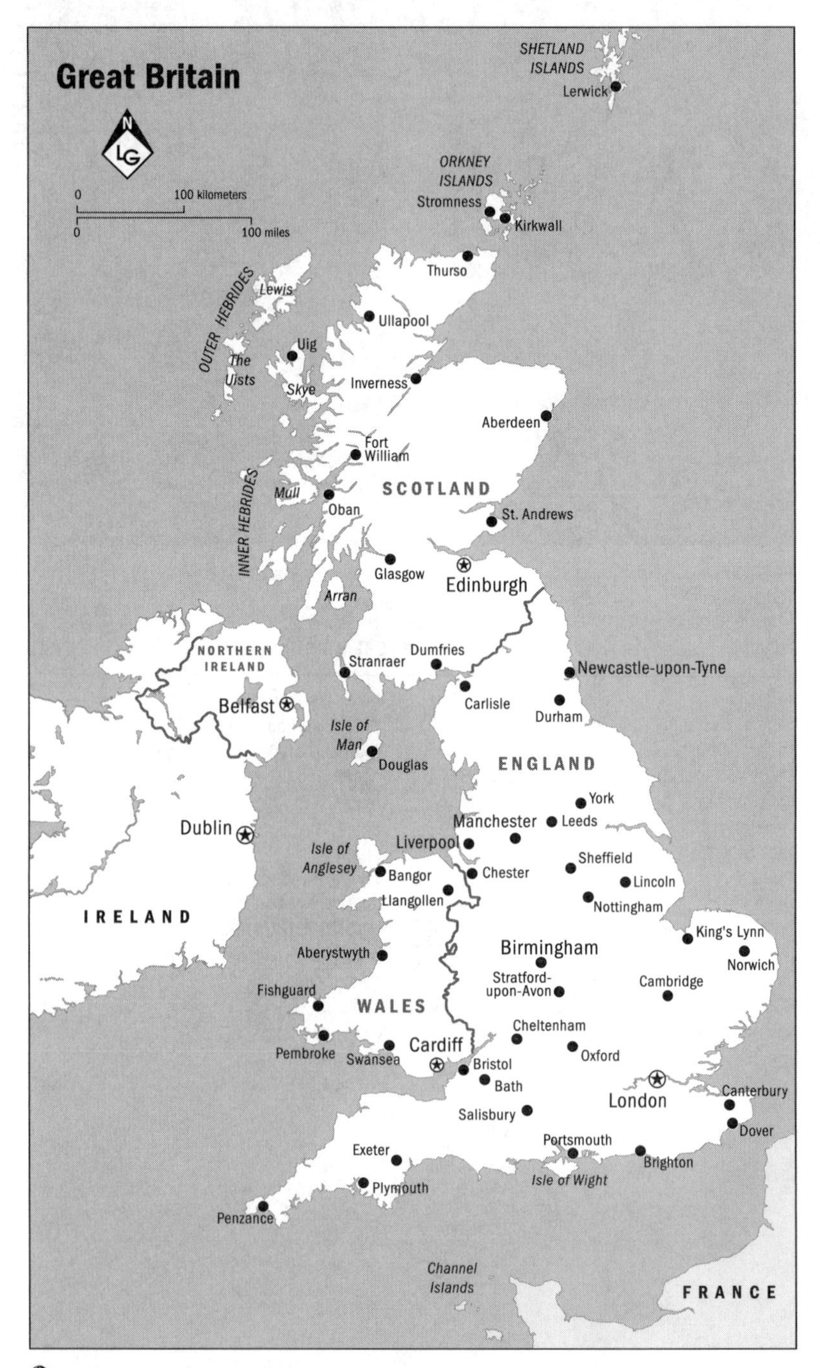
Great Britain
N
LG
0
100 kilometers
0
100 miles
SHETLAND
ISLANDS
Lerwick
ORKNEY
ISLANDS
Stromness
Kirkwall
Thurso
OUTER HEBRIDES
Lewis
Ullapool
Uig
The
Uists
Skye
Inverness
Aberdeen
Fort
William
INNER HEBRIDES
Mull
Oban
SCOTLAND
St. Andrews
Glasgow
Edinburgh
Arran
NORTHERN
IRELAND
Dumfries
Stranraer
Newcastle-upon-Tyne
Belfast
Carlisle
Durham
Isle of
Man
Douglas
ENGLAND
York
Manchester
Leeds
Dublin
Liverpool
Isle of
Anglesey
Sheffield
Bangor
Chester
Lincoln
Llangollen
Nottingham
IRELAND
King's Lynn
Birmingham
Norwich
Aberystwyth
Stratford-
upon-Avon
Cambridge
Fishguard
WALES
Cheltenham
Pembroke
Swansea
Cardiff
Oxford
Bristol
Bath
London
Canterbury
Salisbury
Dover
Exeter
Portsmouth
Brighton
Plymouth
Isle of Wight
Penzance
Channel
Islands
FRANCE

RESEARCHER-WRITERS

ASA BUSH. This *Let's Go* veteran kept us laughing with his witty writing and quirky photos from Scotland and Ireland. From a tour of the Jameson Irish Whiskey Factory to "Bloomsday" celebrations with fellow James Joyce fanatics, Asa's eye for excitement found him plenty of kindred—and distilled—spirits during his stay in Dublin.

RACHEL LIPSON. Britain's confusing accents and dreary weather couldn't put a damper on this New York native and first-time *Let's Go* RW. Whether chatting with Vikings or pretending to be an Oxford student, Rachel showed an incredible thirst for adventure (and cider!) as she traveled all across England.

BENJAMIN NADDAFF-HAFREY. Though some travel to London for prestige and tradition, this feisty freshman came to the British capital with a different mission: to get into his first bar fight. Lucky for us, Ben decided to play it safe while he single-handedly navigated London, even as World Cup mania brought out the hooligan in every Englishman.

GREAT BRITAIN

There once was a country made up of great islands
with peat bogs and moors, great rivers and highlands,
Its people built castles and churches with spires
and started a powerful global empire.
Meanwhile, the hills, filled with white sheep and crofters,
inspired great artists, bold monarchs, and authors.
Today, on a belly of bangers and mash,
the British continue their long, storied past
with Wimbledon, cricket, golf tourneys, and football,
festivals, theatre, and cold pints on pub crawls.
It's time to discover and leave what you know—
boot up in your wellies, grab your pack, and let's go!

when to go

Great Britain's high season tends to be June through August, but expect a steady influx of tourists almost year-round. Low (or at least lower) seasons are spring (April-May) and fall (September-October); during these months, you'll likely find cheaper flights, though be warned that sights and accommodations may have reduced hours.

With few exceptions, weather tends to be mild throughout the central parts of England, Ireland, and Scotland, and climatic extremes are few and far between. In fact, in London, it so rarely snows substantially that if a few inches fall university students frolic outside and make snow angels. Of course, it's a different story in the rest of England, Scotland, and Ireland, where wintery weather can hit pretty harshly. In the spring, expect any green patches to be blanketed by daffodils, though as much as we'd like to tell you it's all flowers and frolicking, there's one element you can't escape: the rain. No matter when you're going to Britain, be sure to bring along your water-proof duds, especially in the summer.

what to do

DOMES, THRONES, AND BONES

Nerds and non-nerds alike must acknowledge the rich history of Great Britain. You can't possibly walk through a bustling city or rural town without stumbling upon a grand stucture commemorating a grander past.

- **INTO PARLIAMENT YOU SHALL GO:** Stop by the **Houses of Parliament** (p. 23) and maybe you too can wear one of those awesome wigs.
- **DEAD POET'S SOCIETY:** Be sure to visit the **Poet's Corner** at **Westminster Abbey,** (p. 54) but you better not step on Alfred Lord Tennyson.
- **WHISPER SWEET NOTHINGS:** The legended **Whispering Gallery** of **St. Paul's Cathedral** (p. 43) has unique acoustics that make it really hard to tell a secret.
- **PILGRIM'S PROGRESS:** Make the trek to **Canterbury Cathedral** (p. 161) and pretend you're a member of Chaucer's motley crew.
- **DUBBED "DUBLIN":** Explore **Dublin Castle** (p. 365), a fortress built on top of a Viking settlement, the city's namesake, *Dubh Linn* ("Black Water").

BRITAIN BY THE BOOK

Even if you've never been to Britain, you've surely read some words, words, words by its literary greats. In fact, you just did.

- **MISERABLE ORPHANS:** Make pitstops at London landmarks like Bernard's Inn and Newgate Prison, famously featured in **Charles Dickens's** novels of the nitty gritty city.
- **MAGICAL ORPHANS: Harry Potter** enthusiasts flock to such London sights as Leadenhall Market, the Boa Constrictor tank at London Zoo, and Platform 9¾ at King's Cross Tube station (you know, if you're out of Floo Powder).
- **BILLY SHAKES:** Hit up a performance at **Shakespeare's Globe Theatre** (p. 51) in London. Then head to **Stratford-upon-Avon** (p. 203) and tour Shakespeare's birthplace and Holy Trinity Church, where the Bard is buried. Good night, sweet prince.
- **WHO'S AFRAID?:** Meander through **Bloomsbury** (p. 18) in London where Woolf

Let's Go
www.letsgo.com

and her Modernist cohorts held intellectual powwows. True Woolfians should make **The Voyage Out** from **Brighton** (p. 149) to Woolf's cottage, **Monk's House** in Rodmell, East Sussex.

- **SPLISH SPLASH:** Visit the city of **Bath,** (p. 137) stomping ground of **Jane Austen** from 1801-1806 and the setting of *Northanger Abbey* and *Persuasion.*
- **ALES AND TALES: JRR Tolkien** and **CS Lewis** contrived wizards and wardrobes over pints at The Eagle and Child in **Oxford** (p. 107).
- **SCOTTY BOY:** Scattered throughout **Edinburgh** (p. 281) you'll find monuments commemorating locals' favorite literary hometown boy, **Sir Walter Scott.**

top five places to throw back ale

5. GLASGOW: For a throwback to a 1920s speakeasy, visit **Buff Club.**

4. DUBLIN: Imagine the cast of *The Jersey Shore* in Dublin and you've got **Tripod.**

3. LONDON: England's capital has everything from classy pubs like **The Chelsea Ram** to frenetic clubs like **Fabric.**

2. NEWCASTLE-UPON-TYNE: Revel in Newcastle's fertile music scene at **The Cluny.**

1. CARDIFF: Legos and alcohol? A winning combination contrived by **Cardiff Arts Institute.**

LET'S GOAL!

Football (soccer, if you must) fanatics are everywhere in Britain: the queen is an Arsenal fan, and the police run a national hooligan hotline. Sports like rugby, cricket, and horseracing also have loyal fans—though they're not nearly as insane as their football counterparts.

- **FOOTBALL:** In London, don **Chelsea** blue at Stamford Bridge or spur on the **"Spurs"** at White Hart Lane. At **Manchester United's** (p. 245) hallowed turf of **Old Tafford** on Sir Busby WaY, you can bend it like **Beckham** (or at least the way he bent it before crossing the pond). Imagine how dangerous it would be for the Red Sox and the Yankees to hail from the same city; well, that's what you've got in the rivalry between Everton and Liverpool, the top two teams in the city of **Liverpool** (p. 224).
- **"THE GENTLEMAN'S GAME":** Men in white play their endless games at Lord's Cricket Ground in St. John's Wood in London. The world's longest cricket marathon was played by the Cheriton Fitzpaine Club in Devon for 24hr. and 34min.
- **40 LOVE:** A fierce competition masquerading as a garden party, Wimbledon (p. 406) is the world's oldest annual tennis tournament.
- **GIDDY-UP!:** Saddle up for the annual **Royal Ascot horse race,** a train-ride or a 1hr. drive away from London. Dresscode depends upon where you're sitting for the events. Want to come looking like a frump? Neigh.
- **TO A TEE:** Called the "Home of Golf," **St. Andrews** attracts plaid-clad enthusiasts from all over. Today, the city has seven coastal "links" golf courses and four golf clubs.
- **STUCK IN THE MUD:** Punting is a popular pastime at **Oxford** (p. 107) and **Cambridge** (p. 181). How does one "punt," you ask? You literally navigate a boat by

jabbing a pole in the mud. As long as you're not the one steering, it's quite a tranquil experience.

TAKE A BOW, BRITAIN

London is known for vibant, sparkling theater, while Edinburgh is renowned for its world-class arts festivals. And who ever said thespians couldn't be studious? Oxford and Cambridge also host hip performing arts scenes, perfect for the theater- and music-hungry traveler.

- **THEATER OUT THE WEST END:** From Billy Shakespeare to *Billy Elliot,* you're bound to find a show that tickles your fancy in **London's West End,** where the bustling theater community rivals that of New York City's Broadway.
- **'TIL THE FAT LADY SINGS:** Classical music aficionados flock to the **London Coliseum,** home of the **English National Opera,** and the **Royal Opera** (p. 88) in Covent Garden.
- **ALL THAT JAZZ:** Head to **Jazz Café** (p. 91) in London's Camden Town for some quality crooning.
- **MUSIC OVER EASY:** There's nothing like music in the morning time. Pry yourself away from the library (yeah right), and attend one of the **Oxford Coffee Concerts** (p. 127), top-notch chamber music performances held every Sunday morning in Holywell Music Hall.
- **BARDY PARTY:** The **Cambridge Shakespeare Festival** (p. 197) takes place every year throughout July and August and features several plays by the man himself.
- **STRATFORDIAN SPOTLIGHT.** True Shakespeare aficionados should head to Stratford-upon-Avon to see a performance by the **Royal Shakespeare Company** (p. 208).
- **FRINGE BENEFITS:** The **Edinburgh Fringe Festival** (p. 306), the world's largest arts festival takes place over the course of three weeks every August.
- **WARBLING IN WALES.** Attend a performance of the Welsh National Opera at the impressively-domed **Wales Millennium Theatre** (p. 177).
- **GLASGOW STANDING-O.** While in Scotland, whet your musical appetite with a show at **Glasgow Royal Concert Hall** (p. 326), which has hosted the likes of Elvis Costello.
- **RIVERDANCE!** These step-dancing superstars perform at Dublin's **Gaiety Theatre** (p. 376) every summer. Quintessentially Irish. Quintessentially un-missable.

student superlatives

- **BEST PLACE TO COUNT SHEEP:** Wales
- **BEST PLACE FOR MONK-Y BUSINESS:** Westminster Abbey
- **BEST PLACE TO GET AN ARSE-ACHE:** Shakespeare's Globe Theatre
- **BEST WAY TO REPLACE YOUR STAIR MASTER:** Climbing to the dome of St. Paul's Cathedral
- **BEST PLACE FOR A PICNIC:** Hampstead Heath
- **BEST PLACE TO—FORE!:** St. Andrews
- **BEST PLACE TO AVOID THE SIRENS:** Dublin

BEYOND TOURISM

Those craving an international adventure that involves more than just sightseeing ought to explore the study, work, and volunteer opportunities available in Great Britain, Ireland, and Scotland. Especially in Anglophone countries, it's possible to dive into academic and professional programs headfirst and get a full immersion experience.

- **STUDY ABROAD:** Whether you're a Shakespearean or a biologist, you're bound to find a titillating program at one of Britain's premiere universities. Get your Econ on at the **London School of Economics** (p. 414), be "supervised" in one of **Cambridge's** (p. 414) small tutorials, or study with the Scottish Parliament at the **University of Edinburgh** (p. 414).
- **VOLUNTEER ABROAD:** If getting in touch with your philanthropic side is more attractive than hitting the books, fear not. There are countless possibilities in Great Britain, Ireland, and Scotland, from offering urban families financial advice to creating **sustainability** projects (see **Volunteering,** p. 416).
- **WORK ABROAD:** If you want to rake in any kind of dough during your time abroad, you should plan ahead. With the right qualifications you might wind up **teaching** your subject of choice at a British grammar school. Events like the **Edinburgh Fringe Festival** (p. 306) are teeming with short-term employment opportunities (see **Working,** p. 418)

discover great britain

suggested itineraries

THE BEST OF GREAT BRITAIN (1 MONTH)

1. LONDON (1 WEEK): First, be inspired to belt out a riveting rendition of "God Save the Queen" at **Buckingham Palace.** At **Westminster Abbey,** pay homage to Tennyson, Dickens, and Hardy in the **Poet's Corner.** While you're in the neighborhood, take a gander at the **Houses of Parliament,** where all those guys in wigs make important decisions. Straddle a lion in **Trafalgar Square.** Then visit the Impressionist exhibit in the **National Gallery.** Next, marvel at **St. Paul's Cathedral,** a domed marble masterpiece. Next, trek over to Bloomsbury and **The British Museum,** where the **Rosetta Stone** isn't even the climax. Enjoy an interactive medieval experience at the **Tower of London**.

2. DOVER (1 DAY): A major WWII bastion boasting a castle and cliffs.

3. SALISBURY (1 DAY): A towering medieval cathedral about 10 mi. from Stonhenge.

4. BATH (1 DAY): How the Romans pampered themselves.

5. OXFORD (2 DAYS): Hit up each of the **colleges** oozing with history—from **Christ Church** to **Queen's** to **Trinity.** Then, hit up each of the pubs oozing with booze.

6. LIVERPOOL (2 DAY): Where the Beatles still top the charts.

7. BELFAST (2 DAYS): Northern Ireland's capital, where the *Titanic* was built.

8.GLASGOW (2 DAYS): The largest city in Scotland is home of the Glaswegians (seriously).

9. EDINBURGH (5 DAYS): The capital of Scotland, where castles and cocktails coexist in perfect harmony.

10. NEWCASTLE (1 DAY): Newcastle-upon-Tyne used to be an industrial center; now it's a party center, with some of the best nightlife in all of Britain.

11. YORK (2 DAYS): Head to York Minster, surrounded by tons of cafes and street entertainers.

12. CAMBRIDGE (2 DAYS): The **colleges** are surprisingly identical to those of Oxford, but with their own pasts to brag about, including Henry VI, Henry VIII, and *Winnie the Pooh.* Care for a punt on the Cam?

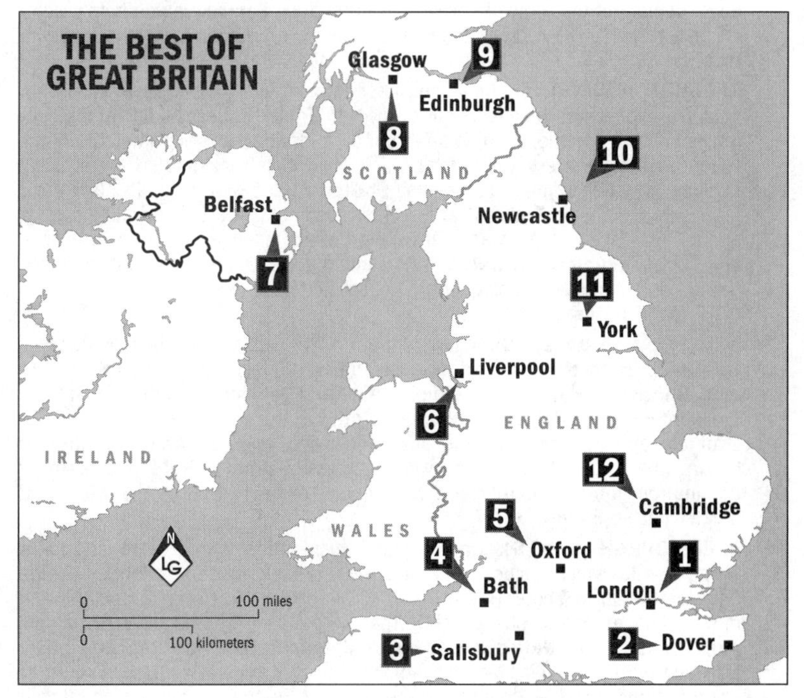

A CITY TOUR OF THE ISLES (3 WEEKS)

1. LONDON (6 DAYS): Start off in **Trafalgar Square** with lions and pigeons and Nelson—oh my! Be sure to spend at least an afternoon roaming around the **National Gallery.** For Gothic architecture, superb sculptures, and tons of buried celebs, mosey on over to **Westminster Abbey.** While you're in the neighborhood, check out the **Houses of Parliament.** Admire—and even climb—Wren's domed marble masterpiece, **St. Paul's Cathedral.** Then, as you'll probably want your fair share of gimicky medieval fun, hit up the **Tower of London,** an interactive experience. During your time in the capital, head over to the **British Museum** in Bloomsbury, which houses everything from Turkish temples to Egyptian mummies. Round out the trip with a visit to **Buckingham Palace;** you definitely won't be able to make them crack a smile, so don't even bother being the fool who tries.

2. DUBLIN (5 DAYS): Channel your inner Joycean scholar and revel in all that Ireland's capital has to offer. Walk on over to **Trinity College,** built by the British in 1592 to "civilize the Irish and cure them of Popery." While away the hours in the **National Gallery,** where Irish, Dutch, and Italian masters converge. While strolling the streets you'll realize that **Grafton Street** is a veritable playground for pedestrians, while **Temple Bar** is full of artistic tourist attractions, like studios and performance venues. Marvel at **Dublin Castle,** the sight of the Easter Rising, and **Christ Church Cathedral,** with its stained glass windows and raised crypts. Castles and churches are nice, but flasks are better, so top it all off with a visit to the **Guinness Storehouse.**

3. BELFAST (5 DAYS): During your time in Belfast, be sure to see **Queen's University Belfast,** designed like Magdalen College at Oxford. You can't miss **Belfast City Hall,** the administrative and geographic center of Belfast. the impressive **Grand Opera House** stands as the third take of a beautiful structure that was bombed and destroyed twice, while **St. Anne's Cathedral** has a built-in shout-out to the working class. Before jet-setting to another destination, journey to **Odyssey,** an arena with hockey games, movies, and meals—but no Sirens.

4. EDINBURGH (5 DAYS): One of your first priorities should be to visit **Edinburgh Castle,** which includes the palace where Mary, Queen of Scots, became Mommy, Queen of Scots. (It's a James!) Climb **Outlook Tower** to see colorful, moving images of the street below. Then, experience an artistic orgy of epic proportions at the **National Gallery of Scotland,** featuring Raphael, Titian, El Greco, Turner, Gaugin, Monet, and Poussin. The exhibits at the **Museum of Scotland and Royal Museum** trace the gamut of Scottish history. Finish off your time in Edinburgh the right way, at the **Scotch Whisky Experience**—like Disney World, with alcohol.

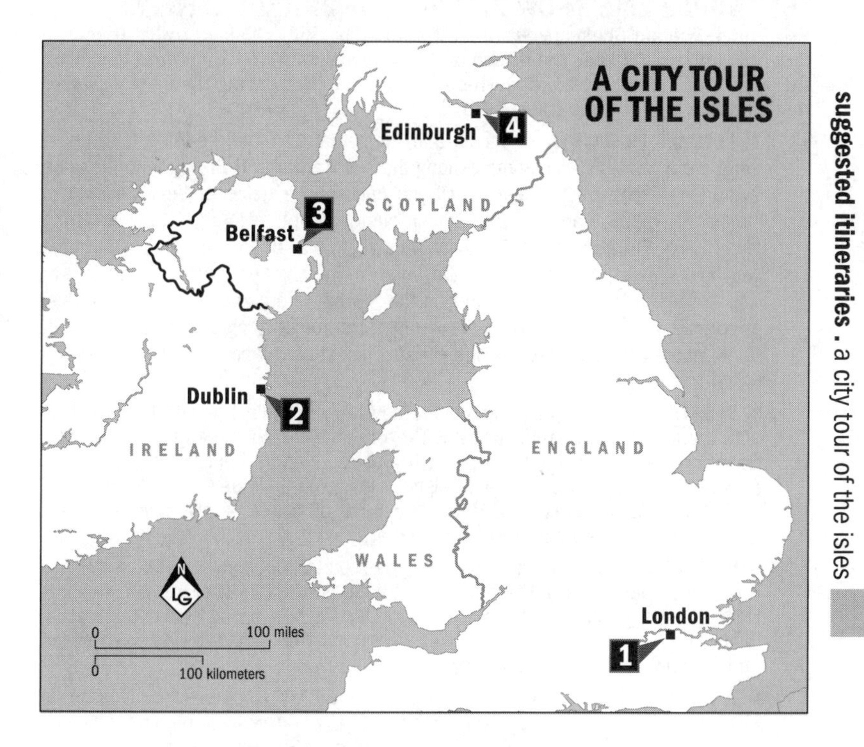
A CITY TOUR
OF THE ISLES
Edinburgh
4
SCOTLAND
3
Belfast
Dublin
2
IRELAND
ENGLAND
WALES
London
1
N
LG
0
100 miles
0
100 kilometers

THE "NO BIZ LIKE SHOW BIZ" TOUR OF BRITAIN (3 WEEKS)

Ever since William Shakespeare—better known as "Billy Shakes" to his friends—first put quill pen to paper, the British Isles have been known for their prominence on the stage. But it's not just London where you can find theater, and it's not just theater that can treat you to a good time.

1. LONDON (6 DAYS): For music and theater aficionados heading to London, there are a few must-see spots. Among them is **Barbican Hall,** where the London Symphony Orchestra resides. See if you can snag a ticket at the **Coliseum,** a staggering venue, home of the English National Opera. In the West End, from **Wyndham's Theatre** to **Shaftesbury Theatre,** you're bound to find a show that gets your toes tappin'. If you "just can't wait to be king," pounce at the chance to visit the Lyseum, a historic theater on the Strand, where *The Lion King* has been performed since 1999 and is still roaring. Don't forget to cross over to the South Bank, where **Shakespeare's Globe Theatre** is just the place to hold the mirror up to nature.

2. DUBLIN (5 DAYS): Take your seat at the **Abbey Theatre,** Ireland's National Theatre, founded by W.B. Yeats and Lady Gregory in 1904. Then, head to the younger **Gate Theatre,** where you can whet both your contemporary and classic theatrical appetites. During July and August, nightly classical music performances are held at the **National Concert Hall.** Meanwhile, open-air concerts take place at Dublin Castle. A concert at a castle? Cheers to that.

3. BELFAST (4 DAYS): Plays, music, comedies, burlesque, balls–the **Black Box** has it all. For something slightly more traditional, hit up the **Lyic Theatre,** which counts Liam Neeson among its esteemed alums. Make a pit-stop at **Waterfront Hall,** a relatively new venue with performances year-round. And definitely don't wait 'til the fat lady sings to visit the **Grand Opera House.**

4. EDINBURGH (6 DAYS): The **Stand Comedy Club** is open for laughs seven nights a week, while **Whistle Binkie's** pub, literally housed underground, offers all flavors of musical performances. If you're here from September to May, be sure to catch a show at the **Royal Lyceum.** And, of course, the **Edinburgh Fringe Festival,** the world's largest arts festival, takes place over the course of three weeks every August.

THE "NO BIZ LIKE SHOW BIZ" TOUR OF BRITAIN
4
Edinburgh
SCOTLAND
3
Belfast
Dublin
2
IRELAND
ENGLAND
WALES
London
1
N
LG
0
100 miles
0
100 kilometers

GREAT BRITAIN: THE SCENIC ROUTE (2 WEEKS)

1. DOVER (1 DAY): Famous chalky white cliffs that face France at the narrowest part of the Channel.

2. LONDON (7 DAYS): One of the Royal Parks of London, **Regent's Park** is complete with gardens, fountains, and the London Zoo. Its cousin, **Hyde Park,** is the Royal Park where you go into the Speaker's Corner for running your mouth. Adjacent to Buckingham Palace, **St. James's Park** is the oldest of the Royal Parks contains a lake and two islands. Finally, the best place in London for simultaneously frolicking on the hills and spotting celebs is Hampstead Heath in the north.

3. STONEHENGE (1 DAY): Religious structure? Calendar? Either way, you probably don't want to miss it.

4. THE COTSWOLDS (2 DAYS): Rolling hills officially labeled an "Area of Outstanding Natural Beauty," less than an hour from Bath.

5. WATERFALL DISTRICT (1 DAY): Walk behind the thundering falls of Sgwd yr Eira, less than 2mi. from Cardiff.

6. LAKE DISTRICT (2 DAYS): The lakes and mountains that turned Wordsworth on.

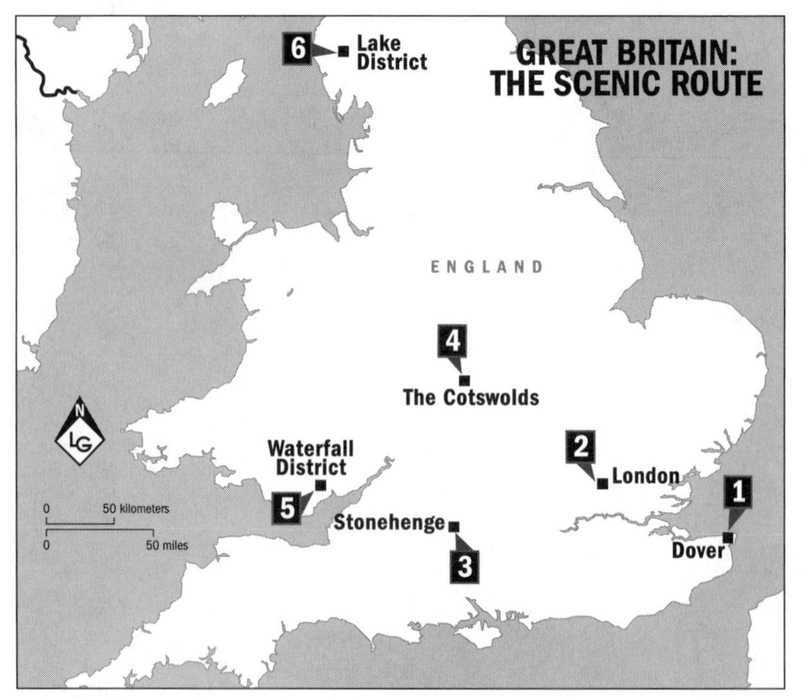

how to use this book

CHAPTERS

In the next few pages, the travel coverage chapters—the meat of any *Let's Go* book—begin with **London.** After a visit to Big Ben and a romp through Hampstead Heath, we venture to **Oxford** to hit the books and the pubs. From Oxford, journey through idyllic **southern England** and **Cardiff,** the cosmopolitan capital of **Wales.** Following that, sweep up to **Cambridge,** then through the fens of **East Anglia** and the countryside of the **Midlands.** Next, continue north, where you may have time to catch a Manchester United vs. Liverpool football match. After that, grab your kilts and golf clubs for a jaunt through **Scotland.** Our adventure next brings us to **Belfast** in **Northern Ireland.** Finally, in true Joycean fashion, we complete our journey in **Dublin,** the Irish capital, chock-full of Guiness and history.

But that's not all, folks. We also have a few extra chapters for you to peruse:

CHAPTER	DESCRIPTION
Discover Great Britain	Discover tells you what to do, when to do it, and where to go for it. The absolute coolest things about any destination get highlighted in this chapter at the front of all *Let's Go* books.
Essentials	Essentials contains the practical info you need before, during, and after your trip—visas, regional transportation, health and safety, phrasebooks, and more.
Great Britain 101	Great Britain 101 is just what it sounds like—a crash course in where you're traveling. This short chapter on Great Britain's history and culture makes great reading on a long plane ride.
Beyond Tourism	As students ourselves, we at Let's Go encourage studying abroad, or going beyond tourism more generally, every chance we get. This chapter lists ideas for how to study, volunteer, or work abroad with other young travelers in Great Britain to get more out of your trip.

LISTINGS

Listings—a.k.a. reviews of individual establishments—constitute a majority of *Let's Go* coverage. Our Researcher-Writers list establishments in order from **best to worst value**—not necessarily quality. (Obviously a five-star hotel is nicer than a hostel, but it would probably be ranked lower because it's not as good a value.) Listings pack in a lot of information, but it's easy to digest if you know how they're constructed:

ESTABLISHMENT NAME type of establishment❶

Address ☎phone number website

Editorial review goes here.

Directions to the establishment. *i* *Other practical information about the establishment, like age restrictions at a club or whether breakfast is included at a hostel.* *Prices for goods or services.* *Hours or schedules.*

ICONS

First things first: places and things that we absolutely love, sappily cherish, generally obsess over, and wholeheartedly endorse are denoted by the all-empowering **Let's Go thumbs-up.** In addition, the icons scattered throughout a listing (as you saw in the sample above) can tell you a lot about an establishment. The following icons answer a series of yes-no questions about a place:

	Credit cards accepted		Cash only		Wheelchair-accessible
	Not wheelchair-accessible		Internet access available		Alcohol served
	Air-conditioned		Outdoor seating available		GLBT or GLBT-friendly

The rest are visual cues to help you navigate each listing:

☎	Phone numbers		Websites		Directions
i	Other hard info		Prices		Hours

OTHER USEFUL STUFF

Area codes for each destination appear opposite the name of the city and are denoted by the ☎ icon. Finally, in order to pack the book with as much information as possible, we have used a few **standard abbreviations.**

PRICE DIVERSITY

A final set of icons corresponds to what we call our "price diversity" scale, which approximates how much money you can expect to spend at a given establishment. For **accommodations,** we base our range on the cheapest price for which a single traveler can stay for one night. For **food,** we estimate the average amount one traveler will spend in one sitting. The table below tells you what you'll *typically* find in Great Britain at the corresponding price range, but keep in mind that no system can allow for the quirks of individual establishments.

ACCOMMODATIONS	BRITAIN	DUBLIN	WHAT YOU'RE LIKELY TO FIND
❶	under £20	under £24	Campgrounds and dorm rooms, both in hostels and actual universities. Expect bunk beds and a communal bath. You may have to provide or rent towels and sheets.
❷	£20-27	£25-39	Upper-end hostels or lower-end hotels. You may have a private bathroom, or there may be a sink in your room and a communal shower in the hall.
❸	£28-34	£40-57	A small room with a private bath. Should have decent amenities, such as phone and TV. Breakfast may be included.
❹	£35-42	£58-73	Should have bigger rooms than a ❸, with more amenities or in a more convenient location. Breakfast probably included.
❺	over £42	over £73	Large hotels or upscale chains. If it's a ❺ and it doesn't have the perks you want (and more), you've paid too much.
FOOD		**RANGE**	**WHAT YOU'RE LIKELY TO FIND**
❶	under £6	under £7	Mostly street-corner stands, food trolleys, sandwiches, takeaway and tea shops. Rarely a sit-down meal.
❷	£6-12	£8-13	Sandwiches, pizza, appetizers at a bar, or low-prices entrees. Most ethnic eateries are a ❷. Either takeaway or a sit-down meal, but only slightly more fashionable decor than a ❶.
❸	£13-18	£14-18	Mid-priced entrees, good pub grub, and more upscale ethnic eateries. Since you'll have the luxury of a waiter, tip will set you back a little extra.
❹	£19-24	£19-26	A somewhat fancy restaurant. Entrees tend to be heartier or more elaborate, but you're really paying for decor and ambience. Few restaurants in this range have a dress code, but some may look down on T-shirts and sandals.
❺	over £24	over £26	Your meal might cost more than your room, but there's a reason—it's something fabulous, famous, or both. Slacks and dress shirts may be expected. Offers foreign-sounding food and a decent wine list. Don't order a PB and J!

ENGLAND AND WALES

LONDON

Most people have a well-defined idea of "London": staid tradition, afternoon tea, stuffy Englishmen with cultured accents, heavy ales, and winding lanes—all of it decorated in styles that were popular back when high foreheads were also fashionable. People with this notion of London can easily complete their vacation in 3min. by working their way to the bank of the Thames and staring pointedly at the gilded heights of **Big Ben,** but to employ this tactic is to miss the true charm of the foggy city.

Despite London's weighty history and culture, the city today is not all **ghost tours, beefeaters,** and **double-decker buses.** In London, there's always an underground scene to be found, and a modern pulse beats behind every beautiful old surface.

History is written on the face of every Blitz-scarred building, but take the time to wander and talk to the people inside them. Immerse yourself in the culture, especially if you're from a superficially similar English-speaking country; the difference will only be more poignant when you realize it. Now, finish your **pint** and *Let's Go.*

greatest hits

- **MAMMA MIA!** Satisfy your *buon appettito* with some of the most epic sandwiches in London at Spianata (p. 65).
- **CHALLENGE THE STATUS QUO.** Or at least hear others with more gumption do so at the Speaker's Corner in Hyde Park (p. 33).
- **DRINK WITH ANIMALS.** Triumph over a fake rhinoceros in the weekly pub quiz at The Three Kings (p. 78).
- **YA DIG IT?** Get your jazz on in the smooth surroundings of Ronnie Scott's in Soho (p. 90).

student life

Face it. Over the past few centuries, the Parliament's lost its funk. If you want to experience the best student life in London, head to Bloomsbury. The home of University College London also hosts countless student backpackers looking for the cheapest hostels in the city. Bloomsbury may not have the best clubs in town, but the bar scene is young and vibrant. Tired of British pub grub? Well, Bloomsbury also has some of the best ethnic restaurants in London, so you can satisfy your craving for tapas and souvlaki without leaving the neighborhood. It also has some of the city's most beautiful gardens, so you and your roommates can make your own picnic and enjoy the scenery (for free!). Throw off your backpack and set up shop in Bloomsbury.

orientation

BAYSWATER

Formerly a watering hole for livestock, Bayswater was built up from a small hamlet in the late 18th and early 19th centuries. In the late 19th century, the neighborhood took on a wealthier set of inhabitants before increased immigration to London spiced up its character and cuisine a bit. It's nestled close to Notting Hill but has much cheaper housing. Get off the Tube at the ⊖**Bayswater** stop for the west of the neighborhood, and at ⊖**Paddington** or ⊖**Lancaster Gate** for the east. Bayswater is east of Notting Hill and west of Marylebone.

BLOOMSBURY

Once famous for the manor houses, hospitals, universities, and museums that made the area a cultural landmark, Bloomsbury is now a haven for student travelers seeking cheap accommodations in a central location. Providing easy access to the British Museum and the rest of London, Bloomsbury is a perfect location from which to see the city. The borough features a wide range of ethnic restaurants, providing a welcome respite from British specialties like the inimitable "bubble and squeak" (fried leftovers). Especially pleasant are the many beautiful gardens and parks sprinkled throughout the neighborhood. Where once you might have seen **Virginia Woolf** and **John Maynard Keynes,** members of the bohemian Bloomsbury Group, you may now see Ricky Gervais. To reach Bloomsbury, west of **Clerkenwell,** take the Tube to ⊖**Tottenham Court Road** or ⊖**Russell Square.**

CHELSEA

Chelsea once gained a reputation as a punk hangout, but there is nothing punk about the neighborhood today. Overrun by rich "Sloanes" (preps, in British parlance), Chelsea now has sky-high prices, expensive clubs, and absurd cars. Just about the only thing that's still edgy about the neighborhood is the **Saatchi Gallery.** Current home of **Mick Jagger** and former home of **Oscar Wilde,** most of the action can be found in **Sloane Square, King's Road,** and **Royal Hospital Road.** Visit for the restaurants and the sights, but find your home and nightlife elsewhere. Chelsea is between **Westminster** and **Hammersmith** and beneath **Kensington.** Take to the Tube to ⊖**Sloane Square** to access it.

THE CITY OF LONDON

One of the oldest and most historic parts of London, the City of London, often referred to as "the City," houses many of London's finest and most crowded tourist attractions, as well as the city's financial center. Written in the histories of many of the buildings are the devastating tragedies of German bombing during the Blitz and the Great Fire of London in 1666. The fire spread rapidly, destroying 80% of the City of London in five days. Much of the current city was rebuilt after both of these tragedies, and its fantastic architecture stands as a monument to the resilient London spirit. "The City" also holds many of London's Roman artifacts, as well as vestiges of the ancient London Wall. It is a neighborhood where the spires of famous churches stretch up with the towers of powerful insurance companies. The City borders the northern bank of the **Thames** and is east of **Holborn.** Take the Tube to **⊖St. Paul's.**

HOLBORN AND CLERKENWELL

In the 18th century, Holborn was home to **Mother Clap's Molly House,** a gay brothel. Today, however, it houses many banks, law firms, and upscale pubs, so things are a little bit different. Clerkenwell is a former monastic center, defined by the Priory of St. John, before Henry VIII began the reformation. It has since become a popular spot for excellent meals and hardy night life. Holborn is west of the City of London; Clerkenwell is north of Holborn, with Charterhouse St. serving as part of its southern boundary. Take the Tube to **⊖Farringdon** or **⊖Temple.**

KENSINGTON AND EARL'S COURT

Once a Saxon settlement, Kensington has since developed into one of the most pleasant parts of London. Known as **The Royal Borough of Kensington and Chelsea,** it is sometimes pretentiously referred to as "The Royal Borough." Filled with some of the best museums, nicest bars and swankiest residences in London, Kensington may have more Lamborghinis, Maseratis, and Ferraris per capita than most London neighborhoods. Notable for its museums, ease of access to **Hyde Park,** and laid-back nightlife, Kensington is well worth a visit. Kensington is south of **Notting Hill** and north of **Knightsbridge.** Use **⊖High Street Kensington** for Kensington High St. and Hyde Park, and **⊖South Kensington** for Old Brompton Rd. and the museums. Earl's Court is just up Old Brompton Rd. from Kensington, but it feels worlds apart, and is a much better neighborhood for a quiet evening out.

KNIGHTSBRIDGE AND BELGRAVIA

Once a dangerous neighborhood, Knightsbridge has since improved its rep. Appealing mostly thanks to its selection of undercrowded and enjoyable sights and fantastic department stores, this neighborhood between **South Kensington** and **Kensington** merits at least a short visit. Use **⊖Knightsbridge** and **⊖Hyde Park Corner** if you travel here. **Belgravia** is a rich neighborhood bordered by **Chelsea** and **Westminster.** It features many fantastic restaurants and a reasonable selection of accommodations, but not much else. Take the Tube to **⊖Sloane Square** or **⊖Victoria** to get to Belgravia.

MARYLEBONE AND REGENT'S PARK

Pronounced (*Mar*-leh-bone), Marylebone is a classic London neighborhood. From the winding, pub-lined **Marylebone Lane** to the gorgeous and romantic **Regent's Park,** the neighborhood offers a complete British experience. The city's diverse population is represented on Edgware Rd., where a predominantly Lebanese community boasts many Middle Eastern restaurants. The area surrounding **Baker Street** features some of the city's more touristy attractions, including the Sherlock Holmes Museum and Madame Tussaud's. Take **⊖Bond Street** to reach the south, **⊖Edgware** for the Lebanese area. **⊖Baker Street** or **⊖Regent's Park** will get you to Regent's Park. Shocking, no?

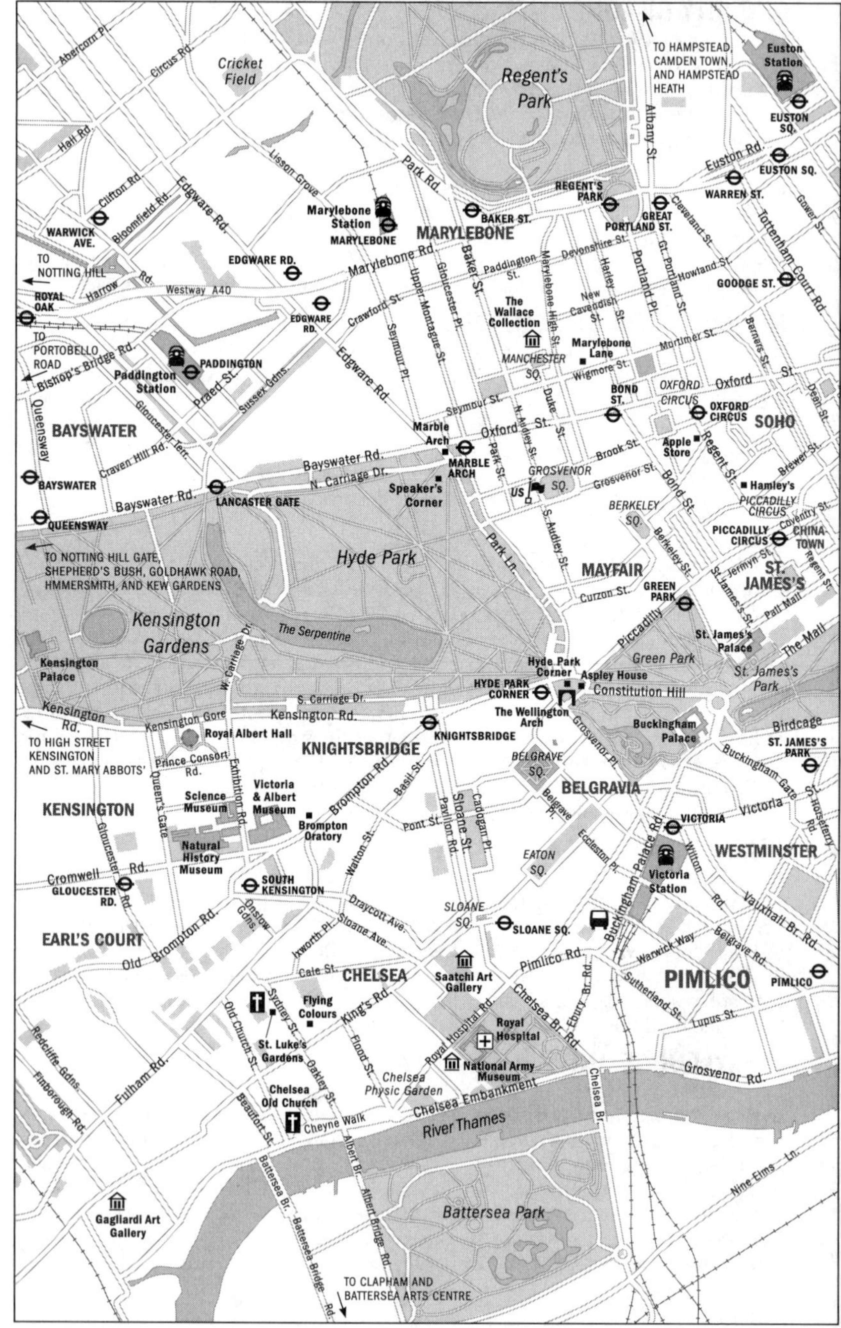
Regent's Park
Cricket Field
TO HAMPSTEAD, CAMDEN TOWN, AND HAMPSTEAD HEATH
Euston Station
EUSTON SQ.
Marylebone Station
MARYLEBONE
MARYLEBONE
BAKER ST.
REGENT'S PARK
GREAT PORTLAND ST.
WARREN ST.
GOODGE ST.
WARWICK AVE.
TO NOTTING HILL
EDGWARE RD.
ROYAL OAK
TO PORTOBELLO ROAD
PADDINGTON
Paddington Station
The Wallace Collection
MANCHESTER SQ.
Marylebone Lane
BOND ST.
OXFORD CIRCUS
SOHO
BAYSWATER
Marble Arch
MARBLE ARCH
Speaker's Corner
GROSVENOR SQ.
US
Apple Store
Hamley's
PICCADILLY CIRCUS
BERKELEY SQ.
LANCASTER GATE
QUEENSWAY
TO NOTTING HILL GATE, SHEPHERD'S BUSH, GOLDHAWK ROAD, HMMERSMITH, AND KEW GARDENS
Hyde Park
MAYFAIR
CHINA-TOWN
ST. JAMES'S
GREEN PARK
Kensington Gardens
The Serpentine
Kensington Palace
Green Park
St. James's Palace
St. James's Park
Hyde Park Corner
Aspley House
HYDE PARK CORNER
Constitution Hill
The Wellington Arch
Royal Albert Hall
KNIGHTSBRIDGE
KNIGHTSBRIDGE
Buckingham Palace
ST. JAMES'S PARK
TO HIGH STREET KENSINGTON AND ST. MARY ABBOTS'
BELGRAVE SQ.
BELGRAVIA
KENSINGTON
Science Museum
Victoria & Albert Museum
Brompton Oratory
VICTORIA
Natural History Museum
EATON SQ.
WESTMINSTER
Victoria Station
GLOUCESTER RD.
SOUTH KENSINGTON
SLOANE SQ.
SLOANE SQ.
EARL'S COURT
CHELSEA
Saatchi Art Gallery
PIMLICO
PIMLICO
Flying Colours
St. Luke's Gardens
Royal Hospital
National Army Museum
Chelsea Physic Garden
Chelsea Old Church
River Thames
Battersea Park
Gagliardi Art Gallery
TO CLAPHAM AND BATTERSEA ARTS CENTRE

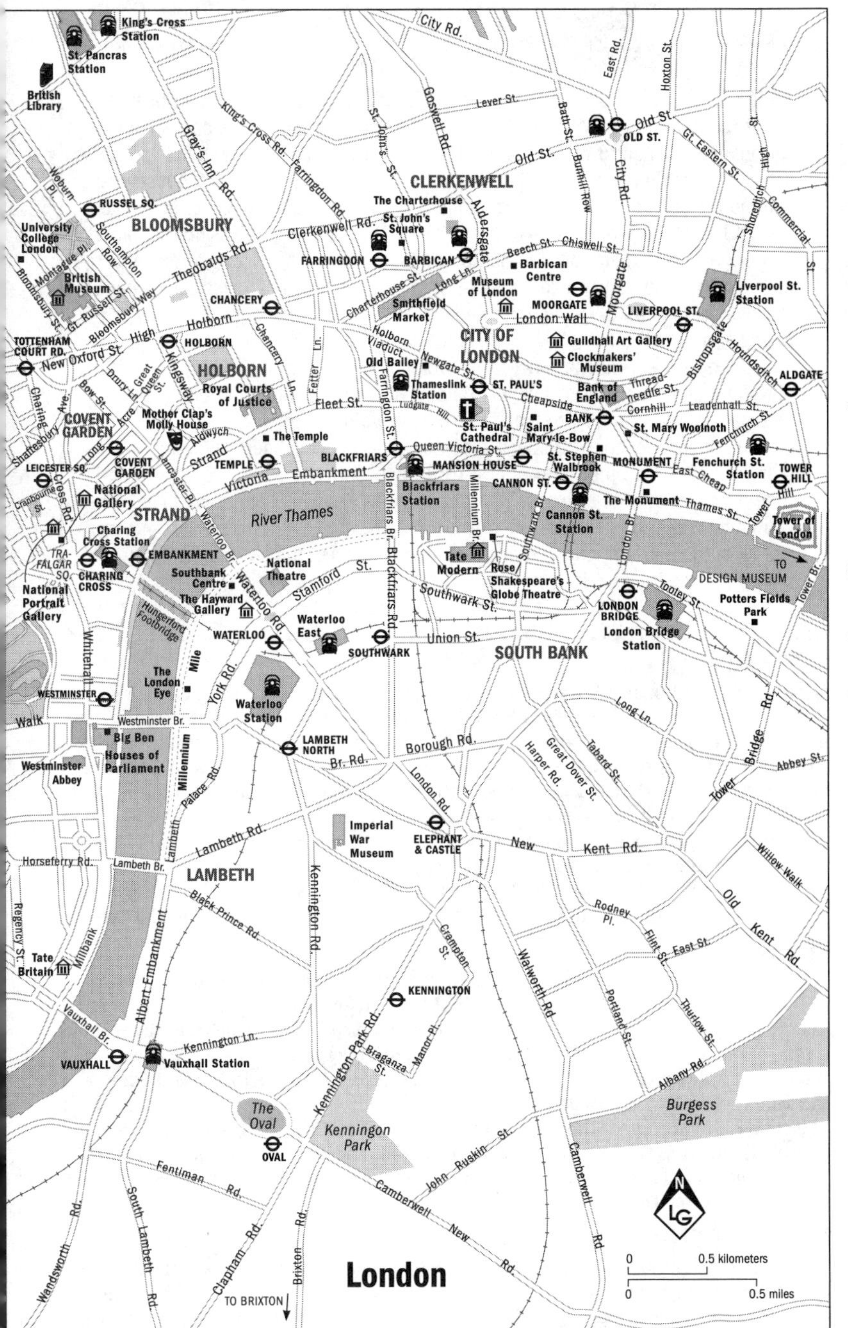
London
King's Cross Station
St. Pancras Station
British Library
City Rd.
East Rd.
Hoxton St.
Lever St.
Goswell Rd.
St. John's St.
King's Cross Rd.
Gray's Inn Rd.
Farringdon Rd.
Bath St.
Bunhill Row
City Rd.
Old St.
OLD ST.
Gt. Eastern St.
Commercial St.
Shoreditch High St.
CLERKENWELL
The Charterhouse
St. John's Square
Clerkenwell Rd.
Aldersgate
Woburn Pl.
RUSSEL SQ.
BLOOMSBURY
University College London
Southampton Row
Theobalds Rd.
Montague Pl.
Bloomsbury St.
British Museum
Gt. Russell St.
Bloomsbury Way
FARRINGDON
BARBICAN
Beech St.
Chiswell St.
Barbican Centre
Museum of London
Long Ln.
Charterhouse St.
Moorgate
MOORGATE
Liverpool St. Station
LIVERPOOL ST.
CHANCERY
Smithfield Market
London Wall
Bishopsgate
Houndsditch
High Holborn
Holborn
Chancery Ln.
Fetter Ln.
TOTTENHAM COURT RD.
New Oxford St.
HOLBORN
Kingsway
Holborn Viaduct
Newgate St.
CITY OF LONDON
Guildhall Art Gallery
Clockmakers' Museum
Old Bailey
Farringdon St.
Thameslink Station
ST. PAUL'S
Bank of England
Threadneedle St.
ALDGATE
Drury Ln.
Great Queen St.
Bow St.
Charing Cross Rd.
Shaftesbury Ave.
HOLBORN
Royal Courts of Justice
Fleet St.
Ludgate Hill
Cheapside
Cornhill
Leadenhall St.
COVENT GARDEN
Long Acre
Mother Clap's Molly House
Aldwych
The Temple
St. Paul's Cathedral
Saint Mary-le-Bow
BANK
St. Mary Woolnoth
Fenchurch St.
COVENT GARDEN
Lancaster Pl.
Strand
TEMPLE
BLACKFRIARS
Queen Victoria St.
MANSION HOUSE
St. Stephen Walbrook
MONUMENT
Fenchurch St. Station
TOWER HILL
LEICESTER SQ.
Cranbourne St.
National Gallery
Victoria Embankment
Blackfriars Station
Millennium Br.
CANNON ST.
East Cheap
The Monument
Thames St.
Tower Hill
STRAND
Waterloo Br.
River Thames
Blackfriars Br.
Southwark Br.
Cannon St. Station
London Br.
Tower of London
Charing Cross Station
EMBANKMENT
TRAFALGAR SQ.
CHARING CROSS
National Portrait Gallery
Southbank Centre
National Theatre
Stamford St.
Tate Modern
Rose/Shakespeare's Globe Theatre
Southwark St.
TO DESIGN MUSEUM
Tooley St.
Tower Br.
LONDON BRIDGE
London Bridge Station
Potters Fields Park
The Hayward Gallery
Waterloo Rd.
Hungerford Footbridge
Waterloo East
WATERLOO
SOUTHWARK
Blackfriars Rd.
Union St.
SOUTH BANK
Whitehall
Mile
The London Eye
York Rd.
Waterloo Station
WESTMINSTER
Walk
Westminster Br.
Long Ln.
Big Ben
Houses of Parliament
Millennium
LAMBETH NORTH
Borough Rd.
Br. Rd.
Great Dover St.
Harper Rd.
Tabard St.
Tower Bridge Rd.
Abbey St.
Westminster Abbey
Lambeth Palace Rd.
London Rd.
Imperial War Museum
ELEPHANT & CASTLE
New Kent Rd.
Lambeth Rd.
Horseferry Rd.
Lambeth Br.
LAMBETH
Willow Walk
Old Kent Rd.
Regency St.
Black Prince Rd.
Kennington Rd.
Crampton St.
Walworth Rd.
Rodney Pl.
Flint St.
East St.
Tate Britain
Millbank
Albert Embankment
KENNINGTON
Portland St.
Thurlow St.
Kennington Park Rd.
Manor Pl.
Braganza St.
Vauxhall Br.
VAUXHALL
Vauxhall Station
Kennington Ln.
Albany Rd.
The Oval
Kennington Park
Burgess Park
OVAL
John Ruskin St.
Fentiman Rd.
Camberwell New Rd.
Camberwell Rd.
Wandsworth Rd.
South Lambeth Rd.
Clapham Rd.
Brixton Rd.
TO BRIXTON
N
LG
0
0.5 kilometers
0
0.5 miles

history lessons

There are, of course, ghost tours, double-decker sightseeing buses, and beefeaters at the Tower of London, and St. Paul's and Trafalgar Square are on everyone's list during their visit to London (with good reason), but the true fabric of the city lies in the people themselves. The population is diverse beyond belief, but several common threads run through all Londoners, regardless of their origin or language: first and most importantly, everyone is a historian, and every pub pundit's history is more accurate than any textbook or guide you'll find. An example: You didn't realize it, but the spot you're standing on now (yes, right now) was once where Dickens sold opium to Queen Elizabeth. It doesn't matter when, or whether you're in England or not, but we have it on good faith that this is, indeed, the spot. The people you'll meet on the Tube, in restaurants and—more likely—in pubs under pints of alcohol and heavy-lids will paint a slurred picture of the city that's so strangely vivid you won't be able to see it as you did before.

Londoners are doggedly persistent under all circumstances. Whether it's a grunting call for another beer after a World Cup bid goes awry or a bizarre and total attachment to the phrase "Keep Calm and Carry On," Londoners believe in continuity and consistency. It's in large part thanks to this conviction that the city has an authentic spirit and essence that feels connected to its history, rather than merely looking back on it.

NOTTING HILL

Notting Hill is a beautiful neighborhood and, while touristy, it's worth a visit—even if you don't bump into Hugh Grant in a local bookstore. Many shopping options are geared towards an older crowd, but Portobello Market (**Portobello Road,** Saturdays from about 6am-6pm) is a blast; you can buy anything from antiques to fresh fruits and vegetables. Aside from the market, the neighborhood's charm lies in its pastel residences, high-end fashion boutiques, and fancy restaurants. These upscale offerings and fantastic houses are what have convinced celebrities like Claudia Schiffer to move to the area. In other celebrity lore, the Clash are rumored to have gotten their start on Portobello Rd. Rock on. Notting Hill is just north of **Kensington,** and organizes itself mainly around Portobello Rd. Take the Tube to **⊖Notting Hill Gate.**

THE SOUTH BANK

Populated with the renovated factories of yore, the South Bank has undergone a renaissance, reinforcing its status as a hub of London entertainment. This status does, of course, have some history to it: both the **Rose** and **Shakespeare's Globe Theatre** resided on the bank. Now, the **Southbank Centre** hosts exciting classical music concerts. Great theaters abound, as do some of the best museums and galleries in London, including the famous **Tate Modern. "Millennium Mile"** stretches from the London Eye in the west and runs eastward along the **Thames,** making for a beautiful walk, especially around sunset. Head to **⊖Waterloo** for inland attractions and to **⊖Southwark** for Bankside. The neighborhood is located in the south of Central London on—you guessed it—the south bank of the Thames.

THE WEST END

The West End is one of the largest, most exciting parts of London. Comprised of **Soho, Covent Garden, Mayfair and Saint James's,** and **Trafalgar Square,** the West End has some of the most affordable shopping in London, as well as arguably the city's best (free!)

public museums, such as the **National Gallery,** and the **National Portrait Gallery,** among others. Known by many as the Broadway of London, the West End offers a host of excellent theater options close to Trafalgar Square, accessible by **⊖Charing Cross.**

Soho, most easily accessed via **⊖Tottenham Court Road** is one of the hipper and seedier parts of London. Home to one of the most prominent gay communities in London, Soho is teeming with nightlife for the GLBT and straight clubgoers alike. During the day, however, Soho is known for its excellent restaurants. **Chinatown** in particular offers many popular options. It's located off Gerrard St. and is easily accessed from Leicester Square or Piccadilly Circus. The **⊖Oxford Circus** Tube stop exits onto Regent St. which is one of the more famous and beautiful streets in London, and is home to many chains and famous shops. Most notable here are the gorgeous Apple store and the famous **Hamley's** toy store, which will help anyone rediscover their inner child.

Covent Garden (accessible via **⊖Covent Garden**, of course) is famous for its shops and the Covent Garden Piazza, recognizable from Hitchcock's *Frenzy* and the opening scene of *My Fair Lady.* Though no longer a Cockney flower market or a place where merchants burst spontaneously into song, Covent Garden is known for its rich history of street performers. One could spend a fulfilling trip in the West End only. It should be noted, however, that as the West End is a prime tourist location as well as a nightlife location, it can be quite dangerous. When going out, people should try to travel in groups and stick to the crowded, well-lit streets. If you get tired of walking on foot, you can also travel by rickshaw. Also note that false store fronts with paper signs inside advertising "model" or "girl" are poorly-concealed brothels. If taken in the right spirit, however, and with proper precautions, the West End's relative sketchiness only adds to its color. We prefer to think of it as Dickensian rather than depressing.

WESTMINSTER

After the City of London, Westminster lays claim to London's most famous sites. Between the **Houses of Parliament, Buckingham Palace,** and **Westminster Abbey** (as well as many of the modern centers of government), Westminster feels like the seat of the royal empire. Be warned that, outside of the sites, however, there isn't a lot to do. South of Victoria lies Pimlico, a residential neighborhood with several accommodation options, many of them on Belgrave Rd. The **⊖Westminster** Tube stop is near most sights, but exit at the **⊖Victoria** or **⊖Pimlico** stops if you're looking for hostels. Westminster is north of the **Thames** and West of **Belgravia** and **Pimlico**.

NORTH LONDON

North London is a sprawling expanse north of central London. **Hampstead** and **Camden Town** are the two most popular draws. Hampstead provides pleasant dining and a properly British small-town feel. It also offers the glorious and meandering **Heath,** a must for all nature-lovers. Camden was once punk central but is now more upscale. Still worth a visit, it contains some underground culture and many upscale restaurants and boutiques. Hampstead is accessible via **⊖Hampstead** and **⊖Golders Green** on the northern line and **⊖Hampstead Heath** via the **National Rail. Camden Town** is accessible on the **Northern Line.** Hampstead is just north of Camden.

SOUTH LONDON

South London has been maligned historically as one of London's dodgier neighborhoods. While the area has enjoyed something of a renaissance in recent years, it's still not as safe as many of the areas in London proper; **Clapham** teems with young professionals patronizing its pub and restaurant scene. Now a cultural center as well, Clapham houses the **Battersea Arts Centre,** renowned for its revolutionary productions. **Brixton** is less quaint than nearby Clapham. Bible-thumpers preach the Apocalypse from convenience store pulpits, and purveyors of all goods at the nearby Afro-Caribbean market make sales despite the overpowering smell of fish. Brixton is also a good place to be if you've been missing fast food. **Stockwell** and **Vauxhall** are less accessible and interesting than the other two neighborhoods in South London, but Vauxhall does claim the **City Farm** in the town park. The local underground stations in many of the southern neighborhoods play classical music, thought by many to be a tactic for keeping young people from accumulating in the Underground, *Clockwork Orange*-style. Access Clapham via **⊖Clapham North, ⊖Clapham Common,** or **⊖Clapham South** or take the **National Rail** services to Clapham Junction. Brixton is accessible via **⊖Brixton** on the **Victoria Line,** and Stockwell can be easily reached via **⊖Stockwell.** Those looking to visit Dulwich can take the P4 bus from **⊖Brixton Station.** Vauxhall is southwest of the **City of London,** Clapham is south of Vauxhall, Brixton is east of Clapham and south of Stockwell.

EAST LONDON

East London, and especially the **East End,** is known for its cutting-edge galleries and its deliciously affordable markets and restaurants. The neighborhood has all of the spark and edge that **Chelsea** used to, and its massive immigrant community rounds out the culinary landscape nicely. **Brick Lane,** named after the brick kilns brought by Flemish immigrants and defined by the waves of Huguenot, French, Russian, Bengali, and Muslim immigrants who came after, is packed to the gills with fantastic and cheap ethnic cuisine as well as some of the most exciting and youthful nightlife in London. Further east, Greenwich features some of London's more famous sites. Use the **Docklands Light Railway (DLR)** to get to Greenwich, Old St., and Liverpool St. for the East End, **⊖Aldgate East** for Brick Lane.

WEST LONDON

West London is one of the more shape-shifting areas of London. **Shepherd's Bush** is a crush of ethnic life, which is evident in the varied restaurants lining **Goldhawk Road,** culminating in the veritable World's Fair that is **Shepherd's Bush Market.** Also unique to Shepherd's Bush is Westfield's, the 43-acre monument to shopping that makes American strip malls look like rinky-dink corner stores. It's essentially a shopping city, and one of those structures where a wavy ceiling constitutes a viable design aesthetic and makes a bold architectural statement. The name Shepherd's Bush is derived from a thorn tree that is deformed by shepherds lying in it while watching their flock. **Hammersmith** is removed from the bustle, feeling more like a seaside

internet cafes

Many restaurants and cafes offer Wi-Fi, but there are a few surefire ways to get Internet in London. Traveling with a laptop has its challenges and its unexpected joys. No matter how heavy the computer, or how total the hard drive crash after your hostelmate spills beer and vodka, which he, for some reason, thought would "taste really good together, bro," few things compare to the thrill of finding cheap Internet somewhere other than the Internet cafe. Some sure bets include chains like Starbucks, but a true laptop adventurer won't stop there. Sure, you can hit up a Starbucks (and, if it has two floors like the one in Victoria Station, you can camp out on the second floor for hours without anyone realizing you're there), but what happens after it closes? That's when you find the cheesiest, most touristy pub you can, and ask if they have Wi-Fi. If they do, you've got internet until 11pm or midnight, plus a killer soundtrack. If, however, that's just not your thing, www.easyinternetcafe.com allows users to search for nearby Internet cafes. Search London for a list of most internet cafes and to add ratings.

resort than a corner of London. The **Thames** provides many water views that would be impossible in the city proper. A good place for a good meal and a quiet day, **Kew** feels like rural London. It is, however, a bit touristy because of the gorgeous **Kew Gardens,** which is the world's largest collection of living plants. (*i Wheelchair-accessible. ⓢ £13.50, concessions £11.50, under 17 free. Open M-F 9:30am-6:30pm, Sa-Su 9:30am-7:30pm.)* Hammersmith is accessible via the **⊖Hammersmith and City Line** (last stop), and Shepherd's Bush is accessible via the **⊖Central Line.** Kew is on the **Richmond** branch of the **⊖District Line** and is the penultimate stop.

accommodations

London is an infamously expensive city, and accommodations are no exception to this rule. The cheapest options are the city's hostels, and there are quite a few, especially in **Bloomsbury, Kensington,** and **Earl's Court** and **Bayswater** (extra emphasis on Bloomsbury). Travelers looking for long-term accommodations should look into rooms at the colleges. Those unwilling to stay in a hostel can stay in bed and breakfasts as they can offer the privacy and comfort of a hotel at close-to-hostel prices.

BAYSWATER

THE PAVILION

THEMED HOTEL ❺

34-36 Sussex Gardens ☎020 7262 0905 www.pavilionhoteluk.com

All you really need to know about the Pavilion is that the most popular room is named "Honky Tonk Afro." Maybe you need to know more. No, the Pavilion is not a blaxploitation film, but rather a themed hotel with rooms ranging from '70s decor to a Casablanca theme. Many famous and half-naked celebrities have posed here, and the hotel is often used by modeling companies.

⊖Paddington. Left onto Praed St., right onto London St., left onto Sussex Gardens. i Continental breakfast delivered to your room. ⓢ Small singles £60, large singles £85, doubles £100, triples £120, family (4 people) £130. 4% extra charge when you pay with a credit card.

ASTOR QUEST

HOSTEL ❷

45 Queensborough Terr. ☎020 7229 7782 www.astorhostels.com

A homey and friendly hostel with a chummy staff that lives on-sight. The rooms are par for the course in hostel-land, but everything is cleaned and beds are made with fresh sheets daily. Breakfast included and served in a room by the kitchen, which is freely available for use. Hostel-weary travelers have the unique experience of dining under Sid Vicious's drugged-out gaze. Be sure to ask the 24hr. receptionist for deals on clubs.

⊖Bayswater. Take right onto Queensway, left onto Bayswater Rd., and left onto Queensborough Terr. i Age limit is 18-35. 4-bed dorms and twins have shared bathroom. Free luggage storage. Padlocks £2. Laundry wash £2.50, dry £1. Hostel renovations should be completed in Jan 2011. ⓢ 4-bed dorm £20, 8-bed £17, 6-bed with ensuite bathroom £19, 4-bed with ensuite £21. 1 female-only room available; 6 beds; £19.

HYDE PARK HOSTEL

HOSTEL ❶

2-6 Inverness Terr. ☎020 7727 9163 www.hydeparkhostel.net

Ramshackle glory seems a fitting description for this aging, battered but grand hostel. Ten-bed dorms have high ceilings with intricate woodwork and lots of open space. While it doesn't seem a particularly convivial hostel, the rooms are well-suited to a debauched weekend in the city.

⊖Bayswater. Take right onto Queensway, left onto Bayswater and left onto Inverness Terr. i Must be above 18. 2-week max. stay. Wi-Fi £1 per hr. Lockers £1.50 per day. Free bed sheets are given daily upon request. Shared bathrooms. ⓢ 14-bed dorm £7.99, 4-bed £14, 6-bed £13, 8-bed £12.50, 12-bed £11, 10-bed £10, singles £40. Reception, kitchen, laundry, TV room 24hr.

GARDEN COURT HOTEL HOTEL ❹

30/31 Kensington Gardens Sq. ☎020 7229 2553 www.gardencourthotel.co.uk

The Garden Court Hotel offers a bed and breakfast level of comfort, cleanliness, and isolation within the bustle of London. The gardens make the Garden Court feel tucked away, but it is actually phenomenally close to Bayswater's attractions. The Garden Court has spacious and reasonably furnished rooms at a price. To save money, you may book a room without a bathroom.

Bayswater. Left onto Queensway, left onto Porchester Gardens, right onto Kensington Gardens Sq. ***i*** *Wi-Fi £1 per hr.* Ⓢ *Singles without facilities £49, with facilities £74; doubles £78/119; triples with facilities £150; family with facilities £170.*

THE ADMIRAL HOTEL HOTEL ❺

143 Sussex Gardens ☎020 7723 7309 www.admiral-hotel.com

Though the art lining the walls tries to be as suave and modern as the blue lights throughout the hotel, the presence of glitter in the paintings sort of ruins the effect. The rooms are modern and sophisticated and are spacious enough, well-furnished, and lit by large windows. The glass door in the lobby leads to a breakfast room where a picture of Sinatra hangs on the wall: yup, **Old Blue Eyes** in Britain.

Paddington. Left onto Praed St., right onto London St., left onto Sussex Gardens. ***i*** *Check-in at 139 Sussex Gardens* Ⓢ *Singles £59-69, doubles £69-79, triples £89-99, quads £99-119.*

BLOOMSBURY

ASTORS MUSEUM HOSTEL HOSTEL ❶

27 Montague St. ☎020 7580 5360 www.astorhostels.com

This is a true backpackers' hostel, quiet but centrally located. The incredibly friendly staff live on-site and are always ready with a pub-crawl, a good song on the reception speakers, a discount on local sights, and themed parties once a week. Astors is welcoming, comfortable, and exciting all at once. The rooms are spacious and clean, the kitchen is open for guest use, and everything is cleaned at least once a day.

Russell Square. Go down Guilford toward Russell Sq., turn left onto the square and follow it around until you reach Montague St. Turn left onto Montague St. i Continental breakfast included. Bring a padlock for the locker under the bed or borrow one with a £3 deposit and a £2 rental. Luggage storage free. Laundry £2.50 to wash, £0.50 dry. Wi-Fi throughout building, 40min. free upon arrival, £5 per day, £8 per week. Recommend booking 2 weeks in advance and 3 weeks in advance for weekends. No ensuite rooms. 4-bed, 6-bed, 8-bed, 10-bed, and 12-bed dorms range £15-25, but prices vary. Doubles/twins £70 for 2 people per night, but price subject to change.

GENERATOR HOSTEL PARTY HOSTEL ❶

37 Tavistock Pl. 020 7388 7666 www.generatorhostels.com

Upon waking up in the Generator Hostel after a night of revelry, you may wonder if you forgot to leave the club. The likely answer is that you never went to a club but stayed in to partake in one of the hostel's nightly parties which occasionally feature DJs. Equipped with a bar open late and a 24hr. reception that plays 24hr. of music, the Generator is generating some very good times. The cafeteria-like common spaces and the fact that the staff doesn't live on-site prevents it from feeling homey, but the neon blue lights and steel panels make it look like a hell of a party.

Russell Sq. Go down Colonnade away from Russell Sq. and turn left onto Grenville St.; follow it onto Hunter St. and turn left onto Tavistock Pl. i Bring your own padlock. Laundry £2 wash, £0.50 per 10min. in dryers. Free Wi-Fi. No private baths. 4-6 bed dorms £20-25; 8-12 bed dorms £17.50-22.50. Singles £55-60; doubles £25-30; triples £17.50-25; quads £17.50-20. Call ahead as prices change. Bar open 6pm-2am. Happy hour 6-9pm.

CLINK 261 HOSTEL ❶

265 Gray's Inn Rd. 020 7833 9400 www.ashleehouse.co.uk

If you dream of a hostel where every night is movie night (and the film is picked by majority vote and watched from comfortable pleather chairs), where cube chairs fill the entry, and where sleek, retro plastic coverings blanket every surface, then you have dreamed of quirky Clink 261. Centrally located in Bloomsbury, Clink 261 has style, relative grace, and clean and simple rooms that are well-suited to hostlers unwilling to commit to grungier options.

King's Cross/St. Pancras. Turn left onto Euston Rd. and follow it as it curves right into Gray's Inn Rd. i Continental breakfast included. Lockers free, but bring your own padlock. Luggage storage and linens included. The hostel is cleaned and fresh sheets are distributed daily. Laundry £2 wash, £.50 per 20min. in the dryer. Wi-Fi £1 per 30min., £2 per hr., £5 per day. Rooms available in 18-bed, 10-bed, 8-bed, 6-bed, 4-bed and private. Shared bath. Dorms £18-25; private rooms £50-60. Call ahead for current prices. Breakfast M-F 7:30-9:30am, Sa-Su 8-10am. Free walking tour daily 10:10am.

YHA ST. PANCRAS HOSTEL ❸

79-81 Euston Rd. 020 7388 9998 www.yha.org.uk

The large YHA is home to guests of all ages, making it feel more like a hotel than a hostel. YHA is clean, efficient, and very modern in its design. Decked out with a few classy lounges filled with books such as Chabon's *The Yiddish Policeman's Union*, YHA is a bit more institutional than the average hostel but also a bit cleaner.

King's Cross/St. Pancras. Turn right onto Euston Rd. i The Meal Deal (breakfast basket and a hot snack) £5. Laundry £4.50. Wi-Fi access from lounges £5 per 24hr., £9 per week. 80% of rooms have ensuite bath. Only 1 room is wheelchair-accessible, so call ahead if you need to use it. Doubles £45-72; quads £79-127; quints £99-159; 6-person rooms £116-191. Breakfast 7:30-10:00am. Bar open 24hr., alcohol served until 1am.

THANET HOTEL HOTEL ❹

8 Bedford Pl. ☎020 7636 2869 www.thanethotel.co.uk

The charm of this hotel lies in its proximity to the beautiful Russell Square Gardens. Rooms are clean and the hotel is quiet. Guests on the lower floors have views through windows that stretch to the ceilings, which in this hotel are quite high. Enjoy breakfast in the pleasant breakfast room decorated with blue and teal curtains and fresh flowers on every table. In short, Thanet is a family-run, budget hotel whose accommodations hardly feel budget.

Russell Square. Turn onto Guilford going toward Russell Sq. Turn left onto Russell Sq. and follow it around until you reach Bedford Pl. i Wi-Fi is not guaranteed in all rooms, but it is free. Singles £82; doubles £110; triples £135; quads £150 Breakfast M-Sa 7:45-9:15am, Su 8:30-9:30am.

THE GEORGE HOTEL ❹

58-60 Cartwright Gardens ☎020 7387 8777 www.georgehotel.com

The rooms at the George are a bit old, but they're quite spacious and well furnished. In a secluded part of busy Bloomsbury, the George is a quiet and cozy hotel that'll keep you rested without keeping you away from the action. All 40 rooms have digital TV and tea and coffee machines. Also, there's a **fish tank.**

Russell Sq. Go down Colonnade away from Russell Sq. and turn left onto Grenville St.; follow it onto Hunter St. and turn left onto Cartwright Gardens i Full English breakfast included. Free Wi-Fi. Singles £55, with bath £75; doubles £68/89; triples £79/99; quads with bath £89. Discounts for stays longer than 5 nights. Breakfast M-F 7:30-9am, Sa-Su 8-9:30am.

THE WARDONIA HOTEL BUDGET HOTEL ❸

46-54 Argyle St. ☎020 7837 3944 www.wardoniahotel.com

Located close to King's Cross, the Wardonia offers Spartan accommodations for correspondingly low prices. Don't come here if you're looking for community or "luxury" amenities like breakfast.

King's Cross/St. Pancras. Cross Euston Rd. and go down Belgrove St. with your back to King's Cross. Turn right onto Argyle St. i Luggage room. Ensuite bath. TV in room. Singles £45; doubles £60-65; triples £80.

CHELSEA

No longer a punk-rock haven, Chelsea is now overrun with Ferraris, Benzes, and Porsches, and the hotels have adjusted accordingly. Budget accommodations here are short-stay apartment rentals.

IES RESIDENCE HALLS STUDENT RESIDENCE HALLS ❶

Manresa Rd. ☎020 7808 9200 www.iesreshall.com

Simple but highly affordable and value-packed (as Chelsea accommodations go), IES Residence Halls fill a large void in the Chelsea housing market, which is dominated by four- and five-star hotels. Three rooms share one spacious kitchen that has chairs, a table, a couch, and a fridge. The style is modern, the concept is simple, and the rates are low. Common rooms on each floor house a TV and the six RAs organize occasional events.

Sloane Sq. Exit the Tube and go straight down Sloane Sq. The street slanting gently left is King's Rd. If you don't want to walk the road (it's manageable but long), the following buses service the area: 11, 19, 22, 211, 319, right on Manresa Rd. i Laundry: washer £2; soap £1.20; dryer £1. No Wi-Fi, but ethernet in every room. Bathrooms cleaned once a week, kitchens cleaned twice a week. Bathrooms ensuite. 1-16 weeks, weekly rates: singles £331-397; twins shared £207. Rates for 16-36 weeks and 36-50 weeks also available. Daily rates: singles £52.86, twins £58.75. Security 24hr.

SYDNEY HOUSE CHELSEA LUXURY HOTEL ❹

9-11 Sydney St. ☎020 7376 7711 www.sydneyhousechelsea.com

A luxury hotel that's graceful rather than obnoxious. The rooms are beautiful and bright, all light wood and clean surfaces. The lobby contains a lovely tapestry and the common spaces are bedecked in cool modern paintings and sketches. The breakfast room is pleasant and lit by lights with a patterned surface that looks like the guys from Tron have been racing on it. Not exactly directed toward students, but a very pleasant, four-star hotel.

Sloane Sq. Exit the Tube and go straight down Sloane Sq. The street slanting gently left is King's Rd., go onto it and turn right at Sydney St. i Breakfast of pastries, poilane bread, and coffee or tea £5.50. English breakfast £11. Everything is cleaned daily. Bathrooms ensuite. Prices change, but rooms range £150-295. Call in advance.

THE SLOANE SQUARE LUXURY HOTEL 4

7-12 Sloane Sq. ☎020 7896 9988 www.sloanesquarehotel.co.uk

These rooms preside over gorgeous (and expensive) Sloane Square with elegance. If you're going for the luxury Sloane experience, might as well go all the way. This hotel provides some rooms with bay windows veiled by soft curtains and some with large bathtubs. They're well furnished and comfortable, each with a free locker, a laptop, and an iPod station. Pay for breakfast separately and enjoy it in the sleek breakfast room.

Sloane Sq. i Discounts at some local restaurants given. Wi-Fi £4.50 per 1hr., £14.99 per day. Singles £147; doubles £173; "superior" £214; club room £239. Rates exclusive of VAT; check online for weekend rates.

CHELSEA CLOISTERS SHORT STAY APARTMENTS 3

Sloane Ave. ☎020 7584 1002 www.chelseacloisters.co.uk

Though a bit old and worn, Chelsea Cloisters offers a viable alternative to the high-cost hotels that might otherwise prohibit a stay in Chelsea. The rooms are clean and efficient, each with its own kitchen and bathroom. It's not the swankiest or brightest building, but the apartments are clean and serviceable. Check carefully what you're paying before you book, as there are a few compulsory charges (cleaning and deposit) not included in the rates. Because of the deposits, it might be wise to book only for very long stays or for stays under a week, in which case no deposit is needed.

Sloane Sq. Exit the Tube and go straight down Sloane Sq. The street slanting gently left is King's Rd., go onto it and turn right onto Sloane Ave. i Luggage room. BT Openzone vouchers (for Wi-Fi) sold at the desk; £40 per month, £27 per 5 days, £10 per 24hr. Book at least a week in advance. Compulsory 5-day maid service and linen change £58.75 for a studio, £70.50 for 1 bed, £82.25 for 2 beds. 1-week prices: large studio apartment £590; 1-bedroom apartment £785. 2-bedroom apartments: doubles and singles £1,025; doubles and twins £1,075. Deposit: studio £600; 1-bedroom £600; 2-bedroom £800.

KENSINGTON AND EARL'S COURT

ASTOR HYDE PARK HOSTEL 1

191 Queen's Gate ☎020 7581 0103 www.astorhostels.co.uk

Built in the 1800s as a grand Victorian House, the Astor Hyde Park was also a hotel once upon a time. The flagship among Astor Hostels, the Hyde Park location is all high ceilings, aged grandeur, and comfort. The hostel is very close to beautiful Hyde Park. The six-floor hostel has no maximum stay, but it's not meant for long-term stays. Everything is cleaned twice a day, and the kitchen is cleaned three times daily. Careful, though—backpackers subject to delusions of grandeur could easily mistake the other residents for servants in their personal mansion. The hostel keeps some of that old grandeur in the teas with live music and the spacious common room.

High Street Kensington. Turn right onto Kensington High St., then turn right onto Queen's Gate. i Free linens; beds are made fresh daily. Laundry: washing machine £2.50, washing powder £1, dryer £1 per 40min. Lockers £1.50 per day, £7 per week. Free Wi-Fi. Coin-operated computers for those without laptops. Every room is ensuite, except 3- to 4-bed rooms, which still have private bathrooms. Ⓢ Winter prices around £15-20. Summer weekday dorm prices £20-£26; doubles £80; twins £70. Weekend rates go up by £5 per dorm bed and £10 per double and twin. ⏰ Reception 24hr.

VICARAGE HOTEL BED AND BREAKFAST ❹

10 Vicarage Gate ☎020 7229 4030 www.londonvicaragehotel.com

Posh and warm, the Vicarage Hotel provides an affordable experience of superb comfort. Each room is individually decorated, and the walls are bedecked with ornately framed, original paintings. The red-and-white-striped chairs on the landings are perfect reading chairs, and the rich red carpet only adds to the comfortable atmosphere of this simple B and B.

⊖High Street Kensington. Turn right onto Kensington High St., left onto Kensington Church St., and continue straight onto Brunswick Gardens and right onto Vicarage Gate. Ⓢ Singles £56, with bath £95; doubles/twins £95/125; triples £120/160; quads £130/176. ⏰ Reception 7:30am-7:30pm. Breakfast 7:30am-9am.

YHA EARL'S COURT LONDON HOSTEL ❷

38 Bolton Gardens ☎020 7373 7083 www.yha.org.uk

In one of the pleasant in-between spaces of London which are central yet oddly removed, YHA Earl's Court London is a fairly spacious hostel which, despite its shared bathrooms, grants everyone their own space. Some of the rooms even have their own areas for storage. Frequented by families as well as backpackers, the hostel is welcoming and affordable.

⊖West Brompton. Turn right on Old Brompton Rd., left onto Earl's Ct. Rd., right onto Bolton Gardens ***i*** *Continental breakfast £2.95. Sheets are included, beds are made daily. Shared bathrooms. Ⓢ Laundry: washer, dryer, and detergent £4.50. Lockers in room, padlocks £3. Internet £5 per 24hr., £9 per week. Check ahead, but generally beds in single-sex 4-, 6-, and 10-bed dorms £20-24.50.*

YHA LONDON HOLLAND PARK HOSTEL ❷

20 Holland Wk. ☎020 7937 0748 www.yha.org.uk

A patchwork hostel of three buildings (one of which used to be a noble's house), the Holland Park YHA doesn't feel like a typical hostel. This bizarre otherness is furthered by its location at the rear of Holland Park, making it feel like a Park Ranger's office. The tranquil garden space, which features a fountain inhabited by fish and weird-looking duck-like creatures, is particularly peaceful when there's a classical music concert in the park. The Hostel frequently hosts school groups, but, despite the crowded rooms, for some it will be a welcome deviation from the norm.

⊖High St. Kensington. Turn left onto Kensington High St. right down Holland Walk in Holland Park. ***i*** *Use night gate at the rear after 10pm as the park closes.* ***i*** *Breakfast included. Linens included. Towels £4. Laundry: washer £1, dryer £.20 per 15min. Wi-Fi £1 per 20min., £3 per hr., £5 per 24hr., £9 per week. Ⓢ £21-27.50 per bed for adults; £16.50-21.50 for under 18. ⏰ Breakfast 7:30-9:30am. Dinner is 5-8pm. Kitchen open until 10pm. 7-day max. stay.*

OXFORD HOTEL HOTEL ❸

16-18, 24 Penywern ☎020 7370 1161 www.the-oxford-hotel.com

A comfortable, simple hotel seconds away from the Tube, the Oxford Hotel provides amenities like fridges, LCD TVs, safes, and ensuite bathrooms with every room. The two breakfast rooms are bright yellow and pleasant. One is sometimes partially used to store luggage, and the other looks out onto a simple back patio with wooden stairs and a few chairs.

⊖Earl's Ct. Right onto Earl's Ct., right onto Penywern. Reception is at 16-18 Penywern. ***i*** *Wi-Fi £5 per 3hr., £2 per 1hr., £8 per 5hr., £20 per 24hr. Luggage room £5 per day per room (to be used within reason). Ⓢ Singles £75; doubles/twins £85; triples £95; quads £105. Rates change, so check in closer to your stay. ⏰ Reception 24hr.*

BADEN-POWELL HOUSE (MEININGER HOSTEL) — HOSTEL ❷

65-67 Queen's Gate ☎020 7590 6900 www.meininger-hotels.com

A clean, simple urban hostel, the Baden-Powell House's Meininger Hostel is located close to the Tube. With a ping-pong table on the roof terrace and a foosball table in the lobby, you might not even need such easy access to the Tube to have a good time.

Gloucester Rd. Left onto Gloucester Rd. Right onto Queen's Gate.. i Continental breakfast £5 per day. Laundry is £2.50 for washing and drying. Linens included. Each room has lockers. Free luggage room downstairs. Wi-Fi £1 per 20min., £5 per 24 hr., £8 per week. Ⓢ Dorms with shared facilities £15; max. 14-bed (coed) dorm £21; Max. 14-bed. Single-sex dorm £23; 3-to-8-bed £24. Singles £69; doubles £45. Breakfast M-F 7-10am, Sa-Su 7:30-11am.

KNIGHTSBRIDGE AND BELGRAVIA

MORGAN GUEST HOUSE — GUEST HOUSE ❷

120 Ebury St. ☎020 7730 2384 www.morganhouse.co.uk

This cozy guest house feels just like a home. Most rooms have a fireplace and all are clean and well decorated, occasionally decked out with chandeliers, huge mirrors, and fresh flowers. In the back, guests can enjoy a patio that's like the Secret Garden. For a pleasant budget stay in Belgravia, you could do worse than the Morgan Guest House.

Victoria. Turn left onto Buckingham Palace Rd. With your back to Buckingham Palace Rd., turn right onto Elizabeth, then left onto Ebury St. Ⓢ Singles £58; doubles £78, with bath £98; triples £98/138; quads with bath £148. Breakfast M-F 7:30-9am, Sa-Su 8-10am.

WEST END

FIELDING HOTEL — HOTEL ❸

4 Broad Ct. ☎020 7836 8305 www.thefieldinghotel.co.uk

Named after the novelist Henry Fielding, who worked next door at Bow St. Magistrate's Court where Oscar Wilde was later tried, the Fielding Hotel is located in pleasant Broad Ct. A short walk from the Royal Opera House, the hotel is in one of the most exciting parts of town, but the Fielding doesn't use that as an excuse for poor rooms or exorbitant prices. Book a room at this comfortable, classy, well-located, and reasonably-priced hotel.

Covent Garden. Right onto Long Acre. Right onto Drury Ln. Right onto Broad Ct. i Book around a month in advance. Ⓢ Singles £90; doubles £115; superior twins/doubles £140, with sitting room £160; 3-person suite £200. Rates do not include VAT. Call ahead because rates change.

YHA OXFORD ST. — HOSTEL ❶

14 Noel St. ☎020 7734 1618 oxford@yhalondon.org.uk

The big appeal of YHA Oxford St. is the location, with prime placement in the West End. There are prettier and friendlier accommodations in this city, but you can't complain about the price. Two washer-dryers service 76 beds, and the rooms begin on the third floor, with a battered lift as an alternative to the stairs; don't buy too much of the alcohol served behind reception, as you might not make it up.

Oxford Circus. Turn left down Regent St., left onto Noel St.. N13, N15, N18, N136, N159 available from the Oxford Circus Station Bus Stop. i £1.60 for washing, £.50 for a 15-20min. drying cycle. 7-night max. stay. Wi-Fi: £1 per 20min., £5 per 24hr., £9 per 7 days, available in the lounge and some of the rooms. Ⓢ 3- to 4-bed dorms £23-32; doubles £56-76; triples £84-117. Alcohol served behind reception: Bottles of beer £2.10-2.75, Irish apple cider £3, Smirnoff Ice £2.85. Alcohol served 10am-11:30pm.

WESTMINSTER

ASTOR'S VICTORIA — HOSTEL ❸

71 Belgrave Rd. ☎020 7834 3077 www.hostelworld.com

A franchise in a chain, Astor's Victoria is especially popular with students.

Rooms feel small and run-down but great to live in. Bathrooms are cleaned twice daily, and linens are changed daily. The walls are covered with friendly tips for travelers and low-cost (and specially discounted) outing opportunities. The staff hosts movie nights and pub crawls, and the hostel's excellent location only makes going out easier.

 # Victoria. Left onto Buckingham Palace Rd. Left on Belgrave Rd. i Breakfast included. Storage available. Personal safes £1.50. Wi-Fi £1 for 40min., £5 for 24hr. Common room open until 1am. Ⓢ Prices for rooms range wildly; call well in advance. Breakfast 8am-10am.

VICTOR HOTEL

HOTEL ❸

51 Belgrave Rd. ☎020 7592 9853 www.victorhotel.co.uk

A basic, clean, and—depending on the day—cheap hotel, the Victor is one of the many townhouse establishments lining Belgrave Rd. Boasting a convenient location near the heart of Westminster, the Victor provides well-kept rooms that, while not large, are not nearly as cramped as those of some of the hotels on the same street.

 # Victoria. Left onto Buckingham Palace Rd. Left onto Belgrave Rd. i All rooms have an en-suite bathroom. All room prices subject to change based on dates, season, and local events, so check online. Ⓢ Doubles M-F £75-85, Sa-Su up to £95. Reception 24hr.

NOTTING HILL

Notting Hill isn't an ideal place to find budget accommodations—although there are many beautiful residences, travelers short on funds aren't welcome to stay in many of them. Prices hover around £80-120 for doubles. Nearby Bayswater is a much better bet for the penny-pinching traveler.

BOWDEN COURT

HOSTEL ❷

24 Ladbroke Rd. ☎020 7727 5665 www.lhalondon.com

This four-floor hostel is just about the only budget-friendly option for people looking to stay in Notting Hill, but luckily, it's close to all the action. In the basement lies a clean and spacious dining room. The food is decent but not terribly healthy. Also in the basement are a laundry room, study room with computers, and TV room. Bathrooms are communal.

 # Notting Hill Gate. Exit north, take a right onto Pembridge Rd., and turn left onto Ladbroke Rd. i Lockers £1 per day, £3.50 per week, £10 per month. Laundry: washers £3; dryers £1. Ⓢ 2-bed dorms £25; 3-bed £23.50. Singles £28-29; doubles £52. Weekly 2-bed dorms £114; 3-beds £94.50. Weekly singles £159.50-179.50; doubles £250. Breakfast M-F 7am-8:15am; Sa-Su and bank holidays 9:30-10:30am. Dinner M-F 6:30-8pm. Lunch Sa-Su and bank holidays 12:30-1:30pm.

THE PORTOBELLO GOLD

HOTEL ❹

97 Portobello Rd. ☎020 7460 4910 www.portobellogold.com

Your life has been incomplete until you discover the Portobello Gold. While expensive, the Portobello Gold has such a good location that it might be worth it—not to mention access to a roof terrace complete with a putting green. Rooms are small but well kept. They might be noisy, since the pub is downstairs, but residents get a special fixed price menu at the pub, as well as an included continental breakfast. If you've come to London but don't actually want to leave your building, this is your deal.

 # Notting Hill Gate. Exit North, turn right onto Pembridge Rd. and left onto Portobello Rd. Ⓢ Doubles £80-£100; 4-poster bed, capacity to fit 3 mattresses on floor £135; apartment £180. Stay over 7 days and get a discounted rate.

THE ABBEY COURT HOTEL

HOTEL ❺

20 Pembridge Gardens ☎020 7221 7518 www.abbeycourthotel.co.uk

If it's raining out—which is likely—cuddle up with a good book in a spacious, clean, and comfortable room at the Abbey Court Hotel. The centrally located ho-

tel boasts a sunlit breakfast room and a lavish lounge that feels properly British.
Notting Hill Gate. Exit South. Singles, doubles, and four poster rooms available, but prices change on a regular basis, so be sure to call ahead.

THE GATE HOTEL ❹

6 Portobello Rd. ☎020 7221 0707 www.gatehotel.co.uk

At the top of busy Portobello Rd., The Gate enjoys the luxury of a centralized location, while maintaining the relative solitude of less active areas. The rooms are simple, with thick carpets and clean facilities.

Notting Hill Gate. Exit North, take right on Pembridge Rd., left onto Portobello Rd. Wi-Fi £10 for your stay. Singles week night £60, weekend £70; doubles £85/95; doubles lux £95/105; triples £115/135.

NOTTING HILL HOTEL HOTEL ❸

2 Pembridge Sq. ☎020 7727 1316 www.nottinghillhotel.com

If you've been traveling for weeks and you are self-conscious about your body odor, stay here—the smell got here hours before you did, and no one will blame you for it. The only appealing thing about this place is its location; the rooms are in disrepair, and aren't that large. Still, if this is your only option, it's very close to the action on Notting Hill.

Notting Hill Gate. Exit North, take right on Pembridge Rd., turn right at Pembridge Sq. Notting Hill Hotel will be on your right. Breakfast included. Midweek rates: singles from £50; doubles or twins from £60; family room for 3 from £80. Weekend and holiday rates: singles from £55; doubles or twins from £70; family rooms for 3 from £90.

sights

From the hints of the city's Roman past at the London Wall to the memories of WWII or the unforgettable Great Fire of London, London's long past has not only been documented in stone but also in its art scene, from the masterworks in the West End's National Gallery and the Tate Modern to the cutting edge galleries of Chelsea and the South Bank. And not to worry—this artistic splendor is totally accessible to travelers on a budget, especially those who carry their student IDs. When trying to see a church, look for service times, as you can frequently get in free during masses, Evensong, etc. If you can't afford to visit all of the sights individually, buy a ticket up to the top of St. Paul's—the view from the Golden Gallery is magnificent and the cathedral itself is worth every pence.

Don't limit your experience to the ticketed sights either. Once you realize that London's history is everywhere, you won't be able to escape it. No matter what path you choose, whether you're strolling down the winding lanes of Marylebone, ducking your way through the growth in Hampstead Heath, or navigating the thousands of roses in Regent's Park, your exploration will be rewarded. There is no wrong turn. Unless you're on the heath and you hear a strange growling noise to your left. In that case, a left turn may be the wrong turn.

BAYSWATER

SPEAKERS' CORNER HISTORICAL SITE, PERFORMANCE SPACE

Hyde Park, Park Ln.

This innocuous corner of Hyde Park is the stage for political, religious, and social debates. Speakers present ideas, challenge each other, and take questions from the audience. There are no set hours, and anyone is welcome to speak. Come watch free speech in action!

Lancaster Gate. Take left onto Bayswater Rd. Go in through Victoria Gate and continue left down Hyde Park. Stay close to Bayswater Rd. Free. Hours vary, but can be 9am-10pm in summer.

ALEXANDER FLEMING MUSEUM MUSEUM

St. Mary's Hospital Praed St. ☎020 7886 6528

Walk the same steps Alexander Fleming walked on the day in 1928 when he discovered Penicillin. The museum is small, but it successfully recreates the original conditions of the laboratory. Worth a visit if only to see the room where a discovery that completely changed the entire last century was made. Informative film and a room with facts about the discovery can be found upstairs.

Edgware Rd. Right on Chapel St. and continue onto Praed St. Look for St. Mary's. There will be a gate and a passageway. The museum is on your left with a picture of the petri dish in which penicillin was discovered. i Tours by request. £4, students and seniors £2. Open M-Th 10am-1pm.

SUBWAY GALLERY GALLERY

Joe Strummer Subway ☎078 1128 6503 www.subwaygallery.com

Bringing a new meaning to the term "underground art" (their joke), the Subway Gallery features installations from local artists often dealing with pop culture or music. Check the website for exhibit information. Exhibits change monthly. If you're in the area, it's definitely worth stopping by this very cool venue, but don't go out of your way to get here. And we wouldn't recommend traveling here at night.

Edgware Rd. Exit, take sharp right down Cabbell St., left before the flyover and then go down the stairs into Joe Strummer Subway. Free. Open M-Sa 11am-7pm.

concessions

The British word "concession" is the equivalent of the American "discount." It usually applies to fees for students, seniors, the unemployed with proof of unemployment and, sometimes, the disabled.

BLOOMSBURY

THE BRITISH MUSEUM MUSEUM

Great Russell St. ☎020 7323 8299 www.british-museum.org

The funny thing about the British Museum is that there's almost nothing British in it. Founded in 1753 as the personal collection of Sir Hans Sloane, the museum juxtaposes Victorian Anglocentricism with more modern, multicultural acceptance. The building itself, in all its Neoclassical splendor, is magnificent; a leisurely stroll through the less crowded galleries is well worth an afternoon visit. The many visitors who don't make it past the main floor miss out—the galleries above and below are some of the museum's best, if not most famous.

The **Great Court** is the largest covered square in Europe, and has been used as the **British Library** stacks for the past 150 years. The blue chairs and desks of the **Reading Room,** set inside a towering dome of books, have shouldered the weight of research by Marx, Lenin, and Trotsky, as well as almost every major British writer and intellectual—and minor ones as well! From the main entrance, the large double doors to the left of the Reading Room lead to the Museum's most popular wing, the **West Galleries.** The **Rosetta Stone** takes center stage in the **Egyptian sculpture** rooms, while the less iconic but enduringly huge monumental friezes and reliefs of the Assyrian, Hittite, and other Ancient Near East civilizations are worth more than a glance. Most famous (and controversial) of the massive array of Greek sculptures on display are the **Elgin Marbles** from the Parthenon, statues carved under the direction of Athens's greatest sculptor, Phidias (Room 18). The Greek government technically bought the Marbles (albeit for a measly price). Other Hellenic highlights include remnants of two of the seven Wonders of the Ancient World: the **Temple of Artemis** at Ephesus and the **Mausoleum of Halikarnassos** (Rooms 21-22).

Upstairs, the **Portland Vase** presides over Roman ceramics and house wares (Room 70). When discovered in 1582, the vase had already been broken and reconstructed, and in 1845, it was shattered again by a drunk museum-goer. When it was put back together, 37 small chips were left over; two reconstructions have reincorporated more and more leftover chips, though some are still missing from the vase. Egyptian sarcophagi and mummies await in the **North Galleries** (rooms 61-66). The newer **African Galleries** display a fabulous collection accompanied by soft chanting, video displays, and abundant documentation (Room 25, lower floor). In Rooms 51-59, musical instruments and board games from the world's first city, Ur, show that leisure time is a historical constant, while Mexico dominates the **Americas** collection with extraordinary Aztec artifacts (Rooms 26-27). **Islamic** art resides in Room 34, and above it, the largest room in the museum holds **Chinese, South Asian,** and **Southeast Asian** artifacts alongside some particularly impressive Hindu sculpture (Room 33). The highlight of the **Korean** display, in Room 67, is a *sarangbang* house built on-site, while a tea house is the centerpiece of the **Japanese** galleries (Rooms 92-94).

In the **South and East Galleries,** the **King's Library** gallery holds artifacts gathered from throughout the world by English explorers during the **Enlightenment.** While the labeling is poor (and in some places nonexistent), the collection itself is spectacular. The upper level of the museum's southeast corner is dedicated to ancient and medieval Europe, and includes most of the museum's British artifacts. A highlight of the collection is the treasure excavated from the **Sutton Hoo Burial Ship;** the magnificent inlaid helmet is the most famous example of Anglo-Saxon craftsmanship. Along with the ship is the **Mildenhall Treasure,** a trove of brilliantly preserved Roman artifacts (Room 41). Next door are the enigmatic and beautiful **Lewis Chessmen,** an 800-year-old Scandinavian chess set mysteriously abandoned on Scotland's Outer Hebrides (Room 42). Collectors and enthusiasts will also enjoy the comprehensive **Clocks and Watches Gallery** (Rooms 38-39) and **Money Gallery** (Room 68).

Tottenham Court Rd., Russell Square, or Holborn. i Tours by request. Free. Small suggested donation. Prices for events and exhibitions vary. Museum open daily 10am-5:30pm. Select exhibitions and displays open Th and F until 8:30pm. Paul Hamlyn Library open M-W 10am-5:30pm, Th 10am-8:30pm, F noon-8:30pm, Sa 10am-7:30pm.

THE BRITISH LIBRARY

LIBRARY

96 Euston Rd. ☎020 7412 7676 www.bl.uk

Castigated by traditionalists during its long constructionfor being too modern and by moderns for being too traditional, the new British Library building (opened in 1998) now impresses all nay-sayers with its stunning interior. The 65,000 volumes of the King's Library, collected by George III and bequeathed to the nation in 1823 by his less bookish son, George IV, are displayed in a glass cube toward the rear. The sunken plaza out front features an enormous and somewhat strange statue of Newton, and also hosts a series of free concerts and events. The heart of the library is underground, with 12 million books on 200 miles of shelving; the above-ground brick building is home to cavernous reading rooms and an engrossing museum. In the **Literature Corner** of the museum, find **Shakespeare's** first folio, **Lewis Carroll's** handwritten manuscript of *Alice in Wonderland* (donated by Alice herself), and **Virginia Woolf's** handwritten notes to *Mrs. Dalloway* (then called *The Hours*). Music-lovers visiting the museum will appreciate **Handel's** handwritten *Messiah*, **Mozart's** marriage contract, **Beethoven's** tuning fork, and a whole display dedicated to the **Beatles,** including the original handwritten lyrics to "A Hard Day's Night"—scrawled on the back of Lennon's son Julian's first birthday card. In the museum, the original copy of the **Magna Carta** has its own room with accompanying Papal Bull that Pope Innocent III wrote in response. **Leonardo da Vinci's** notebooks are in the **Science** section, while one of 50 known **Gutenberg Bibles** is in the **Printing** section.

Euston Sq. or King's Cross St. Pancras. Free Wi-Fi. To register for use of reading room, bring 2 forms of ID—1 with a signature and 1 with a home address. Open M 9:30am-6pm, Tu 9:30am-8pm, W-F 9:30am-6pm, Sa 9:30am-5pm, Su 11am-5pm. Group tours (up to 15 people) Tu and Th at 10:30am and 2:30pm, £85 per group; call 020 7412 7639 to book. Individual tours M, W, and F 11am, free; booking recommended; call 019 3754 6546 to book.

the many haunts of london

If you believe all the stories, London is absolutely infested with ghosts. From the Tower of London to the Underground, here are some of the more interesting ghouls:

- **BACON'S CHICKEN:** Near the spot where Francis Bacon first put his idea of refrigeration to the test, a featherless, panicky chicken phantom, presumably the thing he refrigerated, has been known to roam.
- **THE PHARAOH IN THE TUBE:** The British Museum once had a Tube stop of the same name. However, it closed down in 1933, and if you believe the rumors, the reason was the presence of an escaped museum Egyptian. And that's not the end of the story—later, the comedy/thriller film *Bulldog Jack* included a secret tunnel from the station to the Egyptian room at the museum. The very night the film was released, two women disappeared from Holborn, the next station over from where the British Museum stop used to be.
- **THE SUBTERRANEANS:** Though not technically a ghost story, it's still disturbing: the idea that a group of Londoners who took to living in the subway tunnels have since mutated into half-wild humans who eat discarded junk food and the occasional solo traveler.
- **WAX PHANTOMS:** The Chamber of Horrors at Madame Tussaude's Wax Museum, which boasts replicas of dictators and the decapitated, is regularly reported to be haunted by the spirits of the models (as if a room full of bloody wax heads isn't creepy enough). Some say the perfectly coiffed hair on the wax head of Hitler grows noticeably!

CHELSEA

SAATCHI ART GALLERY — ART GALLERY

Duke of York Sq. — 020 7811 3085 www.saatchigallery.co.uk

It's rare to find a free gallery of this caliber. The rooms are cavernous and bright, providing ample space for each installation. The gallery focuses on contemporary art, all taken from Charles Saatchi's collection. If you see something you really like, be sure to check out the shop where many of the works are condensed into pocket-sized forms. There are three to four shows a year, and the pieces run the gamut from paintings, to sculptures, to really frightening installations of plaster people hunched in corners. If you really want to experience the Saatchi Gallery, stand next to one of the wax/plaster humanoid sculptures and argue with it. Sure, it's weird, but is it art?

Sloane Sq. Go straight once out of the Tube and continue onto King's Rd. Free as the wind. Open M-F 10am-5:50pm, Su-Sa 10am-5:45pm.

CHELSEA PHYSIC GARDENS BOTANICAL GARDENS

66 Royal Hospital Rd. 020 7352 5646 www.chelseaphysicgarden.co.uk

The physic gardens are some of the oldest botanic gardens in Europe. Established in 1673 by a society of apothecaries, the gardens contain pharmaceutical and perfumery plant beds, tropical plant greenhouses, Europe's oldest rock garden, and a total of 5,000 different plants. The garden was also important to the establishment of the tea industry in India, but apart from that, they're simply beautiful, peaceful, and well worth a visit.

Sloane Sq. Left onto Lower Sloane St.; right onto Royal Hospital Rd. i Call ahead to arrange wheelchair-accessible visits. Free guided tours, depending on availability of guides. £8, children, students, and the unemployed £5, under 5 free. Open Apr 1-Oct 31 W-F noon-5pm, Su noon-6pm.

CHELSEA OLD CHURCH HISTORIC CHURCH

64 Cheyne Walk 020 7795 1019 www.chelseaoldchurch.org.uk

Though this church was bombed like so many others in 1941, the story of its rebuilding is slightly different than most; parishioners simply picked up many of the pieces of destroyed plaques and monuments and put them back together, with the cracks and rough edges serving as delicate reminders of the war. The church has also played host to several celebrity worshippers. Henry VIII is rumored to have married Jane Seymour here, while Queen Elizabeth I, "Bloody" Mary, and Lady Jane Gray, the nine-day queen, worshipped here. Henry James also frequented the church, and Thomas Moore prayed in the chapel that is named after him. In 1958, the church was reconsecrated and opened by the Queen Mother. This quiet, removed church isn't an obvious sight, but it rewards those willing to look closely.

Sloane Sq. Left onto Lower Sloane St., right onto Royal Hospital Rd., and right onto Cheyne Walk. i Wheelchair-accessible. Free. Open Tu-Th 2-4pm, Su open for services: Holy Communion 8am, children's service 10am, matins 11am.

ST. LUKE'S GARDENS PARK

Sydney St.

Only one street removed from the bustle of King's Rd., St. Luke's Gardens feels a world apart. Rose gardens of pink, red, white, and yellow fragrant roses arranged in open circles flourish in the summer, lending a sweet fragrance to the whole park. A large mulberry tree in the center of the park casts a shadow over the benches arranged in a semi-circle around it. On the side of the park sits St. Luke's, a magnificent Gothic church. As it is in a quiet part of town, the park can be safely enjoyed while it's light out.

Sloane Sq. Go down King's Rd. away from the Tube. Take a right onto Sydney St. Open daily 7:30am-dusk.

NATIONAL ARMY MUSEUM MUSEUM GALLERY

Royal Hospital Rd. 020 7730 0717 www.nam.ac.uk

Yet another museum with far too many plaster-people for its own good, the National Army Museum answers the question on everybody's mind: what are British soldiers wearing? There are funny hats galore, and the museum is packed with information on British military conquests, even if most of it is directed toward a younger audience. The true gems of this museum are W. Siborn's expansive, 420 sq. ft., 172-year-old model of the battle of Waterloo, and the skeleton of Marengo, Napoleon's favorite horse. Of course, there's the colo(u)ring station and the guns that you can "load" and "fire," but if you want to see what a real gun is like, you might have to wrestle one off an **actual guard.**

Sloane Sq. Left onto Lower Sloane St., right onto Royal Hospital Rd. There is also an art gallery. Free. Open daily 10am-5:30pm.

GAGLIARDI ART GALLERY — ART GALLERY

509 King's Rd. ☎020 7352 3663 www.gagliardi.org

Run by the Gagliardi family, the gallery showcases contemporary artists painting in styles that include abstract, Surrealist, figurative, and landscapes, among others. Works on display range from the late 20th century to the early 21st century. All the art is for sale and goes for about half as much as it would in the galleries on the West End.

Sloane Sq. Exit the Tube and go straight down Sloane Sq. The street slanting gently left is King's Rd. If you don't want to walk the road (it's manageable but long), the following buses service the area: 11, 19, 22, 211, 319. Open daily 1-7pm.

FLYING COLOURS — ART GALLERY

6 Burnsall St. ☎020 7351 5558 www.flyingcoloursgallery.com

When most people commemorate their trip to London, they buy Big Ben keychains, squeezable Teddy Bears that bark "Mind the gap!" and, for those Americans between 17 and 21, Svedka in the duty-free. If you want to step up your souvenir purchasing, check out Flying Colours. All the art is contemporary British, with a specialty in Scottish painting. Exhibitions change once a month. Even if you aren't going to buy, the paintings are still worth seeing.

Sloane Sq. Go down King's Rd. away from the Tube. Take a right onto Burnsall St. Open M-F 10:30am-5:30pm.

HOLBORN AND CLERKENWELL

THE TEMPLE — SIGHT

Between Essex St. and Temple Ave. ☎020 7427 4820 www.templechurch.com

The Temple was a complex of buildings established by the Knights Templar, catapulted into stardom by *The Da Vinci Code*. Established as the English seat for the order in 1185, the buildings were leased to lawyers after the order ended in 1307, and the site is now devoted to legal and parliamentary offices. The medieval church, gardens, and Middle Temple Hall are open to the public. The 1681 Fountain Court is a place for peaceful reflection and was featured in Dickens's *Martin Chuzzlewit*. Also beautiful is Elm Court, the small garden enclosed by stone structures. Originally used as a stable for the Knights Templar, Middle Temple Hall became a bit more distinguished later when Shakespeare acted in the premiere of *Twelfth Night* there. This historic building—which survived WWII—is an excellent example of 16th- and 17th-century Elizabethan architecture with its beautiful double hammer beam roof. On the night of his return from the Spanish Indies in 1586, Sir Francis Drake came to Middle Temple Hall. Today, the temple houses a table known as the "Cup-board" made from the hatch of his ship.

Temple. Go to the Victoria Embankment, turn left and turn left at Temple Ln. 1hr. tours Oct-July T-F at 11am; book tours ahead of time. You can book to stay for lunch if you are appropriately dressed. Church and tours free. Middle Temple Hall open M-F 10am-noon and 3-4pm, except when in use. Su service 11:15am. Hours for church vary, but are posted oustide. Organ recitals W 1:15-1:45pm. No services in Aug and Sept.

ROYAL COURTS OF JUSTICE — SIGHT

Where Strand becomes Fleet St. ☎020 7947 7684

This stunning Neo-Gothic structure was designed by G.E. Street and was opened by Queen Victoria on December 4, 1882. It is home to more than 1000 rooms, and 3.5 mi. of corridor. Justice had better be pretty swift with all the walking it takes to get anywhere in this building. Supposedly, a tributary of the Fleet River, the namesake of Fleet St., runs beneath the building. It is also famous for its large and beautiful mosaic. Guests can sit in the back two rows of the court rooms and listen to the proceedings if court is in session. Order!

Temple. Right onto Temple Pl., left onto Arundel St., right onto Strand. There is a sign with wheelchair accessibility and routes in the entrance to the main building off the Strand. Tours (usually on 1st and 3rd Tu of every month) £10; should be booked in advance. Open M-F 9am-4:30pm.

ST. JOHN'S SQUARE
SIGHT, MUSEUM

St. John's Ln. 020 7324 4005 www.sja.org.uk/museum

This was originally the site of the 12th-century Priory of St. John, former seat of the Knights Hospitallers. The foundation of a round church in the Norman style, built by the Order of St. John, is marked in the square by gray cobblestones. The crypt of the original church is still intact and was probably used as a chapter hall for the early order. William Weston, the last prior, who"died of a broken heart" in the face of the dissolution, has an effigy in the crypt, near an effigy of a Spanish knight of the order who died in 1575 sculpted by famous sculptor Esteban Jordan. The crypt is one of the few surviving examples of Norman architecture in London and is well worth seeing. The fantastic gate which guards the square was originally built in 1504 as the entrance to the priory. (Shakespeare had his plays licensed by the master of the revels at the priory, and William Hogarth lived in the gate, where his father ran a Latin-only cafe.) The order of St. John bought back the gate in 1874, and the modern order of St. John has been an order of chivalry headed by Her Majesty since 1888.

Farringdon. Left onto Cowcross St., left onto St. John St., left onto St. John's Ln. Free. The museum will be finished in fall 2011. Hours to be determined. Check the website. Tours will reopen in Sept.

mind the doors

In many other countries, the train doors for Underground equivalents are pushovers. If you're having a bad hair day and your sleeve is caught in the sensor, the train won't go anywhere. However, things are different in England, and the Brits' gentility is not shared by their train doors. If you try and get on a packed train as the doors are closing, you may wind up leaving your bag and half a limb behind you.

THE CHARTERHOUSE
SIGHT

North on Charterhouse Sq. 020 7253 9503 www.thecharterhouse.org

Built by Thomas Sutton in 1611 on a burial ground for victims of the Black Death, the Charterhouse was a widely acclaimed school and home for the elderly. While the school moved elsewhere, it remains a functional senior citizens home. In 1371, it was a Carthusian priory, but its religious functions were expunged during the Reformation. Elizabeth I stayed at the Charterhouse immediately prior to her coronation.

Barbican. Left onto Carthusian St., right onto Charterhouse Sq. Partially wheelchair-accessible. Tour £10; Apr-Aug W at 2:15pm; must be booked in advance. To book, send a letter with 3 dates and a check to "Charterhouse." Include a contact number and a self-addressed envelope. Send to Tour Bookings Charterhouse Sutton's Hospital, Charterhouse Sq., London EC1M 6AN.

KENSINGTON AND EARL'S COURT

VICTORIA AND ALBERT MUSEUM
GALLERY MUSEUM

Cromwell Rd. 020 7942 2000 www.vam.ac.uk

The V and A is one of the most bizarre and all-encompassing museums out there.

Originally founded because the director, Henry Cole, wanted to promote different design ideas to the British public, the V and A has examples of styles from all around the world and is as much about the making of things as it is about the artifacts themselves. The many galleries include **Asia, Europe, The British Galleries, Modern,** and **The Fashion Gallery.** With such specific topics, who could possibly be interested in the collections? The **Asia** gallery features everything from ornate, gold Buddhist shrines to traditional suits of armor. Especially popular is the beautiful Iranian Ardabil Carpet, which is lit for 10min. every hour. The **Europe** gallery features the gorgeous Hereford Screen, which is 11m long and 10.5m high, and depicts Christ's Ascension. The British Galleries showcase the ever-popular Great Bed of Ware, which, for a bed, was a remarkably big deal back in 1596 when the first mention of it was made. The **Materials and Techniques** gallery details different techniques of art-making. The stained glass collection on the thirrd floor is not to be missed, nor are sketches by Matisse. Those looking for education on the arts or art-making can find it in the **Lecture Theatre** or the famous **National Art Library,** which houses some of Dickens's manuscripts and da Vinci's sketches (register online to see these). When you enter the main rotunda, be sure to look out for the Rotunda Chandelier by Dale Chihuly. It's pretty hard to miss.

South Kensington. Take a right onto Thurloe Pl. and turn left on Exhibition Rd. The museum is to your right across Cromwell Rd. Wheelchair-accessible guides available at the Grand Entrance Information Desk. Exhibit on "Diaghileu and the Golden Age of the Ballets Russes 1909-1929" from Sept 25-Jan 9. Free, with the exception of the special exhibitions which are generally £6-£10. Open M-Th 10am-5:45pm, F 10am-10pm, Sa-Su 10am-5:45pm. National Art Library Tu-Th 10am-5:30pm, F 10am-6:30pm, Sa 10am-5:30pm. Free daily tours available; look at screens in entrances for times.

SCIENCE MUSEUM — MUSEUM

Exhibition Rd., South Kensington — 087 0870 4868 — www.sciencemuseum.org.uk

The Science Museum is an exciting look at the history and cutting edge of the discipline. Featuring tons of cool, interactive displays (granted, many of these are directed at children), the Science Museum has myriad valuable and historic artifacts from all areas of science; including many that you won't even realize you wanted to see until you've seen them. A Newcomen-type atmospheric engine dwarfs its surroundings in the Energy Gallery, and the space galleries remind visitors of all ages of the excitement of space travel through their history of rockets and artifacts like a V2 Engine from 1944, and things like wrist watches used on the Apollo missions. Learn about Charles Babbage English, the man responsible for mechanical calculators and shoes for walking on water (conspiracy theorists will be disappointed once reminded that he lived long after Jesus). And if you were wondering what an inventor's brain looks like (we hope this isn't on your mind), they have one in a **jar!** Charles Babbage English's, in fact. If you want to appreciate how far we've come, pay ERNIE 1 a visit. The Electronic Random Number Indicator Equipment computer is the size of most dorm rooms, and was used to generate random numbers so premium bond owners could win prizes. From brains in jars to men on the moon, the Science Museum has it all.

South Kensington. Take a right onto Thurloe Pl. and turn left onto Exhibition Rd. The museum is to your left just past the Natural History Museum. A climate change exhibit will open in Nov. The museum also features a popular IMAX cinema. Tickets to IMAX 3D shows £8, concessions and children £6.25. Open daily 10:00am-6pm. Last admission at 5:30pm, but it starts closing at 5:40pm.

ST. MARY ABBOTS — CHURCH

High St. Kensington — 020 7937 5136 — www.stmaryabbotschurch.org

This gorgeous and silent church sits on a site where Christians have worshipped for 1000 years. Designed in 1873 by a famous Victorian architect, Sir George Gilbert, the church is known for its beautiful and simple stained glass by Clayton and Bell and the scorch marks of the 1944 bombing that are visible in the pews. Fridays from 1-2pm musicians from the Royal Academy of Music perform for free.

⊖High St. Kensington. Right onto Kensington High St., left onto Kensington Church St. M 8:30am-6pm, T 8:30am-6pm, W-F 7:10am-6pm, Sa 9:40am-6pm, Su 8am-6pm.

church concerts

For free access to churches, be on the lookout for services and concerts. St. Paul's (p.43) gives free organ recitals every Sunday from 4:45-5:15pm, as does St. Stephen Walbrook (p.47) on Fridays at 12:30pm, but access to that church is already free.

NATURAL HISTORY MUSEUM — MUSEUM

Cromwell Road — ☎020 7942 5011 www.nhm.ac.uk

Sure, the museum may be more directed at kids, but who doesn't love a moving T-Rex? Known as the "Cathedral of the Animals," the Natural History Museum houses exhibitions on everything from animal anatomy to histories of scientific research. The Darwin Centre has more than 20 million species in jars. Dinosaurs rule the museum, and the moving T-Rex is especially popular. Watch the parents' faces as they unwittingly lead their kids into the Human Biology section, featuring a red-lit walk-in womb (Freud would have a field day) with a terrifyingly large fetus, and aptly entitled "MORE ABOUT THE PLACENTA." The museum is pretty simple and easy to navigate, so come for a low-investment, reasonable-return trip.

⊖South Kensington. Take a right onto Thurloe Pl. and turn left on Exhibition Rd. The museum is to your left across Cromwell Rd. i Book early for special tours of Darwin's special collections. $ Free. Special exhibits are around £8, and students get discounts. Open daily 10am-5:50pm. Last entry 5:30pm.

KNIGHTSBRIDGE AND BELGRAVIA

APSLEY HOUSE — HISTORICAL SIGHT, MUSEUM GALLERY

Hyde Park Corner — ☎020 7499 5676 www.english-heritage.org.uk

Named for Baron Apsley, the house later known as "No.1, London" was bought in 1817 by the Duke of Wellington, whose heirs still occupy a modest suite on the top floor. The house is a stunning architectural triumph, from the gilded mirrors to the gilded oval spiral staircase. Perhaps the most fantastic of all the valuable collections in the house is Wellington's art collection, much of which he received from monarchs around Europe after the Battle of Waterloo. One of the most sought after pieces is Velazquez's beautiful *The Water Seller of Seville*, which he painted in 1600. Throughout the house you can find various trinkets, such as a silver-gilt dessert plate bearing Napoleon's arms, the key to the city of Pamplona (granted after the Duke captured the city), the death masks of Wellington and Napoleon, and a stunning 6.7m Egyptian service set, given by Napoleon to Josephine as a divorce present. Scholars maintain that the dessert service was meant as a mean joke about Josephine's weight. It's huge.

⊖Hyde Park Corner. i Arch is wheelchair-accessible; house is not. Complimentary audio tours. June 18th is Wellington Day, so check for special events. $ £6, joint ticket with Wellington Arch £7.40; concessions £5.10/6.30; children £3/3.70; family joint £18.50. Open W-Su Apr-Oct 11am-5pm; Nov-Mar 11am-4pm. Last entry 30min. before close.

SERPENTINE BOATING LAKE
LAKE BOATING

Hyde Park ☎020 7262 1330 www.theboathouselondon.co.uk

Created in memory of Queen Caroline between 1727 and 1731, the Serpentine Boating Lake is one of the most beautiful parts of Hyde Park. Rented boats drift lazily across the placid waters as fat waterfowl battle it out on the shore for pieces of bread. Boats can be rented and taken out for any amount of time. Be sure to check out the nearby Rose Garden.

Hyde Park Corner. Hyde Park. Pedal boats and row boats £7 per person per 30min., £9 per person per hr. Open daily Jan-Nov 10am-6pm (earlier in low season). Stays open later depending on weather. Boats don't go out if it's raining. Closed in Dec.

THE WELLINGTON ARCH
HISTORICAL SIGHT

Hyde Park Corner ☎020 7930 2726

Commissioned by King George IV and built between 1828 and 1830 as a back gate to Buckingham Palace, the Wellington Arch is a famous London landmark. Visitors are treated to a history of the arch, which doesn't quite merit the cost, and then a reasonable view from the observation deck, which is more or less tree-level with Hyde Park. The arch was originally topped with a large statue of the Duke of Wellington, but he was taken down in 1883. In 1912, a new statue took its place. The current statue is Quadriga, the angel of Peace, descending on the chariot of war driven by youth. It's an interesting commentary on British society's evolution, but the exhibition and view are most worth it if you also get the well-priced joint ticket with the Apsley House.

Hyde Park Corner. £3.70, joint ticket with Apsley House £7.40, concessions £3.10/6.30; child £1.90/3.70, family joint £18.50. Open W-Su Apr-Sept 10am-5pm; Oct-Mar 10am-4pm. Last entry 30min. before close.

BROMPTON ORATORY
CHURCH

Brompton Rd. ☎020 7808 0900 www.bromptonoratory.com

Built between 1880 and 1884, the Brompton Oratory is named after its founders, the Oratorians. Its nave, wider than St. Paul's, is breathtaking. The architecture of this still-functional church is marble-packed and filled with Baroque flourishes, as well as Soviet secrets: the KGB used the oratory as a drop point for secret messages during the Cold War.

Knightsbridge. Left onto Brompton Rd. i Wheelchair-accessible at side entrance to the left of the church. Free. Open daily 6:30am-8pm. Services: M-F mass at 7, 8, 10am, 12:30, 6pm (Latin); Sa 7, 8, 10am, 6pm.

MARYLEBONE AND REGENT'S PARK

THE REGENT'S PARK
PARK

Regent's Park ☎020 7486 7905 www.royalparks.org.uk

In 1811, the Prince Regent commissioned the parks as private gardens, and hired **John Nash** to design them. However, in 1841, the parks were opened to the public, and the city lives all the better for it. Locals, pigeons, thirty couples of herons, and tourists alike frolic among the 10,000 wild flowers and 50 acres of pitches and courts. **Queen Mary's Garden** houses the national collection of delphiniums as well as a gorgeous collection of 30,000 roses. It is also home to an interesting strain of pink flower known as **Sexy Rexy.** The park's popular open-air theater is the setting for all kinds of shows, the screams from the more dramatic performances intermingling with those of children deprived too long of **ice cream.** The Gardens of **St. John's Lodge** are behind one of the eight villas on the park, and serve as a place for quiet meditation beneath the gorgeous latticed archways—a sort of secret garden which also affords a peek into the back of St. John's Lodge. Be aware that security's tight. Also, be sure to check if the grass is greener on his side of the fence. The **Winfield House** just off the outer circle is the home of the US ambassador.

Regent's Park. Call 020 7486 8117 for information on the deck chairs. Book plays through www.openairtheatre.com. Deck chair £1.50 per hr., £4 per 3hr., £7 per day. Boats £6.50 per 1hr., £4.85 per 1½hr. Park open daily 5am-dusk. Boating lake open Mar-Oct 10:30am-7pm.

THE WALLACE COLLECTION — GALLERY

Manchester Sq. — 030 7563 9552 www.wallacecollection.org

Housed in the palatial **Hereford House,** the Wallace Collection features an array of paintings, porcelain, and armor collected by over five generations of the Wallace family and bequeathed to the nation by **Sir Richard Wallace** in 1897. The mansion's stunning collection is rendered even more dazzling by its grand gilded setting. The ground floor's four **Armoury Galleries** boast scads of richly decorated weapons and burnished suits of armor while the **State Rooms** hold a collection of sumptuous Sèvres porcelain. The East Galleries feature 17th-century masterpieces by **Van Dyck, Rembrandt, Rubens, Ruisdael, Velazquez, Titian** and **Gainsborough** within the **Great Gallery.** One of the collection's most celebrated pieces, Frans Hals's *The Laughing Cavalier* is in here as well.

Marble Arch. Left onto Oxford St., left on Duke St., right onto Manchester Sq. Private tours W, Sa, Su 11:30am and 3pm; call for details. Gallery free. Suggested donation £5. Audio tours £4. Open daily 10am-5pm.

THE CITY OF LONDON

Most stereotypical "London" sights are located here and can't be missed—even if having a camera slung around your neck is practically required for entrance.

SAINT PAUL'S CATHEDRAL — CHURCH

St. Paul's Churchyard — 020 7246 8350 www.stpauls.co.uk

Entering Saint Paul's Cathedral and not taking the Lord's name in vain is a challenge. Like many churches in the area, Saint Paul's was destroyed in the Great Fire of London. Christopher Wren's masterpiece is the fourth cathedral on the site, with the first building dating to 604 CE. From the start, Wren wanted to include the fantastic dome that is now visible throughout London, but the Church of England was hesitant to include a piece of architecture that was characteristically Roman Catholic. Ultimately, Wren won.

INTERIOR. The first thing you see upon entering the Cathedral is the nave. The baptismal font stands next to an elaborately designed wax candle in the south part of the nave. If you can pull your eyes away from the dome, which was painted by Sir James Thornhill, look out for the terrifyingly huge memorial to the **Duke of Wellington** (on your left in the north aisle as you walk through the nave) and William Holman Hunt's *The Light of the World* which can be found in the Middlesex Chapel, a chapel set aside for private prayer dedicated to the members of the Middlesex regimen of the British army. Also look out for Henry Moore's strikingly modern *Mother and Child* sculpture as well as the memorial to American and British service men in WWII.

SCALING THE HEIGHTS. We know what you're thinking—yes, you are allowed to climb to the top of the dome. After 257 short, dizzyingly tight wooden steps, guests find the Whispering Gallery, a seating area around the inner ring of the dome where, under the right conditions, you can whisper and be heard on the other side. Many people try this at the same time, which makes standing at the rim of Wren's magnificent dome feel a bit like one of the scarier whisper segments in *Lost,* but it's worth giving this acoustic novelty a try. The experience of climbing to the top is greatly enhanced if you make the journey while a choir sings in the nave; the acoustics in the Whispering Gallery are incredible. After 376 steps, visitors can climb out onto the Stone Gallery which is open-air, low-stress, and thoroughly enjoyable. Then it's another 152 steps to the Golden

Gallery, an open-air, super high look out onto the city. The army used this gallery in the second World War to spot enemy planes coming from up to 10 miles away. The only drawback to the view is that you can't see the grandeur of St. Paul's itself.

PLUMBING THE DEPTHS. A veritable who's who of famous Britons reside in the loins of St. Paul's. Descend beneath the cathedral to find the tombs and memorials of **Captain John Cooke, Horatio Nelson, Florence Nightingale, the Duke of Wellington** (whose massive tomb is footed by sleeping stone lions), **William Blake, Henry Moore,** and finally **Christopher Wren.** Wren's inconspicuous tomb (to the right of the OBE Chapel) is inscribed *"Lector, si monumentum requiris circumspice"* which translates to "Reader, if you seek his monument, look around." Saint Paul's Cathedral is jaw-droppingly magnificent; there could be no better monument to its visionary architect than the simple words etched on his tomb.

*⊖St. Paul's. There are signs outside the station that will lead you to the Cathedral. **i** Guided tours are 1½hr., and they occur at 10:45, 11:15am, 1:30, and 2pm; £3, children £1. A free multi-media tour will be provided starting mid-July-early Sept 2010. Audio tours available in 8 languages including English £4). £12.50, students £9.50, seniors £11, children £4.50; family (2 adults, 2 kids) £29.50; group rates (10+) adults £11.50, students £8.50, seniors £10.50, children £4. M-Sa 8:30am-4:00pm (last ticket sold). Least crowded early in the day. Get in for free (though you'll have limited access) at one of the church services; 7:30am matins; 8am. 12:30pm Holy Communion; 5pm evensong. Free organ recitals every Su from 4:45-5:15pm.*

MUSEUM OF LONDON

MUSEUM

sacred sights

Many sights will self-advocate based on their superior views of the city. In our opinion, the view from the Golden Gallery atop **St. Paul's Cathedral** trumps all others. There's plenty of room, it's higher than the Monument, and it's more central than the Tower Bridge.

By the London Wall ☎020 7001 9844 www.museumoflondon.org.uk

The Museum of London is an exhaustive celebration of the city, tracing its history from the pre-Roman days, through the fall of that empire (too bad the city's no longer known as Londinium), up to the present through a series of timelines, walk-in exhibits, and artifacts. Among the fascinating pieces of history on display are a walk-in replica of a London Saxon house from the mid-1000s, a beautiful model of the original St. Paul's cathedral, a taxi from 1908, and Beatlemania paraphernalia. Relatively compact for its sheer scope, the Museum of London yields tremendous bang for your buck, especially because it's free!

*⊖St. Pauls. Go up St. Martins and Aldersgate. **i** 45min. tours at 11am, noon, 3, and 4pm. Free. Open M-F 10am-6pm.*

POTTERS FIELDS PARK

PARK

Tooley St. towards Tower Bridge ☎020 7407 4702 pottersfields.co.uk

Providing wide patches of grass for denizens of the park to stretch out on, as well as breathtaking views of Tower Bridge and the Thames, Potters Fields Park is an oasis in such a busy city. It's at the heart of London, but far removed from its bustle. City Hall sits within the park and is just as architecturally magnificent as Tower Bridge. After seeing the park, you may want to check out more of the waterfront and do some shopping in **Hay's Galleria.** Also, be sure to notice the **HMS Belfast,** which is just down the river from the park; a ticket is required to board the vessel.

London Bridge. Walk down Tooley St. towards Tower Bridge. Go through Hay's Galleria and walk along the river towards Tower Bridge. Free.

TOWER BRIDGE SIGHT

Tower Bridge 020 7403 3761 www.towerbridge.org.uk

If Fergie had gone to the Tower Bridge exhibition, she would have known that bascule bridges come down more often than London Bridge. Built between 1886 and 1894, Tower Bridge was created because London Bridge had become too crowded. It is a bascule bridge, meaning that, if you're lucky, you'll get to see it rise (and then come down). The exhibition is enjoyable, though if you're afraid of heights, it might not be for you. Hear fun facts about the bridge as well as enchanting anecdotes such as the story of a 1952 double-decker bus that accidentally jumped the bridge while it was rising—clearly the driver never heard the phrase, "Mind the gap." The bridge is less of a tourist trap than the Tower of London, and just as engaging. Of course, the stunning architecture and eye-popping colors of the bridge can be enjoyed for free.

Tower Hill. Follow signs to Tower Bridge. £7, concessions £5 ages 5-15 £3, under 5 free; 1 adult and 2 children £11; 2 adults and 1 child £14; 2 adults and 2 children £16; 2 adults and 3-4 children £18. Open daily Apr 1-Sept 30 10am-5:30pm; Oct 1-Mar 31 9:30am-5pm.

GUILDHALL ART GALLERY HISTORICAL SIGHT, ART GALLERY

Between Basinghall St. and Coleman St. 020 7332 3700 www.guildhall-art-gallery.org.uk

The entrance to the gallery is through fantastic **Guildhall Yard,** which feels isolated from the city. The gallery specializes in Victorian art but also has a rotating exhibit of art from all periods relating to London (they're currently running an exhibit on the Royal Post). "I'm sold!" you say. But wait. You haven't heard the best part! While constructing the gallery in 1988, archaeologists uncovered an amphitheater from Londinium (Roman London). The intact portions from the site are left as they were found beneath the gallery in an impressive exhibition. Also included in the exhibition is a display of a Roman drainage system.

Bank. Go up Princes St., take left on Gresham St. and right on Basinghall St. Guildhall Yard will be on your right. £2.50, free after 3:30pm and all day F; concessions for students, seniors, and unemployed £1. Open M-Sa 10am-5pm, last entry at 4:30pm; Su noon-4pm, last entry 3:45pm.

TOWER OF LONDON SIGHT

Between Tower Hill and the Thames 084 4482 7777 www.hrp.org.uk/toweroflondon

In its 1000-year history, the Tower of London has been a fortress, a royal palace, a prison, a zoo, a mint, the house of the first royal observatory, and a tourist trap. If tourists were an invading army back in the day of William the Conqueror, he would have surrendered instantly. The Tower has tours led by "Beefeaters," the men and women who guard and live within the tower.

TRAITOR'S GATE. Originally named "Watergate," Traitor's Gate was the passage from the Tower to the River Thames through which prisoners entered the tower.

BYWARD AND WAKEFIELD TOWERS. Byward Tower is part of the Tower's intriguing, if somewhat gimmicky, attempt at living history. Byward Tower currently houses many of the Tower's more than 100 residences. Wakefield Tower is near the home of the famous six ravens. The legend of the ravens claims that if they fly away the white tower will crumble and disaster will befall the monarchy.

BLOODY TOWER. The tower was built in 1225, and the most famous anecdote surrounding it is one of bizarre death (as are most stories surrounding the Tower). Prince Edward V and Richard, Duke of York, were suffocated by pillows in the tower, and their bodies weren't found until 191 years after their deaths. This tale was the inspiration for Shakespeare's *Richard III.*

THE WHITE TOWER. Built by William of Normandy in 1078 as the first structure of the Tower of London, the White Tower was once a royal palace with the top floor reserved for kings and queens, the floor below housing the servants, and the basement serving as a dungeon (and guest house!). Part of it is built on the Roman city wall of London. The White Tower currently houses the "Royal Armoury: Fit for a King" exhibit which features armor from the Normans to the Windsors, with notable sections that feature Henry VIII's personal armor. Be sure to take note of his enhanced codpiece, as well as the chuckling British and cackling Americans pointing at it, while their kids try to figure out what all the fuss is about.

JEWEL HOUSE. The Jewel House contains all of the regalia used for the coronation of British royalty and boasts jewels with enough glitter to induce an epileptic seizure. The gems are the focal point of many people's trips to the tower, so try to go earlier in the day, if possible. Inside, you'll find the sovereign's scepter highlighted by a cross with the world's largest perfect diamond in the world, the **First Star of Africa** (530.2 carats).

TOWER GREEN. The Green is a lovely grass area at the center of the tower, outside the Chapel Royal of St. Peter and Vincula. The eight friends of the monarch who were beheaded by the government had the good fortune to get their heads lopped off on the Tower Green. Whatever happened here, it did **wonders for the grass.**

OUTSIDE THE TOWER. Outside the tower lies **Tower Hill,** the primary execution site. The last execution (that of Lord Lovat) was held here in 1747. Every night for the last 700 years, the Ceremony of the Keys has been performed.

Tower Hill. Buy tickets at the Tube stop or at the Welcome Center, as these places tend to be less crowded. To get a ticket to the Ceremony of the Keys, you must send an application with the names of everyone you hope to bring and two possible dates of attendance at least two months in advance (earlier if you're attending in the summer) inside an envelope with proper stamps (or at least two coupon-response international) to "Ceremony of the Keys Office, Tower of London, LONDON, EC3N 4AB, Great Britain." The Ceremony is free, but you need tickets, and groups are limited to six people max. £17; student, senior, and disabled £14.50; children under 5 free; family (1-2 adults and up to 6 kids) £47. Audio tours available in 9 different languages; £4, students £3. An Individual Membership gives you unlimited, year-round access to all the Royal Palaces for £41, family membership £80. Portions of the site wheelchair-accessible. Mar 1-Oct 31 M 10am-5:30pm, Tu-Su 9am-5:30pm, last ticket sold at 5pm. Nov 1-Feb 28 M-Tu 10am-4:30pm, W-Sa 9am-5:30pm, Su 10am-4:30pm last entry sold at 4pm. Cafe open M 10:30am-5pm, Tu-Sa 9:30am-5pm, Su 10:30am-5pm. Ceremony of the Keys daily 9:30pm.

CLOCKMAKERS' MUSEUM

MUSEUM

Inside Guildhall Library off Aldermanbury ☎020 7332 1868

The one-room Clockmakers' Museum is sort of like the interior of Doc Brown's house from *Back to the Future*, except with more clocks. Each clock, watch, sun dial, and chronometer from the 500 year history of clocks is explained either historically or technically by its accompanying pamphlet. For those less inclined to horological technology, the museum has famous watches and clocks, like the watch worn by Sir Edmund Hillary during his successful 1953 climb of Mount Everest and some of the first mass-produced watches. Worth a brief visit, if only to hear the sound of so many clocks ticking together.

St. Paul's. Go down Cheapside with your back to St. Paul's Cathedral. Turn left on King St., left on Gresham and right on Aldermanbury. Enter through the library. Free. M-Sa 9:30am-4:45pm. Closed Sa on bank holiday weekends.

SAINT MARY-LE-BOW

CHURCH

Cheapside, near Bow Ln. ☎020 7248 5139 www.stmarylebow.co.uk

Though the chapel dates back to 1080 when there was first a church on the site, the church has been restored several times. First, it was burned in the Great

Fire of London in 1666, but it was rebuilt by Christopher Wren. Then, it was bombed during World War II, rebuilt in its modern form, and reconsecrated in 1956. London lore says that if you're born within the sound of Bow bells (which used to ring the 9pm city curfew, signaling all the apprentices to stop working) you're a true cockney. The interior of the church is a masterpiece, filled with gorgeous gold-laced Corinthian columns.

St. Pauls. Walk down Cheapside away from St. Paul's Cathedral. Free. M-W 7am-6pm, Th 7am-6:30pm, F 7am-4pm.

THE MONUMENT SIGHT

Monument ☎020 7626 2717 www.themonument.info

Built between 1671 and 1677, the Monument stands in memory of the Great Fire of London that burned most of the city in 1666. At 202 ft. tall, with an inner shaft containing 311 stairs that must be climbed in order to reach the breathtaking open-air top floor, the Monument is what your Stairmaster would look like in the pre-mechanical age. If you were to lay the tower on its side pointing in a certain direction, it would land on the spot where the fire started. It would also cause mass hysteria. It is the only non-ecclesiastical Christopher Wren building, though some scholars maintain that it was built to worship **rock hard thighs**. Enjoy the view from the top!

Monument. Get off the Tube and it will be directly in front of you as you exit the station. £3, concessions £2, children £1. Combined tickets available with the Tower Bridge exhibition. Combined prices: £8, concessions £5.50, children £3.50. Open daily 9:30am-5pm. Closed on Christmas and Boxing Day.

ST. STEPHEN WALBROOK CHURCH

39 Walbrook ☎020 7626 9000 www.ststephenwalbrook.net

You may wonder about the marshmallow-like object sitting in the center of the room, but this is merely Henry Moore's controversial idea of what an altar should look like. Rumored to have "the most perfectly proportioned interior in the world," St. Stephen Walbrook, a Saxon church originally built in the seventh century, is a beautiful Wren reconstruction. The church used to be bordered by a river, and the structure fights a continuous battle against gravity as it slips downward. Visit toward the end of the day during the summer to bask in the light that floods through the glass windows.

Mansion House. Take right onto Cannon St., then left onto Walbrook. i Eucharist is M at 1pm. Free. M-F 10am-4pm. Organ recitals F 12:30pm.

ST. MARY WOOLNOTH CHURCH

Intersection of King William and Lombard St. ☎020 7626 9701

This church is seated near the center of one of the busiest intersections in the City of London, and was restored by (who else?) Christopher Wren after the Great Fire of London. John Newton (the co-composer of Amazing Grace) was also a rector here from 1779-1807. St. Mary Woolnoth's is an undiscovered piece of history in a city full of crowded gems.

Bank. Intersection of King William and Lombard St. i Free meditation hr. W 6:30pm. Free. M-F 9:30am-4:30pm.

THE SOUTH BANK

IMPERIAL WAR MUSEUM MUSEUM

Lambeth Rd. ☎020 7416 5000 www.iwm.org.uk

Housed in what used to be the infamous Bedlam insane asylum, the Imperial War Museum is mad for history. The exhibits start out right with two massive naval guns guarding the entrance to the imposing building. The first room is cluttered with enough devices of war to make any general salivate. Highlights include a **Polaris A3 Missile,** the first submarine-launched missile, a full-size **German V2**

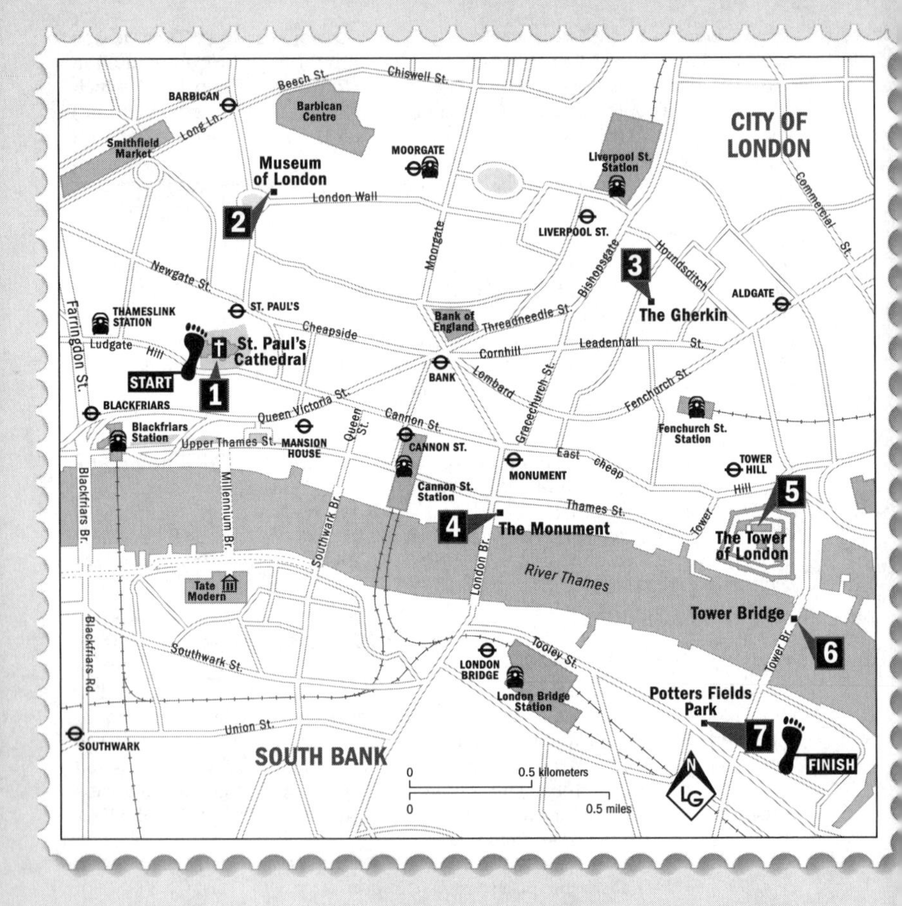

city of london

Let's be real. London's big, and you probably can't experience the entire city in one day. But that doesn't mean you can't experience the City of London in one day. Right in the heart of town, the "Square Mile" packs a ton into one single neighborhood. Back in the Middle Ages, it actually made up the entire British capital, and though many diverse, bustling neighborhoods have come to surround it, "The City" is still the financial and historical center of London today. With its own mayor and separate jurisdiction, The City of London even has sway over the Queen, who must ask permission of the Lord Mayor before entering. Lucky for you, visitors have easier access than Lizzie does, so you can grab your camera and head over there on the Tube. The City has some of London's best sights, so a walking tour won't necessarily be quick. Still, **Let's Go** has a simple plan for you to cover the City of London in seven easy stops.

1. ST. PAUL'S CATHEDRAL. Before you begin your walk through the City of London, get off the Tube at ⊖St. Paul's and follow the signs until you reach St. Paul's Cathedral, London's grandest and most beautiful church. In order to get an early start on your day through the "Square Mile" and avoid the church-going tourist crowds, try to arrive at St. Paul's before 10am. If you really want to catch a tour, the earliest is at 10:45am. If you're not struggling too hard with jet lag, climb to the Golden Gallery atop St. Paul's for the best views of London.

2. MUSEUM OF LONDON. Head north through Paternoster Sq. onto Edward St., which becomes Montague St. Follow it until you reach the roundabout where you'll find the Museum of London. For no money, you'll get the most in-depth lesson on the history of London, from the city's pre-Roman beginnings to its present-day culture. Our walking tour may last you just a day, but a 45min. tour at this museum will take you on a journey through a milenia or two.

3. THE GHERKIN. Walk west along London Wall until it becomes Wormwood St., which then becomes Camomile St. Make a right onto St. Mary Ave. and walk south two blocks. You've arrived at 30 St. Mary Ave., most commonly known as "The Gherkin." Sure, the rounded glass skyscraper may stick out like a sore thumb in the City of London, but it stands its ground among Wren's legendary architecture. Serving as one of London's financial centers, the Gherkin itself isn't open to the public, but be sure to stop and look up at this award-winning mod monument.

4. THE MONUMENT. Continue down St. Mary Ave. and turn right onto Leaderhead St. Then make a left onto Gracechurch St. and walk south until you cross Eastcheap onto Fish St. Hill. In the middle of the street, you'll find the Monument, a 202 ft. stone column commemorating the Great Fire of London in 1666. You can climb to the top for another great view of the city, but that daunting walk up the inner staircase isn't suited to those afraid of heights, enclosed spaces, or exercise.

5. THE TOWER OF LONDON. Walk south on Fish St. Hill and make a left onto Lower Thames St. Walk east several blocks until you reach the Tower of London, right beside the Thames. Though this fortress was once a prison, the scariest thing about it today are the tourists you'll come across when you visit. If you can survive them, you should have no fear being trapped in the Tower of London as you hang out with Beefeaters for an hour or so. The last tickets are sold at 4pm during low season and 5pm during high season, so be sure to get to the tower in time.

6. TOWER BRIDGE. Follow signs to Tower Bridge, directly to the east of the Tower of London. The iconic bascule bridge crossing the River Thames opens and closes daily, but you can get onto it until 5:30 pm during high season (low season 5pm). If you'd like to learn fun facts about the iconic bascule bridge, you'll enjoy the fun and inexpensive tour.

7. POTTERS FIELDS PARK. Once you've crossed Tower Bridge going south, turn right on Tower Bridge Rd. to reach Potters Fields Park. After a long day of walking and sight-seeing, take a breather and stretch out on its peaceful greens. The park offers the best views of the City of London, so you can take one last look at the capital's capital.

WALKING TOUR

Let's Go www.letsgo.com

Rocket, and the shell (not the inner mechanisms, luckily) of a **"Little Boy,"** the type of bomb detonated above Hiroshima. Luckily, the bomb is non-functional, but it gets unnerving when kids whack the casing. The third floor houses the expansive **Holocaust Exhibition.** This haunting exhibit traces the catastrophic injustice of WWII Nazi atrocities with cartographic precision and deep feeling, with miles of film exploring everything from the rhetoric of the Nazi party to a history of anti-Semitism. Of course, many visitors may feel like a visit to a museum would be unbalanced with only such light subject matter, and they'll take solace in the **Crimes Against Humanity** exhibition one floor down.

Art nuts will enjoy **"Breakthrough,"** the museum's fantastic art collection. The first floor houses the exciting, if sensational, "Secret War" exhibit of WWII spy gadgetry, providing a brief history of MI5 and the Special Operations Executive. The popular **Blitz Experience** and **Trench Experience** exhibits recreate the experience of hiding during an air raid and living in the trenches respectively.

Elephant and Castle. Turn right onto Elephant and Castle (roundabout), right onto St. George's Rd., and then left onto Lambeth Rd. Free. Special exhibits £5, students £4. Multimedia guides £3.50. Open daily 10am-6pm. The Blitz Experience daily schedule is downstairs. It lasts around 10min.

TATE MODERN — FAMOUS GALLERY, MODERN

53 Bankside — ☎020 7887 8008 www.tate.org.uk

Located in George Gilbert Scott's Brutalist old Bankside Power Station, Tate Modern defies traditional organizational methods, opting out of the chronological in favor of thematic organization. The permanent collection rotates through two floors. Those desperate to see one work in particular should check out the computers on the fifth floor, which enable users to scan through the entire collection.

Level 3 houses the **Material Gestures** gallery, which focuses mainly on post-war European and American art and showcases works by Monet, Francis Bacon and **Anish Kapoor.** Sculptures by Giacometti can also be found here. **Poetry and Dream,** an area centering on Surrealism and its associated themes, displays the work of **Dali** and **Picasso** among others.

On Level 5, **Energy and Process** looks at Arte Povera, the movement from the 1970s that used everyday materials and natural laws to create art. **States of Flux** focuses on cubism and futurism as well as other important modern movements, displaying the works of **Roy Lichtenstein, Robert Frank, Warhol,** and **Duchamp,** among others.

Southwark. Left onto Blackfriars Rd. Right onto Southwark St., left onto Sumner, left onto Holland St. Free. Multimedia guide £3.50, concessions £3. Open M-Th 10am-6pm, F-Sa 10am-10pm, Su 10am-6pm. Free 10min. talks given around the various galleries; check schedule signs for details.

THE HAYWARD GALLERY — GALLERY

South Bank Centre — ☎084 4847 9910 www.haywardgallery.org.uk

The Hayward Gallery was opened in 1968 and designed by a group of Brutalist architects. The Gallery has been showing cutting edge modern art in its galleries for years. Two to three shows run at once. Check online to see how the space is currently being used.

Waterloo. Head toward York Rd., turn right onto York Rd. and left onto Waterloo Rd. The gallery's left of the bridge and the signage in the center will help you find it. i Mostly wheelchair-accessible. £11, seniors £10, concessions £8, ages 12-18 £6.50, under 12 free. Open M-Su 10am-6pm, F 10am-10pm.

DESIGN MUSEUM — GALLERY

Shad Thames — ☎020 7940 8790 www.designmuseum.org

Though the museum has no permanent collection, it is consistently fascinating.

Featuring a range of installations from architecture to illustration, fashion, product design, and occasional retrospectives and competitions, the Design Museum is an excellent place to come think about the aesthetics of everyday life and to see those of the future.

⇞ ⊖Tower Hill. Cross Tower Bridge. Left onto Queen Elizabeth St., left onto Shad Thames. Ⓢ £8,50, students £5, concessions £6.50. ⏰ Open M-Su 10am-5:45pm. Last entry 30min. before close.

THE LONDON EYE

SIGHT

Minster Ct. ☎087 0990 8881 www.londoneye.com

Also known as the **Millenium Wheel,** the **London Eye** is one of the most popular tourist attractions in London. The massive Ferris wheel takes visitors on a 30min. ride, giving them unparalleled arial views of London. An exciting 4D movie experience opens the entire trip which, while gimmicky, is worth it.

⇞ ⊖Westminster. Cross the bridge heading toward the Eye. Ⓢ £17.95, seniors and disabled £14.30, ages 4-15 £9.50, under 4 free. 10% discount if you book online. ⏰ Hours vary. Call or check the website. In general, Oct-Mar daily 10am-8pm; Apr daily 10am-9pm; May-July daily M-Th 10am-9pm, F-Sa 10am-9:30pm, Su 10am-9pm; July-Aug daily 10am-9:30pm; Sept 10am-9pm.

SHAKESPEARE'S GLOBE

EXHIBITION, HISTORICAL SITE

21 New Globe Walk ☎020 7902 1500 www.shakespeares-globe.org

A recreation of the original **Globe Theatre** which burned down during a performance of *Henry VIII* in 1613—who's idea was it to fire a real cannon toward a thatched roof?—Shakespeare's Globe does a pretty accurate job of recreating the unique, open-air theater, with numerous exhibits and a tour on the history of Shakespeare and area theater. Though short on actual artifacts, the historical overview offered by the exhibit is fascinating and well-designed. Special booths allow visitors to speak lines with automated casts, and other booths enable visitors to hear iconic Shakespearean monologues read by famous actors.

*⇞ ⊖Southwark. Left onto Blackfriars Rd., right onto Southwark St., left onto Great Guildford, right onto Park St., left onto Emerson St. **i** For information on productions, see **Arts and Culture,** p. 87. Ⓢ Exhibition £5; exhibition and tour £10.50; exhibition and bankside tour £7.50, students £6.50, ages 5-15 £4.50, under 5 free. ⏰ Exhibition open daily 9am-5pm. Exhibition and bankside tours T-Sa 1-5pm, Su noon-5pm. Tours stop around 12:30pm, when there's a matinee performance.*

THE WEST END

THE NATIONAL GALLERY

GALLERY

Trafalgar Sq. ☎020 7747 2885 www.nationalgallery.org.uk

The National Gallery presides over **Trafalgar Square** and is nearly as impressive as the Square itself. Founded in 1824 and moved to its current location in 1838, the gallery encompasses all the major traditions of Western European art. The more recent **Sainsbury Wing** was opened in 1991, and it encompasses the 13th through 15th centuries. Often, visitors are in such a hurry to see the master works, that they traverse the main steps without looking at the floor. They are ignoring one of the most impressive artworks in the gallery, Boris Anrep's mosaics. The first landing depicts the awakening of the muses, the top landing depicts the modern virtues such as compassion, humor, open-mindedness, pursuit, wonder, and curiosity, all of which will be evoked in a thorough viewing of the gallery. The **West Vestibule** ponders art, astronomy, commerce, music and sacred love among others, for a start, while the **East Vestibule** celebrates the pleasures of life (Christmas pudding, conversation, cricket, mud pie, profane love, speed). Ask for the pamphlet on the mosaics at the front desk for more details! The gallery is all-encompassing, but here are the highlights from a few rooms:

Room 4. Are there many German fans of *Let's Go*? If so, this is for you: Room

4 has some works by Hans Holbein, one of Germany's best known painters.

Room 6, 7 and 8 showcase works by **Michelangelo** and **Raphael.** If you really want to piss people off, ask them where they're keeping the **Donatellos. Room 18** was donated by Yves St. Laurent. **Room 23** features **Rembrandt.**

Room 30. Focused mainly on religious painting, Room 30 has several famous Velázquez's including *Rokeby Venus*, and *La Tela Real*, which depicts Philip IV hunting wild boar. It is also a must-see for any aspiring mustache-growers, see Velázquez's 1656 *Philip IV of Spain* for curl and the nearby Juan Bautista Martínez del Mazo's *Don Adrián Pulido Pareja* for volume and under-lip work.

Room 32 explores the introduction of naturalism to more traditional styles of painting through works such as Caravaggio's *Boy Bitten by a Lizard*, and Guercino's famous *The Incredulity of Saint Thomas* which shows St. Thomas touching a post-resurrection Christ's wounds out of doubt.

Room 34 is best seen while *Rule Brittania* blares loudly in the background, but the gallery assistants who are posted at each room probably wouldn't take very kindly to that. Showcasing art from Great Britain between 1750 and 1850, Room 34 concerns itself mainly with heroic acts, huge ships and bold, grand landscapes. Especially of note are the several paintings from **Turner.**

Room 43 is a heavy-hitter with **Manet** and **Monet,** so much more distinct than their one-letter difference might lead you to believe. This is the home of some of Monet's **water lilies** paintings and his beautiful *The Grand Canal, Venice* with its soft-hewn domes and gentle brush strokes. *The Gare St-Lazare* from 1877 may rekindle the romance of train stations for tired travelers. As if all this weren't enough, one of **Van Gogh's** famous *Sun Flowers* is also on display in this room.

Room 44 is for people interested in Pointillism and Impressionism, featuring **Pissarro** and still lifes from **Gauguin** as well as **Renoir's** famous *The Umbrellas.* Many people have heard that the best way to view an Impressionist work is by squinting and backing away from it. We share this not to advise you, but rather to explain why three people just backed into you. **Room 46** will make fans of **Degas** happy.

The Sainsbury Wing. Fans of **Botticelli, Van Eyck,** and **Bellini** would be well-served to pay the wing a visit. Many of the paintings are taken from religious structures, so the canvases are often interestingly designed or shaped like arches.

Charing Cross. Free. Audio tours in English £3.50, students £2.50. Maps £1 and are well-worth the purchase as the gallery is huge. Special exhibits cost around £10 on average. Open M-Th 10am-6pm, F 10am-9pm, Sa-Su 10am-6pm.

TRAFALGAR SQUARE

HISTORICAL SIGHT

Trafalgar Sq.

People flock to Trafalgar Sq. like Hyde Park pigeons to bread, and if you're homesick for your native tongue, you'll likely hear it here (yes, American English counts). Designed by Sir Charles Barry, who also designed the Houses of Parliament, Trafalgar Sq/ commemorates Admiral **Horatio Viscount Nelson's** heroic naval victory at the Battle of Trafalgar. The Square serves as a gathering point and has hosted national celebrations and rallies of all sorts. The square is bordered by institutions from many different countries such as the New Zealand House, the Uganda House, the Canada House, and the South Africa House. The National Gallery is north of the Square. Every Christmas, a tree is erected in Trafalgar Square. Norway has given the tree annually since 1947 as thanks for British aid during WWII.

A statue of Nelson tops **Nelson's column,** which is the central point of the square. The four panels surrounding its base celebrate his naval victories at St. Vincent in 1797, the Nile in 1798, Copenhagen in 1801, and Trafalgar in 1805 (the panel for this victory says "England expects every man will do his duty"). A bronze lion rests on each of the four corners of the block supporting the column, and on any given day, you can see children climbing all over them, and occasionally dangling from their mouths.

There are **two beautiful fountains** in the square, each with teal statues of strange merpeople holding fish. To call them strange merpeople may seem redundant, but the two tails will make you double-take. The water in the fountains is so blue that it makes the Thames look black, instead of sickly green.

⊖Charing Cross.

NATIONAL PORTRAIT GALLERY GALLERY

St. Martin's Pl. ☎020 7306 0055 www.npg.org.uk

In London, it's easy to get lost in history. You have to remember names of monarchs, gossip stars, the insanely wealthy, the star-crossed lovers—and we haven't even talked about those outside of the royal family. The National Portrait Gallery is less about the art of the portraits themselves than it is about the people behind the portraits and what they meant for England. In fact, the gallery presents excellent short histories of the subjects and organizes them by room in such a way that it traces British history through its greatest asset—its people. Highlights:

Room 2 displays Queen Elizabeth I circa 1600, and the famous "Ditchley Portrait" in which Her Majesty is depicted standing on a globe.

Room 12 shows greats of the 18th century, such as **Samuel Johnson** and **Johann Christian Bach.**

Room 14 deals with the rise of the British Empire, including a brief mention of the American Revolution in the form of a replica of a **Gilbert Stuart** portrait of **George Washington.** It also has the dramatic *Death of the Earl of Chatham,* who is portrayed mid-collapse after trying to persuade the British government to go easy on America.

Room 16 documents the sordid tale of Lady Jane Grey, the "nine-day queen."

Room 18 has portraits of **John Keats, William Wordsworth,** and **Thomas Paine** as well as a rather romantic depiction of **Byron** who looks like a mixture of **Jake Gyllenhaal** in the *Prince of Persia* and **Captain Jack Sparrow.**

Room 27 features **Charles Darwin** in cartoon and portrait form (in one of them he has the body of an ape) as well as **Michael Faraday,** who discovered electromagnetic induction. The question remains, could he discover what the hell was going on with that damn island?

Room 31 has got all your **Winston Churchill.** Also worth noting is the exhibition dedicated to **D. H. Lawrence** and its history of *Lady Chatterley's Lover.* A priceless photograph of three men on the Tube shows the two men flanking the central figure (who's reading *Lady Chatterley's Lover*) gazing over his shoulder at its "obscene" pages.

Artists and Sitters has modern portraits such as the extra-large portrait of **Paul McCartney.**

The **Ground Floor** features contemporary portraits like Julian Opie's Blur portraits (fans of the band will recognize the images from the cover of the Greatest Hits collection) and his animated self-portrait.

Room 38 houses Marc Quinn's *Self.* The room is set up in such a way that you enter and notice the reddish bust of a man's head sitting in a refrigerated case. Then you read the plaque and realize its made out of the artist's own frozen blood.

⊖Charing Cross. Walk down Strand to Trafalgar Sq. and turn right along the sq. Ⓢ Tickets for small special exhibits £5, large exhibitions £10. Audio tour £3. Open M-W 10am-6pm, Th-F 10am-9pm, Sa-Su 10am-6pm. Guided tours depart from main room T at 3:00pm, Th at 1:15pm, Sa-Su at 3pm. Certain scheduled nights open until 10pm.

ST. MARTIN-IN-THE-FIELDS
CHURCH

Trafalgar Sq. ☎020 7766 1100 www.smitf.org

The beautiful church is notable for its sculptures that sit outside; for its strange, contemporary "East Window"; for its status as the Royal Parish Church which has been frequented by the queen; and for its massive organ. But St. Martin-in-the-Fields is most well-known for its long musical history. Every Monday, Tuesday and Friday at 1pm, they have a 45min. "lunch-time concert," which is a classical recital from students at the musical academies and colleges. In the evening, more renowned artists perform in the beautiful space. Additionally, St. Martin is a charitable organization, feeding and sheltering around 3000 homeless people annually. Known as the "church of the ever-open door" because of its use as a place of refuge for soldiers en-route to France in WWI, St. Martin-in-the-Fields is a must see for any music lover.

Charing Cross. It's to the east of Trafalgar Square. i Audio tour available in English. Brass rubbing £4.50. Reserved ticket for jazz £9, unreserved £5.50. Church open daily 8am-5pm at least, but it stays open later on off-concert days. Shop open M-W 10am-7pm, Th-Sa 10am-9pm, Su 11:30am-6pm. W 8pm is Jazz night.

COVENT GARDEN PIAZZA
HISTORICAL SITE, SHOPPING

Located between a market filled with tasty food and St. Paul's Church, where there is sometimes summer theater, Covent Garden Piazza is instantly recognizable from films such as Hitchcock's *Frenzy* and *My Fair Lady*. The site of the first Punch and Judy performance in 1662, the Piazza still sees many talented street performers. Once host to Mike Myers and Neil Morrissey, Covent Garden Piazza is worth a visit for its history and its entertainment.

Covent Garden. Turn right down James St.

INSTITUTE OF CONTEMPORARY ART
GALLERY

The Mall ☎020 7930 3647 www.ica.org.uk

The Institute of Contemporary Art is a typically British study in contrast. Located just down the road from Buckingham Palace, the ICA puts on some of the most cutting edge, modern work out there. The cinema shows independent and world cinema, has director Q and As, and has gigs with the likes of Devendra Banhart, Joanna Newsom, Amy Winehouse, and M.I.A. The ICA has no permanent collection, so check the website to see what's on.

Charing Cross. Turn left down Strand, under the arch and down the mall. The ICA is on your right. i Partially wheelchair-accessible. Exhibits rotate out every 6-7 weeks. Free. Cinema £9, concessions £8. Hours are likely to change, so check, but they are W noon-7pm, Th noon-9pm, F-Su noon-7pm. Film screenings 6:15pm, 7:30pm and 8:30pm.

SEVEN DIALS
HISTORICAL SITE

At the intersection of Mercer, Monmouth, and Earlham St.

Referring to the intersection of seven streets at the column, Seven Dials is an architectural marvel. Thomas Neale owned the land in the area and wanted to generate a profit. To maximize that, he laid out the streets so he could have the seven converge at that point, maximizing space and allowing for more shops and residences. The sundial, known as the Sundial Pillar, at the center was built in 1694, removed in 1773, and replaced in 1989 at an unveiling by the queen of the Netherlands.

Leicester Square. Turn right onto Long Acre and left down Monmouth.

WESTMINSTER

WESTMINSTER ABBEY
ABBEY, HISTORICAL SITE

Off Parliament Sq. ☎020 7222 5152 www.westminster-abbey.org

Founded in 960, Westminster Abbey became the royals' church after the crowning of William the Conqueror in 1066. Nearly every monarch since William has

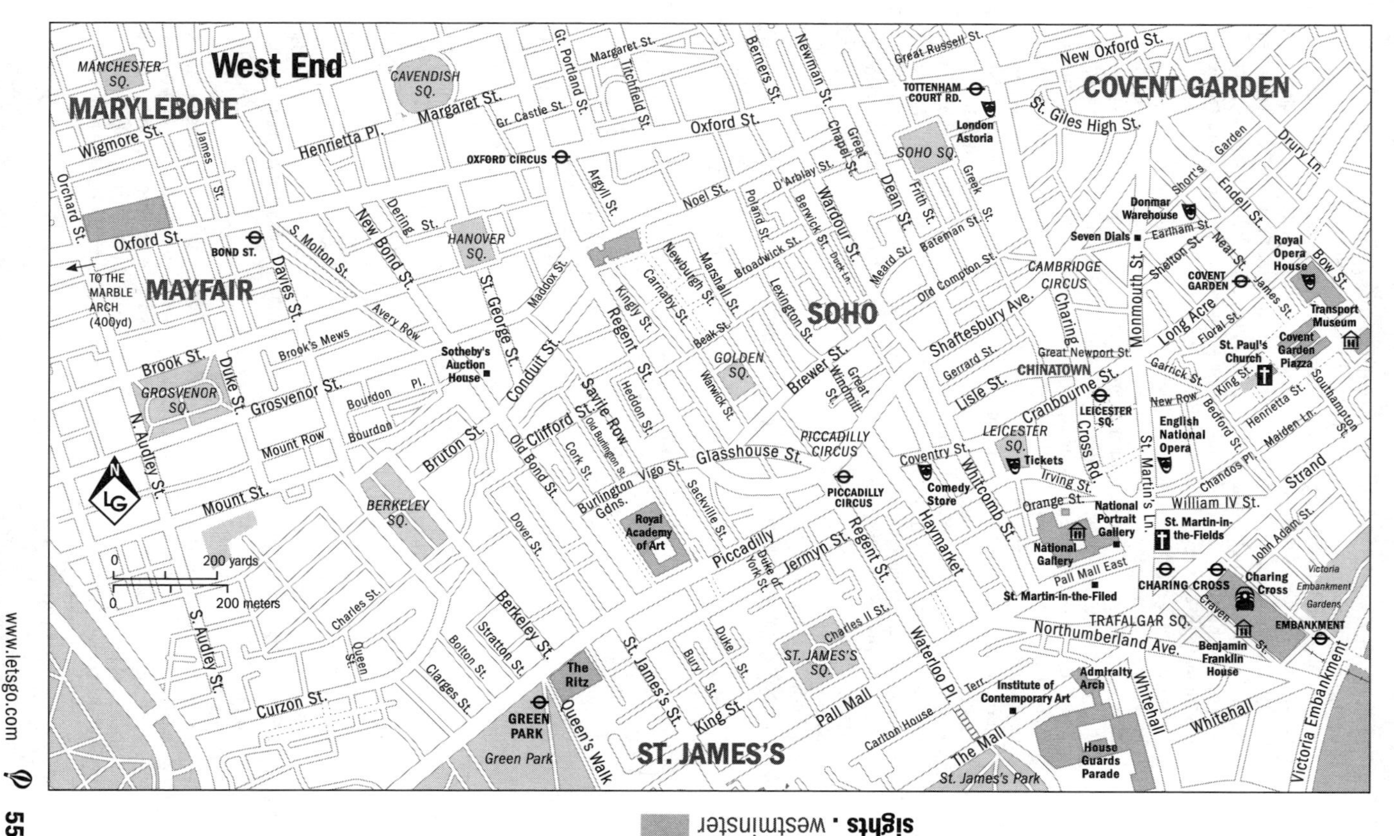

West End
MARYLEBONE
MAYFAIR
SOHO
COVENT GARDEN
ST. JAMES'S
CHINATOWN
MANCHESTER SQ.
CAVENDISH SQ.
HANOVER SQ.
GROSVENOR SQ.
BERKELEY SQ.
GOLDEN SQ.
SOHO SQ.
LEICESTER SQ.
ST. JAMES'S SQ.
TRAFALGAR SQ.
CAMBRIDGE CIRCUS
PICCADILLY CIRCUS
OXFORD CIRCUS
TOTTENHAM COURT RD.
BOND ST.
LEICESTER SQ.
COVENT GARDEN
CHARING CROSS
EMBANKMENT
PICCADILLY CIRCUS
GREEN PARK
Green Park
St. James's Park
Oxford St.
New Oxford St.
Wigmore St.
Orchard St.
James St.
Henrietta Pl.
Margaret St.
Gr. Castle St.
Gt. Portland St.
Titchfield St.
Argyll St.
Berners St.
Newman St.
Great Chapel St.
Wardour St.
Dean St.
Frith St.
Greek St.
Bateman St.
Great Russell St.
St. Giles High St.
Charing Cross Rd.
Shaftesbury Ave.
Old Compton St.
Meard St.
Berwick St.
Duck Ln.
D'Arblay St.
Poland St.
Broadwick St.
Noel St.
Lexington St.
Brewer St.
Great Windmill St.
Marshall St.
Newburgh St.
Carnaby St.
Beak St.
Warwick St.
Kingly St.
Regent St.
Heddon St.
Savile Row
Old Burlington St.
Cork St.
Clifford St.
Burlington Gdns.
Vigo St.
Sackville St.
Glasshouse St.
Piccadilly
Jermyn St.
Duke of York St.
Duke St.
Bury St.
King St.
St. James's St.
Queen's Walk
Berkeley St.
Stratton St.
Bolton St.
Clarges St.
Dover St.
Old Bond St.
Conduit St.
Maddox St.
St. George St.
New Bond St.
Dering St.
Bruton St.
Avery Row
Brook's Mews
Bourdon Pl.
Bourdon
Grosvenor St.
Mount Row
Mount St.
Davies St.
S. Molton St.
Brook St.
Duke St.
N. Audley St.
S. Audley St.
Charles St.
Queen St.
Curzon St.
Haymarket
Coventry St.
Whitcomb St.
Lisle St.
Gerrard St.
Great Newport St.
Cranbourne St.
Irving St.
Orange St.
Pall Mall East
Pall Mall
Waterloo Pl.
Charles II St.
Carlton House Terr.
The Mall
Northumberland Ave.
Whitehall
Craven St.
John Adam St.
Strand
Victoria Embankment
Victoria Embankment Gardens
William IV St.
Chandos Pl.
St. Martin's Ln.
Bedford St.
New Row
Garrick St.
Henrietta St.
Maiden Ln.
Southampton St.
King St.
Floral St.
Long Acre
James St.
Neal St.
Earlham St.
Shelton St.
Monmouth St.
Endell St.
Short's Garden
Drury Ln.
Bow St.
Seven Dials
Donmar Warehouse
London Astoria
Comedy Store
Tickets
English National Opera
Royal Opera House
Transport Museum
Covent Garden Piazza
St. Paul's Church
St. Martin-in-the-Fields
St. Martin-in-the-Filed
National Portrait Gallery
National Gallery
Charing Cross
Benjamin Franklin House
Admiralty Arch
House Guards Parade
Institute of Contemporary Art
Royal Academy of Art
Sotheby's Auction House
The Ritz
TO THE MARBLE ARCH (400yd)
0
200 yards
0
200 meters
N
LG

been crowned here. Henry III built the modern abbey, but Edward the Confessor built the first church on the site. Inside the abbey, you can see the high altar where kings and queens are crowned and where coffins are displayed during funerals. The chapels interspersed throughout the church house gloriously sculpted monuments. Especially impressive is the statue of Lord and Lady Norris in the north chapel. Sunlight floods the Lady Chapel during the day, and it's a sight worth seeing. In the Poets' Corner rests the tomb of Chaucer as well as monuments to W.H. Auden, George Eliot, Dylan Thomas, D. H. Lawrence, Lord Byron, Alfred Lord Tennyson, Lewis Carroll, Jane Austen, Charles Dickens, William Shakespeare, and Laurence Olivier. Also buried in the church are Sir Isaac Newton and Charles Darwin. At the end of the audio tour, you'll come across the Tomb of the Unknown Soldier, as well as the Chapter House, where monks signed the abbey over to the king. Nearby is Britain's oldest door, built around 1050. Outside the main building lies St. Margaret's Church, the "parish church of the House of Commons." This church was built by the abbey because the monks didn't want their worship to be disturbed by the masses of commoners coming to worship there. Sir Walter Raleigh was buried in St. Margaret's in 1618.

Westminster. Walk down Westminster Bridge away from the water on the side of the Westminster Tube stop. Parliament Sq. and the abbey will be on your left. *i* *Audio tours in 11 languages, including English. Definitely take advantage of this free tour (narrated by Jeremy Irons in true Troy McClure fashion), as there aren't many signs around the abbey.* *£15, students and seniors £12, ages 11-18 £6, under 11 (accompanied by adult) free, family ticket (2 adults and 1 child) £30 plus £6 for each additional child.* *Open M-Tu 9:30am-3:30pm, W 9:30am-6:00pm, Th-Sa 9:30am-3:30pm. Abbey Museum 10:30am-4pm daily.*

CHURCHILL MUSEUM AND CABINET WAR ROOMS — MUSEUM, HISTORICAL SITE

Clive Steps, King Charles St. ☎020 7930 6961 www.iwm.org.uk/cabinet

The War Rooms opened in 1938, a week before WWII broke out. They were used as a shelter for important government officers, and Winston Churchill spent almost every day of the war in the windowless, airless subterranean rooms, recreated here and opened for public access. The rooms are tense with wartime anxiety, and the map room, with lights that were not turned off for six years during the war, still burns bright. Connected to the Cabinet War Rooms is the Churchill museum. Visitors can step on the sensors to hear excerpts from some of his most famous speeches and watch videos detailing the highs and lows of his career. Also on display are his alcohol habits, which included drinks with breakfast, lunch, and dinner daily, and his patented "romper," better known as a onesie. The interactive, touch-screen "lifeline" is phenomenally detailed; be sure to touch his 90th birthday and August 6th, 1945, but be prepared to draw stares from the other patrons of the museum. It should be noted that, while a lock of his childhood hair is on display, the heavy security surrounding it makes it impossible to use a voodoo doll or potion to bring the great man back to life.

Westminster or St. James's Park. From Westminster, take a right down Parliament St. and a left onto King Charles St. *i* *Free sound guide available in 8 languages.* *£14.95, students and seniors £12, disabled £9, under 16 free. Special rates available for groups, so call ahead.* *Open daily 9:30am-6pm. Last admission 1hr. before close. Call about scheduling a 2hr. tour.*

ST. JAMES'S PARK — PARK

The Mall.

Despite its proximity to the crowds of Buckingham palace, St. James's Park is a true haven. Established in 1531, St. James's is more natural than its popular, well-tended cousin, Hyde Park. It features a wildlife reserve area reminiscent of a scene from Bambi. The park lake is placid and beautiful, and pelicans feed on the rocks. In fact, the lake and the grassy area surrounding it are an official waterfowl preserve.

St. James's Park. Take a left off Tothill St. onto Broadway. Follow it until you hit the park. Open daily 5am-midnight.*

BUCKINGHAM PALACE

George III bought Buckingham House—which wasn't originally built for the royals—in 1761 for his wife, Queen Charlotte. Charlotte proceeded to give birth to 14 out of her 15 children at Buckingham Palace. The house was expanded by George IV, who commissioned John Nash to transform the existing building into a palace. In 1837, Queen Victoria moved into Buckingham Palace, and it has remained a royal residence since then.

Everyday at 11:30am from April to late July, and every other day the rest of the year, the **Changing of the Guard** takes place. The "Changing of the Guard" is the exchange of guard duty between different regiments. Forget the dumb American movies where an obnoxious tourist tries in every immature way possible to make the unflinching guards at Buckingham Palace move; the guards are far enough away so that tourists can do no more than whistle every time they move 3 ft. and salute. The entire spectacle lasts 40min. To see it, you should show up well before 11:30am and stand in front of the palace in view of the morning guards. The middle of the week is the least crowded time to watch.

THE STATE ROOMS

At the end of the Mall. ☎020 7766 7300 www.royalcollection.org.uk

The Palace opens to visitors every August and September while the royals are off sunning themselves. Visitors are granted limited access and are only allowed in the State Rooms which are used for formal occasions. As a result, these rooms are sumptuous and as royal as you could hope them to be. As you tour them, look for the secret door concealed in one of the White Drawing Room's mirrors, through which royals entered the state apartments. Also not to be missed are the Throne Room and the glittering Music Room. The Galleries feature master works from the royal collections, and the gardens display birds that are marginally prettier than the birds you'd see outside.

Victoria. Turn right onto Buckingham Palace Rd. and follow it onto Buckingham Gate. i Audio guide provided. Wheelchair users should book by calling ☎020 7766 7324. $ £17, students and seniors £15.50, under 17 £9.75, under 5 free, family (2 adults and 3 children under 17) £45. Open daily late July-Oct 9:45am-4pm. Last admission 45min. before close.

THE ROYAL MEWS — MUSEUM, CARRIAGE HOUSE

At the end of the Mall. ☎020 7766 7300 www.royalcollection.org.uk

The Royal Mews functions as a museum, stable, riding school, and a working carriage house. The carriages are fantastic—especially the "Glass Coach," which is used to carry royal brides to their weddings, and the four-ton Gold State Coach which is not, as the name would suggest, a coach dedicated to California. Unfortunately, the magic pumpkin carriage that the royals use to escape evil step-royals is only visible until midnight, but if you're in the Royal Mews past midnight, you have other problems.

Victoria. Turn right onto Buckingham Palace Rd. and follow it onto Buckingham Gate. Entrance to the Mews and Gallery will be on your left. i Wheelchair-accessible. $ £7.75, students and seniors £7, under 17 £5, under 5 free, family (2 adults and 3 children under 17) £20.50. Open Mar 20-Oct 31 M-Th 11am-4pm, Sa-Su 11aam-4pm; Nov 1-Dec 23 M-F 11am-4pm. Last admission 45min. before close.

QUEEN'S GALLERY — GALLERY

At the end of the Mall ☎020 7766 7300 www.royalcollection.org.uk

The Queen's Gallery is dedicated to temporary exhibitions of jaw-droppingly valuable items from the Royal Collection. Five rooms, designed to look like the interior of the palace are filled with glorious artifacts that applaud the sovereign.

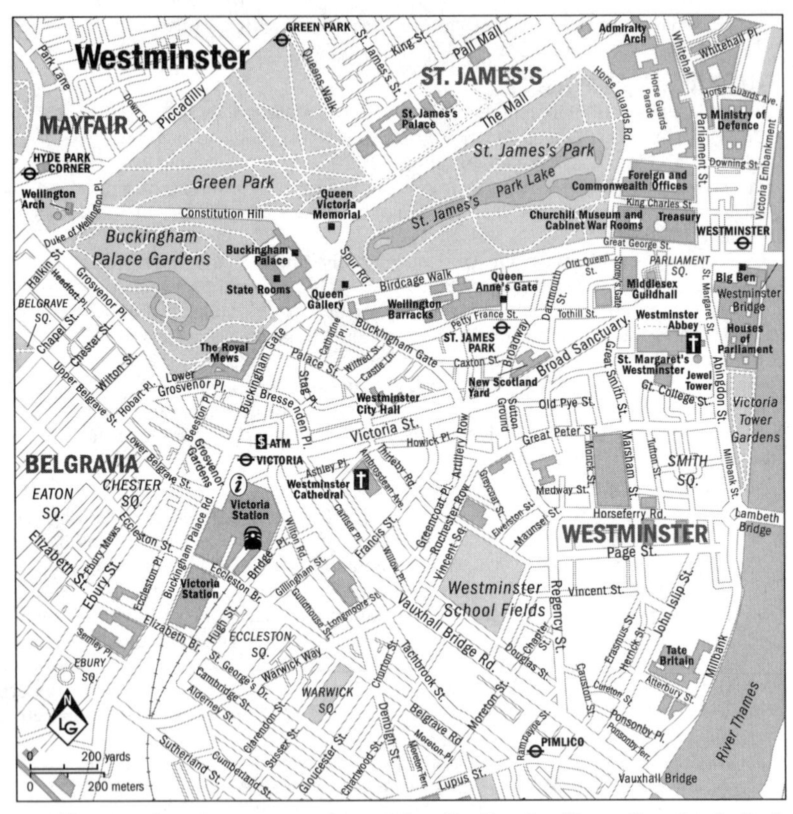

Once purchased, passes can be registered online for 12 months of unlimited access.

Victoria. Turn right onto Buckingham Palace Rd. and follow it onto Buckingham Gate. Entrance to the Mews and Gallery will be on your left. Wheelchair-accessible. Open daily 10am-5:30pm, July 27-Oct 1 9:30am-5:30pm. Last admission 1hr. before close. Closed Nov 1-Apr 14, 2011.

NORTH LONDON

HAMPSTEAD HEATH

PARK

Hampstead

020 7332 3030

Hampstead Heath was initially much smaller than its present 800 acres. After Sir Thomas Maryon Wilson tried to develop and sell off the Heath in the early 19th century, the public began to fight for it, culminating in an Act of Parliament in 1872 that declared the Heath open to the public forever. Now it sprawls gloriously in the heart of Hampstead. The **Hill Gardens** are in the southwest corner of the Heath just off North End Ave. The Hill House was owned by Lord Leverhulme (of Lever Soap), and he modified the surrounding landscapes to create the beautiful, tamer Hill Gardens. A pergola presides over the gardens, its lattice work is entwined with roses, and painters often station themselves around the gardens and pergola. The view through its Georgian columns is best enjoyed around sunset. **Parliament Hill** is one of the higher points in London, offering those willing to climb its deceptively steep sides a glorious reminder that they aren't in the middle of rural England, but are, in fact, only four miles from London proper. Parliament Hill likely derives its name from its use as a point of defense for Parliament loyalists during the English Civil War, but legend has it that Guy Fawkes watched Parliament from the hill as he waited for it to explode. A surfeit of benches strangle the opening that yields the view, but if you stand on one you can keep everyone irritated and your picture intact. Locals say that "gangs of teenagers" roam the Heath at night, so it's best to visit during the day.

Bus #210 will drop you at the north of the Heath, from which you can access Kenwood House and work your way southeast toward Parliament Hill. Alternatively, you can get off at ⊖Hampstead and turn right onto Heath St., up North End Way, left onto Inverforth Close and left onto a path that will take you to the hill gardens. Bus #214 allows easy access to Parliament Hill. Heath open 24hr. Hill Garden open daily May 24-Aug 1 8:30am-8:30pm; Aug 2-May 23 8:30am-1hr. before sunset.

KENWOOD HOUSE

♿ GALLERY

Hampstead Ln. ☎020 8348 1286 www.english-heritage.org.uk

The Kenwood House was the primary residence of Lord Iveagh, a Barrister and Lord Chief Justice who lived in the house during the 18th century. It currently houses his fabulous art collection, and stands as a representation of an upper-class house from that era. Each room is equipped with laminated sheets explaining the function, decor, and art of the space. The Iveagh Bequest fills the house with paintings that are essentially odes to London of yore. Views of the city from the Heath, like Crone's *"View of London from Highgate,"* and an early Turner depicting, per usual, a nautical subject touch upon themes common to the bequest—typical British life. Many come to see Rembrandt's *"Portrait of the Artist"* and Vermeer's *"The Guitar Player."* The Suffolk Collection, composed mainly of portraits, is on semi-permanent exhibition on the first floor (second floor, for American readers).

*Bus #210 will stop on Hampstead Ln. **i** Only ground floor is wheelchair-accessible. Free. Booklets £4. Open daily 11:30am-4pm. Last entry 3:50pm.*

KEATS'S HOUSE

♿ HISTORICAL SITE

Keats Grove ☎020 7332 3868 www.cityoflondon.gov.uk/keatshousehampstead

John Keats lived with his friend Charles Brown in the house from 1818-1820, right before his death. It is also where he fell in love with Fanny Browne, and where he composed some of his famous poems such as "Ode to a Nightingale." Meant more for die-hard fans, the museum doesn't offer much beyond a few sheets in each room, some of which feature angst-ridden love letters, famous poems, and explanations of the history of the house and the functions of the rooms. This museum has recreated the rooms in all their Regency-inspired glory, though, so the site is as much about the building as it is the writing. Still, if you want to be a writer, and you believe in osmosis, this is the place for you.

*⊖Hampstead Heath. Left onto South End Rd., follow it until it hits Keats Grove. **i** Only ground floor is wheelchair-accessible. English audio tour free. £5, concessions £3, under 16 free. Free room guide. Open Apr 6-Oct 31 T-Su 1-5pm; Nov 1-Easter F-Su 1-5pm. Check website for details.*

matching colors

Some Tube tracks run multiple lines. To be sure you're on the correct line, just look at the color of the poles in the train; they'll match the color of the line.

EAST LONDON

WHITECHAPEL GALLERY — CONTEMPORARY ART

77-82 Whitechapel High St. ☎020 7522 7888 www.whitechapelgallery.org

This edgy gallery has been showing important contemporary art since it opened in 1901. Originally an effort of hoity-toity uppity-ups to bring art to the culturally decrepit inhabitants of the East End, the gallery's mission has changed, though its commitment to excellence hasn't. Gallery 7 is dedicated to collections that change four times a year. Gallery 2 features year-long commissioned works, and the rest of the gallery deals with contemporary art and occasional mid-career retrospectives. Art films can be seen running on loop in the cinema space.

Aldgate East. Left on Whitechapel High St. Free. Special exhibits normally under £10, £2 off for students. Open Tu-Su 11am-6pm. Open 1st Th of every month 11am-9pm.

NATIONAL MARITIME MUSEUM — MUSEUM

Romney Rd. ☎020 8312 6608 www.nmm.ac.uk

Housed in the formal training center for boys who dreamt of naval careers, the National Maritime Museum provides a history of the organization that gave credence to the claim that Britannia **rules the waves.** This museum has something for all British naval history fanatics. Exhibits include a recreation of the **Starvation Cove,** where Sir John Franklin froze to death, complete with a **frozen arm** hanging over the ship edge, and the uniform in which Horatio Nelson was shot, including blood-soaked stockings and the fatal bullet wound, the museum has something for all fanatics of British naval history. Especially of note are the stained glass windows from the Baltic Exchange which include the intact half-dome which was recreated after it was destroyed in a terrorist attack. The Bridge Simulator allows visitors to take control of a full-size (simulated) ship.

Greenwich. Left on Kay Way, right down Straightsmouth to Greenwich High Rd., right onto Stockwell St., left onto Nevada St., left onto King William Walk. Right onto Romney Rd. Free. Open daily 10am-5pm. Last entry 30min. before close. Last entry to the Bridge Simulator M-F 4:35pm, Sa-Su 4:30pm.

THE ROYAL OBSERVATORY — HISTORIC SITE, MUSEUM

Blackheath Ave. ☎020 8312 6608 www.nnn.ac.uk

Charles II founded the Royal Observatory in 1675 to "advance navigation and astronomy." Translation: to stop British ships from sinking so frequently. Greenwich now serves as a marker of hemispheres, with its Prime Meridian, or longitude 0° 0'0" lying in the courtyard of the Royal Observatory. Visitors to the observatory can take pictures in two hemispheres simultaneously by straddling the red LED strip and taking pictures of the floor. After seeing the intersection of the hemispheres, visitors choose one of two routes. The **Meridian route** explores the history of time, with most of the exhibition in the Flamsteed House, former home and workspace of John Flamsteed, the first Astronomer Royal. This route features the original Harrison timekeeper intended to solve the longitude problem and more telescopes than should ever be necessary. The **Meridian Building** features a clever "Time Stood Still For Me When..." exhibit which allows visitors to write about moments when, well, time stood still for them. A true tear-jerker reads, "time stood still for me when I came home to see my pet hamster had died. (His name was Lucky, but in the end he was not)." The **Astronomy route** will give you the opportunity to touch a 4.5-billion-year-old piece of the Gibeon meteorite and also provides access to the popular planetarium.

*Greenwich. Left on Kay Way, right down Straightsmouth to Greenwich High Rd., right onto Stockwell St., left onto Nevada St., left onto King William Walk. Right onto Romney Rd., up the hill. **i** Guided tours are free at different times in different languages depending on the day. Check online under events. Handicapped tourists should know that, while there is parking on top of the* *hill, the hill itself is very steep.* Ⓢ *Free. Planetarium £6.50, concessions £4.50. Audio guides available £3.50.* ⏰ *Open daily in summer 10am-7pm; in winter 10am-5pm.*

food

British food doesn't have a great reputation. Yes, it is bad for you and no, it doesn't have complex flavors, but it is so intrinsically a part of British life that to forego it would be a grave error for any visitor to England. **Fish** and **chips, bangers** and **mash, tikka masala** (a British invention), and, of course, **warm ale** are all different names for the same thing: comfort food. Neighborhoods like Bloomsbury and Shoreditch serve up wide varieties of ethnic food (read: Indian), but "pub grub" and British food are inescapable. There's a reason that old war propaganda line, "Keep Calm and Carry On," is plastered all over the place; there's a reason the Queen still rolls down the Mall every June 12th; there's a reason the Brits always think England will win the Cup; and there's a reason fair Albion still has the pound; and for that same reason, British food is what it is. Now eat your mushy peas—the cod's getting cold.

BAYSWATER

Shocking though it may be, most travelers like to take a break from bubble and squeak and bangers and mash. When you get itchin' for a little something from an ethnic kitchen, give Bayswater a shot. A wide range of affordable Middle Eastern and Indian restaurants abound in this neighborhood.

LA BOTTEGA DEL GELATO — GELATO ❸

127 Bayswater Rd. ☎020 7243 2443

Simply put, this gelato, made in-store, is divine. La Bottega Del Gelato fills the hole in the London ice cream scene with a variety of delicious flavors. Enjoy it outside on Bayswater Rd. in their seating area; even in the heart of the city, this gelato will make you feel like you're on a quiet street in Roma. The Ferrero Rocher is especially good.

⊖Bayswater. Right onto Queensway, follow it until you hit Bayswater Rd. Ⓢ *1 scoop £2, 2 scoops £3.50, 3 scoops £4.50; milkshakes £3.50.* ⏰ *Hours change depending on weather, but the store opens daily 10:30am.*

APHRODITE TAVERNA — GREEK ❷

15 Hereford Rd. ☎020 7229 2206 www.aphroditerestaurant.co.uk

Decorated with statues of Aphrodite and a few inexplicable pineapples, Aphrodite Taverna serves up fantastic Greek food at prices that even recession-era Greece can't beat! Too soon? Let's hope not. Come and enjoy a meal of chicken kofta with rice *(£5.90)* or homemade pita *(£4.50)*, and relax as power pop pipes through the store speakers.

⊖Bayswater. Left onto Queensway, left onto Moscow Rd., right onto Hereford toward Westbourne Grove. Ⓢ *Entrees £5.50-6.80.* ⏰ *M-Su 8am-5pm.*

DURBAR RESTAURANT — INDIAN ❸

24 Hereford Rd.

☎020 7727 1947 www.durbartandoori.co.uk

An authentically Indian interior complements the warm smells from the kitchen of Durbar, where the same family has served Indian specialties for the last 54 years. A popular Indian restaurant before Indian restaurants were popular, it has the history and accolades to back it. The menu ranges across India with a collection of favorites and some unexpected dishes. Be sure to try one of the 13 varieties of bread baked fresh daily.

⊖Bayswater. Left onto Queensway, left onto Moscow Rd., right onto Hereford toward Westbourne Grove. Ⓢ *Tikka £6.95.* ⏰ *Open M-Th noon-2:30pm and 5:30-11:30pm, F 5:30-11:30pm, Sa-Su noon-2:30pm and 5:30-11:30pm.*

KHAN'S RESTAURANT INDIAN ❷

13-15 Westbourne Grove ☎020 7727 5420 www.khansrestaurant.com

Dine among the faux palm trees at this affordable Indian restaurant. Nearly 35 years old, this family-run joint serves the traditional tandoori specialties *(chicken tikka £5.80)* as well as other popular Indian dishes.

Bayswater. Left onto Queensway until you hit Westbourne Grove. Entrees around £4.50-5.80. Open M-Th noon-2:45pm and 6-11:45pm, F-Su noon-11:45pm.

THE BATHURST DELI DELI ❷

3 Bathurst St. ☎020 7262 1888

Despite its outrageous orange and green exterior, the Bathurst Deli still manages an authentic deli experience. With a friendly staff serving up lasagna, quiches, cannoli, and toasted sandwiches you can get a good, affordable meal at this down-to-earth eatery.

Lancaster Gate. Take a left onto Westbourne St. and a right onto Banhurst St. Lasagna, quiche, and cannoli £2.20, toasted sandwiches £4-5. Open M-Sa 7am-11pm, Su 8am-11pm.

i want candy

What could be more British than a bar of Cadbury chocolate? Well, in early 2010, Cadbury, the famed UK confectioner that started up in 1824, unfortunately fell victim to a hostile takeover by the US based international conglomerate Kraft Foods. However, any Cadbury chocolate you buy in the UK is still made from a different recipe than its American counterpart, and is generally thought to be far more delicious—according to the British, at any rate. In addition to making the classic Dairy Milk bar, Cadbury enables chocoholics with their Curly Wurly, Crunchie, and Flake bars. The last of these is often added to the top of soft-serve vanilla ice cream to create a British summertime staple known as the "99." While there is debate as to where the name comes from, it is universally agreed that a Flake bar and ice cream is a scrumptious dessert. Visitors to the UK should also sample the Cadbury Crème Egg (not to be confused with a Scotch egg—the latter is an actual hard-boiled egg coated in ground sausage, herbs, and breadcrumbs and then deep-fried).

In the realm of candy, the word "Smarties" may induce unpleasant memories of chalky, pastel colored tablets, but never fear—in Britain, Nestlé Smarties, originally known as "Chocolate Beans," are reminiscent of M and Ms. Those looking for a non-chocolate candy treat can channel their inner Edmund Pevensie from C.S. Lewis's *The Lion, the Witch, and the Wardrobe* and try Turkish Delight. This sugary, gelatinous treat, often flavored with rosewater and rolled in powdered sugar, tends to be rather divisive—people either love it or hate it. Since it is widely available throughout the UK, you can decide for yourself whether Turkish Delight is delectable or disgusting. Be sure to keep in mind that while rosewater is one of the most common flavors, it's also something of an acquired taste; a safer choice might be lemon or mint.

BLOOMSBURY

Riddled with cheap student eats, Bloomsbury is an exciting and accessible culinary neighborhood. Here are some of the true gems.

NEWMAN ARMS BRITISH PIES ❸

23 Rathbone St. ☎020 7636 1127 www.newmanarms.co.uk

Established in 1730, the Newman Arms has been serving succulent British pies about as long as the Queen's relatives have been on the throne. The menu reads like an ode to comfort food, with pies like beef and Guinness, steak and kidney, and lamb and rosemary. The warm upstairs dining room fills up fast, so be sure to reserve a table one day in advance during the summer and much farther in advance during the winter (sometimes even months). This food will warm your heart without shrinking your wallet.

Goodge St. Turn left onto Tottenham Court Rd., left onto Tottenham St., left onto Charlotte St., and right onto Rathbone St. i Enter through the corridor next to the entrance to the pub. Pies £10. Puddings £11. Open M-F noon-2:30pm and 6-9:30pm.

NAVARRO'S TAPAS BAR TAPAS ❸

67 Charlotte St. ☎020 7637 7713 www.navarros.co.uk

It would make sense if, upon entering this restaurant, you began patting yourself for your passport and looking for the customs agent who won't take "I've nothing to declare" as a personal challenge. Bathed in candlelight and strains of Flamenco music, Navarro's boasts an excellent selection of regional wines that will convince you that you're on your way to Spain. The waitresses wear black and red traditional outfits, and the food lives up to the hype. Tapas are small plates of food, and most people order two or three, with three being a typical meal. Don't forget your castanets.

Goodge St. Turn left onto Tottenham Court Rd., turn left onto Tottenham St. and left onto Charlotte St. i Nicer dress is preferable, as is booking in advance. Mainly vegetarian dishes £4.85-4.95, fish and shellfish £5.75-6.10. Open M-F noon-3pm and 6-10pm, Sa 6-10pm.

NORTH SEA FISH RESTAURANT FISH AND CHIPS ❸

7-8 Leigh St. ☎020 7387 5892 www.northseafishrestaurant.co.uk

In a country where you'd think "chips" were a natural part of the fish, North Sea Fish takes the British staple one step further with a wide-ranging menu encompassing dishes such as the Seafood Platter (fried goujons of cod, haddock, plaice, pieces of scotch scampi, squid, and sardines). Basically, most of the menu is fish and chips, and the fact that this is still a good restaurant speaks volumes.

Russell Sq. Go down Colonnade with your back to Russell Sq. Turn left on Grenville St. Follow it onto Hunter St., which will become Judd St. Turn left at Leigh St. i Cheap takeaway available next door to the restaurant. Entrees £14-15. Open M-Sa noon-2:30pm and 5:30-10:30pm.

SAVOIR FAIRE BISTRO ❷

42 New Oxford St. ☎020 7436 0707 www.savoir.co.uk

This place looks a little bit like a New Orleans whorehouse, and we mean that in the best way possible. Handwritten notes on the ceiling advise customers to "make love to every woman you meet." If you get 5% on your outlays, it's a "good investment," while a mural of dancing, drinking French women covers the wall. The ceiling is also partially filled with notes from friends, emphasizing the community feel of the restaurant. What Savoir Faire knows how to make is immediately obvious and is explained by their slogan: "affordable gourmet food." Omelettes are served with fresh baked bread, and sandwiches come on fresh baguettes.

Tottenham Court Road. Turn onto New Oxford St. so that Tottenham Court Rd. is on your left and Charing Cross Rd. is on your right. Omelettes £5-6, sandwiches £4.50. Open M-Sa noon-11pm, Su noon-10:30pm.

ANDREAS GREEK AND MEDITERRANEAN ❺

40 Charlotte St. ☎020 7580 8971 www.andreas-restaurant.com

Andreas is expensive, but some say that Mediterranean cuisine is the healthiest for you; so if you want to live long in poverty, eat here often. Offering well-made Greek and Mediterranean food at correspondingly high prices, Andreas hits all of the classics. The menu features dishes like moussaka, dolmades, and garlic poussin that are chic and upscale, yet accessible.

Goodge St. Turn left onto Tottenham Court Rd., turn left onto Tottenham St. and left onto Charlotte St. Entrees £13-15. Open M-F 11:30am-3:30pm and 5:30-11pm, Sa 5:30-11pm.

CHELSEA

BUONA SERA — ITALIAN ❸

289a King's Rd — ☎020 7352 8827

People haven't eaten like this since our ancestors moved out of the trees and onto the ground. The small restaurant manages to fit 14 tables into its tight space by stacking the booths one atop the other. It's sort of like a game of Tetris, except involving delicious and affordable Italian food. Plants on the upper level make the experience feel like it's taking place in the canopy of a tree, but the food will remind you of the pleasures of civilization.

Sloane Sq. Exit the Tube and go straight down Sloane Sq. The street slanting gently left is King's Rd. If you don't want to walk the road (it's manageable but long), the following buses service the area: 11, 19, 22, 211, 319 Salads £4.50-5.70, lunch entrees £7.90-8.50. Pasta and risotto £8.60-9.80. Meat and fish entrees £14.50-14.80. Pizza £3.80, plus £1.50 per topping set (tuna and onions, ham and mushrooms, etc.). Open M 6pm-midnight, Tu-F noon-3pm and 6pm-midnight, Sa-Su noon-midnight.

GORDON RAMSAY — CELEBRITY, FRENCH ❺

68 Royal Hospital Rd. — ☎020 7352 4441 www.gordonramsay.com

Owned by celebrity chef Gordon Ramsay, this haven for those with cash to drop hides behind a simple black and white facade on a quiet stretch of Royal Hospital Rd. On the curb by the restaurant, you may see the sleeping drivers of the Masters of the Universe who dine within. You can join their charges for dinner only if you book exactly three months in advance. With a prix fixe menu *(£90)* offering three delicious courses of exquisite French food, Gordon Ramsay may be the splurge you're looking for.

Sloane Sq. Straight onto Sloane Sq., left onto Lower Sloane St., right onto Royal Hospital Rd. i See website for dress code. Jeans, T-shirts, or sportswear not accepted. Reservations for lunch do not need to be made as far in advance. Open M-F noon-2:30pm and 6:30-11pm.

LA BOTTEGA — ITALIAN COFFEE ❷

65 Lower Sloane St. — ☎020 7730 8844 www.labottega65.co.uk

Some London cappuccino connoisseurs insist that there's no better cappuccino than the one at La Bottega. Made with Illy Coffee, their cappuccino transcends the health food kick and is always made with creamy whole milk. In addition to fantastic coffee, La Bottega offers handmade breadsticks and Italian favorites like meat lasagna and eggplant parmesan. Most of the ingredients are imported weekly from Italy, and a shelf opposite the counter houses select vinegars and olive oils straight from the culinary king of countries.

Sloane Square. Left onto Lower Sloane St. Entrees from £4.90. Open M-F 8am-8pm, Sa 9am-7pm, Su 10am-5pm.

THE CITY OF LONDON

Many of the culinary offerings in the City of London are geared toward businessmen (expensive) and tourists (expensive but not very good). Fortunately, there are a few promising options for the budget traveler.

SPIANATA — ITALIAN, SANDWICH, PIZZA ❶

73a Watling St. — ☎020 7236 3666 www.spianata.com

Enjoy the delicious taste of Italy in every sandwich served on Spianata's freshly baked bread. The businessmen in the city know that some of the best sandwiches and pizzas in the city are served at this authentically Italian shop, so arrive before the peak lunch hour.

St. Paul's. Go down Cheapside away from St. Paul's Cathedral; turn right at Bread St. and left at Watling St. Sandwiches £3.25-4; pizza £1.60 cold, £1.90 hot. M-F 7:30am-3:30pm.

YE OLDE CHESHIRE CHEESE — PUB 3

145 Fleet St., down Wine Office Ct.

The current Cheese was built in 1667, but a pub has been in its current location since 1538. **Charles Dickens** and **Samuel Johnson,** author of the first dictionary (a copy is upstairs), frequented the pub. Despite its history, Ye Olde Cheshire Cheese remains a personable, old-timey watering hole, serving traditional English "fayre" alongside their phenomenally cheap and excellent Samuel Smith brews from Yorkshire. If you explore the downstairs dining room, be wary of the sign that says "mind your head." They mean it.

St. Paul's. Take a right on New Change, a right onto Cannon St. which becomes St. Paul's Churchyard, Ludgate Hill and then Fleet St. Entrees £9.95-11.95; bangers and mash £3.50. Shots £1.89-2.20; ½ pint of lager £1.14; pint of lager £2.27; ½ pint of ale £1; pint of ale 1.99. M-Sa 11am-11pm, Su 11am-6pm.

CAFE BELOW — CAFE 3

Underneath St. Mary-Le-Bow, in Crypt — 020 7329 0789 www.cafebelow.co.uk

Cafe Below gives those of us alive and kickin' reason to visit the crypt. The cafe serves up delicious, wholesome breakfast, lunch and dinner to visitors and non-visitors alike. With a beautiful dining room that takes full advantage of the church's fantastic architecture, Cafe Below provides food that's uniquely homemade at reasonable prices.

St. Paul. Go down Cheapside with your back to St. Paul's Cathedral. Breakfast, £4.50-5, lunch £7.50-8.50, dinner £10.50. Take-away tends to be roughly £1 less. M-F 7:30am-9pm.

S AND M — BRITISH FOOD 2

28 Leadenhall Mkt. — 020 7626 6646 www.sandmcafe.co.uk

S and M will give you serious pleasure. We're both talking about sausage and mash, right? Dedicated to the preservation of British cuisine, S and M serves authentic British breakfasts in addition to their various varieties of sausage and mash. It gets crowded at lunch, so if you're going to do S and M, come early.

Bank. Walk down Cornhill towards Leaden Hall St. Breakfast from £3.25, S and M dishes £8.50-8.95, entrees £8.95-9.50. Open M-Tu 8am-3pm, W-Th 8am-9pm, F 8am-3pm.

HOLBORN AND CLERKENWELL

Holborn offers standard fare plus a few high-class restaurants and bistros mixed in with typical take-away sandwich joints. Clerkenwell has a lot more in the vein of hip, light, and interesting restaurants.

THE CLERKENWELL KITCHEN — HEALTHY, BRITISH, SEASONAL 3

31 Clerkenwell Close — 020 7101 9959 www.theclerkenwellkitchen.co.uk

Normally when a restaurant advertises "soft drinks," they mean cola and root beer. At the Clerkenwell Kitchen, a "soft drink" means a taste-bud-exploding concoction like their elderflower cordial *(£2).* The closest they come to Coke is their organic cola. Cooking with locally grown ingredients and organic, free-range meat, the Clerkenwell Kitchen welcomes guests to the lighter side of British fare. In the summer months, bask in the light that fills their terrace; in the winter, enjoy dishes like slow-roast pork belly with braised lentils, chard, and quince aioli. The menu changes daily based entirely on which fresh and local ingredients they receive, but if one thing is consistent, it's the high quality of this hidden restaurant.

Farringdon. Right onto Cowcross St., right onto Farringdon, right onto Pear Tree Ct., right

onto Clerkenwell Close. Walk straight as if still on Pear Tree Ct. If you see the church, backtrack. Entrees £9-10. Teas and coffees £1.50-1.85. Open M-F 8am-5pm and noon-3pm.

DANS LE NOIR FRENCH 5

30-31 Clerkenwell Green ☎020 7253 1100 www.danslenoir.com/london

Remember that Halloween game you played when you were a kid? Someone's mom would bring out a bowl of spaghetti and you would put your hands in it and squirm at the thought that you were touching real human intestines. Dans le Noir recreates that experience, only this time, once you're done sticking your hand in your plate, you eat the intestines. Served by blind waiters, patrons of the restaurant dine in a pitch black dining room, getting served a surprise meal of meat, fish, vegetarian, or "surprise" varieties. It may be expensive, but you're paying for a full sensory experience as well as the fantastic food.

Farringdon. Left onto Cowcross St., left onto Turnmill St., and a right at the Vine St. Bridge. It's across the green. Surprise 2-course meal £39, surprise 3-course menu is £44. You can book for a 6:30-9pm meal or a 9pm-whenever your meal ends (by midnight) meal.

BLEEDING HEART TAVERN FRENCH, TAVERN 3

Entrance to Bleeding Heart Yard ☎020 7242 2056 www.bleedingheart.co.uk/tavern

Bleeding Heart Tavern takes the challenge of reinventing pub food and succeeds. While holding onto its status as an excellent tavern that'll get you "drunk for a penny, and dead drunk for two pence," the Bleeding Heart Tavern also produces mouth-watering pub food, like its salt beef sandwich served on delectable homemade bread with a side of delicious coleslaw. From homemade pork sausages to spinach and three cheeses roulade, Bleeding Heart Tavern does it all with a French twist, and they do it well.

Farringdon. Take a right onto Cowcross St., and continue onto Greville St. Open M-F noon-2:30pm and 6-10:30pm, Sa noon-3pm and 6-11pm.

BLEEDING HEART BISTRO FRENCH BISTRO 4

Bleeding Heart Yard www.bleedingheart.co.uk/bistro

A classic and classy bistro experience, the Bleeding Heart Bistro takes excellent tavern fare (mentioned above) to the next level. With an adventurous menu featuring more than 450 wines, the Bleeding Heart Bistro offers an atmosphere that, despite the anti-smoking laws in the UK, manages to seem romantically smoke-filled at all times.

Farringdon. Take a right onto Cowcross St. and continue onto Greville St. Entrees £10.95-11.95. Open M-F noon-2:30pm and 6-10:30pm, Sa noon-3pm and 6-11pm.

MARYLEBONE AND REGENT'S PARK

THE GOLDEN HIND FISH AND CHIPS 2

73 Marylebone Ln. ☎020 7486 3644

The Golden Hind might just have the best fish and chips in London. With a wide selection of fish and a selection of classic sides, the menu will challenge you in ways you never thought fish and chips could.

Bond St. Left onto Davies St., right onto Oxford St., left onto Marylebone Ln. Fish (fried or steamed) £4.70-5.70. Chips £1.50. Peas £1. Open M-F noon-3pm and 6-10pm, Sa 6-10pm.

PATOGH PERSIAN 2

8 Crawford Pl ☎020 7262 4015

Patogh is the definition of hole-in-the-wall. Small and crowded but nicely decorated and exquisitely scented, Patogh provides traditional Persian food like minced lamb and huge servings of sesame flatbread in a highly atmospheric setting.

Edgward Rd. Right onto Chapel St., left onto Edgware Rd., left onto Crawford Pl. Entrees £8-9. Open daily noon-11pm.

LE RELAIS DE VENISE L'ENTRECOTE — STEAK *FRÎTES* ❹

120 Marylebone Ln. ☎020 7486 0878 www.relaisdevenise.com

Amid the warm decor and wall-size paintings of canals that decorate this restaurant, hungry diners just in from a queue that typically stretches around the block feast on one thing and one thing only: L'entrecote's fantastic *steak frîtes.*

Bond St. Left onto Davies St., right onto Oxford St., left onto Marylebone Ln. Open M-Th noon-2:30pm and 6-10:45pm, F noon-2:45pm and 6-10:45pm, Sa 12:30pm-3:30pm and 6:30-10:45pm, Su 12:30pm-3:30pm and 6:30-10:30pm.

ROYAL CHINA — DIM SUM ❸

24-26 Baker St. ☎020 7487 4688 www.royalchinagroup.co.uk

This micro chain is a good place to find Dim Sum if you're craving it. Though the decor walks the fine line between elegant and cheesy, the restaurant is quiet and pleasant, and the selection is expansive.

Baker Street. Left Baker St. Most dim sum items £2.65-3.15. Noodles £7.50-8. Entrees £8.50-9.20. Set meals for 2+ people £30 per person. Open M-Sa noon-11pm. Dim Sum M-Sa noon-5pm, Su 11am-5pm.

THE WEST END

MÔ CAFÉ — CAFE, TEA, NORTH AFRICAN ❷

23-25 Heddon St. ☎020 7434 4040 www.momoresto.com

When juxtaposed with the absurd decadence of nearby Absolut Icebar (yes, that is a bar...made of ice), the Mô Café's own absurd conceit feels a little less ridiculous. With waiters wearing bright red shirts and black pants, chandeliers that are draped in tassels and strings and bronze table tops surrounded by low chairs, the Mô Café looks like it's trying too hard. However, try the hummus or the mint tea (made with tea imported from Morocco, obviously), and you'll feel your skull tingle where your fez once was. The restaurant is a true experience, especially when the other patrons are enjoying £18 hookah in your general vicinity. That's right, hookah. Only in Soho would that just as easily be a mispronunciation of another commonly purchased service.

Piccadilly Circus. Turn left onto Regent St. and left onto Heddon St. Cold mezze £4.50-4.75. Hot mezze £5.50-5.80. M-Sa noon-1am, Su noon-11pm.

FERNANDEZ AND WELLS CAFE — CAFE, SANDWICHES ❸

73 Beak St. ☎020 7287 8124 www.fernandezandwells.com

Yuppified to the max, Fernandez and Wells knows its crowd and it serves them well. A bright space with simple wood and thin counters for eating, the restaurant prides itself on its coffee and gives out a map to all the good coffee spots in London, serving the yuppy desire to be "cool" and "in-the-know." Providing ready-made, delicious sandwiches with well-prepared ingredients, Fernandez and Wells is a good spot for a fast and easy lunch.

Piccadilly Circus. Turn right down Shaftesbury Ave. and left onto Lexington St., left onto Beak St. Croissaints £1.65-1.80. Chelsea bun £2.45. Coffee £2.20-2.50. Sandwiches £4.25-5.50. Open M-F 7:30am-6pm, Sa 9am-6pm, Su 9am-5pm.

KOYA — JAPANESE ❸

49 Frith St. ☎020 7434 4463 www.koya.co.uk

Unlike many Japanese restaurants, where Chinese or British cooks pretend to make authentic Japanese dishes, Koya is the real deal. Through the cloth that guards the front door lies a dining room where only the most authentic and delicious *hiya-atsu* and *atsu-atsu* (cold and hot udon) is served. This place is good, and Soho knows it, so try to come sometime other than 6:30pm, as they don't take reservations, it gets crowded, and the starving people you'll stand outside with may or may not be very pleasant.

Tottenham Court Rd. Turn down Oxford St. with your back to Tottenham Court Rd and then left onto Soho St. Go around Soho Sq. to the left and turn left onto Frith. Ⓢ Udon is around £8.50-9. ⏰ Open M-Sa noon-3pm and 5:30-10:30pm.

BAR ITALIA COFFEE BAR ❸

22 Frith St. ☎020 7437 4520 baritaliasoho.co.uk

Bar Italia is about as close as you'll get to what would've happened if Ed Hopper had painted the *Nighthawks* in Soho. Its simple, unassuming decor is as authentic as the coffee is strong, and photos of its storied past (replete with coffee drinkers of yore) line the walls. On a nice day, many sit outside and watch the parade of altered life that is Soho. The clientele runs the gamut—hip or unhip, it matters not: they belly up to the same counter for Bar Italia's classic coffee.

Tottenham Court Rd. Turn down Oxford St. with your back to Tottenham Court Rd. and then left onto Soho St. Go around Soho Sq to the left and turn left onto Frith. Ⓢ Espresso £2.50-3.80. Cappuccino is £2.80-3.80. Caffe latte £3-4. Pizzas around £11.50. Panini £6.20-6.80.

SOFRA ♿ MEDITERRANEAN ❹

18 Shepherd St. ☎020 7493 3320 www.sofra.co.uk

Sofra has a brightly lit, wide open dining room that somehow feels like it's sitting on the edge of a Mediterranean beach where men in three-button-undone shirts seduce women in red dresses. Is that just us? Well, either way, this pleasant dining space provides fairly high-priced Mediterranean classics like Lamb Tagine, kebabs, and salmon stew.

Hyde Park Corner. Go down Piccadilly Arcade staying to the left of the Wellington Arch with your back to Hyde Park. Turn left onto White Horse St. Ⓢ Entrees around £11.95, but there's a wide range. ⏰ Open daily 8am-11pm.

NORTH LONDON

LA CRÊPERIE DE HAMPSTEAD ♿ CRÊPES, STREET STAND ❶

Around 77 Hampstead High St. www.hampsteadcreperie.com

Walking down Hampstead High St. from the underground station, a traveler may notice several people lining the bus stop benches, ravenously eating crêpes out of small conical cups. Walk a bit further down, and you'll see La Crêperie de Hampstead. Serving the community since 1929, the crêperie is not the average street vendor's booth. The crêpes are expertly crafted—a perfect balance of light and doughy—and the ingredients, sweet or savory, are well-blended to create crêpes that burst with flavor.

Hampstead. Left onto Hampstead Heath St. i No seating available, but check the nearby benches. Ⓢ Savories £4.30-4.65. Sweets £3.40-3.90. ⏰ Open M-Th 11:45am-11pm, F-Su 11:45am-11:30pm.

MANGO ROOM CARIBBEAN ❸

10-12 Kentish Town Rd. ☎020 7482 5065 www.mangoroom.co.uk

Located near bustling Camden Town, the Mango Room is the perfect place to escape the excitement. The cool room decorated with bright paintings that nicely complement the food is perfect for anyone who regrets choosing rainy London over the sunny Caribbean for a vacation. Serving Caribbean dishes like ackee and saltfish with scallions and sweet peppers *(£11)*, the Mango Room is about as escapist and pleasant as the name suggests.

Camden High St. Left onto Camden High St., left onto Camden Rd., Left onto Kentish Town Rd. i Minimum £10. Ⓢ Dinner entrees £10.50-11. Lunch entrees £7-8.50. Mixed drinks £4 during happy hour. ⏰ Open daily noon-11pm. Bar open until 1am F-Sa. Happy hour 6-8pm.

CARMELLI BAKERY ♿ KOSHER BAKERY ❶

128 Golders Green Rd. ☎020 8455 2074 www.carmelli.co.uk

Carmelli Bakery is overfilling with delicious kosher foods—everything from fresh made bagels to delicious chollas and chocolate eclairs. While there's no seating in the store, the nearby bus stop has a bench.

Golders Green. Cross Finchley Rd. to Golders Green Rd. Bagels £2-2.20 closed, £1.40-1.50 open (with toppings like cream cheese, chopped herring, salmon and cream cheese). Eclairs £.85. Chocolate mousse £.90. Open daily 6am-1am.

MARINE ICES GELATO ❷

8 Haverstock Hill ☎020 7482 9003 www.marineices.co.uk

Though it looks like someone decided to move part of the Jersey Shore to London, Marine Ices serves some of the finest quality Italian ice in London at affordable prices. They make it all in-house and then serve it in hearty portions to regular patrons and local restaurants alike. While there isn't much else to do at Chalk Farm, Marine Ices is right near the Tube and, if you're in the area, might just be worth a stop.

Chalk Farm. Credit card min. £5. Wheelchair-accessible through the window (where they serve ice cream on nice days), not through restaurant. 1 scoop £1.90, 2 scoops £3.50, 3 scoops £4.90. Each topping £.60. Open Tu-Su noon-11pm.

EAST LONDON

Most of East London's culinary offerings are packed into the unbeatable **Brick Lane.** If you're looking for curry, you'd have to be blind and smell-challenged not to find it. However, if you want to partake in the Shoreditch scene but can't handle the pressure of choosing just one curry restaurant, here are a few good alternatives.

NUDE ESPRESSO CAFE ❸

26 Hanbury St. ☎078 0422 3590 www.nudeespresso.com

Most good cafes pride themselves on buying exotic coffee beans, but Nude Espresso takes their gimmick a step further, actually roasting the coffee beans themselves. Serving up some of the best coffee in London, the hip Nude Espresso is a welcome break from the myriad curry restaurants hawking their wares on Brick Ln. With its aluminum cups and stylish interior, Nude Espresso gets the aesthetic right while never forgetting what its clients came for: damn good coffee.

Aldgate East. Left onto Whitechapel Rd., left onto Osborn St., continue onto Brick Ln.; left onto Hanbury. Credit card min. £6. Wi-Fi available, but they don't allow plugins. Breakfast and lunch entrees £6-7.50. Espresso £2-2.50. Specialty coffee drinks around £3.60. Open M-F 7:30am-6pm, Sa-Su 10am-6pm.

CAFE 1001 CAFE ❷

91 Brick Ln. ☎020 7247 9679 www.cafe1001.co.uk

Under the overhang connecting Cafe 1001 to the Truman Ale factory, hip East Enders bask in the British sun's occasional appearances and share in the good coffee served from the cafe's year-round outdoor cart. Inside the cafe, numerous patrons listen to music from the likes of Caetano Veloso and kick back in the warehouse-like space. At night, the salad bar turns into a real bar, and the back room becomes a venue for up-and-coming bands and DJs, and sometimes it even serves as a classroom for aspiring swing dancers. Basically, this cafe is as close as a cafe comes to being a cultural center. Incidentally, Jack the Ripper killed someone out behind the back room, so prostitutes might want to take their business elsewhere. Bloc Party also filmed their video for "The Prayer" here. "East London is a vampire," as the boys would say.

Aldgate East. Left onto Whitechapel Rd., left onto Osborn St., continue onto Brick Ln. Credit card min. £4. F, Sa, and Su are club nights from 7pm-midnight, with DJs playing in the back room. Live bands every T (rock) and W (folk and jazz). Swing dancing classes Th 11am-5pm. Coffee £1.20-1.70 for a small, £.40-£2 for a large. Cover charge £3-5 after midnight. Free Wi-Fi. Open daily 7am-midnight, sometimes no closing F-Su (as in, it stays open continuously).

BEIGEL BAKE

BAGELS ❶

159 Brick Ln. ☎020 7729 0616

This sparse-looking bakery may not seem appealing to the casual observer, but once the sweet and heavy perfume of their classic, fresh-made bagels has enveloped you, you'll have a harder time passing it by.

Aldgate East. Left on Whitechapel Rd, left on Osborn St., continue onto Brick Ln. Filled bagels £.80-1.50. Open 24hr.

OTHER NEIGHBORHOODS

POILÂNE

BAKERY ❸

46 Elizabeth St. ☎020 7808 4910 www.poilane.com

Poilâne is one of the most famous bakeries from Paris, which means that, by London standards, it's ungodly good. The commitment to excellence at Poilâne is unparalleled. Many of the bakers live above the shop, baking the bread all through the night to ensure that it's fresh for the morning crowd. They use only the oldest, most time-honored traditions and techniques when creating their sourdough masterpieces, and the *pain au chocolat* is to die for. Also worth noting is the fact that they bake in wood-fired ovens of the type that started the Great Fire of London—but don't worry, Poilâne is both safe *and* delicious.

Victoria. Left onto Buckingham Palace Rd., right onto Elizabeth St. Walnut bread £4. Pain au chocolat £1.20. Sourdough bread £4.40. Custard tart £16. Open M-F 7:30am-7pm. Sa 7:30am-6pm.

DA SCALZO

ITALIAN ❸

2 Eccleston Pl. ☎020 7730 5498 www.dascalzo.com

You should really be wary of Italian restaurants, especially ones in close proximity to train and bus stations, like da Scalzo, but da Scalzo defies all odds. The food is well-priced and fantastically portioned, making for a real Italian feast to be savored. Their pastas and pizzas are especially delish, but they do amazing things with the preparation of other dishes that'll make you double take when you see the bill (which, for food of this caliber, is strikingly low). More important than all of this, however, is the atmosphere at da Scalzo. The waiters and waitresses pal around with each other, putting on informal shows with pizza dough, and they have the incredible ability to make you feel that, though you may have just gotten off the plane, you've been dining at da Scalzo for your whole life.

Victoria. Left onto Buckingham Palace Rd., right onto Elizabeth St. Pasta and risotto £6-7. Stone baked pizza £8.50-9. Meat £12.50-14. Fish £12.50. Open M-Sa 8am-11pm, Su 8am-8pm.

BAKER AND SPICE

NEW EUROPEAN PASTRIES ❸

54-56 Elizabeth St. ☎020 7730 3033 www.bakerandspice.uk.com

Baker and Spice is the *part deux* of the one-two pastry punch on Elizabeth St. The street boasts Poîlane, and, less than a block away, the equally good Baker and Spice. Serving freshly made pastries; strong, delicious coffee; and a wide variety of ready-made meals and salads, Baker and Spice is gourmet on the go. Ideal for takeaway, but delicious enough to be savored slowly in the al fresco dining areas, Baker and Spice does it all with ample style and grace.

Victoria. Left onto Buckingham Palace Rd., right onto Elizabeth St. Open M-Sa 7am-7pm, Su 8am-5pm.

THE KENSINGTON CRÊPERIE

CRÊPES ❸

2-6 Exhibition Rd. ☎020 7589 8947 www.kensingtoncreperie.com

Close to the museums off Exhibition Rd., the Kensington Crêperie serves fantastic and affordable crepes and less affordable, equally fantastic ice cream sundaes. Along with delicious crêpes like the garlic, spinach, and cream cheese option, the Kensington Crêperie produces ice cream sundae masterpieces such as the Stone Age. (hazelnuts, walnuts, peanuts, coconuts, flaked almond, two scoops of ice cream, sauce of choice, honey, and walnuts). With al fresco dining on Exhibition Rd., each delicious savory and sweet crêpe only tastes better.

South Kensington. Turn right onto Thurloe St., left onto Exhibition Rd. Crepes £7.75-8.30. Sundaes £5.95. Open daily 8am-11pm.

THE GATE — VEGETARIAN, VEGAN, GLUTEN FREE ❹

51 Queen Caroline St., 2nd fl. ☎020 8748 6932 www.thegate.tv

Tucked away down Queen Caroline St. in the lofty, sunlit studio of a former puppet-maker, The Gate has been serving a menu composed almost entirely of vegetarian, vegan, or gluten-free dishes for the last 20 years. Everything is made from seasonal ingredients, and the massive window that illuminates the dining room is bordered by sunflowers. If you like what you eat, you can buy their own cookbook, too.

Hammersmith. Take the south exit from the Hammersmith shopping center toward the London Apollo and follow Queen Caroline St. i Reservations recommended 3 days in advance. Entrees £12.50-13.50. Open M-F noon-2:30pm and 6-10pm, Sa 6-11pm.

PATIO — POLISH, ENGLISH ❷

5 Goldhawk Rd. ☎020 8743 5194

Patio is literally buried in the numerous accolades and press given to the restaurant over its 24-year career. Owned by a former Polish opera singer, Patio is filled with warm carpets and stuffed upholstered chairs, meant to create a casual but pleasant dining experience. Diners enjoy traditional English and Polish fare (the menu is filled with veal), and selections from the Polish menu come with complimentary Polish vodka. There's also a dusty-sounding piano which any guest can play. Come and enjoy and then catch a show nearby.

Shepherd's Bush. Cross Uxbridge Rd. and turn right onto Shepherd's Bush Green. Follow it until it becomes Goldhawk Rd. Entrees £8.50-11. Seafood £8.50-9.50. Open M-F noon-3pm and 5-11pm, Sa-Su 6-11:30pm.

JENNY LO'S TEAHOUSE — ASIAN TEA ❷

14 Eccleston St. ☎020 7259 0399 www.jennylo.co.uk

Thought you'd never hear about J. Lo again? This unassuming teahouse serves delicious Asian classics like Vietnamese-style vermicelli rice noodles, Thai-style lamb in green curry, and wok noodles. They have their own herbalist (Dr. Xu) and a terrific selection of delicious teas. Come here for a quick, quiet, and delicious meal.

Victoria. i Min. £5 per person. Takeaway available. Entrees £7.50-8.50. Therapeutic teas £2. Mint tea £3.50. Chinese teas £2. Open M-F noon-3pm and 6-10pm.

CHARLIE'S PORTOBELLO RD. CAFE — BRITISH CAFE ❸

59A Portobello Rd. ☎020 7221 2422 www.charliesportobelloroadcafe.co.uk

Tucked away in a small alcove off busy Portobello Rd., Charlie's Portobello Road Cafe is a hidden gem in one London's most over-exposed areas. Light streams into the spacious, authentically worn dining space through the huge French windows which are thrown open to a plant-lined patio. An atmospheric restaurant, Charlie's is a great place for a good, old-fashioned English breakfast.

Notting Hill Gate. Take a right onto Pembridge Rd. and then left onto Portobello Rd. i Free Wi-Fi. Full English breakfast £9.50. Open M-Sa 9am-5pm, Su noon-2:30pm.

THE HUMMINGBIRD BAKERY — PASTRY ❸

133 Portobello Rd. ☎020 7229 6446 www.hummingbirdbakery.com

Priding themselves on bold, simple, American-style baked goods, the Hummingbird Bakery serves up their popular cupcakes and cakes in a simple space decorated by paintings of (surprise!) hummingbirds.

Notting Hill Gate. Take right onto Pembridge Rd. and then left onto Portobello Rd. Credit card min. £5. Takeaway cheaper than eat-in. Cupcakes £1.75-2. Open M-F 10am-6pm, Sa 10am-6pm, Su 11am-5pm.

BON GUSTO SANDWICHES, ITALIAN ❶

75-77 Buckingham Gate ☎020 7222 7185

London, and Westminster especially, is teeming with touristy, budget restaurants that advertise themselves as *"Ristorante Italiano,"* but serve up the most British Italian food ever. Bon Gusto advertises as such, but anyone passing the front door will find it hard to turn away. The restaurant unleashes a gust of hearty Italian smells on any passerby, and the toasted sandwiches on ciabatta and focaccia are delicious at unbeatable prices.

Victoria. Right on Victoria St., left onto Buckingham Gate. Sandwiches £3.85-3.90. Open M-Sa 7am-10pm, Su 7am-3pm.

nightlife

If you seek the club scene of say, Barcelona, go to Barcelona. The elitist impulse often rears its head in British club life—this is especially evident in Kensington and Chelsea where many clubs are "members only," meaning they'll make you ask to have your name put on a guest list. That doesn't mean that there's no nightlife. Visitors can find evening kicks in bars that serve some exciting drinks (check out Soho for lessons in **mixology**). Music venues like the **Troubadour** in Kensington provide killer atmospheres and young crowds late at night.

Still, pubs are the fabric of British life. Most are open daily 11am-11pm with some variation in regards to the weekend. Pubs are where Brits come to eat and drink too much. At lunchtime, the pubs in Westminster and the City of London fill with men in matching suits. The best are the ones that claim residence in the oldest drinking locations in London, meaning that people have been drunk there since the dawn of time. Be wary of the "George Orwell drank here" or the "Dylan Thomas drank here" line—you will see those names everywhere, because not only were they fantastic drunks, they were also prolific walkers. Parliament even passed the **Defense of the Realm Act** during WWI to limit pub hours in order to keep the munitions workers sober. This law was in effect until 1988, and many pubs still retain the early hours. Always bring cab fare or plan your **night bus** route home as the **Tube** closes early.

stags and hens

Especially young travelers to Britain should note that "stag" and "hen" parties refer to bachelor and bachelorette parties, respectively. It's literally the husband- and bride-to-be's last time to be party animals.

BLOOMSBURY

VATS WINE BAR WINE BAR

51 Lambs' Conduit St. ☎020 7242 8963 www.vatswinebar.com

The epitome of a warm, British restaurant, Vats imports much of its wine while keeping the feel of the place properly British. With a menu boasting around

160 vintages from all over, Vats is an upscale and pleasant evening experience. Upscale pub food like venison sausages with creamed mash, broccoli florets, belotte beans, bacon sauce, and a garnish of cranberries are par for the course. Dine downstairs or outside between the two latticework fences that shield the restaurant's facade. The food is hearty and delicious, and the wine flows freely.

Russell Square. Left onto Colonnade, right onto Grenville St., left onto Guilford St. and right onto Lambs' Conduit St. Sides £3.75. Entrees £13-15. Open M-F noon-2:30pm and 6-9:30pm.

THE FITZROY TAVERN FAMOUS TAVERN

16A Charlotte St. 020 7580 3714

Many pubs try to ensnare tourists by claiming they are the oldest pub in England or telling bizarre perversions of famous stories ("and that penny that **Dickens** gave to the little boy was spent on whiskey in our pub...") that lend a historical grandeur to what is actually just a decrepit pub with bad ales. The Fitzroy Tavern actually has a published book about its history, and artifacts from that history coat the walls. Famous for the charitable program instated by the tavern to send kids on outings to the country and for the authors who frequented the pub, most notably **Dylan Thomas** and **George Orwell,** The Fitzroy Tavern is the real deal. Pints are cheap, the history's free, and there's a comedy night too.

Goodge St. left on Tottenham Ct. Rd., left on Tottenham St., left on to Charlotte St. Credit card min. £10, 1.5% surcharge. Most pints under £3.15; £2.50 is the average. Open M-Sa noon-11pm, Su noon-10:30pm. Comedy night W 8:30pm.

THE COURT PUB

108a Tottenham Court Rd. 020 7387 0183

A true-blue student pub for a student neighborhood, The Court boasts loud music, cheap beers, juke boxes, and a hip crowd. In the upstairs area, there's a pool table, but most of the pubgoers sit outside or inside the brightly-lit pub area, under hanging strings of lights, devouring cheap and tantalizing burgers.

Warren St. Left on Warren St., right on Tottenham Court Rd. Pints £3. Burgers £4.95-5.95. With student discount (you qualify if you buy the yellow student discount card at the pub), the pints are around £2.50. Open M-W 11am-midnight, Th-Sa 11am-1am. Kitchen open M-Sa 11am-9pm.

PRINCESS LOUISE PUB

208 High Holborn 020 7405 8816

A student-packed local hang, the Princess Louise has a classic interior filled with elaborately-designed fogged glass, worn leather seats, and various other pieces of ornate decor. Perhaps the most beautiful things in the pub are the (figurative) price tags on the beers, which are much cheaper than what you'll find in most pubs in the area. A fun atmosphere with a young crowd, the Princess Louise is a neighborhood favorite.

Holborn. Left onto High Holborn. Pint of bitters £1.99. Pint of lager £2.27. Open M-F 11:30am-11pm, Sa-Su noon-11pm.

THE OLD CROWN PUBLIC HOUSE PUB

33 New Oxford St. 020 7836 9121 www.theoldcrownpublichouse.com

Old Crown meets young crowd. The pub is filled with old, beat-up wood tables and worn leather-backed chairs. The pipes from an ancient organ appear distorted through the bottles of hard alcohol behind the bar, and nicely framed, goofy pictures line the walls. In addition to the pub, there's a function room with another bar and space for dancing.

Holborn. Left onto High Holborn right onto New Oxford St. Pint £3.80. Open M-W noon-midnight, Th-Sa noon-3am, Su noon-midnight. DJs F-Sa 9pm-3am.

QUEENS LARDER PUB

1 Queen Sq. ☎020 7837 5627 www.queenslarder.co.uk

Queen Charlotte, the wife of George III, stored special treats for her hubby in the cellar beneath this pub. Now, the larders are stocked with other sorts of special treats perfect for today's student-aged Englishmen, and you won't find Queen Charlotte hanging here anymore. The pub is bustling, with outdoor seating and a pleasant upstairs lounge.

Russell Square, right onto Colonnade, left onto Herbrand St. right onto Guilford St., left onto Russell Sq., continue onto Southampton Row left onto Cosmo Pl. Pint £3.55. Open M-Sa 11am-10:30pm. Lunch served noon-3pm.

CHELSEA

Chelsea is now one of the more exclusive and pretentious places to find nightlife in London. Many clubs advertise as members-only private establishments, but for many, you only have to call to get on the guest list. There are a few excellent pubs and many clubs, but if you're looking for an easily accessible, young scene, look elsewhere.

THE CHELSEA RAM PUB

32 Burnaby St. ☎020 7351 4008

A classy neighborhood pub that's more of a quiet hang than it is a rowdy party, The Chelsea Ram specializes in cultivating a pleasant atmosphere. With loads of regulars congregating under the pub's high, bright ceilings, the pub provides friendly staff, good books, fun board games, and interesting art that's for sale (if you tend to buy art when drunk, beware). Any pub with the love poetry of John Donne is a good pub. It's near the rougher section of King's Rd. though, so it may be best to enjoy it earlier or take a cab home.

Sloane Square. Exit the Tube and go straight down Sloane Sq. The street slanting gently left is King's Rd. If you don't want to walk the road (it's manageable but long), the following buses and night buses service the area: 11, 19, 22, 211, 319, N11, N19, N22. Left on Lots Rd., left on Burnaby St. Pints £4. Entrees £11.50-12.95. Open M-Sa noon-11pm. Su noon-7pm. Kitchen open M-Sa noon-3pm and 6-10pm.

HENRY J. BEAN'S BAR AND GRILL PUB

195-197 King's Rd. ☎020 7352 9255 www.henryjbeans.co.uk/chelsea

Henry J. Bean's attitude toward nightlife is very much embodied in its license-plate map of the states: really cool but a little mixed-up (why is Delaware in the Midwest?) Henry J. Bean's is jam-packed with a super loud young crowd grooving to a wide range of blaring music. The good times await.

Sloane Square. Exit the Tube and go straight down Sloane Sq. The street slanting gently left is King's Rd. If you don't want to walk the road (it's manageable but long), the following buses and night buses service the area: 11, 19, 22, 211, 319, N11, N19, N22. Pints £3.80. Open M-W 11am-11pm, Th-Su 11am-midnight.

THE CADOGAN ARMS PUB

298 King's Rd. ☎020 7352 6500 www.thecadoganarmschelsea.com

At the bottom of The Cadogan Arms' fantastic menu, there's a little note that many diners unfortunately miss: "Please note that game dishes may contain shot." In summary: The Cadogan Arms is classy, but it's still a pub. With more horns on the wall than there are known horned animals, The Cadogan Arms is high on atmosphere. Meals best enjoyed with excellent company and conversation, drinks best shared with friends.

Sloane Square. Exit the Tube and go straight down Sloane Sq. The street slanting gently left is King's Rd. If you don't want to walk the road (it's manageable but long), the following buses and night buses service the area: 11, 19, 22, 211, 319, N11, N19, N22. Entrees £15-17. Open M-F noon-3:30pm and 6-10:30pm, Sa noon-10:30pm, Su noon-9pm.

EMBARGO 59 CLUB

533b King's Rd. ☎020 7351 5038 www.embargo59.com

Climbing the steel steps to Embargo (when referring to it, you drop the 59), it's hard to know what to expect. Suddenly, guests enter the pink backlit reception area from the cold staircase. Then, the main room has a long bar, a lengthy cushion-backed bench with small tables and a dance floor composed of panels that change light. There is also a gorgeous smoking terrace with its own cocktail bar, and a roof made of string lights that look like especially bright stars. Though the club caters to a 20-something professional crowd, like most clubs in Chelsea, W nights, intended for students, feature cheaper drinks.

Sloane Square. Exit the Tube and go straight down Sloane Square. The street slanting gently left is King's Rd. If you don't want to walk the road (it's manageable but long), the following buses and night buses service the area: 11, 19, N11, N22. Turn left onto Lots Rd. Cash only for the cover, MC/Visa at the bar. Cover W-Th £5-10, F-Sa £10-15. Bottles of beer W-Th around £2.50, F-Sa £3-4. Mixed drinks W-Th £5, F-Sa £6.95-8.95. Open W-Th 10pm-2am, F-Sa 10pm-3am.

THE ANTELOPE PUB

22-24 Eaton Terr. ☎020 7824 8512

Established in 1827, The Antelope enjoyed a brief stint as a celebrity pub in the '60s, hosting such rising stars as Roman Polanski. More recently, Prince William came in to drink, but these days The Antelope is otherwise a quiet, small, and cozy neighborhood bar with a Scrabble set, and a worn couch that sits by a lamp and under a bookshelf.

Sloane Sq. Take a right onto Sloane Sq. and another right onto Eaton Gate. Take a left onto Eaton Terr. Free Wi-Fi. Credit card for purchases over £10. Pints £3.50. Open M-Sa noon-11pm.

THE CROSS KEYS PUB

1 Lawrence St. ☎020 7349 9111 www.thexkeys.co.uk

Tucked away among Chelsea's beautiful residences. The Cross Keys is recognizable thanks to the gigantic, crossed gold keys which are embedded in the perfectly circular hedge on the building's facade. There has been a pub on the site since 1708, when the river ran right up to its wall. The dining room is James Bond meets Vermont ski lodge, with a sliding roof and uniquely-cut rustic wood tables. Beautiful art lines the walls, stained mirrors decorate the ground floor, and a graceful, billowing chandelier dangles from the top floor to illuminate your pint *(£3.40).*

Sloane Square. Exit the Tube and go straight down Sloane Sq. The street slanting gently left is King's Rd. If you don't want to walk the road (it's manageable but long), the following buses and night buses service the area: 11, 19, 22, 211, 319, N11, N19, N22. Turn left onto Glebe Pl. and then right onto Lawrence St. Pints £3.40. Open M-Sa noon-midnight, Su noon-11:30pm. Kitchen open M-F noon-3pm, and 6-10:30pm.

THE PHOENIX PUB

23 Smith St. ☎020 7730 9182 www.geronimo-inns.co.uk

The Phoenix is a case study in the power of understatement. Down a quiet street off of King's Rd., The Phoenix sits behind a quiet exterior, calmly offering reasonably-priced drinks (for Chelsea anyway) and fine food. It caters to a definitively local crowd, and most of the patrons are over 30. Chalkboards around the bar offer words of wisdom from famous drunkards.

Sloane Square. Exit the Tube and go straight down Sloane Sq. The street slanting gently left is King's Rd. Left at Smith St. Pints £3.30-3.75. Entrees £12-14 Open M-Sa 11am-11pm, Su noon-10:30pm.

151 CLUB CLUB

151 King's Rd. ☎020 7351 6826

Right in the middle of posh King's Rd., the 151 Club offers a fairly standard and pleasant club space to a wide variety of people six nights a week. The club is decorated with oversized bottles, and leather chairs abound. The ceiling above the dance floor has tiny white lights that shift in intensity, creating a mesmeric effect. Expect to hear top-of-the-chart songs and cheesy club classics.

Sloane Square. Exit the Tube and go straight down Sloane Sq. The street slanting gently left is King's Rd. If you don't want to walk the road (it's manageable but long), the following buses and night buses service the area: 11, 19, 22, 211, 319, N11, N19, N22. i Most crowded W-Sa. Drink deals M-W. Credit cards 5% surcharge. Cover Th £5, F-Sa £10. Beer £4.50, M-W £2.50. Open M-Sa 11pm-3am.

QUEEN'S HEAD PUB GLBT PUB

25-27 Tryon St. ☎020 7589 0262 www.the1440.co.uk

Over a 100 years old, The Queen's Head (make of that what you will) is one of the oldest gay pubs in London. A friendly and convivial watering hole with an older clientele of both gay and straight patrons. Bingo once a month, karaoke every other week, and quiz night weekly.

Sloane Square. Exit the Tube and go straight down Sloane Sq. The street slanting gently left is King's Rd. If you don't want to walk the road (it's manageable but long), the following buses and night buses service the area: 11, 19, 22, 211, 319, N11, N19, N22. Turn right onto Tryon St. Pint of lager £3-4.50. Bitters £3.15+. Pub grub £6.95-7.25, all-day breakfast £6.95. Open M-Th noon-11:00pm, F-Sa noon-midnight, Su noon-10:30pm.

MARVEL LONDON CLUB

196-198 Fulham Rd. ☎020 7351 1711 www.marvellondon.com

A cool, chilled-out club, Marvel caters to 25-35-year-old Chelseans. The back room has a bean bag, striped pillows, and, of course, glass cases with killer robot toys. Pretty relaxed, but nothing that exciting. Week nights feature quiet couples' PDA on the sofa near the bar.

Sloane Square. Exit the Tube and go straight down Sloane Square. The street slanting gently left is King's Rd. If you don't want to walk the road (it's manageable but long), the following buses and night buses service King's Rd: 11, 19, 22, 211, 319, N11, N19, N22. Turn right onto Park Walk and then left onto Fulham Rd. i Credit card for purchases over £10. Be warned, sometimes when it gets busy, a 21+ rule is instated. White wine 175ml £4.50-39. Classic mixed drinks £7.50-8, martinis £7.50-8.50. Open daily 11am-1am, DJ F-Sa from 9pm on. Live music Sa 2-5pm and 9-11pm.

CHELSEA POTTER PUB

119 King's Rd. ☎020 7352 9479

Though serving a slightly older crowd, Chelsea Potter provides a comfy, open space in which to drink with friends. Comfortable benches sit outside the pub, providing an excellent angle for people-watching, and few roads could provide better subject matter.

Sloane Square. Exit the Tube and go straight down Sloane Sq. The street slanting gently left is King's Rd. If you don't want to walk the road (it's manageable but long), the following buses and night buses service the area: 11, 19, 22, 211, 319, N11, N19, N22. Pint £3.50, different guest ale every few weeks. Entrees £7.45-8.25. Sandwiches £4.75-4.95. Open M-Th 11am-11pm, F-Sa 11am-midnight, Su noon-10:30pm.

HOLBORN AND CLERKENWELL

Holborn is a pub town, and Clerkenwell is on the up-and-up. Look out for a mix of pleasant, old pubs and hip clubs, most of which can be found on Charterhouse St.

THE THREE KINGS

PUB

7 Clerkenwell Close

☎020 7253 0483

On warm evenings, patrons of The Three Kings line the curbs outside and drink their pints *(£3.30-3.50)* of Timothy Taylor, Staropramer, and Beck's. Inside, customers sit in the arm chairs under the watchful gazes of luminaries like Woody Allen, Hunter S. Thompson, Smokey Robinson, and that fake rhino the pub has on the wall. Strings of colored lights swoop down over a sign that says "Stop Bush," and sausage sandwiches are made on ciabatta bread with basil oil *(£4.50)*. This is a bar with character, grace, and an easy-going vibe. Classic rock, soul, and jazz pipe out of the speaker system, originating in the pub's trusty record player which sits atop a vast record collection. Weekly music quizzes are Mondays at 9pm; poetry night is the first Tuesday of every month at 8pm.

Farringdon. Right onto Cowcross St., right onto Farringdon, right onto Pear Tree Ct., right onto Clerkenwell Close. Open M-F noon-11pm, Sa. 5pm-11pm.

YE OLDE MITRE

PUB

Ely Court

☎020 7405 4751

You're only going to get to Ye Olde Mitre if you're looking for it. It's a pub with history (it was established in 1546 and sits to the side of an ancient church), but it doesn't equate "historic" with run-down. The downstairs and upstairs areas are bright, clean, and pleasant. While it caters to an older audience, it has an easy-going atmosphere and a good selection of relatively cheap beers and what they refer to as "English Tapas," including toasted sandwiches *(£2)*. Also, *Snatch* with Brad Pitt was filmed here—proof that good-looking people drink in this pub, too. While the pub seems safe, it's down a small, removed alley, so women especially may not want to travel here alone.

Farringdon. Right onto Cowcross St., left onto Farringdon Rd. right onto Charterhouse St., right onto Ely Pl. Most pints £3.20. Pints of lager £3.30. Open M-F 11am-11pm; closed on bank holidays.

THE 3 TUNS

STUDENT PUB

Houghton St.

☎020 7955 7156

While this place is not rich in the atmosphere department, the 3 Tuns customers are rich in the money department, thanks to this pub's dirt-cheap pints. This London School of Economics pub is frequented by (you guessed it) LSE students and is a good place to come if you want to meet university-aged people or play a game of pool in a sparsely furnished room where people drink beer from plastic cups.

Temple. Right onto Temple Pl., left onto Surrey St., cross the Strand. Continue onto Melbourne Pl., left onto Aldwych, right on Houghton St. Pints £2.10. Term-time hoursM-Tu 10am-11pm, W 10am-midnight, Th 10am-11pm, F 10am-2am, Sa 9pm-3am. During school holidays, call for hours.

THE JERUSALEM TAVERN

PUB

55 Britton St.

☎020 7490 4281 www.stpetersbrewery.co.uk

A truly ancient tavern, the Jerusalem Tavern was originally in St. John's Gate before it was reopened at its present location on Britton St. The tavern is homey and warm and—more importantly—the only tavern in London to offer all of the St. Peter's ales. These fantastic and specialized ales have brands like "Golden Ale," "Ruby Red Ale," "Honey Porter," and "Cream Stout." All of them are worth trying, but we're not saying you should try all of them at once...that would be irresponsible and would probably lead to the **craziest night ever.**

Farringdon. Left onto Cowcross St., left onto Turnmill St., right onto Benjamin St., left onto Britton St. Pints around £3.10, ½ pints £1.55. Open M-F 11am-11pm. Lunch served noon-3pm.

FABRIC CLUB

77a Charterhouse St. ☎020 7336 8898 www.fabriclondon.com

Do you go to dances and stand to the side clutching your drink? Do you frequently call the police at parties to report a mass epidemic of seizures? Do you not find "September" by Earth, Wind, and Fire irresistibly funky? Worry not! Fabric has the cure to this fatal disease. The club, which inhabits an abandoned meat packing warehouse, boasts Europe's premier "bodysonic dancefloor," a floor which, because of the subwoofers that line its rubbery surface, vibrates in time with the music. Yes, the floor does it for you. The club is a true phenomenon, and its three dance floors are sure to be packed with 20-somethings. The queue starts getting really long around 11pm, and the peak hour is 2am.

Farringdon. Left onto Cowcross St. Continue until you hit Charterhouse St. £15, students £11. After 3am discount £6. Bottle of Stella £4. Open F 10pm-6am, Sa 11pm-8am.

FULLER'S ALE AND PIE HOUSE PUB

194 Fleet St. ☎020 7430 2255

Fuller's Ale and Pie House traces English history: once a tavern, then a bank, now a pub. Make of that what you will. The pub plays up the grandeur of the old Bank of England. Though more upscale than a traditional pub, Fuller's has an exciting atmosphere, and any drink there feels unique. Additionally, it sits between Sweeney Todd's barber shop on Fleet St. and his girlfriend's pie shop, so be sure to try one of their pies if you're feeling adventurous.

Temple. Right onto Temple Pl., left onto Arundel St., right on Strand, continue onto Fleet. Pints £3.45-3.65. Shots £2-3. Open M-F 11am-11pm.

KENSINGTON AND EARL'S COURT

JANET'S BAR BAR

30 Old Brompton Rd. ☎020 7581 3160 janetsbar@yahoo.com

Janet's Bar is all about spirits, in both senses of the word. Run by Janet herself, who knows most of the people in the bar and has organized something of a lively ex-pat community around the place, Janet's Bar is a well-formed but instantly welcoming community. This joint features baseball memorabilia, photos of club regulars, and Red Sox and Yankees pennants so close you can practically touch them. If the atmosphere doesn't make you feel welcome, the Beatles sing-alongs will.

South Kensington. As you exit, Old Brompton Rd. will be across from you. i Though not wheelchair-accessible, a ramp can be arranged if you call in advance. Credit card min. £3. Bottle of beer around £4.50. Pint £5.95. Shots around £5. Mixed drinks £6.50-8.50. Bottle of wine from £18.50. M-W 11:45am-1am, Th 11:45am-1:30am, F 11:45pm-2:30am, Sa noon-2:30am, Su 2pm-1am. Live music Tu-Su after 9:30pm.

PIANO PIANO BAR

106 Kensington High Street ☎020 7938 4664 www.pianokensington.com

If you ever dreamed of lying atop a piano in a dimly lit room while someone played sultry jazz, blues, rock, and sing-along music, Piano will do you one better: you can eat on the piano, and there's a different pianist every night of the week. Piano is a classy joint loaded with pictures of **Old Blue Eyes** (Frank Sinatra) and New York, as well as photos from shoots that have happened in the bar, such as the one with Estelle and John Legend or the one with an ex-Sugar Babe.

High Street Kensington. Turn right on Kensington High Street. i Credit card min. £5. Most entrees £6.50-7. Bottle of beer £4.50. Glass of house red or white £4.50. Tu-Sa 11am-midnight, Su 4:30-11:30pm. Music starts T-F 6pm, Sa 8pm. Jazz trio Su 8pm.

THE DRAYTON ARMS PUB

153 Old Brompton Rd. ☎020 7835 2301 www.thedraytonarmssw5.co.uk

The Drayton Arms is a comfortable, well-kept pub with high ceilings and white string lights that amble up the tree trunk and soft red lights that border the ceiling. Enjoy affordable beers around the fire place, and then go see a film or play in the black box theater on the second floor. Check the site for theater, sporting, and film events in the upstairs theater.

Gloucester Rd. Turn right onto Gloucester Rd., turn right onto Old Brompton Rd. Average pint £3.20. Burgers £7-8.25. Sandwiches £4.25. Entrees £7.50-8.25. Open M-F 11am-midnight, Sa-Su 10m-midnight.

THE PEMBROKE PUB

261 Old Brompton Rd. 020 7373 8337 www.thepembroke5.co.uk

Spacious and easy-going, The Pembroke is a solid neighborhood pub in the typical Kensington style: lofty ceilings and clean decoration. Chandeliers dangle from the ceiling on the second floor and people stand on the terrace when it's nice out. There are DJs at the pub *(F-Sa from 8:30pm on).*

West Brompton. Turn right onto Old Brompton Rd. Average pint £3.80. Open M-Sa noon-midnight, Su noon-11pm.

THE SCARSDALE TAVERN PUB

23a Edwardes Sq. 020 7937 1811

Bottles upon bottles line the window sills and ceiling trimmings, and old, tasseled, and worn curtains drape beside large windows. Edwardes Sq. was initially meant as a living space for the French officers who would arrive when Napoleon invaded, and The Scarsdale cheerfully revisits history with its warm French style.

High Street Kensington. Turn left onto Kensington High St., left onto Edwardes Sq. Entrees £9-11. Average pint £3.30-3.50. Open M-Sa noon-11pm, Su noon-10:30pm.

MARYLEBONE AND REGENT'S PARK

THE GOLDEN EAGLE PUB, MUSIC

59 Marylebone Ln. 020 7935 3228

The Golden Eagle is one of the most special pubs in London. Though aesthetically basic, it has some of the friendliest patrons and staff that can be found around town. Three nights a week, the bespectacled Tony "Fingers" Pearson rolls out an old stand-up piano and proceeds to hammer out classics like "La Vie En Rose," "Tenderly," "I'm Confessing I Love You," and "Just One of Those Things." There's no better way to feel welcome in the country than by catching a rousing, boozy chorus of "Consider Yourself." Between the alcohol-induced golden haze, the music, and the unbelievably friendly company, the Pub is a living Capra film, and in no way is that a bad thing.

Bond St. Right onto Oxford St., left onto Marylebone Ln. Average pint £3.50. Open M-Th 11am-11pm, F-Sa 11am-midnight, Su noon-7pm. Music Tu, Th, and F 8:30pm.

THE SOCIAL CLUB, BAR

5 Little Portland St. 020 7636 4992 www.thesocial.com

Though the upstairs looks like a typical hip bar with its exposed light bulbs and bare wood floor (however, there are DJs on the first floor most nights), the downstairs space at The Social is where the action is. Here is where the ragingly popular hip-hop karaoke night happens every other Thursday as well as other events like club nights and live performances. Many nights have no cover charge. Check online to see what's happening at this popular and exciting hangout.

Oxford Circus. Right onto Regent St., right on Little Portland St. i Credit card min. £10. Pints around £3.70. Mixed drinks around £7. Cover £5-7 on club night. Student cards will get you discounts on most covered nights. Open M 5pm-midnight, Tu-W noon-midnight, Th-F noon-1am, Sa 7pm-1am.

THE COCK

PUB

27 Great Portland St. ☎020 7631 5002

Crowds of students gather beneath the red patterned ceiling, crowding the bar for some of the cheapest pints in London. Traditional decor rounds out the great deals at this pub—and there's nothing obscene about it.

Oxford Circus. right on Oxford St., left on Great Portland St.. i Credit card min. £5, small surcharge. Bitters £2. Pint of lager around £2.27-3.10. Open M-Sa noon-11pm, Su noon-10:30pm.

THE COACH MAKERS OF MARYLEBONE

PUB

88 Marylebone Ln. ☎020 7224 4022 www.thecoachmakers.com

The Coach Makers of Marylebone, unsurprisingly, used to be the offices of coach makers in Marylebone. Now the place is an upscale pub, featuring music on weekends *(from 7pm)*, old gilded mirrors, and deep leather couches that rest beside a fireplace. Simple and elegant, The Coach Makers is a pleasant pub.

Bond St. Right onto Oxford St., left onto Marylebone Ln. Pints £3.70. Entrees £11.50-12.50. Open M-Th noon-11:30pm, F-Sa noon-midnight, Su noon-10:30pm.

NOTTING HILL

Notting Hill is not an ideal neighborhood for nightlife. The pubs thrive on daytime tourists, and many of the locals are young professionals who tend to frequent other spots. The neighborhood can feel deserted at night, and while it's a safe area, the emptiness isn't conducive to late-night revelry.

PORTOBELLO STAR

BAR

171 Portobello Rd. ☎020 7229 8016 www.portobellostarbar.co.uk

If cafes could have superhero alter egos, the Portobello Star would be Superman. By day, it's a pleasant cafe with internet access; by night, it's a bustling bar... with internet access. It's popular but not too crazy, sophisticated but with fun drinks *("Rock the Kasbah," Grey Goose vodka with lemon juice, mint tea syrup, orange flower water, and egg white £10)*. You'll hear your favorite classic rock, soft rock, R and B, soul, and hip-hop from the bar or the leather couches in the calmer chill-out room on the second floor of the building. The crowd is in their early 20s to early 30s, and the place is hopping.

Notting Hill Gate. Take a right onto Pembridge Rd. and then left onto Portobello Rd. Mixed drinks £7.50-8. M-Th 10am-midnight, F-Sa 10am-1am, Su 10am-midnight.

RUBY AND SEQUOIA

BAR

6-8 All Saints Rd. ☎020 7243 6363 www.ruby.uk.com/sequoia

Upscale, chic, bright, and with a painting of firefighting nuns (clearly the highlight here), Ruby and Sequoia is a pub filled with many local, young professionals enjoying hearty meals and lengthy drinks. Dress up a bit, but nothing too fancy. Just prime yourself for a relatively glamorous yet relaxed night on the town. There's a lounge downstairs with a DJ starting at 9pm. Bring friends to sit with, as people tend to come in groups. The street leading to the bar isn't that well lit, and the area is a bit deserted. Regardless, the warmth of the bar keeps the dark from the street at bay.

Notting Hill Gate. Take right onto Pembridge Rd. and then left onto Portobello Rd.; take right on Westbourne Park Rd. and then left on All Saints Rd. Mixed drinks £8-8.50. Shots £4-5. Large glasses of wine £6. M-Th 6pm-12:30am, F 6pm-2am, Sa 10am-2am, Su 10am-12:30am.

SUN IN SPLENDOUR

PUB

7 Portobello Rd. ☎020 7792 0914 www.suninsplendourpub.co.uk

A fun, typical pub with a young crowd (20s-30s). The major draw is the fantastic beer garden in the back. The garden has benches and wood tables, lattices with ivy and primrose, lanterns, and heaters. It closes at 9:30pm, so try and get out there early.

Notting Hill Gate. Take right onto Pembridge Rd. and then left onto Portobello Rd. Small glass of white wine £3.95-4.25; small glass of red wine £3.85-4.10; pint of draught £3.15-3.95. M-Th noon-11pm, F noon-midnight, Sa 9am-12am, Su 9am-10:30pm. Kitchen open M-F noon-10pm, Sa-Su limited hours.

PRINCE ALBERT — PUB

11 Pembridge Rd. 020 7727 7362 www.the-prince-albert.co.uk

Prince Albert pub blares rowdy, retro indie music and serves veggie plates with olive, falafel, tomato, hummus, crudites, mozzarella, cherry tomato salad, garlic flatbread, and chips *(£10)*. Fun, young, and crowded (but its size accommodates).

Notting Hill Gate. Take right onto Pembridge Rd. 8 oz burgers £8-9. Sandwiches £4.50. Entrees £7-8. M-F 10am-midnight, Sa-Su 10:30am-midnight.

PORTOBELLO GOLD — PUB

95 Portobello Rd. 020 7229 8528 www.portobellogold.com

An old-fashioned pub with a crowd that will sing along to the classic rock that's playing. The clientele represents the whole age spectrum—from students to 70-something locals. The pub is endearingly ragged, bright, and just what you'd think an English pub should look like. There's a full service restaurant with pub grub in the back. The peak hours on Saturday are after 11pm.

Notting Hill Gate. Take right onto Pembridge Rd. and then left onto Portobello Rd. Live music Su 6:30-10pm. ½ pints £1.90-2.60; full pints £3.60-4.10; bottles £3.60-4.80. Glass of red wine £4.20-4.60; glass of white wine £3.80-5.60; Cuban cigars £10.50. M-Th 10am-noon, F-Sa 10am-12:30am, Su 10am-11:30pm.

MAU MAU — BAR

265 Portobello Rd. 020 7229 8528 www.maumaubar.com

Mau Mau rests at the bottom of Portobello Rd., and though on Notting Hill's main drag, it feels totally removed from the touristy bustle of the street outside. The cool reds and greens of the walls reflect the smooth tones of the music, which is mainly jazz, trip-hop, and soul. If you're into pool, there's a table, but look out for a long queue by 10:30pm, the bar's peak hour. Clientele tends to be 40-something locals.

Notting Hill Gate. Take right onto Pembridge Rd. and then a left onto Portobello Rd. Live music Th 8:30-10:30pm and Su 8:30-10pm. Shots £3.50-5. ½-pint £1.75; full pint £3.30; bottles £3. M-Th noon-10:30pm, F-Sa noon-midnight, Su 1-10:30pm.

THE WEST END

ABSOLUT ICEBAR — BAR

31-33 Heddon St. 020 7478 8910 www.absoluticebarlondon.com

This bar is absurd in the best way possible—the way where everything is made out of ice imported from the Torne River in Sweden. Located in the former wine vault for the monarchy, Absolut Icebar is the perfect place to escape all that British...er, cold. Before entering the hip, "cool" bar, visitors are given designer thermal wear. Each stay is 40 minutes, during which time you drink as much as possible so you don't feel your face as it slowly freezes off. All drinks are served in glasses made of ice. Chipping ice off the wall and into your drink is frowned upon. Highly.

Piccadilly Circus. Turn left onto Regent St. and left onto Heddon St. Tickets include first vodka cocktail. Refills £6. Reserve for weekends around 2 weeks in advance. Reservations are taken up to 28 days in advance. M-W £13.50 (£12.50 if booked in advance), Th until 6:30pm £13.50 (£12.50 if booked in advance), Th night-Sa £15, Th-Sa all day £16 without reservation, Su £13.50 (£12.50 if booked in advance). Open M-W 3:30-11pm, Th 3:30-11:45pm, F noon-1:15am, Sa 12:30pm-1:15am, Su 3:30-11pm. Last entry 45min. before close. DJs F and Sa from around 8pm.

GORDON'S WINE BAR

WINE BAR

47 Villiers St. ☎020 7930 1408 www.gordonswinebar.com

Once down the narrow staircase visitors come upon what looks like a cave. Bottles draped in melted wax and rough, irregularly sloping walls lit by flickering candles fill the space between people sharing bottles of wine from around the world. Out on Watergate Walk, winos sip the fine wines of London's oldest wine bar if the weather permits.

Charing Cross. Upon exiting, turn 180 degrees and go down Villiers. Wine £16-17 per bottle, around £4.50 per glass. Hot meals £9-11, items from the grill are around £6.65. Open M-Sa 10am-11pm, Su noon-10pm.

FREUD

BAR

198 Shaftesbury ☎020 7240 9933 www.freudliving.com

You wouldn't find Freud unless you were looking for it. With original art decorating the otherwise spare space, Freud is a study in successful understatement. The young and hip come to Freud and get a seat wherever they can, enjoying the reasonably priced drinks.

Piccadilly Circus. Exit with Haymarket on your right and Regent to your left. turn right around the triangular intersection and right at Shaftesbury. i Credit card min. £10. Beer £3.15-3.65. Mixed drinks £5.55-6.50 on average. Open M-Sa 11am-11pm, Su noon-10:30pm.

KU

GLBT

25 Frith St. ☎020 7287 7986 www.ku-bar.com

A more relaxed alternative to some of the more pulsing gay clubs on the Soho scene, Ku serves up well-priced drinks with a friendly staff. Located above the bar is the gay tourist office *(open daily noon-6pm)*, providing tips for gay travelers. A comfortable and fun bar (and accompanying club downstairs) with a good heart, Ku is the place to be.

Tottenham Court Road. Turn left onto Oxford St., turn left onto Soho St., left around Soho Sq., left onto Frith St. i Free Wi-Fi. Single+mixer £3.50, double shot+mixer £6. Pints £3.50. Bar open daily noon-midnight. Nightclub open daily 7pm-midnight.

CAFE PACIFICA

MEXICAN BAR TEQUILA

5 Langley St. ☎020 7379 7728 www.cafepacifico-laperla.com

Though at first glance Cafe Pacifica may seem a typical Mexican restaurant, its 130 varieties of tequila beg to differ. Though you have to order food to drink, the atmosphere is pleasant, with light Latin music piping through the speakers and classic Mexican entrees like enchiladas. If you're feeling like a real taste in exorbitant spending, pick up a shot of the Cuervo Coleccion *(£125)*. If you buy it, you'll get your name on a board in the restaurant and also possibly on the IRS's auditing list.

Covent Garden. Left on Long Acre, right on Langley. Shots of tequila £3-15. Enchiladas around £9.50. Open M-Sa noon-11:45pm, Su noon-10:45pm.

LAB

BAR

12 Old Compton ☎020 7437 7820 www.labbaruk.com

LAB, which is short for the London Academy of Bartenders, is known for its bartenders, who compete as drink makers, sometimes internationally. When off the circuit, they serve up affordable cocktails that fill up 32 pages of a menu. With drinks ranging from the Aviation *(Plymouth gin, maraschino liqueur shaken hard with freshly squeezed lemon juice, served straight up with a cherry £7)* to the Hemmingway Daiquiri, Death in the Afternoon, and the playful Satan's Whiskers, LAB does it all in a pleasant, retro 70s bar space.

Tottenham Court Road. Turn right down Charing Cross Rd. and turn right on Old Compton St. Most cocktails £7-7.50. Open M-Sa 4pm-midnight, Su 4-10:30pm. Table service downstairs Th-Sa. DJs W-Sa 8pm-midnight.

THE EDGE GLBT, MIXED

11 Soho Sq. ☎020 7439 1313 www.edgesoho.co.uk

With four floors, The Edge is a full clubbing experience. Disco balls and a crazy light-changing chandelier that looks like an exploding atom decorate the space. The first floor has a quieter lounge bar filled with couches. The second floor is the al fresco lounge, serving up massages every night where the recipient pays however much he or she feels it's worth. The third floor has fake trees with climbing blue lights and a dance floor with tiles that change color.

Tottenham Ct. Rd. Turn left onto Oxford St., turn left onto Soho St., Edge is on your right. Pints £3. Open M-Sa noon-1am, Su noon-10:30pm. Dance floor open F-Sa 8pm.

THIRST BAR

53 Greek St. ☎020 7437 1977 www.thirstbar.com

A hip, spare space where the music's always funky and it's always either "Stupid" hour, where the drinks are almost half price, or happy hour (the two never coincide, so ignorance is never bliss). Thirst is stylish with its candles, spray-painted signs and stainless steel tables. Ask for a student discount. Dancing is downstairs whenever your feet start to move uncontrollably.

Tottenham Court Road. Turn left onto Oxford St., turn left onto Soho St., left around Soho Sq., left onto Greek St. i Credit card min. £10. "Stupid" prices are £4.25-4.50, "happy" are around £6, "normal" £8. Open daiiy 5pm-3am. Stupid hour 5-7:30pm daily. Happy hour M-W 7:30pm-3am, Th-Su 7:30-10:30pm. Downstairs bar open Th-Sa, as well as busy nights.

SOHO VILLAGE MIXED CLUB, BAR

81 Wardour St. ☎020 7434 2124 www.village-soho.co.uk

Walking down Wardour St., it's hard to miss Soho Village, even if you aren't looking for it. A typical night has crowds of giggling spectators of all sexual orientations whose faces are lit by occasional flashes of light in time to pulsing music. Inside, "Gogo Boys" *(Th-Sa from 8pm)* might be dancing on platforms, and hot and sweaty dancers abound. Down the steel staircase is another dance floor, bordered by cool blue-lit booths, where people of all sexual orientations come to have a good time. Though the club is primarily gay, it is definitely straight-friendly.

Tottenham Ct. Rd. Turn down Oxford St. with your back to Tottenham Ct. Rd., turn left onto Wardour St. Open M-Sa 4pm-1am, Su 4-11:30pm.

PROFILE GLBT BAR

84-86 Wardour St. ☎020 7734 3444 www.profilesoho.com

With one of the brightest yellow interiors in Soho, Profile practically screams good time. Serving up American diner food and providing events like Bingo at 6pm on Sundays and psychic Sundays on off-bingo weeks (get your fortune read!), Profile is a great GLBT bar. Downstairs is the cleverly-titled Low Profile, the bar's corresponding nightclub.

Tottenham Ct. Rd. Turn down Oxford St. with your back to Tottenham Court Road, turn left onto Wardour St. Mixed drinks £6-7. Beer £3.50. Profile M-Sa 11am-11pm, Su 11am-10:30pm. Low Profile T 10:30pm-2am, F-Sa 10:30pm-4am. Bar closes at 3am. DJs upstairs F 7pm, Sa 8pm. Happy hour at Profile daily 5-7pm.

BAR RUMBA CLUB

36 Shaftesbury Ave. ☎020 7287 6933 www.barrumbadisco.co.uk

Boasting a very young crowd, Bar Rumba is one of the more popular clubs in the area. In a spare space with low ceilings, booths, and tables, the dance floor is where all the action takes place among the flashing lights and young crowd. Watch out for the long queue, though! Themed Saturdays are advertised on the website, and if you dress in theme you get in free. Check the website for details.

Piccadilly Circus. Turn left onto Great Windmill St. and follow it to Shaftesbury Ave. *i* Credit card min. £10. Up until 10:30pm guys get in for £5, girls get in free. 10:30-11:30pm, guys £10, girls £5. After 11:30pm, everyone £10. Cash only for cover. Open daily 8:30pm-3am.*

22 BELOW BAR

22 Great Marlborough ☎020 7437 4106 www.22below.co.uk

A simple bar in every way, 22 below is, appropriately, in the basement of the 22nd building on Great Marlborough St. Seasonal themes dominate the decoration, but the space is small, bright, and relaxed. The drinks menu includes award winning recipes, and many of the drinks are associated with authors. The Thai Sorbet *(£8.50)* nearly won the Bacardi Capital Cocktail Competition, so drink it slow.

Oxford Circus. Turn left onto Regent St., left onto Great Marlborough St. Cocktails £7.50-8.50. Open M-F 5pm-midnight, Sa 7pm-midnight.

G-A-Y BAR GLBT BAR

30 Old Compton St. ☎020 7494 2756 www.g-a-y.co.uk

Bringing in an eccentric and eclectic clientele, G-A-Y Bar serves up cheap drinks and loud chart music throughout the whole space. Decked out with tons of TVs embedded in the walls, pink walls and just the right number of flashing lights, G-A-Y is a solid bar.

Tottenham Ct. Rd. Turn right down Charing Cross Rd. and turn right on Old Compton St. Some drinks available for £1.59 M-F noon-8pm. M-Th and Su noon-midnight house, red, or white wine is £1.60.. Open daily noon-midnight.

ALPHABET BAR

61-63 Beak St. ☎020 7439 2190 alphabet@a3bars.com

Alphabet is the kind of pub that can mix soul, funk, top forty and Frank Sinatra without it seeming incongruous. Between the stylish decor, the sharing boards of meat and cheese, and the graffiti-covered walls, Alphabet covers "stylish" from several different angles, and its customers are all the better for it. The downstairs area is spacious and replete with leather couches and stools. As you descend, heed the wall's warning to "Mind yer bloody head!!"

Oxford Circus. Left down Regent St., left onto Beak St. i Credit card min. £5. Mixed drinks £6.50. Entrees £8-8.20. Shooters £3.60. Pints £4. Open M-Sa noon-11pm. Kitchen open noon-9pm.

MADAME JOJO'S LIVE ENTERTAINMENT VENUE

8-10 Brewer St. ☎020 7734 3040 www.madamejojos.com

Built on the cabaret and live entertainment traditions of yore, Madame Jojo's is not your average club. Every night begins with some form of entertainment before the cabaret tables disappear and the dance floor gets hopping. Dress is smart casual, music is smoking and, when the curtain goes down, the dancing begins.

Piccadilly Circus. Go down Shaftesbury and turn left on Wardour St., turn left on Brewer St. i Sometimes cover is cash only. Tu is indie night (which is also pretty much a student night). Show finishes around 9:30, and then club night begins with DJs. F is northern soul and funk. Sa is 1950s rockabilly and drive. Su is Latin, house, and bebop. W is Trannyshack night, aimed at the transgender community. Tickets £10-52.50 depending on event, so check website. Single measure spirits+mixer, bottles of beer and glasses of the house red or white £4.50. Open daily 7pm-3am. 7-9pm is live music, burlesque, comedy, magic, or variety show.

CANDY BAR GLBT

4 Carlisle St. ☎020 7287 5041 www.candybarsoho.co.uk

Though open only to women and their male friends, Candy Bar is otherwise a pretty standard bar. There are occasional student nights featuring a student DJ and a female pole dancer every other week on Friday or Saturday around 10pm (check online). Karaoke happens on Tuesdays and open mikes will be on Thursdays.

Tottenham Court Road. Turn onto Oxford St. with your back to Tottenham Ct. Rd., turn left onto Dean St. Credit card min. £5. M-Th and Su 20% off everything: mixed drinks become £5. Pints £3.30. Mixed drinks average £7. Open daily noon-3am.

ESCAPE DANCE BAR GLBT BAR

10a Brewer St. 020 7734 2626 www.escapesoho.co.uk

This stylish gay bar has a wide open dance floor with flashing lights and wallpaper with horses on them. Speakers with excellent quality sound thump out hits from the charts, and, on Wednesdays and Saturdays, karaoke reinterpretations of said tunes.

Piccadilly Circus. Go down Shaftesbury and turn left on Wardour St., turn left on Brewer St. Credit card surcharge £.50. Pint of Stella £2. Other pints around £3.80. Open M-Sa 5pm-3am. Karaoke W 8pm-midnight, Sa 5-8pm.

THE CHANDOS PUB

60 Chandos Pl. 020 7836 1401

A classic, Sam Smith's pub near Trafalgar Square, the Chandos is a welcome change from the bar and club culture of the West End. Welcoming guests graciously into its open space, The Chandos has booths that are very secluded, and which keep visitors bathed in colored light from the stained glass that looks out onto the street. It also boasts some of the cheapest pints in town.

Charing Cross. Turn left onto Strand, right onto St. Martin's Ln. and right onto William IV St. Credit card min. £5. Pints £2. Burgers £4.50-5. Entrees £6-6.30. Open M-Sa 11am-11:30pm, Su noon-10:30pm. Kitchen open M-Sa 11am-7pm, Su noon-7pm.

BOX CAFE BAR GAY-FRIENDLY MIXED

32-34 Monmouth St. 020 7240 5828 www.boxbar.com

This gay-friendly bar has a very mixed crowd. Decorated with glittering paintings of stars such as Marilyn Monroe and lit by orange, blue and green hanging lights, The Box Cafe Bar is an exciting and friendly place to drink. They have a different promotion every day, so check ahead to find out how you an save!

Covent Garden. Turn left onto James St., left on Long Acre. Turn right onto Upper Mercer St. and then left onto Monmouth. Free Wi-Fi with purchase. Average pint £3.50-3.80. Open M-Th noon-11pm. F-Sa noon-midnight, Su noon-11pm.

DOG AND DUCK PUB

18 Bateman St. 020 7494 0697

Formerly one of George Orwell's favorite pubs, the Dog and Duck is a standard pub in the middle of Soho's otherwise off-the-wall nightlife scene. The interior is decorated with elaborate mirrors, and every Thursday night from 5-10pm is Sausage night, with sausage and mash and a beer *(£8)*.

Tottenham Court Road. Turn down Oxford St. with your back to Tottenham Ct. Rd., turn left onto Soho St., right around Soho Sq. and right onto Frith St. and right onto Bateman St. Pints £3-3.50. Open M-Th 10am-11pm, F-Sa 10am-11:30pm, Su noon-10:30pm.

WESTMINSTER

Westminster isn't an ideal location for nightlife, pubs, or clubs. Enjoy it during the day, and then take the party elsewhere, old sport.

THE BUCKINGHAM ARMS PUB

62 Petty France 020 7222 3386 www.buckinghamarms.com

When the lawmen and -women who keep order in this country need to unwind, they can come here: it is right down the street from the Ministry of Justice. Partially lit by a cool skylight, the pub has comfy armchairs and large windows, so homey charm abounds. It is also worth noting that the Ministry of Justice is on a street named "Petty France." Coincidence? We think not.

Victoria. Right onto Grosvenor Pl. Continue onto Victoria St., left onto Buckingham Gate, right on Petty France. Pint of Youngs £3. Open M-F 11am-11pm, Sa-Su noon-6pm.

THE CASK AND GLASS PUB

39 Palace St. ☎020 7834 7630 www.shepherd-neame.co.uk

A small pub hidden in the concrete and brick facades of Westminster, The Cask and Glass imports a bit of that old 1698, the year of the brewery's founding, charm to which pubs in other parts of town aspire. The beer is good but a bit expensive in this pleasant, neighborhood joint.

Victoria. Right onto Grosvenor Pl. Continue onto Victoria St. Left on Palace St. Pints £3.35-3.85. M-F 11am-11pm, Sa noon-8pm.

THE PHOENIX PUB

14 Palace St. ☎020 7828 8136 www.geronimo-inns.co.uk

A basic, slightly posh pub, The Phoenix is well located and filled with 30-something professionals. Enjoy the relaxed beer garden or a dinner of upscale pub grub served in the Yalumba room upstairs. Even if you're bored by this pub, you'll be able to say you're eating in the Yalumba room. Try saying Yalumba 10 times fast.

Victoria. Right onto Grosvenor Pl. Continue onto Victoria St. Left on Palace St. Pints £3.55-3.85. Ales £3.25. M-F 11am-11pm, Sa 11am-11pm, Su noon-10:30pm.

arts and culture

You might wonder if the city that brought the world Shakespeare and Harold Pinter has lost its theatrical edge. Not to fear, however—the London theater scene is as vital as ever. From the perennial hard-hitters at the Royal Court to daring musical fare like *Enron: The Musical*, the London stage remains packed with the dramatic flare that put it on the map in the first place.

For those weary of Coldplay, who fear that the country that brought you the Rolling Stones, The Sex Pistols and The Clash hit a roadblock, turn your ears from the arenas and put them to the ground—underground, in fact—to city hotspots where young bands committed to their fans are not interested in seeing their names in gaudy lights. There's that famed British wit making audiences chuckle from the gut in basements everywhere.

CINEMA

London is teeming with traditional cinemas, the most dominant of which are **Cineworld** and **Odeon,** but the best way to enjoy a film is in one of the hip repertory or luxury cinemas. *Time Out* publishes show times, as does **www.viewlondon.co.uk.** Americans will find the cinema in London to be particularly illuminating, as most films are about a certain kind of American—namely, the stupid, stereotypical kind that would make Europeans hate Americans.

BFI SOUTHBANK THE SOUTH BANK

Belvedere Rd. ☎020 7928 3232 www.bfi.org.uk

Hidden under Waterloo Bridge, the BFI Southbank is one of the most exciting repertory cinemas in London. Showcasing everything from art to foreign, British to classic, the BFI provides a range of styles to keep all cinema lovers happy. It runs in seasons, with a different theme each month featuring different elements of film. (For example, a season could be on a director or cinematographer or actor.) The **Mediatech** is free for anyone and allows people to privately view films from the archives.

Waterloo. i Call ☎020 7815 1329 for details on Mediatech hours. Evenings M-F £9, concessions £6.65, under 16 £5. Tu £5. Mediatech open T-Su noon-8pm.

ELECTRIC CINEMA NOTTING HILL

191 Portobello Rd. ☎020 7908 9696 www.electriccinema.co.uk

This 100-year-old theater is the epitome of a luxury viewing experience. With a bar inside the auditorium and luxury leather arm chairs that come equipped with a table, a footstool and a wine cooler, it almost doesn't matter what films are showing. The Electric shows some vintage films but sticks mainly to big, new releases.

Notting Hill Gate. Turn right onto Pembroke Rd., then left onto Portobello Rd. i Tickets must be booked at least 2 weeks in advance, but some shows sell out faster than that. Discounts for children. £7.50-14.50. Appetizers £4.50. Pints £3.75. Wine £4.25-7. Open M-Sa 9am-8:30pm, Su 10am-8:30pm.

RIVERSIDE STUDIOS WEST LONDON

Crisp Rd. ☎020 8237 1111 www.riversidestudios.co.uk

Riverside Studios derives its name from its close proximity to the Thames. Frequently showing films in old-school double-bill packages, Riverside Studios specializes in foreign films, art house flicks, and old gems. The building itself is a hotbed for culture, featuring an exhibition space and occasional live theater performances.

Hammersmith. Take south exit and pass the Hammersmith Apollo. Continue to follow Queen Caroline St. and turn left onto Crisp Rd. i Book ahead for wheelchair access. Ethernet in cafe. Tickets £7.50, concessions £6.50. Pints £3.70. Open daily noon-9pm. Shows are normally M-F 6:30pm and 8:30pm, Sa-Su 1:30pm, 3:30pm, 6:30pm, 8:30pm. Bar open M-Sa noon-11pm, Su 11am-10:30pm.

COMEDY

The English are famous for their occasionally dry, sophisticated wit and often ridiculous ("We are the knights who say Ni!") sense of humor. This humor continues to thrive in the standup and sketch comedy clubs throughout the city. Check *Time Out* for listings, but be warned that the city virtually empties of comedians come August when it's festival time in Edinburgh.

COMEDY STORE THE WEST END

1a Oxendon St. ☎0844 847 1728 www.thecomedystore.co.uk

This comedy venue offers everything from stand-up to the Cutting Edge, a show every Tuesday that does up-to-date topical humor.

Piccadilly Circus. Turn left onto Coventry, then right onto Oxendon. Tickets £14-20. Box office open M-Th 6:30-9:30pm, F-Sa 6:30pm-1:15am, Su 6:30-9:30pm. Doors open daily 6:30pm.

DANCE

As with everything else artistic in London, the dance scene here is diverse, innovative, and first-rate. Come for the famous ballets at older venues like the Royal Opera House or stop by one of the smaller companies for some contemporary dance.

SADLER'S WELLS CLERKENWELL

Rosebery Ave. ☎0844 412 4300 www.sadlerswells.com

Encapsulating all forms of dance, Sadler's Wells puts its belief in the power of dance to good use in wide-ranging and always exciting presentations. The site holds 300 years of dance history.

Angel. Left onto Upper St., then right onto Rosebery Ave. i Some shows offer student discounts. Tickets £10-£55. Open M-Sa 9am-8:30pm.

ROYAL OPERA HOUSE THE WEST END

Bow St. ☎020 7304 4000 www.roh.org.uk

The Royal Opera House (ROH) may be opera-oriented in name, but in repertoire, it's split between opera and ballet.

Covent Garden. Right onto Long Acre, right onto Bow St. Tickets £5-150. Booking office open M-Sa 10am-8pm.

MUSIC

Clubs are expensive, and pubs close at 11pm. Especially during the current recession, fewer young people are willing to shell out the £10-15 it takes to get into a club, especially since beers cost £4-5 on top of that. Much of the London nightlife scene thus lies beyond pub-and club-hopping in the darkened basements of bars everywhere and the glaringly bright, seismically loud music clubs. With a musical history including **The Beatles, Radiohead,** and **The Clash,** all of the bands from the infamous "British Invasion," and most of the best bands from '90s anthemic pop, London has always had a fantastic music scene. Frequently, English musicians respond to American tropes and take them to the next level: where America had the blues, England had **Eric Clapton** and the **Stones,** and when America learned rock, England fired off **The Clash** and **The Sex Pistols.** The London music scene is very much intact, and makes for both a great night out and an excellent way to forge lasting travel friendships. The London music scene is not to be missed.

Classical

There are several large organizations that supply the city with some of the most renowned classical performances in the world. For free chamber and classical music, check out some of London's churches, where students from famous music schools often give free, professional-quality recitals.

ROYAL OPERA HOUSE — THE WEST END

Bow St. ☎020 7304 4000 www.roh.org.uk

Though the glorious glass facade of the Royal Opera House makes it look more like a train station than a theater, patrons of the opera enjoy all of the great works of opera and some of the more contemporary pieces too. Though no discounts are offered, students can try to get standby tickets by going online and selecting "student standby" from the website. Top-price seats are available for £10 if you get lucky. Booking opens around two months before each performance, so try and book early. The ROH also sponsors free outdoor film screenings, so look out for those on their website.

Covent Garden. Right onto Long Acre, then right onto Bow St. Tickets £5-150. Booking office open M-Sa 10am-8pm.

PERFORMANCES AT ST. MARTIN-IN-THE-FIELDS — WESTMINSTER

Trafalgar Sq. ☎020 7766 1100 www.smitf.org

Every Monday, Tuesday, and Friday at 1pm, they have a 45min. **"lunch-time concert"** in which conservatory students perform classical recitals. In the evening, more renowned artists perform in the space. Known as the "Church of the Ever-Open Door" because of its use as a place of refuge for soldiers en route to France in WWI, St. Martin-in-the-Fields is a must-see for any music lover.

Charing Cross. To the east of Trafalgar Sq. Jazz night W 8pm. Reserved jazz ticket £9, unreserved jazz ticket £5.50. Open daily 8am-5pm, but it stays open later on off-concert days. Gift shop open M-W 10am-7pm, Th-Sa 10am-9pm, Su 11:30am-6pm.

ROYAL ALBERT HALL — KENSINGTON

Kensington Gore ☎0845 401 5045 for box office www.royalalberthall.com

Deep in the heart of South Kensington, the Royal Albert Hall was commissioned by Prince Albert in order to promote the arts, and has been in continuous operation since 1871. Offering some of the biggest concerts in London, the famous **BBC Proms** classical festival, and a range of other phenomenal musical events, the hall is an experience in history and culture that's not to be missed.

Knightsbridge. Turn left onto Knightsbridge and continue onto Kensington Rd. From £10. Open daily 9am-9pm.

THE LONDON COLISEUM WESTMINSTER

33 Saint Martin's Ln. 087 1472 0600 www.eno.org

Home of the English National Opera, The London Coliseum shows opera in English translation. Showcasing mostly new, cutting-edge ballet and opera, the Coliseum is a must for anyone who's ever wondered what exactly the fat lady is singing when she closes out the show.

Charing Cross. Go along the east side of Trafalgar Sq. up Charing Cross Rd., turn right onto Chandos Pl., and left onto Saint Martin's Ln. i Sometimes students and other concessions can get discounted tickets 3hr. before the performance. Tickets £15-90. Open on performance days M-Sa 10am-8pm, non-performance days M-Sa 10am-6pm.

SOUTHBANK CENTRE THE SOUTH BANK

Belvedere Rd. 084 4847 9915 www.southbankcentre.co.uk/classical

The gorgeous classical music played at the riverside Southbank Centre may clash with its Brutalist design, but that's no reason to skip it. The Queen Elizabeth and Purcell rooms provide much more intimate spaces, while the Royal Festival Hall aims for a grander, classically classical experience.

Waterloo. Right onto York Rd. and left onto Waterloo Rd. i Call 084 4847 9910 for wheelchair access. Tickets £9-45. Students can get 50% off all sorts of tickets to some concerts. Available by phone daily 9am-8pm. Royal Festival Hall Ticket office open daily 10am-8pm.

Jazz

RONNIE SCOTT'S SOHO

47 Frith St. 020 7439 0747 www.ronniescotts.co.uk

Ronnie Scott's has been defining "hip" in Soho for the last 51 years. It's hosted everyone from **Tony Bennett** to **Van Morrison,** and **Chick Corea** to the **Funk Brothers.** The venue is all flickering candlelight and dulcet reds and blues. Pictures of jazz greats line the walls in black and white, and a diverse crowd imbibes such creations as Jazz Medicine, Jagermeister, sloe gin, Dubonnet, fresh blackberries, angostia bitters *(£8).* The venue's cool, but the jazz is hot. Stop by if the Soho scene gets overwhelming.

Tottenham Court Rd. Turn down Oxford St. with your back to Tottenham Ct. Rd. and turn left on Soho St. turn right onto the sq. and then right onto Frith St. £10 cover, more for big acts. Champagne £8-10. White wine £4.80-5.30. Red wine bottles £22-26. Mixed drinks £8.50-9. Open M-Th 7:15pm-late, F-Sa 6pm-1:30am, Su noon-4pm and 6-10:30pm. Box office open M-F 10am-6pm, Sa noon-5pm.

THE 606 CLUB KNIGHTSBRIDGE

90 Lots Rd. 020 7352 5953 www.606club.co.uk

On quiet Lots Rd., opposite what appears to be a rather foreboding abandoned factory, the 606 Club has been quietly hosting the best of the UK music scene since 1969. Properly underground (it's in a basement), the club itself is candlelit and dim. The musicians play on a marked patch of floor that serves in place of the stage as the diners, frequently musicians, who are sitting in on the jams, surround them at tables. Musical styles run the gamut from jazz, Latin, soul, gospel, R and B, and rock, and while the artists may be relatively unknown, they're worth hearing. And be sure to satisfy your stomach, as well as your ears: entrees range from linguine *(£9.40)* to Cajun-style roast chicken breast *(£14).* Note that the area around the club is residential and fairly abandoned at night, so it might be safest to take a cab there and back.

Sloane Sq. Exit the Tube and go straight down Sloane Sq. i Non-members have to eat in order to drink. Check website for special Su afternoon lunch and show. Cover M £10, Tu-W £8, Th £10, F-Sa £12, Su £10. Entrees £9-18. Bottled beers from £3.45. Open M 7:30pm-midnight, Tu-Th 7pm-midnight, F-Sa 8pm-1:30am, Su 7-11pm.

JAZZ CAFÉ NORTH LONDON

5 Parkway ☎020 7688 8899 www.jazzcafe.co.uk

One of the most well-known jazz venues in London, the Jazz Café often surprises people with the expansiveness of its repertoire. It has hosted De La Soul and GZA as well as jazz luminaries, and every Saturday night starting at 10:30pm they have DJs playing '80s hits, followed by '90s nights on Fridays, and karaoke hairbrush nights on the third Friday of every month (they're songs you would sing into your hairbrush.) While no student discount is offered by the club, some of the outside promoters who hire it out occasionally offer student discounts.

Camden Town. Left onto Camden High St., and right onto Parkway. i £1 credit card surcharge for purchases under £12. Tickets £5-40. Average £25 at door and £17.50 in advance. Pints around £3.80. Drink deals on club nights £2 for vodka, mixer, Carlsberg pint. Box office open 10:30am-5:30pm. Shows generally start at 7pm. Some nights are double-bills with the late show starting at 11pm.

Pop and Rock

THE TROUBADOUR CAFE KENSINGTON

263-267 Old Brompton Rd. ☎020 7370 1434 www.troubadour.co.uk

Many famous acts have graced the Troubadour's small stage since its founding in 1954. Its hanging string lights and stage lights illuminated **Bob Dylan, Jimi Hendrix,** and **Joni Mitchell,** and pictures of some of these artists are plastered into the tops of the tables. To this day, The Troubadour is a community of aspiring and acclaimed artists bound by great music, good drinks, and the intoxicating atmosphere of artistic promise. Come here to see some of the city's most exciting acts before they break.

Gloucester Rd. Turn right onto Gloucester Rd., then turn right onto Old Brompton Rd. i Most nights feature several bands. Every other M poetry night. Cover is cash only. Open M-W 8pm-midnight, Th-Sa 8pm-2am, Su 8pm-midnight. Happy hour Tu-Su 8-9pm.

KOKO NORTH LONDON

1a Camden High St. ☎087 0432 5527 www.koko.uk.com

Koko's lodgings are not typical of a rock and roll venue. Originally a theater, then a cinema, then one of the first BBC radio broadcasting locations, and then the famous Camden Palace Nightclub, Koko holds all its 110 years of history within its beautiful red walls and its gilded, curved wrought-iron fences guarding the balconies from which music-lovers can look down to the stage. Bringing in mostly big-name indie acts, but also some celebs in pop and rock (they've had everyone from Madonna to the Hold Steady and Andre Bird; James Blunt, Kanye West and Usher to Devendra Banhart and Justice), Koko is one of the premier venues in London.

Mornington Crescent. Right onto Hampstead Rd. It's to your right. i Cash only for in-person purchases. Tickets sold through various outlets online. Indie night (indie music and dancing) F 9:30pm-4am. Credit card min. £10. Concert tickets £10-30. Beer £3.50-4. Mixed drinks £4. For indie night, the first 100 people get in free. Cover: students £5 up to midnight, students £7 after midnight. Non-students £7. Box office open noon-5pm on gig days.

BORDERLINE SOHO

Orange Yd. 16 Manette St. ☎084 4847 2465 www.venues.meanfiddler.com/borderline

A simple venue that, despite its lack of the outlandish Art Deco, theatrical trappings of other similar London concert halls, oozes the spirit of rock and roll from every beer-soaked wall and ear-blowing speaker. Often, big name artists will play the Borderline when starting solo careers. Townes Van Zandt played his last show at the Borderline, Eddie Vedder, Jeff Buckley, and Rilo Kiley have played there, and **Spinal Tap** played the Borderline right after the movie came out. The amps go to eleven, the music's piping hot, and the location is prime.

Tottenham Ct. Rd. Right on Charing Cross. Club nights W-Sa 11pm-3am. Tickets £6-20. Pints £3.40. Doors open for shows daily 7pm. Tickets available at the Jazz Cafe box office M-Sa 10:30am-5:30pm.

HMV APOLLO WEST LONDON

15 Queen Caroline St. 020 8563 3800 www.hmvapollo.com

Like many of the big, architecturally stunning venues in London, the Art Deco HMV Apollo was originally a cinema. It was formerly known as the Hammersmith Odeon and hosted **Bruce Springsteen** in his 1975 Hammersmith Odeon film (he would go on to play there four times). It has hosted huge acts like Oasis, R.E.M, Elton John, the Rolling Stones, and even The Beatles once.

Hammersmith. Opposite the Broadway Shopping Centre. Call in advance about wheelchair accessibility. Call 084 4844 4748 for tickets. Tickets depend on the event, check online. Box office open 4pm-start of the show on performance days.

02 ACADEMY BRIXTON SOUTH LONDON

211 Stockwell Rd. 020 7771 3000

Home to Europe's largest fixed stage, the 02 Academy Brixton's set list is rife with the big names of our generation. Past acts include MGMT, Echo and the Bunnymen, Plan B, Pavement, LCD Soundsystem, and the Gaslight Anthem. They also occasionally have club nights (which aren't on a fixed schedule, so check the website). The area can be a bit rough, so you may want to take a cab.

Brixton. Right onto Brixton Rd., then left onto Stockwell Rd. Bars are cash only. Call in advance for wheelchair accessibility. Ticket prices vary, most £20-35. Pints £4. Box office opens 2hr. before doors on gig nights.

london

HMV FORUM NORTH LONDON

9-17 Highgate Rd. 020 7428 4099 www.kentishtownforum.com

One of the most famous venues in London, the HMV Forum gets some of the most famous acts to come to town. The 75-year-old theater has hosted N.E.R.D., Slayer, Limp Bizkit, Wolf Parade, and the Decemberists on its massive stage. The hall holds 2350 people, and is just right for a big show.

Kentish Town. Right onto Kentish Town Rd., then left onto Highgate Rd. Cash machine. Gigs are 14+. Tickets £10-60. Pints £4. Box office open on show days 5-9pm. Doors open 7pm.

02 EMPIRE WEST LONDON

Shepherd's Bush Green 020 8354 3300 www.02shepherdsbushempire.co.uk

A popular space hosting large rock acts, the 02 Empire is one of the big names on the London music scene. With a classic feel greatly augmented by the bold stonework and old-fashioned hand-placed letters on the awning out front, the Empire hearkens to the heyday of rock and roll.

Shepherd's Bush. Right onto Uxbridge Rd. then left at the end of Shepherd's Bush Green. Call 084 4477 2000 for tickets. Box office open on show days 4-6pm and 6:30-9:30pm.

HAMMERSMITH IRISH CULTURAL CENTRE WEST LONDON

Blacks Rd. 020 8563 8232 www.irishculturalcentre.co.uk

Located on a quiet, unassuming street in Hammersmith, the Irish Cultural Centre is shockingly full of life within. Families—both Irish and otherwise—congregate in the main room before consulting reception and going to different parts of the building to participate in such varied events as clog lessons, concerts from Irish folk artists, book readings, free jams (participation encouraged), film screenings, and storytelling. Check the website for details on prices and events, but come prepared with a love for the Emerald Isle.

Hammersmith. Black's Rd. is just off of Queen Caroline St. near where it intersects with Beadon Rd. Monthly movie screening £1.50. "The Session" (Irish jam) Th 6-8pm. Movies are shown the 1st Th of every month. Hours vary. Box office open M-F 9am-1pm. If something is happening in the afternoon, box office open 1-3pm.

THEATER

Ah, "theatre" in London. While in London, many people choose to see a show because the city is renowned for its cheap theater. Tickets for big musicals on the **West End** go for as cheap as £25 the day of, which is pittance compared to the $100 tickets sold on Broadway, the American equivalent. In the West End, the main theater district, you'll find the bigger musicals that are produced in only one theater. For instance, *Phantom of the Opera* is entering its 25th year at Her Majesty's Theatre. Other theaters in the area and throughout London put on more cutting-edge or intellectual plays. Many pubs have live performance spaces in the back where theater groups rehearse and perform for an audience that, thanks to a few pints, always finds the second act more confusing than the first. Also, many churches, such as St. Paul's in Covent Garden, put on summer theater, and there are ways to get your culture for free. Always check discount prices against the theater itself. Only buy discounted tickets from booths with a circle and check mark symbol that says **STAR** on it. This stands for the Society of Tickets Agents and Retailers, and it vouches for the legitimacy of a discount booth.

ROYAL COURT THEATRE — KNIGHTSBRIDGE

Sloane Sq. ☎020 7565 5000 www.royalcourttheatre.com

Famous for pushing the theater envelope, the Royal Court is the antidote to all the orchestral swoons and faux-opera sweeping through the West End. The Royal Court's 1956 production of John Osborne's *Look Back in Anger* (not to be confused with the Oasis song of a similar title) was largely credited with launching Modern British drama. Royal is known as a writers' theater, purveying high-minded works of great drama for audiences that will appreciate them.

Sloane Square. Tickets M £10, Tu-Sa £12.18-25. Student discounts available on day of performance, preview and Sa matinees. Open M-F 10am-6pm or until the doors open, Sa open 10am-curtain on performance days.

THE NATIONAL THEATRE — THE SOUTH BANK

Belvedere Rd. ☎020 7452 3400 www.nationaltheatre.org.uk

Opened in 1976 by appointment of the monarchy, the National Theatre shows great new and classic British drama on its three stages, of which the Olivier is largest. It also revives lost classics from around the world. Special Travelex shows mean half the seats are available for £10 only.

Waterloo. Right onto York Rd. then left onto Waterloo Rd. Tickets £10-44. Box office open M-Sa 9:30am-8pm, Su noon-6pm.

THE OLD VIC — SOUTH LONDON

The Cut ☎084 4871 7628 www.oldvictheatre.com

This famous theater was built in 1818 and has hosted the likes of **Laurence Olivier.** Though dealing in a huge range of styles, the Old Vic is predominantly a traditional theater showing the classics. Fans of Kevin Spacey will want to visit now, since he is the theater's current artistic director.

Southwark. Right onto The Cut. Tickets £10-47. Open M-Sa on non-show days 10am-7pm, on show days 10am-6pm.

THE YOUNG VIC — SOUTH LONDON

66 The Cut ☎020 7922 2922 www.youngvic.org

Formerly the studio space for the Old Vic, the Young Vic puts on a variety of shows, most of which are edgier, more exciting, and newer than the more traditional Old Vic down the road. They frequently do reinterpretations of classic works as well as newer stuff. The three spaces in the theater allow for great versatility, with one main house and two studio spaces.

Southwark. Right onto the Cut. Tickets £10-22. Open M-Sa 10am-6pm.

DONMAR WAREHOUSE THE WEST END

41 Earlham St. ☎084 4871 7624 www.donmarwarehouse.com

The warehouse puts on everything from Shakespeare to contemporary works, occasionally by little known artists. Though it is a mainstream theater, it rotates in new plays once every two months. The space has a studio feel, with cushioned red benches facing the stage.

Covent Garden. Turn right onto Long Acre, left on Endell St., left onto Shelton St., right onto Neal St., and then left on Earlham St. Tickets £15-29, students £12 tickets 30min. before the show if it's not sold out. Ticket office open M-Sa 10am-showtime.

SHAKESPEARE'S GLOBE SOUTH LONDON

21 New Globe Walk ☎020 7401 9919 www.shakespeares-globe.org

Though the original Globe theater burnt down in 1613 during a performance of *Henry VIII*, this accurate reconstruction was opened in 1997. Much like the original Globe, it has an open roof and standing area for the "groundlings." Steeped in historical and artistic tradition, the theater stages Shakespeare as well as two new plays a year.

Southwark. Left onto Blackfriars Rd., right onto Southwark St., left onto Great Guildford, right onto Park St., left onto Emerson St. Standing £5, seats £35. Box office open M-Sa 10am-8pm, Su 10am-7pm. Telephone open M-Sa 10am-6pm, Su 10am-5pm.

BATTERSEA ART CENTER SOUTH LONDON

176 Lavender Hill, Old Town Hall ☎020 7223 2223 www.bac.org.uk

Located in the old Clapham Town Hall, the Battersea Art Center is automatically a strange theater experience. Throw in the BAC's reputation for hosting young producers, new companies, and some of the most cutting-edge and bizarre theater when deemed too young to be "on the scene," and you have a night of some wild shows ahead of you. The BAC boasts 72 rooms that host everything from closets to more traditional spaces. In a famous performance at the BAC, an Italian theater company put on a show where the audience had to pretend to be dogs. This resulted in audience members rolling around on wheel trays with oven mitts on their hands and eating scraps off a table while tennis balls were thrown at them. One of the best parts about the BAC is the SCRATCH program, in which artists show a work in development and get feedback from the audience. This famous program only cements the BAC's status as a hip, young, unconventional theater.

*Clapham Common. Take bus #345 headed toward South Kensington and it will let you out nearby on Lavender Hill. Min. at bar £10. **i** Under 26-ers should also note that the BAC is part of "A Night Less Ordinary." Ticket prices vary. Pints £3.20. Check the website for details, and look out for the occasional "pay what you can Tuesday!" Box office open M-F 10am-6pm, Sa 3-6pm.*

rail penalty

On many of the stations used in the National Rail and DLR system, the stations are not guarded by gates, and passengers are forced to remember to touch in and out at small stands. Don't forget to do this—it's easy to get on the train, but it's not easy to pay the penalty. And they do check.

THE BUSH THEATRE

WEST LONDON

Shepherd's Bush Green ☎020 8743 5050 www.bushtheatre.co.uk

Located on the edge of Shepherd's Bush Green in an old building, The Bush Theatre's repertoire is in stark contrast to its old London surroundings. Presenting new writing in its unique, intimate theater space, which rarely looks the same between two shows, The Bush is the place to come for some of the most forward-thinking theater in London.

Shepherd's Bush. turn right down Shepherd's Bush Green. Tickets £20, concessions are £10. Matinees £15/7.50. The Bush is part of "A Night Less Ordinary." Box office open M-Sa on non-show days 10am-6pm, on show days noon-8pm. Shows are normally M-Sa 7:30pm. Sa matinees 2:30pm.

HACKNEY EMPIRE

EAST LONDON

291 Mare St. ☎020 8985 2424 www.hackneyempire.co.uk

With great, bold sandstone letters announcing its presence on an otherwise normal block, the Hackney Empire looks just as an old variety theater that once showcased the likes of **Charlie Chaplin** and **Harry Houdini** should. All faded grandeur and vaudeville-esque decor, the Hackney puts on everything from comedy gigs to productions from the Royal Shakespeare Company.

Take the overline to Hackney Central (in East London). Left onto Graham Rd., right onto Mare St. Tickets £10-22.50, student discount £2 off. Box office open M-Sa 10am-6pm, show days M-Su 10am-9:30pm.

OPEN-AIR THEATRE

REGENT'S PARK

Regent's Park ☎084 4826 4242 www.openairtheatre.com

Housed inside the beautiful Regent's Park, the Open-Air Theatre puts on a variety of shows best enjoyed in the warm summer months. After the show, take a stroll around the park and enjoy observing the less-dramatic lives of the herons who reside therein.

Regent's Park. Tickets M-Th evening £10-43, F-Sa £19-46. Standby £15 for best available. Telephone box office open M-Sa 10am-6pm.

FESTIVALS

BBC PROMS

KNIGHTSBRIDGE

Kensington Gore ☎0845 401 5045 www.bbc.co.uk/proms

BBC Proms is a world famous classical music festival put on by the BBC in the Royal Albert Hall. What in the world is a "Prom," you ask? "Prom" stands for "Promenade Concert"—a performance at which some of the audience stands on a promenade in the arena. During the Proms, there is at least one daily performance in London's Royal Albert Hall, in addition 70-odd events and discussions. Note that performances are broadcast for free.

Knightsbridge. Turn left onto Knightsbridge, continue onto Kensington Rd. i Check website for specific wheelchair-accessibility information. From £10. July-Sept.

GLASTONBURY FESTIVAL

SOMERSET

Pilton, England Festival Office ☎01458 834 596 www.glastonburyfestivals.co.uk

One of the most famous rock festivals in the world, the Glastonbury Festival explodes onto the scene every June. Possibly as close as you will ever get to going to Woodstock, it's essentially a bunch of festivals jam-packed into one, distributed through the Dance Village, Green Field, Circus and Theatre fields, and the Park.

Festival office: 28 Northload St., Glastonbury, Somerset BA6 9JJ. i National Express has routes to Glastonbury. Bristol and Glastonbury town shuttles provide transportation to the festival. Disabled patrons must register in order to use the festival's accessible facilities; to get a registration form, request a disabled-access packet, which includes information on the site's accessible facilities. Standard ticket £185 + £5 booking fee per ticket + £5 P and P per booking. June. Performance dates and times vary.

BLAZE THE CITY OF LONDON

Barbican Centre, Silk Street London, EC2Y 8DS ☎020 7638 8891 www.barbican.org.uk/blaze

An annual festival that features major international artists in the Barbican and open-air performance spaces throughout London. Blaze makes for a full-immersion arts experience, as audience participation is encouraged.

Barbican. i The main entrance to the venue is wheelchair-accessible, and all venues have seating for wheelchair users. The Barbican Centre requests that patrons inform them of access requirements upon booking their tickets. Annual membership £20. Event prices vary. June-July.

LONDON LITERARY FESTIVAL THE SOUTH BANK

Southbank Centre Belvedere Road, SE1 8XX ☎0844 847 9939 www.londonlitfest.com

Some of the world's hottest thinkers and writers assemble at the South Bank Centre every July. This literary extravaganza has featured poets, novelists, musicians, and scientists. Visit the website to download podcasts of the events.

Waterloo; Embankment. i For complete wheelchair-accessibility details, see "Access Information" on website. Check website for ticket prices. Online booking transaction fee £1.45. Telephone booking transaction fee £2.50. Call between 9am-8pm daily. Book through Royal Festival Hall Ticket Office daily 10am-8pm.

shopping

London is known as one of the shopping capitals of the world. With its famous department stores (like **Harrods** and **Harvey Nichol's**) keeping the old flame of shopping as spectacle alive over in Knightsbridge, London has kept some of its old shopping class and the prices that come with it. Vintage stores and hip, independent record stores fill Soho, and the East End has lots of fun boutiques. Notting Hill is famous for **Portobello Market**, but even in off-market days, the road has a host of cute boutique shopping options. Chelsea is for those with a bit more money and a serious commitment to shopping. For you literary junkies, **John Sandoe's** is our favorite bookstore in the city. Shopping is a significant part of tourism in London, so if you aren't broke and have some extra room in your backpack, shop the day away.

WESTMINSTER

Westminster is filled with chains. The area is worth seeing for the sights, but die-hard shoppers might be best served by looking elsewhere.

WESTMINSTER BOOKSHOP BOOKSTORE

8 Artillery Row ☎020 7802 0018 www.westminsterbookshop.co.uk

The last independent bookstore in Westminster, this little shop is fighting the chains with an excellent and specialized selection. In case experiencing London first-hand isn't enough for you, you can utilize the store's impressive British history, British politics, biography, political thought, and London sections for a full English intellectual experience. Just be sure to swing by the classics for some Austen, Dickens, or Woolf (among many, many others) on your way out. If you're looking to pick up the 5000th Bourne book that you saw advertised on the subway, this is not the store for you

Liverpool St. Take a right onto Liverpool St., a left onto Bishopsgate, right onto Artillery Lane, and then right onto Artillery Row. M-F 9:30am-5:30pm, Sa 11am-4pm.

HOTEL CHOCOLAT CHOCOLATE

133 Victoria St. ☎020 7821 0473 www.hotelchocolat.co.uk

One of a chain, Hotel Chocolat is one of the more exciting accommodations in Westminster. The inside is sleek, like a more efficient version of Willy Wonka's

Chocolate Factory. Seventy percent of the chocolate here is made in Britain, and it's packaged into ridiculous items like framed chocolate portraits and chocolate dipping sets, all for sale. For anyone who's ever felt that a chocolate "slab" is preferable to a chocolate bar, you have found your store.

Victoria. Take right onto Grosvenor Pl. and follow it onto Victoria St. Open M-F 8:30am-7pm, Sa 9:30am-6pm, Su 11am-5pm.

MARYLEBONE AND REGENT'S PARK

IT'S ONLY ROCK 'N' ROLL — ROCK PARAPHERNALIA

230 Baker St. ☎020 7224 0277 www.itsonlyrocknrolllondon.co.uk

London is known for its rich musical history, and It's Only Rock 'N' Roll exploits that fact as much as possible. Filled with paraphernalia both gimmicky and original, like gold and platinum records, binoculars from the Stones' "Bridges to Babylon" tour, Pink Floyd shower slippers, a Coldplay calendar, and a signed vinyl cover of the Who's *Rock Opera Quadrophenia*, It's Only Rock'N Roll is a must for any visiting rock fan.

Baker St. Right on Baker St. Open daily 10am-6:30pm.

BAYSWATER

Bayswater is full of quirky little shops, though it's not a major shopping center like Notting Hill.

BAYSWATER MARKET — MARKET

Bayswater Rd.

Every Sunday, local artists of all media and skill levels decorate the Hyde Park Fence with their wares, making it look like an art gallery with commitment issues. It's open all afternoon, so join the crowds as they move from touristy London pictures to more original works from rising stars in the London art scene. Art is for sale at all prices, so come with an open mind and be ready to dig a sizeable hole in your wallet.

Lancaster Gate. Open Su late morning through the afternoon.

CHELSEA

Shopping in Chelsea runs the gamut, with stores from the neighborhoods punk-rock salad days to a stifling amount of kitchen and home shops. Still, if you want to trick out your hostel room, we've seen some lovely linoleum.

JOHN SANDOE BOOKS — BOOKSTORE

10 Blacklands Terr. ☎020 7589 9473 www.johnsandoe.com

While taking the stairs to the fiction section on the second floor, one remembers the joy of independent bookstores. There's barely space for peoples' feet as half of each stair is taken up by a pile of carefully selected books. On the crammed second floor, a cracked leather chair presides over shelves so packed with masterworks and little known gems that they are layered with moving shelves. There are books everywhere in this store, and the knowledgeable staff is personable and ready to offer excellent suggestions. Book lovers beware: it would be easy to spend the day in this shop.

Sloane Sq. Exit the Tube and go straight down Sloane Sq. The street slanting gently left is King's Rd. Go straight onto it and turn right at Blacklands Terr. Open M-Sa 9:30am-5:30pm, Su noon-6pm.

TASCHEN — ART BOOKSTORE

12 Duke of York Sq. ☎020 7881 0795 www.taschen.com

If you've ever heard of Taschen, or the art-book-publishing company, you'll want to see this store. Packed with high quality, well-written, high-culture art books about everything from Impressionism to logo design and some low-culture books such as those pertaining to big butts, breasts, penises, and, of course, architecture. Taschen's got everything a self-respecting art aficionado could want...except the originals.

Sloane Square. Exit the Tube and go straight down Sloane Sq. The street slanting gently left is King's Rd. go onto it and turn left onto Duke of York Sq. (it's the one by the Saatchi Art Gallery). Prices vary, but the books can be surprisingly inexpensive. Open M-Tu 10am-6pm, W 10am-7pm, Th-F 10am-6pm, Sa 10am-7pm, Su noon-6pm.

AD HOC — WOMEN'S CLOTHING, SEX TRINKETS

153 King's Rd — 020 7376 8829 www.adhoclondon.co.uk

If you have an inescapable yet reasonably innocuous fascination with breasts and penises (and really, who doesn't), then Ad Hoc might be the shopping experience you've been missing. There are tassels, flashing breast lights, grow your-own willies, inflatable boobs, bouncing boobs, and glow-in-the-dark cock straws. There are also shirts, hats, adventurous tights, and sunglasses. Randomly, Fllann's tattoo parlor is a part of the shop. Sex and tattoos, what more convincing do you need?

Sloane Square. Exit the Tube and go straight down Sloane Sq. The street slanting gently left is King's Rd. Open M-Tu 10am-6pm, W 10am-7pm, Th-Su 10am-6pm.

KENSINGTON AND EARL'S COURT

BOOKTHRIFT — BOOKS

22 Thurloe St. — 020 7589 2916

Advertising "Quality Books at Bargain Prices," Bookthrift buys overstock books off publishers, meaning they can sell new books at used prices. Featuring a wide selection of Art books, History, and Fiction, Bookthrift has fun deals like 3 books for the price of two in Military History or the three for £2 on £2.99 paperback fiction. The selection isn't as good as it is in other bookstores, but if you look closely, you're likely to find a good read at a great price.

South Kensington. Take a right down Thurloe St. Open M-F 10am-8pm, Sa 11am-7pm, Su noon-7pm.

TRINITY HOSPICE BOOKSHOP — BARGAIN BOOKS MUSIC DVDs EQUIPMENT

31 Kensington Church St. — 020 7376 1098

With all proceeds going to charity, the Trinity Hospice Bookshop is a good place for any socially-conscious traveler who wants a book that's cheap enough to abuse guilt-free. All the products are donated, and since the store gets them for free, they sell them at next to nothing. The selection ranges wildly, so set aside some time for digging and you just might find a cheap, vintage gem.

High Street Kensington. Turn right onto Kensington High St. and left onto Kensington Church St. Paperbacks £2. Hardcovers £3. CDs £2. All vinyls (with the exception of rare jazz records) £1. Open M-Sa 10:30-6pm, Su 11am-5pm.

WHOLE FOODS — GROCERY STORE

63-97 Kensington High St. — 020 7368 4500 www.wholefoodsmarket.com

For those living nearby who have the hankering for some health-food cookin', look no further than this centrally-located Whole Foods location. This store is also a good antidote to homesickness for those coming from the States and Canada.

High St. Kensington. Turn right onto Kensington High St. Open M-Sa 8am-10pm, Su noon-6pm. Restaurant open Mo-Sa 8am-9:45pm, Su 10am-5:45pm.

KNIGHTSBRIDGE AND BELGRAVIA

Mostly posh shops and chains, Knightsbridge isn't the most friendly place for shopping, price-wise. However, the spectacle of its famous department stores make browsing enjoyable.

HARRODS — DEPARTMENT STORE

87-135 Brompton Rd. ☎020 7730 1234 www.harrods.com

An ode to the shopping experience, Harrods is probably the most famous department store on the planet. Packed with faux-hieroglyphs, a room named "Room of Luxury" or its sequel, "Room of Luxury II," Harrods is just as much a sight to see as it is a place to shop. Especially entertaining are the prices and the people who pay them. Be sure to check out the toy section—it's hard not to rediscover your inner child. Also worth seeing is the candy section of the food court, which is where they sell chocolate shoes *(£84 per pair)*. On the bottom floor, they sell "Personalised Classics" which enable you to insert names in place of the ones already in a given book. Who needs "Romeo and Juliet" when you could have "Fred and Agnes?"

Knightsbride. Take the Harrods Exit. Open M-Sa 10am-8pm, Su 11:30am-6pm.

PANDORA — CONSIGNMENT DRESSES

16-22 Cheval Pl. ☎020 7589 5289 www.pandoradressagency.com

If you get tired of the prices at the more expensive department stores, come to Pandora and see the same designer clothes second-hand at lower prices! Clothe yourself in Chanel, Dior, Yves St. Lauren, and Gucci and be sure to save money for accessorizing.

Knightsbridge. Turn left onto Brompton Rd., right onto Montpelier St. and left onto Cheval Pl. Open M-Sa 10am-7pm, Su noon-6pm.

HARVEY NICHOLS — DEPARTMENT STORE

109-125 Knightsbridge ☎020 7235 5000 www.harveynichols.com

Whoever was looking for the Fountain of Youth clearly never checked out the ground floor of Harvey Nichols. The entire level is packed with women arming themselves for the battle against age. In fact, four floors of the great department store are taken up by fashion, cosmetics, beauty, and accessories. After that, there's menswear, food, and hospitality. Most high-end designers are sold here. Foreigners can shop tax-free if they go to the fourth-floor customer services and fill out a form. The store is upscale, densely populated with women, and a little less of a scene than nearby Harrods.

Knightsbridge. Open M-Sa 10am-9pm, Su 11:30am-6pm (browsing only 11:30am-noon).

NOTTING HILL

Like we said, Portobello Rd. is truly where it's at. Otherwise, shopping options in Notting Hill consist mainly of antique stores, souvenir sellers, and high-end clothing shops.

MUSIC AND VIDEO EXCHANGE — MUSIC

42 Notting Hill Gate www.mveshops.co.uk

Though part of a chain, this Music and Video Exchange will entertain any audiophile endlessly. The staff engage in Hornby-esque conversations oozing with musical knowledge, while customers browse through the vinyls, CDs, and cassettes in the bargain area. Upstairs in the rarities section, you can find anything from original vinyl of the Rolling Stones' *Get Yer Ya-Ya's Out! (£12)* to the original German sleeve for the Beatles' final record, *Let it Be.* Customers can trade in their own stuff in exchange for cash or—in a move betraying MVE's cold-hearted understanding of a music lover's brain—twice the cash amount in store vouchers.

Notting Hill Gate. Walk out the south entrance and go down Notting Hill Gate. Open daily 10am-8pm.

THE TRAVEL BOOKSHOP BOOKS

13-15 Blenheim Crescent ☎020 7229 5260 www.thetravelbookshop.com

You may be tempted to disregard this bookstore as soon as you figure out why Americans are taking their pictures in front of it, but that would be a mistake. The inspiration for the "Travel Book Company" in the film *Notting Hill*, the shop has all the charm the filmmakers thought it had. The shelves are piled high with travel literature, travel guides, and maps. You can even find stylish postcards, children's books, and historical literature. We're sure you're perfectly content with the travel book you're currently using, but the shop's worth a browse.

Notting Hill Gate. Exit the station from the north exit. Turn right onto Pembridge Rd. and then left onto Portobello Rd. Follow Portobello down and turn left on Blenheim Crescent. Open M-Sa 10am-6pm, Su noon-5pm.

a sohovian conversation

I was in Soho (yes, there is a Soho in London, too) the other day when I noticed a high number of rickshaws circling the area. Thinking it would make good fodder for a tip, I approached one of the drivers. The following conversation ensued:

Me: Excuse me, I was wondering what your rates are.

Rick: Get in.

Me: No, that's alright, I just wanted to know how much you charge per block or so.

Rick: You want to go where?

Me: I don't want to go anywhere, but if I were to take your rickshaw, how much would it cost me to get to the other side of Soho Square?

Rick: I'll give you a ride, sure.

Me: How much?

Rick: Alright, let's go.

Me: No thanks, I'll just walk.

Rick: So you want go to a strip club then?

Ah, Soho.

Benjamin Naddaff-Hafrey

THE SOUTH BANK

MARCUS CAMPBELL ART BOOKS

ART BOOKS

43 Holland St. ☎020 7261 0111 www.marcuscampbell.co.uk

Close enough both in theme and proximity to the **Tate Modern** (p. 50) to be its unofficial bookstore, Marcus Campbell Art Books sells a wide variety of what you might expect. Cheap catalogues are on sale *(£1-£2)*, and rare and expensive books run the gamut, with some coming in at over £3000. A fun store for browsing and shopping alike.

⊖Southwark. Left onto Blackfriars Rd. Right onto Southwark St., left onto Sumner, left onto Holland St. Open M-Sa 10:30am-6:30pm, Su noon-6pm.

SOUTHBANK PRINTMAKERS

ART SHOP

Unit 12 Gabriels Wharf, 56 Upper Ground ☎020 7928 8184 www.southbank-printmakers.com

Every five minutes, someone in London is sold a cheap work of bad, tourist-trap art. Southbank Printmakers have a chance to put a stop to this grave injustice. This artist cooperative has been around for 10 years, producing quality lino cuts, wood cuts, etchings, and monoprints at affordable prices. Many of the prints are London-themed, making them perfect, original, and affordable souvenirs.

⊖Southwark. Left onto Blackfriars Rd., left onto Stamford St., right onto Duchy St. Open in summer M-F 11:30am-6:30pm, Sa-Su 10am-8pm, in winter M-F 11:30am-5:30pm, Sa-Su 10am-7pm.

TATE MODERN BOOKSHOP

ART BOOKS

53 Bankside ☎020 7401 5167 www.tate.org.uk/shop

Located just off Turbine Hall in the fabulous Tate Modern, the Tate Modern Bookshop has everything for the art lover. Sketch pads, high-art postcards, art theory books, kids' books, books on film, and films are all sold in this comprehensive bookshop which lies close to its inspiration.

⊖Southwark. Left onto Blackfriars Rd. Right onto Southwark St., left onto Sumner, left onto Holland St. Open M-Th 10am-6pm, F-Sa 10am-10pm, Su 10am-6pm.

THE WEST END

Shopping in the West End is more student-oriented than most areas in London. Filled with cool independent stores, most of them selling books, CDs, vinyls and more vintage clothes than the Motown stars ever wore, the West End is a fun shopping district that tends to emphasize the cheap. Break out the chucks, Ray-Bans and tight black jeans—your wallet must lighten.

SISTER RAY

INDEPENDENT RECORDS AND CDS

34-35 Berwick St. ☎020 7734 3297 www.sisterray.co.uk

An old school record shop of the best kind, Sister Ray has every sort of genre, from constant chart-toppers to one-hit wonders. The stellar staff is adept at creating musical matches-made-in-Heaven, directing listeners to artists. Hip, cheap books about music line the check-out counter, and listening stations are throughout the store.

⊖Tottenham Court Rd., left on Oxford St. left on Wardour St., left on Berwick St. i Wheelchair access at the top of the store, ramp available on request. Open M-Sa 10am-8pm, Su noon-6pm.

THE SCHOTT MUSIC SHOP

SHEET MUSIC, PRACTICE ROOMS

48 Great Marlborough St. ☎020 7292 6090 www.schottmusic.co.uk

This quiet and spacious shop is one of the oldest sheet music shops in London. Open since 1857, The Schott Music Shop sells everything from the Beatles to Bartok and Muse to Mendelssohn. Especially of note to musical travelers are the three **practice rooms** beneath the shop which are available for 1hr. rehearsal times. There you'll find two baby grand Boston pianos and one Steinway, all of which are tuned every two months. They also hold recitals for young performers *(£8-10).*

Oxford Circus. Left on Regent St., left on Great Marlborough St. Students get 10% discount on print music. Upstairs only wheelchair-accessible. £10 per hr. before noon, £12 per hr. noon-6pm, £15per hr. after 6pm. Open M-F 10am-6:30pm, Sa 10am-6pm.

BM SOHO MUSIC — DJ RECORD STORE

25 D'Arblay St. — 020 7437 0478 www.bm-soho.com

A favorite for many local DJs, BM (known to those in the know as **Black Market**) has all things House and drum and bass. Most striking is just how many subgenres of house there are. DJ gear like slip mats and cases for records are on sale in the back, and regular customers get discounts *(£1-3)*, but you have to ask for it. Check the website for the occasional in-store appearance of a famous DJ who'll jam out while patrons enjoy free cider.

Tottenham Ct Rd., left on Oxford St. left on Wardour St., left on Berwick St., right on D'Arblay. You have to ask a clerk to take records down for you. Most records £5-10. Open M-W 11am-7pm, Th-F 11am-8pm, Sa 11am-7pm, Su noon-6pm.

essentials

PRACTICALITIES

- **TOURS: Big Bus Company** *(48 Buckingham Palace Rd. Victoria. 020 7233 9533 www.bigbustours.com Buses leave every 15min. 8:30am-6pm)* offers a **Red Tour** (history) which stops at the Green Park Underground, Hyde Park Corner, Trafalgar Square, Whitehall, Westminster Bridge, London Eye, Tower of London, Buckingham Palace, and Victoria. **Original London Walks** *(020 7624 9255 £8, 65+ and students £6)* has themed walks like "Jack the Ripper Walk" and "Alfred Hitchcock's London." Check the website for schedules. **Britain Visitor Centres** *(1 Regent St. Piccadilly Circus. www.visitbritain.com Open M 9:30am-6:30pm, Tu-F 9am-6pm, Sa 9am-5pm, Su and Bank Holidays 10am-4pm.)* **London Information Centre.** *(Leicester Sq. Leicester Sq. 020 7292 2333 M-Su 8am-midnight.)*
- **US EMBASSY:** *(24 Grosvenor Sq. Bond St. 020 7499 9000 www.usembassy.org.uk.)*
- **CREDIT CARD SERVICES: American Express** *(www.amextravelresources.com)* locations at *(78 Brompton Rd. Knightsbridge.* 084 4406 0046 *Open M-T 9am-5:30pm, W 9:30am-5:30pm, Th-F 9am-5:30pm, Sa 9am-4:00pm)* and *(30-31 Haymarket. Piccadilly Circus. 084 4406 0044 Open M-F 9am-5:30pm.)*
- **GLBT RESOURCES: Boyz** *(www.boyz.co.uk)* lists gay events in London as well as an online version of its magazine. **Gingerbeer** *(www.gingerbeer.co.uk)* is a guide for lesbian and bisexual women with events listings.
- **POST OFFICE: Trafalgar Square Post Office.** *(24-28 William IV St., Westminster. Charing Cross. 0207 484 9305 Open M 8:30am-6:30pm, Tu 9:15am-6:30pm, W-F 8:30am-6:30pm, Sa 9am-5:30pm.)*

EMERGENCY!

- **POLICE:** Call **City of London Police** *(020 7601 2000)* or **Metropolitan Police** *(030 0123 1212).*
- **PHARMACY: Boots** *(www.boots.com)* and **Superdrug** *(www.superdrug.com)*, the most popular drugstores in London, are scattered throughout the city.

Zafash Pharmacy. *(233-235 Old Brompton Rd. ⊖Earl's Court. ☎020 7373 2798 🖳www.zafash.com.)* **Bliss Pharmacy.** *(107-109 Gloucester Rd. ⊖Gloucester Rd. ☎020 7373 4445.)*

- **HOSPITAL: St.Thomas's Hospital.** *(Westminster Bridge Rd. ⊖Westminster. ☎020 7188 7188.)* **Royal Free Hospital.** *(Pond St. ⊖Hampstead Heath. ☎020 7794 0500.)* **Charing Cross Hospital.** *(Fulham Palace Rd. ⊖Hammersmith. ☎020 3311 1234.)* **University College Hospital.** *(235 Euston Rd. ⊖Warren St. ☎0845 155 5000.)*

GETTING THERE

By Plane

The main airport in London is **Heathrow** *(☎084 4335 1801 🖳www.heathrowairport.com).* There are five terminals at Heathrow, which is commonly regarded as one of the busiest international airports in the world. Terminal 2 is closed, and there are exceptions to the rules concerning the location of airlines. The best way to find your terminal is through the **"Which terminal?"** function on the Heathrow website. This tool enables you to search via airline and destination as well as specific flight number.

The cheapest way to get from London Heathrow to Central London is on the Tube. The two Tube stations servicing the four terminals of Heathrow form a distressing looking loop at the end of the **⊖Piccadilly** line which runs between Central London and the Heathrow terminals *(⏰ 1hr., every 5min. M-Sa 5am-11:54pm, Su 5:46am-10:37pm.)*

Heathrow Express *(☎084 5600 1515 🖳www.heathrowexpress.com)* runs between Heathrow and Paddington four times per hour. The trip is significantly shorter than many of the alternatives, clocking in at around 15-20min. *(⏰ M-Sa 1st train from terminals 1, 2 and 3 5:12am; Su 5:08am. daily first train from Terminal 5 5:07am),* but the £16.50 *(when purchased online; £18 from station; £23 on board)* makes it a little less enticing. The **Heathrow Connect** also runs to Paddington but is both cheaper and longer because it stops at five places on the way to and from Heathrow. There are two trains per hour, and the trip takes about 25min.

The **National Express** bus runs between Victoria Coach Station and Heathrow three times per hour. Though cheap and often simpler than convoluted Underground trips, the buses are subject to that great parasite of the Queen's country: traffic. There are naysayers roaming the halls of Heathrow moaning terrifying tales about people spending vacations on buses, but if you're looking for a cheap thrill and you're from anywhere with normal driving laws, you can look forward to that first time when they pull onto the highway and your travel-addled mind instructs you to wrench the steering wheel from the driver's mad hands. *(☎08717 818 178 🖳www.nationalexpress.com).* Posing a similar traffic threat, **taxis** from the airport to Victoria cost around £60 and take around 45min. In short, they aren't worth it.

Getting to **Gatwick Airport** *(☎084 4335 1802 🖳www.gatwickairport.com)* takes around 30min., making it less convenient than Heathrow but less hectic too. The swift and affordable train services that connect Gatwick to the city make the trip a little easier. The **Gatwick Express** train *(☎084 5850 1530 🖳www.gatwickexpress.com ⑤ 1-way £15.20; round-trip £25.80, valid for a month)* runs non-stop service to Victoria station *(⏰ 35min., every 15min., 5:50-12:35am).* Buy tickets in terminals, at the station, or on the train itself.

National Express runs services from the North and South terminals of Gatwick to London. The National Express bus *(☎08717 818 178 🖳www.nationalexpress.com)* takes approximately 1½hr., and buses depart for London Victoria hourly. Taxis take about 1hr. to reach central London. **easyBus** *(☎084 4800 4411 🖳www.easybus.co.uk)* runs every 15min. from North and South terminals to Earls Court and West Brompton *(Tickets from £20. 65min., every 15min.)*

London also offers several ways to easily reach other European destinations. **Eurolines** *(☎08717 818 181 www.eurolines.co.uk Open 8am-8pm)* is Europe's largest coach network, providing service to 500 destinations throughout Europe. Many buses leave from **Victoria Coach Station,** which is at the mouth of Elizabeth St. just off of Buckingham Palace Rd. Many coach companies, including **National Express, Eurolines,** and **Megabus** operate from Victoria Coach. National Express *(☎087 1781 8178 www.nationalexpress.com)* is the only scheduled coach network in Britain and can be used for most intercity travel and for travel to and from various airports. It can also be used to reach Scotland and Wales. **Greenline** *(☎087 1200 2233 www.greenline.co.uk)* provides services throughout London. One of its stops is by **Eccleston Bridge,** right next to Victoria, but it also reaches such convenient areas as **Hyde Park Corner** and **Baker Street.**

GETTING AROUND

Though there are daily interruptions to service in the Tube (that's right, not the metro, not the subway, but the Tube or the Underground), the controlling network, **Transport of London,** does a good job of keeping travelers aware of these disruptions to service. Each station will have posters listing interruptions to service, and you can check service online at **www.tfl.gov.uk** or the 24hr. travel information service at ☎0843 222 1234. Most stations also have ticket booths and informed TFL employees who can help you and guide you to the proper pamphlets.

Though many people in the city stay out past midnight, the Tube doesn't have the same sort of stamina. When it closes around midnight, night owls have two choices: a cab or **nightbuses.** Most nightbus lines are prefixed with an **N,** (N13, for instance) and some stops even have 24hr. buses.

Travel Passes

Travel Passes are almost guaranteed to save you money. The passes are priced based on the number of zones they serve (the more zones, the more expensive), but zone 1 encompasses central London and you will not likely need to get past zone 2. If someone offers you a secondhand ticket, don't take it. There's no real way to verify whether it's valid—plus, it's illegal. Those under 16 get free travel on buses and trams. Children under five rule the public transportation system, getting free travel on the Tube, tram, **Docklands Lights Railway (DLR),** overground, and **National Rail** services (though they must be accompanied by someone with a valid pass). Passengers ages 11-15 enjoy reduced fares on the Tube with an Oyster photocard. Students eighteen and older must study full-time *(at least 15hr. per week over 14 weeks)* in London to qualify for the Student Photocard, which enables users to save 30% on adult travel cards and bus and tram passes. You can apply for one online but you need a passport-sized digital photo and an enrollment ID from your school. It's worth it if you're staying for an extended period of time. (Study abroad kids, we're looking at you...)

Oyster Cards store everything you need and enable you to pay in a variety of ways. Fares come in peak *(M-F 4:30am-9:29am)* and off-peak *(any other time)* varieties and are, again, distinguished by zone. In addition to letting you add Travelcards, Oysters enable users to "pay as you go," meaning that you can store credit on an as-needed basis. The cards have price capping that will allow you to travel as much as you want, while ensuring that you don't pay above the cost of the day Travelcard you would otherwise have purchased. Register your card, especially if you put a lot of money on it. That way, you can **recover everything if it's lost.** Weekly, monthly, and annual Oyster Cards can be purchased at any time from Tube stations. They yield unlimited *(within zone)* use for their duration *(Weekly rates for zones 1-2 £25.80. Monthly £99.10. Day off-peak £5.60. Day anytime is £7.20.)*

By Underground

Most stations have **Tube maps** on the walls as well as free pocket maps. Please note that the Tube map barely reflects an above-ground scale, and should not be used for even the roughest of walking directions. Platforms are organized by line, and will have the **colors** of the lines serviced and their names on the wall. The colors of the poles inside the trains correspond with the line, and trains will often have their end destination displayed on the front. This is an essential service when your line splits. Many platforms will have a digital panel indicating ETAs for the trains and sometimes type and final destination. When transferring in stations, just follow the clearly marked routes. Yellow **"WAY OUT"** signs point toward exits.

The Tube runs Monday to Saturday from approximately **5:30am** (though it depends on which station and line) to around **midnight.** If you're taking a train within 30min. of these times (before or after), you'll want to check the signs in the ticket hall for times of the first and last train. The Tube runs less frequently on Sunday, with many lines starting service after 6am. Around 6pm on weekdays, many of the trains running out of central London become packed with the after-work crowd. It's best to avoid the service at this time.

You can buy **tickets** from ticket counters (though these often have lines at bigger stations) or at machines in the stations. You need a ticket to swipe in at the beginning of the journey and also to exit the Tube. If your train is randomly selected, you will need to present a valid ticket to avoid the £50 penalty fee, which is reduced to £25 if you pay in under 21 days.

By Bus

While slower than the Tube for long journeys (traffic and more frequent stops), **buses** can be useful for traveling short distances covered by a few stops (and several transfers) on the Tube. For one-stop distances, your best bet may be walking.

Bus stops frequently have lists of buses servicing the stop as well as route maps and maps of the area indicating nearby stops. Buses display route numbers.

Every route and stop is different, but buses generally run every 5-15min. beginning around **5:30am** and ending around **midnight.** After day bus routes have closed, **Night Buses** take over. These routes are typically prefixed with an N and operate similar routes to their daytime equivalents. Some buses run 24hr. services. If you're staying out past the Tube closing time, you should plan your nightbus route or bring cab fare.

Singles for adults and students cost £2; fare is only £1.20 with Oyster pay-as-you-go. Sixteen and up Oyster Photocard users get £.60 rates on pay-as-you-go. 11-15-year-olds are free with Oyster Photocards. Under 11s are free regardless of Oyster photocard.

OXFORD

Oxford has **prestige** written all over it. The renowned university has educated some of the most influential players in Western civilization, serving as a home to intellectual royalty, royal royalty, and at least a dozen saints. Students from all around Britain and the world aspire to join the ranks of **Adam Smith, Oscar Wilde,** and **Bill Clinton**... but if you can't join 'em, visit 'em. Swarms of tourists descend on Oxford throughout the year, so don't expect everybody you see to be a local (or a genius). The town is rich in history, and it's not very cheap either. Accommodations are notoriously pricey, and a visit to most of the colleges will even cost you. Still, from the university lore to the town pubs, there's something for everybody on the breathtaking grounds of Oxford. Make room in your budget for some extra-credit **college knowledge.**

greatest hits

- **GO ASK ALICE.** At Christ Church College (p. 114) wander the winding walkways where Lewis Carroll first met the Alice.
- **BIRDY BONES.** Head to the Oxford Museum of Natural History (p. 121) for your first ever encounter with dodo bones.
- **VEGGIES AT VAULTS.** Snack on organic vegetables while overlooking a world-famous university at Vaults and Garden (p. 123).
- **BOOKS AND BOOZE.** Stop by the Eagle and Child (p. 126) to find that some of England's greatest writers were also some of its greatest boozers.

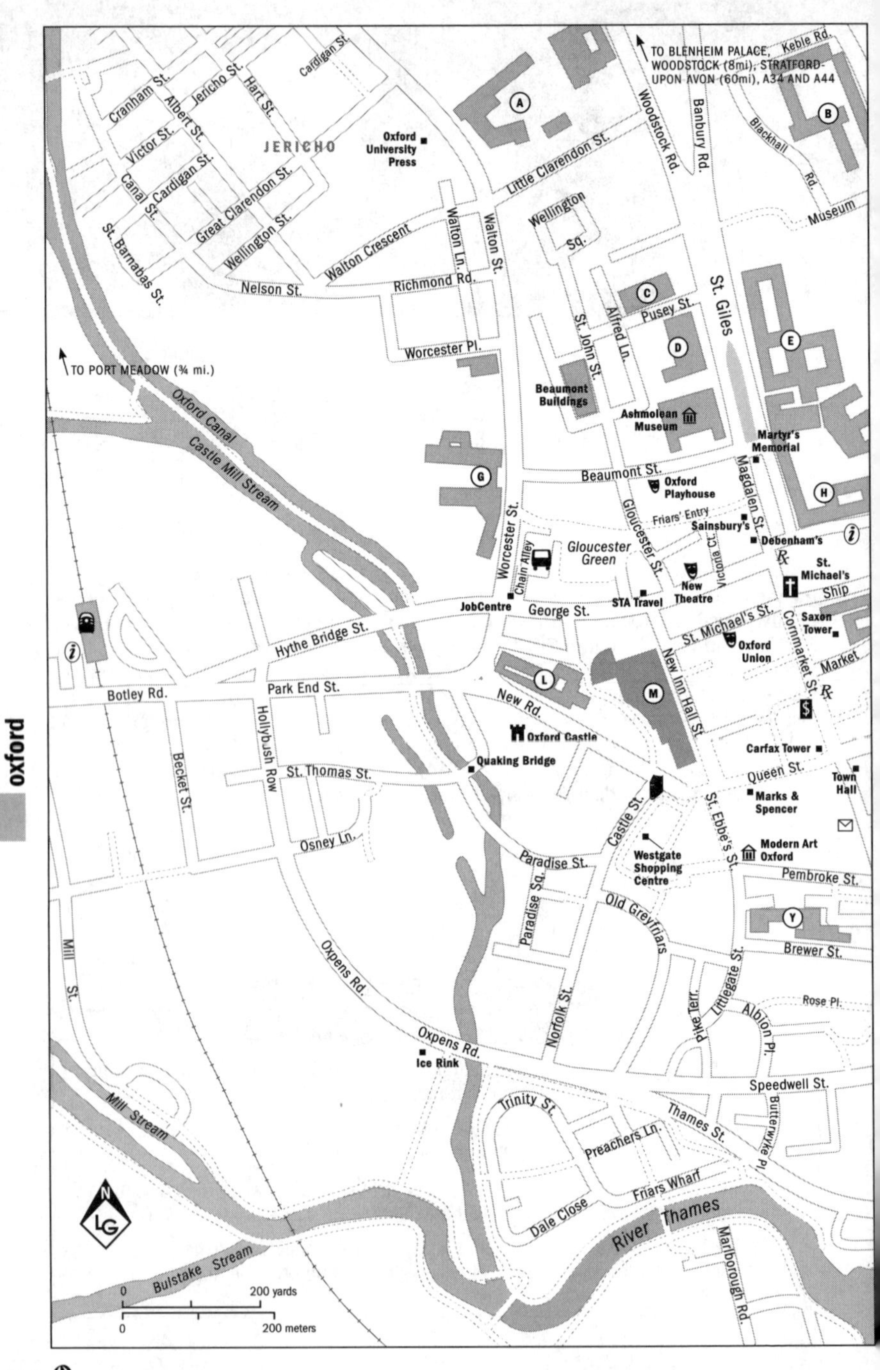
TO BLENHEIM PALACE, WOODSTOCK (8mi), STRATFORD-UPON AVON (60mi), A34 AND A44
JERICHO
Oxford University Press
TO PORT MEADOW (¾ mi.)
Beaumont Buildings
Ashmolean Museum
Martyr's Memorial
Oxford Playhouse
Sainsbury's
Debenham's
Gloucester Green
St. Michael's
New Theatre
STA Travel
JobCentre
Saxon Tower
Oxford Union
Oxford Castle
Quaking Bridge
Carfax Tower
Town Hall
Marks & Spencer
Westgate Shopping Centre
Modern Art Oxford
Ice Rink
River Thames
Oxford Canal
Castle Mill Stream
Mill Stream
Bulstake Stream
Hythe Bridge St.
Botley Rd.
Park End St.
George St.
New Rd.
Queen St.
St. Giles
Woodstock Rd.
Banbury Rd.
Cornmarket St.
Oxpens Rd.
200 yards
200 meters

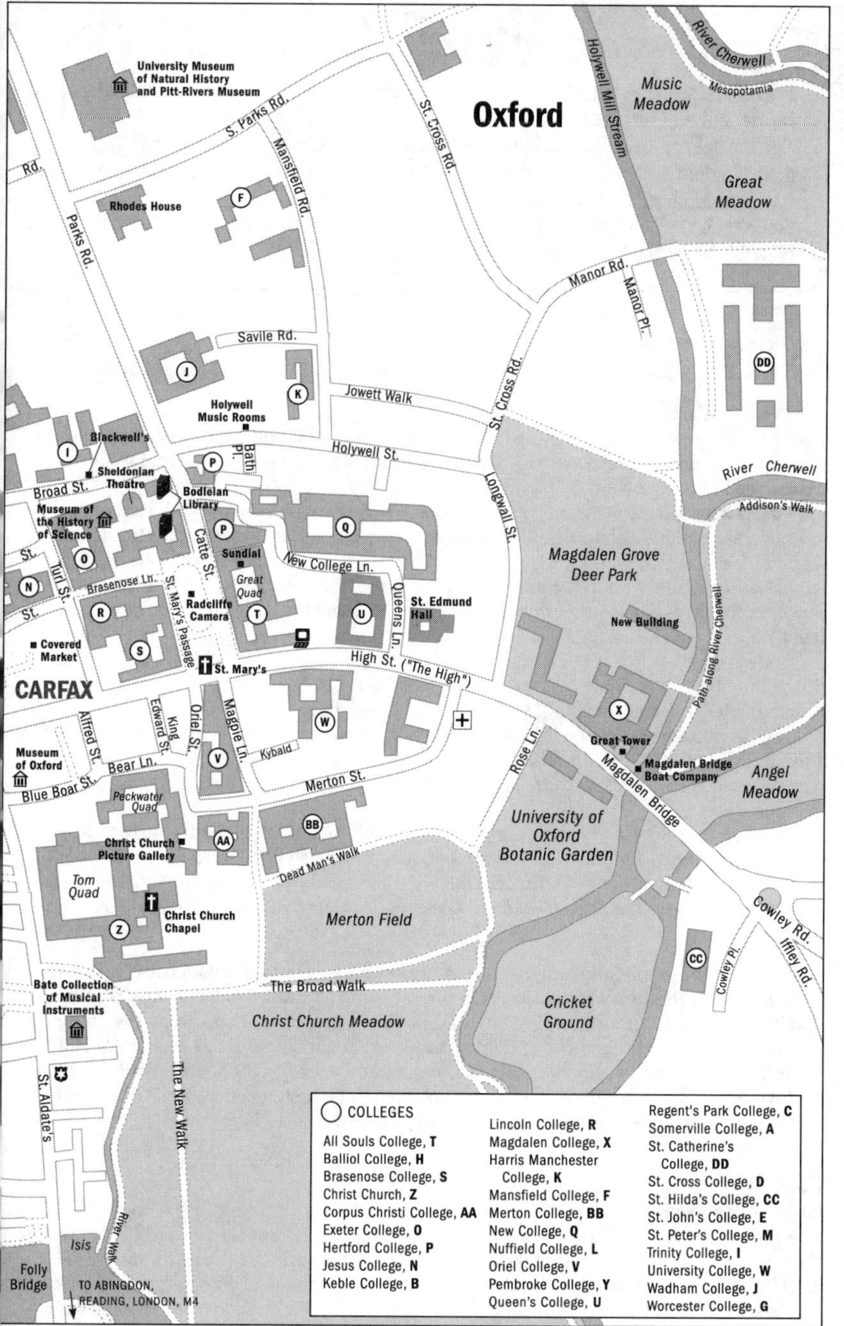
Oxford
University Museum of Natural History and Pitt-Rivers Museum
S. Parks Rd.
Rd.
Mansfield Rd.
St. Cross Rd.
Holywell Mill Stream
River Cherwell
Music Meadow
Mesopotamia
Great Meadow
Rhodes House
Parks Rd.
Manor Rd.
Manor Pl.
Savile Rd.
Jowett Walk
Holywell Music Rooms
Blackwell's
Holywell St.
Bath Pl.
Sheldonian Theatre
Broad St.
Bodleian Library
Museum of the History of Science
Longwall St.
River Cherwell
Addison's Walk
St.
Turl St.
Catte St.
Sundial
New College Ln.
Magdalen Grove Deer Park
Brasenose Ln.
St. Mary's Passage
Great Quad
Queens Ln.
St. Edmund Hall
New Building
Radcliffe Camera
St.
Covered Market
St. Mary's
High St. ("The High")
Path along River Cherwell
CARFAX
Alfred St.
King Edward St.
Oriel St.
Magpie Ln.
Kybald
Great Tower
Museum of Oxford
Bear Ln.
Rose Ln.
Magdalen Bridge Boat Company
Magdalen Bridge
Angel Meadow
Blue Boat St.
Merton St.
Peckwater Quad
University of Oxford Botanic Garden
Christ Church Picture Gallery
Dead Man's Walk
Tom Quad
Christ Church Chapel
Merton Field
Cowley Rd.
Iffley Rd.
Cowley Pl.
Bate Collection of Musical Instruments
The Broad Walk
Christ Church Meadow
Cricket Ground
St. Aldate's
The New Walk
River Walk
Isis
Folly Bridge
TO ABINGDON, READING, LONDON, M4
COLLEGES
All Souls College, T
Balliol College, H
Brasenose College, S
Christ Church, Z
Corpus Christi College, AA
Exeter College, O
Hertford College, P
Jesus College, N
Keble College, B
Lincoln College, R
Magdalen College, X
Harris Manchester College, K
Mansfield College, F
Merton College, BB
New College, Q
Nuffield College, L
Oriel College, V
Pembroke College, Y
Queen's College, U
Regent's Park College, C
Somerville College, A
St. Catherine's College, DD
St. Cross College, D
St. Hilda's College, CC
St. John's College, E
St. Peter's College, M
Trinity College, I
University College, W
Wadham College, J
Worcester College, G

student life

The college scene at Oxford isn't exactly reminiscent of the college scene in **Animal House,** but that doesn't mean the town can't party. Nightlife gets rowdiest just outside the heart of campus, with clubs surrounding **Hythe Street** in Carfax. Rumor has it all of Oxford's nightclubs are right by the bus and train station because that area was already considered too noisy. Whether that's true or not, you can rest assured that you won't disturb any students grinding out papers in their dorms. After all, you'll probably be busy with your own **grinding** on the dance floor.

orientation

COWLEY ROAD

If you're looking for an interesting change of pace from blue-blood, tourist-crammed Oxford, take an excursion across **Magdalen Bridge,** then follow the roundabout to **Cowley Road.**

Cowley Road is Oxford's shopping hub that provides a glimpse into the rich diversity thriving outside the touristy High St. and Cornmarket shops. Cowley Rd. leads through inner-city East Oxford, and into the suburb of Cowley, which **William Morris,** the automobile tycoon, transformed into one of Britain's most significant mass production plants à la Henry Ford. This industry brought a steady flow of immigrants from Wales from the early 1900s.

Today, Cowley Rd. reveals its diversity through its food: in just a quick stroll down the street, you'll see everything from halal groceries to Chinese woks, from Italian dishes to Polish specialties, from tapas to shishas.

A vibrant annual Cowley Rd. **carnival** shuts the streets down for a full day each July. Booths of ethnic food are rampant, there's live music and a parade, and debauchery ensues. Check with the TIC or www.cowleyroadfestival.co.uk for dates and details.

Modern Cowley Rd., however, is not only a rich mix of cultures; it's also chockfull of natives and students. For example, current **Prime Minister David Cameron** spent part of his student years at Oxford living here, and used to frequent the notoriously quirky Jamaican eating house, **Hi Lo** *(70 Cowley Rd. ☎01865 725 984).*

JERICHO

Jericho is Oxford's bohemian student neighborhood. Home to the **Oxford Canal** with its walking paths, the **Oxford University Press,** and a young, vibrant nightlife (mostly pubs and bars), this part of town is up-and-coming. Bikes, and bike shops are everywhere and have become the favorite mode of transport for many Jericho residents. But never fear—Jericho is easy walking distance from Oxford's city center. Walk north up **Saint Giles** (Cornmarket St. becomes Magdalen St., which leads into St. Giles) and make a left onto **Little Clarendon.** The main Jericho drag, **Walton Street,** runs off of Little Clarendon.

CARFAX

Carfax is the pulsing heart of the city of Oxford, with both ancient and modern ties. The name comes from the French word *carrefour,* meaning "crossroads." Today, Carfax is at the crossroads of Oxford's main shopping district: **High Street, Saint Aldate's, Cornmarket Street,** and **Queen Street** are the busiest thoroughfares of this tourist-mobbed district. (Cornmarket is pedestrian only, but that doesn't mean its not equally packed.) **Carfax Tower** and **Saxon Tower,** two ancient structures in the city center, serve as convenient orientation points. Meanwhile, the magnificent looming spires of the most centrally-located colleges hover over Carfax, dominating the skyline.

accommodations

COWLEY ROAD

HEATHER HOUSE — BED AND BREAKFAST ❹

192 Iffley Rd. ☎01865 249 757 www.heatherhouse.plus.com

This cozy home is a good value in otherwise pricey Oxford, with clean, comfortable rooms and a welcoming guest living room, with a homey couch and books about Britain and Oxford, plus the free advice of a local host. Heather House is located on a residential main street about a 10min. walk from the colleges. Tea lovers will be pleased that there's a wide selection of herbal teas included with breakfast.

*10-15min. walk from the Magdalen College, but a good 30min. from the train station. Walking: cross the Magdalen Bridge and bear right at the roundabout onto Iffley Rd. From train station, take bus # 4 (A, B, or C) from New Rd. bus stop. Get off opposite the Greyfriars Church bus stop. **i** Includes full English breakfast. Free internet use on a communal computer. Discounts for longer stays. Ⓢ Singles with private bath £38-48; ensuite twins £68-80; doubles £70-80. Open 24hr.*

ACORN GUEST HOUSE — BED AND BREAKFAST ❹

260 Iffley Rd. ☎ 01865 247 998 www.oxford-acorn.co.uk

Comfy, family-run guest house with selection of singles, twins, doubles, and family rooms, with windows and a sunny ambiance. Singles are shared bath but with wash basins in the room. Full breakfast and free Wi-Fi help justify the price jump.

*Walking: cross the Magdalen Bridge and bear right at the roundabout onto Iffley Rd. By bus: Take bus # 4 (A, B, or C) from New Rd. bus stop. Get off at Iffley Rd. adjacent Magdalen Rd. **i** Breakfast included. TVs and tea and coffee in all rooms. Discounts for longer stays. Ⓢ Singles shared bath £35; twins (with private or shared baths) from £63; doubles £70-75; triples £90. Open 24hr.*

THE ISIS — BED AND BREAKFAST ❹

45-53 Iffley Rd. ☎01865 613 700 www.isisguesthouse.com

Owned and operated by St. Edmund's Hall, one of Oxford's colleges, the guest house is only open in July, August, and September. Less than a 5min. walk from the colleges and 10min. to downtown shopping, with nearby cafes and bars on Cowley Rd., this large Victorian house offers simple basic rooms, some with bathrooms and some without.

*Walking: cross the Magdalen Bridge and bear right at the roundabout onto Iffley Rd. By bus: take bus # 4 (A, B, or C) from New Rd. bus stop. Get off at The Plain, on Iffley Rd. **i** Breakfast included. Laundry facilities included. TVs in all rooms. Ⓢ Basic singles £37, ensuite singles £45; basic doubles and twins £74/80; family basic £37/40 per person. Open July-Sept. Reception 24hr.*

CARFAX

CENTRAL BACKPACKERS — HOSTEL ❷

13 Park End St. ☎01865 24 22 88 www.centralbackpackers.co.uk

The relaxed rooftop garden with couches and a big screen is the perfect place to kick back and watch a game while throwin' back a pint. The only drawback to a prime downtown location are the sounds of Beyoncé from nearby clubs at 10pm every night. Think of it as motivation, though—shouldn't you be out enjoying Oxford? For those who don't agree, the hostel handily provides free earplugs.

Short walk from Train station; Botley Rd. becomes Park End St. Continental breakfast included. Free luggage storage. Free lockers. Self-catering kitchen. Laundry £3.50. Beers on the terrace £1. 4-bed dorms £21, 8-bed £19, 6-bed female £20, 12-bed £18. £1 per debit/credit transaction. Reception open 8am-11pm.

YHA OXFORD

HOSTEL ❷

2A Botley Rd. ☎01865 727 275 www.yha.org

Don't let the less-than-stylish exterior deceive you: YHA Oxford is recently renovated, with modern facilities and spotlessly clean rooms. Special amenities include an intimate library perfect for cozying up to a good book, a "Boathouse" restaurant, an outdoor seating area, and snacks for sale at reception. Like at many YHAs, however, the guest list is made up of significant numbers of schoolkids and other large groups, so you might not find people kicking back and relaxing. If you're lonely, try debating philosophy with the famous Oxfordians in picture frames on the walls. Still and lifeless as they are, they'll give you a run for your money.

Next to train station. Breakfast not included, £4.95 for full English breakfast. Self-catering kitchen. Internet £1 per 15min. Wi-Fi £5 per day. Library and TV lounge. All rooms ensuite, plus extra bathrooms in hallways. Dorms £16-22; singles £28; doubles/twins £45-55. £3 charge for non-YHA members. Reception open 24hr.

OXFORD BACKPACKERS

HOSTEL ❷

9A Hythe Bridge St. ☎01865 721 761 www.hostels.co.uk

The self-proclaimed "Funky Backpackers" hostel has brightly colored walls, and you'll have a colorful experience there. The big-screen projector in the lounge makes for a lively communal space for its international crowd. The dorms, though adequately clean, are less than spacious.

Hythe Bridge St., down the road from the bus station. Small continental breakfast included. Free lockers, but bring your own padlocks. Luggage storage £1 per item for guests. Laundry £2.50. Wi-Fi £2 per day, £5 per week. Ethernet cables free for use in common area. Self-catering kitchen. Dorms £15-19.50; £75 per week. Discounts online. Reception open 8am-11:30pm.

WESTGATE HOTEL

HOTEL ❹

1 Botley Rd. ☎01865 726 721 www.westgatehoteloxford.co.uk

This simple hotel, right next to train station, is nothing luxurious, but has all the basic amenities you'd need. The decor is a little old-fashioned, but rooms are clean and fairly large, with mostly ensuite bathrooms. Come prepared for nighttime noise: trains abide by no curfew, and the nearby clubs mean that people are out and about at night.

2min. walk from train station down Botley Rd. Full breakfast included. Free Wi-Fi in main building, not in annex. Singles £48-58; doubles/twins £82-86, family (ensuite, sleeps 3-4) £88-£120. Possible discounts in off-season. Reception open 7am-11pm.

UNIVERSITY ACCOMMODATIONS

The University of Oxford's conferencing website, **www.conference-oxford.com** lists some individual email contacts for B and B accommodations at the colleges. The process can be a hassle, but worth it if you'd like to stay in the medieval digs of one of Oxford's prestigious colleges.

In addition, **www.universityrooms.co.uk** has a simple online booking service for the nine colleges that offer B and B options for individual travelers: **Balliol College, Keble College, Lady Margaret Hall, Mansfield College, The Queen's College, St. Hugh's College, Trinity College, University College,** and **Wadham College.** Book in advance, as all of these usually fill up quickly. Prices vary and follow the rules of Balliol College attendee Adam Smith: price is determined by supply and demand, and therefore the prices at the more historic colleges generally run higher. You'll also pay some extra quid for ensuite rooms.

LINCOLN HALL BED AND BREAKFAST DORMS, BED AND BREAKFAST ❸

Museum Rd. beckie@internal.linc.ox.ac.uk

Lincoln College offers up to 60 single ensuite rooms with shared kitchens in historic, brightly-colored Victorian townhouses. Centrally located to university sites, like the **Bodleian Library** (p. 119) and Pitt Rivers Museum.

Near the University science area. Continental breakfast included. Must pay in full before stay. £10 key deposit. Internet access via Ethernet port. Ensuite singles £40. Open July-Aug. Reception 24hr.

accepted

It happens sometimes in my travels that I'm mistaken for a student.

Well, after all, I am one. I walk around town, too-cool-for-school in my sunglasses, with a simple tote bag, sometimes a computer, sometimes a notebook, on a mission, looking like I know where I'm going. Some days I'm a bit grungier than I should be, but I think that's pretty normal too.

Yesterday afternoon was my first day in Oxford, and within three hours, I had already been asked four times for directions to various university buildings and sights. Let me clarify. I've discovered that I've actually come to Oxford at the perfect time. The University is hosting a huge annual program for potential applicants, across all the colleges.

Witnessing the whole scene made me realize how very glad I am to be past that stage of life. I thought it was only American parents who were ridiculously intense and overbearing about the college process. I thought wrong. These British parents were just as bad, if not worse, peppering every possible student they saw with a rapid stream of questions—"Which A-Levels did you take?" "What kind of school did you come from?" "How many other people do you think you were competing with for your engineering spot at Trinity in your year?"

But I digress. The reason this whole "Open Days" program is great for me is that I could breeze through the doors of any college I wanted, free of charge, free of hassle. Not only that, but there were loads of student guides around in bright colored T-shirts, giving tours, offering to show us the bedrooms and the dining halls and libraries and all those other things that you normally need a swipe card to access. I went college-hopping and tour-hopping, switching between guides when I would spot something interesting and leaving when they would start talking too much. I amused myself with the various courses I was interested in studying when asked, starting off with closest-to-the-truth, P.P.E. (Politics, Philosophy and Economics) and then getting more adventurous with law, chemistry, and Russian.

I wound up with a free lunch at Somerville College via a voucher, a good pub recommendation, and my own collection of informational pamphlets. It had been a productive day. Now, time to be 20 again.

Rachel Lipson

CARFAX

Colleges

The **Tourist Information Centre** on **Broad Street** sells the *Oxford What to See and Do Guide* for £.60, which lists all of the colleges' visiting hours and prices and has a handy map. Hours can also be accessed online at **www.ox.ac.uk.** Note that hours and the list of sites open to tourists can be changed at any given time without explanation or notice. Some colleges charge admission, while others are accessible only through the official blue badge tours, booked at the TIC (see **Practicalities**), and a few are generally off-limits. Take this as warning that it's not worth trying to sneak into Christ Church outside open hours. College bouncers in bowler hats, affectionately known as "bulldogs," will squint their eyes and promptly kick you out.

One of the best ways to get into the colleges for free (and also to witness a beautiful, historic ritual) is to check out one of the church services in the college chapels during term-time, for "Evensong" in particular. Usually, this takes place around 6pm. Show up 15min. before it starts and tell the people at the gate that you'd like to attend the service; they generally let you in for free.

Christ Church

CHRIST CHURCH — COLLEGE

St. Aldates — ☎01865 276 492 www.chch.ox.ac.uk/college

Oxford's most famous college has the university's grandest quad and some of its most distinguished alumni, including 13 saints and past prime ministers. During the English Civil War, "The House" was also the home to **Charles I** and the royal family, who used the Royalist-friendly university as a retreat during Cromwell's advance, and escaped Oxford dressed as servants when the city came under threat. The college is also notable as the place where Lewis Carroll first met **Alice,** the young daughter of the college dean, before she headed to Wonderland. In other cultural references, the dining hall and central quad serve as shooting locations for many *Harry Potter* films (tourists mob to see the site of Hogwarts' dining hall). In the early summer months, don't judge the students if they seem somewhat moody as they navigate their way through the crowds of visitors: while you're snapping pictures, they're taking exams.

Through an archway to your left as you face the cathedral is **Peckwater Quad.** The chalk markings on the wall are the standings for rowing competitions among the colleges, and certain corners will honor past Christ College teams that have finished the season with success. Also look out for Christ Church's library—perhaps the most elegant Palladian building in all of Oxford. Though it's closed to visitors, its exterior is impressive in itself.

Perhaps the most peaceful part of the college grounds is **Christ Church Meadow,** which stretches east and south from the main entrance. This attempt to compensate for Oxford's lack of "backs" (the riverside gardens in Cambridge) seems pretty successful to us: not only are the meadows beautiful, with flower-adorned views of the college, but they are also free, so those guarding their wallets can still enjoy a piece of the Christ Church atmosphere.

Down St. Aldates from Carfax. £6.30, concessions £4.80, family ticket £12. Open M-Sa 9am-5:30pm, Su 1-5:30pm.

CHRIST CHURCH CHAPEL — CHAPEL

St. Aldates — ☎01865 276 492 www.chch.ox.ac.uk/cathedral

Christ Church Chapel is the only church in all of England to serve as both a cathedral (for the archdiocese of Oxford) and college chapel. The church was founded

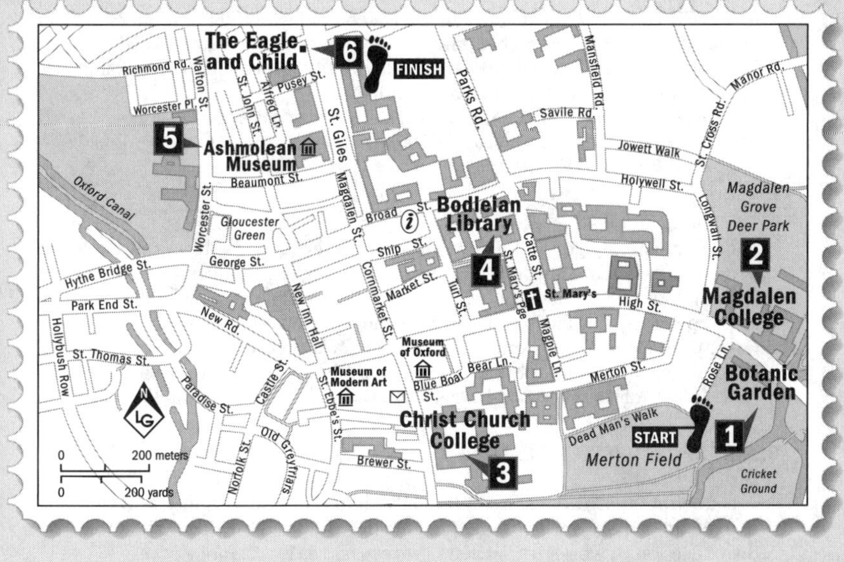

oxford

Oxford may not be as large or imposing as London, but don't take that the wrong way; it's still full of gems you won't want to miss. In case you're crunched for time and need to experience the city in just a single day, **Let's Go** has consolidated some of Oxford's highlights into a six-step plan. So tie up your laces and let's get going!

1. UNIVERSITY OF OXFORD BOTANIC GARDEN. Start off with a whiff of the oldest botanic garden in Britain, located on High Street in the eastern part of campus.

2. MAGDALEN COLLEGE. Once you're sufficiently high on nature, simply cross High St. to get to Magdalen College. Arguably the sexiest of Oxford's colleges, Magdalen has churned out such superstars as Cardinal Wolsey, Oscar Wilde, and Seamus Heaney.

3. CHRIST CHURCH COLLEGE. From Magdalen, make your merry way along High St. in an westward direction for a few blocks, before turning left onto Aldate St., where Christ Church College is located. Maybe you'll be lucky enough to hear the world-famous cathedral choir sing a little ditty.

4. BODLEIAN LIBRARY. Next, head north onto St. Aldate St., which will become Cornmarket St. Turn right onto Market St., left onto Turf St., and right onto Broad St., where you'll find the famed Bodleian Library—but probably no talking caterpillars or a Queen of Hearts.

5. ASHMOLEAN MUSEUM. Walk eastward along Broad St. before turning right onto Magdalen St. E. Use caution, as these streets are busy and may be missing walkways. Turn left at Beaumont St., where the Ashmolean Museum is located. Guy Fawkes' lantern is among its treasures.

6. THE EAGLE AND CHILD. Travel north along St. Giles St. (again, exercising caution) and finish your day off right at the 17th-century Eagle and Child. After a few pints, you may either feel like you've sprouted wings or reverted to infancy.

WALKING TOUR

Let's Go
www.letsgo.com

in 730 CE by Oxford's patron saint, **St. Fridesweide,** who built a nunnery here in honor of two miracles: the blinding of her persistent suitor and his subsequent recovery. A stained-glass window, c. 1320, depicts **Thomas à Becket** kneeling moments before his death in Canterbury Cathedral.

Down St. Aldates from Carfax. Admission £6.30, concessions £4.80, family ticket £12. Hall and cathedral open M-F 10:15am-11:45am and 2:15-4:30pm, Sa-Su 2:30-4:30pm. Chapel services M-F 6pm; Su 8, 10, 11:15am, 6pm.

TOM QUAD — QUAD

Tom Quad adjoins the chapel grounds, but more importantly, it is the site of undergraduate lily-pond dunking. The quad takes its name from **Great Tom,** the seven-ton bell that has rung **101 times** (the original number of students) at 9:05pm, the original undergraduate curfew, every evening since 1682. The bell rings specifically at 9:05pm because, technically, Oxford should be 5min. past Greenwich Mean Time. Christ Church keeps this time within its gates. Nearby, the college hall displays portraits of some of Christ Church's famous alums—**Sir Philip Sidney, William Penn, John Ruskin, John Locke,** and a bored-looking **W.H. Auden** in a corner by the kitchen.

CHRIST CHURCH PICTURE GALLERY — GALLERY

Canterbury Quad ☎01865 276 172 www.chch.ox.ac.uk

Architecture and gardens aren't the only source of visual beauty in Oxford. At this picture gallery, generous alumni gifts have allowed for a small but noteworthy collection of works by **Tintoretto, Vermeer,** and **da Vinci,** among others.

Entrances on Oriel Sq. and at Canterbury Gate; visitors to the gallery should enter through Canterbury Gate. £3, concessions £2. Open Apr-Sept M-Sa 10:30am-1pm and 2-5:30pm, Su 2-5pm; Oct-Mar M-Sa 10:30am-1pm and 2-4:30pm, Su 2-4:30pm.

Other Colleges

Oxford's extensive **college system,** distributing its 20,000 students among 38 official colleges and 6 permanent private halls of the university—each with its own structure and rules—means that there are plenty of beautiful grounds to stroll year-round. We've picked out a few of the most frequented to save you the purchase of a guide—well, *another* guide. Full books, however, are published on just single colleges. For information on others, pick up one of the many guides found at the TIC or the paperback books found in souvenir shops all over town.

ALL SOULS COLLEGE — COLLEGE

Corner of High and Catte St. ☎01865 279 379 www.all-souls.ox.ac.uk.

All Souls College (founded in 1438) is so exclusive that admission is solely offered on an invitation-only basis: the graduate fellows who live here are engaged in intense academic research and are rumored to rarely leave their rooms because of it. You might notice that the **Great Quad,** with its carefully manicured lawn and two spires, is also one of the quietest, with hardly a living soul passing over. Check out the unusual **sundial** designed by **Christopher Wren,** moved here from the Front Quad in 1877.

Rumor has it that All Souls currently serves as a think-tank of sorts for the British Department of Defense. How does one join this premier group of scholars? Candidates who survive the admission exams to All Souls are invited to a dinner, where the dons repeatedly confirm that they are "well-born, well-bred, and only moderately learned." As further reward for admission, All Souls is also reported to have the best wine cellar in the city. Once every century, a bizarre torchlight procession takes place here with the **"Mallard Society."** During the ceremony, the Mallard Song is sung and a "Lord Mallard" is hoisted high in an ancient chair. No one really knows how the Mallard came to be affiliated with All Souls, but the song is sung frequently at college **gaudies,** or feasts, and the ritual on the Quad has been going strong for centuries.

i The next processions will happen on January 14th, 2011. Ⓢ Free. ⏰ Open Sept-July M-F 2-4pm.

BALLIOL COLLEGE COLLEGE

Broad St. ☎01865 277 777 🖳www.balliol.ox.ac.uk

Along with Merton and University, **Balliol,** founded in approximately 1263, has a legitimate claim to being the oldest college in Oxford. According to tradition, the story of Balliol begins with the story of a lord and a princess: John Balliol married Dervorguilla, a Scottish princess. Shortly thereafter, a land dispute with the Bishop of Durham compelled Balliol, father of John Balliol, future and short-lived King of Scotland, to rent out a house just outside of the Oxford town walls for 16 poor scholars to live in as penance. When he died, his wife made the community permanent. Matthew Arnold, Gerard Manley Hopkins, Aldous Huxley, Adam Smith, three British prime ministers, and **six members of the Obama administration** were products of Balliol's mismatched spires.

Ⓢ £2, students £1, under 18 free. ⏰ Open daily 10am-5pm or dusk.

MAGDALEN COLLEGE COLLEGE

High St. ☎01865 276 000 🖳www.magd.ox.ac.uk

Many consider Magdalen (MAUD-lin), with its winding riverbanks, flower-filled quads, and 100 acres of grounds, to be Oxford's best-looking college. Magdalen boys have also been traditionally quite a catch: they've produced seven Nobel Prizes, Dudley Moore, and **Oscar Wilde.** The college has a **deer park,** where deer have grazed aimlessly for centuries (the first written record of the deer is from 1705) in front of students playing (also aimlessly?) croquet. The path following the river brings you back around to the college's **New Building,** where "New" means 1733, when this building was erected.

The college skyline is ruled by the 144 ft. **Great Tower,** built by **Cardinal Wolsey,** a former bursar of the college, and used as a vantage point during the English Civil War. Since the days of Henry VII, each year on May Day at 6am, the choir members from Magdalen and its sister school meet on the roof of the tower to sing together, culminating with "Te Deum patrem colimus." This a well-known and popular Oxford tradition that consistently brings throngs of crowds and is followed by much revelry, including champagne breakfasts and Morris dancing.

Ⓢ £4.50, concessions £3.50. ⏰ Open daily Oct-June 1-6pm or dusk; July-Sept noon-6pm.

MERTON COLLEGE COLLEGE

Merton St. ☎01865 276 310 🖳www.merton.ox.ac.uk

Though Balliol and University were endowed before it, **Merton** has the earliest formal college statutes (1274), so it can boast of being the oldest college in its own right. Merton's library houses the first printed Welsh Bible. **JRR Tolkien** was the Merton Professor of English, inventing the **Elven** language and writing some minor trilogy in his spare time. The college's 14th-century **Mob Quad** is Oxford's oldest and one of its least impressive—the "little" quadrangle was where the junior members of the college were housed after the grander Fellows' Quadrangle was built in 1610—but nearby St. Alban's Quad has some of the university's best gargoyles.

Ⓢ Grounds free. Library tours £2. ⏰ Open M-F 2-4pm, Sa-Su 10am-4pm.

NEW COLLEGE COLLEGE

New College Ln. ☎01865 279 555 🖳www.new.ox.ac.uk

Apparently, New College is said to have been the model that **Henry VI** had in mind when he founded King's College, Cambridge. The college was set up to replace all the ministering men who died of the **Black Death** in the 14th century, when the country was in desperate need of new clergy. New College boasts **Kate Beckinsale** and **Hugh Grant** as attractive alums. The college's cloisters were used in **Harry Potter.**

i Easter to mid-Oct enter via New College Lane; mid-Oct to Easter enter via Holywell St. Gates. Ⓢ £2, students and children £1, seniors £1.50. ⏰ Open daily from Easter to mid-Oct 11am-5pm; mid-Oct to Easter 2-4pm.

the most curious thing i ever saw

Today was Alice Day in Oxford.

That means little girls dressed up like Alice in Wonderland, a few not-so-little girls dressed up like the Queen of Hearts, and everyone enjoying picnics, plays, and all the fanfare that comes with celebrating Lewis Carroll's most famous heroine in her, and his, old stomping grounds of Oxford. The real Alice, Alice Liddell, was the daughter of a former dean of Christ Church College and Carroll (real name: Charles Dodgson) used to tell her stories about turtles and ducks and the Jabberwocky out on the Thames River while he was a Professor of Mathematics here at the college.

Unlike my grandfather, who can recite lines of Alice's Adventures in Wonderland from memory, I don't think I ever quite finished the book. (I hate that I'm one of those people who have seen the movie but never read the book. Terrible.)

Still, I was curious to see what all the fuss was about. First, I tried to talk to the costumed characters standing outside of Blackwell's bookstore, but they had run out of leaflets and weren't sure where the next event was taking place. Then, I followed a family of face-painted children and wound up at the National History Museum. Outside there was a man with a guitar singing Alice verses to mobs of clapping and giggling toddlers. I was just about to head out and give up on Alice shenanigans completely when I saw a sign for the lecture hall. (You know you've been out of school for too long when you start gravitating towards the mention of lectures.)

The room was packed to the brim with Alice fans of all (well, 16+) ages, everyone there to listen to the president of the Lewis Carroll Society (yes, there is such a thing) give a free lecture on "Carroll and Surrealism." I plopped down in one of the few empty chairs and eagerly pulled out my notebook.

The lecturer read off his notes for about a half hour, and the climax of the presentation (aka the final slides of the PowerPoint) was supposed to be Salvador Dali's famous surrealist paintings of Alice in Wonderland. Just as he's about to switch over to the slide, though, the projector freezes and then turns blue. The man fiddled for a few seconds with the computer, but with no luck. I felt bad for whomever the tech guys working in the museum were: as the Queen of Hearts would say, "Off with their heads!"

Rachel Lipson

QUEEN'S COLLEGE COLLEGE

High St. ☎01865 279 120 ■www.queens.ox.ac.uk

Though the college was founded 1341, Queen's was rebuilt in the 17th and 18th centuries in the distinctive Queen Anne style. Queen's College has a strange Christmas tradition of ushering in a boar's head. The ceremony apparently pays homage to the time when a Queen's student, with his head stuck in a book of Aristotle on a country walk, ran into a savage wild boar and saved himself by ramming the philosopher's book down the boar's throat. Meanwhile, in a dinnertime ritual here, students are called to all formal dinners by the sounds of a trumpet. How melodious.

Open to blue-badge tours only.

TRINITY COLLEGE — COLLEGE

Broad St. ☎01865 279 900 www.trinity.ox.ac.uk

Trinity was the home of some of Oxford's most eccentric college presidents. One of them, Ralph Kettell, elected in 1599, would allegedly come to dinner with a pair of scissors to chop off anyone's hair that he deemed too long. To keep them out of trouble in town, he made it his duty to ensure that Trinity had some of the best beer in Oxford at its table, keeping the students at home and comparatively sober. Check out the hall named after him in the front quadrangle. Kettell was also known for great achievements in fostering a sense of community and making architectural improvements and expanding the college.

Founded in 1555, the college itself has a Baroque chapel with a limewood altarpiece, cedar latticework, cherubim-spotted pediments, four large quads, a spacious lawn and gardens, and a small area of woodland. It was founded by **Sir Thomas Pope,** a devout Catholic who, with no surviving children, wanted to find a way ensure that someone would still remember and pray for him and his family. Why not start a college at Oxford?

£2, concessions £1. Open M-F 10am-noon and 2-4pm, Sa-Su 2-4pm.

UNIVERSITY COLLEGE — COLLEGE

High St. ☎01865 276 602 www.univ.ox.ac.uk

Built in 1249, this soot-blackened college is known by many as **"Uni"** and is where **Bill Clinton** spent his Rhodes Scholar days. Other notable students and fellows include **Bob Hawke,** a former prime minister of Australia who set the Guinness world record for downing a yard of beer during his Oxford days, **CS Lewis, Stephen Hawking,** and Prince Felix Yusupov, the assassin of **Rasputin.** The famed Romantic poet **Percy Bysshe Shelley** came here in 1810, but he was expelled a year later after the dissemination of a pamphlet he had written entitled **"The Necessity of Atheism."** Today, though, the college honors him with a prominent statue that you can see on your right as you enter.

Entry for groups by prior arrangement with the domestic bursar. Entry for individuals and families at the discretion of the lodge porter, and to blue badge tours only.

Museums

ASHMOLEAN MUSEUM — MUSEUM

Beaumont St. ☎01865 278 000 www.ashmolean.org

Oxford University's Museum of Art and Archeology is newly reopened after a multi-million-pound renovation that added 39 new galleries and doubled its display space. The Ashmolean collection (named for 17th-century English antiquary, politician, and wealthy collector Elias Ashmole) is the oldest public museum in Europe, with seriously world-class exhibits from every region of the world. In addition to beautiful exhibits that shed light on how world cultures developed through contact with one another, Oxford's only rooftop restaurant lies upstairs. Though the restaurant is pricey, it has excellent views of the city. Pick up a free Ashmolean *What's On* booklet to find out about upcoming lectures and special exhibitions.

Opposite the Randolph Hotel. Free lunchtime gallery talks for first 12 interested Tu-F 1:15-2pm. Pick up tokens from the information desk. Free. Open Tu-Su 10am-6pm.

BODLEIAN LIBRARY — LIBRARY

Broad St. ☎01865 277 178 www.bodleian.ox.ac.uk

As you enter through the Great Gate into the Old Schools Quadrangle, you'll be in good company—in spirit, anyway. Five kings, 40 Nobel Prize winners, 28 British prime ministers, and writers like Oscar Wilde, CS Lewis, and JRR Tolkien also entered this gate at some point. Included in the large complex is Oxford's Divinity School, the oldest teaching room in the university, completed in 1488 and seen as a masterpiece of English Gothic architecture with its elaborate fan-vaulted ceiling. The standard and mini guided tours include stops here and at Duke Humfrey's medieval library. The 1hr. tour also enters the 17th-century Convocation House and Court, where Parliament was held during the Civil War. Extended tours include entry to the Radcliffe Camera, the first rotunda library built in Britain, and the underground tunnels and passages leading to the book stacks where millions of volumes of the Oxford collection are stored.

Entrances on Broad St., Cattle St. and Radcliffe St. Entrance to the courtyard free. 30min. tour of Library and Divinity Hall £4.50, 1hr. tour £6.50, extended tour £13.50. Audio tour £2.50. Entrance to Divinity Hall £1. Open M-F 9am-5pm, Sa 9am-4:30pm, Su 11am-5pm.

Other Sights

OXFORD CASTLE

CASTLE

44-46 Oxford Castle ☎01865 260 666 www.oxfordcastleunlocked.co.uk

As you wander around the serious students and mobs of tourists, it's easy to forget that Oxford had a history that involved people and things a little more scandalous than philosophers, books, and elegant churches. Oxford Castle reminds one of Oxford's darker past: stories of escapes, betrayal, and romance are told within the walls of the city's 11th-century castle and prison. Tours include a climb up Saxon St. George's tower and a trip down to a 900-year-old underground crypt.

Off New Rd. £7.75, concessions £6.50. Tours daily 10am-4:20pm.

CARFAX TOWER

TOWER

Junction of St. Aldates/Cornmarket St. and High St./Queen St. ☎01865 792 633

This was the site of the former City Church of Oxford (St. Martin's Church). However, in 1896, university leaders decided that the church needed to be demolished to widen the roads and make room for more traffic in the downtown area. Still, the tower was left untouched. Look for the church clock on the east side of the facade: it is adorned by two "quarter boys," who hit the bells every 15min.

£2.20, under 16 £1.10. Open daily Apr-Sept 10am-5:30pm; Oct 10am-4:30pm; Nov-Mar 10am-3:30pm.

SAXON TOWER

TOWER

St. Michael's Church, North Gate ☎01865 240 940 www.smng.org.uk

Out of all of Oxford's ancient and medieval spires, this is actually the city's oldest building, dating back to the Late Saxon period, or about 1040. Later on, this same tower was attached on the west side to the Bocardo Prison, where the famous Oxford Martyrs, **Bishops Latimer, Ridley,** and **Cranmer** were burnt at the stake by Queen Mary for refusing to convert to Catholicism. Though the North Gate, where the prison was located, was later demolished because of congestion concerns, the door to their former cell is still inside the tower.

Church free. Tower £2, concessions £1.50. Open daily Apr-Oct 10:30am-5pm; Nov-Mar 10:30am-4pm.

UNIVERSITY OF OXFORD BOTANIC GARDEN

GARDEN

Rose Ln. ☎01865 286 690 www.botanic-garden.ox.ac.uk

Back in the day (meaning, of course, the 1600s), this garden, though created to enhance the glory of God and the learning of man, actually had a practical purpose as well: they sold fruit grown in the garden to pay for its upkeep. Today, the garden has another useful purpose: a peaceful haven to resort to if you get overwhelmed by the mobs of tourists on High St. Stay for at least an hour to justify paying to see flowers. The oldest botanic garden in the UK, it lies outside of the city walls, and it happens to be on top of an ancient Jewish cemetery.

Off High St. £3.50, concessions £3. Year-long season ticket £12, students £10. Open daily May-Aug 9am-6pm; Sept-Oct and Mar-Apr 9am-5pm; Nov-Feb 9am-4:30pm. Glasshouses open at 10am.

OXFORD MUSEUM OF NATURAL HISTORY — MUSEUM

Parks Rd. ☎01865 272 950 www.oum.ox.ac.uk

Animal-bone lovers will rejoice at this 150-year-old museum: the collections of zoological, entomological, and geological specimens include dinosaur bones found in the Oxford area, **Charles Darwin's** crustaceans, and the most complete remains of a **dodo** found in the world. A famous debate on evolution that took place inside the building in 1860 between Thomas Huxley and Bishop Sam Wilberforce. The building itself is pretty memorable, with admired Neo-Gothic architecture and statues of famous figures like **Aristotle, Bacon,** and **Darwin.** Attached is the **Pitt-Rivers Museum** (Archeology and Anthropology), also worth a visit for its collection of lifestyle objects from across the globe—and for its shrunken heads *(☎01865 270 927 www.prm.ox.ac.uk).*

Off Broad St. Free. Open daily 10am-5pm. Pitt-Rivers Museum open M noon-4:30pm, Tu-Su 10am-4:30pm.

food

Here's one major perk of living in a student town: **kebab trucks** line High St., Queen St., and Broad St. (we recommend **Hassan's,** on Broad St.) and stay open until 3am during the week and 4 or 4:30am on weekends to fulfill late-night cravings. People think kids here have better things to do, like study? Please.

COWLEY

KAZBAR — TAPAS ❷

25-27 Cowley Rd. ☎01865 202 920 www.kazbar.co.uk

They say this is where southern Spain meets Northern Africa. Granted, Cowley Rd. is very ethnically diverse... but we think their geography might be a little off. Still, the authentic atmosphere almost makes us forget it. Meat, fish, cheese, and vegetable tapas are enjoyed on Moorish-style cushioned benches, with burning incense, colorful tiles, patterned rugs, and an open ceiling. On nice summer days, hip people sip glasses of wine *(£3.25-4.50)* outside in the sun.

Across from Magdalen Bridge. i ½-price tapas M-F 4-7pm, Sa-Su noon-4pm. Tapas £3.10-4.60. Open M-Th 4pm-midnight, F 4pm-12:30am, Sa noon-12:30am, Su noon-midnight.

ATOMIC BURGER — BURGERS ❷

96 Cowley Rd. ☎01865 790 855 www.atomicburger.co.uk

A "far-out" selection of homemade beef, chicken, and veggie burgers *(£6.50-8.75),* including a "burger of the week," in a funky outer-space-themed restaurant. If the hanging figurines and comic-book-covered walls don't get you in a cosmic mood, maybe a milkshake with "spacedust" sprinkled on it will do the trick *(£3.50).*

i All burgers come with free side order. 10% discount on takeaway. Weekend breakfast options include waffles, muffins, pancakes, and huevos rancheros. Gluten-free options. Entrees £4.50-10.50. Double your burger and choose 2 side orders for £5 more. Open M-F noon-2:30pm and 5-10:30pm, Sa-Su 9:30am-10:30pm.

GRAND CAFE — BURGERS ❷

84 High St. ☎01865 204 463 www.thegrandcafe.co.uk

Grand Cafe contends with across-the-street neighbor Queens Lane Coffee Shop

for claim to the site of the first coffee house in England (according to Samuel Pepys' diary, 1650). No matter, the cafe has much else to boast about, especially when it comes to tea. Afternoon teas are available 2-5pm, ranging from a simple leaf tea in a pot *(£2.50 per person)* to a cream tea, which comes with scones, butter, jam, and clotted cream *(£7.50)*, to the grand high tea, which includes smoked salmon with cream cheese and egg mayonnaise sandwiches, scones with jam and clotted cream, handmade chocolate truffles, and a glass of champagne *(£16.50)*. The classy decor of marble pillars and gold borders, gives your tea time an authentic Victorian feel. And if you've enjoyed your tea so much that you'd like to recreate the experience, teacups and saucers are available for purchase.
At intersection of High St. and Queen's Ln. Open M-Sa 9am-11pm, Su 9am-7pm. Kitchen open 9am-6pm.

JERICHO

G AND D'S — CAFE ❷

55 Little Clarendon St. ☎01865 516 652 www.gdcafe.com
94 St. Aldate's ☎01865 245 952
104 Cowley Rd. ☎01865 727 111

G and D's is a favorite Oxford haunt, with a Ben-and-Jerry's-caliber obsession with cows. Known for their bagel combinations and their natural, homemade ice cream. Bagels and ice cream—what better combination is there?
Three locations. i Lunchtime meal deal M-F noon-2pm: Bagels £3.50. Greek/Caesar salad, regular filter coffee, tea, and pack of chips or piece of fruit. Cow night Tu 7pm-midnight. Get 20% off with anything cow-related. Bagels £2-5. Ice cream from £2. Open daily 8am-midnight.

FREUD — PIZZA, COCKTAILS ❷

119 Walton St. ☎01865 311 171 www.freud.eu

Beneath the vaulted ceilings of a 19th-century Greek Revival church sits a local club/bar/cafe/art gallery. The disco ball may seem out of place (and a little unholy) among stained glass windows, and you sit on old pew benches while eating your whole-wheat pizzas with marinated olives *(£3.25)* or hummus with pita *(£3.85)*, but on nights when there's live jazz, they say the music can make the church's old ghosts come alive.
Next to Radcliffe Infirmary. i Vegetarian options. Organically grown food. Express lunch: pizza slice of day with side salad £5.25. Mains £5.55-10. Cocktails from £5. Open M-Th 5-11pm, F 5pm-2am, Sa 10am-2am, Su 10am-11pm. Kitchen open daily until 10pm.

JERICHO CAFE — CAFE ❷

112 Walton St. ☎01865 310 840 www.thejerichocafe.co.uk

This cozy neighborhood cafe is a staple of Walton St. Offers breakfast, salads *(£7-£8.55)*, melts *(£5.25)*, and filling entrees, many of them fish dishes (like fish pie with salmon, haddock, and prawns) or eggplant parmesan. Free newspapers and yummy pastries. If you're new to Oxford and looking for things to do, check out the wall next to the staircase: it's blanketed with fliers advertising various musical and other cultural events.
Next to Radcliffe Infirmary. i Vegetarian options. Takeaway available. Entrees £7-12. Open M-W 8am-9:30pm, Th-Sa 8am-10pm, Su 9am-8pm.

THE STANDARD TANDOORI — INDIAN ❷

117 Walton St. ☎01865 553 557

The decor might look a little dated, but the Indian food is fresh, and the service is friendly. Students say they make one of the best curries in all of Oxford. Many items are £2 cheaper to take out than to eat in, so if you're looking to save a few quid, you might want to call in, stroll over, and pick up.
Next to Radcliffe Infirmary. i Vegetarian options. Takeaway available. Mains £3.65-12. Open daily noon-2:30pm and 6-11:30pm.

GREEN'S CAFE CAFE ❶

50 St. Giles ☎01865 316 878 www.greenscafeoxford.co.uk

This student-friendly coffee shop has a relaxed upstairs seating area filled with friends having a drink or breakfast and individuals with their laptops Facebook-stalking... or, rather, studying. There's a a selection of British newspapers available if you're looking for some reading material.

Next to the Eagle and Child.

CARFAX

THE VAULTS AND GARDEN CAFE ❷

St. Mary's Church, Radcliffe Sq. ☎01865 279112 www.vaultsandgarden.com

In the summertime, this is possibly the best setting in Oxford for lunch. Based out of the University Church of St. Mary the Virgin, the large garden eating area offers picturesque views of the Bodleian Library, Radcliffe Camera, and nearby colleges. There are even picnic blankets on the grass to stretch out and sunbathe with your coffee, meal, and book. The menu changes daily, with buffet-style serving and fresh salads, sandwiches, and soups, along with coffees, yogurt, and pastries. All vegetables come from the nearby organic garden.

Turn up St. Mary's Passage off Queens St. or High St. i Menu changes daily for breakfast and lunch. 10% student discount. Lunch entrees £4.50-9. Open daily 8:30am-6:30pm.

BEN'S COOKIES COOKIES ❶

108-109 Covered Market ☎ 01865 247 407 www.benscookies.com

Yes, you might have seen a few of these quaint little cookie stands in London, but this was the original, around for over 25 years in Oxford's 18th-century covered market. This tiny little stall sells what are most definitely the best cookies in town. They come in 10 delicious flavors, like white chocolate chip and triple chocolate chunk, and are served basically fresh out of the oven, nice and gooey.

By High St. Cookies £1 and up. Sold by weight. Tins of 3 £5.50, tins of 8 £11.50. Open M-Sa 9:15am-5:30pm, Su 11am-4pm.

CHIANG MAI KITCHEN THAI ❷

130A High St., Kemp Hall Passage ☎ 01865 202 233 www.chianmaikitchen.co.uk

It might seem a bit incongruous inside a classic 16th-century English building, but the herbs and spices flown in weekly from **Bangkok** give the food a deliciously tangy flavor and pack this two-story restaurant with hungry people every night. Wash down your chicken, beef, pork, or veggies with the authentic Thai iced tea *(£3.50)*.

Hidden in an alley to the right of the Starbucks at 127 High St. Look for signs pointing you back behind the street. Entrees £6.30-11.50 Open M-Sa noon-2:30pm and 6-10:30pm, Su 6-10:30pm.

QUEEN'S LANE COFFEE HOUSE MEDITERRANEAN ❷

40 High St. ☎01865 240 082 www.queenslanecoffeehouse.co.uk

On this spot in 1654, Cirques Jobson is said to have started selling a revolutionary new drink called coffee; thus, Queen's Lane Coffee House claims itself to be the oldest coffeehouse in Europe (though Grand Cafe across the street seems to reserve the honor for itself). Meanwhile, its prime location also made it a supposed favorite retreat for 17th-century scholars who debated issues of the day. Today, though, the large, laid-back restaurant is a good place for a solo traveler to eat a meal without feeling self-conscious. Full breakfasts *(£3.50-£7.45)*, pastries *(£1.50)*, lasagna, Turkish pizza *(lahmacun)*, Kiev, moussaka, and spicy Turkish sausage on ciabatta *(£5.45)* are all available. Typical coffee house fixtures, mixed with Mediterranean and Turkish specialties.

High St. begins right after Magdalen Bridge. Restaurant on the right coming from the direction of Magdalen College. i Credit card min. £5. Entrees £6.45-9. Open M-Sa 8am-9pm, Su 9am-9pm.

THE KING'S ARMS

PUB ❷

40 Holywell St. ☎01865 242 369

For at least 350 years, this was a gents-only pub. By 1973, this was the last male-only pub in Oxford, and after a fire that conspiracy theorists say was started by radical feminists, they re-opened with the doors clear for the ladies as well. Today this is one of the popular spots for students in the nearby colleges, with large cozy wooden tables for patrons, a rotating selection of Young's cask ales, and classic pub fare. The King's Arms is especially known for its **Pimms** and late-night snacks. After the kitchen closes you can still grab yummy bar snacks like olives, popcorn, and candy bars up until closing. If you're more ambitious, come earlier while the kitchen's still running and try the traditional faggots, braised in red onion gravy.

Intersection with Broad St. Holywell St. is parallel with High St. Longwall St. connects the 2. Open daily 10:30am-midnight. Kitchen open 11:30am-9:30pm.

GEORGINA'S COFFEE SHOP

CAFE ❶

Ave. 3, Covered Market ☎01865 249 527

This bohemian coffee shop is one of the only places in town where any self-respecting hippie can feel safely hidden from the prepsters and mobs of tourists. With old-school movie posters on the ceilings, charmingly shabby tables and chairs, yummy vegetarian wraps and pastries, and peaceful alternative background music, this is a place worth checking out.

Above Brothers in the Covered Market. Takeaway available. Entrees £5-6. Open M-Sa 8:30am-4:30pm.

THE NOSEBAG

ORGANIC CAFE ❸

6-8 St. Michaels St., 2nd fl. ☎01865 721 033  www.nosebagoxford.co.uk

Piping-hot home-cooked dishes in a cozy and relaxed, but informal, setting (don't expect elegance but rather economical service). The second-floor location in a 15th-century building means nice views of the quaint street below. Healthy organic options, along with vegetarian alternatives. Pastries and wine top off the casseroles, pies, salads, and fish. Menu changes daily.

Vegetarian options available. Entrees £8-£10. Open M-Th 9:30am-10pm, F-Sa 9:30am-10:30pm, Su 9:30am-9pm. Last orders taken 30min. before close.

EDAMAME

JAPANESE ❷

15 Holywell St. ☎01865 246 916 www.edamame.co.uk

This tiny, hip Japanese restaurant is one of the hottest spots in town, beloved by students and 20-somethings. Thursday sushi nights are particularly popular; arrive on the early side to avoid waiting in lines. Other favored menu items include ramen *(£7-8)*, sake *(£3.50-6)*, and of course, some of those weirdly addictive green baby soy beans for which the restaurant is named *(£2)*.

Holywell St. is parallel with High St. Longwall St. connects the 2. Vegetarian options available. Lunch cash only. Dinner credit card min. £10. Lunch entrees £5-9. Evening entrees £3-8. Sushi night sets £6-9. Open W 11:30am-2pm, Th-Sa 11:30am-2pm and 5-8:30pm, Su noon-3:30pm.

nightlife

The main clubbing area in Oxford is near the train station, on **Park End Street** and **Hythe Bridge Street.** Maybe they figured that there was enough noise already with the trains going by, so a little bit of blasting music couldn't hurt. Both of these streets split off from **Botley Road** (the train station's home). From the center of town, George St. turns into Hythe Bridge St. as you head eastward, and New Rd. likewise becomes Park End.

CARFAX

THE BRIDGE

CLUB

6-9 Hythe Bridge St. ☎01865 242 526 www.bridgeoxford.co.uk

This mainstream club is very popular with Oxford's crowds of students, English or foreign, especially for their frequent student nights *(M and Th; international student night W)*. The modern art on the walls may seem out of place at this pretty conventional venue, or it might be welcomed as a nice alternative touch. Either way, come prepared for R and B and the biggest pop hits of the month. If you're not into that mass-produced... "stuff," this might not be your cup of tea.

Down the road from the bus station. No shorts, no hats, no ripped jeans, no white sneakers. Cover £3-8. Open M 10pm-2am, W 10pm-2am, Th-Sa 10pm-3am.

THIRST

BAR, CLUB

7-8 Park End St. ☎01865 242 044 www.thirstbar.com

This lounge bar is hopping all nights of the week because of its blasting DJs, free cover on weeknights, and spacious outdoor garden, where those who are so inclined can share a hookah (better known as shisha here) to complement their cocktails. Not classy, but not trashy either.

Down the road from the bus station. Cover Th-Su £3. Open M-W 7:30pm-2am, Th-Sa 7:30pm-3am, Su 7:30pm-2am.

LAVA AND IGNITE

CLUB

Cantay House, Park End St. ☎01865 250 181 www.lavaignite.com/oxford

Perhaps the most popular club in Oxford, the space is newly refurbished and packed with partying packs of patrons. There are three separate and distinct

livin' the pub life

I have to admit that one of my favorite things about the UK is the pub culture.

Cliché as it might be, I've rarely felt as distinctly British as when I sit down in a 16th-century pub in the middle of the afternoon with a pint of cider. On cloudy days, I sit inside and admire the fine woodwork and the idiosyncratic wall decorations. On sunny days, I like sitting out in the beer garden and basking in the summer sunshine with whatever ale the bartender has recommended. This kind of relaxed, communal space is something that we Americans are seriously lacking (along with an appropriate legal drinking age).

Oxford has some of the best pubs I've seen so far. Not only are they old, and oozing with character, but they all have great stories behind them.

Last night a friend and I tried out the King's Arms. Until 1973, this was the last male-only pub remaining in Oxford. The bartender was proud to tell me that Hugh Grant (Oxford alum) had stopped by just last week. Right nearby was the Turf Tavern, where former Australian Prime Minister Bob Hawke set a Guinness World Record for finishing off a yard glass of ale in just 11 seconds. As local legend has it, this was also the site where a young Bill Clinton, during his days as a Rhodes Scholar, purportedly "didn't inhale."

Today I stopped by The Eagle and the Child. Here, CS Lewis, JRR Tolkien, and other members of the "Inklings," a little club of writers, used to meet weekly to drink, discuss and debate the issues of the day. They say that the *Chronicles of Narnia* and *The Hobbit* were first read aloud in the back "Rabbit Room."

Rachel Lipson

dance floors, plus a separate "chill-out" space for sitting, drinking and talking (three plus one equals four bars), so if you get tired of the scenery, feel free to rotate. Call ahead to be put on the guest list and skip the lines on weekends.
*Across the street from Thirst and Central Backpackers. **i** Student night W. Covers £3-8. Open W 9:30pm-2am, Th-Sa 10pm-3am.*

JERICHO

THE EAGLE AND CHILD — PUB
49 St. Giles ☎01865 302 925

This brick-and-wood pub might be a stop on Oxford's literary trail, but that doesn't mean it shouldn't be on your pub crawl as well. Around as a public house since 1650, this was a former playhouse for Royalist soldiers during the English Civil War and then, four centuries later, a favorite watering hole of **JRR Tolkien, C.S. Lewis** and the group of writers who dubbed themselves the "Inklings." Have a drink in what used to be the back room (before the garden area was incorporated into the pub), the **Rabbit Room,** where the group had what Lewis referred to as "golden sessions" with drinks in hand and philosophy and literary genius spilling from mouths. There's a letter hung up by the bar bearing witness to the writers' presence, with their signatures and a statement that the men have drunk to the landlord's health.
Down St. Giles, north of the Ashmolean Museum. Entrees £6.45-10. Open M-Th 11am-11pm, F-Sa 11am-11:30pm, Su midnight-10:30pm.

JERICHO TAVERN — TAVERN

56 Walton St. ☎01865 311 775 www.thejerichooxford.co.uk

Radiohead first made its debut here back in 1984; since then, it has been sold, bought, remodeled, and rebranded, but thankfully the Jericho Tavern remains a good place to find live music in Oxford. The heated outdoor beer garden is also a plus—especially if you get a Fruli Strawberry Beer *(£3.50)* to enjoy out there—the spacious inside is good for big groups of friends, and there are board games for your entertainment on nights without music. Live acoustic on Sunday nights from 8pm. Check out the music listings on the tavern's website.
Near the Phoenix cinema. Entrees £6.50-11. Open daily noon-midnight. Kitchen open noon-10pm.

arts and culture

THEATER

NEW THEATRE — CARFAX
George St. ☎01865 320 760, 0844 847 1588 for booking www.newtheatreoxford.org.uk

It's showtime. Formerly known as the **Apollo Theater,** this is the main commercial theater in Oxford. The Art Deco building is home to many visiting concerts, musicals, and dramas.
From the bus station, follow Hythe Bridge St. to Worcester St. Make a right and follow down George St. Tickets £17.50-42.50. Occasional concessions for weekday showings. Occasional £11 student standbys on day of performance. Inquire at box office. Box office open M-W 10am-5pm, Th 10am-5:30pm, F non-performance days 10am-6pm, performance days 10am-3min. before curtain, Sa 10am-5pm.

OXFORD PLAYHOUSE — CARFAX
11-12 Beaumont St. ☎01865 305 305 www.oxfordplayhouse.com

Oxford's independent theater, better known to locals as simply "The Playhouse," puts on British and international drama, family shows, contemporary dance and music, student and amateur shows, comedy, lectures, and poetry. The Playhouse also produces and tours its own shows and hosts Artists in Residence.

Down Beaumont St. from the Ashmolean Musem. Advance concessions £2 off ticket prices. Student standbys available day of show at box office for £9.50. Box office open M-Sa 10am-6pm or until 30min. before curtain, Su performance days 2hr. before curtain. Cafe open on non-performance nights 10am-5:30pm, on performance nights 10am-11pm.

MUSIC

One of the most popular outlets for music lovers visiting Oxford are the university colleges' **choirs.** These choirs are professional quality—many of them go on international tours, (hopefully) a clear marker of success, and also have CDs that are available for purchase. Many tourists take full advantage of the opportunity to hear them in their natural environment at **Evensong.** Better yet, Evensong is always free. Generally during term time at Oxford *(Oct-Dec, Jan-Mar, and Apr-June)*, the college choirs are present at daily evening services, usually held at 6pm *(show up about 15min. beforehand and tell the porter or security that you've come for Evensong)*. However, confirm the choir performance information on the college website or with the porters' lodge during the day before showing up for the service.

OXFORD COFFEE CONCERTS — CARFAX

Holywell Music Room ☎01865 305 305 www.coffeeconcerts.com; www.ticketsoxford.com

This is one of the premier chamber music series in the country. Concerts held weekly on Sunday mornings feature string quartets, ensembles, and other classical duos and trios. Though you can't actually bring coffee inside, it's served beforehand at the nearby Turf Tavern, Vaults and Garden Cafe, and King's Arms. The concerts take place in the historic 1748 Holywell Music Hall, the oldest purpose-built concert hall in Europe.

Located on Holywell St., past the King's Arms and before Mansfield Rd. Tickets £11, concessions £10. Season tickets £96, concessions £84. Tickets can be purchased online or in person at the Oxford Playhouse Box Office, Beaumont St. Oxford Playhouse Box offce open M-Sa 10am-6pm or until 30min. before curtain. Tickets can also be bought in person at the door on the day of the performance starting at 9:45am. All concerts start at 11:15am.

OXFORD PHILOMUSICA — CARFAX

Various Venues ☎020 8450 1060 www.oxfordphil.com

Oxford's professional symphony orchestra is the first-ever orchestra in residence at the University of Oxford. It has established itself as a top-rate orchestra in the region.

i Held at Christ Church Cathedral, Chipping Norton Theatre (2 Spring St.), Holywell Music Room (Holywell St.), Jacqueline du Pre Music Building (St. Hilda's College, Cowley Pl.), Oxford Town Hall (St. Aldate's), Sheldonian Theatre (Broad St.), University Church of St. Mary (High St.), and Wyvern Theatre (Theatre Sq.). Tickets available through www.ticketsoxford.com or at Oxford Playhouse, Beaumont St. Tickets £10-37, students £5, under 18 ½-price. Oxford Playhouse Box Offce open M-Sa 10am-6pm or until 30min. before curtain. Box Office at each venue opens for door sales and ticket collection 2hr. before each concert.

DANCE

BURTON TAYLOR STUDIO — CARFAX

11 Beaumont St. ☎01865 305 305 www.oxfordtickets.com

The Burton Taylor Studio or BT Studio puts on occasional dance performances in its theater space, hosting visiting companies of contemporary dance. Ask at the box office of the Oxford Playhouse (above).

Across from Ashmolean Museum. Open M-Sa 10am-6pm or until 30min. before curtain. Su performance days from 2hr. before curtain.

shopping

Cornmarket St. is Oxford's chain-happy heaven, turning into Magdalen St. You will find many of the department stores in this area. Jericho has more alternative shopping, while High St. and St. Aldates, with their historic-looking decor, are generally aimed at tourist shopping (i.e. souvenir-hunting). High St. begins directly off Magdalen Bridge, passing colleges and meeting up with Cornmarket St. and St. Aldates to the East before becoming Queen St.

CLOTHING

JACK WILLS
CARFAX

125 High St. ☎01865 794 302 www.jackwills.com

The "University Outfitters" pride themselves on being "fabulously British." While you won't be able to afford a new wardrobe, it's worth a quick peek inside the store on ritzy High St., if only to pat yourself on the back and leave satisfied that there do exist people who fit that stereotype you had of Oxford before arriving. Check out the old memorabilia from Oxford-Cambridge matches, then outfit yourself in British attire of choice. You'll never feel more British.

From Carfax Tower, walk down High St. Open M-Sa 9:30am-6pm, Su 11am-5pm.

DEBENHAMS
JERICHO

Magdalen St. ☎0844 561 6161 www.debenhams.com

Department stores are always a convenient one-stop shop for all the essentials you've forgotten to bring. Though not always the most affordable, there are some deals to be had. Debenhams is a typical British department store: massive size, attempt at grandeur, lots of cooking supplies and home furnishings, and then the clothing. There's a restaurant and bus information on the upper floors.

Magdalen St. begins where Beaumont St. and Saint Giles St. meet, not by Magdalen College or Bridge. Open M-W 9:30am-6pm, Th 9:30am-8pm, F 9:30am-7pm, Sa 9am-7pm, Su 11am-5pm.

HABIBI
JERICHO

21 Little Clarendon St. ☎01865 558 077

This small, independent shop features a mishmash of accessories, including jewelry, scarves, handbags, and earrings. There are also plenty of mirrors—for sale—but also good for checking out whether those sunglasses look cute or not.

Down the road from St. John's College. Open M-Sa 10am-5:30pm, Su 11am-4pm.

UNCLE SAMS
JERICHO

25 Little Clarendon St. ☎01865 510 759

It's not surprising that Oxford's funkiest neighborhood has its own vintage clothing shop to serve all its hippies, past and present. What is a little more unexpected, though, is that the outlet features all American-themed items. That might seem to imply that American shoppers should feel right at home, but a lot of the merchandise consists of velvet and jean vests from the '60s and '70s—so it might be a little before your time. If you're into that sort of thing, though, it's perfect.

Down the road from St. John's College. Open M-Sa 10am-5:30pm, Su noon-4pm.

HOBBIES AND GAMES

ALICE'S SHOP
CARFAX

83 St. Aldates ☎01865 723 793 www.aliceinwonderlandshop.co.uk

Alice's Shop, located across the road from Lewis Carroll's old stomping grounds, is in the spot where the real Alice, Alice Liddell the Dean's daughter, used to buy her sweets back in Carroll's day. There's even a drawing of the shop in the original Alice book. Like Wonderland, the store is "full of all manner of curious things," with Alice in Wonderland Christmas ornaments, chess sets, teacups, Mad Hatter key racks, and Cheshire Cat tea cozies.

Open daily July-Aug 9:30am 6:30pm; Sept-June 10:30am-5pm.

HOYLES
CARFAX

72 High St. ☎01865 203 344 www.hoylesonline.com

An endearing specialty shop for all kinds of nifty games, puzzles, juggling, and magic accessories. Pick up one of over 50 different kinds of chess sets, **Monopoly the Oxford Edition,** or Stonehenge playing cards. Tired of studying and need a toy to distract yourself with? Scrabble, Disney version? Oh yeah.

Open in summer daily 9:30am-6pm; in winter M-Sa 9:30am-6pm.

BOOKS

THE ALBION BEATNIK
JERICHO

34 Walton St. ☎01865 511 345 www.albionbeatnik.co.uk

In this independent bookstore, almost half of the space is dedicated to an impressive collection of Beat poets and music books and general things related to the "Beat" lifestyle. Open up the coolly decorated cupboard in the back corner: inside you'll find hundreds of jazz CDs. There's also a cafe of sorts inside, so you can enjoy a cup of tea *(£1.50)* in an armchair with your book while Dylan and Coltrane play on in the background.

North on St. Giles Rd.; left into Little Clarendon St. At the end turn right. New and second-hand books from £1. Open M-W noon-7pm, Th-Sa 1-11pm, Su 3-5:30pm.

OXFORD UNIVERSITY PRESS
CARFAX

116-117 High St. ☎01865 242 913 wwww.oup.com/uk/bookshop

The OUP Bookshop is the official retailer for the largest university publisher in the world. The prestigious Oxford University Press is actually a department of the University of Oxford, and it printed its first book way back in 1478. The shop, though, has only been around on the High St. site since 1872—so practically yesterday in Oxford time. There are five levels, but the most unique section is the dictionary area, obviously. The Oxford English Dictionary is sold here in sizes ranging from 20 volumes to "shorter" to "concise" to "compact" to "pocket" to "little," and to, finally, "mini." Meanwhile, you can find Oxford Dictionaries of Quotations, Proverbs, British Place Names, and Dentistry, among others. There's such a selection, we're at a loss for words. Any suggestions?

i Ask about 10% student discount. Catalogs free. Open M-Sa 9:30am-6pm, Su 11am-5pm.

BLACKWELL'S
CARFAX

48-51 Broad St. ☎01865 792 792 www.blackwell.co.uk

Blackwell's is a popular British chain bookstore, but its roots are firmly staked in Oxford. The flagship store at 48-51 Broad St. was started back in 1879. Originally, the Broad St. shop at number 50 was only 12 sq. ft., but the store quickly grew to incorporate the upstairs, cellars, and next door storefronts. Many famous writers saw their first books sold at Blackwell's. One such literary is **JRR Tolkien,** who in 1915 saw his first poem, "Goblin's Feet," published here. Today, the shop includes a coffeeshop if you'd like to nosh while you read, and the **Norrington Room,** built beneath the quad of Trinity College. This room, with 3 mi. of shelving, holds the Guinness Book of World Records award for housing the largest display of books for sale in one room anywhere in the world. Check the posters on the walls for listings of author visits, literary walking tours (see **Practicalities,** p. 130), and signings. Art fans and music aficionados should definitely check out the nearby sister Blackwell shops on Broad St.: Blackwell Art and Poster shop *(27 Broad St. ☎01865 333 641)* featuring a wide selection of prints, art books, photography, and Blackwell Music *(23-25 Broad St. ☎01865 333 580)* with its vast collection of sheet music, classical CDs, and musical literature.

Holywell St. becomes Broad St. Open M 9am-6:30pm, Tu 9:30am-6:30pm, W-Sa 9am-6:30pm, Su 11am-5pm.

THE LAST BOOKSHOP — JERICHO

126 Walton St.

It's a tiny little place, with a correspondingly small and random collection; there's also little room to move around, and certainly no room for sitting. However, you don't need to sit, just buy: all books are £2!

Open M-Sa 9am-5:45pm.

LIQUOR STORES

THE WHISKY SHOP — CARFAX

7 Turl St. ☎01865 202279 www.whiskyshop.com

Come here for your fix of Jack Daniel's... and so much more. The wooden shelves are stuffed to the ceilings with the finest whiskeys in the worlds, plus old malts, single malts, Bailey's, and Captain Morgan. If you're admittedly clueless when it comes to whiskey, that's OK too: there are tiny sample 50mL bottles for experimentation *(from £3.20)*, Jack Daniel's fudge for the faint-hearted, and even little reviews from the the *Whisky Bible* and *Malt Whisky Companion* taped above the bottles to help you make your decision.

Behind Covered Market. Open Tu-Sa 10am-5:30pm.

essentials

PRACTICALITIES

- **TOURIST OFFICE:** The Tourist Information Centre is crowded with mobs of tourists during the summer. Ask for a free *In Oxford What's On* guide and free restaurant and accommodation guides. Also sells discounted tickets to local attractions. Books rooms for free with a 10% deposit. *(15-16 Broad St. ☎01852 252 200 www.visitoxford.org Open M-Sa 9:30am-5pm, Su 10am-4pm.)*
- **STUDENT TRAVEL: STA Travel.** *(Threeways House, 36 George St. ☎0871 702 9839 www.statravel.co.uk Open M-Th 10am-7pm, F-Sa 10am-6pm, Su 11am-5pm.)*
- **TOURS:** The 2hr. official **Oxford University Walking Tour** leaves from the TIC and provides access to some colleges otherwise closed to visitors. The 2hr. tours allow only up to 19 people and are booked on a first come, first served basis, so get tickets early in the day at the TIC, by phone, or online 48hr. in advance. *(☎726 871, 252 200 to book tickets. visitoxford.org Daily in summer 10:45, 11am, 1, 2pm; in winter 10:45am, 2pm. £7, children £3.75.)* Themed tours, like the CS Lewis and JRR Tolkien Tour and Garden run on a varied schedule. *(£7.50, children £4.)* Check with the TIC or pick up an Official Guided Walking Tours Brochure. **Blackwell's Walking Tours** *(☎01852 333 606)* run from April through October and leave from Canterbury Gate at Christ Church. The company runs a number of walking tours throughout the university town, including the General Literary University and City Tour *(Tu 2pm, Th 11am. £7, concessions £6.50)*, the Literary Tour of Oxford *(Tu 2pm, Th 11am)*, the "Inklings" Tour about CS Lewis, JRR Tolkien, and cohorts *(W 11:45am. £7, concessions £6.50.)*, and the Chapels, Churches, and Cathedral Tour. *(F 2pm. £9, concessions £8.)* **Oxford Walking Tours** runs 1½hr. walks through the colleges, leaving from Trinity College Gates. *(☎07790 734 387. www.*

oxfordwalkingtours.com ⏰ *Apr-Oct M-F 11am, 1, 3pm, Sa-Su every hr. 11am-4pm; Nov-Mar M-F noon, 2pm, Sa-Su every hr. 11am-3pm.* Ⓢ *£7.50, concessions £7.)* They also offer Ghost Tours. *(⏰ Apr-Oct 7:30pm; Nov-Mar 4, 7pm.* Ⓢ *£7.)* **Bill Spectre's Ghost Tours** leave every F-Sa evenings from Oxford Castle Unlocked at 6:30pm for 1¾hr. tour or from the TIC at 7pm for a 1¼hr. tour. *(☎07941 041 811* 🖳*www.ghosttrail.org* Ⓢ *£6, children £3.)* **City Sightseeing** offers hop-on, hop-off bus tours of the city with 19 stops, running every 10-15min. *(Starting at Bay 14 of the bus station. Pick up tickets from bus drivers or stands around the city. ☎01852 790 522* Ⓢ *£12.50, students £10.50, children £6.)*

- **CURRENCY EXCHANGE:** Banks line **Cornmarket Street. Marks and Spencer** has a bureau de change with no commission. *(13-18 Queen St. ☎01852 248 075 ⏰ Open M-W 8:30am-6:30pm, Th 8:30am-7:30pm, F 8:30am-6:30pm, Sa 8:30am-6:30pm, Su 11am-4:30pm.)* There is also a bureau of change attached to (but not affiliated with) the TIC, with no commission.
- **INTERNET:** Free at **Oxford Central Library,** but there is often a wait during prime hours; some stations are open to pre-booking if you know exactly when you'd like to use it. *(Westgate. ⏰ Open M-Th 9am-7pm, F-Sa 9am-5:30pm.)* **C-Work Cyber Cafe.** *(1st fl. of Nash Bailey's House, New Inn Hall St. ☎722 044* Ⓢ *£1 per 50min. ⏰ Open M-Sa 9am-9pm, Su 9am-7pm.)*
- **POST OFFICE:** *(102-104 St. Aldates. ☎08457 223 344 Bureau de change inside. ⏰ Open M 9am-5:30pm, Tu 9:30am-5:30pm, W-Sa 9am-5:30pm.)*
- **POSTAL CODE:** OX1 1ZZ.

EMERGENCY!

- **POLICE:** *(St. Aldates and Speedwell St. ☎505 505.)*
- **HOSPITAL: John Radcliffe Hospital.** *(Headley Way. Take bus #13 or 14. ☎741 166.)*

GETTING THERE

By Train

Botley Road Station *(Botley Rd., down Park End. ☎01865 484 950 ⏰ Ticket office open M-F 5:45am-8pm, Sa 7:30am-8pm, Su 7:15am-8pm.)* offers trains to **Birmingham** *(Ⓢ £27. ⏰ 1hr. 10min., every 30min.)*; **Glasgow** *(Ⓢ£98.50. ⏰ 5-7hr., every hr.)*; **London Paddington** *(Ⓢ £20. ⏰ 1hr., 2-4 per hr.)*; and **Manchester** *(Ⓢ£61. ⏰ 3hr., 2 per hr.)*

By Bus

Gloucester Green Station has **Stagecoach** buses *(☎01865 772 250* 🖳*www.stagecoachbus.com)* running to **London Buckingham Road** *(Ⓢ £14, students £11. ⏰ 1¼hr., 5 per hr.)* and **Cambridge.** *(Ⓢ £10.90. ⏰ 3hr., 2 per hr.)* Buy tickets on the bus and enjoy free Wi-Fi.

The Oxford Bus Company *(☎01865 785 400* 🖳*www.oxfordbus.co.uk)* runs the **Oxford Express** *(i Free Wi-Fi.* Ⓢ *£13, students £10. ⏰ 1¾hr., every 15-30min.)* and the **X70 Airline** services to **Heathrow.** *(i Free Wi-Fi.* Ⓢ *£20. ⏰ 1½hr., every 30min.)* Also runs the **X80** service to **Gatwick's** north and south terminals. *(i Free Wi-Fi.* Ⓢ *£25. ⏰ 2½hr., every hr.)* All leave from **Gloucester Green.** Tickets can be bought on the bus or at the **National Express** office *(£1 booking fee)*. However, the only way to secure a spot in advance on a particular bus is on the website.

National Express Bus 737 *(☎08717 818 178* 🖳*www.nationalexpress.com ⏰ Ticket office open M-Sa 8:30am-6pm, Su 8:30am-5:30pm)* goes to **London Stansted,** *(Ⓢ £19.30. ⏰ 3½hr., 8 per day.)*, **Birmingham** *(Ⓢ £13.40. ⏰ 2½hr., 1 per day.)*, and **Bath.** *(Ⓢ £9.50. ⏰ 2hr., 1 per day.)*

GETTING AROUND

Public Transport

Oxford Bus Company (*01865 785 400 www.oxfordbus.co.uk*) provides many services within the city. Fares vary depending on distance traveled. (*DayPass £3.70, weekly pass £13.*) Week passes can be purchased at the Oxford Bus Company office. (*3rd fl. of Debenham's department store on corner of George and Magdalen St. Open M-W 9:30am-6pm, Th 9:30-8pm, F 9:30am-6pm, Sa 9am-6pm.*) **Stagecoach** (*01865 772 250 www.stagecoach-bus.com*) also runs buses in the city and to some surrounding villages. One-way-tickets within the city usually cost £1.80. Be careful when buying Day Passes because they don't apply to both companies (if you buy an Oxford Bus DayPass, it only works on Oxford Bus Company buses). For real-time information on buses in Oxford, use www.oxontime.com, which can also text to your cell phone.

By Taxi

Call **Radio Taxis** (*01865 242 424*) or **ABC** (*01865 770 077*) for taxis. There are taxi ranks at **Oxford Station, Saint Giles, Gloucester Green,** and **Carfax** in the evening. Taxis (like London black cabs) can be hailed in the street.

By Bike

Bike Rental: Cycloanalysts (*150 Cowley Rd. 01865 424 444 www.cycloanalysts.com £17 per 24hr., £25 per 2 days, £50 per week. Includes locks. Open M-Sa 9am-6pm, Su 10am-4pm.*)

By Boat

Magdalen Bridge Boat House (*Cross bridge from city center and turn left; down by the banks. 01865 202 643 www.oxfordpunting.co.uk Open daily 9:30am-dusk.*) Rents punts (*£20 per hr., up to 5 people*) and offers chauffeured punts. (*£23 per 30min. for up to 4 people.*)

SOUTHERN ENGLAND AND WALES

From Roman ruins to debauched nightlife, Southern England has it all. Visitors can enjoy a spa day in **Jane Austen's hometown,** a romp on the nudie beach in **Brighton,** or a walk through **Canterbury** in all its cobblestoned quaintness. While you're in the southern region of the island, why not head over to **Wales,** England's oft-neglected neighbor? The Welsh proudly cling to their Celtic heritage, determined to assert their national independence. And a visit to **Cardiff** will teach you that the Welsh know how to do more than count sheep; they can party hearty better than anyone on the island.

greatest hits

- **AUSTENIAN APPETITE.** Have "Tea with Mr. Darcy" at Regency Tea Room (p. 142) in Bath.
- **BE A BEACH BUM.** From the pier to the beer, **Brighton** (p. 149) is a blast.
- **SAUCY CHAUCEY.** Enact Chaucer's playful tales in **Canterbury** (p. 160).
- **(W)ALES.** Revel in **Cardiff's** extraordinary nightlife (p. 175) scene along St. Mary St.

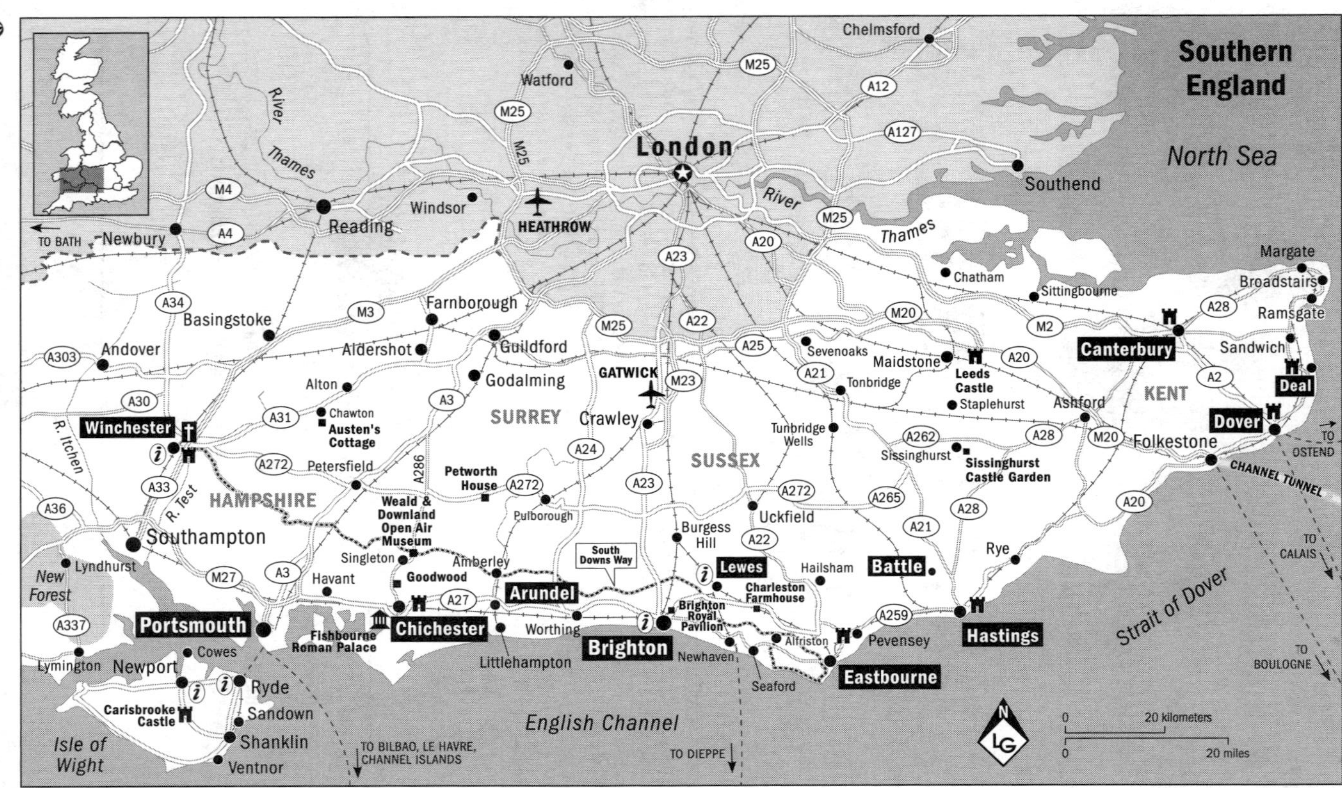
Southern England
North Sea
English Channel
Strait of Dover
London
HEATHROW
GATWICK
KENT
SUSSEX
SURREY
HAMPSHIRE
Canterbury
Dover
Deal
Hastings
Battle
Eastbourne
Lewes
Brighton
Arundel
Chichester
Portsmouth
Winchester
Margate
Broadstairs
Ramsgate
Sandwich
Folkestone
Ashford
Sittingbourne
Chatham
Southend
Chelmsford
Maidstone
Leeds Castle
Staplehurst
Sissinghurst
Sissinghurst Castle Garden
Rye
Pevensey
Tonbridge
Sevenoaks
Tunbridge Wells
Uckfield
Hailsham
Alfriston
Seaford
Newhaven
Charleston Farmhouse
Brighton Royal Pavilion
Burgess Hill
Crawley
Pulborough
Worthing
Littlehampton
Amberley
Goodwood
Petworth House
Weald & Downland Open Air Museum
Singleton
Havant
Fishbourne Roman Palace
Guildford
Godalming
Farnborough
Aldershot
Alton
Chawton
Austen's Cottage
Petersfield
Watford
Windsor
Reading
Basingstoke
Newbury
Andover
Southampton
Lyndhurst
New Forest
Lymington
Isle of Wight
Cowes
Newport
Carisbrooke Castle
Ryde
Sandown
Shanklin
Ventnor
River Thames
R. Itchen
R. Test
South Downs Way
CHANNEL TUNNEL
TO OSTEND
TO CALAIS
TO BOULOGNE
TO DIEPPE
TO BILBAO, LE HAVRE, CHANNEL ISLANDS
TO BATH
0 20 kilometers
0 20 miles
M25
M20
M23
M2
M3
M4
M27
A2
A3
A4
A12
A20
A21
A22
A23
A24
A25
A27
A28
A30
A31
A33
A34
A36
A127
A259
A262
A265
A272
A286
A303
A337
LG

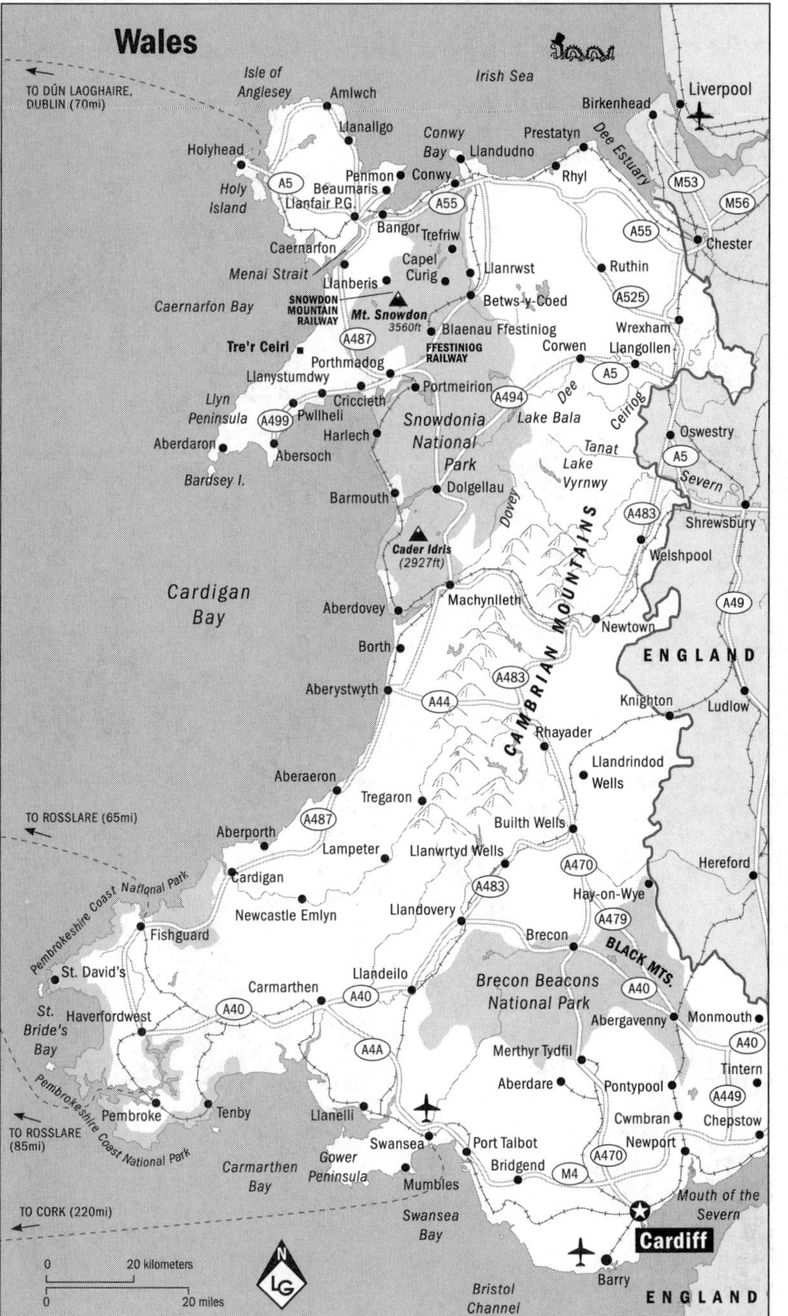
Wales
Irish Sea
Isle of Anglesey
TO DÚN LAOGHAIRE, DUBLIN (70mi)
Amlwch
Llanallgo
Holyhead
Holy Island
Penmon
Beaumaris
Llanfair P.G.
Conwy Bay
Llandudno
Conwy
Prestatyn
Rhyl
Dee Estuary
Birkenhead
Liverpool
Chester
Bangor
Trefriw
Caernarfon
Menai Strait
Capel Curig
Llanberis
Llanrwst
Ruthin
Caernarfon Bay
SNOWDON MOUNTAIN RAILWAY
Mt. Snowdon 3560ft
Betws-y-Coed
Wrexham
Blaenau Ffestiniog
FFESTINIOG RAILWAY
Tre'r Ceiri
Porthmadog
Llanystumdwy
Corwen
Llangollen
Portmeirion
Criccieth
Llyn Peninsula
Pwllheli
Abersoch
Aberdaron
Bardsey I.
Harlech
Snowdonia National Park
Lake Bala
Dee
Ceiriog
Oswestry
Tanat
Lake Vyrnwy
Severn
Barmouth
Dolgellau
Dovey
Shrewsbury
Welshpool
Cader Idris (2927ft)
CAMBRIAN MOUNTAINS
Cardigan Bay
Machynlleth
Aberdovey
Newtown
Borth
ENGLAND
Aberystwyth
Knighton
Ludlow
Rhayader
Llandrindod Wells
Aberaeron
Tregaron
TO ROSSLARE (65mi)
Aberporth
Builth Wells
Lampeter
Llanwrtyd Wells
Hereford
Cardigan
Pembrokeshire Coast National Park
Newcastle Emlyn
Llandovery
Hay-on-Wye
Fishguard
Brecon
BLACK MTS.
St. David's
Llandeilo
Carmarthen
Brecon Beacons National Park
St. Bride's Bay
Haverfordwest
Abergavenny
Monmouth
Merthyr Tydfil
Tintern
Aberdare
Pontypool
Pembroke
Tenby
Llanelli
Cwmbran
Chepstow
TO ROSSLARE (85mi)
Swansea
Port Talbot
Newport
Pembrokeshire Coast National Park
Carmarthen Bay
Gower Peninsula
Bridgend
Mumbles
Mouth of the Severn
TO CORK (220mi)
Swansea Bay
Cardiff
Barry
0
20 kilometers
20 miles
Bristol Channel
ENGLAND
A5
A55
M53
M56
A525
A487
A494
A499
A483
A49
A44
A470
A479
A40
A4A
A449
M4

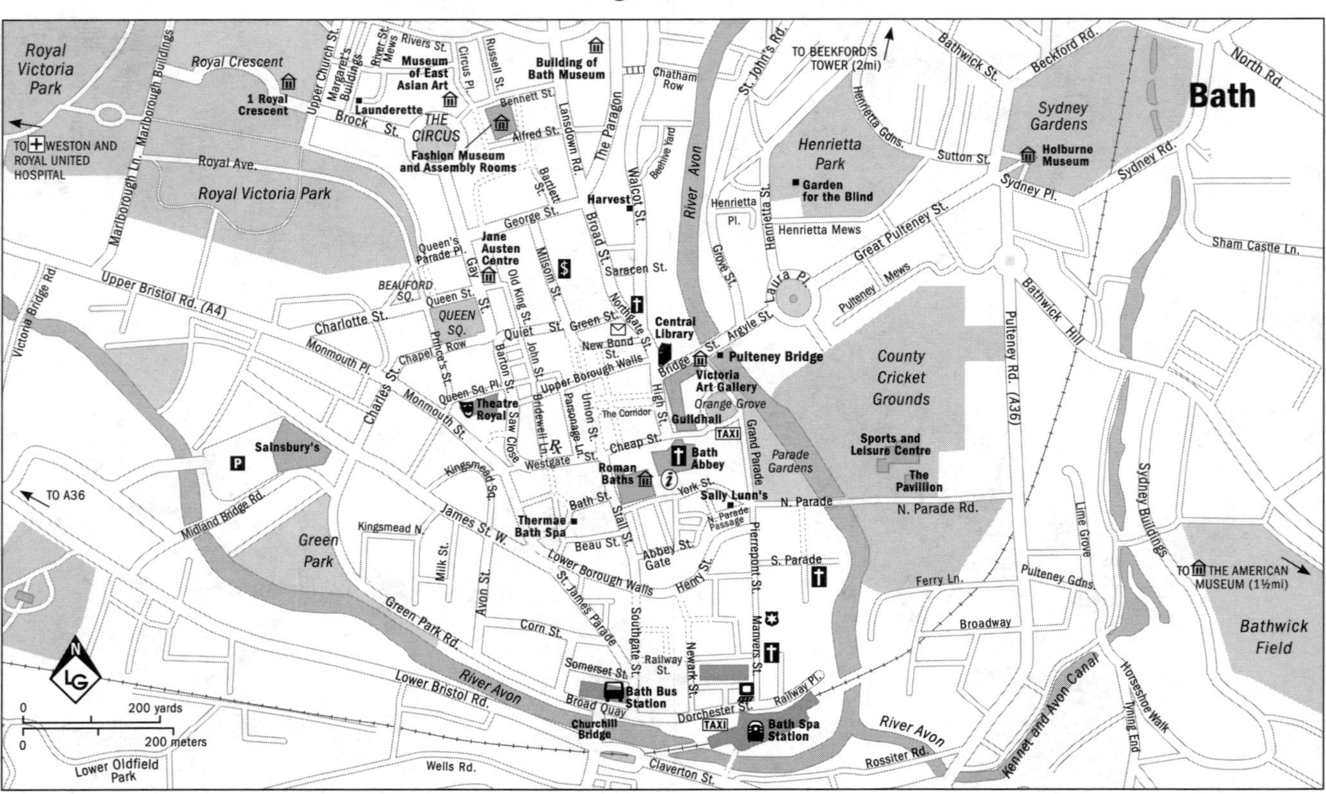
Bath
Royal Victoria Park
Royal Crescent
1 Royal Crescent
Upper Church St.
Margaret's Buildings
River St. Mews
Rivers St.
Museum of East Asian Art
Launderette
Circus Pl.
Russell St.
Building of Bath Museum
Chatham Row
St. John's Rd.
TO BEEKFORD'S TOWER (2mi)
Bathwick St.
Beckford Rd.
North Rd.
Sydney Gardens
Holburne Museum
Sydney Rd.
Sydney Pl.
Sutton St.
Henrietta Gdns.
Henrietta Park
Garden for the Blind
Henrietta Pl.
Henrietta St.
Henrietta Mews
Great Pulteney St.
Sham Castle Ln.
TO WESTON AND ROYAL UNITED HOSPITAL
Marlborough Buildings
Marlborough Ln.
Brock St.
THE CIRCUS
Bennett St.
Alfred St.
Fashion Museum and Assembly Rooms
Lansdown Rd.
The Paragon
Beehive Yard
River Avon
Royal Ave.
Bartlett St.
Harvest
Walcot St.
Broad St.
George St.
Queen's Parade Pl.
Jane Austen Centre
Gay St.
Milsom St.
Saracen St.
Grove St.
Laura Pl.
Pulteney Mews
Bathwick Hill
Upper Bristol Rd. (A4)
Victoria Bridge Rd.
BEAUFORD SQ.
Queen St.
QUEEN SQ.
Old King St.
Northgate St.
Charlotte St.
Quiet St.
Green St.
Central Library
Argyle St.
Pulteney Bridge
County Cricket Grounds
Pulteney Rd. (A36)
Monmouth Pl.
Chapel Row
Princes St.
Barton St.
John St.
New Bond St.
Upper Borough Walls
Bridge St.
Victoria Art Gallery
Orange Grove
Queen Sq. Pl.
Charles St.
Theatre Royal
Saw Close
Bridewell Ln.
Parsonage Ln.
Union St.
The Corridor
High St.
Guildhall
Monmouth St.
Cheap St.
Grand Parade
Parade Gardens
Sports and Leisure Centre
Sainsbury's
Westgate St.
Bath Abbey
Roman Baths
The Pavilion
Kingsmead Sq.
York St.
Sally Lunn's
N. Parade
N. Parade Rd.
TO A36
Bath St.
Midland Bridge Rd.
James St. W.
Thermae Bath Spa
Stall St.
N. Parade Passage
Lime Grove
Sydney Buildings
Kingsmead N.
Beau St.
Abbey St.
Abbey Gate
Pierrepont St.
Green Park
S. Parade
TO THE AMERICAN MUSEUM (1½mi)
Milk St.
Avon St.
Lower Borough Walls
Henry St.
Ferry Ln.
Pulteney Gdns.
St. James Parade
Corn St.
Broadway
Bathwick Field
Green Park Rd.
Southgate St.
Newark St.
Manvers St.
Somerset St.
Railway St.
Kennet and Avon Canal
Horseshoe Walk
Tyning End
Lower Bristol Rd.
River Avon
Bath Bus Station
Railway Pl.
Broad Quay
Dorchester St.
0
200 yards
200 meters
Churchill Bridge
Bath Spa Station
River Avon
Rossiter Rd.
Lower Oldfield Park
Wells Rd.
Claverton St.

student life

It's a shame that some students only associate Wales with its seemingly unreadable language. The Welsh capital of **Cardiff,** a veritable haven for partying students, houses the hidden hip-ness of the island. There are shindigs happening all year-round. And we're not just talkin' about your usual cramped and claustrophobic clubs. This city offers unique options, including the **Cardiff Arts Institute,** a funky and colorful spot covered in unlikely decorations, like knick-knacks and childhood toys. The venue also hosts poetry readings and other delightfully artsy events.

bath ☎01225

In many ways, Bath is the quintessential idyllic English town—it's got rolling green hills, classic architecture, charming pubs, and historic churches. For that very reason, foreigners have trekked here for centuries. A luxurious destination throughout its history, Bath was once a meeting place for the Roman elite who migrated here to frequent the city's healing mineral baths which they dedicated to the goddess Minerva. Later, Britain's upper-class social set, featured in novels by **Jane Austen** and **Charles Dickens,** vacationed to Bath, the hip reatreat of the day. Austen's aristocratic heroine in *Northanger Abbey* claims that, "Bath is a charming place, sir; there are so many good shops here." Indeed, with the brand-new Southgate shopping center, Bath serves today's visitors just as it did those in Austen's time.

Though Bath might be home to England's hottest springs, it's not known for its steaming nightlife. However, a modern influx of students plus the constant comings-and-goings of young travelers, now add a bit of spice to the mix of local Bathonians and older tourists that typically roam its Georgian streets.

ORIENTATION

The **Roman Baths,** the **Pump Room,** and **Bath Abbey** sit at the center of Bath's touristy, bustling city center, which is bounded by **York Street** and **Cheap Street.** The River Avon lies just to the east of them and swerves around the southernmost part of town near the train and bus stations. The legendary **Pulteney Bridge,** which crosses the river, is disguised by the shops that lie on both sides. It is one of only four bridges in the world with this kind of design.

Bath borders **Cotswolds'** southern fringes, and the city limits are hilly. As you head north, you'll find that the streets get progressively steeper and exhausting for travelers. Nevertheless, the view of honey-colored Georgian buildings hovering over the slopes is still gorgeous. The famed buildings of the **Royal Crescent** and **Circus** sit on these hills.

ACCOMMODATIONS

It may not be Jane Austen's Bath anymore—women don't walk around in corsets, and the balls have basically seen their end. Still, well-to-do visitors have kept this a fashionable place to spend time and therefore, prices have stayed high. Budget accommodations, however, are out there if you look for them, and the steady flow of backpackers that leave London for Bath or make it a base for Stonehenge have kept the four city hostels in business. Meanwhile, bed and breakfasts, some of them affordable and some of them less so, cluster on **Pulteney Road** and **Pulteney Gardens. Marlborough Lane** and **Upper Bristol Road,** west of the city center, also offer accommodations.

YMCA

HOSTEL ❷

International House, Broad St. Pl. ☎01225 325 900 www.bathymca.co.uk

This large and spacious complex has the best of both worlds when it comes to location: and near the nightlife of George St. for prime bar-hopping action also set off from the street with its own scenic courtyard and picnic tables for restful nights. The lounge of the old Victorian building is modern and comfortable, with flatscreen TV and Internet. The dorms are clean and fairly spacious, though beds are a bit creaky. A cheesy but comforting mural of the world winds around the staircase, hoping to provide tired travelers with a little taste of home.

From the bus or train station walk north up Manvers St. Pass Bath Abbey on your left and, keeping the River Avon on you right, continue via Orange Grove (on left) and High St. to Walcot St. or Broad St. There are entrances to the YMCA, which is within a courtyard, from Broad St. (next to a haridresser's) or Walcot St. (close to Harvest Food Shop) up a flight of steps. Look out for signs pointing to YMCA. ***i*** *Continental breakfast included. Laundry: wash £2, dry £1. Luggage storage at reception £1 per 24hr. Lockers available for purchase. Free Wi-Fi downstairs. Internet £1 per 30min. Bike racks. Health and fitness center available for guest use, £4 for full-day access. Tea and coffee £.70 per cup. Single-sex dorms available.* *Dorms £17-£19; singles £28-32; doubles £23-26; triples £20-23; quads £18-21. Weekly rates available by phone booking.* *Reception 24hr. Restaurant open daily for breakfast and M-F noon-2pm.*

BATH BACKPACKERS

HOSTEL ❶

13 Pierrepont St. ☎01225 446 787 www.hostels.co.uk

Bath's most colorful hostel is made memorable by the bright paintings on its walls, its dark late-night "dungeon" (a.k.a. window-less basement), and unique room names ("Divas," "Brutus"). This is definitely a true backpackers' home—and that means you shouldn't expect luxury: rooms are less than spacious, and weekends mean late (and possibly loud) comings-and-goings. Those with aching backs should take note, though; the hostel is only a 3min. walk from the bus and train stations.

From train station, go straight down Manvers Street for 400m, past the police station and church on the right side. The hostel is on the left side, just before the 2nd set of traffic lights on the same street. ***i*** *Breakfast included. Laundry £3.50. Luggage storage £1. Wi-Fi £2.50 for full stay. Internet £1.20 per 30min. Self-catering kitchen. Single-sex dorms available. Online and weekly discounts available.* *Dorms £12-19.* *Reception 7am-midnight.*

ST. CHRISTOPHER'S INN

HOSTEL ❷

9 Green St. ☎01225 481 444 www.st-christophers.co.uk

Centrally located to Bath's major sites with a young crowd of partiers. These are simple dorm rooms that don't have room for much else other than the beds. However, there's a 10% discount on food and alcohol at the downstairs bar, which is bustling on days of popular sporting events, and an upstairs common area with TV, movies, and a microwave.

Past the Podium, Green St. is to the left. On top of Belushi's Bar. Reception is at the bar. ***i*** *Laundry service available. Discounts when you book online. Free Wi-Fi downstairs at the bar. Internet £1 per 30min.* *Dorms £16-26.*

THE WHITE GUEST HOUSE

BED AND BREAKFAST ❸

23 Pulteney Gardens ☎01225 426 075 www.whitehguesthouse.co.uk

Only a 5-10min. walk from downtown Bath and the main attractions, this cozy B and B is ideal if you're looking for a reasonably priced stay in a quiet neighborhood that is still close to all the action. The rooms are tastefully decorated, each with its own distinct personality, and all have TVs, coffeemakers, and ensuite baths.

Take N. Parade Rd. over the river (away from downtown) and make a right onto Pulteney Rd. Pulteney Gardens is a left off Pulteney Rd. after the overpass. ***i*** *Full English breakfast included.* *Ensuite singles £45; doubles £50-70.*

UNIVERSITY OF BATH UNIVERSITY CAMPUS ❸

The Ave., Claverton Down ☎01225 386 622 www.haatbath.com

The university's very green (both aesthetically and environmentally) campus is located about a 1½ mi. outside the city center. Single rooms with shared bath are available for student-friendly prices during the summer.

Take the U18 bus from the bus station (every 10min.). i Laundry. Free Internet. Self-catering kitchens. Ⓢ Singles from £21. Reception 24hr.

Bathwick

YHA BATH HOSTEL ❷

Bathwick Hill ☎0845 371 9303 www.yha.org.uk

Disguised in an elite neighborhood of gorgeous Georgian mansions, you'd never guess from the front that this was a YHA. It's a trek: up a substantial hill, hidden off the road, around a curving driveway, set apart a beautiful patch of greenery, but worth the trip. Also named "Fiesole," the building dates from 1848, was designed by a local architect for well-to-do members of the Bath elite, then to the sick and injured officers from the second World War. Today, the beautiful structure and grounds remain virtually unchanged. Dorms and private rooms in the main building are spacious and bright, many with antique, though non-functioning, fireplaces and great views of the scenic surroundings. Rooms in the add-on building, however, are much more standard and lack the character of the main building. If you're looking for a double, call in advance and request one of the Tower rooms—the views of the city and surrounding hills are spectacular from the top.

1 1/2mi. from train station (uphill). Take the #18 or #418 buses from the Bus Station. Ask for the youth hostel. i Breakfast £5, continental £3. Laundry. Lockers in rooms. Wi-Fi £8 for 24hr. Internet £1 for 15min. Free bike and luggage storage. Bar, open noon-midnight. Restaurant on-site. Towels for rent £2. Ⓢ Dorms £16-£20. Private twins £40-£45, quads £70-£79, 5-person rooms £88-£104, 6-person £105-£118. £3 charge per night for non-YHA members. Reception 7am-11pm. 24hr access.

SIGHTS

The city's oldest house once belonged to a young French refugee who arrived in England over three centuries ago. **Sally Lunn's,** located at 4 North Parade Passage, is built on the site of an old monastery and serves portions of the famed round and rich bread better-known as the Sally Lunn Bun. The downstairs restaurant offers a quaint candelit evening dinner starting nightly from 5pm, but if you're not a big fan of buns, you can check out the museum which displays the building's ancient "faggot" oven, and even older Roman and medieval foundations. *(☎01225 461 634 www.sallylunns.co.uk. $ Museum free. Open M-Sa 10am-6pm, Su 11am-6pm.)*

In the city's residential northwest corner are the Georgian rowhouses, built by famed architects John Wood the elder and John Wood the younger. Bath's **Circus** isn't a home for exotic animals; rather, it's a classical circle of large townhouses, inspired by the Roman Colliseum. This is widely considered the crowning masterpiece of John Wood the Elder, who died before he could see them completed. The 30 houses of the nearby Royal Crescent just up Brock St., designed by John Wood the Younger, are, naturally, laid out in a crescent shape, and are widely hailed as some of the finest examples of Georgian and Palladian architecture in all of Britain. The interior of 1 Royal Crescent, originally inhabited by Thomas Brock, has been lovingly restored by the Bath Preservation Trust to its 1770 form, after years of disrepair and a brief stint as a guesthouse. *(From the city center, take a No. 18 or 418 or a No. U18, to the University of Bath via Bathwick Hill, and get off at The Avenue. From the entrance to the University campus follow the signs approximately ½ mi., downhill to the museum. ☎01225 428 126 www.bath-preservation-trust.org.uk. Ⓢ £6, concessions £5. Open Tu-Su mid-Feb-Oct 10:30am-5pm; Nov 10:30am-4pm. Last admission 30min. before close.)*

ROMAN BATHS

BATHS

Abbey Church Yard ☎01225 477 785 www.romanbaths.co.uk

In 1880, sewer diggers accidentally stumbled across an extraordinary feat of Roman engineering. No, the Romans didn't invent the toilet. Instead, for 400 years, the Romans harnessed Bath's bubbling natural springs which spew 264,000 gallons of 115°F (46°C) water everyday. Since the 1800s, the Baths have been the city's biggest tourist attraction. The city even erected an elaborate Roman-style balcony around them, complete with statues of the Roman gods, to recreate a sense of Bath's elite heritage. The entrance price is high enough to make you squirm. There are really no alternative ways to witness Bath's signature sight: views of the actual baths are inaccessible from the city streets. After all, they *are* the only thermal springs in the entirety of the UK. Sadly, visitors haven't been allowed to swim since 1939, but we doubt you'd want to anyway—because of natural processes and algae, the water is a lovely shade of bright green. Make sure you hold onto your ticket and head over to the elegant Pump Room next door: entrance to the site includes a free glass of mineral water (not the green stuff) coming directly out of the fountain from the Baths. It might not be the best-tasting aqua you've ever tried—it's at least 10,000 years old—but it's a requisite part of the experience.

In the center of Bath. Entrance in Abbey Church Yard. ***i*** *Tickets include audio tour and free guided tours of the Bath area; depart hourly. £11.50, concessions £10; joint ticket with the Museum of Fashion £15/13. Open July-Aug 9am-10pm, Sept-Oct 9am-6pm, Nov-Feb 9:30am-5:30pm, Mar-June 9am-6pm. Last admission 1hr. before close.*

BATH ABBEY

ABBEY

12 Kingston Buildings ☎01225 422 462 www.bathabbey.org

Occupying the site where **King Edgar** was crowned the first king of all England in 973 CE (check out the Edgar window, which depicts the ceremony of his crowning), the 140 ft. Bath Abbey stands in the city center. This is the most-visited parish church in the UK, with about 300,000 visitors each year, and if you come in the summer, you'll believe it. It may seem crowded already, but that's nothing when you think about what goes on underground: there are believed to be 3000-4000 bodies squished together and buried directly underneath the abbey floor. For a hefty price, wealthy believers could have their remains placed in the church up until an 1853 Act of Parliament prohibited the practice on the grounds of danger to public health. The abbey itself is the fourth place of worship to stand on the site, and the heritage vaults show fragments of these prior inhabitants from the post-Roman, Saxon, later-Saxon, and Norman periods. In 1499, Bishop Oliver King followed through on a command he heard from God in a dream: "Let an Olive establish the Crown and a King restore the Church." Hence, the crowned olive tree. Perhaps the most captivating pieces of the church are the numerous memorial plaques—test your history knowledge by noting how many you can recognize.

The Abbey is next to Orange Grove, off of Manvers/Pierrepoint St., and on the other side of the Roman Baths. Suggested donation £2.50. Tower tours £5. Open Apr-Oct M-Sa 9am-6pm, Su 1-2:30pm and 4:30-5:30pm; Nov-Mar M-Sa 9am-4:30pm, Su 1-2:30pm and 4:30-5:30pm.

FASHION MUSEUM AND ASSEMBLY ROOMS

MUSEUM

Bennett St. ☎01225 477 173 www.fashionmuseum.co.uk

The museum hosts a vivacious parade of four centuries of catwalk styles. Thematic exhibits chart the evolution of everything from pockets to gloves, and interactive pieces let visitors try on an authentic corset and hoop skirt. Also on display is the famed silver tissue dress, an exquisite survivor from the 1660s, and a mini-replica of an 18th-century court dress. The museum tries hard to keep current with rapidly-changing fashion trends; annually since 1963 they have annually honored a Dress of the Year. Recent selections have included pieces by **Giorgio Armani, John Galliano,** and **Alexander McQueen.** The museum hides in the basement of the Assembly Rooms, which once held *fin-de-siècle* balls and concerts. Today's visitors, dressed somewhat less elegantly, can still take tea. Bombing during WWII ravaged the rooms, but a renovation has duplicated the originals.

In the Assembly Rooms, next to the Royal Crescent and Circus in Bath's Upper Town. Follow Black pedestrian signs. £7, concessions £6.25; joint ticket with the Roman Baths £15/13. Audio tours included. Open daily Mar-Oct 10:30am-6pm; Nov-Feb 10:30am-5pm. Last admission 1hr. before close.

VICTORIA ART GALLERY — GALLERY

Next to Pulteney Bridge ☎1225 477 233 www.victoriagal.org.uk

Bridge St. holds a diverse collections stretching from the 15th century to the present day. Better yet, it's free to enter. Named to commemorate Queen Victoria's 60 years on the throne in 1900—check out the attractive statue of her outside, financed by the admiring women of Bath—it includes sculptures in plaster by Gainsborough, dramatic works by Thomas Barker, probably Bath's most famous painter, and local scenes by Walter Sickert. Rotating exhibits take place on the ground floor.

Free. Open Tu-Sa 10am-5pm, Su 1:30-5pm.

JANE AUSTEN CENTRE — MUSEUM

40 Gay St. ☎01225 443 000 www.janeausten.co.uk.

Jane Austen is one of Bath's most famous residents, though ironically she loathed living here—she found the city to be the leading cause of a five-year period of writers' block, a span of time over which she managed only one attempt at a novel, *The Watsons*, abandonded after 17,000 words. Even though Austen wrote of "happy feelings of escape" when she departed Bath for good in 1806, the city had notable influences on her work and was referenced in many of her novels, partciularly in *Persuasion* and *Northanger Abbey.* The Jane Austen Centre Stands just a few blocks from her former dwellings. Exhibits tell the story of Austen's experiences in Bath, and also explain the atmosphere of Bath during her day. note the Language of the Fan Wall display: a fan that is open, held behind the head means "Do not forget me."

£6, concessions £5. **i** Tours of Bath sights mentioned in Austen's books and her family's homes are also available. *Open July-Aug M-W 9:45am-5:30pm, Th-Su 9:45am-7pm; Nov-Mar M-F and Su 11am-4:30pm, Sa 9:45am-5:30pm. Last entry 50min. before close. Walking tours Sa-Su 11am.*

BUILDING OF BATH MUSEUM — MUSEUM

Countess of Huntingdon's Chapel, the Vineyards ☎01225 338 895 www.bath-preservation-trust.org.uk.

Architecture buffs will fawn over the Building of Bath Museum, which chronicles the story of Bath's legendary Georgian design, and of the people who morphed a sleepy backwater village into an elite Spa/resort town. Even the less aesthetically-inclined can appreciate the effort put into the detailed model of the city—it took 10,000 hours to perfect its layout at a 1:500 scale.

£4, concessions £3.50. Open mid-Feb-Nov Sa-M 10:30am-5pm.

MUSEUM OF EAST ASIAN ART — MUSEUM

12 Bennett St. ☎01225 464 640 www.meaa.org.uk.

This museum might seem a little out of place in white-as-porcelain Bath, but it displays an impressive collection of objects dating back to 5000 BCE, with jade, ceramics, metalwork, and amulets from a wide variety of cultures.

£4, concessions £3.50, families £9. Open Tu-Sa 10am-5pm, Su noon-5pm. Last admission 4:30pm.

AMERICAN MUSEUM — MUSEUM

Claverton Manor ☎01225 460 503 www.americanmuseum.org..

The American Museum is a little piece of the Stars and Stripes in the Motherland. Started by two American citizens in the 1950s (one a psychiatrist, and the other a British-born antiques dealer), it might just be the reason why the Yanks seem to love Bath so much? Check out the extensive collection of American quilts and make sure to take a look aroud hilly grounds, with its river views.

£7.50, concessions £6.50. Grounds admission £5.50/4.50. Open mid-Mar.-Oct. Tu-Su 2-5:30pm. Last admission 5pm. Gardens and tearoom open Tu-Su noon-5:30pm.

FOOD

BATH GUILDHALL MARKET — MARKET

High St. ☎01225 460 808 www.bathguildhallmarket.co.uk

Bath's historic market (dating to the 16th century) boasts a slew of delicious eats, including a cheese shop, an espresso snack bar, a fruits and veggies specialty shop, and the "Bath Humbug" shop featuring a selection of snacks and chocolates. While you're here, check out the market's original 1863 design: the impressive dome, created by Hicks and Isaac, contains intricate floral moldings and high iron framed windows.

High St., between Northgate St. and Grand Parade. Open M-Sa 8am-5:30pm. Individual shop hours may vary.

REGENCY TEA ROOM — TEA ROOM ❷

Jane Austen Centre, 40 Gay St. ☎01225 443 000 www.janeausten.co.uk/tearooms

The best place in town to take authentic afternoon tea is the lovely Georgian townhouse that hosts the Jane Austen Center: the Regency is an acclaimed winner of the Tea Guild's rare Award of Excellence. Unlike the Jane Austen Center's exhibits, however, entrance to the Tea Room is free. *Pride and Prejudice* fans must try the "Tea with Mr. Darcy" *(£11.50)*, which, as high tea, includes cheese and cucumber finger sandwiches, cakes, scones with cream and jam, and a tea of your choice from the 15 varieties of loose-leaf on the menu. If you're looking for a quicker and cheaper option, stop by before 12:30pm for the morning "Tea and Cake" deal *(£4.50)*. As some character or other probably said at some point in every single Jane Austen novel, "You must drink tea with us." Ah, you must.

Enter the Jane Austen center, then head upstairs to the 2nd floor. i 10% off voucher available on website. Sandwiches £5.50. Toasties £6. Cakes £3.75. Teas £2.25-2.75. Open Apr-Oct daily 9:45am-5:30pm, Nov-Mar M-F 11am-4:30pm, Sa 9:45am-5:30pm, Su 11am-4:30pm.

THE EASTERN EYE — INDIAN ❸

8a Quiet St. ☎01225 422 323 www.easterneye.com

Previously a casino, ballroom, and auction house, this polished Georgian building is now the long-time home to an award-winning Indian Restaurant. Check out the intricate murals coloring the walls and the famous three-domed ceilings. Zesty tandoori, meat, poultry, seafood, and vegetarian dishes are available.

Green St. and Wood St. become Quiet St. Entrees £8-17 Open daily noon-2:30pm and 6-11:30pm.

CAFE RETRO — CAFE, TAKEOUT ❷

18 York St. ☎01225 339 347 www.caferetro.co.uk

Retro is housed in an Old Georgian building with large windows that allow patrons to watch the tourist-filled streets. Menu inclues specialty teas, ground coffee, milkshakes, smoothies, organic burgers*(£6.10-7.50)*, and fresh salads.

From train station, left off Pierrepoint. Entrees £6.10-7.50. Open daily 8am-4pm.

SCOFFS SANDWICHES, DELI ❶

9 Terrace Walk ☎01225 471 137

This local sandwich shop sells sandwich creations completely crafted on-site (with the exception of the fresh bread, which comes from a bakery up the street). Grab a fish, veggie, or meat sandwich of choice and a slice of cake and sit outside on the nearby green of Orange Grove or by the River Avon, just a 2min. walk away.

East on York St., toward North Parade. Open M-Sa 8am-5pm, Su 9am-4pm.

BOSTON TEA PARTY CAFE ❷

19 Kingsmead Sq. ☎01225 313 901 www.bostonteaparty.co.uk

Boston Tea Party brews the best coffee in Bath and dishes out meals to acompany it. Pleasant outdoor seating looking over the busy square completes the picture here. Check out the full breakfast menu that features Belgian waffles. Maybe order one for your dog—well-behaved pooches welcome.

Kingsmead Sq. is at the intersection of Avon, Westgate, and Monmouth Streets. i Free Wi-Fi. Salads £5.50-6.50. Burgers £5.25-7.25. Open M-Sa 7:30am-7:30pm, Su 9am-7:30pm.

JAMIE'S ITALIAN ITALIAN ❸

10 Milsom Pl. ☎01225 510 051 www.jamieoliver.com

Celeb chef Jamie Oliver's Bath restaurant is a balanced mix of hip and casual. Considering the chef's famous name, the prices are reasonable, the food is fresh and rich, and the atmosphere is bustling, and unabashadly stylish. Outdoor tables on a balcony have views overlooking Bath's streets and churches. Plus, avid fans can pick up their very own Jamie's oven gloves *(£12)* or apron *(£12)* for purchase. Reservations are recommended on weekends.

Milsom Pl. is off of Milsom St. between George St. and Quiet St. Pasta £6-13.50. Entrees from £10. Open M-Sa noon-11pm, Su noon-10:30pm.

HARVEST ORGANIC ❶

37 Walcot St. ☎01225 465 519 www.harvest-bath.coop

A local and well-established organic food cooperative. Deli sections stock all-local products, and other aisles feature many vegetarian options and yummy and organic sweet snacks. Healthy alternative to the same-old supermarkets.

Next to Bath YMCA. Open M 9am-6pm, Tu 10am-6pm, W-Sa 9am-6pm.

MAI THAI THAI ❷

6 Pierrepont St. ☎01225 445 557 www.maithai.co.uk

Mai Thai's a classy Thai restaurant with impressively affordable meal prices and tasty authentic dishes. The menu is over six pages long, so indicisive eaters beware. At the end of the meal, enjoy the specially-wrapped Mai Thai chocolate that comes with the bill, and pat yourself on the back for the find.

Pierrepont St., between North Parade and Parade. i Takeaway available. Entrees £6-8. Open M-Th noon-2pm and 6-10:30pm, F-Sa noon-2pm and 6-11:30pm, Su noon-2pm and 6-10:30pm.

YAK YETI YAK NEPALESE ❷

12 Pierrepont St. ☎01225 442 299 www.yakyetiyak.co.uk

You might never get to Mt. Everest, but you can get a little taste of Nepal from this unique, authentic restaurant. Head down the steps to the basement venue where local music plays in the background and the owners display a diverse mix of items and decorations picked up from years of travel around the Himalayas, including a pair of boots that reached the summit of Everest. The dishes have a distinct and unusual spice to them, and the prices are very reasonable. If you're feeling like getting into the atmosphere, try the *kukharako thukpa*, the national dish of the Sherpas, and request seating in the side room. Its low-lying tables allow customers to sit and enjoy their meals on floor cushions. There's also a pleasant garden eating area out back.

Next to Bath Backpackers. Underground. Vegetarian options available. Entrees £4.90-8.60. Open M-Sa noon-2:30pm and 5-10:30pm, Su noon-2:30pm and 5-10pm.

RIVERSIDE CAFE CAFE ❷

17 Argyle St. ☎01225 480 532 www.riversidecafebath.co.uk

A dear and charming small riverfront venue with fresh salads, soups, and sandwiches. If all the outdoor tables are taken, check out the takeout menu and grab a sandwich to-go for a pleasant picnic lunch at the nearby riverside park.

Below Puteney Bridge. Takeaway available from separate menu. Entrees £5-10. Open M-F 8am-7pm, Sa-Su 9am-7pm.

NIGHTLIFE

Bath might not be known as the nightlife capital of England, but a steady influx of tourists, young and old alike, brings a reliable stream of revenue to the city's pubs, bars, and clubs. Meanwhile, two universities help bring some needed youthful vigor to this ancient town. After 11pm, most of the older tourists go back to the hotels to sleep and the tamer pubs close down, but the younger segments of the population keep the late-night clubs rocking until 2am and later on weekends. Almost all clubs charge covers, so party-seekers should be prepared to shell out a fiver to keep their night going. **George Street** is a major nightlife thoroughfare. To get there, take Broad St. (from High St.) or Milsom St.

THE PORTER PUB, BAR, MUSIC VENUE

15 George St. ☎01225 424 104 www.theporter.co.uk

The Porter is a comfortable, all-vegetarian pub and bar that also plays host to live music gigs Monday through Thursday in their dark and mysterious downstairs cellar. The upstairs is much brighter and airier, but no less popular, with young and old alike coming in for good tunes, a mellow vibe, and tasty fare. Sunday nights are popular comedy nights starting at 8pm *(£5 for students if you purchase in advance).*

From the direction of the train station, George St. is a left off of Broad St. Cover free-£7 on comedy nights. Open M-Th 11am-midnight, F-Sa 11am-1am, Su 11am-11:30pm. Kitchen open 11am-9pm.

THE PIG AND THE FIDDLE PUB

2 Saracen St. ☎01225 460 868 www.thepigandfiddle.co.uk

This stone-faced, classic pub is well-frequented for its massive streetside (and heated!) beer garden, lively atmosphere, and meal deals—like a full hearty English meal plus a pint of beer or glass of wine *(£6).* The intimate all-wooden interior is often filled with backpackers and local students alike. Mondays at 8pm are quiz nights; Tuesdays at 8pm are open-mike nights.

Off Broad St. Free Wi-Fi. Credit cards accepted for food only. Meals £4.50-6.95. Pints from £2.60. Open M-Th 11am-11:30pm, F-Sa 11am-midnight, Su noon-10:30pm. Kitchen open M-F 11am-6:30pm, Sa 11:30am-6pm, Su noon-6pm. Happy hr. M-F 3-7pm.

BACK TO MINE! BAR, CLUB

7 Bladud Buildings ☎01225 425 677 www.backtomine.co.uk

Bath's younger residents flock to this chilled-out club to listen to a mix of DJs and live music. The combination of colored lights and wooden fixtures make it feel like a pimped-out forest hut. Can anyone say cabin fever? Best seat in the house is the table in the middle. Steps lead down from it on all sides, and you'll be the highlight of everyone's attention.

Roman Rd. Free entry M-Th. F-Sa free before 11pm, £5 11pm-1am, £3 after 1am. Mixed drinks £6-7.50. Open daily 10pm-2am.

COEUR DE LION PUB

27 Northumberland Pl. ☎01225 333 639

Bath's self-proclaimed smallest pub is hidden off an alley in a corner. However, it takes advantage of its pocket-sized interior nicely, outfitting it with snug, red-velvet-covered wooden booths, and mirrors that make the room look bigger, to create a cozy atmosphere. Try a pint of Abbey Ales' Bellringers *(£3)*—this is one of Bath's only locally brewed beer brands.

Open M-Th 10:30am-11pm, F-Sa 10:30am-late. Kitchen open M-Th 10:30am-3pm and 5:30-8:30pm, F-Sa 10:30am-5pm.

ADVENTURE CAFE BAR BAR

5 Princes Building, George St. ☎01225 462 038

During the day, this is a sophisticated, civilized cafe, but at night, blasting music and cocktails bring out the wild sides in their young clientele. It's a good place to pre-game before heading to a club, especially in the relaxed outdoor seating area.

6-9pm pizza £6. Open daily 8am-midnight. Kitchen open until 9pm.

MOLES MUSIC CLUB

14 George St. ☎01225 404 445 www.moles.co.uk

This cavern-like underground club is filled up with young indie Bath students. "Cheese nights" are Tuesday nights featuring fittingly "cheesy" music, while Thursday nights are indie nights with live music, but sounds ranging from house to funk to soul can be heard from the speakers on a given night. Its restaurant and independent record shop are located upstairs, and there's happy hour at the bar from 10pm to midnight on weekends.

Cover £4-8. Open M-Th 9pm-2am, F-Sa 9pm-4am, Su 11:30am-midnight. Restaurant open 11am-9pm.

THE SALAMANDER PUB

3 John St. ☎01225 334 617 www.bathales.com

Classy and simple with wooden, paneled walls that give the place a boat house feel, The Salamander used to be "steak and chop house." Today, it's still very popular for Sunday roasts, and for its local Bath ales.

Off Queen Sq. Open M-Th 10am-11pm, F-Sa 10am-midnight, Su 10am-11pm. Kitchen open M-Th 10am-3pm and 6:30-9pm, F-Sa 10am-3pm and 6:30-9:30pm, Su 10am-3pm and 6:30-9pm.

THE BELL BAR

103 Walcot St. ☎01225 460 426 www.walcotstreet.com

The Bell is one of the best beer gardens in town combined. With nine quality ales *(£2.70-3.20)* and an eclectic mix of music that plays on Monday and Wednesday evenings and Sundays at lunchtime, it's pretty hippy-ish, but the staff's not abashed and you shouldn't be either. The Bell has DJs on Saturday night, but don't worry, only vinyl is allowed. Check out the bar billiards table in the back.

Free Wi-Fi. Free. Open M-Sa 11:30am-11pm, Su noon-10:30pm.

MANDAYLNS GLBT, BAR

13 Fountain Buildings, Landsown Rd. ☎01225 425 403 www.mandalyns.com

Bath's most popular gay pub. Average drinks and a leopard-print sofa are spiced up by weekly karaoke nights *(Th and Su)*, quiz nights *(Tu, with drag queens)*, and cocktail nights *(F)*.

Just past the intersection with George St., on the left. Credit card min. £10. Open Tu-W 6pm-midnight, Th-Sa 6pm-2am, Su 6pm-1am.

ARTS AND CULTURE

Theater

LITTLE THEATER CINEMA ST. MICHAEL'S PLACE

St. Michael's Pl. ☎ 330 817 www.picturehouses.co.uk

This local theater has two screens showing art house films and recorded operas.

Take a break from sightseeing and relax in this building which is owned by the same Bath family that opened the cinema in 1936.

Corner of St. Michael's Pl. and Bath St. Tickets £7.50, concessions £6.50. £1.50 fee for online and phone bookings. Box office open 15min. before 1st curtain, closes 15min. after last curtain. Generally M-Th 9:30am-11:15pm, F-Sa 12:30-11:30pm, Su 9:30am-11:15pm.

Comedy

KOMEDIA — CITY CENTER

22-23 Westgate St. ☎0845 293 8480 www.komedia.co.uk/e

Bath's new comedy club features a large stage and modern technology with classic architecture. Also features music, cabaret, club nights, and even sports matches on the big screen. Book in advance by phone, online, or in person.

Balcony seats £10, downstairs £15, lower level including food £26.50. Sa nights are most expensive. Student discounts available. Box office open F-Sa 11am-5pm.

Classical Music

THEATRE ROYAL — CITY CENTER

Sawclose ☎01225 448 844 www.theatreroyal.org.uk

This highly vaunted theater sees pre-West End tours come to Bath as well as dramas, music performances, operas, and classical music.

i Standby tickets available in person starting at noon. £6 for specific areas in the theater. Tickets £15-35. Student concessions available M-Th evening shows and Sa matinees; usually £1 off. Box office open M-Sa 10am-8pm, Su noon-8pm.

Festivals

BATH INTERNATIONAL MUSIC FESTIVAL — CITY CENTER

☎01225 462 231 www.bathmusicfest.org.uk

Since 1948, this two-week-long festival has brought world-class symphony orchestras, chamber ensembles, classical music, contemporary jazz, and more to Bath. Performances generally take place in city venues, though the festival also includes an outdoor event that is free to the public.

May-June.

SHOPPING

Books

MR. B'S EMPORIUM — CITY CENTER

14-15 John St. ☎01225 331 155 www.mrbsemporium.com

Mr. B. knows best. He'll give you top-notch recommendations through his specially set-aside "Delightful Lists of Good Reads" and through the individual commentary posted on the shelf next to selected novels. And whoever said you can't buy peace and quiet? If hostel-living has made you desperately crave some "me" time, test out Mr. B's Sumptuous Reading Booth: you'll receive 30min. of serenity and tranquillity in your own cozy armchair closed off from the main room, a cup of tea, and cookies *(£3.50)*. If you don't feel like shelling out a few pounds, then try the bathroom instead—covered from floor to ceiling with articles, poems, and covers of the London Review of Books.

Behind Jolly's, opposite the "Salamander" pub. Open M-Sa 9:30am-6:30pm.

TOPPING AND COMPANY BOOKSELLERS OF BATH — NORTH OF CITY CENTER

The Paragon ☎428111 www.toppingbooks.co.uk

One of Bath's most well-known independent booksellers hosts multiple events a week with featured authors. A knowledgable staff helps give an personal touch to the endless rows of books, and a sizable travel section could be helpful for the wandering souls (but what else could you need besides your copy of *Let's Go?*).

Near intersection of George St. and Roman Rd. Open daily 9am-8pm.

Souvenirs

THE GLASSHOUSE CITY CENTER

1-2 Orange Grove ☎01225 463 436 www.bathaquaglass.com

Glassy is classy. A unique Bath souveneir can be found in the beautiful craftsmanship of this store's glasswork. All the pieces—jewelry, panels, blown glass, mirrors, hangings—were handmade in local bath factories. Glassblowing demonstrations are also available at the company's "Theatre of Glass," *(☎01225 428 146)* on 105-107 Walcot St., which offers interactive presentations Monday through Sunday at 11:15am and 2:15pm *(£4, concessions £2.50)* and production viewing at 10:15am, 12:15pm, , 3:15pm, and 4pm *(£2, concessions £1).*

Orange Grove. Open M-Sa 9:30am-6pm, Su noon-6pm.

ESSENTIALS

Practicalities

- **TOURIST OFFICES:** The TIC is at Abbey Chambers, Abbey Yard. Town maps and mini-guide are for sale for £1. Use of books rooms is free with a 10% deposit.*(☎0906 711 2000 ☎0870 420 1278 for accommodation bookings. www.visitbath.co.uk. Open June-Sept M-Sa 9:30am-6pm, Su 10am-4pm, Oct-May M-Sa 9:30am-5pm, Su 10am-4pm.)*
- **TOURS:** Several companies run tours with diverse themes to introduce tourists to the city. **Bizarre Bath** tours leave from Huntsman Inn, North Parade Passage.This isn't your most accurate history lesson, but the guides will keep you smirking with their tricks and ad-libbing as they poke fun at their own city. *(☎01225 335 124 www.bizarrebath.co.uk £8, concessions £5. Nightly 90min. tours leave at 8pm.)* **Ghost Walks of Bath** tours leave from Garrick's Head Public House, next to Theatre Royal. Bath's paranormal past comes to life on these walking tours. *(☎01225 461 888 www.ghostwalksofbath.co.uk £7, concessions £5. 90min. tours Th, F, and Sa at 8pm.)* **Jane Austen's Bath** tours, in coordination with the Jane Austen Centre, walk you through the author's hometown. *(40 Gay St. ☎01225 448 206 www.janeausten.co.uk £7, concessions £5. 90min. tours July-Aug leave every F at 4pm, Sa at 11am and 4pm, Su at 11am.)* **Mayor of Bath** tours leave from outside the Pump Room in Abbey's Church Yard. The volunteer guides impart details about Bath's history and architecture. *(☎01225 448 206 www.janeausten.co.uk Free. 2hr. tours May-Sept Tu 7pm; F 10:30am, 2, 7pm; Sa 10:30am; Su 10:30am, 2pm. Oct-Apr F 10:30am, 2pm; Sa 10:30am; Su 10:30am, 2pm.)*
- **LAUNDRY:** **Spruce Goose**, Margaret's Building off Brock St. *(☎01225 483 309 Open M-Sa 8am-9pm, Su 8am-8pm. Last wash 1hr. before close.)*
- **BANKS:** **Barclays** on Manvers St. *(Intersection with Henry St. Open M-F 9:30am-4:30pm.)*
- **INTERNET:** Free Wi-Fi at **Central Library** and throughout the Podium Shopping Center. You can also get access at **Internet Cafe.** *(13 Manvers St. ☎01225 312 685 £1 per 20min. Open daily 9am-9pm.)*
- **POST OFFICES:** Visit 27 Northgate St. *(☎08457 223 344 Open M 9am-5:30pm, Tu 9:30am-5:30pm, W-Sa 9am-5:30pm.)*
- **POSTAL CODE:** BA1 1AJ.

Emergency!

- **PHARMACY:** **Boots** in Southgate Shopping Centre. *(New Marchant Passage. Open M-Sa 8am-7pm, Su 11am-5pm.)*

- **HOSPITAL: Royal United** at Coombe Park in Weston. *(Take bus #14 ☎01225 428 331).* For Non-emergencies, visit the **NHS Walk-In Centre** in Riverside Health Centre. *(James St. ☎01225 478 811 ⏰ Open daily 8am-8pm.)*

Getting There

By Bus

Bus Station has **National Express** buses going to **London** *(Ⓢ £19.70. ⏰ 3hr., every 2hr.)* and **Oxford** *(Ⓢ £10.60. ⏰ 2hr., 1 per day).* National Express bus #X39 runs to **Bristol.** *(Ⓢ £4.70,. ⏰ M-Sa every 15min.)* The ticket office is open Monday-Saturday 9am-5pm.

By Train

Trains run from **Bath Spa Station** on Manvers Street to **Cardiff** *(Ⓢ£16. ⏰ 1hr. 10min., 2 per hr.)*; **Bristol** *(Ⓢ £5.80. ⏰ 20min., every 10-15min.)*; **London Paddington** *(Ⓢ £34, ⏰ 2½hr., 1-2 per day.)*; **Chippenham** *(Ⓢ £4.40. ⏰ 10min., 2 per hr.)*; **Birmingham** *(Ⓢ £94. ⏰ 2hr., 2 per hr.)*; **Salisbury** *(Ⓢ £13.80,. ⏰ 1hr., 1-2 per hr.)*; and **Oxford** *(Ⓢ £16.50. ⏰ 1½hr., every hr. with change at Didcot Parkway).* Buy at the ticket office *(⏰ Open M-F 5:30am-8:30pm, Sa 6am-8:30pm, and Su 7:30am-8:30pm. Advance tickets M-F 8am-7pm, Sa 9am-6pm, and Su 9:30am-6pm.)*

Getting Around

Part of what makes Bath so charming is its old-school compact layout; the city is easily navigated by foot, as the Victorians and Edwardians did before you. But lazy butts, fear not—other transport options *are* available.

By Bus

First buses *(☎0871 200 2233)* run throughout the city and to the surrounding areas. Day Passes *(Ⓢ £4.30 peak, £4 off-peak)* are available for purchase on the bus for unlimited travel within Bath. **FirstDay South West** passes *(Ⓢ £7.10)* cover a full day of travel within the region. Single fares vary depending on the distance traveled. Most buses depart from **Bath Bus Station** *(Churchill Bridge. ⏰ Office open M-Sa 9am-5pm.)*

By Taxi

For a taxi call **Abbey Radio** *(☎01225 444 444)* or **V Cars** *(☎01225 464 646).* There's also a taxi stand outside of Bath Spa Station.

Getting to Stonehenge

There is no public transportation that runs from Bath to **Stonehenge National Heritage Site** *(☎01722 343 834 🖥www.english-heritage.org.uk/stonehenge Ⓢ £6.90, £5.90 concessions. Price includes a guided audio tour. ⏰ Open daily June-Aug 9am-7pm; Sept-Oct 9:30am-6pm; Oct-Mar 9:30am-4pm; Mar-May 9:30am-6pm.)* The vast majority of visitors who decide to make a Stonehenge stop to take one of the tour companies from in town. They run every day of the year and prices include full transport to and from the site, along with guides and commentary. Generally, though, prices do not include the cost of entering the actual site.

MAD MAX TOURS

Leave Glass Shop, Orange Grove, behind Bath Abbey ☎07990 505 970 🖥www.madmaxtours.co.uk

Afternoon tours stop at Stonehenge and Lacock National Trust Village, a quaint old village mantained to historic image, home of **Harry Potter's** parents and Professor Slughorn's house, among others. Full-day tours include stops at Lacock Vilage, Avebury Stone Circles, and the Cotswold village of Castle Combe, voted prettiest village in England.

i Leave from outside the Glass Shop, Orange Grove, behind Bath Abbey. Ⓢ £15. ⏰ 4hr. tours depart at 1:15pm; full-day tours depart at 8:45am.

SCARPER TOURS

Leave Glass Shop, Orange Grove, behind Bath Abbey ☎07990 644 155 www.scarpertours.com

Head to Stonehenge on Scarper Tours' purple mini-buses.

i Leave from outside the Glass Shop, Orange Grove, behind Bath Abbey. Book tours in advance, especially during the summer as they will often fill up with eager international tourists. $ £14. 3hr. tours daily June-Aug 9:30am; Mar-June and Sept-Oct 10am, 2, and 4:30pm; Oct-Mar 1pm.

brighton ☎01273

Brighton (pop. 250,000) is one of Britain's largest seaside resorts. **King George IV** came to Brighton in 1783 and enjoyed the anything-goes atmosphere so much that he transformed a farmhouse into **The Royal Pavilion,** his headquarters for debauchery, in a historical move roughly equivalent to an episode of "MTV Cribs." A regal rumpus ensued. Since then, Brighton continues to turn a blind eye to some of the more scandalous activities that occur along its shores as holidaymakers and locals alike peel it off—all off—at one of the more popular beaches in England (fist-size rocks aside). **Kemp Town** has a thriving gay and lesbian population as well as a profusion of bed and breakfasts. The huge student crowd and flocks of foreign youth feed the notorious clubbing scene of this "London-by-the-Sea," the history of which, thanks to the teenage Mods and Rockers of the 1960s, is centered predominantly on sex, drugs, and rock and roll. Perhaps it's time you added to that tradition. And Brighton-bound tourists better be fans of The Who's *Quadrophenia*—both the rock opera and the gem of a film.

ORIENTATION

Brighton is on the southeast coast of England with **Hove** to the west and **Kemp Town** to the east. **Queen's Road** runs straight down the middle of it, from the train station at the top of the hill to the waterfront at the bottom. Kemp Town is the gay district of the nightlife scene, and it also hosts many upscale guest houses. **Marlborough Place, Gloucester Place, Grand Parade,** and **Old Steine** run north from the pier through town and can be used as main access roads to the middle of town. The **Lanes** can be accessed from **Prince Albert Street. North Road** is sort of like a main street, boasting many banks, and providing access to the Lanes.

ACCOMMODATIONS

BAGGIES BACK-PACKERS — HOSTEL ❶

33 Oriental Pl. ☎01273 733 740 www.baggiesbackpackers.co.uk

Baggies is, quite simply, one of the best hostels in England. From its cobbled-together but clean rooms to the comforters that everyone gets (some of which are race-car-patterned) to the two acoustic guitars that provide a quieter alternative to the speaker system that resides in the music room. Plus, the kitchen serves complimentary tea and coffee 24hr.

Go down King's Rd. with the water on your left and turn right onto Oriental Pl. i Free towels and linens at the start of your stay. Laundry wash £1, dry £0.40. $ Dorms £12; family rooms £13. Weekly dorms £77. Reception 9am-9pm.

KIPPS — HOSTEL ❷

76 Grand Parade ☎01273 604 182 www.kipps-brighton.com

With a maximum capacity of only 40, Kipps nurtures community. Between the beautifully furnished common room, which is equipped with acoustic guitars, Wii games, and a small but pleasant terrace, Kipps is an unexpectedly upscale living experience for the price.

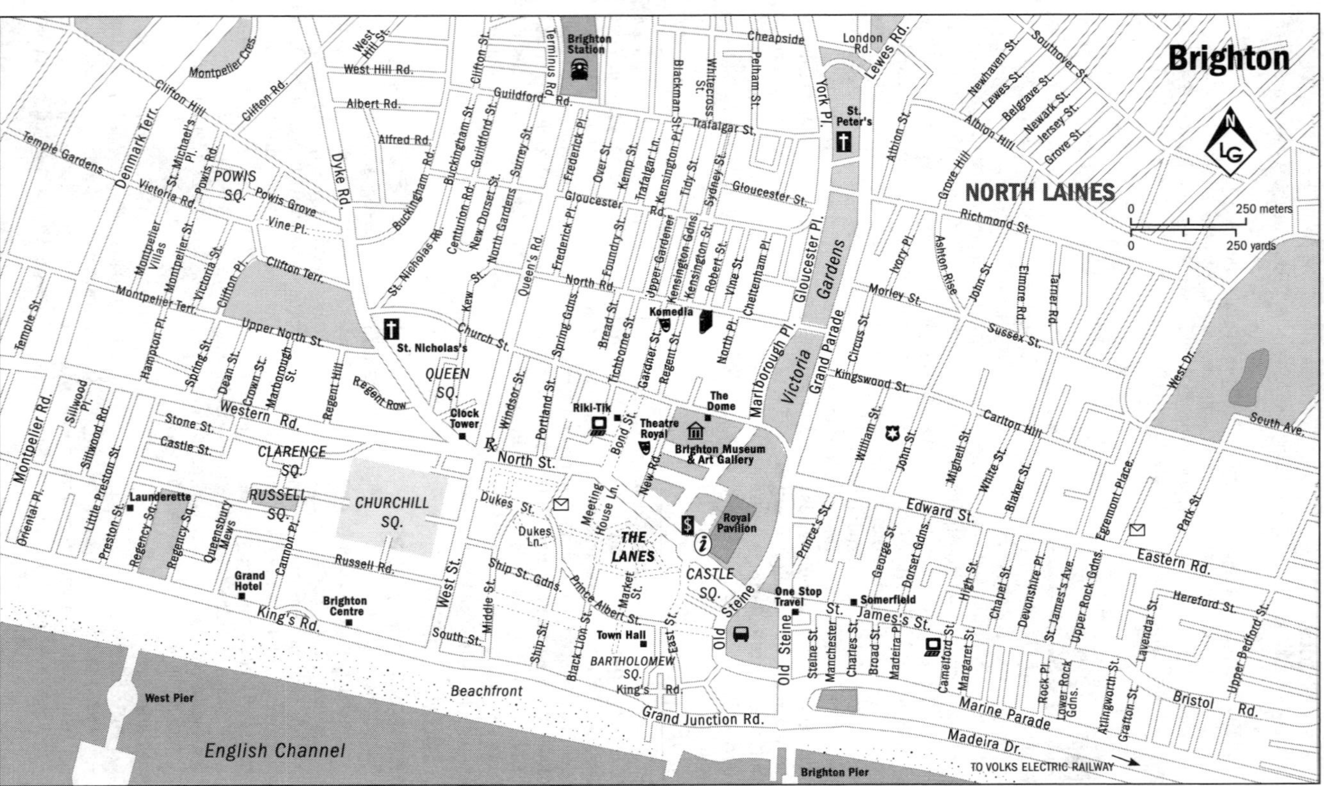
Brighton
0
250 meters
250 yards
NORTH LAINES
THE LANES
CASTLE SQ.
QUEEN SQ.
CHURCHILL SQ.
CLARENCE SQ.
RUSSELL SQ.
POWIS SQ.
BARTHOLOMEW SQ.
English Channel
Beachfront
Brighton Pier
West Pier
TO VOLKS ELECTRIC RAILWAY
Brighton Station
St. Peter's
St. Nicholas's
Clock Tower
Royal Pavilion
Brighton Museum & Art Gallery
The Dome
Theatre Royal
Komedia
Riki-Tik
Town Hall
One Stop Travel
Somerfield
Brighton Centre
Grand Hotel
Launderette
Victoria Gardens
Grand Parade
Marlborough Pl.
Gloucester Pl.
York Pl.
London Rd.
Lewes Rd.
Cheapside
Pelham St.
Whitecross St.
Blackman St.
Trafalgar St.
Gloucester St.
Gloucester Rd.
Terminus Rd.
Guildford Rd.
Clifton St.
Guildford St.
Buckingham St.
Buckingham Rd.
Alfred Rd.
Albert Rd.
West Hill Rd.
West Hill St.
Dyke Rd.
Clifton Rd.
Montpelier Cres.
Clifton Hill
Denmark Terr.
Temple Gardens
Victoria Rd.
St. Michael's Pl.
Powis Rd.
Powis Grove
Vine Pl.
Clifton Terr.
Upper North St.
Clifton Pl.
Victoria St.
Montpelier St.
Montpelier Terr.
Montpelier Villas
Hampton Pl.
Spring St.
Dean St.
Crown St.
Marlborough St.
Regent Hill
Regent Row
Western Rd.
Stone St.
Castle St.
Sillwood Pl.
Sillwood Rd.
Montpelier Rd.
Temple St.
Oriental Pl.
Little Preston St.
Preston St.
Regency Sq.
Queensbury Mews
Cannon Pl.
King's Rd.
Russell Rd.
West St.
South St.
Middle St.
Ship St.
Ship St. Gdns.
Dukes St.
Dukes Ln.
Meeting House Ln.
Black Lion St.
Prince Albert St.
Market St.
King's Rd.
East St.
Grand Junction Rd.
Old Steine
Steine St.
Manchester St.
Charles St.
Broad St.
Madeira Pl.
Camelford St.
Margaret St.
Marine Parade
Madeira Dr.
Rock Pl.
Lower Rock Gdns.
Grafton St.
Attingworth St.
Lavendar St.
Hereford St.
Bristol Rd.
Upper Bedford St.
Eastern Rd.
Park St.
Egremont Place
Upper Rock Gdns.
St. James's Ave.
Devonshire Pl.
Chapel St.
High St.
Dorset Gdns.
George St.
St. James's St.
Edward St.
Prince's St.
William St.
John St.
Mighell St.
White St.
Blaker St.
Carlton Hill
Kingswood St.
Circus St.
Morley St.
Ivory Pl.
Ashton Rise
Sussex St.
Richmond St.
Tarner Rd.
Elmore Rd.
West Dr.
South Ave.
Albion St.
Grove Hill
Albion Hill
Newhaven St.
Lewes St.
Belgrave St.
Newark St.
Jersey St.
Grove St.
Southover St.
Church St.
New Rd.
North St.
Bond St.
Gardner St.
Regent St.
Tichborne St.
Bread St.
Spring Gdns.
Portland St.
Windsor St.
Queen's Rd.
North Rd.
Foundry St.
Frederick Pl.
Frederick St.
Surrey St.
North Gardens
New Dorset St.
Centurion Rd.
St. Nicholas Rd.
Kew St.
Over St.
Kemp St.
Trafalgar Ln.
Kensington Pl.
Upper Gardener St.
Tidy St.
Kensington Gdns.
Kensington St.
Sydney St.
Robert St.
Vine St.
North Pl.
Cheltenham Pl.

Go up Old Steine with the water at your back and keep right at the fork. i Most rooms have ensuite bath. Laundry £5. Dorms M-F £17.50, Sa-Su £22.50. Reception open 8:30am-11pm. Breakfast 8:30-10:30am.

roughin' it

As I sat in my hostel in Brighton, trying to book my stay for the next three days in Canterbury, I berated myself for not realizing that everywhere under 60 pounds a night would be booked full.

When I called my fifth hostel, things began looking up.

"Yeah! We have a bed!" chirped a cheery receptionist.

Immediately I relaxed, having the knowledge that I'd have a place to sleep for one more night.

"...and the tent's just in the backyard." She finished.

"Oh, cool! Is that where dinner is or something?" I asked, enthralled by the idea of eating outside with a bunch of people my own age.

"No, sorry—the accommodation, your bed, is in the tent."

"Excuse me?"

And she slowly explained once again how there were no beds left, but that they had tents in the backyard, one of which would house me for the night.

I arrived the next day and proceeded to check in. This was difficult for a number of reasons, the first being that I had a computer and several valuable objects that I didn't want lying in the backyard all night. Grumpily, I signed the papers, trying to indicate with my eyebrows the extent of my frustration. She thanked me cheerfully once again.

I turned to go and she called me back, "Wait a minute!" There was a rustling under the counter and she slammed a lantern down on the desk. "You'll need this."

"Thanks," I muttered and began trekking out to the tent.

A few things about the tent: 1) Yesterday was, supposedly, the hottest day of the year in Canterbury. 2) The "gate" to the tent area did not close. 3) The blankets were, I think, mattress pads.

So it was that I passed a night clutching my backpack to my chest, sleeping fully clothed in someone's backyard. I woke up a bit after the sun rose, removed the four mattress pads I had piled on top of myself, and checked out of the hostel, a well-rested man.

Benjamin Naddaff-Hafrey

SEADRAGON BACKPACKERS HOSTEL ❶

36 Waterloo St. ☎01273 711 854 www.seadragonbackpackers.co.uk

Located just off the waterfront, Seadragon Backpackers is a small, clean, and pleasant hostel. There are two rooms per floor with a bathroom on each floor, and no room has more than four beds. This makes for a more personal, less oppressive experience than some hostels offer.

Go down the King's Rd away from Brighton Pier with the water on your left and turn right onto Waterloo St. i Towels and fresh linen included whenever you want. Dorms £15-35. Weekly £105. Reception M-Th 10am-2pm and 4-6pm, F 6-10pm, Sa-Su 10am-2pm and 4-6pm.

HOTEL PELIROCCO

HOTEL ❸

10 Regency Sq. ☎01273 327 055 www.hotelpelirocco.co.uk

This themed hotel, one-time host of the Beastie Boys is perfect for wannabe rockstars. Equipped with many awesome rooms with gimmicks and a logo designed by Jamie Reid, the artist responsible for the Sex Pistols' art, and one of the later check-out times in town (just in case you were burning the night oil), the Hotel Pelirocco is the perfect place to crash.

Head down King's Rd. with the water on your left and turn right onto Regency Sq. Breakfast included. Rooms M-F £50-230, Sa-Su £60-250. Reception 24hr. Breakfast M-Th 8-10am, F-Sa 9-11am, Su 8-10am.

AMBASSADOR

BED AND BREAKFAST ❸

22-23 New Steine ☎01273 676 869 www.ambassadorbrighton.co.uk

This upscale bed and breakfast offers four-star comfort at three-star prices. The breakfast features a vegan option and comprises mainly local and organic produce. Wi-Fi is free and the location is prime.

Head away from Brighton Pier with the water on your right and turn left onto New Steine. Singles M-F £55-65, Sa-Su £65-75; doubles £89-109/98-125; triples £105-120/141-156. Reception 24hr.

JOURNEYS

HOSTEL ❷

33 Richmond Pl. ☎01273 695 866 www.visitjourneys.com

Journeys is a clean and standard hostel located close to the heart of Brighton. Though the three-bed bunks may give it less of a homey feel than some other hostels in the area, the rooms are clean, as are the bathrooms—one of them even has a poster of The Who's *Quadrophenia* in it. Though the rooms fit a lot of people, the beds have small curtains that yield some privacy.

Head up Grand Parade with the water at your back. Laundry wash £1, dry £1. Shared bathrooms. 18-bed dorms £15; 12-bed dorms £17; 6-bed dorms £18. Private rooms £30. Reception 24hr. Breakfast M-Th 8-10am, F-Su 8-11am.

AMHERST BRIGHTON

BED AND BREAKFAST ❹

2 Lower Rock Gardens ☎01273 670 131 www.amhersthotel.co.uk

One of the nicer small guesthouses in Brighton (which is saying something), the Amherst Brighton offers easy class and beautiful rooms in a building built in the Regency style popular throughout Brighton.

Walk away from Brighton Pier with the water on your right and turn left onto Lower Rock Gardens. Continental breakfast included. Doubles M-F £79, Sa-Su £105. Call 9am-9pm.

CHRISTINA'S GUEST HOUSE

BED AND BREAKFAST ❸

20 St. George's Terr. ☎01273 690 862 www.christinaguesthousebrighton.co.uk

This small guesthouse is located close to the action in Kemp Town. Some of the rooms share bathrooms.

Head down St. James's St. and contine onto Bristol. Turn left at St. George's Terr. Singles £35-40; small doubles £55, with bath £70. Reception 10am-10pm. Breakfast 8-9:30am.

SIGHTS

THE ROYAL PAVILION

HISTORIC SITE

Pavilion Buildings ☎01273 290 900 www.royalpavilion.org.uk

Built in 1787, the Royal Pavilion is a bit strange for Brighton. It is neither kitschy and flashy like the Brighton Pier, nor is it tiny and ramshackle like the lanes. It is, instead, a glimpse of the Far East. The Prince of Wales asked Henry Holland to design it in the style of the Regency period, which is why the interiors of this holiday home are mostly Chinese-influenced. He later hired John Nash to enlarge it around Indian architecture. It is notable for its history as a military hospital for Indian troops between 1914 and 1916. The audio tours, available in English,

French, German, Spanish, Italian, Mandarin, Cantonese, and child-level English, are well worth their free cost, as there is little text throughout the sight—making the average visit feel a little like you're breaking into someone's summer home. (And we all know how that feels.) Especially of note are the fantastic organ of the music room, the horrible, gaudy statues of Asian men in the entry hall, and the banqueting room's elegant **dragon** chandelier.

Left off Old Steine with your back to the water. £9.50, concessions £7.50, ages 5-15 £5.40. Official Guide in English, French, and German £6. Open daily Apr-Sept 9:30am-5:45pm; Oct-Mar 10am-5:15pm. Last entry 45min. before close.

BRIGHTON MUSEUM AND ART GALLERY MUSEUM

Royal Pavilion Gardens www.brighton-hove-museums.org.uk

The Brighton Museums and Art Gallery features many movements from contemporary art to present, highlighting things like Aestheticism and Surrealism, most notably in the form of Salvador Dali's *Mae West's Lips*, which is a sofa. Art from around the world is shown, including textiles from Japan. A tribute to Egyptologist and Brightonian Francis Llewellyn Griffith is found in the Egyptian gallery, which hosts a few mummies. The Brighton Museum follows some of the more salient details in Brighton's history, helpfully explicating the phrase "dirty weekend" and showing a real Lambretta Li 150 from 1962, the type of scooter the Mods used to ride.

In the heart of the city center within the Royal Pavilion estate. Free. Special exhibitions are generally around £5. Open T-Su 10am-5pm. Last entry 45min. before close.

BRIGHTON BEACHES BEACHES

No "dirty weekend" in Brighton would be complete without a trip to the handful of beaches. Brighton's nude beach in particular is surrounded by a mound of gravel and marked by a green sign. It's about 20 minutes from the pier towards the marina. Pro: you won't find sand clinging to your clothes. Con: there are fist-size rocks everywhere—which you may trip over, while being distracted by the larger-than-fist-size attractions.

Many concentrated around Madeira Dr. From the dawn of time until it eventually erodes.

BRIGHTON PIER ATTRACTION

Waterfront

Brighton Pier imports a bit of sleazy seaside kitsch to the Brighton seaside, lighting the night away with its famous sign and making people wince during the day with its disco balls and terrifying music choice. The pier is gimmicky, loud, flashing, and bright and is a must-see for any visitor to Brighton. Between the arcade, the rides, and the various restaurants, there's a lot to do on the pier that may or may not be worth it, but you should at least see it.

Rides £1-2. Pier open daily 10am. Palace of Fun open M-F 10am-10pm, Sa-Su 10am-11pm. Dome open M-F 11am-7pm, Sa-Su 10am-9pm. Rides open M-F noon-7pm, Sa-Su 11am-10pm.

THE LA(I)NES HISTORIC SITE

Sandwiched between Prince Albert St., North St., and East St., the Lanes are one of the more historic areas in Brighton. In the 17th century, the area was home to most of the fishermen, whose cottages thronged the twisting and turning lanes, some of which are a mere 3 ft. wide. Now, quirky boutiques, cafes, and fun independent shops sell items well out of any 17th-century fisherman's price range. North of the Lanes, the North Laines provide a fresh take on shopping too, as well as ample opportunities to get lost. Fans of *Quadrophenia* should look out for the alley of the same name!

VOLKS ELECTRIC RAILWAY RAILWAY

285 Madeira Dr. ☎01273 292 718 www.volkselectricrailway.co.uk

The world's oldest operating electric railway, the Volks Electric Railway was invented by Magnus Volk and built in 1883. Providing transport from Aquarium Station by the pier toward the marina, the Volks Railway is actually a viable mode of transportation, since that walk is rather long. Trains run every 15 minutes. *£1.80, round-trip £2.80; child £0.90/1.40. Open Apr 11-Sept 30 M-F 10am-5pm, Sa-Su 10am-6pm.*

FOOD

Though greasy-spoon burgers and fish and chips places abound, Brighton is chock-full of fantastic cafes and specialty restaurants that serve up healthy, classic food at great prices. Try the Lanes and North Laines for some of the more offbeat, upscale cafes. If you want greasy fish and chips and the like, the waterfront is the place for you.

TIC TOC — FRENCH ❷

53 Meeting House Ln. ☎01273 770 115 www.tictoc-cafe.co.uk

Written across the front of this cafe tucked away on the outskirts of the winding Lanes is the following quote: "*Probablement* the best coffee in Brighton—Napoleon Bonaparte." Now, we haven't checked the historical accuracy of this attribution, but its claim is good. Tic Toc is one of the best cafes in Brighton, with delicious sandwiches ranging from warm BLTs *(£5)* to chicken, peanut butter, red pepper, and chili on toasted chunky bread *(£4.20)*. Inventive smoothies like melon, watermelon, and mint are best sipped at the old, sunbathed tables with flowers bowing out of soft-drink bottles. The outdoor seating also gives an excellent vantage point from which to watch confused tourists stumble out of the Lanes looking as if they came from the heart of the jungle.

Walk down Prince Albert St. with the water on your left and turn right onto Meeting House Ln. Sandwiches around £5. Open M-F 7:30am-6:30pm, Sa 10am-6pm, Su 10am-4pm.

crash landing

Brighton used to be one of the more prominent fishing villages in England. The fishermen used to live in tiny cottages in an area now populated with boutiques, where the price of the average product is more than a fisherman would make in a lifetime. The area is called the Lanes and North Laines, and some of the streets are a mere three-feet wide.

I was eating in a cafe in the Lanes, enjoying the feeling of claustrophobic isolation. An Australian man was explaining to his companion the history of the Lanes when suddenly a shadow grew over us.

There was a loud squawk and then a large seagull ran straight into the man's back, causing him to emit a loud "Crikey!" The seagull spun out, shook itself, and, realizing there wasn't enough space to take off, began a mad dash towards the end of the lane. When it was just a few feet away, it spread it's wings and took off into an old woman. Recovering once again, it flew away, and everyone went back about their business, trying to forget the absurdity of what had just happened.

Benjamin Naddaff-Hafrey

CLOUD 9 — BAKERY GELATO ❸

15 Brighton Pl. ☎01273 723 020 www.cloud9brighton.co.uk

Though it's hidden among the Lanes, it's hard to miss the flaming pink facade and tables of this bakery. The gelato meets typical British pricing standards, but excels in two ways: first, this is some of the best gelato you will ever have, and second, two scoops is more ice cream than should ever be ingested in one sitting. Try the coconut with Belgian chocolate sauce.

In the portion of the Lanes off North St. Credit card min. £5. 1 scoop £2, 2 scoops £3, 3 scoops £4. Open M-Th 10:30am-9pm, F-Sa 10:30am-11pm, Su 10:30am-9pm.

NIA MODERN EUROPEAN ❸

87-88 Trafalgar St. ☎01273 671 371

The shabby-chic Nia is a welcome break from the greasy-spoon cuisine that dominates the Brighton scene. Serving classic European meals with a fresh twist, the cheery staff at Nia regularly delivers their entirely organic or locally sourced products to crowds of enthusiastic locals. Get the roast pigeon on a herbed risotto cake with plum and red onion jam and rocket and green bean salad *(£12)*. It's a small price to pay for one less pigeon.

Go up York Pl. with your back to the water and turn left onto Trafalgar St. Dinner entrees £11-12. Open M 9am-5pm, Tu-Th 9am-9pm, F-Sa 9am-10:30pm, Su 9am-5pm.

FOOD FOR FRIENDS VEGETARIAN ❹

17-18 Prince Albert St. ☎01273 202 310 www.foodforfriends.com

Food for Friends specializes in delicious, carefully prepared vegetarian food and homemade delicacies. Children at heart roam Brighton looking for two things: alchohol and ice cream, and Food for Friends combines the two in their homemade Bailey's ice cream. The restaurant is bright, open, and welcoming, and the food is excellent.

Go up East St. with your back to the water and turn left onto Prince Albert St. Entrees £11.45. Afternoon tea from £5. Open M-Th noon-10pm, F-Sa noon-10:30pm, Su noon-10pm. Afternoon tea daily 3-6pm.

BILL'S PRODUCE STORE EUROPEAN ❷

100 North Rd. ☎01273 692 894 www.billsproducestore.co.uk

Tucked into an abandoned warehouse space, Bill's is known for their excellent ingredients. They are carefully selected from around the world, feeding the international menu, which includes many British classics as well. Some of the ingredients are available for individual purchase on the shelves around the store, and various menu items are posted on chalkboards hanging above diners.

Go up Marlborough Pl. with your back to the water and turn left onto North Rd. Sandwiches £4.15-5.65. Dinner entrees £9-10.50. Open M-Sa 8am-10pm, Su 9am-10pm.

THE HOP POLES UPSCALE PUB ❸

13 Middle St. ☎01273 710 444

The Hop Poles looks like a typical pub, with two noticeable differences. The first: the villainous, red-eyed octopus made out of hubcaps that hangs from the ceiling as if half-submerged in the ocean. The second: the adventurous food such as the goat cheese, sun-blushed tomato, and pesto mushroom burger with chips and homemade coleslaw *(£7.50)* and the meat *meze serrano* and *milano salami*which comes with various other delicacies *(£8)*. Enjoy your meal to the tune of jazz, blues, and indie in the pleasant pub space, or take it out back to the garden and dine beneath the strung lights.

Go down Grand Junction Rd. with the water on your left, turn right onto Middle St. Credit card min. £10. Entrees £7.50-8. Open M-Th noon-midnight, F-Sa noon-1am, Su noon-midnight. Kitchen open daily noon-9pm.

SOLERA D TAPA TAPAS ❷

42 Sydney St. ☎01273 673 966 www.d-tapa.com

Tucked away among the graffitied Sydney St., Solera D Tapa imports most of its ingredients directly from Spain. It follows the same tactic with its intimate and traditional setting, complete with an open-air room in the back with a red polka-dot table cloth.

Go down Gloucester Pl. with your back to the water and turn left onto North Rd. and right onto

Kensington St. which will become Sydney St. Ⓢ Each item £3.75-4. Tablas (platters) £5.50-7.50 on average. ⏰ Open M-Sa noon-midnight.

NIGHTLIFE

THE FORTUNE OF WAR — PUB

157-159 King's Rd. Arches ☎01273 205 065

Located right on the beach with an interior designed to look like the hull of a ship, The Fortune of War is sort of like what would have happened if a massive Spanish ship commanded by DJs (Friday and Saturday) carrying gallons of beer, plastic cups, and various other alcohol had washed up on the beach. Take the beer onto the beach and enjoy. Watch the sunset if you like, or just pretend it's any other pub and drink.

Off King's Rd. on the beach. i Credit card min. £5. Ⓢ Average pint £3.70. ⏰ Open M-Th 11am-midnight, F-Sa 11am-3am, Su 11am-midnight.

YE OLD KING AND QUEEN — PUB

18 Marlborough Pl. ☎01273 607 207 www.kingandqueen.co.uk

Built in 1779 as a farmhouse, the pub has more grandeur than the average watering hole, even if it has a fair amount of gimmick to it as well. With cheap beers and karaoke nights, Ye Old King and Queen is a fun place to grab a pint.

Go up Old Steine with your back to the water, then take the left fork around the green onto Marlborough Pl. i Credit card min. £10. Ⓢ Average pint £3. ⏰ Open M noon-11pm, Tu noon-midnight, W noon-11pm, Th-Sa noon-midnight, Su noon-11pm.

CHARLES STREET AND ENVY — BAR, CLUB

8 Marine Parade ☎01273 624 091 www.charles-street.com

Above the bar Charles Street, the club Envy rages with pulsing dance beats, beautiful views of the pier, and a variety of themed nights. The upstairs club has more disco balls than John Travolta has seen in his lifetime.

Head down Old Steine toward the water, then turn left onto Marine Parade. Ⓢ Cover Th 8-10pm £1, after 10pm £2. ⏰ Club open Tu-W noon-midnight, Th 10pm-3am, F-Sa noon-3am, Su noon-midnight. Bar open Tu-W noon-midnight, Th-Sa noon-3am, Su noon-midnight.

AUDIO AND ABOVE AUDIO — CLUB

10 Marine Parade ☎01273 606 906 www.audiobrighton.com

This hip club is beneath the aptly titled bar "Above Audio." Hosting live bands and DJs alike, the club and bar hold a variety of events in this spare and cool space.

Head down old Steine toward the water, then turn left onto Marine Parade. i Tu Indie nights, Th charts music, Sa live bands 8pm. Ⓢ £4 cocktail menu every M-W and F-Sa. ⏰ Open M-Tu 1pm-1am, W-Sa 1pm-late, Su 1-11:30pm.

THE FISHBOWL — PUB

73 East St. ☎01273 777 505

This pub has a reputation for being quite busy come the wee hours. There is, rather predictably, a fishbowl the size of a small planet on the bar. There's also live music on Wednesdays from 8-11pm.

Down Old Steine toward the water, turn right on Grand Junction Rd. and right onto East St. i Credit card min £5. Ⓢ Pints under £3 available, but £3.70 is the average. ⏰ Open M-W noon-2am, Th noon-3am, F-Sa 11pm-3am, Su noon-2am.

FONT — BAR

Union St.

Not "font" like "Comic Sans," but "font" like the part of a church where people are baptized. In fact, this establishment is sort of like what would happen if the communion wine were a lot more hardcore and if the church were backlit with pink lights. Yup, the bar is actually a converted church built in 1608.

With the water on your left, go up North St. and turn left on Ship St., or then left on Union St. Credit card min. £5. Cheap night on Tu, with pints and a vodka mixer at £1.25. Average pint £3. Open M 11am-midnight, Tu 11am-1am, W 11am-midnight, Th-Sa 11am-1am.

REVENGE GLBT CLUB
32-34 Old Steine ☎01273 606 064 www.revenge.co.uk
This pulsing dance club has two dance floors, each playing its own unique style of music for the dancing masses. Check the website for events and special nights.
Old Steine is just off the water, close to the Pier. Credit card min. £10. Cover is almost always under £8, generally around £3-4, some student discounts, depending on the night. Average pint £2.30. Tu 10:30pm-late, Th-Sa 10:30pm-late, Su 10pm-5am.

COALITION CLUB
171-181 King's Rd. Arches ☎01273 772 842 www.brightoncoalition.co.uk
Restaurant by day, nightclub by...night. Coalition rests on the beach, attracting crowds of students during the week who come for the tunes and stay for the dancing.
King's Rd. Arches are on the beach, running parallel to King's Rd. Cover is cash only. Cover varies, but generally £2-15, and some club nights offer student discounts. Average pint £3.65.

SEVEN STARS PUB
27 Ship St. ☎01273 258 800 www.sevenstarsbrighton.co.uk
This old, warm pub is bedecked in regal old decor and packed with locals. To add to the community feel of the place, there are movie nights every Tuesday at 8pm and live music on Sundays at 4pm.
Turn right off Grand Junction with the pier behind you. Credit card min. £5. Average pint £3.50. Open M-Th 12:30-11pm, F-Sa noon-1am.

ARTS AND CULTURE

Brighton doesn't just provide a geographic escape for vacationers. Its varied and exciting entertainment scene runs the gamut from impressive street performers who frequent the Pavilion Gardens, to more traditional modes of entertainment on the stage, to spectacularly enormous parades. Brighton, home of Fat Boy Slim, is also unique in that DJ-ing is practically considered a high form of art there.

THEATRE ROYAL BRIGHTON VARIETY THEATER
New Rd. ☎084 487 17650 www.ambassadortickets.com/brighton
This theater was commissioned by **King George IV,** the same king who commissioned the Pavilion. Though less garish, it's just as entertaining. The entertainment here is varied but excellent, and patrons can come to the Theatre Royal Brighton for everything, including comedy, plays, opera musicals, and drama.
Right off North St. when coming with your back to Old Steine and the waterfront on your left. Tickets roughly £15-30. Students M-Th £2 discounts for week-long shows. Standby rate £11 for unsold tickets 1hr. before showtime. Box office open M-Tu 10am-8pm, W 11am-8pm, Th-Sa 10am-8pm, Su 2hr. before the start of the performance. Available via telephone M-Sa 9am-10pm, Su 10am-8pm.

BRIGHTON DOME MUSIC
29 New Rd. for box office; main entrance on Church St. ☎709 709 www.brightondome.org.uk
Many of the biggest acts who come to Brighton come here. The Brighton Dome has hosted everyone from ABBA to Jimi Hendrix to Jane's Addiction. Come for pop, rock, jazz, classical, and even comedy, and be sure to inquire about discounts.
Off Marlborough Pl. Walk onto it with the waterfront on your left and Marlborough Pl. behind you. Tickets £4-100. Box office open M-Sa 10am-6pm.

BRIGHTON FESTIVAL FESTIVAL
☎01273 709 709 www.brightonfestival.org
This massive arts festival hosted every May is one of Brighton's biggest events,

celebrating a range of art forms. In 2010, Brian Eno was the guest artistic director.

Victoria Station on the Southern Railway. May 7-29, 2011.

BRIGHTON PRIDE ▼ FESTIVAL

6 Bartholomews, Brighton, BN1 1HG ☎01273 775 939 www.brightonpride.org

This festival is the biggest free pride festival in the UK. The finale, a carnival parade and party in Preston Park, is not to be missed!

Pride events late July-Aug. Parade usually early Aug.

ESSENTIALS

Practicalities

- **TOURIST OFFICE: Visitor Information Centre.** *(Royal Pavilion Shop, 4-5 Pavilion Bldg. ☎01273 290 337 www.visitbrighton.com Open daily in summer 9:30am-5:30pm; in winter 10am-5pm.)*
- **TOURS: CitySightseeing** offers tours visiting the Brighton Marina, the Sea Life Centre and the Royal Crescent, among other Brighton sights. *(Leave from Grand Junction Rd., opposite Coach Station. ☎01273 886 200 www.city-sightseeing.com £8, student £7, seniors £6, 5-15 £3. 50min.+ tours every 30min.)*
- **CURRENCY EXCHANGE: Brighton Coin Shop.** *(38 Ship St, Brighton. ☎01273 733 365 No commission charged. M-Sa 9:30am-5:15pm.)* **Western Union** in **Jennifer's Shop.** *(11 St. James's St. ☎01273 622 291.)*
- **GLBT RESOURCES: Lesbian and Gay Switchboard.** *(☎01273 204 050 Lines open daily 5pm-11pm.)*
- **INTERNET ACCESS: Starnet.** *(94 St. James's St. ☎01273 621 921 £1 per hr. Open M-Sa 9:30am-8pm, Su 11am-5pm.)*
- **POSTCODE:** BN1 1BA.

Emergency!

- **POLICE:** *(John St. ☎0845 607 0999 Open 24hr.)*
- **PHARMACY: Boots.** *(129 North St., Brighton. ☎01273 207 461 Open M-Sa 8am-midnight, Su 11am-5pm.)*
- **HOSPITAL: Royal Sussex County.** *(Eastern Rd. ☎01273 696 955.)*

Getting There

By Train

Trains leave from **Brighton Station.** *(Uphill at the northern end of Queen's Rd., perpendicular to King's Rd. ☎08451 272 920,24hr. helpline for National Rail ☎08457 484 950.)* Trains from Brighton to **Arundel** *(£8.30. 1hr., 2 per hr.)*; **London Victoria** *(£14-20.70. 2 fast trains, and 1 slow train every hr.)*; **Portsmouth** *(£13.90. 1hr., every hr.)*; and **Rye** *(£14.70. 1hr., every hr.).* National Rail sold at the Visitor Information Centre at the Royal Pavilion.

By Bus

Bus tickets and information available at **1 Stop Travel.** There are two locations in Brighton, at **16 Old Steine** *(Open in summer M-Tu 8:30am-5:45pm, W 9am-5:45pm, Th-F 8:30am-5:45pm, Sa 9am-5pm, Su 9:30am-3pm; in winter M-Tu 8:30am-5:45pm, W 9am-5:45pm, Th-F 8:30-5:45pm, Sa 9am–5pm.)* and **Brighton Station.** *(Open M-F 8am-5pm, Sa 9am-5pm, Su 9:30am-7pm; in winter open M-F 8am-5pm, Sa 9am-5pm.)* Buses leave from Preston Park for **London Victoria** *(£11.70. 2hr. 20min., every hr.)* Tickets are sold on board when not sold out. Local bus and National Express tickets sold at the Visitor Information Centre at the Royal Pavilion.

Getting Around

Taxis

Call **Brighton and Hove Streamline Taxis** (☎01273 202 020) or **Brighton and Hove Radio Cabs** (☎01273 204 060).

Public Transportation

Local **buses** operated by **Brighton and Hove** (☎01273 886 200 www.buses.co.uk) congregate around Old Steine. 1 Stop Travel can give information on routes and prices, and they distribute a magazine with all of the information. Nightbuses operate on Thursday, Friday, and Saturday nights (£2.20).

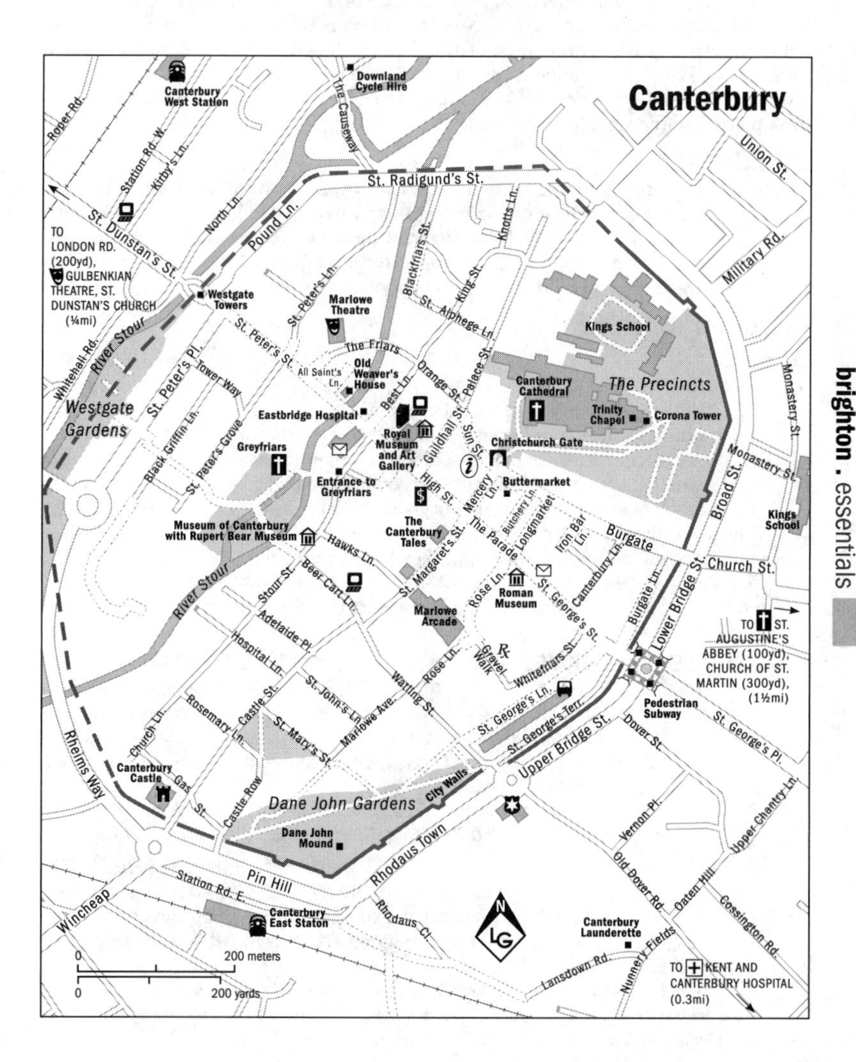

canterbury ☎01227

It's safe to say Canterbury never got over the murder of **Thomas Becket.** Residents in denial may argue against that claim, but here's easy proof: the murder occurred, and Becket was subsequently buried and sainted because everyone thought he was responsible for the mass miraculous healings that were occuring. For this reason, masses of people began making pilgrimages to Canterbury, so he's probably the main reason the cathedral is so famous. While many claim *The Canterbury Tales* by **William Chaucer** as an independent claim to fame, the entire book is comprised of stories told by pilgrims...on a pilgrimage to Becket's tomb. Suffice it to say he had an impact. Now, the town is part tourist trap, part quaint, south England town. The center of the city is closed off to cars, making for a pleasant walking experience down cobbled lanes. Watch out for those irregular stone areas, though—they look about as harmless as burning sand, and you'll look as ridiculous walking over them.

ORIENTATION

Canterbury's center is roughly circular, defined by the eording medieval city wall. The main street crosses the city northwest to southeast, changing names from **Saint Peter's Street** to **High Street** to **The Parade** to **Saint George's Street.** Butchery Ln. and Mercury Ln., each only a block long, run north to the **Cathedral Gates,** while numerous other side streets lead to hidden pubs and chocolatiers.

ACCOMMODATIONS

KIPPS — HOSTEL❶

40 Nunnery Fields ☎01227 786 121 www.kipps-hostel.com

One of the nicest and cheapest accommodations in Canterbury, Kipps charges crappy-hostel prices for pleasant B and B levels of comfort. Between the beautiful backyard and the elegant and spacious common space (with its deep leather chairs and big-screen TV), Kipps is incredibly liveable. The staff goes the extra mile with events like a barbecue out back on Saturdays, pasta night on Fridays, and Rock Band Night on Tuesdays (which involves free pancakes). Traveling guitarists will appreciate the guitar they have available.

Right off St. Georges Pl. onto Upper Chantry Ln. Follow onto Oaten Hill and then Nunnery Fields. Dorms in summer from £16; in winter from £13. Reception 7:30am-11pm, but someone is on-site 24hr.

CLARE ELLEN GUEST HOUSE — BED AND BREAKFAST❷

9 Victoria Rd. ☎01227 760 205 www.clareellenguesthouse.co.uk

Though not terribly central to Canterbury, the Clare Ellen Guest House provides beautiful, bright rooms, flexible service (their full English breakfast, which is included in the price, meets special dietary needs on request), and a small swimming pool for low prices. Take a dip.

Head down Wincheap away from Canterbury East Station and turn Left onto Victoria Rd. i Free Wi-Fi. Singles £32-50; doubles £60-70; triples £75-110. Reception daily 7am-10pm.

ALEXANDRA HOUSE — BED AND BREAKFAST❷

1 Roper Rd. ☎01227 786 617 www.alexandrahouse.net

This is a fairly standard but pleasant guesthouse whose prices are better than most in the area. Cozy up on their lime-green couches to get a break from your sightseeing.

With your back to town center, go down St. Dunstan's and turn right onto Roper Rd. i Full English breakfast included. Singles £38-48; doubles £65-70; triples £80-85; families £90-95. Reception 8am-10pm. Breakfast M-Sa 8-9am, Su 8:30-9:30am.

VICTORIA HOTEL
HOTEL❸

59 London Rd. ☎01227 459 333 www.thevictoriahotel.co.uk

Located a little outside of town, the Victoria Hotel provides a pleasant, self-contained experience. All the rooms have ensuite baths, and there's a full restaurant on the ground floor. Oh, and did we mention that they have not one, but two beer gardens? *Danke!*

Go down St. Dunstan's St. away from town center and turn left onto London Rd. i Free Wi-Fi. 2-night min. stay F-Sa. Ⓢ Singles £65; doubles £79; triples £89; families £109.

YHA CANTERBURY
HOSTEL❶

54 New Dover Rd. ☎01227 462 911

Located in the former mansion of a German officer, the YHA Canterbury is old and grand, though its interior is more or less average for a hostel. In the warmer months, large tents are available in the backyard for backpackers willing to brave the Canterbury wilderness.

Go down St. George's Pl. away from town center and continue onto New Dover Rd. i Laundry: wash £2, dryer £0.75, soap powder £0.75. Wi-Fi £5 per 24hr. Computer £1 per 20min. Ⓢ Dorms £12-20. £20-35 per tent. Reception 5-11pm.

SIGHTS

CANTERBURY CATHEDRAL
HISTORIC SITE, CATHEDRAL

The Precincts ☎01227 762 862 www.canterbury-cathedral.org

Built in 597 CE after the King of Kent learned the error of his pagan ways and converted to Christianity, Canterbury Cathedral would not become famous until centuries later. The Archbishop of Canterbury is the leader of the worldwide Anglican community, so it is an important religious seat. However, it been a site of religious pilgrimage since 1170, when there was murder in the cathedral. Becket, the then-Archbishop of Canterbury, was installed in the position by his friend King Henry II in the hopes of bringing the church under the thumb of the state. However, Becket began defending the church, and was exiled. After he returned from exile, Henry misspoke and four knights took it upon themselves to kill Thomas Becket. After his death, Becket was entombed in the crypt. Then, miraculous healings (depicted in the miracle windows) began to take place, precipitating the canonizing of Becket that occured a mere three years after his death. After he was sainted, his shrine was moved out of the crypt and into a more prominent location in the Trinity Chapel, and the miraculous healings promptly stopped. Henry VIII destroyed the tomb in 1538, much like he destroyed most other things in England.

Trinity Chapel houses the Chair of St. Augustine, which is where the Archbishop sits during services. A lit candle on the floor of the chapel marks the place where Becket's shrine was before Henry VIII went on his massive power trip. As you walk up the steps, note how they are worn. This is the product of centuries of pilgrims kneeling as they approached the shrine, a process which is long-windedly described in the *Canterbury Tales.* Trinity Chapel houses the **Miracle Windows,** stained glass windows depicting the incredible healings that took place after the death of Thomas Becket. Note the green boxes in each scene: these represent the money that families would bring to the shrine of Becket after their loved ones were healed.

Corona Tower, at the eastern end of the cathedral, this tower is known as "Corona" because it's where a piece of the crown of Becket's head was encased in silver. William the English built it after a fire destroyed the original in 1174. The beautiful Redemption window depicts Christ on the cross, the entombment, resurreçtion, and ascension. To the right of the Corona Tower are the Jesse Panels, two 13th-century works of stained glass.

Finally, you can stand in the very place that made Canterbury something other than your average sheep-filled British town. It was here that the four knights killed Becket as he prayed. A statue of two swords cast two shadows, representing the four swords that killed him. The spot where the martyrdom took place is on your left as you approach the Trinity Chapel.

i Audio guides available in English, French, German, Spanish, Italian, and Japanese and last 40min. ⑤ £8, students and seniors £7, under 5 free. Guidebook £2. Audio tours £3.50, students £2.50. Guided tours £4.50, students £3.50. ⏰ Open in summer M-Sa 9am-5:30pm, Su 12:30-2:30pm, in winter M-Sa 9am-5pm. Last entry 30min. before close. Check times for guided tours at the Welcome Center and nave pulpit. Tours1¼hr. M-Sa.

GREYFRIARS ♿ HISTORIC SITE

6A Stour St. ☎01227 471 688

Built in 1267, the first English Franciscan Friary was destroyed between 1538 and 1547. Only the present-day chapel, which was initially a watermill, remains. The grounds are beautiful, complete with a lazy river that slips under the watermill and a densely packed wildflower meadow. If you sit near the water during the summer, prepare to hear the pigeons hidden in the walls that border the water cooing at amplified volumes. They think you can't see them, so they're extra loud. It's kind of like singing in the shower.

Heading toward the river down High St., turn left onto Stour St. i The gardens are wheelchair-accessible, but the chapel isn't. ⑤ Free. ⏰ Chapel open M-Sa 2-4pm. Gardens open daily 6:45am-5pm.

WESTGATE TOWERS HISTORIC SITE

St. Peters St. ☎01227 789 576 www.canterbury-museums.co.uk

These magnificent 60-drum towers were built in 1380 in order to defend Canterbury against France in the **Hundred Years' War.** It later served as a town prison. Now there's a museum there. An excellent view of Canterbury is available from the top.

Just down St. Peter's St. by the water. ⑤ £2. ⏰ Open daily 10am-4:30pm.

ST. DUNSTAN'S CHURCH CHURCH

St. Dunstan's St.

St. Dunstan's dates from before 1066 and is one of the many local sites that have been tied into the web of history surrounding the cathedral. In 1174, Henry II stopped at St. Dunstan's to don a hair shirt and pilgrim's cloak. He proceeded to walk barefoot to the cathedral where he was flogged. Basically, it was as hard as apologizing ever is. The church is a static snapshot of history, with pieces of it being added in almost every century. The nave is 15th-century, the bells are 14th-century, the stained glass is modern, and the porch is 17th-century.

Go down High St. toward the Westgate Towers and continue onto St. Dunstan's St. ⑤ Free. ⏰ The hours aren't fixed, but the church is generally open sunrise-sunset.

ST. MARTIN'S CHURCH CHURCH

North Holmes Rd. ☎01227 768 072 www.martinpaul.org

In 580 CE, the pagan King of Kent married a Christian princess from France. Showing a depth of religious understanding otherwise lacking in that century, the King granted her a Roman building to use as a chapel, making St. Martin's Church the oldest church in England. The entrance to the church is guarded by ancient, slanted tombstones, and the church itself is beautiful and silent.

Left off of Longport onto North Holmes Rd. ⑤ Free. ⏰ Open Tu, Th, Sa 11am-4pm.

MUSEUM OF CANTERBURY WITH RUPERT BEAR MUSEUM ♿ MUSEUM

18 High St. ☎01227 475 202 www.canterbury-museums.co.uk

When this museum says it shows exhibits on the whole history of Canterbury, it really means the whole history—to the point where it begins with with the dawn of time. It then works its way through fossils, the Roman city of Durovernum

Cantiacorum that stood on the site of modern-day Canterbury, and an exhibit on Joseph Conrad, who lived in Kent. Conrad's study is recreated, and a bust of Conrad by Sir Jacob Epstein resides there as well. One-quarter of the city was bombed during the Blitz, and the period of the war is commemorated in the World War II exhibition. Of course, there's attention paid to Thomas Becket, mostly in the form of a 60 ft. frieze by Oliver Postgate and Naomi Linnell, retelling his story in medieval-cartoon fashion. The end of the museum features brief displays on two children's entertainment enterprises based out of Canterbury: Bagpuss (the psychedelically pink-striped cat) and Rupert the Bear, who is shown in one picture posing with an obnoxious-looking Paul McCartney.

i There is a free multimedia guide in Japanese, German, French, and English. $ £3.60, children and concessions £2.30, families £9.20. Open June-Sept M-Sa 11am-5:30pm; Su 1:30-4pm; Oct-May daily 11am-4:30pm. Last entry 30min. before close.

ST. AUGUSTINE'S ABBEY — RUINS, HISTORIC SITE

Longport ☎01227 767 345

To the layman, St. Augustine's Abbey looks like a pile of rocks. To the informed visitor (that means you), St. Augustine's Abbey is a pile of rocks with history. Founded by St. Augustine in 597 CE in an attempt to conver the Anglo-Saxons into good ol' God-fearing Christians, the abbey was one of the first Christian burial grounds for monarchs. As with most English religious structures that have strangely been reduced to rubble, Henry VIII was the man behind the wreckage. He destroyed it partially because of his anti-Catholic tendencies but also because he believed the Spanish and French were going to invade, and he needed the stone to build the Deal Castle near Dover. St. Augustine was buried here, but nobody knows where, so bring a shovel.

On Longport, left onto Lower Chantry Ln. off St. George's Pl. i Partially wheelchair-accessible. Free audio tour. $ £4.50, concessions £3.80, children £2.30. Open Apr-June W-Su 10am-5pm; July-Aug daily 10am-6pm; Sep-Oct Sa-Su 10am-5pm; Nov-Mar Sa-Su 10am-4pm. Last entry 30min. before close.

EASTBRIDGE HOSPITAL — HISTORIC SITE

25 High St. ☎01227 471 688

Founded in 1180 to accomodate the high volume of pilgrims attempting to stay in Canterbury (kind of like the original hostel, or trying to find a bed on graduation weekend), Eastbridge Hospital was closed by the great closer Henry VIII in 1538. It was opened 40 years later as an almshouse and has been just that for the last 426 years. Ten people currently live here. Admittance lets you see the old slanted columns, roof beams that date as far back as 1285 and ancient pews that are throughout the hospital. The Chantry Chapel was opened in 1365 and functioned until it was sealed by Henry VIII in 1547 and reopened in 1969.

High St. $ £1, students £0.75. Open M-Sa 10am-5pm. Last entry 30min. before close.

CANTERBURY CASTLE — CASTLE

Castle St.

Built by William the Conqueror (who took Canterbury without having to fight), this was one of the first royal castles along with the ones built in Dover and Rochester. As with many castles, it is partially built along the Roman town wall. In the late 12th century, it served as a prison for Kent and was used much later as a facility for the Canterbury Gas Light and Coke Company.

Turn left onto St. Margaret's St. off High St. and continue onto Castle St. $ Free. Open daily 8am-dusk.

THE CANTERBURY TALES — REENACTMENT SIGHT

23 Hawk's Ln. ☎01227 479 227 www.canterburytales.org.uk

Though ridiculously gimmicky, the Canterbury Tales does an admirable job of translating the famous stories into a walk-in medieval Canterbury with accompanying audio tour, which, if you think about it, was how the tales were meant to be heard in the first place. After a selection of five tales, you wind up at Thomas Becket's shrine.

Left onto St. Margaret's St. off High St. and right onto Hawk's Ln. i Call for wheelchair-accessibility details. Audio tours are in English, Italian, French, German, Spanish, Japanese, and Dutch (as well as children's English). £7.75, students £6.75, senior £6.75. Open daily Mar-June 10am-5pm; July-Aug 9:30am-5pm; Sept-Oct 10am-5pm; Nov-Feb 10am-4:30pm.

FOOD

CAFÉ BELGE

BELGIAN ❸

89 St. Dunstan's St. ☎01227 768 222 www.cafebelge.co.uk

How many ways do you think there are to prepare mussels? Café Belge offers 52 different ones, including mussels with goat cheese, pine nuts, spinach, wine, cream garlic and nutmeg *(£11.95)* with Belgian *frîtes* and bread. This Belgian cafe is covered in Magritte reprints and Lichtenstein-esque blow-ups of Tintin panels and offers the largest selection of Belgian beer in the UK. The upstairs dining room looks like the residence of someone named Hans with its exposed dark wood beams and slanted roofs.

Walk down High St. towards the river, cross it and continue onto St. Dunstans St. Entrees £10-11. Mussels generally £12. M-F 11am-3pm and 6pm-late, Sa-Su 11am-3:30pm and 6pm-late.

CAFÉ DES AMIS DU MEXIQUE

MEXICAN❸

95 St. Dunstan's St. ☎01227 464 390 www.cafedez.com

Though the name may be geographically confused, the food is not. This is straight-up, delicious Mexican food, served among candlelit tables, painted tile walls, and colorful sculptural paintings that pop out of the wall. The cafe pumps out the kind of jazz that sounds best accompanied by happy chatter while diners enjoy a range of traditional Mexican food and a selection of Mexican beers.

Follow High St. toward the river with your back to the cathedral. It becomes St. Dunstan's after you cross the river. The restaurant is on your left. i Student discount M-F noon-5pm (buy 2 entrees and get 1 free). Early evening menu available M-F 5-6pm (2 courses and a drink for £11.95. Lunch specials £7.25. Entrees £10-11. Open M-Th noon-10:30pm, Su noon-9:30pm.

CAFÉ MAURESQUE

MEDITERRANEAN❹

8 Butchery Ln. ☎01227 464 300 www.111.cafemauresque.com

Café Mauresque provides an effective culinary metaphor for globalization, serving up North African and Spanish food in equally heaping, delicious portions. Between the red lights, low-slung chairs, and the elaborate shades placed over the lights, Café Mauresque more than matches the high quality of its food with the relaxed atmosphere.

Right off High St. when heading toward the river from the roundabout (intersection of Upper Bridge St., Lower Bridge St. and St. George's Pl.). i Student discounts of 20% on meals on M and Su. Tagines £13.75-15. Tapas £3.25-5.25 per plate. Lunch entrees £6.50-8. Early evening menus, 2 courses M-F 5pm-6:30pm, £11. Open M-Th noon-10pm, F-Sa noon-10:30pm, Su noon-10pm.

AZOUMA

ARABIAN, MEDITERRANEAN❸

4 Church St. ☎01227 760 076 www.azouma.co.uk

Azouma feels like a different country. The restaurant occasionally has belly dancers *(Th 8pm)*, and hungry diners are served an array of Arab and Mediterranean dishes by a befezzed waitstaff.

Right off Lower Bridge St. when town center is on your left. i Arabian Student Nights on W (buy 1 meal, get 1 50% off). Lunch buffet £7. Entrees £9.25-10.95. Open M-F noon-3pm and 5-11pm, Sa-Su noon-midnight or 1am.

THE CANTINA

AMERICAN ❸

61 Dover St. ☎01227 450 288 www.shedcantina.co.uk

Tucked just outside central Canterbury, The Cantina brings a slice of laid-back California cuisine to the already international Canterbury culinary scene. The bright blue and orange walls and sun-dappled upstairs dining room are as Californian as the wine list.

Upper Bridge St. runs west off the roundabout just outside town (on the other side from the river). Take this road and turn left onto Dover St. Ⓢ Entrees £9.50-11. Ⓞ M-F noon-2pm, Sa noon-3pm, and 6-10pm.

CITÉ CRÊPES

CREPES ❶

On High St. in front of Nasons Memorial Garden www.citecrepes.com

Unlike many crepe stands in touristy areas, Cité takes itself seriously, delivering honest-to-goodness delicious crepes to the throngs that move slowly down High St. Though it offers no seating, the Nasons Memorial Garden right behind it is a fantastic place to enjoy some of the delicious savoury crepes like ham and cheese or salami and cheese or the fantastic sweet crepes such as the nutella and banana or apple, sultana, and cinnamon crepe.

High St. Ⓢ Sweet £2.30-2.50. Savory £2.50-2.75. Ⓞ Open in summer M-Sa 10:30am-6pm, Su 11am-5pm; in winter M-Sa 10:30am-5pm, Su 11am-5pm. Closed during rain.

NIGHTLIFE

BRAMLEY'S

BAR

15 Orange St. ☎01227 379 933 www.bramleysbar.com

From the outside, Bramley's looks like a house, and passersby will surely miss it. This is its charm. Inside the small, unassuming doorway, Bramley's inexplicably bustles with pool tables, sewing machines, typewriters, and highbacked comfy chairs. With comedy nights on the first Monday of each month and a jazz pianist at the elegant grand every Thursday, Bramley's makes sure its guests are entertained.

Down Guildhall St. off High St.; left on Orange St. i £0.50 credit-card charge for purchases under £10. Ⓢ Pints £3.20-3.60. Ⓞ Open M-Th noon-11:30pm, F-Sa noon-12:30am.

PENNY THEATRE

PUB

30-31 Northgate ☎01227 812 850

The Penny Theatre is a perennial favorite among the masses of students looking to get drunk in Canterbury. The outdoor beer garden makes this a hot spot in the summertime. Though relatively spare in decoration (except for the bare colored bulbs shielded by welders' masks), the alcohol is cheap and the crowds are young.

Go down Lower Bridge St. away from town, turn left onto Union St. and right onto Northgate. i They sell a yellow card for £1, which gives £.35 off all pints. Ⓢ Pints £2.20. Beef and burger £4 after 3pm. Ⓞ Open M-W 11:30am-midnight, Th-Sa 11:30am-1am, Su 11:30am-midnight.

THE LADY LUCK

PUB

18 St. Peters St. ☎01227 763 298 www.theladyluck.co.uk

The Lady Luck is themed on classic rock and roll, which is, of course, the ideal drinking music. Offering cheap pints and a mostly student crowd, the Lady Luck is a good place to begin or end any night on the town.

High St. becomes St. Peters St. Ⓢ Pints £3. Most mixed drinks £5. Ⓞ Open M-Th noon-1am, F-Sa noon-2am, Su noon-11pm.

THE CANTERBURY TALES

PUB

12 The Friars ☎0782 444 3933

Though it feels wrong to encourage the fetish this town has with *The Canterbury Tales*, this relaxed, warm pub merits a visit. With wax-coated Jack Daniel's bottles serving as candle holders and logs piled high in the corner of the back room, the Canterbury Tales feels like a comfortable old-country pub. Try the Addlestones cloudy cider *(pint £3.30)* for some of that old-country libation.

Follow Orange St. toward the river. Pints £3.30. Open M-Sa from mid-afternoon to 1am.

THE BISHOP'S FINGER — PUB

13 St. Dunstan's St. — ☎ 01227 768 915

This elegant, old-fashioned pub plays into a traditional idea of what a Canterbury pub should be, which is, perhaps, why it's on one of the main drags. However, between its large brick fireplace and the wrought-iron screen that guards bottles of alcohol and its guilded mirror, the atmosphere merits the touristy nature of its decor. Try a cocktail shot of "Brokeback Mountain" *(chocolate vodka, Bailey's float; £2.80).*

Head down High St. toward the river. It becomes St. Dunstans St. Pints £3.20. Open DAILY noon-midnight.

CHILL — CLUB

St. George's Pl. — ☎01227 761 276 www.chill-nightclub.com

Chill imports a bit of the Brighton club scene into sleepy, pubby Canterbury. With loads of special events (including occasional UV parties), Chill is a hot club in a town where such a thing is pretty rare.

Just off the roundabout heading toward New Dover Rd. away from town. Cover M and W-Th £4; F-Sa before 10:30pm £6, After 10:30pm £7pm. Every drink £1.50 until midnight, certain drinks £1.60 after. Open M 9:30pm-2am, W 10pm-2am, Th 10pm-2:30am, F-Sa 9:30pm-3am.

SEVEN STARS — PUB

1 Orange St. — ☎01227 786 934

A simple, studenty neighborhood pub equipped with a pool table. Karaoke nights break out at 8pm on Wednesdays, and who doesn't want to see drunk people blow out their voices while straining for the high notes in "Take on Me?" That's right. No one.

Down Guildhall St. off High St., left on Orange St. Pints £3.10. Open M-Th 11am-11pm, F-Sa 11am-1am, Su 11am-10:30pm.

CASEY'S — PUB

5 Butchery Ln. — ☎01227 463 252

Casey's is a warm yet spacious, neighborhood pub. With small areas segmented off by wood framing, the pub provides intimate spaces in which to enjoy the relatively cheap pints. The pub occasionally hosts live music and DJs on the weekends.

Right off of High St. when heading toward the river. Pints £3.20. Open daily noon-midnight.

ARTS AND CULTURE

ORANGE STREET MUSIC CLUB — MUSIC

15 Orange St. — ☎01227 760 801 www.orangestreetmusic.com

Housed on the second floor of 15 Orange St., this warehouse-like music club has high ceilings and a hodgepodge of comfy-looking chairs cluttering the space. At the back, there's a large stage which hosts a variety of musical acts from blues every Tuesday (Bluesday) to local amateur songwriters on Mondays.

Down Guildhall St. off High St., left on Orange St. Cover W-Sa £2-15. Pints £3.30. Cosmos £4. Open M-Sa noon-midnight. Live music generally 8:30-11pm.

THE GULBENKIAN — THEATer

University of Kent — ☎01227 769 075 www.kent.ac.uk/gulbenkian

This University of Kent theater does everything from master classes with famous musicians to theatrical productions to concerts. The cinema provides lesser-known cinematic fare.

Off University Rd. Go down Whitstable Rd. away from town and continue onto St. Thomas Hill; turn right onto University Rd. Cinema Tickets £7, concessions £6. Theater tickets £12-15, but vary depending on the event. Open M-Sa 11am-5pm (until curtain on show nights), Su 2-9pm.

THE MARLOWE THEATRE — Theatre

The Friars — ☎01227 787 787 www.newmarlowetheatre.org

Christopher Marlowe, the famous contemporary of Shakespeare (some think he actually *was* Shakespeare—blasphemy!), lived in Canterbury, and this theater is named after him. Though currently under construction, it hopes to be open in 2011 and promises to be spectacular.

Right onto Best Ln.; left onto The Friars. i The box office is currently in the Visitor Information Centre at 12-13 Sun St. Contact box office for access information. Box office open M-Sa 9:30am-5pm. Phone booking M-Sa 9am-6pm.

STOUR MUSIC FESTIVAL — MUSIC FESTIVAL

All Saints' Boughton Aluph — www.stourmusic.org.uk

Held in the old countryside church All Saints' Boughton Aluph, the Stour Music Festival has been providing beautiful classical music in a pastoral setting every June since 1962.

Located just off the A28, about 4 mi. from Ashford (exit 9 from M20), and 10mi. from Canterbury. End of June.

ODEON CANTERBURY — CINEMA

43-45 St. George Place — ☎08712 244 007 www.odeon.co.uk

Yes, you can see the latest popcorn flicks in Canterbury. The Odeon is a good old blockbuster cinema showing most of the new, hot films.

Walk down St. George Pl. heading out of town. £6.85-8.10, students £5.75-6.80. Varies by week, so check showtimes online.

ESSENTIALS

Practicalities

- **TOURIST OFFICES: Canterbury Visitor Centre.** *(12-13 Sun St., The Buttermarket. ☎01227 378 100 www.canterbury.co.uk They book beds for a £5 charge. Open M-Sa 9am-5:30pm, Su 10am-5pm; hours are subject to change.)*
- **TOURS:** Walking tours leave from the Canterbury Visitor Centre daily. *(£6, students £5.50. Lasts 1½hr. Leaves July-Aug 11am and 2pm; leaves Sept-June 11am.)*
- **LAUNDROMATS: The Canterbury Launderette.** *(4 Nunnery Fields. ☎01227 452 211 M-F 9am-6pm, Sa 9am-5pm.)*
- **POST OFFICE: Post Office and Bureau de Change.** *(19 St. George's St. M-Sa 9am-5:30pm.)*
- **POSTCODE:** CT1 2BA.

Emergency!

- **POLICE:** Station. *(Old Dover Rd. ☎01227 762 055 for non-emergencies.)*
- **HOSPITAL: Kent and Canterbury Hospital.** *(Ethelbert Rd. ☎01227 766 877.).*

Getting There

By Train

Canterbury has two central train stations. **Canterbury West** *(Station Rd. W. off St. Dunstan's St. ☎0845 748 4950 www.southeasternrailway.co.uk. Open M-Sa 6:15am-7:30pm, Su 8:30am-5pm.)* Trains to **Brighton** *(£17.90 off-peak. 1hr., 3 per hr.)*, **Central London** *(£27.80. 1hr., 3 per hr.)* and **Charing Cross** *(£27.80. 2hr.)*. **Canterbury East** (*Open M-Sa 6:10am-8:20pm, Su 7:40am-7:20pm)* has trains to **Cambridge** *(Connects through London. £34. 3hr., every 30min.)*

By Bus

Bus station at St. George's Ln. *(☎087 1781 8181. ⏰ Open daily 8:15am-5pm)* sends buses to **London** *(Ⓢ£6. ⏰ 2hr., every hr.)* **Stagecoach** *(☎0845 600 2233)* operates the local buses, which go to the surrounding areas.

Getting Around

Most of the center of Canterbury has been shut off to motor vehicles, making it an ideal walking city. Most side roads can be accessed off High St. and St. Dunstan's. Stagecoach buses (see above) operate buses to surrounding areas.

By Taxi

Tudor Cars offers 24hr. service in Canterbury *(☎01227 451 451).*

By Bike

Downland Cycle Hire is at Malthouse *(St. Stephen's Rd. ☎01227 479 643 www.downland-cycles.co.uk. Ⓢ £15 per day; helmets £5 per day, tandems £35 per day. Must be booked and paid for in advance. ⏰ Open M-Sa 9:30am-5:30pm.)*

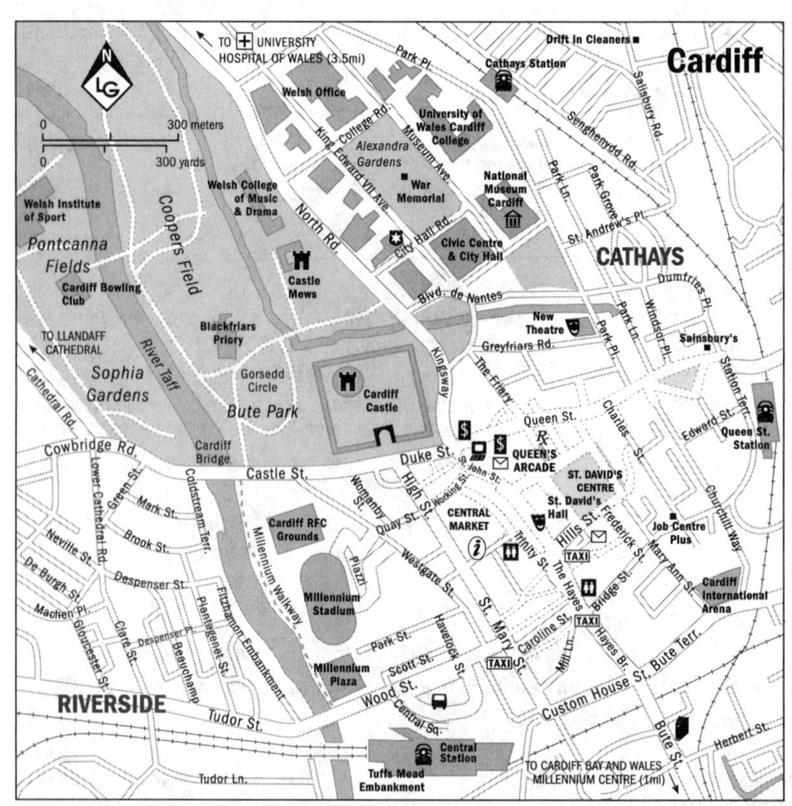

Cardiff is the capital of Wales and infinitely proud of it. What's refreshing for visitors after forays into self-deprecating England is the Welsh's casually confident sense of pride: not just of their city or of their language, or even of their legendary castle, but mostly of their sports teams. The colossal Millenium Stadium, which stands as a spectacular piece of the city skyline, is symbolic of Cardiffians' fierce sports fanaticism.

Cardiff is known as "Europe's Youngest Capital." What its residents lack in number, however, they make up for in youthful spirit and vigor.

ORIENTATION

Sprawling **Cardiff Castle** used to be the center of the ancient city, but today, Cardiff's busy shopping districts have superceded the Castle as the center of action. The city center's perimeter is roughly guided by the **Edwardian Civic Centre** (Cathays Park) to the north, **Central Rail Station** to the south, **Queen Street Station** to the east, and the **River Taff** to the west. The river runs next to the massive Millenium Stadium, dividing the residential section from the more commercial downtown and flowing directly into Cardiff Bay, a reinvigorated waterfront area, located about a mile south of Central Station.

While the city center is quite urban and industrialized, the edges of development in Cardiff border directly on greenery, so it's easy to flee the hustle and bustle of cosmopolitan life. Picturesque **Pontcanna Fields, Sophia Gardens,** and **Bute Park** stretch out from the walls of Cardiff Castle. Roath Park, with a 30-acre lake, is to the north of the city center.

ACCOMMODATIONS

Cardiff's legendary nightlife scene makes this city a magnet for young backpackers and also for visitors from other UK cities. They flood southern Wales on the weekend, so many hostels will fill up on Friday and Saturday nights. Book in advance for weekends, especially during summer. The same goes for important rugby matches at 75,000-seat Millenium Stadium (all those drunk fans have to find somewhere to crash after the game). **Cathedral Road,** which runs towards **Llandaff** (and, not surprisingly, its large cathedral) has scores of B and Bs, many of them on the pricier side. Hunt around on the side streets for better deals.

THE RIVER HOUSE BACKPACKERS — HOSTEL ❷

59 Fitzhamon Embankment ☎02920 399 810 www.riverhousebackpackers.com

This backpackers' favorite is situated within a beautiful house overlooking the River Taff. Pristine private-stall style bathrooms, a state-of-the-art kitchen, lovely outdoor patio area, and free nightly communal snacks give this place a truly homey vibe. The brother-sister pair that own and run the place are eager to please. Make sure you drag yourself out of bed before 10am to catch the included morning meal—it will probably be the very best hostel breakfast you'll ever have.

*Facing Millenium Stadium, across the River. Leave Central station to left and cross river bridge. Turn right and walk up the river bank toward the next bridge in the distance. River House if right before Despenser St. on the left. **i** Laundry £3. Free luggage storage. Towels included. Free large lockers in rooms. Free Wi-Fi. Internet £1 per 30min. Free tea and coffee 24hr. Fully equipped self-catering kitchen. Lounge with Wii, DVDs, books, and a 42in. LCD TV. Garden and outdoor seating area. Ⓢ Dorms from £17.50. Reception 24hr.*

NOS DA STUDIO HOTEL — HOSTEL, BUDGET HOTEL ❷

53-39 Despenser St. ☎02920 378 866 www.nosda.co.uk

Nos Da provides comfortable digs in a great riverside location. The full-service popular bar downstairs gives the building a lively, youthful vibe, and sweet facilities like a snazzily-decorated common area with hammocks, an HDTV, and a brand-new gym, come as added perks. Given all the other luxuries, you may be surprised to find dorms outfitted with standard bunks rather than king-sized beds. Young couples spring for the affordably priced private rooms, while 20-something gangs of Brits have made this a **stag** and **hen** (bachelor and bachelorette party) haven on weekends.

Facing Millenium Stadium, across the River. Leave Central Station to left and cross river bridge. Turn right and walk up the river bank toward the next bridge in the distance. Make a left at Despenser St. It's on the corner on your right. i Laundry. Free Wi-Fi. Self-catering kitchen. Gym for guests £3.50 per 2hr. 10% guest discount at downstairs restaurant and bar. Ⓢ 4-, 6-, 8-, 10-person dorms £16-30. Singles £30, with bath £40; doubles £43/55. Reception 24hr.

CARDIFF BACKPACKER
HOSTEL ❷

98 Neville St. ☎02920 345 577 www.nosda.co.uk

Nos Da's funkier sister is more geared toward the traditional backpacker, like the solo international travelers. A private bar offers cheap drinks at night, and the brightly-colored walls give the place an upbeat mood. The hammocks atop the roof are prime places to relax after a long day on the road.

Leave Central Station to left and cross river bridge. Turn right and walk up the river bank towards the next bridge in the distance. Make a left at Despenser St. and follow it straight, turns into Neville St. i Breakfast included. Internet £1 per 30min. Self-catering kitchen. Only open F-Su.

NOMAD
HOSTEL ❶

11 Howard Gardens, Roath ☎02920 256 826 www.nomadcardiff.co.uk

This new addition to Cardiff's hostel scene is simple, but offers good value for a young clientele. Plus, there's a TV and game room with pool table, communal bar, outdoor BBQ area, and self-catering kitchen.

1 mi. from train station and bus station. Head east at Central Sq. and make a right onto Great Western Ln., then a left at Saunders Rd. Take a right onto A4160/Custom House St., which becomes A470/Bute Terrace; take a slight right onto A470/Adam St. and continue to follow this until it becomes Moira Terr., after which you'll turn left at Howard Gardens. i Continental breakfast included. Laundry £6. Free Wi-Fi. Bar and games room. Female-only dorm available. Ⓢ Dorms £11-17; quads £56-72; quints £70-90.

YHA CARDIFF
HOSTEL ❷

2 Wedal Rd., Roath Park ☎02920 462 303 www.yha.org.uk

Two miles, or a 15min. bus ride from the city center, YHA Cardiff is a large brick house in the middle of a residential neighborhood. The dorms are standard but fairly spacious, and the communal facilities are adequate, though they certainly won't be winning any awards for their decor. Backpackers can't be picky, though.

Bus # 28, 29, or 29B depart from St. Mary's St. and Westgate St. Ask the driver to let you off at the bus stop for Wedal Rd./Lake Rd. West (hostel is 1min. away from stop). 15min. ride to city center. i Full breakfast included. Wi-Fi £4 per hr., £8 per 24hr. Internet £1 per 15min. Bar. Parking. All dorms are single-sex. Family rooms available. Ⓢ Dorms £14-24. £3 charge per night for non-YHA members. Doubles £52-90. Reception open 7:30am-11pm.

AUSTIN'S
BED AND BREAKFAST ❷

11 Coldstream Terr. ☎02920 377 148 www.hotelcardiff.com

Austin's is an affordable B and B option with standard rooms and breakfast. It's handily located close to Cardiff's Millenium Stadium, Bute Park, and the downtown area. River views are available if you get lucky!

Facing Millenium Stadium, overlooking the river. Leave Central Station to left and cross river bridge. Turn right and walk up the river bank toward the next bridge in the distance. Fitzhamon Embankment becomes Coldstream Terr., before the next bridge. Ⓢ Dorms £16.

PENRHYS HOTEL
BED AND BREAKFAST ❸

127 Cathedral Rd. ☎02920 387 292 www.penrhyshotel.com

A large, pleasant guesthouse in a tree-lined residential neighborhood, with tastefully-decorated, albeit dark, bedrooms with ensuite baths. Of the B and Bs on Cathedral Road, this is where you'll find the best value.

Take the Castle St. bridge over the River (second bridge from train station, past Millenium Stadium, right before Bute Park). Make a right on Cathedral Rd. Hotel is on left. i Breakfast included. Towels provided. Free Wi-Fi. Tea- and coffeemakers. TVs and telephones in each room. Singles £35; doubles £55.

ANCHORAGE GUESTHOUSE BED AND BREAKFAST 3

45 Fitzhamon Embankment, Riverside 02920 228 904

Riverside B and B has a mix of standard and ensuite rooms. The luckiest clientele gets especially large windows and river views, but all are provided with a flatscreen TV, floral bedspreads, and breakfast. If internet or laundry are requirements for you, look elsewhere.

Leave Central Station to left and cross river bridge. Turn right and walk up the river bank towards the next bridge in the distance. Anchorage guesthouse is on the left, overlooking the river i Breakfast included. Standard singles £25, with bath £35; doubles with bath £55.

CARDIFF CARAVAN PARK CAMPSITE 1

Pontcanna Fields 02920 398 362

This campsite, run by a bike company, is close to park grounds and ballfields, and within 15min. of the main downtown area. Hot showers and bathrooms are located on-site, along with a cafe that serves snacks and hot meals during the day.

Turn into the National Sports Centre off Cathedral Rd., pass the Swalec Stadium (cricket grounds), and follow signs to Caravan Park. i Cafe on-site. Bike rental on-site. Handicapped facilities. Electricity available. £9.50-22 per night for caravan and caravan rallies. Tents £16-21.50 per night.

ACORN CAMPING AND CARAVANING CAMPSITE 1

Ham Ln. South 01446 794 024 www.acorncamping.co.uk

This 4.5 acre site is surrounded by farmland and located right on the water. It's an hour away from Cardiff's Central Station and within 1 mi. of the beach at Wales's Heritage Coast. A children's play area will bring out your inner child, but the 11pm quiet time will silence your inner party animal.

Rosedew Farm, Ham Ln. S., Llantwit Major. 1hr. by bus #X91 from Central Station; 15min. walk from the Ham Ln. stop. i 1 mi. from Llantwit Major and the beach. 105 pitches. Can accommodate touring caravans, motor homes, and tents. The pitches are individually marked, some with trees and hedgerows providing extra privacy and shelter. £8.75 for 1 adult, unit, and car. £10.60 for 2 adults, unit, and car. £4.50 for each additional adult. Quiet time 11pm-7am.

SIGHTS

CARDIFF CASTLE CASTLE

Castle St. 02920 878 100 www.cardiffcastle.com

"Cardiff wouldn't be Cardiff without its castle," boasts a brightly-colored sign in the modern video viewing room. That's true indeed. The castle holds a dear place in the history of the Welsh, as its origins date back to Roman times (0-50 CE) and it has played an important role in every major period of rule from those Romans to the Normans to Victorians. Barraged by both sides during the English Civil War, the castle was left in ruins. A 19th-century refurbishment has restored it to glory, unearthing the historic moat around the castle's keep and erecting a stately home for one of Wales's most important families.

i Premium tours start at 10am and run every hr. Open Mar-Oct 9am-6pm, Nov-Feb 9am-5pm. Last audio tour distributed 30min. before close. Last video 1hr. before close.

NATIONAL MUSEUM CARDIFF MUSEUM

Cathays Park 02920 397 951 www.museumwales.ac.uk

The flagship institution of the Wales' National Museums, Cardiff's beautiful Edwardian gallery has exhibitions that explore Welsh heritage. The permanent exhibit, the "Evolution of Wales," traces the region's roots all the way back to the Big Bang. The upstairs galleries are beautiful and peaceful, highlighted by the

Impressionists exhibit, featuring pieces by the likes of Monet, Manet, Cezanne, Pisarro, and Degas, among others. In the Welsh Art exhibit, keep an eye out for the portrait of **Katheryn of Berain.** The granddaughter of Henry VII's illegitmate son, she married four times and became one of the richest and most powerful women Wales has ever seen.

*Civic Centre. **i** Pick up a site-specific What's On pamphlet at the information desk for special events. Free guided tours daily at 12:30pm. Free. Open Tu-Su 10am-5pm.*

LLANDAFF CATHEDRAL — CATHEDRAL

Cathedral Green — www.llandaffcathedral.org.uk

The Cathedral sits on the site of an ancient religious site and former sixth-century monastery; people have worshipped here since at least 500 CE. Proof lies in the ancient Celtic cross that stood on the grounds, which now stands on display near the door of the Chapter House. The current building dates from 1130, but the cathdral has fallen into disarray at various points in its history. It was used by Cromwell's men as an alehouse, as an animal shelter during the Reformation, and as German target practice in 1941. All of this turmoil accounts for its amalgamation of styles—even the official church descriptions can't think of a more-apt classification than "mostly Gothic," because it has had Norman, Tudor, and modern additions. Today, the cathedral is in perhaps its best shape ever, enjoying a brand-new handmade £1,500,000 organ, which, at 26 ft. was the largest to be built in Britain in over 40 years.

Take the 24 or 25 bus from Central Station (15min. ride). Get off at the Black Lion. Follow signs to cathedral. Free. Volunteers staff the cathedral daily 10am-4pm. Guided tours available if booked in advance (and with donation).

CARDIFF BAY — WATERFRONT

The 21st century's attempt to duplicate the 19th-century civic center has taken the form of completely revitalized waterfront area. You probably won't be able to afford much more than an ice cream or a coffee, but on a lovely summer day, it's still worth the trek to see the scenery and people-watch.

Walk 1 mi. down Lloyd George Ave., or take the # 1 or 2 bus from Central Station, or the # 66, 35, or 36 from Wyndham Arcade. Alternatively, you can take a boat shuttle from Cardiff Castle.

ARCADES — SHOPPING DISTRICT

The shopping kind, not the ones with tokens and video games. Cardiff's famed Victorian arcades provide needed relief from the invasion of big chain stores that has hit the city in the last couple of years. While perusing the main shopping district, keep an eager eye out for the small hole-in-the-wall entrances—then, walk in and enjoy the music stores, independent booksellers, vintage clothing shops, and quaint cafes. Though they might be older, each is still well-kept and sparkling.

Royal Arcade and Morgan Arcade, between St. Mary's St. and The Hayes. Castle Arcade, off Castle St., connecting to High St. Duke St. Arcade, off Duke St. High St. Arcade, between High St. and Working St. Wyndham Aracade, off Westgate St. Dominions Arcade, off Greyfriars St. Queens' Arcade. Most shops open 8am-5pm.

FOOD

Mill Lane is the best place to find traditional British and pub fare. For more ethnic, but mostly chain options, the **Old Brewery Quarter** features a circle of mid-range and more expensive options. The historic arcades of the city center offer many small, local cafes, each with their own distinct flavors. Clubbers and partiers, meanwhile, will almost certainly find their way to **Caroline Street** for a late-night fourth meal—the takeout shops here stay open selling fish and chips, kebabs, burgers, and all of those greasy favorite weekend treats until the wee hours of morning. Other take-away joints are congregated in the university area of town, a bit out of the main city center by **Salisbury Street.** The **Cardiff Bay** area is a popular food and drink spot with

mid-20s yuppies, but most of the restaurants are outsite the average backpacker's price range.
Historic **Cardiff Market,** dating from 1891, *(Open M-Sa 8am-5:30pm)* has food stands of every possible genre on the bottom floor, and cheap cafes on the balcony level. The main entrance is on St. Mary's St. The **Riverside Farmer's Market** is held every Sunday from 10am-2pm on Fitzhamon Embankment and features gourmet Welsh specialties like cheese and Welshcakes. **Tesco Express,** is on St. Mary's St. *(Open daily 6am-11pm),* while **Sainsbury Central** is located at the corner of Queen St. and Dumfires Pl. *(Open M-F 7:30am-8:30pm, Sa 11am-5pm).*

MADAME FROMAGE — DELI, CAFE ❷

21-25 Castle Arcade ☎02920 644 888 www.madamefromage.co.uk

Tucked inside the narrow halls of charming Castle Arcade, Madame Fromage is a combination delicatassen and patisserie with an elegant touch. A casual observer would think, "French, definitely," but Welsh and Breton cuisine is also available. Fine cheese, featured in delicacies like crepes and filled baguettes, is the specialty, but the menu also includes traditional Welsh specialities, lasagna, desserts, and milkshakes.

There are entrances to Castle Arcade from High St. and Castle St. Madame Fromage is on the corner where the arcade switches direction. Entrees £4.50-7.75. Open M-Sa 10am-5:30pm, Su 11am-4pm.

GWDIHŴ — MEDITERRANEAN AND BRITISH ❶

6 Guildford Crescent ☎02920 397 933 www.gwdihw.co.uk

You might be far from home, but a visit to this Log cabin-ish living room space will instantly make you feel comfortable. This alternative hangout offers various types of sandwiches that come with fresh salads and chips *(£5-6).* Other meals are also served in the vintage digs (check out the animal hides, family portraits, and various heirloom-type objects hanging out around the fireplace and mantle). At night, live music or indie-spinning DJs are the norm. Special theme nights like flamenco and micro-festivals that can go on all day long complement the regular entertainment lineup.

Guildford is off Churchill Way. i 15% student discount on food, 5% on drinks. Entrees £5-7. Open M-Th 11am-midnight, Sa 11am-2am, Su noon-midnight.

PANCAKE HOUSE — CREPES ❷

18 Caroline St. ☎02920 644 954

Surrounded by overpriced chains, a glass cube in the middle of the quarter is a magical oasis of both sweet and savory crepes. Those seeking a decadent experience might try the chocolate fondue with fruit and marshmallows *(£4.50).* Trashy newspapers and magazines are available for the traveler's perusing. The glass cube can get a little stuffy, though, so take your crepe outside to a metal table.

In the Brewery Quarter, off St. Mary St. Open M-Th 10am-10pm, F 10am-11pm, Sa 9am-11pm, Su 9am-10pm.

VEGETARIAN FOOD STUDIO — INDIAN, VEGETARIAN ❶

109 Penarth Rd. ☎02920 238 222 www.vegetarianfoodstudio.co.uk

Largely removed from Cardiff's downtown area, this small Indian vegetarian restaurant is a hidden gem. A long list of healthy meatless and vegan options come in large portions and with distinctive spices. Contemporary Gujarati (southern Indian) cuisine is the specialty. Try the *Barfi* in flavors like chocolate-chip, mango, almond, pistachio,cherry, or mixed-nut for dessert.

Grangetown. Walk down the Embankment, and make a right on Penarth. i Vegan options. Takeaway and delivery available. Bring your own alcohol with £1 corkage charge per person. Open Tu-Th 10am-9:30pm, F-Su 10am-10pm.

CAFE CITTA ITALIAN ❷

4 Church St. ☎02920 224 040

A warm, small Italian restaurant with fresh pasta *(£6.50-8.50)* and 12" pizzas *(£5-8.50)* made on a log-burning oven, Cafe Citta boasts excellent quality for decent prices. The lunchtime special served from noon-6pm includes your choice of pasta, lasagna, or 9 in. pizza with a salad or garlic bread *(£5.50)*.

Near St. John's Cathedral. Open Tu-Sa 11am-9pm, Su noon-5pm.

THE PLAN DELI, CAFE ❷

28-29 Morgan Arcade ☎02920 398 764

Good coffee, a friendly neighborhood feel, and free newspapers should you feel right at home in this cozy cafe. The Plan takes advantage of local produce in its fresh sandwiches and breakfasts.

Morgan Arcade is between St. Mary's St. and The Hayes. Open M-Sa 8:45am-5pm, Su 10am-3:30pm.

NEW YORK DELI DELI, BAGELS, TAKEOUT ❶

High St. Arcade ☎02920 388 388

There aren't too many places in the UK to get a decent bagel, so you've got to cherish them when you find them. Enjoy one toasted with the nosh of your choice *(£1.25-3.70)* or try a hoagie *(£4.30-6.20)* or a sandwich off the "Especially American" menu and appreciate the tastefully tacky American kitsch and Big Apple posters that cover the walls.

High St. Arcade is between High St. and Working St. i 10% Student Discount. Takeaway and delivery available. Entrees £1.25-6.20 Open M-Sa 8am-5pm.

CHAPTER CAFE CAFE ❶

Chapter Arts Centre, Market Rd. Canton ☎02920 304 400

A local treasure, Chapter Cafe is located within the Chapter Arts Centre in Canton. All food is freshly prepared and healthy, with locally sourced organic ingredients. Plus, it's all surprisingly affordable. The menu changes seasonally, but Chapter Cafe is known for their breakfast. Meat-lovers should try the Welsh bacon.

Canton, behind Cowbridge Rd. east, between Llandaff Rd. and Market Rd. Accessible from the city center by # 17, 18, and 31 buses every 5min. from Cardiff Central. i Gluten-free and dairy-free options. Entrees 5-7. Open M-Sa 8:30am-9:30pm, Su 9:30am-9:30pm.

EURASIAN TANDOORI INDIAN, INDONESIAN ❷

66 Cowbridge Rd. E. ☎02920 398 748 www.eurasiantandoori.co.uk

The large, varied menu features vegetarian options along with seafood, traditional tandoori, and curry cooked in a wide variety of different styles. Takeout is cheaper, and delivery saves the trip out of the way.

From town, take the bridge from Castle St., which becomes Wellington St. Cowbridge is a right off Wellington. i Delivery 6-11pm. Free delivery for orders over £10.50. Entrees £5.25-14.95. Open M-Th 6pm-12:30am, F-Sa 6-11pm, Su 6pm-12:30am.

POSH NOSH DELI ❶

53a Cowbridge Rd. E. ☎02920 398 055 www.posh-nosh.co.uk

Posh Nosh isn't a place to sit and relax (it's way too tiny), but it does serve up excellent sandwich for a day on-the-go—better yet, at rock-bottom prices. Watch out for crowds in suits during lunch hour.

Junction of Cathedral Rd. and Cowbridge Rd. Sandwiches and baguettes £1.85-2.15. Open M-F 10:30am-2pm.

NIGHTLIFE

Cardiff nightlife is buzzing all year long, so it only makes sense that *Buzz*, a publication available for free at the TIC, comes out monthly and has all the live music listings for the upcoming month.

The major nightlife drag is **Saint Mary Street.** On weekends, its sidewalks are packed with young people ready to spend a long night out on the town. The major gay area is concentrated around **Churchill Way** and **Charles Street,** but on any given night you'll see a wide range of gay and straight clientele hitting up the clubs here.

While Cardiff is safe and there are always people out, especially on weekends, it has its share of sketchy characters who roam the streets at night. Hail a cab in front of the bus station during late hours, especially if you're shacking up outside of the main downtown areas.

CARDIFF ARTS INSTITUTE — CLUB

29 Park Pl. ☎02920 231 252 www.cardiffartsinstitute.org

This funky hotspot for Cardiff's artists has a decor that is infinitely eclectic, with an entire wall is lined with multi-colored kitchen gloves and another with legos that you might start fiddling with after grabbing a few too many drinks from the in-house "Mojito Bar." Check out the old-school telephones and bean bag chairs, and then venture outside with your camera to snap a shot of your head in one of the cutouts. Events include festivals, film screenings, exhibitions, and poetry readings. The weekends are louder, with DJs on Friday nights and live music starting at midnight on Saturdays.

*Near the National Museum, in between Park Ln. and Park Rd. **i** Free Wi-Fi. Cover free-£5. Open M-Th noon-1am or 2am, F-Sa noon-4am, Su noon-1am or 2am.*

10 FEET TALL — DELI, RESTAURANT, BAR, CLUB

12 Church St. ☎02920 228 883 www.thisis10feettall.co.uk

Cardiff partiers flock to this unique club and restaurant. Three stories, each with their own vibe, crazy-colored lighting, good DJs and North African cuisine make this the place to be seen in town. If you're feeling scholarly, recline in the mezzanine "library" with couches and black-and-white bookshelf-themed wallpaper. If you're feeling more energetic, check out the upstairs dance floor club area or the Rock Room, which hosts live music acts, comedy shows, and even films.

*Church St. is off of High St. **i** Free Wi-Fi. Cover F-Sa £5. Open daily noon-4am. Kitchen open M-F noon-9pm, Sa-Su noon-10pm.*

CLWB IFOR BACH (THE WELSH CLUB) — CLUB

11 Womanby St. ☎02920 232 199 www.clwb.net

This is the signature club on legendary Womanby St. In its early days, only Welsh-speakers were allowed, but the club opened its doors to all in the '90's to become one of the biggest hotspots in the Cardiff music scene. The history remains, though, and they'll definitely appreciate those who attempt to thank the bartender in Welsh. On the three diverse floors, you'll hear everything from indie to hip-hop to dubstep to reggae and electro. If you're lucky enough, you might even get to catch some authentic Welsh music. Student night is every Wednesday.

From the river, take Castle St. and make a right onto Womanby St. Club is on your left. Cover £3-6, higher when big names come to play (up to £15). Open W until 2am, Th-Sa until 3am. Opening times vary, so call ahead or check the website.

MILGI LOUNGE — BAR, MUSIC VENUE, CAFE

213 City Rd. ☎02920 473 150 www.milgilounge.com

This funkily decorated local and independent venue is brightly colored and vibrant, a great spot to grab a drink with friends in a unique atmopshere. Live music, much of it experimental, is featured several times a week, often in the outdoor tent area. (Did we mention there's a hot tub? And beds in sheds?) Milgi also features comedy shows and an affordably priced and healthy food menu, with all vegetarian and some vegan options. Note the unusual decorations: many of them are designed on sight by members of Milgi's "art club."

Take the # 38/39 bus from Wyndham Arcade; there's a stop right outside Milgi, on City Rd. Free Wi-Fi. Cover free-£5. Open M-Th 11am-11:30pm, F-Sa 11am-12:30pm, Su 11am-11:30pm.

PULSE GLBT, BAR, CLUB

3 Churchill Way ☎02920 647 380 www.pulsecardiff.com

Pulse advertises itself as "gay, but straight-friendly." Recline in the blue booths and enjoy the mellow vibe during the day, then wait for the music to get pulsing at night. Wednesday nights are student nights *(students £2, non-students £4).* Drinks are £1.20 from 5-8pm. On Friday nights, drinks are only £.99 in the downstairs club.

From the city center, Churchill Way is accessible by taking Charles St. to a right onto Heol Y Frenhines, and a right onto Churchill Way. You can't miss the outdoor tables. All meals £2.99. Cover free before 11pm, up to £5 (Sa). Open M 11am-4am, Tu 11am-8pm, W 11am-4am, Th 11am-8pm, Sa-Su 11am-4am. Kitchen open daily 11am-5:30pm.

WOW BAR BAR, CLUB

4 Churchill Way ☎02920 666 247 www.wowbarcardiff.com

Theme nights are every night in this zebra-motif (with splashes of orange thrown in) gay bar. Downstairs, a club with its own separate bar area rocks on weekends. Wednesday nights are student nights *(all drinks £1.50 all night long)* and every day during Cheeky Hour all drinks are £1.50.

From the city center, Churchill Way is accessible by taking Charles St. to a right onto Heol Y Frenhines, and a right on Churchill Way. Again, you can't miss the outdoor tables. Food served 10am-5pm (Su 10am-4pm). Separate VIP room available for rent. Open M-Th 10am-2am, F-Sa 10am-3am, Su 10am-2am.

TAFARN BAR

53-59 Despenser St. ☎02920 37 88 66 www.nosda.co.uk/tafarn

The downstairs Bar (or "Inn" as Tafarn means in Welsh) of Nos Da is open to the public, who have definitely taken advantage of its young atmosphere and waterfront perks. For affordable prices, you can try out authentic Welsh beers and ciders, all while reclining outside on the heated porch and admiring the banks of the River Taff. Crowds come in the masses before major matches at nearby Millenium Stadium.

Leave Central Station to the left and cross river bridge. Turn right and walk up the river bank toward the next bridge in the distance. Make a left at Despenser St. It's a 3min. walk. Tafarn is inside of Nos Da Hostel. Free Wi-Fi. Open M-Th noon-11:30pm, F-Sa noon-12:30am, Su noon-11:30pm. Kitchen open daily noon-10pm.

FAT CAT BAR

Grosvenor House, Greyfriars Rd. ☎02920 228 378 www.fatcatcafebars.co.uk

Fat Cat is modern and sophisticated, with tasseled red lampshades, comfortable booths, armchairs, and couches, and classy cocktails. Drinks aren't the cheapest you'll find, but Mondays and Wednesdays are student nights, with £1 tequila and two-for-one drink deals. Students always get 20% off all food.

From the National Museum and Gallery, make a right onto Park Pl. past Blvd. de Nantes. Greyfriars Rd. will be to the right. Bar is on left. . Open M-Th 11am-midnight, F-Sa 11am-2am, Su 11am up to midnight. Kitchen open M-Sa 11am-10pm, Su noon-4pm.

BARFLY CLUB, MUSIC VENUE

The Kingsway ☎396 590 www.barfly.com/cardiff

One of Cardiff's favored sites at night, Barfly puts on a ton of events for club-hoppers, ranging from "Hammertime" '90s nights on Tuesdays to techno and house. Generally speaking, Saturday nights are the dance nights for getting your groove on, whereas Fridays are more typical of the alternative rock gigs that originally gave Barfly its name.

Across from Cardiff Castle. Student discounts on club nights. Bring student ID. Cover £2-9. Tickets for music gigs £5-15. Purchase at the door and in-person cash only. Tickets can be purchased in-person at the club M-F 10am-6pm. Open M 7:30-11pm, Tu-Th 7:30pm-2am, F-Sa 7:30pm-3 or 4am, Su 7:30-11pm.

LIVE LOUNGE — BAR/CLUB

9 Greyfriars Rd. ☎0750 307 9825 www.theliveloungecardiff.co.uk

This young venue features live cover bands seven nights a week. They set the stage for a DJ who plays the best indie, rock, and chart tunes until 4am. Live Lounge gets crowded right around midnight, so try to show up early to avoid the line, no matter how cheesy the tribute bands might be.

From the National Museum and Gallery, make a right onto Park Pl. past Blvd. de Nantes. Greyfriars Rd. will be to the right. Live Lounge is on the left. Open daily 11am-4am. Food served until 9pm.

THE PEN AND THE WIG — PUB

1 Park Grove ☎02920 371 217

A large beer garden combined with cheap prices makes this a popular place for students in town during term time, and a prime summer pub for locals. Look out for special nightly deals, like curry Thursdays *(£5)* and grill Wednesdays *(grill of choice + drink, £6)*. The beer might not be the most unique or best quality you've ever had, but you can get a bottle of Coors Light *(£2)* or a decent glass of wine *(from £1.09)*.

Cathays. Front entrance on Park Grove, back entrance on Park Ln., both off of St. Andrew's Pl. Open M-Th 10am-midnight, F-Sa 10am-1am, Su 10am-11:30pm. Kitchen open 10am-10pm.

REVOLUTION — BAR, CLUB

9-11 Castle St. ☎02920 236 689 www.revolution-bars.co.uk

This is the new and trendy place to be in town. Revolution has sleek, modern decor, signature chandelier lamps, and big-screen TVs for your favorite sports action. This is definitely a liquor-specialty place, so if you're starting your night here, you're going hard.

Across from Cardiff Castle. Free Wi-Fi. Shots £2. Mixed drinks £5.50-6. Open M-Sa 11am-2am, Su noon-2am. Kitchen open M-Sa 11am-9pm, Su noon-9pm.

ARTS AND CULTURE

ST. DAVID'S HALL — CITY CENTER

The Hayes ☎02920 878 444 www.stdavidshallcardiff.co.uk

The National Concert Hall of Wales hosts bands and comedians throughout the year, and is the home of the BBC National Orchestra and Chorus of Wales. It also gains fame for hosting the BBC Cardiff Singer of the World competition, held every two years, and the Welsh Artist of the Year Competition,which recognizes and exhibits the work of top local contributors to the arts.

Next to St. David's shopping center, opposite the TIC. Book in advance. No standbys. Tickets from £5.50. Box office open M-Sa 9:30am-8pm, Su 1hr. before perfromance.

WALES MILLENNIUM THEATRE — CARDIFF BAY

Cardiff Bay, Bute Pl. ☎02920 636 464 www.wmc.org.uk

An impressive architectural structure, the Wales Millenium Theatre is most famous for its large bronze dome, made of the same materials that used to be so important to Cardiff's seafaring livelihood. It also features a multi-colored slate facade, inscribed with words "In These Stones Horizons Sing" written by **Gwyneth Lewis,** one of Wales's premier poets. The theater has become home to Welsh National Opera and to the BBC National Orchestra of Wales. The main theater can seat almost 2000 people.

Walk ¾ mi. down Lloyd George Ave. (on your left) or take a bus (every 10min.) from the city center to Cardiff Bay. i Backstage tours 11:30am and 2:30pm; must book in advance. Tickets £5-45. Some offer concessions. Welsh National Opera offers £10 tickets for some shows to those under 26; check on website. Backstage tours £5.50, concessions £4.50. Ticket office open M-F 10am-30min. after last curtain; Sa 11am-late, Su performance days only from 5pm.

NEW THEATRE — CITY CENTER

Park Pl. ☎02920 878 879 www.newtheatrecardiff.co.uk

Back when this theater was being built, smashed-up bottles were used for the foundation to stop rats from gnawing at the timbers of the building. Miraculously, though, the theater has survived on this foundation since 1906, though it was recently refurbished. Popular musicals and dramas come to town, and the annual pantomime is much-loved by Cardiff locals.

1 block past Boulevard de Nantes, on your right. i "Student Specials" available for dramas only for evening performances (except Sa). For musicals and ballets, student standby tickets are available; cash-only. Concessions are also available for weekday performances, usually about £3.50 off normal ticket price. Musicals £9-31.50, dramas £8-25. Box office open M-Sa non-performance days 10am-6pm, performance days 10am-8pm. Su only open on performance days.

CHAPTER ARTS CENTRE — CANTON

Market Rd., Canton ☎02920 304 400 www.chapter.org

This internationally renowned art-house features a variety of music, theater, cinema, and dance from around the world. Chapter Arts Centre is home to many of Cardiff's most creative citizens, and also hosts gallery space for modern art.

Canton, behind Cowbridge Rd. E., between Llandaff Rd. and Market Rd. Accessible from the city center by # 17, 18, and 31 buses every 5min. from Cardiff Central. Films £3-12, concessions available. Theater £3-35. Gallery free. Box office open M-Sa 11am-8:30pm, Su 3-8:30pm. Gallery open Tu-Sa 10am-8pm, Su 2-8pm.

ESSENTIALS

Practicalities

- **TOURIST OFFICES: The Hayes** is in the newly renovated Old Library. *(☎02920 873 573 www.visitcardiff.com i Luggage storage available. Books rooms for £2 plus 10% deposit. Internet £1 per 30min. Open M-Sa 9:30am-5:30pm, Su 10am-4pm.)*
- **TOURS: City Sightseeing Cardiff** runs a 12-stop hop-on, hop-off open-top bus tour throughout the city center, starting from Cardiff Castle. *(☎02920 473 432 www.city-sightseeing.com £9, concessions £7. Runs daily March-Oct daily.)* **Aquabus** offers a 45min. guided boat cruise leaving from the dock at Cardiff Bay *(£5, children £3)* and circling around the nature reserve and the Bay.
- **BANKS:** Banks with ATMs line Queen St. and St. Mary St. One of the major banks in the city is **NatWest.** *(117 St. Mary St. Open M-F 9am-4:30pm.)*
- **LUGGAGE STORAGE:** Store your luggage at the tourist office. *(Small locker £3, medium locker £5. Key deposit £3.)*
- **LAUNDROMATS: Drift In.** *(104 Salisbury Rd. ☎02920 239 257 www.drift-in.*

co.uk ⏰ Open M-Th 9am-6pm, F 9am-9pm, Sa 9am-6pm, Su 10am-9pm.)

- **INTERNET ACCESS:** The central library, **The Hayes,** offers free Wi-Fi and free internet. *(⏰ Open M-W 9am-6pm, Th 9am-7pm, F 9am-6pm, Sa 9am-5:30pm, Su 11am-3pm.)*

Getting There

By Plane

Cardiff International Airport*(☎01446 711 111 💻www.tbicardiffairport.com)* is a 30min. train ride away from the city center. A rail link connects the terminal to Cardiff Central via a free shuttle bus to and from **Rhoose Cardiff International Station**. Trains run in each direction every hour to Cardiff Central Station. Cardiff Bus X91 operates between Cardiff (Central Station) and Cardiff International Airport hourly *(£3.40)*.

By Train

Trains run from Central Station, Central Sq., south of the city center and behind the bus station, to **Bath** *(Ⓢ £15.90. ⏰ 1hr., 2 per hr.)*; **Birmingham** *(Ⓢ £51.50. ⏰ 1 per hr., 2hr.)*; **Bristol** *(Ⓢ £9.30. ⏰ 45min., 2 per hr.)*; **London Paddington** *(Ⓢ £25. ⏰ 2 per hr., 2hr.)*; and **Edinburgh** *(Ⓢ £130.50 ⏰ 6½-8hr., 2 or 3 per hr.)*. Buy tickets at the ticket office. *(⏰ Open M-Sa 5:45am-9:30pm, Su 7:30am-9:45am. Advance Tickets sold M-Sa 9am-6pm, Su 1-5:30pm.)*

By Bus

National Express *(☎08717 81 81 81 💻www.nationalexpress.com)* buses run from Central Station on Wood St. to **Birmingham** *(Ⓢ £26.90. ⏰ 2¾hr., 4 or 5 per day)*; **London** *(Ⓢ £25.20. ⏰ 3hr. 35min., every hr.)*; **London Gatwick** *(Ⓢ £50.50. ⏰ 3¾hr., every 2hr.)*; and **Manchester** *(Ⓢ £38.30, ⏰ 5hr., 4 or 5 per day)*. The National Express Booking Office and Travel Centre is located on Wood St. next to Central Station *(⏰ Open M-Th 8am-5:15pm, F 8am-5:45pm, Sa 7am-5:45pm, Su 8am-5:45pm)*. **Megabus** *(☎0871 266 3333 💻www.megabus.com)* also runs cheap buses leaving from the Kingsway to **London Victoria** *(Ⓢ from £5. ⏰ 3½hr., 10 per day)*.

Getting Around

By Bus

Cardiff Bus *(☎0871 200 22 33 💻www.cardiffbus.com)* is the main operator in the city. The Travel and Customer Service Centre is in St. David's House on Wood St. opposite the Central Bus and Rail Stations *(⏰ Open M-F 8:30am-5:30pm, Sa 9am-4:30pm)*. Cardiff Bus only accepts exact fare *(Ⓢ single £1.50, day pass £3)*, so make sure you have enough change before you step on a bus or purchase your day pass beforehand in the Travel Centre.

By Train

Regular trains run from Cardiff's Queen Street station to Cardiff Bay and city stops including Cathays, Ninian Park, and Llandaff *(Ⓢ £1.70)*.

By Taxi

For a taxi in Cardiff, call **Delta Taxi** *(☎02920 201 010)* or **Dragon Taxi** *(☎02920 333 333)*. The best place to hail a cab if you're out on the town at night is in front of Central Station. Other stations on Wood St. and St. Mary St.

By Boat

The **Waterbus** *(☎07940 142409 💻www.cardiffwaterbus.com)* and **Aquabus** run shuttle services between the Millenium Stadium, Mermaid Quay, and Penarth and from Cardiff Bay to Cardiff Castle. *(☎07500 556 556 💻www.aquabus.co.uk Ⓢ Single £3, round-trip £5.)*

By Bike

PedalPower is located in Pontcanna Caravan Park, off Dogo St. in the city center *(☎02920 390 713 www.cardiffpedalpower.org.uk ⑤ £5 per 1hr., £7.50 per 2 hr., £15 per 24hr. £20 deposit per bike. ⏰ Open Apr-Sept M-F 9am-6pm and Su 10am-4pm, Oct-Mar 10am-4pm)* and in Cardiff Bay, just beyond Norwegian Church, over the footbridge, and 100 yards on your right in Cardiff Marina Boat Yard. *(⑤ £5 per 1hr. £7.50 per 2 hr., £15 per 24hr. £20 deposit per bike. ⏰ Open Sa-Su 11am-5pm.)*

CAMBRIDGE

One of the more student-oriented cities in England, Cambridge is packed with pubs, clubs and intimate cafes. Winding lanes twist and turn between the age-old colleges of the university, each one a path through the town's fascinating history. It was here that **Watson** and **Crick** discovered the double helix, **Newton** discovered gravity, **Byron** and **Milton** wrote their famous poetry, and **Winnie the Pooh** was born. If you're looking for a simplified Cambridge experience, the "P and P" formula is perhaps best: Punting and Pimm's (in other words, boating and boozing, although the two together could be a disaster waiting to happen). In the summer, multitudes of foreign exchange students come to Cambridge to learn English, making for a congested, multilingual street scene.

greatest hits

- **SWIM AND BARE IT.** Visit the fountain at Trinity College (p. 184) where Lord Byron used to skinny-dip.
- **WHIMSICAL WINDOWS.** Meditate in King's College Chapel (p. 185), perhaps the only place on campus with both **dragons** and unicorns.
- **A HEADLINING PUB.** Extra! Extra! Drink all about it!...at the Free Press pub (p. 193).
- **ROLLIN' DOWN THE RIVER.** Rent a punt from Scudamore's (p. 196) and cruise down the Cam.
- **GO FOR JOE.** For cheap coffee and lively debates, head to Indigo Coffee House, a favorite among "uni" students (p. 189).

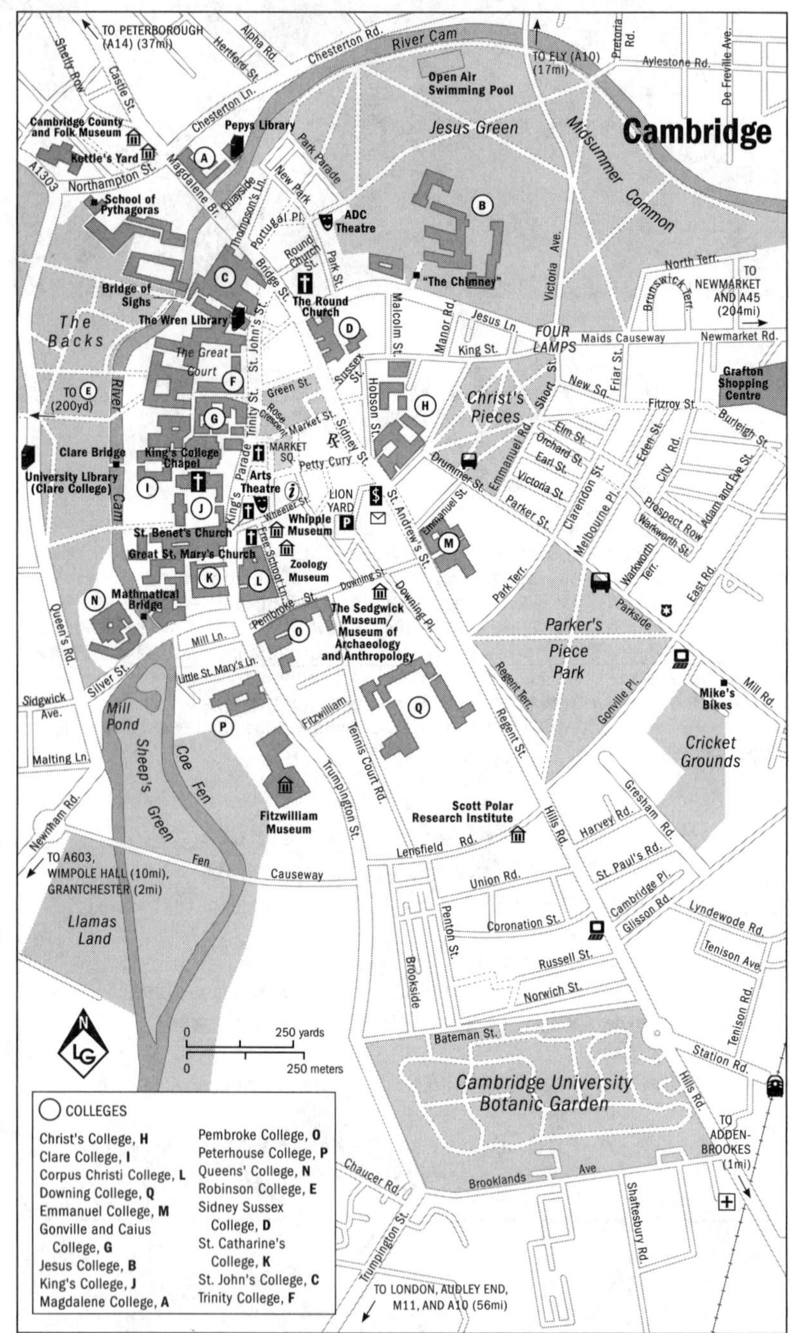
Cambridge
TO PETERBOROUGH (A14) (37mi)
TO ELY (A10) (17mi)
TO NEWMARKET AND A45 (204mi)
TO A603, WIMPOLE HALL (10mi), GRANTCHESTER (2mi)
TO LONDON, AUDLEY END, M11, AND A10 (56mi)
TO ADDENBROOKES (1mi)
TO E (200yd)
River Cam
Open Air Swimming Pool
Jesus Green
Midsummer Common
Cambridge County and Folk Museum
Kettle's Yard
Pepys Library
School of Pythagoras
ADC Theatre
"The Chimney"
Bridge of Sighs
The Wren Library
The Round Church
The Backs
The Great Court
FOUR LAMPS
Christ's Pieces
Grafton Shopping Centre
Clare Bridge
University Library (Clare College)
King's College Chapel
MARKET SQ.
Arts Theatre
LION YARD
Whipple Museum
St. Benet's Church
Great St. Mary's Church
Zoology Museum
Mathmatical Bridge
The Sedgwick Museum/ Museum of Archaeology and Anthropology
Parker's Piece Park
Mike's Bikes
Cricket Grounds
Mill Pond
Sheep's Green
Coe Fen
Fitzwilliam Museum
Scott Polar Research Institute
Llamas Land
Cambridge University Botanic Garden
Chesterton Rd.
Chesterton Ln.
Alpha Rd.
Hertford St.
Shelly Row
Castle St.
Pretoria Rd.
Aylestone Rd.
De Freville Ave.
A1303
Northampton St.
Magdalene Br.
Quayside
Thompson's Ln.
Park Parade
New Park
Portugal Pl.
Round Church St.
Park St.
Bridge St.
St. John's St.
Trinity St.
Green St.
Rose Crescent
Market St.
Sidney St.
Sussex St.
Hobson St.
Malcolm St.
Manor Rd.
Jesus Ln.
King St.
Victoria Ave.
North Terr.
Brunswick Terr.
Maids Causeway
Newmarket Rd.
New Sq.
Friar St.
Short St.
Fitzroy St.
Burleigh St.
Emmanuel Rd.
Elm St.
Orchard St.
Earl St.
Victoria St.
Drummer St.
Parker St.
Clarendon St.
Melbourne Pl.
Eden St.
City Rd.
Prospect Row
Warkworth St.
Adam and Eve St.
Warkworth Terr.
East Rd.
Parkside
Petty Cury
King's Parade
Wheeler St.
Free School Ln.
Emmanuel St.
St. Andrew's St.
Downing St.
Downing Pl.
Park Terr.
Pembroke St.
Mill Ln.
Little St. Mary's Ln.
Fitzwilliam
Tennis Court Rd.
Trumpington St.
Regent Terr.
Regent St.
Gonville Pl.
Mill Rd.
Queen's Rd.
Silver St.
Sidgwick Ave.
Malting Ln.
Newnham Rd.
Fen Causeway
Lensfield Rd.
Hills Rd.
Gresham Rd.
Harvey Rd.
St. Paul's Rd.
Union Rd.
Cambridge Pl.
Glisson Rd.
Lyndewode Rd.
Tenison Ave.
Tenison Rd.
Coronation St.
Penton St.
Brookside
Russell St.
Norwich St.
Bateman St.
Station Rd.
Chaucer Rd.
Brooklands Ave
Shaftesbury Rd.
0 250 yards
0 250 meters
N
LG
COLLEGES
Christ's College, H
Clare College, I
Corpus Christi College, L
Downing College, Q
Emmanuel College, M
Gonville and Caius College, G
Jesus College, B
King's College, J
Magdalene College, A
Pembroke College, O
Peterhouse College, P
Queens' College, N
Robinson College, E
Sidney Sussex College, D
St. Catharine's College, K
St. John's College, C
Trinity College, F

student life

There's no cooler place to be a young intellectual than Cambridge. After all, the pub where Watson and Crick announced their discovery of **DNA** is still a popular spot for cheap pints and stimulating debates. In the warmer months, though, you're more likely to find young people in the **parks** than the pubs. The beautiful gardens behind the colleges are perfect for reading a book, hanging out with students, and avoiding the tourist rush in the center of town. If you're really craving some nightlife after sunset, celebrate youth at the **Fountain Inn** or climb the **Soul Tree,** a popular three-story club with graffiti-covered walls. You're more likely to discover a hangover than the double helix, but hey, we won't judge.

orientation

Cambridge has two central avenues: the main shopping street starts at **Magdalene Bridge** north of the River Cam and becomes Bridge Street, Sidney Street, Saint Andrew's Street, Regent Street, and Hills Road. The other main thoroughfare begins as **Saint John's Street** (just off Bridge St.), becoming Trinity Street, King's Parade, and Trumpington Street. To get into town from the Drummer St. bus station, take **Emmanuel Rd.** This leads to **St. Andrew's St.**, and a bank-heavy block with loads of cash machines. To get to the center of town from the train station, follow **Station Rd.** and turn right onto **Hills Rd.** Then follow it straight until it becomes St. Andrew's St. and turn left on Downing St. and follow to Pembroke St. and turn right onto King's Parade, which will take you past King's College and onto Trinity St. by Trinity College.

accommodations

The Cambridge lodging scene is notoriously bad. There are few affordable rooms anywhere near the town center, and an excess of overpriced, occasionally sketchy bed and breakfasts fill the north and south of town, particularly on **Arbury Road** and **Chesterton Road** to the north. Several can be found closer to town on **Tenison Road.**

WARKWORTH HOUSE BED AND BREAKFAST ❹

Warkworth Terr. ☎01223 363 682 www.warkworthhouse.co.uk

Warkworth House is truly a cozy bed and breakfast. It's been owned by the same people for 33 years, and the beautiful rooms are all well furnished. Breakfast is not included... psych! Of course it is.

Walk down Parkside away from town center and turn left onto Warkworth Terrace. Ⓢ Singles from £60; doubles from £80; family rooms from £100.

TENISON TOWERS BED AND BREAKFAST ❸

148 Tenison Rd. ☎01223 363 924 www.cambridgecitytenisontowers.com

With more affordable prices than most bed and breakfasts, Tenison Towers offers small, bright, and clean rooms as well as delicious homemade muffins and jams with the complimentary hot breakfast.

From the station, go down Station Rd. and turn right onto Tenison Rd. Ⓢ Singles £40; doubles £64.

YHA CAMBRIDGE HOSTEL ❶

97 Tenison Rd. ☎0845 371 9728

Though rather worn, the YHA Cambridge is unbeatable for the prices it offers.

It's one of the few truly budget accommodations in Cambridge.

From the station, head down Station Rd. and turn right onto Tenison Rd. Internet £1 per 20min., £5 per 24hr., £12 per 3 days, £15 per 7 days. Reservations taken daily 7am-11pm. Dorms £14-20. Reception 24hr.

A. AND B. GUESTHOUSE BED AND BREAKFAST ❸

124 Tenison Rd. ☎01223 315 702 www.aandbguesthouse.co.uk

A pleasant, relatively centrally located B and B with clean and bright rooms. A. and B. has a full English breakfast, but can also satisfy vegetarian and gluten-intolerant customers upon request.

From the station, walk down Station Rd. and turn right onto Tenison Rd. Singles £50, doubles £70, family £90. Reception 7am-noon and 6pm-midnight; self check-in after midnight.

LYNWOOD HOUSE BED AND BREAKFAST ❸

217 Chesterton Rd. ☎01223 500 776 www.lynwood-house.co.uk

The Lynwood House offers home-style comfort in an affordably priced B and B. Though Chesterton Rd. is outside the city center, it's not unbearably far.

Walk up Victoria Ave. away from town center and turn right onto Chesterton Rd. Doubles ensuite. Singles from £40; doubles from £75; twins ensuite from £75.

THE CASTLE BED AND BREAKFAST ❹

37 St. Andrew's St. ☎01223 307 477 www.thecastlecambridge.co.uk

Just above the stylish bar of the same name, the Castle may not be exactly what you'd expect from a place called "The Castle." It's also not quite what you'd expect from a guest house above a bar, though the noise is noticeable some nights. It is, however, hard to get closer to the center of town, especially for the rates offered here.

Head north on Regent St. until it becomes St. Andrew's St. Shared bathrooms. Doubles £68, but prices vary. Reception daily 8am-11pm.

ACORN GUEST HOUSE BED AND BREAKFAST ❸

154 Chesterton Rd. ☎01223 353 888 www.acornguesthouse.co.uk

This small guest house provides relatively affordable housing. Visitors can take buses into town.

Head up Victoria Ave away from town center and turn right onto Chesterton Rd. Singles £50-75; doubles £70-95.

ASHLEY HOTEL HOTEL ❹

74 Chesterton Rd. ☎01223 350 059 www.arundelhousehotels.co.uk

The Ashley is the more affordable sister hotel to the Arundel, which is a little further up Chesterton Rd. The rooms are simple and clean, and stained-glass windows cast color on the bright entry hall.

Head up Victoria Ave away from town center, turn right onto Chesterton Rd. Breakfast included. Singles £65; doubles £75; family rooms £95. Reception open 7am-2pm and 5-10pm.

ARUNDEL HOUSE HOTEL HOTEL ❺

Chesterton Rd. ☎01223 367 701 www.arundelhousehotels.co.uk

More upscale than most of the B and Bs that line Chesterton, the Arundel House Hotel has the luxuries of a standard hotel and a restaurant.

Head up Magdalene St. from Sidney St. and turn right onto Chesterton Ln., which becomes Chesterton Rd. Singles £75-95; doubles £95-140. Reception 24hr.

sights

TRINITY COLLEGE COLLEGE

Trinity Ln. ☎01223 338 400

Trinity is perhaps the most popular of the colleges, drawing phenomenal numbers of tourists. **Henry VIII** intended for Trinity College to be the largest and richest in Cambridge, and with the modern-day college holding its own as third largest landowner in Britain (after the Queen and the Church of England), his wish has clearly been fulfilled. Trinity is famous for its illustrious alumni, including literati Dryden, Byron, Tennyson, and Nabokov; atom-splitter Ernest Rutherford; philosopher Ludwig Wittgenstein; and Indian statesman Jawaharlal Nehru. Perhaps most famously, **Sir Isaac Newton** lived there for 30 years. **The Great Court** in the center of the college is the world's largest enclosed courtyard. Visitors enter the courtyard through the Great Gate, which is guarded by a statue of Henry VIII clutching a wooden chair leg—a substitute for the oft-stolen original scepter. The apple tree near the gate is supposedly a descendant of the tree that inspired Newton's theory of gravity; in the north cloister of Neville's court, Newton calculated the speed of sound by stamping his foot and timing the echo. Lord Byron used to bathe **nude** in the college's fountain. Byron also kept a **pet bear** because college rules forbade cats and dogs. **The Wren Library** is home to alumnus A.A. Milne's handwritten copies of **Winnie the Pooh** and Newton's personal copy of his **Principia.**

Turn left onto Trinity Ln. off of Trinity St. £3, children £1.50. Courtyard open daily 9:30am-4:30pm. Wren Library open M-F noon-2pm. Hall open daily 3-5pm.

KING'S COLLEGE — COLLEGE

King's Parade ☎01223 331 100 www.kings.cam.ac.uk

Founded by **Henry VI** in 1441, King's College was originally a partner school to **Eton** until it slackened its admission policy in 1873 to accept students from other public schools. These days, King's reputation is significantly changed, and it is one of the more socially liberal of the Cambridge colleges, drawing more of its students from state schools than any other. Many visitors come for the Gothic **King's College Chapel,** where the spidering arches and stunning stained glass will stun even the most church-weary tourist. Inside the chapel, the period when Henry's mason left off and the Tudors began building is marked by a change in color of the stone. Note the roses, **dragons,** and unicorns repeated throughout the church's interior, even on its ceiling. These were the symbols of the **Tudors,** and it's a good thing for the church's decor that their coats of arms weren't all skulls, cross-bones, and vampire bats. King's alumni include: **John Maynard Keynes, EM Forster,** and **Salman Rushdie.**

Trumpington becomes King's Parade. £5, concessions and children 12-18 £3.50, under 12 free. During term time open M-F 9:30am-3:30pm, Sa 9:30am-3:15pm; during breaks open M-Sa 9:30am-4:30pm, Su 10am-5pm. Chapel during term time M-Sa 5:30pm evensong (enter through the front gate at 5:15pm). Su Eucharist 10:30am, Evensong 3:30pm.

THE POLAR MUSEUM — MUSEUM

Lensfield Rd. ☎01223 336 540 www.spri.cam.ac.uk/museum

Founded in 1920 to memorialize **Captain Robert Falcon Scott** and his crew after they died on a return trip from the South Pole in 1912, The Polar Museum has reopened in a sleek, modern renovation packed with memorabilia from various polar expeditions, such as the barrel organ from an 1819 winter trip to the Arctic (it has 40 tunes spread across a five-barrel system) and John Ross's memoirs and narratives which are written in absurdly fine print. Especially of note is the fantastic gallery of Inuit art at the back.

Head down Regent St. away from the city center and turn right onto Lensfield Rd. Free. Open Tu-Sa 10am-4pm.

THE FITZWILLIAM MUSEUM — GALLERY

Trumpington St. ☎01223 332 900 www.fitzmuseum.cam.ac.uk

Named after Richard Fitzwilliam, this beautiful museum was opened in 1848. Through the Corinthian landings of the main hall, visitors will find a variety of paintings, antiquities and applied arts. Among the numerous highlights are paintings by Monet, Pissaro, and Renoir and sculptures by Rodin. There is also a beautiful **John Constable** painting of the Heath upstairs. The museum features Impressionist artwork, Turkish pottery, and objects from everyday Egyptian life on the ground floor.

Trumpington is one of the main roads. Off Pembroke if coming from the east and Silver St. if from the West. Free. Audio Guides £3, students £2. Guided tours £4. Open Tu-Sa 10am-5pm, Su noon-5pm. Guided tours depart Sa at 2:30pm from the courtyard entrance.

CLARE COLLEGE

COLLEGE

Trinity Ln. ☎01223 333 200 www.clare.cam.ac.uk

Though initially founded by the **Chancellor of England,** it was refounded by **Lady Elizabeth de Clare** when the chancellor ran out of money. The thrice-widowed, 29-year-old Elizabeth's pain is bluntly referenced in the Clare coat of arms which features golden teardrops ringing a black border. The college has lush gardens of dangling ivy and weeping willows, and you can regularly hear the sound of punts hitting the riverbed. The elegant **Clare Bridge** dates from 1638 and is the oldest surviving college bridge. In wandering through Christopher Wren's Old Court, one can see the **University Library,** where **150 mi.** of shelving house **eight million volumes.**

Turn left onto Senate House Passage off of Trinity St. (a continuation of King's Parade). £2.50, under 12 free. Open daily 10:45am-4:30pm.

MAGDALENE COLLEGE

COLLEGE

Magdalene St. ☎01223 332 100

Magdalene (pronounced MAUD-lin) College is housed in a fifteenth-century hostel for Benedictine monks that was, in all probability, nicer than most of the hostels you've been staying in. It's famous for the **Pepys Library,** which holds several diaries by **C.S. Lewis** who, despite his status as an Oxford man, lived in Magdalene occasionally.

Bridge St. becomes Magdalene St. i Wheelchair access in courtyard but not library. Open daily until 6pm. Library open daily Oct 6-Dec 5 2:30-3:30pm; Jan 12-Mar 13 2:30-3:30pm; Apr 20-Aug 31 11:30am-12:30pm and 2:30-3:30pm.

CHRIST'S COLLEGE

COLLEGE

St. Andrews St. ☎01223 334 900 www.christs.cam.ac.uk

When it was in its original location, **Christ's College** was known as "God's-house," but it moved in 1448 to the current site where it was known as "Jesus College." Either way, it's holy. The Hall pays homage to two of the most famous residents of the college—**John Milton** and **Charles Darwin**—in the form of a bust and portrait respectively. New Court is a modern concrete building constructed in 1970.

St. Andrew's St. is a continuation of Regent St. i Wheelchair access in the church but not tower. Free. Open daily 9:30am-noon.

JESUS COLLEGE

COLLEGE

Jesus Ln. ☎01223 339 339 www.jesus.cam.ac.uk

Visitors walk down a pathway known as "The Chimney" to get to the college. The arms of Bishop Alcock, the man who founded the College on the grounds of an abandoned Benedictine nunnery, are of a cock standing on an orb, a rather regal-looking visual pun. Stroll through the gardens and courts thronged by roses and enjoy the 25-acre grounds.

Go north on Sidney St. and turn right onto Jesus Ln. i Wheelchair access in the church but not the tower. Open daily 8am-dusk.

ST. JOHN'S COLLEGE

COLLEGE

St. John's St. ☎01223 338 600 www.joh.cam.ac.uk

Through the green arches of the entrance lies the paved plaza of St. John's college, founded in 1511 by Lady Margaret Beaufort, the mother of Henry VII. Take note of the **Bridge of Sighs,** which is designed on the same pattern as a Venetian bridge of the same name. The **School of Pythagoras** dates to the 12th century and is thought to be the oldest complete building in Cambridge. **The Fellows' Room** in Second Court, which spans an impressive 93 ft.—making it the longest room in the town—was the site of some D-Day planning.

Head north on Sidney St. Turn left off of Bridge St. onto St. John's St. i Credit card min. £5. Ⓢ £3.20, students £2, ages 12-16 and seniors £2. Open daily Mar-Oct 10am-5pm; Nov-Feb 10am-3:30pm.

QUEENS' COLLEGE

COLLEGE

Off Silver St. ☎01223 335 537 www.queens.cam.ac.uk

Queens' College derives its name from its two founders: Queen Margaret of Anjou in 1448 and Elizabeth Woodville (the queen consort of Edward VI) in 1465. Though it's notable for having the only unaltered Tudor courtyard in Cambridge, the main attraction of the college is the **Mathematical Bridge** which is both the only bridge in Cambridge and supposedly the most perfectly structured bridge. We can't tell why, but it was designed by William Etheridge in 1749 and put in place in 1905.

Silver St. is off Trumpington St. i Partially wheelchair-accessible. Ⓢ £2.50. Open daily Mar-Oct 10am-4:30pm.

WHIPPLE MUSEUM OF THE HISTORY OF SCIENCE

MUSEUM

Free School Ln. ☎01223 330 906 www.hps.cam.ac.uk/whipple

This university museum is named after Robert Whipple, who donated a collection of roughly 1000 scientific devices to the university, many of which are on display here, such as the *Gömböc* (a strangely shaped object that, despite its homogeneous consistency, will return to the same resting position no matter where you place it), and **Fred,** a 19th-century anatomical model whose parts have been mercilessly scattered across the museum. Several intriguing planetariums, microscopes, telescopes and a wealth of pocket calculators round out the fantastic collection.

Turn left off of St. Andrew's St. onto Downing St., follow it until it becomes Pembroke and make a right onto Free School Ln. i Call ahead for wheelchair access. Ⓢ Free. Open M-F 12:30-4:30pm.

MUSEUM OF ZOOLOGY

MUSEUM

Downing St. ☎01223 336 650 www.museum.zoo.cam.ac.uk

This museum is packed to the gills with fantastic animals (dead, of course). Come for the giant spider crab, and stay for the birds. Some of these guys are enough to make you believe in creationism. Consider the Gorgeted Bird of Paradise: was the Don King hair style necessary for flight? How did the Raggi's Bird of Paradise fly with wings that look like he got in a fight with a Hoover? These are important questions to ask, best followed by a visit downstairs where there's a little history of the fateful 1831 voyage of the HMS Beagle.

Turn left off of St. Andrew's St. onto Downing St. Ⓢ Free. Open M-F 10am-4:45pm, Sa 11am-4pm.

THE SEDGWICK MUSEUM

MUSEUM

Downing St. ☎01223 333 456 www.sedgwickmuseum.org

Adam Sedgwick was a famous geologist who believed firmly in creationism, once writing to his pupil, Charles Darwin, that he read **Origin of Species** with "more pain than pleasure." The museum houses one of the world's leading collections of paleontology. The Whewell gallery is named after Professor Whewell, coiner of the term "scientist" and collector beautiful minerals. A collection of rocks collected by Darwin on the HMS Beagle journey is also on display.

Turn left off of St. Andrew's St. onto Downing St. Free. Open M-F 10am-1pm and 2-5pm.

MUSEUM OF ARCHAEOLOGY AND ANTHROPOLOGY MUSEUM

Downing St. ☎01223 333 516 www.maa.cam.ac.uk

The MAA is one of the eight university museums, and it features art and artifacts from various indigenous populations across the world. The archaeological displays trace the beginnings of humanity through Roman and medieval Britain, and the fantastic, towering **Haida Totem Pole** from British Columbia blows just about everything else away.

Turn left off of St. Andrew's St. onto Downing St. Free. Open Tu-Sa 10:30am-4:30pm. Closed for renovations from Sept 2010-Feb 2011. Check the website when planning your visit.

CAMBRIDGE UNIVERSITY BOTANIC GARDEN GARDENS

1 Brookside ☎01223 336 265 www.botanic.cam.ac.uk

The rolling 40 acres of these lush gardens contain over 10,000 plants. Perfect for anyone with a green thumb, or those who want to bask in the sun or sit by a pond that induces poetic contemplation, the Botanic Gardens are well worth a visit. The scented garden is, unsurprisingly, fantastically fragrant.

Go down Trumpington Rd. away from town and turn right onto Bateman St. £4, concessions £3.50, under 16 free. Open daily Apr-Sept 10am-6pm; Oct 10am-5pm; Nov-Feb 10am-4pm; Mar 10am-5pm.

THE ROUND CHURCH CHURCH

Bridge St. ☎01223 311 602

The simple round church, founded circa 1130 CE, is the second oldest building in Cambridge and is one of four surviving circular churches in England. Its intriguing Norman architecture is based on the Holy Sepulchre in Jerusalem.

A continuation of Sidney St. closest to the River. £2. Open Tu-Sa 10am-5pm, Su 1-5pm.

KETTLE'S YARD GALLERY

Castle St. ☎01223 748 100 www.kettlesyard.co.uk

Kettle's Yard is composed of two parts: the house and gallery. The gallery rotates through innovative exhibitions while the house, which was the former home of gallery-founder and Tate Curator Jim Ede, contains early 20th-century art and sculpture.

Take Magdalene St. over the river until it becomes Castle St. at the intersection with Chesterton Ln. i House is partially wheelchair-accessible. Free. Open Apr-Sept Tu-Su 1:30-4:30pm; Oct-Mar Tu-Su 2-4pm.

CAMBRIDGE COUNTY AND FOLK MUSEUM MUSEUM

2-3 Castle St. ☎01223 355 159 www.folkmuseum.org.uk

Housed in the old White Horse Inn, the Cambridge County and Folk Museum provides a social history of Cambridge. Themed exhibits every few months range from Dickens-themed to '60s-themed, but generally explore Cambridge through unique lenses. Note the stunning collection of pipes, many of which are bone-white and in the suspicious shape of skulls.

Take Magdalene St. over the river until it becomes Castle St. at the intersection with Chesterton Ln. £3.50, concessions £2, children £1. Open Tu-Sa 10:30am-5pm, Su and Bank holidays 2-5pm. Last entry 30min. before close.

ST. BENET'S CHURCH CHURCH

Benet St. ☎01223 355 146

St. Benet's Church has been a site of worship for almost 1000 years (founded circa 1020). It's even older than the Round Church.

Turn right off of King's Parade when heading north on it from Trumpington St. Free. Open daily 7:30am-6:30pm.

GREAT ST. MARY'S CHURCH — CHURCH

King's Parade — ☎01223 741 716 www.gsm.cam.ac.uk

The tower of the university church of Cambridge is the highest point in town, providing views of most of the glorious colleges. Make use of the church below to pray the bells don't start clanging madly as you gingerly make your way up the 123 steps.

King's Parade. Church free. Tower £3, students £2.40. Church open M-Sa 9:30am-4pm, Su 12:30-4pm. Tower opens M 10:30am. Tower closes earlier than the rest of the church. Try to come before 3:30pm.

Though a student town, Cambridge has a lot of upscale dining. The cafes are nestled in its nooks and crannies and often provide delicious, cheap food and excellent coffee. Cambridge is also something of an ice cream town, so look out for the homemade ice cream and gelato that abound. Late-night food is available in the **Market Square** area.

INDIGO COFFEE HOUSE — CAFE ❷

8 St. Edward's Passage — ☎01223 295 688

A student favorite, the Indigo Coffee House has two tiny floors that are sociable out of necessity. With its popular, inexpensive coffee and sandwiches, the cafe is host to a thousand eager, undergraduate debates.

Head toward Trinity on King's Parade and turn right onto St. Edward's Passage. Bagels with toppings £1.75-4. Small coffees £1.40-1.85, large coffees £2.65. Sandwiches on ciabatta £4.80 to eat in, £3 to take away. Open M-F 10am-6pm, Sa 9am-6pm, Su 10am-5pm.

CB1 — CAFE ❶

32 Mill Rd. — ☎01223 576 306

Claiming to be the "oldest internet cafe in U.K.," CB1 has modern convenience with pre-inflation charm and prices. The sandwiches are delicious and unbelievably cheap, and the creaky wooden bookshelves are bursting with classic novels. Alcohol served with food.

Go southeast on Parkside until it becomes Mill Rd. Sandwiches £2.80. Toasted ciabattas £3.50. Milkshakes £2.60-2.70. Open M-Th 8:30am-8pm, F 8:30am-9pm, Sa 9:30am-8pm, Su 10:30am-8pm.

CLOWNS CAFÉ — ITALIAN CAFE ❷

54 King St. — ☎01223 355 711

This cafe feels like a scene out of an old Italian movie. The effervescent staff playfully jeer at familiar customers and tell regulars they can swing by later to pay the rest of their cash-only bill, while tons of students sit around sipping coffee and tucking into Mediterranean food. There's outdoor seating on the small but pleasant roof terrace.

Turn right off Sidney St. onto Jesus Ln.; turn right onto Malcolm St. and you'll hit King St. Entrees £4-6.50. Full English breakfast £6. W 5-10pm penne carbonara with wine £8.50. Open daily 8am-11pm.

BENET'S — ICE CREAM ❸

20 King's Parade — ☎01223 329 068

With the soul music blaring, the students chatting, and the homemade ice cream slowly melting in the summer heat, Benet's is a Cambridge summer staple. Their milkshakes are especially delicious.

King's Parade. i Credit card min. £5. 1 scoop £2.20, 2 scoops £3.50, 3 scoops £4.40. milkshakes £3.50. Open daily 8am-9pm.

MICHAEL HOUSE CAFÉ

CAFE ❸

Trinity St. ☎01223 309 147 www.michaelhousecafe.co.uk

Meals in the Michael House Café are truly transcendent experiences. Between the light that streams through the stained glass and the hearty mains like slow-roasted lamb shoulder with Merguez spices served with oil olive bread, the only thing keeping you from floating with happiness will be the essentially unchanged weight of your wallet.

Go up King's Parade until it becomes Trinity St. Bread £7-9. Open M-Sa 8am-5pm.

DOJO'S NOODLE BAR

NOODLES, ASIAN ❷

1-2 Millers Yd. (off Mill Ln.) ☎01223 363 471

Dojo's boasts noodle dishes from all sorts of Asian cuisines, including Japanese, Chinese, Thai, and Malaysian. The quick service, large portions, and low prices make this a popular student haunt.

Turn left onto Mill Ln. off of Trumpington St. and then left onto Millers Yard. Fried entrees £6.45-6.50. Rice dishes £7.15-7.20. Soup entrees £7.20-7.50. Open M-F noon-2:30pm and 5:30-11pm, Sa-Su noon-11pm.

RAINBOW CAFÉ

VEGETARIAN, VEGAN, GLUTEN-FREE ❸

9A Kings Parade ☎01223 321 551 www.rainbowcafe.co.uk

Down a small, white-walled alley and under the rainbow arch, vegetarians find their pot of gold: an affordable, exciting, and fast restaurant. Forego the veggie burgers in favor of Libyan Couscous with spinach, chick-peas, zucchini, onion, garlic, green beans and carrot *(£8.95)* or explore a wealth of vegan and gluten-free dishes. Rainbow Café is a true blessing for any vegetarian roaming the meaty wilderness of British cuisine.

King's Parade. Entrees £9-16. Open M 10am-4pm, Tu-Sa 10am-10pm, Su 10am-4pm.

CAMBRIDGE CRÊPES

CREPES ❶

Corner of Sidney and Market St. www.cambridgecrepes.co.uk

This popular crepe stand is packed throughout the day during the summer. With delicious classic sweet crepes and more inventive fare throughout the menu, Cambridge Crêpes is a solid dining option. Note the finesse with which they make a Nutella crepe: they don't just lather on the stuff, but fling it on until it looks like a Jackson Pollock and tastes 5,000 times better. Trust us.

Sidney St. Sweet crêpes £2.50; savory crêpes £3.50-3.80. Open Tu-Su 11am-5pm.

MASSARO'S

ITALIAN GELATO, SMOOTHIES ❸

85 Regent St. ☎01223 314 236

Massaro's specializes in delicious sandwiches that almost live up to the impossible hype created by their exotic ingredients lists. Between the great sandwiches, the homemade gelato, and the delicious iced drinks (iced coffee with vanilla gelato shaken, not blended), we're sold.

Regent St. Sandwiches in-store £7-7.50, take-away £5-5.50. Iced coffee £1.20-1.50. Open M-F 8am-6pm, Sa-Su 10am-6pm.

FUDGE KITCHEN

CARDIAC ARREST ❸

11 King's Parade ☎01223 350 191 www.fudgekitchen.co.uk

Though Fudge Kitchen is a chain, that doesn't change the fact that employees here wear awesome hats and make the fudge fresh in front of throngs of people between 11am and 3pm daily before distributing samples of freshly-made chocolates. Get a Student Loyalty card—after three stamps, you get free fudge. An insider **tip:** pick up the card on your first purchase (any day but Friday) and get one stamp. Then, come in on Friday, buy a slice and say "fudge Friday." This gets you two stamps and then an extra slice of fudge. You're welcome.

King's Parade. 1 slice of fudge £4.25-4.85. Open M-Sa 10am-6pm, Su 10am-5:30pm.

AUNTIE'S TEA SHOP BRITISH TEA ❷

1 St. Mary's Passage ☎01223 870 144 www.auntiesteashop.co.uk

If you're searching for an authentic British tea, look no further than the calming quietude and lace table cloths of Auntie's Tea Shop. This is probably what your aunt's living room would look like if she liked tea and wanted you to call her "auntie."

Go up King's Parade toward Trinity St. and turn right onto St. Mary's Passage. Full tea £7.65. Sandwiches £4-4.50. Panini £5.50. Open M-F 9:30am-6pm, Sa 9:30am-6:30pm, Su 10:30am-5:30pm.

COPPER KETTLE BRITISH ❷

4 King's Parade ☎01223 365 068

A cozy breakfast place with traditionally English fare. Enjoy a full English breakfast (veggie option available) while basking in the beautiful architecture of King's College.

King's Parade. Lunch £7.50-8. Full English breakfast £5.

LA MARGHERITA GELATO ❷

15 Magdalene St. ☎01223 315 232

Though also an Italian restaurant, La Margherita excels at serving the largest section of delectable gelato in Cambridge. The Amaretto is especially fantastic.

Go up Bridge St. Small £1.70, medium £2.50, large £3.80. Open M-F 10am-4pm and 6-10:30pm, Sa 10am-11pm, Su 10:30am-8pm.

CHOCOLAT CHOCOLAT GELATO, CHOCOLATE ❹

21 St. Andrew's St. ☎01223 778 982

Chocolat Chocolat serves, surprisingly, a wealth of delicious, hand-crafted, French chocolate. They also have fantastic gelato. Try the Hazelnut—it's so legitimate you may even bite into a nut now and then. They're also known for their extra-thick hot chocolate and handmade chocolate sheets. It's *delicieux delicieux!*

Go up Regent St. until it becomes St. Andrew's St. Cash only for ice cream. 1 scoop £2, 2 scoops £3, 3 scoops £4. Open M-Tu 9am-6pm, W 9am-8pm, Th-F 9am-6pm, Sa 9am-7pm, Su 10:30am-6pm.

CB2 ITALIAN BISTRO ❹

5-7 Norfolk St. ☎01223 508 503 www.cb2bistro.com

Though a little far from the center of town, CB2 is a great place to catch the occasional concert and the more consistent coffee. Come here if CB1 (see above) just ain't enough.

Go up East Rd. away from town and turn right on Norfolk St. Cover usually £4-8. Entrees £12-14. Pasta £7.50-8.25. Beer £3.20 per bottle. Open M-Th 10am-10:30pm, F-Sa 10am-11pm, Su noon-10:30pm. Breakfast served M-Sa 10am-noon. Th-Sa live music starts 8pm.

THE CAMBRIDGE CHOP HOUSE BRITISH FOOD ❹

1 King's Parade ☎01223 359 506 www.chophouses.co.uk

For anyone who wants to prove that British cuisine can be taken seriously, the Chop House is a necessary stop. The mostly local, fresh ingredients are brought together into carefully-prepared dishes like sausage and mash *(£10.50)* and roast chicken, sugar snaps, peas and carrots, poultry sauce and mash *(£14)*.

King's Parade. Entrees £10-19. M-F 11am-7pm 2 courses £11. Open M-Th 11am-10:30pm, F-Sa 11am-11pm, Su 11am-9:30pm.

t.g.i.f.

Fridays are often turn-around days for tour groups. Take advantage of the diminished crowds to see some of the busier sights.

LA TASCA TAPAS ❹

14-16 Bridge St. ☎01223 464 630 www.latasca.co.uk

Though a chain restaurant, La Tasca manages all the warm, candlelit intimacy of any good local Spanish restaurant and truly delivers on the delicious food. The frequent deals only sweeten the entire package.

Go up Sidney until it becomes Bridge St. i Daily until 5pm 5 tapas for 2 people £10. Ⓢ Tu-W 5-9pm all-you-can-eat £10. Tapas £3.75-4.35, recommended for 3-4 people. Open daily noon-11pm.

ANATOLIA TURKISH ❹

30 Bridge St. ☎01223 362 372 www.anatolia.uk.com

Within the very British town of Cambridge, Anatolia is a refreshingly ethnic treat priding itself on authentic Turkish cuisine. The set lunch, available until 2:30pm, provides a three-course meal *(£11.95).*

Go up Sidney St. until it becomes Bridge St. Ⓢ Entrees £12.50-12.95. Open daily noon-midnight.

DE LUCA'S ITALIAN ❺

83 Regent St. ☎01223 356 666 www.delucacucina.co.uk

A modern Italian restaurant featuring mostly locally-sourced ingredients, an exposed kitchen, and a greenhouse-esque back dining area, De Luca's is a unique and pleasant dining experience. Those looking to save money should take full advantage of the bread, olive oil, and vinegar given free of charge to the table. Come during the express lunch times or order some of the cheaper pastas to feast well for cheap.

Regent St. Ⓢ 2-course express lunch £10, 3-course express lunch £14. Pasta £9.95-10.95. Entrees £16.95-17.95. Open M-Sa noon-10pm, Su noon-8pm. Express lunch M-F noon-4pm.

THE COW PIZZA ❸

Corn Exchange St. ☎01223 308 871 www.barroombar.com

Housed in an alternative bar, The Cow provides cheap, delicious pizzas in the heart of the city. If Cambridge weather behaves itself, you can enjoy your slices in the outdoor seating.

Go down Downing St. and turn right on Corn Exchange. Ⓢ 12 in. pizzas £8-8.25. Wraps £5-5.25. Burgers £8-8.25. Open M-Tu noon-11pm, W-Sa noon-1am, Su noon-11pm.

CHARLIE CHAN CHINESE RESTAURANT CHINESE ❸

14 Regent St. ☎01223 359 336

This calm, simple Chinese restaurant is a delicious place for a highly customizable and enjoyable Chinese meal. Select from a list of rice and noodles and choose an accompanying meat or seafood dish.

Regent St. Ⓢ Chicken, pork, and beef dishes £5.80-7.50. Seafood £7.80. Rice and noodles £1.80-6. Fried rice £3. Boiled rice £1.80. Open daily noon-11pm.

CÔTE BRASSERIE FRENCH ❸

21-24 Bridge St. ☎01223 311 053 111.cote-restaurants.co.uk

One of a chain of restaurants, Côte Brasserie offers up fantastic French food in a pleasant environment for reasonable prices, especially if you come in for one of their lunch or early evening deals.

Go up Sidney St. until it becomes Bridge St. Ⓢ 2-course lunch and early evening deal £10. Open M-F 8am-11pm, Sa 9am-11pm, Su 8am-10:30pm. Lunch and early evening deal noon-7pm.

MAI THAI THAI ❸

Park Terr. ☎01223 367 480 www.mai-thai-restaurant.co.uk

Mai Thai is seated on the edge of a popular cricket pitch, making for a bizarre and highly enjoyable cultural mashup in a calming atmosphere of clean white walls, floors and tabletops.

Go south on St. Andrew's St. toward Regent St. and turn left onto Park Terr. Ⓢ Lunch entrees £6.50. Dinner entrees £8. Open daily noon-3pm and 5:30-11pm.

THE FREE PRESS
PUB

Prospect Row ☎01223 368 337 www.freepresspub.com

This small pub is bursting at the seams with character. Cell phones and music are banned, making space for idiosyncratic, pubby conversation that's missing at many modern establishments. Deriving its name from its former life as a newspaper printing shop, the Free Press is a classic watering hole that's well worth the visit for any pub culture fanatic. Get some sun (or clouds) in the beer garden.

Left off Parkside (when heading away from town center) onto Warkworth Terrace. Left onto Warkworth St., right onto Prospect Row. Pints £3. Open M-F noon-2:30pm and 6-11pm, Sa noon-11pm, Su noon-3pm and 7-10:30pm.

THE EAGLE
PUB

8 Benet St. ☎01223 505 020

On a cool February 28th in 1953, **Francis Crick** and **James Watson** burst into the Eagle and announced to the scientists who were slowly killing their Nobel-prize-winning brain cells that they had discovered the "secret to life," the **double helix.** The history of this charming bar doesn't stop there. Toward the back, messages and squad numbers remain scorched on the ceiling where RAF men burnt them with lighters on the evenings before missions during the war. Furthermore, it's only a short distance from where the atom was first split. For your purposes, the bar has history, charm, and affordable alcohol.

Head toward Trumpington on King's Parade and turn left onto Benet St. i Credit card min. £5. Pints £3. Open M-Sa 10am-11pm, Su 11am-10:30pm.

CHAMPION OF THE THAMES
PUB

68 King St. ☎01223 352 043

The Champion of the Thames is the sort of pub with comfortably low ceilings and lamps that seem to shed only the warmest, most orange light. Decorated in oars and leather chairs and boasting two rotating guest pints which trend towards excellence, the Champion of the Thames is a great place to grab a brew.

Turn right off Sidney St. onto Jesus Ln., then turn right onto Malcolm St. and you'll hit King St. Carlsberg and IPA pints £2.45. Open M-Th noon-11pm, F-Sa 11am-11pm.

THE ANCHOR
PUB

Silver St. ☎01223 353 554

Situated near the river, The Anchor has beautiful bay windows that look onto the water. Get a beer and watch self-punters slowly crash into each other and occasionally sink. The stained glass in the pub is also nice.

Off Trumpington. Pints £3-4. Open M-Th 10am-11pm, F-Sa 10am-midnight, Su 10am-11pm.

THE SALISBURY ARMS
PUB

76 Tenison Rd. ☎01223 576 363 www.thesalisburyarms.com

The Salisbury Arms is packed with eight exciting different lagers as well as unique bottled beers (banana bread beer, anyone?) High on local charm, the bar also has one of the more popular pub dogs in the area, Max, an adorable pooch with hair completely covering his eyes. Check out his page on the website where other dogs write in and he responds, elucidating the pub rules. It's a little strange and highly entertaining.

Go down Mill Rd. away from town center and turn right onto Tenison Rd. i Credit card min. £10. Pints £3. Open M-Th noon-2:30pm and 5-11pm, F noon-2:30pm and 5pm-midnight, Su noon-2:30pm and 7-10:30pm.

MILL PUB

14 Mill Ln. ☎01223 357 026

Mill is a great old-fashioned pub with excellent river views. They're known for their specialty sausages, all delicious local concoctions like lamb and rosemary. Choose your own sausage and then your own mash *(£6.50).*

Go up Trumpington St. toward King's Parade and turn left onto Mill Ln. Pints £3.50. Open daily noon-11pm. Kitchen open M-Sa noon-5pm.

SOUL TREE CLUB

1-6 Corn Exchange St. ☎01223 303 755 www.soultree.co.uk

Soul Tree is the biggest club in Cambridge, with an impressive three floors of stylishly-graffitied walls. Come enjoy the loud music and dancing in the hip environment.

Go down Downing St. and turn right onto Corn Exchange. i Cover cash-only. Credit card min. £10. M international student night: cover £3-4, tequila shots £1, bottled beer £1.80. F before 11pm cover £4, after £6. Sa before 11pm £6, after £8. Mixed drinks £6. Bottled beer £3.50. Open M 10am-4pm, F 10am-4pm, Sa 10pm-4am.

FEZ CLUB CAMBRIDGE CLUB

15 Market Passage ☎01223 519 224 www.cambridgefez.com

The Fez Club hosts the largest student night in Cambridge. With a striped cloth ceiling and faux-cave walls, it's exotically decorated and hopping with activity.

Left onto Market St. off of Sidney St., right onto Market Passage. i Cover cash-only. Inquire about a free membership card from inside and ask about student discounts. M is the biggest student night in Cambridge. Tu is R and B. W is International. Th is Underground. F is a basic club night. Sa is house night. Cover M before 11pm students £3, after £4; adults £4/5. Tu before 11pm £3; 11pm-midnight £4, after midnight £5. W before 11pm £3, after £4; international students £1/3. Th £6-8. F before midnight £5, after £7. Open M-Sa 10pm-3am, Su during term-time 10pm-3am.

HIDDEN ROOMS BAR, CLUB

7a Jesus Ln. ☎01223 514 777 www.hiddenthing.com

Tucked away under Pizza Express, the Hidden Rooms, while not as secretive as the name would suggest, is a hotspot for nightlife, especially for the more soul-oriented clubbers. With a killer laser light show and state of the art sound system, Hidden Rooms provides all the essentials. The curtained booths hearken back to the days when it was host to numerous clandestine meetings (included a heavily rumored meeting between Stalin and Churchill). It's the former site of the University's Pit Club which currently resides on the top level.

Head north on Sidney St. and turn right onto Jesus Ln. i Credit card min. £10. Th is jazz night, F is soul night, Sa is house music. Cover for jazz £2 before 10pm, after £5. Open M-Sa 3pm-12:30am. Club open Th-Sa.

THE GRANTA PUB

14 Newnham Terr. ☎01223 505 016

The Granta has gorgeous river views, riverside outdoor seating, and, perhaps most beautiful of all, occasional deals on burgers and pints. Punting available from the dock just next to the pub.

Left onto Silver St. off of Trumpington, left onto Queen's Rd. i Credit card min. £5. Pints £3. Burger and pint £7. Open M-Th 11am-11pm, F-Sa 11am-midnight, Su 11am-11pm. Kitchen open M-Sa noon-10pm, Su noon-8pm.

THE MITRE PUB

17 Bridge St. ☎01223 358 403

Founded in 1754, The Mitre wears its history with worn grace. Decorated by flickering candles and an ornately carved fireplace, The Mitre's happy customers sprawl out on thick leather couches as well as more traditional chairs. Between the warm atmosphere and the cheap pints, the Mitre's a great place to drink.

A continuation of Sidney St. Credit card min. £5. Pints £2.60. Open M-W 10am-11pm, Th 10am-midnight, F-Sa 10am-1am, Su 10am-11pm.

KING STREET RUN
PUB

86-88 King St. ☎01223 328 900

A bustling pub where the music is as it should be: loud. The juke box offers customers choices from rock, hip-hop and soul, with albums from the likes of Muddy Waters, The Smiths, and the White Stripes.

Turn right off Sidney St. onto Jesus Ln., turn right onto Malcolm St. and you'll hit King St. Pints £3.30. Open M-Th 11am-11:30pm, F-Sa 11am-12:30pm, Su noon-11:30pm. Happy hour M-F 5-7pm.

THE CRICKETERS PUB
PUB

18 Melbourne Pl. ☎01223 305 544

The Cricketers Pub is a good old-fashioned Irish pub by day, even hosting the occasional Irish Jam session. By night, it hosts live music of different varieties, including jazz. Come for the music and stay for the pool and ale.

Turn right off Park Terr. onto Parkside and then left onto Melbourne Pl. Credit card min. £5. Pints £3.40. Open M-Th 11am-midnight, F-Su 11am-1am. Live music M and Th.

THE FOUNTAIN INN
BAR

12 Regent St. ☎01223 366 540 www.fountaincambridge.co.uk

Though it strongly resembles a pub from the outside, the Fountain Inn stays open later and hosts a much younger, more excited crowd than most pubs. Couches in the back and cube chairs dotted around the spacious interior provide relief for club-weary feet.

Regent St. Credit card surcharge under £10. Pints £3.50. Open M-Th 11:30am-2am, F-Sa 11:30am-3am, Su noon-1am.

THE PICKEREL INN
PUB

30 Magdalene St. ☎01223 355 068

The first licensed pub in Cambridge, The Pickerel Inn is a solid, old-fashioned pub with **Being John Malcovich**-esque archways that lead from one part of the bar to the next. A worn old barrel keeps the door to the beer garden open.

Go up Sidney St. until it becomes Bridge St. Follow Bridge until it becomes Magdalene St. Pints £3. Open M noon-11pm, Tu-Sa noon-midnight, Su noon-11pm.

REVOLUTION
CLUB, BAR

3-8 Downing St. ☎01223 364 895 www.revolution-bars.co.uk

Even with several floors, Revolution is one of Cambridge's most crowded clubs. Be sure to catch the Monday night "Tossers" deal, where you order a round, flip a coin, and, if you called it correctly, get an extra round free! There's a screen in the back of the bar area that projects a trippy montage of pop culture images. Plus, stone-baked pizzas are served whenever the place is open. Viva la Revolution!

Left off St. Andrew's St. onto Downing St. Cover cash-only. Sa is 21+ night. Cover M £3; Tu-Th free; F students £3, adults £4; Sa £5-6; Su free. Pints £3.80. Open M-Sa 11:30am-2am, Su noon-2am. Upstairs open Sept-May Tu-Sa.

THE ZEBRA
PUB

80 Maids Causeway ☎01223 308 465 www.thezebracambridge.com

The Zebra frequently hosts live music and DJ nights in its cluttered, alternative space. The curtains are zebra print, there's a picture of a zebra, and there are a few skeletal decorations lying around, all of which contribute to the off-beat feel of this solid pub.

Follow Newmarket Rd. toward town center; it will become Maids Causeway. Credit card min. £3. Pints £3.20. Open M-Su noon-midnight. Last call 30min. before close.

THE BUN SHOP
PUB

1 King St. ☎01223 327 274

This pub is a study in incongruities. An old punting boat named "The Oak Joke" rests retired in the wooden rafters. The juke box has a most-played playlist that features "Rockstar" by Nickelback, "Best of You" by the Foo Fighters, and an M.I.A. song. A fun pub with good alcohol, the contradictions only get better with ale.

Turn right off Sidney St. onto Jesus Ln., turn right onto Malcolm St. and you'll hit King St. Pints £3.20. Open M-F 11am-11pm, Sa-Su 11am-midnight.

THE COUNTY ARMS
PUB

Castle St. ☎01223 361 695

This pleasant neighborhood pub is brightly lit by the sun during the day, and features high-backed benches and a courtyard out back for the outdoorsman that sometimes comes out after your third pint.

Take Magdalene St. over the river until it becomes Castle St. at the intersection with Chesterton Ln. Credit card min. £5. Ale £3, lager £3.50. Open M-F 11am-midnight, Sa 11:30am-midnight, Su noon-6pm.

CLARENDON ARMS
PUB

35-36 Clarendon St. ☎01223 353 640

Another pub with quotes about being drunk on the walls, the Clarendon Arms is a solid neighborhood watering hole with a frequently changing selection of ales and a quiz night every Thursday. You can be drunk too!

Go down Park Terr. toward Parkside and continue onto Clarendon St. Credit card min. £5. Ale £3.10. Open M-Th noon-11:30pm, F-Sa noon-midnight, Su noon-11pm.

arts and culture

SCUDAMORE'S
RIVER CAM

Quayside ☎01223 359 750 www.punting.co.uk

Punting is one of those classic Cambridge activities that can't be skipped—not unlike getting soused on Pimm's and falling in the Cam. These vaguely rectangular boats (punts) can be rented for chauffeured tours up and down the river Cam. More adventurous (or possibly idiotic) boaters can try their hand at punting. Simply stand at the back of the boat and thrust the pole into the bottom of the river. As you remove the pole (quant, in the old lingo, though if you're whipping out *that* vocabulary, you might also want to get your French navy sweater, corncob pipe, and massive harpoon, just in case you see Moby), twist it to ensure it doesn't get stuck and drag you into the water as your boat moves on without you. If you're reading this while a passenger in a self-powered boat, don't tell the punter, and watch in amusement as he or she figures it out. Scudamore's on Quayside offers both types of punting experiences.

Right off Bridge St. underneath Magdalene Bridge. Self-hire £18 per hr. plus a £90 deposit taken in the form of an imprint of your credit or debit card. With student card £14 and a £90 deposit. Guided tours £15, concessions £13.50, under 12 £7.50, no deposit. Open daily May-Aug 9am-10pm; Sept-Nov 9am-8pm; Nov-Easter 9:30am-5pm; from Easter to mid-May 9am-6pm.

ARTS PICTURE HOUSE
CENTRAL CAMBRIDGE

38-39 St. Andrew's St. ☎0871 902 5720 www.picturehouses.co.uk

Just above one of the raging bars of Cambridge, the Arts Picture House screens art flicks, lesser known independent films, classics, and more popular films while its downstairs partner serves alcohol to kill the brain cells the APH's films would otherwise cultivate.

A continuation of Regent St. Off-peak M-F until 5pm. Adults M £7; Tu-F before 5pm £7, after £8; Sa-Su £8. Students £1 off. Box office opens 30min. before first show, closes 15min. after the start of the last. Line open 9:30am-8:30pm daily for phone booking.

ADC THEATRE CHESTERTON

Park St. ☎01223 300 085 www.adctheatre.com

Short for "Arts Dramatic Club," the ADC was a student-run theater for a long time, specializing in new writing and university productions, including frequent performances by the Cambridge Footlights, the comedy group that launched **Hugh Laurie, Steven Fry,** and **John Cleese.** Both **Ian McKellen** and **Sam Mendes** played here while at Cambridge. It still hosts university performances as well as touring shows.

Left off Jesus Ln. when you're heading away from town center. M-F adults £8, concessions £6. Sa-Su adults £10/8. Prices subject to change. Box office open Tu 12:30pm-showtime, W 3pm-showtime, Th 12:30pm-showtime, F-Sa 3pm-showtime.

CAMBRIDGE ARTS THEATRE CHESTERTON

Peas Hill ☎01223 503 333 www.cambridgeartstheatre.com

This popular Cambridge theater puts on a mix of music, straight plays, comedies, operas, ballet, contemporary dance, and occasional shows from the Cambridge Footlights. Basically, everything. The in-house pantomime group is also very popular.

Head towards Trumpington St. on King's Parade, turn left onto Benet St. and left onto Peas Hill. Tickets £12-35. Students £2 off. Open M-Sa in summer noon-6pm; in winter noon-8pm.

CAMBRIDGE CORN EXCHANGE CHESTERTON

Wheeler St. ☎01223 357 851 www.cornex.co.uk

Probably the largest music venue in Cambridge, the Cambridge Corn Exchange presents many big name musical acts coming through Cambridge.

Head toward Trumpington St. on King's Parade, turn left onto Benet St., and go straight until Benet becomes Wheeler St. Prices vary. Occasional student discounts, depending on the show. Open M-Sa 10am-6pm.

MAY WEEK CENTRAL CAMBRIDGE

This is a Cambridge festival that originally marked the end of exams. May Week originally took place in May, but is now in June, lasting for ten days. Seven days just weren't enough to contain the revelry.

10 days in June.

CAMBRIDGE FOLK FESTIVAL EDGE OF TOWN

☎01223 357 851 www.cambridgefolkfestival.co.uk

Paul Simon played at the first Folk Festival in 1965. Since then, this popular mid-July festival has gone on to include the likes of **Lucinda Williams, Mavis Staples, James Taylor,** and **Elvis Costello.** The festival is popular, so book in advance!

Full festival £108, concessions £80, 1-day only £30-50. In July.

HEART OF THE WORLD FESTIVAL VARIOUS LOCATIONS

☎01223 457 555 www.cambridge.gov.uk/public/hotw

Relatively new to the Cambridge festival scene, the Heart of the World Festival features arts from cultures around the world and happens in mid-July. It's a multimedia experience featuring live music, film screening, art exhibitions, and more from international artists.

Mid-July.

CAMBRIDGE SHAKESPEARE FESTIVAL CENTRAL CAMBRIDGE

☎07955 218 824 www.cambridgeshakespeare.com

Running from mid-July through August, the Cambridge Shakespeare Festival features the works of David Mamet. Kidding!—it's a Shakespeare festival. Many of the plays are performed in the colleges' beautiful gardens.

Tickets £14, concessions £10. From mid-July to Aug.

STRAWBERRY FAIR CENTRAL CAMBRIDGE

Midsummer Common www.strawberry-fair.org.uk

Begun in 1974, the Strawberry Fair is a free-wheeling music and arts festival held on Midsummer Common in the first week of June. It is an alternative to the May Week festivities, full of entertainment, arts, and crafts. The 2010 Strawberry Fair was unfortunately canceled, but the 2011 fair is in the works. Phew.

Midsummer Common. 1st week of June.

MIDSUMMER FAIR CENTRAL CAMBRIDGE

Midsummer Common www.cambridge-summer.co.uk

One of the oldest fairs in the country, with a history reaching back to 1211. Midsummer Fair takes place in late June and involves carnival rides. We're in.

Midsummer Common. Late June.

shopping

BOOKS FOR AMNESTY BOOKS

46 Mill Rd. ☎01223 362 496 www.amnesty.org.uk/bookshops

This second-hand charity bookshop is cluttered with an eclectic selection of donated books. The prices are low, making this an excellent place to stock up on road reads. The shelf near the counter houses rare or unique books and is worth a look.

Mill Rd. Open M-F 11:30am-6pm, Sa 9:30am-6pm.

BRIAN JORDAN MUSIC BOOKS FACSIMILES SHEET MUSIC, BOOKS ON MUSIC

10 Green St. ☎01223 322 368 www.brianjordanmusic.co.uk

An old music store, Brian Jordan specializes in elegant editions of classical sheet music as well as a fantastic selection of musical literature.

Go up King's Parade until it becomes Trinity St. and follow it until it becomes St. John's St., turn right onto Green St. Open M-Sa 9:30am-6pm.

HAUNTED BOOKSHOP BOOKS, ANTIQUITIES

9 St. Edward's Passage ☎01223 312 913 www.sarahkeybooks.co.uk

Legend has it that a woman in white smelling of violets paces the stairway of the Haunted Bookshop. Fact has it that the bookshop contains a massive collection of age-old, elegant editions of a wide variety of literature and children's books. Well worth a look for any bibliophile.

Go up King's Parade toward Trinity St. and turn right onto St. Edward's Passage. Open M-Sa 10am-5pm.

ONE WORLD IS ENOUGH CLOTHING

31 Bridge St. ☎01223 361 102 www.one-world-is-enough.net

Probably the only store in the world to simultaneously promote fair trade while directly contradicting James Bond, One World is Enough ships in clothes from fair trade organizations in India, Nepal, Indonesia, and Thailand. The owner personally checks the establishments to make sure all producers of the goods are paid properly. Many of the items, such as silk saris, are handmade or totally unique.

A continuation of Sidney St. Open M-Sa 10:30am-6pm, Su 11am-5:30pm.

ARK VINTAGE CLOTHING

2 St. Mary's Passage ☎01223 363 372 www.arkcambridge.co.uk

There's always old-fashioned, prohibition-style jazz on an Ark, right? Hip retro and vintage clothes, home and garden items, and everything from old school icing pens to funny post cards and comfortable wool travel blankets grace the shelves here.

Go up King's Parade toward Trinity College, turn right onto St. Mary's Passage. Open M-Sa 9:30am-5:30pm, Su 11am-5pm.

TINDALL'S ART AND GRAPHICS ART SUPPLIES

15-21 King St. ☎01223 568 495 www.tindalls.co.uk

Tindall's has a comprehensive collection of notebooks and all things artistic. Come and stock up for the moment when the River Cam strikes inspiration in your nomadic, artistic heart.

Turn right off Sidney St. onto Jesus Ln., turn right onto Malcolm St. and you'll hit King St. Open M-Sa 9am-5:30pm.

KEN STEVENS AND MILLERS MUSIC CENTRE INSTRUMENTS

12 Sussex St. ☎01223 367 758 www.kenstevens.co.uk

A haven for any musician, Ken Stevens and Millers Music Centre (formerly two separate stores, now one fantastic joint) offer a wide selection of excellent instruments and gear that could readily serve any wandering minstrel.

Go up Sidney St. and turn right onto Sussex St. Open M-Sa 9:30am-5:30pm.

TALKING T'S T-SHIRTS

37 Bridge St. ☎01223 302 411 www.t-shirts.co.uk

If you're looking for a shirt that will simultaneously call everyone's attention to your torso and pick a fight with them, this is your shop. With T-shirts running the gamut from sassy to clever to official (Cambridge University shirts), Talking T's is an excellent place to shop for casual wear.

A continuation of Sidney St. Open M-Sa 9:30am-5:30pm, Su 10:30am-5:30pm.

THE MAGIC JOKE SHOP NOVELTY MAGIC

29 Bridge St. ☎01223 353 003 www.jokeshop.co.uk

The Magic Joke Shop is essentially a depository for things that couldn't really fit in any other store. Packed with novelty items like jumping putty, joke biscuits and golf-ball stickers that make it look like you shattered your window, The Magic Joke Shop provides loads of time-wasting items for the discerning customer.

A continuation of Sidney St. Open M-Sa 9am-5:30pm, Su 11am-5pm.

MOOK VINTGE CLOTHES

2a King St. ☎01223 316 001 www.mookvintage.com

Your one-stop, everything shop for vintage clothes and accessories. Come and check out the shoes, handbags, and sunglasses as well as the selection of track jackets.

Turn right off Sidney St. onto Jesus Ln., turn right on Malcolm St. and you'll hit King St. Open M-Sa 10:30am-6pm, Su 11am-4pm.

MARKET SQUARE MARKET OPEN-AIR MARKET

Market Hill

Keeping Market Sq. honest, the Market Square Market is open every day with different stands, serving a wide variety of tooth-melting sweets, instruments, shirts, food, and most other things you can imagine.

Turn right onto St. Mary's St. off of King's Parade. Open M-Su 9am-4pm.

SPICE GATE MARKET

14 Mill Rd. ☎01223 513 097

Spice Gate is a delectable and excellent Middle Eastern Market. Its products include date-filled cookies and juices hailing from the Mid-East.

Mill Rd.

essentials

PRACTICALITIES

- **TOURIST OFFICE: Tourist Information Centre** at Peas Hill sells National Express tickets, discounted punting tickets, sightseeing bus tickets and accommodations bookings. Disabled visitors to Cambridge can get an access guide for the city from the TIC. (☎*0871*

226 8006 www.visitcambridge.org *Open M-Sa 10am-5pm, Su 11am-3pm.)*

- **TOURS:** Several walking tours leave from the Tourist Information Centre. The Guided Tour features King's College and Queens' College. (*£11, concessions £9.50, children £6. Leaves M-Sa 11am, 1pm, Su and Bank Holidays 1pm.)* **CitySightseeing** runs a bus with commentary available in nine languages *(Leaves from Silver St. 01223 423 578 www.city-sightseeing.com £13, concessions £9, children £7, family £32. Tours 1hr. 20min., in summer leave every 20min., in winter leave every 40min.)*
- **BUDGET TRAVEL OFFICE: STA Travel.** *(38 Sidney St. 0871 702 9809 www.statravel.co.uk Open M-Th 10am-7pm, F-Sa 10am-6pm, Su 11am-5pm.)*
- **BANKS: Banks** and **ATMs** line St. Andrew's St.
- **INTERNET ACCESS: Jaffa Net Cafe.** *(22 Mill Rd. 01223 308 380* £1 per hr. *Open daily noon-midnight.)*
- **POST OFFICE: Bureau de Change.** *(9-11 St. Andrew's St. Open M 9am-5:30pm, Tu 9:30am-5:30pm, W-Sa 9am-5:30pm.)*
- **POSTAL CODE:** CB2 3AA.

EMERGENCY!

- **POLICE: Parkside Police Station** on Parkside *(0345 456 4564).*
- **HOSPITAL: Addenbrookes Hospital.** *(Hills Rd. by the intersection of Hills Rd. and Long Rd. 01223 245 151.)*

GETTING THERE

By Train

Trains depart from **Station Road** *(National Rail Enquiries 0845 7484 950 Ticket office open M-Sa 5:10am-11pm, Su 7am-10:55pm.)* Nonstop trains to **London King's Cross** *(£19.10. 48min., 2 per hr.)* and to **Ely** *(£3.70. 20min., 4 per hr.).*

By Bus

Bus station is on Drummer St. *(Ticket office open M-Sa 9am-5:30pm.)* Airport Shuttles run from Parkside. Trains to **London Victoria** *(£14.40. 2hr., every hr.)*; to **Gatwick** *(£32. 4hr., every 2hr.)*; to **Heathrow** *(£29.70. 3hr., every hr.)*; to **Stansted** *(£13. 50min., every hr.)*; to **Oxford** *(Stagecoach Express £11. 3hr., every 30min.).*

GETTING AROUND

By Bus

Buses run from **Stagecoach** *(01223 423 578).* **CitiBus** runs from stops throughout town, including some on **St. Andrew's Street, Emmanuel Street,** and the train station. **Dayrider Tickets** *(Unlimited travel for 1 day. £3.40)* can be purchased on the bus, but for longer stays, you can buy a **Megarider** ticket *(Unlimited travel for 7 days. £11.50.).*

By Bike

City Cycle Hire rents'em. *(61 Newnham Road. 01223 365 629 www.citycyclehire.com £6 per 4 hr., £9 per 8hr., £10 per 24hr., £15 per 2-3 days, £20 per 4-7 days, £30 per 2 weeks, £65 per 9 weeks. Open Easter-Oct M-F 9am-5:30pm, Sa 9am-5pm; Nov-Easter M-F 9am-5:30pm.)*

By Taxi

For a taxi, call **Cabco.** *(01223 525 555 Open daily 24hr.)*

MIDLANDS AND EAST ANGLIA

Hop on a train in London and zip through the countryside to the Midlands and East Anglia, and don't be cowed by the grandiose smoke stacks. Be wooed by a sonnetizing Shakespearean at the bard's Birthplace in **Stratford-upon-Avon.** Next, make your way to **Birmingham.** Second only to London in population, this industrial city boasts an enticing culinary mish-mash.

greatest hits

- **BILLY'S BIRTHPLACE.** Take a stroll through the home where the legendary Stratford chap was reared (p. 205).
- **THE PLAYERS.** In Stratford, catch a performance of the Royal Shakespeare Company (p. 208), either in the Courtyard Theatre or their soon-to-be-open indoor venue.
- **TWEET TWEET.** Revel in dulcet tunes at The Yardbird Jazz Club (p. 218) Birmingham.
- **IKONIC.** Birmingham's contemporary art haven, Ikon Gallery (p. 220), causes a stir; get it on the action.

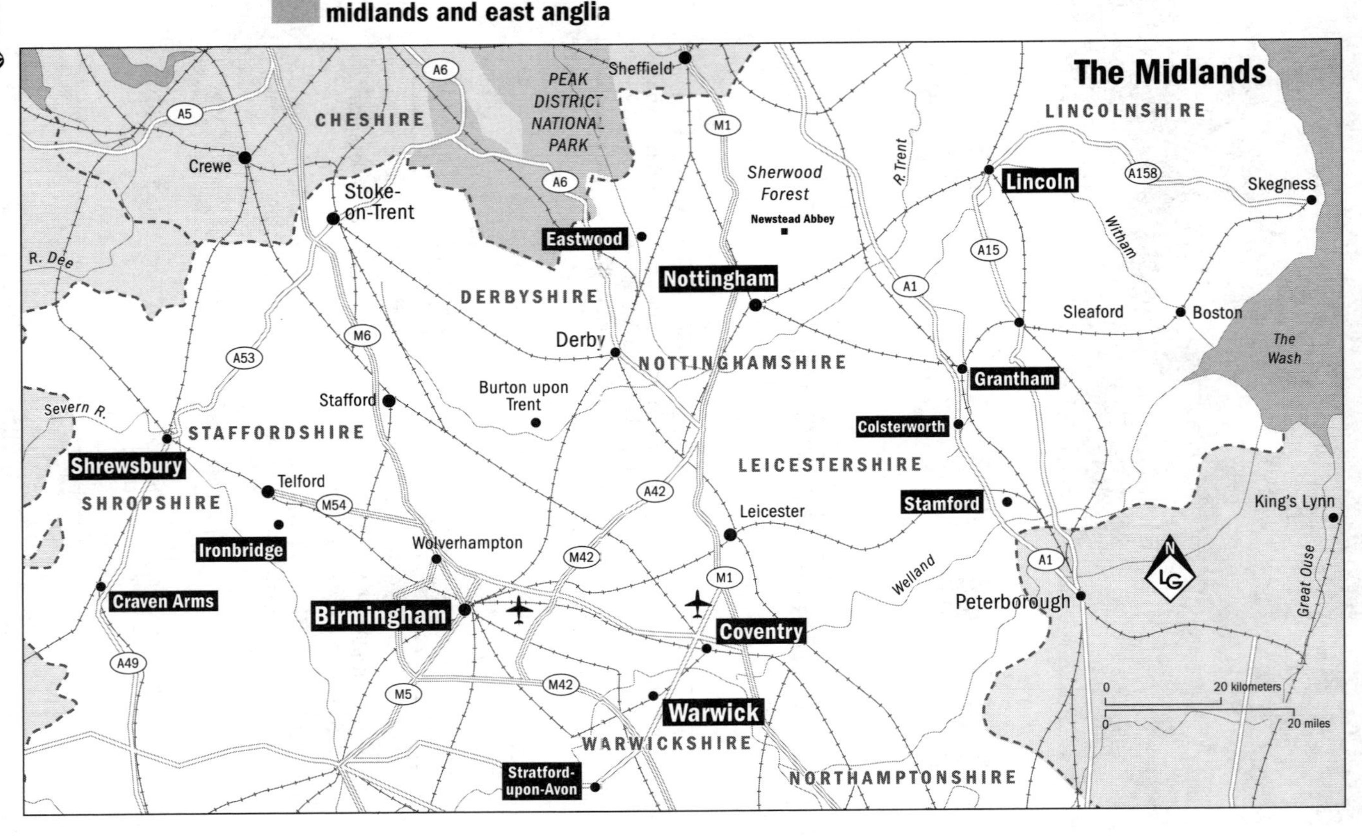
The Midlands
LINCOLNSHIRE
CHESHIRE
PEAK DISTRICT NATIONAL PARK
Sheffield
A6
A5
M1
Crewe
Stoke-on-Trent
A6
Sherwood Forest
Newstead Abbey
R. Trent
Lincoln
A158
Skegness
Witham
Eastwood
R. Dee
A15
Nottingham
A1
DERBYSHIRE
Sleaford
Boston
The Wash
M6
Derby
NOTTINGHAMSHIRE
A53
Grantham
Burton upon Trent
Stafford
Severn R.
Colsterworth
STAFFORDSHIRE
Shrewsbury
LEICESTERSHIRE
Telford
SHROPSHIRE
M54
A42
Stamford
King's Lynn
Leicester
Ironbridge
Wolverhampton
M42
A1
Welland
M1
Great Ouse
Craven Arms
Birmingham
Peterborough
Coventry
A49
M42
M5
0 20 kilometers
0 20 miles
Warwick
WARWICKSHIRE
Stratford-upon-Avon
NORTHAMPTONSHIRE
N
LG

student life

Students visiting **Birmingham** should always have their university IDs easily accessible. Many restaurants and nightclub hotspots offer discounts upon presentation of student IDs. Yup, all they need is tangible proof that we're scrounging scholars.

stratford-upon-avon ☎01789

Stratford-upon-Avon's all-time luckiest fluke was that the **Bard** was born here. This little twist of fate has kept a centuries-long steady stream of tourists flowing through town. Stratford-upon-Avon's population is only about 20,000, but during summer high season, it balloons to over 100,000 with all the tourists. Fivefold increase? Whoa, this guy William must've been pretty important or something. His birthplace alone welcomes over a half million visitors each year; while the Royal Shakespeare Company attracts a million patrons annually to its performances. These visitors primarily belong to an older demographic and seem to abide by Shakespeare's words, "There is money; spend it, spend it; spend more." Never fear, though: the budget traveler can still find free

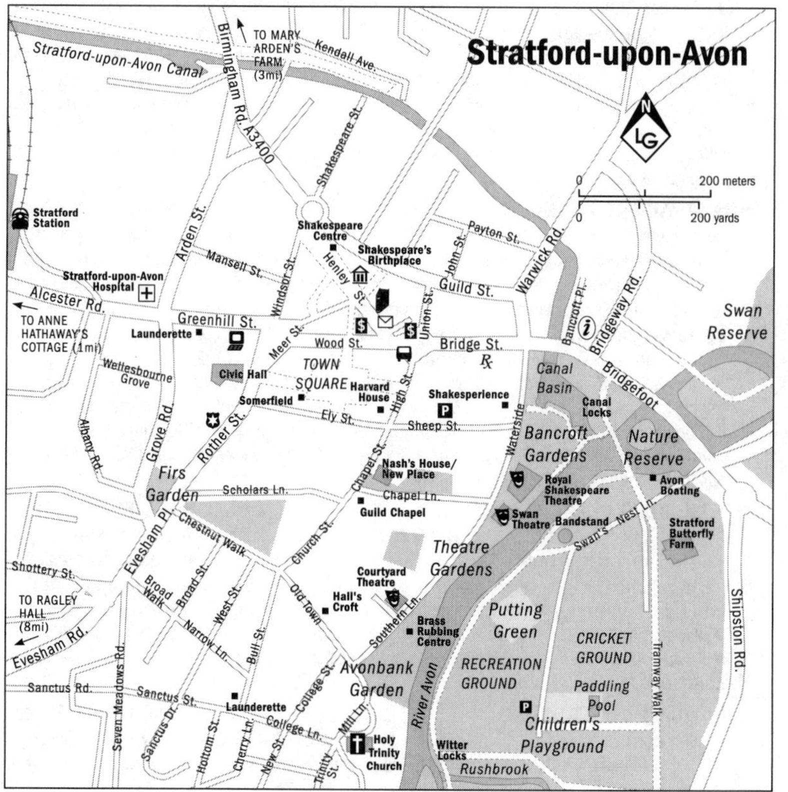

stratford-upon-avon

fun for folly in others' foible—while the Shakespeare sites are frequented by throngs of tourists, Stratford's beautiful countryside and riverfront walks often go blissfully ignored. A wander off into the sunset is the perfect way to end your day.

BY INDIRECTIONS FIND DIRECTIONS OUT

Stratford-upon-Avon is best explored by foot. The train station is located to the west of town but is within easy walking distance of the heart of the downtown. The **River Avon** runs alongside the town, bordering the Royal Shakespeare theaters, and tempts visitors into boat rides and peaceful walks. **Wood Street** and **Bridge Street** are the busiest streets in the town center.

TO SLEEP, PERCHANCE TO DREAM

In Shakespeare's day, visitors to Stratford-upon-Avon probably slept on the floor with the rest of the family. These days, the options are better for visitors to this small part of town. Bed and Breakfasts line Evesham Pl., Evesham Rd., Alcester Rd., and Shipston Rd. (across the river, a 15-20min. walk from the station). The places that are in town tend to run at higher rates. If you're looking for a good deal in Stratford, come during the winter off-season many of the guesthouses in town will lower their charges by £10 or more. However, they're all expecting a big boost in business once the new Royal Shakespeare Company Theatre opens up its doors again for good in Spring 2011.

LINHILL GUEST HOUSE — BED AND BREAKFAST ❸

35 Evesham Pl. ☎01789 292 879 www.linhillguesthouse.co.uk

Tidy, welcoming, and cozy, this family-run B and B offers friendly service and affordable prices, good food, and a location that's a 5min. walk from town, the theaters, and the train station. You'll like the big rooms, but you'll love the huge closets.

From the train station, take a left onto Alcester Rd. then a right onto Grove Rd., which becomes Evesham. i Laundry available. Free Wi-Fi. Flat screen TVs ensuite. Most rooms with ensuite bath. Singles £30; doubles £60. £30 per extra person. Evening meals available: 1-course £5, 2-courses £8.50.

YHA STRATFORD-UPON-AVON — HOSTEL ❸

Hemmingford House, Alveston ☎01789 371 9661 www.yha.org.uk

This large Georgian mansion has sprawling, scenic property and clean rooms, but its location about 2½mi. outside of the main part of town means it is isolated from main attractions and less convenient than the B and B options. Check out the large game room with Shakespearean anecdotes (surprise, suprise), and the theater posters in the dining room.

From Stratford-upon-Avon, at Clopton Bridge take B4086 Wellesbourne Rd; follow hostel signs. Hostel 1.5 m on left. By bus: #18, 18A or 15 from Stratford town center to the hostel. i Full English breakfast included. Laundry. Restaurant. Self-catering kitchen and TV room. Internet £1 per 15min. Wi-Fi £8 per 24hr. Family rooms available. Dorms £14-27; doubles £35-67. £3 fee for non-YHA members. Reception open 7am-midnight.

SALAMANDER GUEST HOUSE — BED AND BREAKFAST ❸

40 Grove Rd. ☎01789 294 770 www.guesthouseinstratforduponavon.com

The Salamander is only a 5min. walk from the train station and close to the town center. A hospitable host, clean rooms, and availability of a single make this a good deal among the pack of bed and breakfast places in Stratford.

i Towels provided. Free Wi-Fi. Non-smoking. All rooms with ensuite bath. TVs, hairdryers, and tea- and coffee-makers. Free parking. Singles £25-35; doubles £40-70; triples £60-90; quads £80-110. Reception 24hr.

SUNNYDALE GUEST HOUSE — BED AND BREAKFAST ❹

64 Shipston Rd. ☎01789 295 166 www.sunny-dale.co.uk

About a 15min. walk away from the city center, this spacious guest house offers a varied selection of comfortable and spotless rooms at affordable prices. The outdoor patio is the perfect place to relax on sunny summer days.

From Stratford city center, cross the Clopton Bridge. Shipston Rd. verges off slightly to the right. i Towels included. Free Wi-Fi. Outside garden area. TVs in each room. Singles £25-40; doubles £40- 70.

THE GILDED MONUMENTS

Stratford's Will-centered sights are best seen before the daytrippers and buses full of schoolchildren arrive at 11am, or after 4pm, when the "Lear-ing" crowds disperse, and the seniors head back for an afternoon nap before nighttime theater. The five official Shakespeare properties in Stratford are operated by the **Shakespeare's Birthplace Trust,** a private charity. These are: **Shakespeare's Birthplace, Mary Arden's House, Nash's House and New Place, Hall's Croft,** and **Anne Hathaway's Cottage.** Visitors can buy packages to get into all five, or just the three that are in the immediate city center. Get the three in-town houses (the Birthplace, Hall's Croft, and Nash's House and New Place) Pass *(£12, concessions £11).* Diehards should get the five-houses ticket *(£17, concessions £16).* Keep in mind that admission to the in-town attractions cannot be purchased separately, so entrance to the Shakespeare Birthplace effectively buys you admission to Nash's House and Hall's Croft, as well.

SHAKESPEARE'S BIRTHPLACE

HISTORIC SIGHT

Henley St. ☎01789 204 016 www.shakespeare.org.uk

The childhood romping grounds of the genius himself has long been a mandatory stop for any lover of literature. Don't feel too ashamed of doing something so undeniably touristy—fellow visitors have included the likes of Charles Dickens, John Keats, Alfred Tennyson, Ralph Waldo Emerson, Henry Wadsworth Longfellow, and Mark Twain (some of whom have left a sign of their visit on the engraved window). The 16th-century building includes guides dressed in all-out Tudor garb, a recreation of Shakespeare's father's glove-making business (you can even try on the fancy ladies' gloves that he would've made), a lovely flower garden, and the requisite walk-through of the Bard's documented life in an exhibit that features, a First Folio and records of his father's illegal refuse dumping. Video demonstrations along with a few artifacts and possessions that have been excavated at the site over the years, lead you through the life and times of Shakespeare. Out in the courtyard, actors battle off in iambic pentameter and will perform your favorite Shakespearean soliloquy upon request.

i Admission includes free presentations by staff and video/audio introduction. Guidebooks £4. Open daily July-Aug 9am-6pm; Sept-Oct 9am-5pm; Nov-Mar 10am-4pm; Apr-June 9am-5pm.

NASH'S HOUSE/NEW PLACE

HISTORICAL SIGHT

Chapel St. ☎01789 292 325 www.shakespeare.org.uk

All of us are mortal, as Shakespeare's plays so bloodily showed us, and so the great one had to die at some point too. These are the grounds where Shakespeare spent the final 19 years of his life and ultimately died in 1626. Once the grandest house in Stratford, this was Will's retirement home of sorts. Unfortunately, because of a disgruntled 19th-century owner named Gastrell who grew sick of the masses of Bard tourists, razed the building, and cut down Shakespeare's mulberry tree in spite, all that remains are the foundation and gardens. Nash's House, the building in which the exhibits are contained, was the home of Thomas Nash, wealthy local property owner and the first husband of Elizabeth Shakespeare, the Bard's granddaughter and last descendent.

Open Apr-Oct 10am-5pm; Nov-Mar 11am-4pm.

HALL'S CROFT ♿ HISTORIC HOME

Old Town ☎01789 292 107 www.shakespeare.org.uk

The 17th-century home of Shakespeare's oldest daughter, Susanna, and her hot-shot physician husband Dr. John Hall. The elegant rooms feature clear signs of wealth and high status, while a beautiful garden teems with roses and herbs that Dr. Hall mentions in his medical notes.

Open daily Apr-Oct 10am-5pm; Nov-Mar 11am-4pm.

ANNE HATHAWAY'S COTTAGE SHAKESPEARE SITE

Cottage Ln. ☎01789 292 100 www.shakespeare.org.uk

This scenic thatched farmhouse is believed to be the childhood home of Shakespeare's wife, Anne Hathaway, thus it's also where young William wooed his beloved. (By the way, Anne Hathaway was eight years older, and three months pregnant when she married William. Cougar much?) Lovely grounds and gardens, a hedge maze, and original Hathaway furniture, including William's "courting chair" near her bed. Entrance entitles you to sit on a bench Will may or may not have also rested his tush upon.

1mi. from Town Centre. Take the hop-on, hop-off tour bus or head west out of town onto Alcester Rd. and look for the sign to the left of the cottage. Part of the 5-house package, or £7.50, concessions £6.50. Open daily Mar-Oct 9am-5pm; Nov-Feb 10am-4pm.

MARY ARDEN'S FARM SHAKESPEARE SITE

Station Rd. Wilmcote. ☎01789 293 455 www.shakespeare.org.uk

This farmhouse in Wilmcote, a village 3 mi. from Stratford, was only recently determined to be the childhood home of Mary Arden, Shakespeare's mother and daughter of a well-to-do yeoman farmer. Historians thought she grew up in the more hoity-toity building next door, but as often happens with the study of history, they were wrong. The working Tudor farm remains in authentic condition, with roaming cattle, Cotswold sheep, Gloucester Old Spot pigs, and women working in the kitchen. A display recounts how Mary fell in love with the elder Shakespeare.

Connected by footpath to Anne Hathaway's Cottage, or take the train from Stratford 1 stop north. Part of the 5-house package, or £8.50, concessions £7.50. Open Apr-Oct 10am-5pm; Nov-Mar 11am-4pm.

HOLY TRINITY CHURCH (SHAKESPEARE'S GRAVE) SHAKESPEARE SITE

Parish Office, Old Town ☎01789 263 316 www.stratford-upon-avon.org

I come not to praise thee but to bury thee... Pay your respects at Shakespeare's final resting place and see the font where he was baptised. Tread carefully near the grave; they say the bard left a poem warning of a curse should his bones ever be moved from the site at Stratford-upon-Avon. Rumor also has it that Shakespeare was buried 17 ft. underground by his request—he thought the extra-deep grave would help him sleep undisturbed. Be sure to look for the large bust of Shakespeare and his birth and death records. The remains of wife Anne and daughter Susanna rest next to William.

Free, but £1.50 donation requested to see grave. Open Apr-Sept 8:30am-5::40pm; Oct M-Sa 9am-4:40pm; Nov-Feb M-Sa 9am-43:40pm, Su 12:30-4:40pm; Mar M-Sa 9am-4:40pm.

STRATFORD BUTTERFLY FARM ♿ FARM

Tramway Walk, Swan's Nest Ln. ☎01789 415 878 www.butterflyfarm.co.uk

You might have come to see the Bard, but why not ogle some beautific butterflies while you're in town. The expert staff are on hand to guide you through the UK's largest collection of tropical butterflies and the world's largest display of live insects. Along with butterflies, there are spiders and scorpions and snails (oh my).

South bank of River Avon, opposite the Royal Shakespeare Theater. £6, concessions £5.45. Open daily Apr-Sept 10am-6pm; Oct-Mar 10am-dusk.

IN THE CAULDRON BOIL AND BAKE

Many of the restaurants in town are fairly upscale and aim to please the theater-going crowd. However, there are affordable baguette stores, tea shops, and bakeries scattered around the town center. Cheapest fare is available from **Somerfield** supermarket *(Town Sq., 1 Fountain Way. Open M-Sa 8am-7pm, Su 10am-4pm)*, and there's a traditional town market with fruits, veggies, pastries, and fish for purchase, held in Market Pl. on Rother St. every Friday. Farmer's Markets are held in the same location every first and third Saturday of the month.

THE DIRTY DUCK — PUB ❷

Waterside ☎01789 297 312

With an ideal location over looking the River Avon and close to the theaters, the Dirty Duck is arguably the best spot to grab a drink and a bite in Stratford. Especially on nice days, the outside terrace and back gardens are packed with young and old, enjoying quality ale and large portions of fine pub fare. Back in the day, The Dirty Duck was known as the Black Swan, but the American GIs who camped over the river during WWII and played darts with the local brewery families dubbed it the "Dirty Duck," and the name stuck. Even more exciting: actors from the Royal Shakespeare company are known to frequent the place before and after performances, so patrons can have a celebrity sighting of sorts.

About 100 yd. down the Waterside from the Royal Shakespeare Theater. Vegetarian options available. Dinner £7.25-14. Open daily 11am-midnight.

OSCAR'S — DELI, BAR, CAFE ❷

13-14 Meer St. ☎01789 295 705

Oscars is cheerful and casual, and concocts totally yummy desserts. The building with white walls and wood panels may be old, but the fare, like quiche, omelettes, and salads, is fresh and served quickly. Upstairs is a popular bar that fills with Stratford's smallish youth population on weekends.

Takeaway available. Gluten-free options. Entrees from £6.

MUST GO — CHINESE ❷

21 Windsor St. ☎01789 293 679 www.mustgroup.co.uk

To say you "must" go here might be a bit of an overstatement, but Must Go is still worth a shot. After appraising the 4 ft. long menu outside, choose between the "Eat Out" door for takeaway (and cheaper prices) or the "Eat In" entrance for table service and comfy seating. The "Must meal deals" *(£4.70-6.70)* are combos of drinks, noodles, entrees, rice, and crackers.

Delivery available. Vegetarian options. Open in summer M-Th noon-midnight, F-Sa noon-12:30am, Su noon-midnight; in winter M-Th noon-2pm and 5pm-midnight, F-Sa noon-12:30am, Su noon-2pm.

HUSSAIN'S — INDIAN ❸

6A Chapel St. ☎01789 267 506

Curry fans cram into Hussain's, generally known as the best Indian restaurant in Stratford. The restaurant is a popular pre-theater haunt, with an Anglo-Indian menu boasting vegetarian options and reasonable prices and a classy atmosphere.

Takeout available. Entrees from £7. Open daily 12:30-2:30pm and 5pm-midnight.

COURTYARD THEATRE CAFE — CAFE ❷

Courtyard Theatre ☎01789 403 415 www.rsc.org.uk

On the site of the Royal Shakespeare Company's second-fiddle theater sits a first-rate place for a cheap eat. Jacket potatoes *(£6)*, handmade fishcakes *(£7)*, quiche *(£6)*, and light meals *(£4-6)* offer the perfect intermission meal, so if you're headed to a show, you don't have to worry about squeezing in a bite beforehand.

Courtyard Theatre, Waterside. Open M-Sa 9:30am-8:30pm, Su 10:30am-5pm.

OPPO BISTRO ❸

13 Sheep St. ☎01789 269 980 www.theoppo.co.uk

Oppo boasts gourmet cuisine that is popular with the theater-goers and which feels right at home in this beautiful venue with an artistic blend of modern and decor and 16th century-style ceilings. Try the spinach and feta cheese pie *(£9.50)* and a glass of wine from the extensive list.

Entrees £11-20 Open M-Th noon-2pm and 5-9pm, F-Sa noon-2pm and 5-10:30pm, Su 6-9pm.

MCKECHNIE'S COFFEESHOP ❶

37 Rother St. ☎01789 299 575 www.mckechniescafe.co.uk

This independent coffee shop is about as alternative as stuffy, Stratford will get. An extensive selection of fruit teas, green teas, coffee, and dainty sandwiches can be eaten at funky tables inside, on a back patio, or out front. The gazpacho *(£5)* is refreshing on the rare warm summer day.

i Free Wi-Fi. Takeaway available. Open M-F 8am-5:30pm, Sa 8:30am-5:30pm, Su 9:30am-4:30pm.

THE BEAR PUB, ENGLISH FARE ❷

Bridgefoot ☎01789 265 540 www.thebearfreehouse.co.uk

Contained within the Swan's Nest Hotel, this pub has a friendly, informal atmosphere, river views, and an excellent selection of drafts, plus a selection of "guest ales" that stop in for a visit every month. The food is on the upper end of the quality scale for pub fare and is affordably priced too. Try the honey-glazed chorizo with olives, hummous, salmon, and crab meat to share *(£10)*.

Open M-Sa noon-midnight, Su noon-11pm.

BENSON'S RESTAURANT TEA ROOM ❷

4 Bard Walk ☎01789 261 116 www.bensonsrestaurant.co.uk

The same owners of a local tea shop also run this popular spot, featuring Danish pastries, smoked salmon, and eggs Benedict, among other options. The cream teas are top-notch, and the setting is comfy cozy. Voted one of the 50 best places in the country for a cup of tea.

Entrees £8-10. Open M-Th 10am-5pm, F 9am-5pm, Sa 8:30am-5pm, Su 10:30am-4:30pm.

THE GARRICK INN PUB ❷

25 High St. ☎01789 292 186 www.garrick-inn-stratford-upon-avon.co.uk

This, the oldest pub in town, was first known as "The Reindeer," but Rudolf and Co. were ditched in favor of famed Shakespearan actor David Garrick in 1769. He held a jubilee in Stratford that year.

Next to Harvard House. Sandwiches and wraps £4.85-5.45. Lunch menu £6.85-8.45. Open daily 11am-11pm.

ALL THE WORLD'S A STAGE

Sure, setting foot in the room where the Bard was born is a thrill in its own right, but the real reason why so many theater-philes make the pilgrimage to Stratford-upon-Avon every year is this legendary mecca of the dramatic arts. As one of the world's most acclaimed repertories, the Royal Shakespeare Company (RSC) sells well over one million tickets each year. Stratford is their permanent base and home.

ROYAL SHAKESPEARE COMPANY (RSC) WATERFRONT

Waterside ☎0844 800 1110 ww.rsc.org.uk

The Royal Shakespeare Theatre, dating from 1932, is finally finishing up with a £112 million renovation that should yield a revolutionary new facility in 2011.

The new theater will boast a 1000-seat auditorium, improved views, and a theater square for outdoor performances. The adjacent Swan Theatre will also reopen in 2011. In the meantime, the show must go on, of course, and plays have continued at the nearby Courtyard Theatre, which will continue to stay open even when the flagship theater reopens its doors.

Ⓢ Tickets £5-£45. Stand-by rate £15 for best available seats. Understudy performances £5. 50 tickets are reserved for 16-25-year-olds for purchase for £5, 40 can be bought in advance and 10 are sold on the day of performance. Under the Program "A Night Less Ordinary," 16-25 year olds can reserve free tickets in advance for Tuesday performances until February 2011. Call the Box Office for more info. ⏰ Courtyard Theatre Box Office open performance days M 9:30am-8pm, Tu 10am-8pm, W-Sa 9:30am-8pm; non-performance days M 9:30am-6pm, Tu 10am-6pm, W-Sa 9:30am-6pm.

NEED YOU MY HELP?

WHO IS'T THAT CAN INFORM ME?

- **TOURIST OFFICES: Bridgefoot** *(☎0870 160 7930)* or *(62 Henley St. ☎01789 264 293 www.shakespeare-country.co.uk ⏰ Open daily 10am-4pm).* Sells **maps** *(Ⓢ £1-1.50)* and guidebooks and books accommodations (10% deposit).
- **TOURS: CitySightseeing** runs a 12-stop, hop-on/hop-off bus tour that stops at all the major Shakespeare sites. *(☎01789 412 680 www.city-sightseeing.com Ⓢ £11.50, concessions £9.50; 48hr. ticket £17, concessions £14. ⏰ Departs every 30min.)* **Stratford Town Walk** offers 1½-2hr. walking tours of all the major sites. *(Meets on Waterside, opposite Sheep St and near the Royal Shakespeare theater. ☎07855 760 377.) www.stratfordtownwalk.co.uk Ⓢ £5, concessions £4. ⏰ Open M-W 11am, Th-Su 2pm.)*
- **CURRENCY EXCHANGE:** Banks are clustered around Wood Street. and Bridge Street. **Barclays** is at the intersection of Henley and Wood St.
- **LAUNDROMATS: Greenhill Launderette.** *(34 Greenhill St. Ⓢ Wash £3.50; dry £1 per 10min. ⏰ Open daily 8am-10pm. Last wash 9:15pm.)*
- **INTERNET ACCESS: Stratford-upon-Avon Library** offers internet service. *(Ⓢ £2.50 per 30min. ⏰ Open M 9am-5:30pm, Tu 10am-5:30pm, W-F 9am-5:30pm, Sa 9:30am-5pm, Su noon-4pm.).* Internet access also available at **Cyber Junction.** *(28 Greenhill St. ☎01789 263 400 Ⓢ 1hr. for £3.50. ⏰ Open M-Th 10:30am-8pm, F 10:30am-5pm, Sa 10:30am-8pm, Su 10:30am-4:30pm.)* Free Wi-Fi is available at some coffeeshops in town, including McKechnies, Wetherspoons, and Starbucks.
- **POST OFFICE:** *(2-3 Henley St. ☎08457 223 355. ⏰ Open M 9am-5:30pm, Tu 9:30am-5:30pm, W-Sa 9am-5:30pm.)*
- **POSTAL CODE:** CV37 6PU.

ALARUM!

- **PHARMACY: Boots.** *(11 Bridge St. ⏰ Open M-Sa 8:45am-5:30pm, Su 10:30am-4:30pm.)*
- **POLICE:** *(Rother St. ☎01789 414 111).*

Hence, Away!

By Train

Stratford-upon-Avon's railway station is located to the west side of town, and sends trains to **Birmingham** *(Ⓢ £6.30 ⏰ 50min., 1-2 per hr.),* **London Marylebone** *(Ⓢ £30.90 ⏰ 2hr. 20min., 5 per day),* and **Warwick** *(Ⓢ £5.20 ⏰ 30min., every 2hr.).* Ticket Office open daily 6am-8:30pm.

By Bus

Coach buses depart from Riverside Coach Park *(off Bridgeway Rd., near the Leisure Centre).* **National Express** buses *(☎08717 818 181 www.nationalexpress.com)* run to **London** *(£17.50 3-4hr., 3 per day)*, **Oxford** *(£9.70 1hr., 2 per day)*, and **Birmingham** *(£7.60 1hr., 2 per day.).*

Get Thee to a Nunnery

While Shakespeare's spirit may loom large, his hometown is relatively tiny. Therefore, the downtown area and most of the major sites in Stratford-upon-Avon are easily accessible by foot and public transportation is limited. Cycling and boat rides are the ideal way to get around on nice days and allow you to take full advantage of the surrounding beautiful countryside.

By Bus

Stagecoach *(☎01789 263 464 www.stagecoach.co.uk)* and **Johnsons** *(☎01564 797 070 www.johnsonscoaches.co.uk)* run bus routes through the city center and to the surrounding towns *(Single trip £2.45, day pass £7).* The major bus stops in town are on Bridge St. and Wood St.

By Taxi

For taxis, call **007 Taxis** *(☎01789 414 007)* or **Ideal Taxi** *(☎01789 290 444).*

Bike Rental

Rent a bike at **Stratford Bike Hire.** *(The Stratford Greenway, Seven Meadows Rd. ☎07711 776 340 www.stratfordbikehire.com Half-day £7, full-day £13. Helmets, locks, and pump included.)*

By Boat

Boat rentals available at **Avon Boating.** *(Swan's Nest Ln. ☎01789 267 073 www.avon-boating.co.uk By Clopton Bridge. Open daily Apr-Oct 9am-dusk. River trips last 30min. Rowboats £4 per hr. Motorboats £25 per hr. River trips £4.50, concessions £3.50.)*

birmingham ☎0121

Birmingham ("Brum" for short) has always gotten somewhat of a bad rap in England. The Brummie accent consistently places last in accent polls that, we kid you not, rate styles of speech on their attractiveness and intelligence. Londoners have stuck their noses up at dirty, dangerous Brum for years. Modern reinvigoration projects, however, have drastically changed the landscape of the UK's second largest city, transforming the town piece by piece with classy post-modern architecture and brand-new, shiny shopping districts. Even the old industrial canals have been transformed into an upscale waterfront area. Despite this extreme facelift, the massive blocks of concrete and highways are unlikely to disappear anytime soon. And so, amid a thriving cosmopolitan scene, Brimingham's industrial past peaks through.

ORIENTATION

Birmingham's city center is surrounded by the **A540,** or the **Ring Road,** which, logically, makes a circle around the city's main downtown area. The central part of town is highlighted by **Victoria Square,** a pedestrian-friendly, European-style plaza that's home to Birmingham's Town Hall and Council House and is an easy meeting place. Adjacent to Victoria Sq. is **Chamberlain Square,** which contains the Birmingham Musuem and Central Library. Chamlerlain Square also holds the Paradise Forum whose bars, shops, and restaurants sit in a pedestrian-friendly area. The city's four major shopping centers are hard to miss, with the **Bullring** bordered by the elaborately modern metal Selfridges building, the **Pallasades** located above New St. Station, the **Mailbox,** a massive new building which reigns over Commercial St., and the **Pavilion,** a modern, glass structure adjacent to the Bullring. New St. links the Bullring to Victoria Square, with New St. Station sitting in the middle. Finally, **Brindleyplace,** off of Broad St., encompasses the scenic and upscale canal area.

ACCOMMODATIONS

Birmingham has two quality hostels. After that, though, options for budget accommodations become decidedly more limited. Many choose to splurge on moderately priced chain hotels like Holiday Inn and Premier Inn located in the city center near major nightlife areas. Others choose to rent out rooms in the upstairs of pubs on the edges of town. For reasonable prices, you can get a single room with a TV, breakfast, and often Wi-Fi. Be forewarned, however, that the crowd of guests at many of these establishments might be different from the typical crowd you'll see in a hostel; many of these rooms are rented out by temporary workers who have come to Birmingham for a few days, few weeks, or even few months for jobs.

BIRMINGHAM CENTRAL BACKPACKERS — HOSTEL ❶

58 Coventry St. ☎0121 643 0033 www.birminghamcentralbackpackers.com

Birmingham is home to the coolest hostel common area you'll ever find. Fluorescent colors, with hanging decorations, lava lamps, tinted windows, a thousand plus movies for the taking, a huge screen with projector, a satisfying board game selection, and Playstation and Nintendo make this a backpacker's heaven. The friendly staff, large certified bar, nightly snacks, and comfy seating make this a true communal space. You'll rarely walk in without seeing at least 10 people just hanging out. Dorms are bright and colorful, albeit a bit cramped, with large lockers.

From Coach Station, take a left onto Oxford St. and turn right onto Coventry St. i Breakfast included. Free nightly snack. Some rooms have showers. Theme Nights and social events. $ Beds from £12.

HATTERS BIRMINGHAM — HOSTEL 2

92-95 Livery St. ☎0121 236 4031 www.hattersgroup.com

Hatters Birmingham is located in the up-and-coming Jewellery Quarter in an old silversmith factory. The factory's accomplishments include the crafting of the FA Cup won by local club Aston Villa and the casting of the medals used in the 1908 Olympics. The dorms are impeccably clean and the downstairs basement has a large common area with a self-catering kitchen, flatscreen TVs, and comfy couches. Hatters is convienent 15min. walk from the main shopping area at Bullring and another 10min. from Broad St.

From New St. Station, leave the station through the shopping mall and turn left onto New St., then turn right up Bennets Hill. Continue onto Newhall St., crossing the main Queensway bypass, then turn right onto Charlotte St. Continue past St. Paul's Sq. then turn left onto Livery St. On your left. i Breakfast included. Laundry facilities. Free Wi-Fi. All rooms with bath ensuite. Self-catering kitchen. Outdoor smoking area. $ Dorms £14.50-23.50; doubles £40-65. Weekends more expensive. Reception 24hr.

THE OLD CROWN — PUB, RESTAURANT, BED AND BREAKFAST 3

188 High St., Diritend ☎0121 248 1368 www.theoldcrown.com

Birmingham's oldest inn dates back to 1368, and the lovingly mantained rooms, tastefully decorated and still held up by the original beams and plaster, have kept much of their traditional character. In 1575, Queen Elizabeth I spent a night here in Room Seven; her seal remains engraved on the wall to mark her presence. A Tudor historian called the place "a fair mansion of tymber" in 1538, and as a friendly, family-run, and comfortable place to spend the night, it remains quite the fair deal for the budget traveler. The charming pub and restaurant downstairs serves food daily until 10pm. The fresh full English breakfast is homecooked by the chef.

From Bullring, follow High St., Digbeth straight for about 10min. until it turns into Deritend. The Old Crown is on your left. i Towels and linens included. Laundry. Free Wi-Fi. TV ensuite. Free parking. Outside patio area. $ Singles £30, without breakfast £25; doubles £60/50. 5-person family room £75. 24hr. access. Breakfast 6:30-10:30am.

THE MOSELEY ARMS — PUB, BED AND BREAKFAST 3

105 Ravenhurst St. ☎0121 766 8467 www.the-moseley-arms.co.uk/accommodation

Moseley Arms, about a 20min. walk from downtown, offers modern and clean ensuite doubles, twins, and singles. The downstairs bar serves food all day and has a big TV and couch for sports-watching.

Take Digbeth High St. (turns into Deritend). Take the right off at Alcester St., and a quick left onto Cheapside. Moseley Arms is on the corner of Cheapside and Moseley Rd. i Breakfast or evening meal included. Towels and linens included. Free Wi-Fi downstairs. Parking available. $ £30 per person. 24hr. access.

THE PARAGON HOTEL — HOTEL 3

145 Alcester St. ☎0121 627 0627 www.theparagonhotel.co.uk

This Victorian Gothic buiding dates back to 1903, and much effort has been made to restore its former glory and yet retain the quaint feel. The top floors of the building offer simple but bright, airy, and clean hotel-quality rooms with bathrooms that are budget-friendly for travelers.

Digbeth. Corner of Alcester St. and Moseley St. If walking, Alcester St. is a right off of Digbeth High St. (Deritend). About a 15min. walk from the bus station and 20-25min. from New St. Station. By bus, take #50 to Bradford St./Alcester St. and head straight on Alcester in direction of the church. Hotel is on your left. i Breakfast £5. Free luggage storage. Towels and linens provided. Laundry service available (through external company). Elevators. Coffeemakers. Telephones and small TVs in each room. Free Wi-Fi on ground floor. Bar, lounge, and restaurant. $ Small singles with windows and ensuite bathrooms £25; doubles/twins £40- £60. Reception 24hr.

NITE NITE HOTEL ❸

18 Holliday St. ☎0121 631 5550 www.nitenite.com

There might not be much more space left after you, your sleeping partner, and your luggage cram into the tiny rooms of this micro-boutique hotel, but you're guaranteed a good night's rest on the luxuriously comfortable beds with free blockbuster movies on a large HDTV screens to lull you into sleep. Besides, if you're feeling claustrophobic, you can always head downstairs to relax in the posh and much more spacious lobby or adjoining classy cafe-bar, or even head out for the night to nearby Broad St., the nightlife hotspot.

Holliday St. is off of Suffolk St. Queensway. From New St. Station, the Queensway is a right off Navigation St. Nite Nite is on the left, attached to Centenary Plaza Apartments. i Breakfast available in cafe; continental £4.50, full £7.50. Laundry service available (picked up by outside company). Free Wi-Fi. Free internet access in lobby. $ Rooms £30-80.

UNIVERSITY OF BIRMINGHAM DORMS ❸

The Vale Student Village, Edgbaston Park Rd. ☎0121 415 8400 www.has.bham.ac.uk

From the middle of July until the middle of September, accommodations are available on the Vale, the University of Birmingham's park-like "student village" which is about a 30min. walk from the main downtown area. The rooms are all single ensuite, with a shared kitchen facility available for guest use.

Take the #1 Bus from Paradise St., Town Hall, to Church Rd. opposite Chamberlain Hall, and follow the Vale towards the canal. Or take the train to Five Ways Station (15min. walk). Easiest way is probably a short taxi ride. Reception is located in the Shackleton building (The Hub), which is next to the Canal and across Vale Rd. from Maple Bank. i Laundry. Free Wi-Fi. Self-catering kitchen. Tea- and coffeemakers. Parking available. $ £31.50 per night. Reception 24hr.

BIG BULL'S HEAD PUB, BED AND BREAKFAST ❸

75 Digbeth ☎0121 643 6790 www.bigbullshead.co.uk

Upstairs from a neighborhood pub, Big Bull's Head offers modern and nicely decorated single and double rooms for reasonable rates. Rooms have large HDTVs and windows, comfortable beds, and free Wi-Fi.

Corner of Milk St. and Digbeth High St. i Free Wi-Fi. £10 key deposit required. $ Singles £30; doubles £50. 24hr. access. Food served downstairs until 9pm.

THE BULL PUB, BED AND BREAKFAST ❷

1 Price St. ☎0121 333 6757 www.thebull-pricestreet.com

Decently-sized doubles, twins, and singles can be found at this aggressively named bed and breakfast. As an added bonus, each room comes with a TV and large windows which make the rooms seem even bigger. Penny-pinchers should be sure to take advantage of the self-catering kitchen available for use upon request.

Corner of Loveday and Price. From New St. station, about a 20min. walk. Take Hill St. north, then make a right onto Navigation St. and a left onto Temple St. A right onto Colmore Row (becomes Colmore Queensway) will take you to the Snow Hill Queensway. At St. Chad's Cathedral, take a right onto Shadwell St. Then, right on Loveday, and left onto Price St. Pub is on your right. i Food available in pub/restaurant downstairs. Towels included. Free Wi-Fi downstairs. All rooms have ensuite bathrooms. $ Rooms £25 per person; doubles £35. Advance booking recommended.

THE KERRYMAN — PUB, BED AND BREAKFAST ❸

80-81 High Street, Digbeth — ☎0121 643 3578 www.thekerryman.co.uk

About 15min. from the main downtown area, this traditional Irish bar offers seven simple but adequate singles, doubles, and quads at reasonable prices. All rooms have ensuite baths.

Follow Digbeth High St. straight from the Bullring. The Kerryman will be on your left. i Continental Breakfast included. TVs in each room. Ⓢ Singles £29.50; doubles £39.50; quads £49.50.

SIGHTS

BIRMINGHAM MUSEUM AND ART GALLERY — MUSEUM

Chamberlain Sq. — ☎0121 303 3129 www.bmag.org.uk

Built in 1884, this Victorian building holds over 40 galleries. The museum's pride and joy is its Pre-Raphaelite collection, the largest in the UK. Other galleries encompass the whole gamut of art history, from the Renaissance to 9000 years ago, mummies to Buddhas. The Waterhall Gallery of Modern Art is first-rate, and the impressive Round Room from the original gallery designed by H. Yeoville Thompson still exists. The Edwardian Tea Room is a particularly beautiful example of the era's ornate design and architecture.

Chamberlain Sq., just behind Victoria Sq. Behind giant water fountain and statue. i Free tours Sa or Su 1pm. Free curatorial talk 3rd Tu of every month at 1pm. Ⓢ Free. Open M-Th 10am-5pm, F 10:30am-5pm, Sa 10am-5pm, Su 12:30-5pm.

THE CUSTARD FACTORY — GALLERY, RESTAURANTS, SHOPS

30 Floodgate St., Digbeth — ☎0121 224 7777 www.custardfactory.co.uk

The 100-year-old Bird's Custard Factory was taken over in the early 90s with promises to provide a home for Birmingham's best young creative and media talents. Since then, the area has turned into a mini-urban oasis of sorts, with over 500 artists, galleries, bars, clubs, retro shops, and restaurants, all of which are interspersed with fountains, sculptures, and green spaces.

From the Bullring, take Digbeth High St., and follow the signs. Ⓢ Free.

NATIONAL SEA LIFE MUSEUM — AQUARIUM

3A Brindley Pl. — ☎0871 423 2110 www.sealife.co.uk

Whet your appetite with the world's only 360° transparent, underwater walk-through tunnel. As you stroll through, you'll think you're in the middle of the ocean as white sharks and Japanese spider crabs swim right past you.

Waters Edge. i Live demonstrations throughout day. Check listings. Ⓢ £17.50, concessions £17. Save money by booking online. Open M-F 10am-5pm, Sa-Su 10am-6pm. Last admission 1hr. before close.

ST. PHILIP'S CATHEDRAL — CHURCH

Colmore Row — ☎0121 262 1840 www.birminghamcathedral.com

St. Philip's, the cathedral of Birmingham and the seat of the Bishop of Birmingham, was built in 1715 and designed by Baroque architect Thomas Archer. Its tower dominates the city center landscape from Colmore Row. Its convenient location in the middle of the city and amid green surroundings make this an ideal location for eating lunch on sunny days.

Walking down New St., turn right onto Tesco St. Ⓢ Free. Open M-F 7:30am-6:30pm and Sa-Su 8:30am-5pm.

EDWARDIAN BATHS (MOSELEY ROAD BATHS) — HISTORICAL SITE

Balsall Heath — ☎0121 464 0150

Housed in one of the city's best-preserved Edwardian buildings that dates from 1907, this is the oldest Edwardian public swimming pool still in use in the UK. Only one of the two pools is currently open for swimming, but the building is a sight unto itself.

Take Bus #50 from the city center. Spectators free. Swim £3.30. Open M 7am-8pm, Tu 7am-4pm, W 7am-3:30pm, Th 7am-8pm, F 7am-1pm, Sa noon-4:30pm, Su 7am-12:30pm. M women-only 3:30-8pm. W over 60s swimming lessons 11:30am-12:30pm.

CANNON HILL PARK PARK

2 Russell Rd., Moseley ☎0121 442 4226 www.birmingham.gov.uk/cannonhillpark

This is Birmingham's most-admired park, having been awarded Green Flag Status, an honor bestowed upon the best parks in the country. There are paddle boats, beautiful picnic spots, and award-winning tulips. The park is home to the newly-reopened Midland Arts Centre or "Mac" (*☎0121 446 3232 www.macarts.co.uk Open daily 9am-11pm.*) which showcases arts, music, film, theater, and dance performances and displays, so you can check out an independent film while you've made the trip. There's also a walking and bicycling route that cuts across the grounds and a range of concerts and performances offered throughout the year.

Take bus #1 to Edgbaston Rd., or bus #45 or 47 to Pershore Rd., all leaving from outside New St. Station. Free. Open daily dawn-dusk.

ASTON VILLA F.C. FOOTBALL STADIUM

Villa Park ☎0800 612 0970 www.avfc.co.uk

Birmingham's oldest and most storied football franchise offers tours of its famed grounds.

Take the train from Birmingham New St. to Aston Station. i Tours W, F, and some Su. No tours on match days, the days immediately preceding match days, or the morning after match days. Tours run daily in summer. M-F tours £10, with lunch £17. Su tours £22.50.

FOOD

Birmingham has no shortage of quality restaurants; however, finding something that's within your budget isn't as simple if you don't know where to look.

Chinatown, located on the south side of the city around Pershore St. and Ladywell Walk, has many lunch buffet deals. **Martineau Place** and the upstairs food court of the Pavillion Shopping Centre offer some surprisingly unique and healthy budget options. The city's indoor and outdoor markets, located on Edbaston and Upper Dean St., display tons of cheap, though not necessarily classy, options (beware the smell of fish). Pricier chain restaurants are clustered around **Brindleyplace, Broad St.,** the **Mailbox,** and the **Arcadian Centre,** flaunting outside seating areas and modern decor. If supermarkets are your venue of choice, there's a **Tesco Metro** on New St., between Temple St. and Needless Alley (*Open M-F 6am-midnight, Sa 6-10pm, Su noon-6pm*). On the last Friday of every month, Central Sq. in Brindleyplace showcases a local **produce market,** selling fruits, vegetables, wines, pastries, and cheeses.

Finally, Birmingham is famous for its **balti,** a Kashmiri dish containing spices, meat, and vegetables and cooked over a high flame. These meals are quite cheap and available at the many establishments in the Balti Triangle area of South Birmingham; Moseley and Balsall Heath create the three points of the triangle.

CANALSIDE CAFE CAFE, VEGETARIAN ❷

35 Worcester Bar ☎0785 441 9862

Literally Canalside, this former lockkeeper's cabin features light vegetarian cuisine, excellent beer, and tons of character. On nice days, people congreate outside under umbrellas with an after-work drink (*high-quality ciders, lagers, draft ales; £3-£3.50 per pint*). The narrow interior is lovingly decorated with quaint mismatched wooden chairs and tables, old-fashioned mirrors, a collection of portraits of canals from around the world, unusual beer labels, and a brick fireplace.

From the city center, take a left off Broad St. onto Gas St. Worcester Bar is hidden off to the left, past the opening in the brick walls directly alongside the canal. You'll see signs for the bridge across Gas St. basin. Entrees £4-7. Beer from £2.50. Open daily 11am-11pm.

WAREHOUSE CAFE VEGETARIAN ❸

54-57 Allison St. ☎0121 633 0261

This classy vegetarian restaurant offers unique gourmet dishes created with all-organic ingredients, combined in skillfull mastery. The menu changes daily, but think potato wedges instead of french fries, goat cheese instead of American. If you have the extra money, try a dessert—the savory cheesecake is delicious. Make a reservation in advance citing a "Student Tuesday" deal, show your student IDs, and buy one meal, get one free *(max. 4 vouchers)*.

Off of Digbeth. i Vegan options available. Free Wi-Fi. Ⓢ Entrees £6.50-8.95. 2 courses £12.50. 3 courses £16.50 Open M-Sa 11am-10pm, Su 11am-6pm.

CAFE SOYA VIETNAMESE, CHINESE ❷

Unit B106 Arcadian Centre, Hurst St. ☎0121 683 8350 www.cafesoya.co.uk

Cafe Soya makes excellent pan-Asian cuisine at low prices. Don't leave without trying the specialty soy milk or soy bean dessert. Many of the delicious treats are prepared by hand daily.

Inside of Arcadian Center. i Takeaway available. Vegetarian options. Ⓢ Entrees £6.50-8. Lunch specials £5.50. Takeaway meal boxes £5. Open M-Tu noon-10pm, Th-Su noon-10pm.

MATTHEW'S OF BIRMINGHAM GRILL ❸

16-17 The Greenhouse, Gibb St. ☎0121 224 7730 www.matthewsofbirmingham.com

Funky and classy at the same time, Matthew's is the perfect culinary counterpart to the Custard Factory's too-cool-for-school artsy vibe. Dinner is definitely pricey, but the lunch menu with affordable meat and vegetarian options and special deals like a sandwich, kettle chips, fruit and a drink combo *(£4.75)* is excellent.

Digbeth. i Takeout options. Pre-order online available. Vegetarian options. Ⓢ Lunch entrees £5.50-9.50. 2-course dinner £25.95. Open M 8:30am-8pm, Tu-F 8:30am-11pm, Sa 10am-11pm.

URBAN PIE PIES ❶

Bullring Shopping Centre ☎0121 643 0040 www.urbanpie.co.uk

Choose from a tasty selection of chicken, steak, kidney, and vegetable pies *(£4)*, try some handmade mash on the side *(£1.75)*, and if you have enough room left, add an apple and cinnamon-sweet pie *(£2.65)*. Top it all off with a "pie"nt- Beers and pies are ½-price Monday through Friday from 5pm until close. It's picnic style: wooden tables with attached benches and outdoor seating to watch the bustling shoppers passing by.

Bullring Shopping Centre. i Halal and vegetarian options. Seasonal specials available. 10% student discount with Student ID. Ⓢ Pies £4. Sweet pies £2.65. Open M-Sa 10am-8pm, Su 10am-6pm.

HANDMADE BURGER CO. BURGERS ❷

14 The Water's Edge ☎0121 665 6542 www.handmadeburger.co.uk

Don't be deceived by the word "burger " in the title—this is 100% gourmet local prime beef, offered in stylish digs, with thick-cut chips or golden onion rings. It's the best budget option in classy Brindley place, with outdoor seating right on the charming canals.

Near the Sea Life Centre. From Broad St. headed away from the shopping areas, make the first right in Brindleyplace (you'll see Pizza Express and your first glimpse of the Canal). i 15% discount with student ID. Open M-Th noon-10:30pm, Su noon-10:30pm.

MR. EGG FASTFOOD ❶

22 Hurst St. ☎0788 839 8110

This delightfully greasy local institution is a late-night must. Open daily until 4am (except Sundays), this is one of the only places in town where you can fulfill your drunken cravings. The fare is perfect for that kind of mood: chips, sausage, kebabs, curry, and burgers. If caffeine is really what you need, there's coffee too *(£1)*. And all this for less than a fiver. You won't be able to miss the giant egg on the ceiling.

From St. Martin's Circus Queensway, make a left onto Hurst St. On your left. i Special deals for bulk orders (so bring your friends). Open M-Sa 11am-3pm and 4pm-4am.

THAI EDGE
THAI ❸

7 Oozelis Sq. ☎0121 643 3993 www.thaiedge.co.uk

Flashy and trendy, this won't be a cheap plate of Pad Thai. They call it Thai with a "contemporary twist." This exotic venue is worth a stop; the lunch menu offers tasty stir-fried dishes at pocketbook friendly prices *(£5.95-6.50)*.

Oozelis Sq. Brindleyplace. Follow pedestrian markers to Brindleyplace. Off of Broad St. Opening times vary. Lunch from noon. Dinner from 5:30pm.

CAFFE GUSTO
SANDWICHES ❷

Top floor, The Mailbox, 103 Wharfside St., Unit C Level 7 ☎0121 665 6555 www.caffegusto.

Awarded Coffee Shop and Sandwich Bar of the Year by the British Sandwich Association in 2009, this member of the small chain offers fresh soup, sandwiches, panini, and toasties at a snip of the price of neighboring coffee giants. It gives us great satisfaction to be snubbing the rest and spending our hard-earned cash here. In Italian, *gusto* means flavor; in English, gusto means pleasure, passion, zest—all words that we feel fully justify the price of a toastie and coffee *(£2.95)*. They ain't stingy either; you can have any coffee on the menu, not just filter. Make that a cheese and bacon toastie and mocha then.

Follow Pedestrian signs to the Mailbox, which is off of Suffolk St. Queensway. i Open daily 7am-7pm.

NATA CAFE
PORTUGUESE, MEDITERRANEAN ❷

25 Martineau Place ☎0871 962 5372

Small and tucked away off of busy New St., this simple Portuguese lunch joint offers a varied selection of tapas—like *piri piri* with Portuguese salad *(£6)*—sandwiches, panini, soups, and wraps at reasonable prices *(£2.75-6)* and with a colorful Mediterranean feel. Cheaper takeout options are available.

Martineau Pl. is enclosed by Corporation St., Bull St., and Union St. i Takeout available. Halal options. Sandwiches, wraps, baguettes, tapas £2.40-6. Open M-F 8am-5pm, Sa 9am-5:30pm.

MAHARAJA
INDIAN ❷

23-25 Thorp St. ☎0121 622 2646 www.maharajarestaurant.co.uk

This award-winning northern Indian restaurant is a good value, with large portions, unique spices, and waiters that are dying to please. The specialties are tandoori dishes and spiced curries, but don't leave without breaking bread: naan and *kulcha* are only a little extra.

Corner of Hurst St. and Thorpe St. i Vegetarian options. Takeaway available. Entrees £5.45-11.05. Naan and kulcha £5.45-11. Open M-Sa noon-2pm and 6-11pm.

CHEZ JULES
FRENCH ❸

5a Ethel St. ☎0121 633 4664 www.chezjules.co.uk

This classy French restaurant is a good deal for the price. With red-checked tablecloths and live, authentic music on special nights...was there ever really such thing as the Seven Years' War? How could the British fight the French when their food is so good? Fish, sandwiches, and *soupes du jour* are all available within cheaper lunch deal options.

Off New St. Tu from 5pm 3 courses and ½ bottle of wine £15. M-F 5-7pm 2 courses £11. 2-course lunch menu £9. Open daily noon-3pm and 5-10pm.

NIGHTLIFE

Birmingham's nightlife is one of its strongest redemptive qualities (when it's dark out, everything looks prettier). As England's second largest city, its diverse mix of residents have created a wide variety of after-hours options to entertain themselves. **Gay Village** is located around the Hurst St. area. Nearby, **The Arcadian** also features a collection of centrally-located (albeit bland and expensive) bars. **Brindleyplace** is where the classiest Birminghamites head for a scenic drink alongisde the canal. Nearby, **Broad Street** is synonymous with nightlife in Birmingham, famous for its lively and international crowd, clubs, and restaurants. Smart attire is required for entry to most clubs: no sneakers, and collared shirts required for guys. Come prepared for long lines and high cover charges, especially on weekends. To get to club central, take Hill St. (off Queens Dr.), make a left onto Paradise St., which turns into the Paradise Circus Queensway, and a quick slight left onto Broad St.

THE YARDBIRD JAZZ CLUB — JAZZ CLUB

Paradise Pl. ☎0121 212 2524

This jazz club is refreshingly cool, modern, and intimate. It's a different kind of place than anywhere else in Birmingham—and it knows it—but it's down-to-earth all the same. Yardbird is funky, with dark red lighting and a unique ambience. Live music is usually jazz and funk, but folk and acoustic nights are also featured.

Next to Central Library, between Copthorne Hotel and Paradise Forum. Food menu available. Pints £2.30-2.40. Open M-W noon-midnight, Th-Sa noon-2am, Su noon-midnight.

SUNFLOWER LOUNGE — BAR, LIVE MUSIC

76 Smallbrook Queensway ☎0121 632 6756 www.thesunflowerlounge.co.uk

With a 1960's Mod theme to it and many customers who dress the part, Sunflower Lounge is the trendy place for the Brummies that are into the rock and indie music scene. Live music, a decent drink selection, and great people-watching potential make it well-worth the trip to Smallbrook Queensway.

Cover free-£5. Open daily noon-late.

ROCOCO LOUNGE — RESTAURANT, BAR

260 Broad St. ☎0121 633 4260 www.rococolounge.co.uk

The scene at Rococo changes drastically depending on when you decide to make your appearance. The venue transforms from a daytime restaurant and pub with a good selection of snacks and meals, to a chill evening bar, then to a crazed dance locale. The venue is split-level, with a lounge section, a bar, and an eatery. Strict rules for the dress code: no sneakers, no Burberry, and no big brands.

Saturday cover £2. Mixed drinks from £3.20. Open M-Th noon-2am, F-Su noon-3am. Kitchen open daily noon-9pm.

BARFLY — CLUB, BAR, MUSIC

78 Digbeth High St. ☎0121 633 8311 www.barflyclub.com

Always on the lookout for new music, this trendsetting indie music venue highlights some of the up-and-coming acts on the Birmingham scene.

Head down Digbeth High St., on the left before the Custard Factory. Open M–Th 7:30-11:30pm, F 7:30pm–2am, Sa 7:30pm–3am, Su 7:30-11:30pm.

NIGHTINGALE

Essex House, 18 Kent St. ☎0121 622 1718 www.nightingaleclub.co.uk

A staple of Birmingham's Gay Village since 1969, the days of Vietnam and Neil Armstrong, Nightingale is not just your standard gay bar: it also hosts live music performances and showcases its very own ensemble of almost-bare muscle men in spandex. In a UK clubbing capital, this is one of the favorite haunts for gay and straight alike. Beat the lines by booking online.

Kent St. is off of Hurst St. Cover free-£7. Open M 9pm-4am, Tu-W 10pm-4am, Th 9pm-4am, F changes weekly (approx. 10pm-4am), Sa 9pm-6am.

GATECRASHER CLUB

182 Upper Broad St. ☎0121 633 1520 www.gatecrasherbirmingham.co.uk

Broad St.'s major dance club blasts tunes all night long. Long lines and high charges are standard, but if you'd prefer to fork out the dough, you're guaranteed big crowds and drunken revelry.

By intersection with Ryland St. Cover free-£12. Student entry £5 on Sa. Special student drink offers. Opening times vary weekly but usually range from 9:30pm-3:30am, and until 6am on weekends.

OH VELVET BAR

200 Broad St. ☎0121 248 0500

As one of only two independent bars on Broad St., Oh Velvet is dedicated to trying to provide that comfortable neighborhood aura that is harder to find in large chain bars. The inside features pool tables, fruit machines, and boxing machines. The music during the week is old-school, with '70s, '80s, and '90s tunes, but the live DJ on weekends spins R and B, house, and pop.

Broad St. No hoods, no sportswear, and no trainers in Sugar Suite upstairs. Purchase a wristband on F night for all £2 drinks. Open M-Th noon-1am, F-Sa noon-2am, Su noon-1am. Kitchen open daily noon-5pm. Sugar Suite open F until 3am and Sa until 4am.

BAR RISA BAR

Quayside Tower, Broad St. ☎0121 632 4936 www.risa-birmingham.co.uk

Bar Risa is an ultra modern establishment that boasts two levels, six rooms, and seven bars. It's also home to Jongleurs, the UK's biggest comedy club. Expect to find a young crowd at Risa.

Broad St. i Kitchen open daily noon-8pm. Open M-Tu noon-1am, W-Th noon-2am, F-Sa noon-3am, Su noon-1am.

AIR CLUB

49 Heath Mill Ln. ☎0121 766 6646 www.airbirmingham.com

The real raging ravers love this rockin' club. Techno, house, and trance is cranked up by the DJ, against a background of glow sticks and big flatscreen TVs. Air is also home to Godskitchen, an internationlly-renowned nightclub with its own music label.

Off Digbeth High St. i Cover cash only. Cover £10-25. Open M-Th 9pm-2am, F-Sa 9pm-6am, Su 9pm-2am.

EQUATOR GLBT BAR

123 Hurst St. ☎0121 622 5077 www.equatorbar.co.uk

Stylish yet unpretentious, this classy gay bar has a decent and affordable, selection of beers and wines, as well as a chill atmosphere.

Hurst St., between Claybrook and Bromsgrove. Open M-Th noon-11pm, F-Sa noon-2am, Su noon-11pm.

ARTS AND CULTURE

INTERNATIONAL JAZZ FESTIVAL VARIOUS LOCATIONS

Across Birmingham ☎0121 454 7020 www.birminghamjazzfestival.com

This huge event offers hundreds of performances across the city in coffeeshops, shopping centers, and concert venues. Better yet, most performances are free.

July.

BIRMINGHAM HIPPODROME CITY CENTER

Hurst St. ☎0870 730 2050 www.birminghamhippodrome.com

This prestigious theater, dating from 1895, is home to the UK's most popular panto and the renowned Birmingham Royal Ballet. It also shows visiting operas, musicals, and dramas.

Tickets £15-46. Concessions vary by performance, often only apply M-Th, and are £3 off normal

prices. Student standbys available 24hr. in advance, best available seats at lowest cost, subject to availability. ⏰ Ticket office open performance days M-Sa 10am-8pm; non-performance days M-Sa 10am-6pm.

02 ACADEMY
CITY CENTER

16-18 Horsepair, Bristol St. ☎0844 477 2000 www.o2academybirmingham.co.uk

Part of the larger 02 UK chain, this venue puts on acts by new and developing talent and also holds shows with major international names in its 3000-fan capacity main auditorium.

A pedestrian link is via a subway at Holloway Circus roundabout (known locally as Chinese Pagoda Island). There are two entry/exit points. One is via the top of Smallbrook Queensway (on the opposite side of the Radisson Hotel by the takeaway food outlets) and the other at Holloway Head (by Clydesdale and Cleveland Towers). $ Booking fee for credit cards. Tickets sold the night of a show are cash only. $ Tickets £3-25. ⏰ Ticket office open M-F 11:30am-5pm and Sa 11:30am-3:30pm.

BIRMINGHAM REPERTORY THEATRE
CENTENARY SQUARE

Centenary Sq. ☎0121 236 4455 www.birmingham-rep.co.uk

The "Rep," as it's better-known, puts on plays primarily, though the occasional musical does make an appearance, and place particular emphasis on staging new pieces. There are two theaters, the Main House and the Theatre Door.

i On F evenings 16-26-year-olds can get a limited number of free tickets through "A Night Less Ordinary" program. Call in advance, and pick up at the door. M and F 16-26-year-olds can get £6.99 tickets in advance. Student standby tickets available after 1pm day of performance M-Th evenings and Th-Sa matinees, £7. $ Tickets £10-32. ⏰ Box office open M-Sa non-performance days 10am-8pm, non-performance days 10am-6pm.

IKON GALLERY
CITY CENTER

1 Oozells Sq. ☎0121 248 0708 www.ikon-gallery.co.uk

This internationally acclaimed contemporary art venue is housed in the neo-Gothic Oozells Street School. The art is directly controversial and often political. On display are international artists using a wide variety of media, including sound, film, mixed media, photography, painting, sculpture, and installation.

From New St. station, walk to Chamberlain Sq., then up toward Central Library, through Paradise Forum and Centenary Sq. Bear left onto Broad St., then turn right onto Oozells St. i Free events and tours. $ Free. ⏰ Galleries open Tu-Su 11am-6pm.

THE ELECTRIC CINEMA
CITY CENTER

47-49 Station St. ☎0121 643 7879 www.theelectric.co.uk

The Electric is the UK's oldest working cinema dating from 1909). Back then, when most people didn't have elecricity in their homes, the word Electric was like magic. It comes complete with soft sofas named for stars from the golden age of cinema, that include waiter service and the ability to text in your orders to the bar. This is one of Birmingham's only independent cinemas, so get your tickets early for the couches—they go like hotcakes.

i Can reserve sofas online. $ Tickets £6.50, concessions £4.50. Sofas £12 per person. ⏰ Opens 30min. prior to first performance of the day.

THE CRESCENT THEATRE
CITY CENTER

Sheepcote St., Brindleyplace ☎0121 643 5858 www.crescent-theatre.co.uk

The Crescent Theatre with a reputation for providing high quality entertainment at affordable prices is one of Birmingham's oldest theater companies. They put on over 15 of their own performances each year, and host outside companies both small and large.

Brindleyplace, by Sheepcote St., just off Broad St. i Online purchase available. $ Tickets £5-16.50. Concessions available, generaly £1 off. Su matinee £5. ⏰ Box office open M-F noon-8pm, Sa noon-4pm and 4:30-7pm. Open Su for performances only, noon-8pm.

ESSENTIALS

Practicalities

- **TOURIST OFFICES: The Rotunda** distributes free copies of *What's On*, free city mini-guides, and free *Birmingham at Day* (sights) and *Birmingham at Night* (restaurants and nightlife) maps. Additionally, The Rotunda books accommodations for free and books tickets for shows and sights for free and sometimes at discounted prices. *(150 New St. ☎0844 888 3883 www.visitbirmingham.com Open M 9:30am-5:30pm, Tu 10am-5:30pm, W-Sa 9:30am-5:30pm, Su 10:30am-4:30pm).* You can also find a small information center at the junction of New and Corporation St. *(Open M 9am-5pm, Tu 10am-5pm, W-Sa 9am-5pm, Su 10am-4pm.)*
- **TOURS: Birmingham Tours** offers themed walking tours, guided walks along the canals, pub walks, and ghost tours, among others. *(☎0121 427 2555 i Purchase tickets in advance at the TIC or at ☎0844 888 4415. www.birmingham-tours.co.uk Tickets £8.)* They also offer 1hr. open-top, hop-on, hop-off bus tours Saturdays in summer. *(Leaving from Church St, opposite St. Philip's Cathedral. £10. Tours Sa May-Sept 10:30am, noon, 1:30, and 3pm.)*
- **BEYOND TOURISM: JobCentre Plus** in Centennial House. *(100 Broad St. ☎0121 480 3800 Open M-Tu 9am-5pm, W 10am-5pm, Th-F 9am-5pm.)*
- **LUGGAGE STORAGE:** *(New St. Station. £3 per bag for up to 3hr., £5 for 3-6hr., £7 for up to 24hr.)*
- **BANKS: Barclays.** *(79-84 High St. Open M-F 9am-5pm, Sa 10am-4pm.)*
- **INTERNET ACCESS: Pavillion Internet Lounge** in the loft level of Pavillion Shopping Center. *(☎0121 636 6172 £2 for 30min., £2.50 for 1hr.)* The Studio *(7 Cannon St. ☎0800 079 0909 £1 for 15min., £2 for 1hr. Open M-F 7:30am-6pm.)* Free Wi-Fi at many coffeeshops around Bullring and New St. Station, and even at McDonald's.
- **POST OFFICE:** The post office is at the intersection of New St. and Victoria Sq. *(1 Pinfold St. ☎0845 722 3344 Open M 9am-5:30pm, Tu 9:30am-5:30pm, W-Sa 9am-5:30pm.)*
- **POSTCODE:** B2 4AA.

Emergency!

- **POLICE:** Steelhouse Lane *(☎0845 113 5000).*
- **PHARMACY: Boots,** Bullring is across from New St. Station. *(Open M-F 8am-8pm, Sa 9am-8pm, Su 11am-5pm.)*
- **HOSPITAL: Queen Elizabeth Hospital,** Mindelsohn Way *(☎0121 627 2000).* For non-emergencies, **NHS Walk-In Centre,** Lower Ground Floor of Boots *(66 High St. ☎0121 255 4500 Open M-F 8am-7pm, Sa 9am-6pm, Su 11am-4pm.)*

Getting There

By Plane

Birmingham International Airport *(☎0844 576 6000 www.birminghamairport.co.uk)* offers flights to and from other UK cities, and European cities in Spain, France, Germany, and Italy. A train ticket from Birmingham New St. to Birmingham International station costs £3.10 and takes 10min. From there, a free shuttle links to the airport terminals.

By Train

New Street Station *(☎08457 48 49 50 ⏰ Ticket office open M-Sa 24hr., Su 12:30am-7pm. Travel Centre sells advance tickets M-Sa 7:15am-9pm and Su 9am-9pm.)* sends trains to most major cities including **Liverpool** *(Ⓢ £27.50. ⏰ 1.½hr., 2 per day)*; **Manchester Piccadilly** *(Ⓢ £28.10. ⏰ 1¾hr., 2 per hr.)*; **Oxford** *(Ⓢ £27. ⏰ 1hr.15min., 2 per hr.)*; and **Sheffield** *(Ⓢ £32. ⏰ 1hr. 20min., 2 per hr.)*. Travel to **London Euston** from New Street Station via speedy **Virgin** trains *(Ⓢ £70. ⏰ 1.5hr., 3 per hr.)* or **London Midland** trains *(Ⓢ £25. ⏰ 2½hr., 2 per hr.)*. You can also travel to London Euston via Chiltern from **Moor St. Station.** *(Ⓢ £31, ⏰ 2½hr., 2 per hr.)*

By Bus

Digbeth Coach Station *(High St.)* offers **National Express** buses *(☎08717 818 181)* to **Cardiff** *(Ⓢ £27. ⏰ 2½hr., 4 per day)*; **Liverpool** *(Ⓢ £10.20. ⏰ 3hr., 4 per day)*; **London Victoria** *(Ⓢ £17.10. ⏰ 2-3hr., 1-2 per day)*; **Manchester** *(Ⓢ £14.60. ⏰ 2hr., 4 per day)*; **Oxford** *(Ⓢ £13.40. ⏰ 1¾hr., 4 per day)*; and **Stratford-upon-Avon** *(Ⓢ £7.60. ⏰ 1hr., 2 per day.)*

Getting Around

By Train

Birmingham New Street, Birmingham Moor Street, and **Snow Hill** stations are the three main train stations in the city station. You can travel from one to the other, or walk. Birmingham New St. is in the middle, with the other two about ½mi. from it.

By Bus

Main local bus stations in town are located at **Corporation Street, Colmore Row,** and **Moor Street. Public Transportation Information Centre** at Centro has all information you'll need *(☎0871 200 2233 💻www.travelinemidlands.co.uk)* in New St. Station. **Traveline** *(☎0871 200 22 33)* has up-to-date information about buses in the area. Bus routes denoted with the letter A head around the city in an anti-clockwise direction, while those with the letter C head clockwise.

By Taxi

Call for a cab at **TOA Taxi** *(☎0121 427 8888)*.

NORTHERN ENGLAND

In the midst of all your London schmoozing and Oxford pubbing, don't forget to trek to the nether regions of the island, starting in **Liverpool** where native Scousers root tirelessly for their football team. Oh, and the Beatles are pretty big, too. In Manchester, head to a football match, joining the droves of fans who root tirelessly for the "Red Devils." Nearby **York** is supposedly "the most haunted city in the world." We can't necessarily attest to that, but we *can* say that this city bounded by medieval walls is a cool place to visit. When it comes to party stamina, size does *not* matter, as proven by small but bustling **Newcastle-upon-Tyne.** Finish off your tour of the north by exploring the castle and cathedral of **Durham**—just be a kinder visitor than the Vikings were, please.

greatest hits

- **NUDITY IN NUMBERS.** Head to the shore in Liverpool to see Anthony Gormley's controversial cast-iron display, *Another Place* (p. 228).
- **FROM THE TROF.** From eggs to kegs, Trof (p. 247) in Manchester is multi-functional, open morning 'til night.
- **FOR REELS.** If you're dying to see an old-fashioned movie, hit up Hyde Park Picture House (p. 255) in Leeds.
- **THE CLUNY.** No, not George (different spelling—duh!). But this popular club in Newcastle-upon-Tyne, featuring live music, is a different kind of hot (p. 271).

student life

Though London is intoxicating and exciting, young travelers to Britain should not discount the smaller towns in northern England. Sometimes the most vibrant party scenes are where you least expect them. Little **Newcastle-upon-Tyne,** for instance, has countless clubs and pubs to satisfy its student population. A new establishment, **The Gate,** combines a club, bar, restaurant, movie theater, and casino—so even if you blow your budget, you can try to win it back. (Note: *Let's Go* does not condone excessive gambling.)

liverpool ☎0151

People hear Liverpool and they think Penny Lane, ports, and impossible-to-discern accents, but there's a whole lot more to this young and thriving city. Named the **European Capital of Culture** in 2008, Liverpool in its prime and beginning to reap the full benefits of its ambitious reinvigoration projects of the '80s and '90s that began the redevelopment trend in Great Britain's old industrial cities. With world-class museums, a legendary music scene, two major universities, and a fierce football rivalry, Liverpool challenges long-time cultural competitor Manchester in a friendly rivalry. A small tidal inlet with a big history, Liverpool oozes with an unwaveringly creative spirit. It is, after all, the hometown of **John Lennon, Paul McCartney,** and **George Harrison.** Today, outsiders flock to Liverpool en masse to soak up its creative juices and see who will be the next great to leave a mark on the city.

ORIENTATION

Liverpool's central district is pedestrian-friendly. There are two main clusters of museums: one on **William Brown Street,** near **Lime Street Station** and the urban oasis of **St. John's Garden,** and the other at **Albert Dock,** right on the pier. These flank the central shopping district, which is enclosed within **Bold, Church,** and **Lord Streets,** and largely consists of walkways and plazas. The area of shops, cafes, and nightclubs between Bold St. and Duke St. is called the **Ropewalks.** The most tourist part of town, **Cavern Quarter,** located on famous **Mathew Street,** houses the major Beatles sites and gift shops. **Liverpool One** is a sparkling new shopping area, containing **Peter Lane** and **Paradise Street** (pedestrian shopping), **South John Street,** a road with over 160 shops, and a brand-new bus station. To the south of the city, over **Nelson Street,** a glittering arch—recently imported from Shanghai as a gift from the People's Republic—marks the entrance to the **oldest Chinatown in Europe.**

ACCOMMODATIONS

A wide selection of affordable hostels makes shackin' up in Liverpool is easy to do. **Beatles Week** is especially popular, so if you're stopping in when it takes place at the end of August, make sure to book in advance. The hostels in town often fill up on weekends and therefore charge higher rates on these nights. Also expect croweded accommodations on nights before major football matches (Liverpool F.C. and Everton F.C.). See hordes of eager fans flood Liverpool hostels in groups larger than the teams themselves. If you forgot to book and are feeling panicked, the TIC's Accommodation hotline *(☎0844 870 0123)* can help you find a bed just in the nick of time.

EMBASSIE BACKPACKERS — HOSTEL ❷

1 Falkner Sq. ☎0151 708 7193 www.embassie.com

All you need is love, and this cozy hostel has lots of it to give. Located in the digs

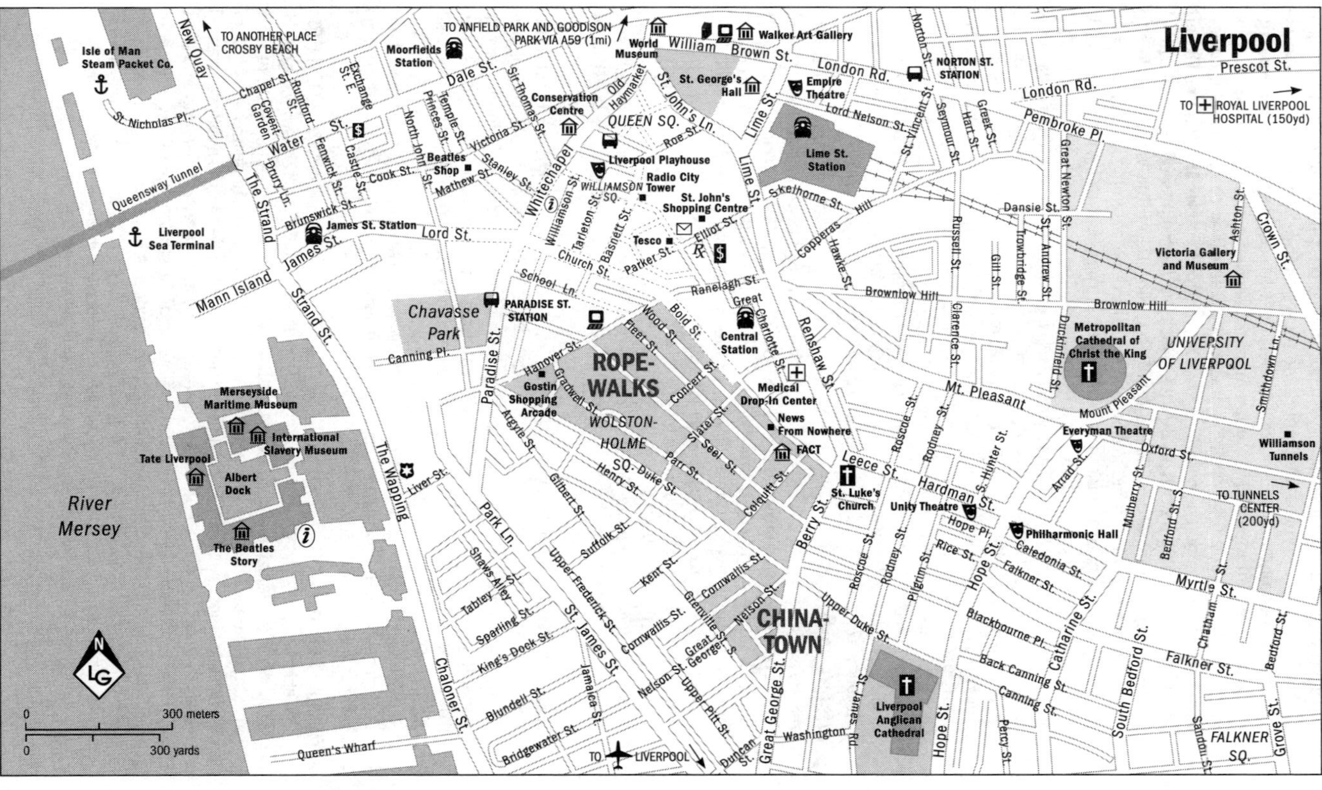
Liverpool
Prescot St.
TO ROYAL LIVERPOOL HOSPITAL (150yd)
TO ANFIELD PARK AND GOODISON PARK VIA A59 (1mi)
TO ANOTHER PLACE CROSBY BEACH
TO TUNNELS CENTER (200yd)
TO LIVERPOOL
Isle of Man Steam Packet Co.
New Quay
St. Nicholas Pl.
Chapel St.
Covent Garden
Rumford St.
Exchange St. E.
Water St.
Moorfields Station
Dale St.
Fenwick St.
Castle St.
North John St.
Princes St.
Temple St.
Sir Thomas St.
Victoria St.
Conservation Centre
Old Haymarket
World Museum
William Brown St.
Walker Art Gallery
St. George's Hall
St. John's Ln.
QUEEN SQ.
Roe St.
Lime St.
Empire Theatre
London Rd.
NORTON ST. STATION
Norton St.
Lord Nelson St.
St. Vincent St.
Seymour St.
Hart St.
Greek St.
Pembroke Pl.
Lime St. Station
Queensway Tunnel
The Strand
Drury Ln.
Cook St.
Beatles Shop
Mathew St.
Stanley St.
Whitechapel
Liverpool Playhouse
WILLIAMSON SQ.
Radio City Tower
St. John's Shopping Centre
Skelhorne St.
Williamson St.
Tarleton St.
Basnett St.
Tesco
Elliot St.
Parker St.
Church St.
Brunswick St.
James St. Station
James St.
Lord St.
Liverpool Sea Terminal
Mann Island
Strand St.
School Ln.
Ranelagh St.
Copperas Hill
Hawke St.
Great Newton St.
Dansie St.
St. Andrew St.
Trowbridge St.
Gill St.
Russell St.
Brownlow Hill
Ashton St.
Crown St.
Victoria Gallery and Museum
Chavasse Park
Canning Pl.
PARADISE ST. STATION
Paradise St.
Wood St.
Bold St.
Fleet St.
Great Charlotte St.
Central Station
Renshaw St.
Clarence St.
Duckinfield St.
Metropolitan Cathedral of Christ the King
UNIVERSITY OF LIVERPOOL
Smithdown Ln.
Hanover St.
Gostin Shopping Arcade
ROPE-WALKS
Gradwell St.
Concert St.
Medical Drop-In Center
Mt. Pleasant
Mount Pleasant
Everyman Theatre
Williamson Tunnels
Merseyside Maritime Museum
International Slavery Museum
Tate Liverpool
Albert Dock
The Beatles Story
River Mersey
The Wapping
Liver St.
Argyle St.
WOLSTON-HOLME SQ.
Slater St.
Seel St.
News From Nowhere
FACT
Roscoe St.
Rodney St.
S. Hunter St.
Oxford St.
Arrad St.
Duke St.
Henry St.
Parr St.
Colquitt St.
Leece St.
St. Luke's Church
Hardman St.
Unity Theatre
Hope Pl.
Philharmonic Hall
Mulberry St.
Bedford St. S.
Gilbert St.
Park Ln.
Berry St.
Rice St.
Caledonia St.
Hope St.
Shaws Alley
Suffolk St.
Kent St.
Cornwallis St.
Pilgrim St.
Falkner St.
Myrtle St.
Tabley St.
Sparling St.
Upper Frederick St.
Grenville St. S.
Nelson St.
CHINA-TOWN
Upper Duke St.
Blackbourne Pl.
Catharine St.
King's Dock St.
St. James St.
Great George St.
Back Canning St.
South Bedford St.
Chatham St.
Bedford St.
Chaloner St.
Blundell St.
Jamaica St.
Nelson St.
Upper Pitt St.
Liverpool Anglican Cathedral
Canning St.
Bridgewater St.
Queen's Wharf
Duncan St.
Washington
St. James Rd.
Percy St.
Sandon St.
FALKNER SQ.
Grove St.
0
300 meters
0
300 yards
N
LG

of the former Venezuelan Embassy (hence the name), this beautiful old Georgian house becomes a home away from home for its multinational guests. Embassie Backpackers combines warm, friendly service with excellent facilities—a large room area, an outdoor area for communal barbecues, a downstairs social area, and a self-catering kitchen fully equipped with all kinds of dishes, tea, coffee, and bread 24hr. daily. The owner's father is a native Scouser and Beatles Expert extraordinaire—he offers free Beatles tours on Thursday nights to all guests and is always up for a chat at the family-style kitchen table where he likes to relive the good old days; he holds the claim to fame of facing off against (and beating) John Lennon's band in a skiffle (think rock and roll with washboards and banjos) band competition back in the '50s.

Take the 80A, 86A, or 86N bus from Lime St. Station. Ask the driver to drop you off at the corner of Catharine St. and Canning St. If walking, exit station toward The Crown Pub. Turn left onto Lime St. and follow through Renshaw St. At St. Luke's Church, turn right onto Berry St. and at the Chinatown arch, take a left onto Upper Duke St. Keep straight past the Liverpool Cathedral, crossing over Catharine St., continuing onto Canning St. until you reach Falkner Sq. The hostel is on your left, facing the park. i Laundry facilities. Towels and sheets included. Lockers available in rooms for £5 deposit. Free coffee, tea, and toast with jam, peanut butter, and marmalade, 24hr. Self-catering kitchen. Satellite TV. Free Wi-Fi and free internet use. Scenic backyard with BBQ. Single-sex dorms available. Dorms M-Th £15, F £17.50, Sa £20, Su £15. Reception 24hr.

INTERNATIONAL INN — HOSTEL ❷

4 S. Hunter St. — ☎0151 709 8135 www.internationalinn.co.uk

This converted warehouse provides a friendly aura, 24hr. service, and guests from all of the world (your first hint are the 20-plus flags hanging around reception). It's also conveniently located near the cheap eats of Hardman St. and the city center. Rooms are bright, cheery, and very clean, with ensuite bathrooms. The attached storefront internet cafe (Sam Joe's Cafe) offers breakfast *(from £2.75)*, Internet *(£1.50 per 30min.)* and live music on some nights.

Off of Hardman St. (Cultural Quarter). i Free Wi-Fi. Free tea, coffee, and toast 24hr. Game room with pool table and free movies. Laundry. Dorms M-Th £15, F-Sa £20, Su £15. Reception 24hr.

COCOON @ INTERNATIONAL INN — HOSTEL ❸

4 S. Hunter St. — ☎0151 709 8135 www.cocoonliverpool.co.uk

In the basement of the International Inn lies the new Budget Pod Hotel. For reasonable prices, couples (or 2 friends) can obtain private hotel-like rooms with HDTVs, blow-dryers, fresh towels, and king-sized beds. However, remember that basement means no windows.

Off of Hardman St. (Cultural Quarter). i Tea- and coffee-makers in rooms. Safety deposit boxes in all rooms. Games room with pool table. Only doubles available. Free Wi-Fi. Doubles M-Th from £43 per room, F-Sa from £53, Su £43.

YHA LIVERPOOL — HOSTEL ❷

25 Tabley St. — ☎0151 0845 371 9527 www.yha.org/uk

Otherwise standard and non-descript, this YHA tries to lend itself some character by staying in touch with its local roots, as the hallways and lounge areas play off of Beatles themes (rock and roll statues, paintings of the Fab Four) a hallway named after "Penny Lane." It is located close to main attractions (museums at Albert Dock), but removed from the hustle-and-bustle of the student nightlife areas (about a 15min. walk to the city center). Almost all the dorms have ensuite bathrooms.

Close to Albert Dock. From the Dock, follow Wapping. Tabley St. is off of Wapping, past Baltic Fleet Pub, to the left. You'll see big signs for YHA. i Breakfast in on-site restaurant for £5; restaurant available for breakfast and dinner. Laundry facilities. Free luggage store. Internet £1 per 15min. Wi-Fi £8 per day, £15 for 3-day pass. Dorms £16-23; private doubles from £41; triples from £52. £3 charge for non-YHA members. Reception 7am-11pm.

HATTERS HOSTEL

HOSTEL ❷

56-60 Mt. Pleasant ☎0151 709 5570 www.hattershostel.com/liverpool

With an organic vegetable garden, historic Gothic building, barbecue area, big movie screen, and helpful staff, this member of the super-popular Hatters hostel chain tries to add some character and intimacy to a huge residence of about 200 beds. Otherwise non-descript dorm rooms have modern and very clean ensuite bathrooms. Situated close major nightlife, Hatters is only a 5min. walk from the train station. Book in advance for weekends, or for a Cathedral view.

*From train station, head south on Lime St., then make a slight left at Brownlow Hill. Right on Mt. Pleasant. Hostel on right. **i** Light breakfast included. Laundry facilities. Internet access in lobby £1 per 15min. Lobby Wi-Fi £5 per day. 7-day WiFi access (in lobby and rooms) £15. Free luggage storage. Bike storage. Self-catering kitchen. Group bookings (6 or more people) require 15% deposit and should be made 2 weeks in advance. Ⓢ Dorms M-Th £16.50-17.50, F-Sa £17.50-£18.50, Su £16.50-17.50; singles £40-60; doubles £27.50-35; triples £25. Reception 24hr.*

THE NIGHTINGDALE LODGE

HOSTEL ❶

1 Princes Rd. ☎0151 943 2378 www.thenightingalelodge.co.uk

The rooms in this hostel (about a 15min. walk from the city center) feel a bit small and stuffy, but they're clean with adequate amenities for the price. The recently refurbished building includes some nice communal features and facilities like a comfortable TV lounge, pool tables *(£1 per game)*, self-catering kitchen, backyard garden, and free tea and coffee. Prices vary depending on availability and day of the week.

*From Lime St. Rail Station, take Lime St. South. Make a left onto Myrtle St., and a right onto Catherine St. When Catherine St. crosses Parliament St., it turns to Princes St. Hostel on left. Or, take the 80A or 86A bus. **i** Continental breakfast included. Free tea and coffee. Lockers and luggage store. Laundry. Lounge area with TV and pool tables. Free Wi-Fi. Self-catering kitchen. Ⓢ Dorms £13-£18; doubles from £30. Reception 24hr.*

REGENT HOTEL

HOTEL ❸

4-8 Mt. Pleasant ☎0151 709 1514

This family-run hotel's dated decor is quaint (if not basic), but private rooms are a plus for the price. Plus the place is a 2min. walk from the train station.

*Across the street from Adelphi Hotel. **i** Breakfast included. Linens included. Color TVs in each room. Some rooms have bathrooms. Licensed bar. Deals for week-long stays. Ⓢ Single from £23; doubles from £46. Reception 24hr.*

EPSTEIN HOUSE

GUEST HOUSE❸

27 Anfield ☎07810 100 900 www.brianepsteinguesthouse.com

Epstein House is the beautiful family home of fames Beatles manager Brian Epstein. Plus, Paul McCartney's father lives on the same road! The house has been converted into a splendid guesthouse. Beatles decor is scattered throughout, and the downstairs lounge area carefully documents Brian Epstein's life story. The facilities and nine guest rooms are top-notch: each room is large with a TV, tea- and coffeemakers, a full bathroom, and memorabilia. Downstairs you can find a guest lounge, a large patio and garden, a licensed bar, and a dining area. Epstein House lies three miles from the city center, but you can easily take the bus or a cab *(£4 fare to/from train station)* to the heart of things.

*From train station, follow signs to Paradise St. bus station. Take the 26 or 27 bus from Paradise St. bus station to Anfield. **i** Continental breakfast £3, full English breakfast £5. Towels, hairdryers, tea- and coffee-makers ensuite. Parking available. Free Wi-Fi. Ⓢ Private rooms from £20 per person. M-F £34 for ensuite room for 2-3 people.*

STRAWBERRY HOUSE

HOSTEL ❶

86 Anfield Rd. ☎07810 100 900

These spacious dorm rooms are good deals. Enclosed within a small row house, the hostel is intimately small with six rooms, a common kitchen, nice patio area, and large common room. Each room has a combination of bunk beds and double beds for three to six people, TVs, and a basin sink.

Anfield. Reception is in the Epstein House, 27 Anfield Rd (see above). Head there first to pay and pick up keys. Look out for number 86; there are no outer markings for the hostel. i Self-catering kitchen with tea- and coffee-makers. Free Wi-Fi. Common area with TV. Ⓢ Dorms £10-12.

BEECH MOUNT BED AND BREAKFAST ❸

1-3 Beech St. ☎0151 264 9189 www.beechmountexecutive.co.uk

Newly opened and about 2 mi. from the city center, this B and B offers large and luxurious business-class furnishings and impeccably clean rooms with bathrooms. If comfort and privacy is important to you, this is a good option. However, the surrounding area is not the safest place to be out and about, and you'll have to schlep out to the city center.

The 10A, 10B bus runs from Lime St. Station to Prescot Rd./Sheil Rd. Head straight; cross Kensington/Prescot Rd. Sheil Rd. becomes Beech St., B and B on your left. The 8 bus runs to Kensington/Sheil Rd. Beech St. is a right off Kensington. B and B is right on your left. i Cots available. TVs in each room. All bathrooms ensuite. Free Wi-Fi. Ⓢ Doubles from £50; "family rooms" (sleep 4 with potential for extra cots; kitchen included) from £85. Ⓣ Reception 24hr.

SIGHTS

THE BEATLES STORY MUSEUM

Britannia Vaults, Albert Dock ☎0151 709 1963 www.beatlesstory.com

Even the most hardcore Beatles fanatic will learn something new about the biggest band that ever was (or, in the words of Lennon, the band that was "bigger than Jesus"). From the group's post-war beginnings to the shag haircuts to the solo careers, the audio guide (included in admission price) will escort you through the quartet's history. You'll hear the voices of Paul McCartney, Alan Williams, Cynthia Lennon, and others, giving the experience an authentic feel. Learn about the initial meeting of McCartney and Lennon and Sir George's near rejection of the Beatles (that would have been a kicker!). Recreations are all the rage here: wander through the streets of Hamburg, where the Beatles had their first overseas tour, discover the Cavern Club of the 1960s. And maybe you won't be as tripped out as groupies were in the '60s, but exhibits on Sgt. Pepper's Lonely Hearts Club Band will still make for a pretty psychadelic experience.

Albert Dock (Follow signs from city center). i Headsets available in multiple languages. Ⓢ £12.50, concessions £8.50. Includes audio tour and admission to 2 sites. Ⓣ Open daily 9am-7pm. Last entry 2hr. before close.

LIVERPOOL ANGLICAN CATHEDRAL CHURCH

St. James Mount ☎0151 709 6271 www.liverpoolcathedral.org.uk

The UK's largest cathedral is surprisingly the product of 20th-century handiwork. Completed in 1978, Liverpool Cathedral has the world's highest and widest Gothic arches, and highest and heaviest peal of bells (you can see them on the tower tour). On Thursday nights in the summer, take a tower tour *(£5)* at dusk and get spectacular views of the Liverpool cityscape.

From the city center, take Mt. Pleasant St., then right onto Rodney St. i Late-night tours of the tower are available Th nights Mar-Oct until 8pm; July-Aug until 10pm. Cafe with free Wi-Fi. Ⓢ Free. 2-day attraction pass, tower climb, and a film and audio tour £5, concessions £3.50. Ⓣ Open daily 8am-6pm.

ANOTHER PLACE OUTDOOR SCULPTURES

Crosby Beach

At the edge of a sleepy seaside town and just a few miles down the shore from old industrial plants, famed sculptor Anthony Gormley has set up an unusual and controversial display of over 100 cast-iron naked figures, nestled in the sand. Made in the form of Gormley's own body, the sculptures weigh 650kg each and stare directly out to sea, supposedly symbolizing the emotions associated with emigration. After earlier trips to Germany, Norway, and Belgium, the display has been approved to stay in Crosby for good. For the most striking views, come by at sunset and at high tide, when the waves lap up against the iron men's bodies.

Take the Merseyrail from Liverpool Central Station to Blundellsands and Crosby (toward Southport, 20min. ride). Trains run every 15min. From the train station, the beach is a 5min. walk. Non-bathing beach. No lifeguards. Free. Open daily.

WALKER ART GALLERY — MUSEUM

William Brown St. ☎0151 478 4199 www.liverpoolmuseums.org.uk

A display of over six centuries of fine and decorative art means that items like Napoleon's toothbrush holder and a post-modern espresso coffee maker sit in the same building as pieces by **Monet** and **Degas.** Gallery also features a collection of British art from the last several decades, much culled from Liverpool's own biennial painting competition.

Close to Lime St. Station, off Victoria Rd. Special events and exhibitions offered; check website for details. Free. Open daily 10am-5pm.

MERSEYSIDE MARITIME MUSEUM — MUSEUM

Albert Dock ☎0151 478 4499 www.liverpoolmuseums.org.uk

Once upon a time, Liverpool was a small fishing village. Before long, though, it had rapidly developed into one of the most important cities in the British Empire, thanks to its position as a major port and center for exports. Liverpool's role in the shipping industry had major social effects on the city that often get overlooked. Fortunately, this museum explores not only the history of Liverpool at sea but also the characters who drive forward its evolution as a major sea power. From the recreation of a Liverpool ship's journey to a Welsh colony in Patagonia (who knew such a thing existed?) to the stories of the Titanic, Lusitania, and Empress of Ireland disasters, to Liverpool as a site in the bombing raids of WWII, the Museum thoughtfully untangles the role of the sea in Liverpool's story. Meanwhile, the downstairs area offers a unique exhibit on the British Agency of Border and Customs that shows the relevance of Liverpool in the present. Test out your instincts and judge who is a smuggler and who is a legit traveler.

Albert Dock. Free Wi-Fi. Lockers on ground floor. Free. Open daily 10am-5pm.

INTERNATIONAL SLAVERY MUSEUM — MUSEUM

Albert Dock ☎0151 478 4499 www.liverpoolmuseums.org.uk

Props to Liverpool: rather than deny its strong ties to the slave institutions of the past, the city owns up to them, mourns the evils of its past, and then seeks to more forward in this unique museum. The exhibits here celebrate black heroes and their achievements. Examining the impact of the slave trade on the world and more specifically, the slave-trade capital of Liverpool. (Many of Liverpool's famed streets were named after residents who were somehow tied to the slave trade—even Penny Lane.)

3rd floor of the Merseyside Maritime Museum. Free. Open daily 10am-5pm.

METROPOLITAN CATHEDRAL OF CHRIST THE KING — CHURCH

Mount Pleasant ☎0151 709 9222 www.liverpoolmetrocathedral.org.uk

Designed by Sir Frederick Gibbard and the older of Liverpool's two towering cathedrals (1967), this contoversially "modern" structure looks like an alien ship from the outside and like a dance club on the inside. The multi-colored glass, modern art, and 3000-seat capacity are certainly striking. The Lutyens Crypt, however, remains from the earlier, more traditional (and even grander) plans for the Church. As one of the largest crypts in the world, it stands as a reminder of the "greatest building never built."

On the end of Hope St. Purchase crypt tickets at the gift shop or Golden Book office. Free.

Crypt £3. Open in summer daily 8am-6pm; in winter M-Sa 8am-6pm, Su 8am-5pm.

FACT

ART, FILM

88 Wood St. ☎0151 707 4464 www.fact.co.uk

Housed in a shimmering metallic building, this state-of-the-art facility features film showings, galleries, and exhibitions of new media arts. There is also a cafe, bar, and lounge area.

Chinatown. Galleries free. Films £7.40, concessions £5.90. Center open M-Sa 10am-11pm, Su 11am-10:30pm. Galleries open M-Tu 10am-6pm, W 10:30a,-6pm. Th-F 10am-6pm, Sa-Su 11am-6pm. Ticket office open M-F 5pm until 15min. after start of last screening, Sa 10:45am-15min after start of last screening.

TATE LIVERPOOL

MUSEUM

Albert Dock ☎0151 702 7400 www.tate.org.uk/liverpool

This staple of the Albert Docks is part of the legendary Tate institution and features special exhibitions as well as some of the finest modern art in the world. In 2010, for example, a much-heralded Picasso exhibition arrived in town. Permanent galleries feature works from the year 1500 to the present day, including works of **Warhol** and **Pollock.** For some years, this was the largest gallery of modern and contemporary art in the UK outside of London.

Follow signs to Albert Dock. Free; some exhibtions charge. Open June-Aug daily 10am-5:50pm, Sept-May Tu-Su 10am-5:50pm.

VICTORIA GALLERY AND MUSEUM

MUSEUM

Ashton St. ☎0151 794 2348 www.live.ac.uk/vgm

This beautiful museum is hosted in the Gothic, picturesque old library of the **University of Liverpool.** The collection ranges from fine art, sculpture, and ceramics to early X-rays, including a fully re-created dentist's surgery room from the 1930's, dinosaur footprints discovered in this region, hippo skulls, and python skeletons.

*From Lime St., continue onto St. George's Pl. and make a left onto Brownlow Hill. Museum is reddish building with clock tower on the corner with Ashton St. **i** Free guided tours every Tu and Th at 12:30pm. Free. Open Tu-Sa 10am-5pm.*

WILLIAMSON TUNNELS

MUSEUM, ATTRACTION

The Old Stable Yard, Smithdown Ln. ☎0151 709 6868 www.williamsontunnels.co.uk

This underground kingdom of winding tunnels and caverns was built in the 1820s and 1830s by **Joseph Williamson,** also known as the "The Mole of Edge Hill." The impressive network of subterranean tunnels was actually just a rich man's folly; Williamson, a wealthy local, didn't believe in charity and rather thought that people should work for their money. So, for 30 years he employed what is believed to be at least half of the local population (men, women, and children alike) to build completely pointless tunnels underneath the city. After his death, the underground passages became smelly rubbish dumps, as people tossed all of their waste through the openings to be hidden underground. The subterranean labyrinth stayed this way until recent years when a group of local volunteers began to extricate the long-time local mystery from all the trash.

*Walking: Take Mt. Pleasant; it becomes Oxford St. Then follow signs to Williamson Tunnels. Bus: The 76, 76A, 77, 139 and 207 stop at Oxford St. East. The 6, 116, 7, 7A, 14, 14C, 61, and 161 all stop at Archbishop Blanche School. **i** 45min. tours run approximately every 20min. Parking available. £4, concessions £3.50. Open Apr-Sept Tu-Su 10am-5pm. Oct-Mar Th-Su 10am-5pm. Tours begin 10:30am. Last entry 1hr. before close.*

FOOTBALL

ANFIELD (LIVERPOOL F.C.)

FOOTBALL CLUB

Anfield ☎0151 260 6677 www.liverpoolfc.tv

In the '70s and '80s, Liverpool F.C. tore up the European football scene, winning four European cups between 1977 and 1984, and a whole generation of English fans from across the country grew up worshipping the ground on which they played. The club is infamous for disaster (96 fans were crushed to death at a Liverpool game in 1989), but fortunately, the stadium itself isn't cursed, as these tragedies happened elsewhere. Tours will take you around the pitch and into the locker room, where you can relive the glories of Istanbul 2005, the most recent European Cup victory for this successful club.

By Bus: 26 or 27 from Paradise St. Interchange, 17 or 217 from Queen Square bus station. Stops directly at the grounds. i Tours run approximately every 30min.; 15min. during peak season. Mini-tours (stadium only, no dressing rooms) are offered the day before a televised home game. No tours on match days. Tour and museum £14, concessions £8; ,useum only £6/4; mini-tours £8/6. Advanced booking recommended. Museum open daily 10am-5pm. Last entry 30min. before close.

GOODISON PARK (EVERTON F.C.) FOOTBALL CLUB

Everton ☎0871 663 1878 www.evertonfc.com

Back in the day, Everton and Liverpool used to be the same team, and Everton played at Anfield. Back then, a heated argument about rent prompted Everton to move away and build its own stadium. Meanwhile, the nephew of the team's beloved sugar daddy, John Moores (the one the university is names after), switched allegiances and transferred the family money to Liverpool, the other club in Merseyside. Ever since, Liverpool has been the more successful club. However, Everton fans will proudly tell you that your stadium is the first football ground ever visited by a monarch; it was christened by King George V and Queen Mary in 1913.

By Bus: #19 from Paradise St. stops directly in front of stadium. Walk across the park from Anfield. i Tours must be booked in advance. Tours £8. Tours M, W, F, 11am, 1pm; Su 11am. No tours on match days.

FOOD

As a university town, Liverpool is blessed with a healthy endowment of cheap eats. Cheap and classy are hardly synonyms, however, and fast-food dumps are practically as common as Beatles posters. **Hardman St.** (veering off from St. Luke's Church, leading into downtown) is full of low-priced pizza, kebab, and burger joints that live off business from the large student population living in the area. If anyone is feeling homesick for America, Liverpool is a particularly good place to pick up all of your old favorite chain restaurants. **St John's Shopping Centre** in the city center has its own "food hall" (a.k.a. food court) featuring many American favorites. Once you reach **Bold Street,** prices will have risen by a few pounds, but food options will have a bit more character. Liverpool's **Chinatown** is the oldest Chinatown in Europe and boasts numerous affordable buffet and lunch specials. Your best bet for a cheap eat might be at one of Liverpool's pubs, many of which offer quality traditional English fare. You can also take advantage of the self-catering kitchens offered at many local hostels. Check out **Tesco Express,** *(97 Bold St. Open daily 7am-11pm).* If you're really feeling strapped for cash and are looking for an affordable snack, try Britain's version of the Dollar Store, **Pound World,** where everything's (you guessed it) just £1 *(66-68 Church St.).*

EVERYMAN BISTRO BISTRO ❷

5 Hope St. ☎0151 708 9545 www.everyman.co.uk

Everyman serves up gourmet, tip-top quality food in a great setting, and is still mighty cheap. The food is all fresh, made from healthy, local ingredients. Customers head up to the front to order and choose from the twice-daily changing menu of scrumptious treats, that's adjusted for the season to take advantage of local produce. The restaurant is always filled with a diverse collection of students, professors, tourists, and locals who come to relish the great quiche and lively atmosphere. Don't skip out on the delicious desserts, like lemon cheesecake or scones *(£1.20-£3.90)*. It's located right beneath the Everyman Theatre. Gluten-free and vegetarian options available.

Underneath Everyman Theatre, next to Metropolitan Cathedral. Entrees £7.50-£9. 3 courses £15. Open M-Th noon-midnight, F noon-2am, Sa 11am-2am.

EGG CAFE VEGETARIAN ❶

16-18 Newington ☎0151 707 2755

Hidden off of Bold St., this local vegetarian restaurant offers healthy and homemade dishes for reasonable prices. The funky atmosphere (large wooden communal tables, local artwork for sale on display in boxes, and purple walls with vines painted on them) is indicative of its quirky clientele. Main meal menu changes daily but includes tasty dishes like quiche, hummus, and pita. Vegan options are available.

*Up 2 flights of stairs, Newington is a side street off of Renshaw St. **i** Breakfast served until noon (except Su, when it's served until 5pm). Entrees £4.95. Open M-F 9am-10:30pm, Sa-Su 10am-10:30pm.*

THE SHIPPING FORECAST PUB GRUB ❷

15 Slater St. ☎0151 706 8045 www.theshippingforecastliverpool.com

This self-proclaimed "Alehouse and Eatery" offers good old comfort food in the form of "Pots of Goodness"—like mac and cheese and vegetable goulash *(£4.60)*, traditional pie and mash with creamy mash, peas, and gravy, and homemade burgers *(from £4.50)*. Live music plays most Thursday, Friday, Saturday, and Sunday nights in the downstairs basement music venue area. It's charming in a "pub meets club" kind of way.

***i** Advance tickets available on ticketweb.co.uk. Cover free-£10 when music plays. Open M-Th 11am-midnight, F-Sa 11am-3am, Su 11am-midnight.*

THE OLIVE PRESS ITALIAN ❸

25-27 Castle St. ☎0151 227 2242 www.heathcotes.co.uk/olivepress

The Financial Quarter isn't the best area to get a cheap eat, but the Olive Press is probably the best value for your pound that you'll get in this area (a neighborhood swamped by businesspeople and wealthy shoppers). A relaxing aura is produced by a brick-fired oven that churns out Italian favorites. The "Healthy Lifestyles" 400 calorie menu offers options for those watching their waists *(£7.20-11.20)*. Mondays are "Happy Mondays"—get 50% of any pizza or pasta after 5pm.

From Albert Dock, take Strand St. and make a right onto James St. Castle is a left off of James. Down flight of stairs. Pizza £6.10-13.50. Open M-Th 11:45am-10pm, F-Sa 11:45am-11pm, Su 11:45am-9pm.

THE QUARTER ITALIAN, CAFE, BAR ❷

7 Falkner Street ☎0151 707 1965 www.thequarteruk.com

This classy cobblestone, street-side cafe offers tasty pasta and stone-baked pizzas for moderate prices. Always abuzz with young professionals, tourists, and students (and even **Yoko Ono**), the setting is perfect for a sunny meal outside with a glass of wine, plate of ravioli, and good friends. Sandwiches and salads are also available.

*Near John Moores University; corner of Hope St. **i** Special menus of the day available. Pasta £6-8.75. Pizza £5-7. Cakes £2-2.85. Open M-F 8am-11pm, Sa 10am-11pm, Su 10am-10:30pm.*

TEA GATHER CAFE CAFE, CHINESE ,ENGLISH, AMERICAN ❶

12 Myrtle St. ☎0151 703 0222

Combination English, Chinese, American deli food may not sound appealing at first, but this hidden cafe off the beaten track has a wide and varied selection of budget meal options from chicken fried rice *(£6.95)* to burgers *(£4-6)* and jacket potatoes that will totally change your mind. The service is fittingly simple and sweet for the students who patronize this establishment: quick, polite, but not overly attentive. Try the authentic Chinese tea in at least one of the 11 flavors *(£1- £1.50)*. It also offers takeout.

Right off Catherine St. on Myrtle St., by intersection with S. Bedford St. Open daily 9am-10pm.

BAGELS LTD — DELI ❶

40 Brunswick St. ☎0151 236 5996 www.bagelsltd.co.uk

Start spreading the news. They call themselves "New York style" bagels, and this is probably as good as they get in Britain. Cheap deals: bacon or sausage on a bagel *(£2)* or tea and a toasted bagel *(£1)*. Notice all the photos of the Statue of Liberty and you'll feel like you're state-side.

Ground fl. of India building. Open M-F 7:30am-2:30pm.

HEMINGWAYS — DELI/COFFEE SHOP/BAR ❶

52-60 Duke St. ☎0151 707 6363

This comfortable coffee house and sandwich bar is a favorite among the locals. With a sizable eating area, Hemingways also features tasty fish sandwiches, jacket potatoes, and a salad bar *(£3.75)*. The coffee is top-notch.

By the corner of York St. 2nd location on Tithebarn St. Free W-Fi. Open M-W 7:30am-4:30pm, Th-F 7:30am-Late, Sa 9am-6:30pm. Last orders 30min. before close.

CAFE TABAC — CAFE, BAR ❶

126 Bold St. ☎0151 709 9502 www.cafetabac.co.uk

During the day, Tabac serves a popular breakfast menu, and customers lounge back against their red cushioned chairs, admiring its lighting, funky wallpaper, and stools, all a striking shade of red. At night, the lights go down and the venue transforms into a comfortable, relaxed bar with live performers and weekly film clubs. Check the website for listings.

Edge of Bold St., across from St. Luke's. Breakfast served 9am-5pm, Lunch and dinner noon-10pm. Free Wi-Fi. Breakfast £3.25-5.50. Sandwiches £4-5. Salads £5.50-6.50. Shots £1-2. Beer £1.80-5. Open M-W 9am-11pm, Th-Sa 9am-11pm, Su 9am-11pm.

SOUL CAFE — CAFE, BAR ❶

114 Bold St. ☎0151 708 9470

Soul music plus soul food equals a full stomach and an excellent mood. This cheap Bold St. joint offers all-day breakfast (with yummy American-style pancakes), milk-shakes, and homemade soups along with other "soul-warming favorites" and light bites. For the occasionally-needed break from Beatlemania, check out the photos and record covers of soul legends like Otis Redding and hum along to the R and B classics playing in the background on Soul FM, the radio station of choice.

Bold St., corner of Colquist St. Breakfast £3-£4.50. Sandwiches from £2.50. Open M-W 11am-6pm, Th 11am-9pm, F-Su 11am-6pm.

KIMOS CAFE — CAFE, EATERY ❸

38-44 Mt. Pleasant ☎0151 707 8288

This casual hang-out offers a unique hybrid of English, Arabic, Mediterranean, and vegetarian cuisine. Keep an eye out on the menu for specials like *baba ghanoush*, kebabs, salads, and Moroccan *harira (lentil and tomato soup, £5.50-7.50)*. Kimos gets crowded at lunch time, so you might have to wait for a table.

Mt. Pleasant St. links Lime St. to city center. Halal. Entrees £6.50-10.50. Open daily 10am-11pm.

LEAF TEA SHOP AND BAR — TEA SHOP, CAFE, BAR ❶

27 Parliament St. ☎0151 707 7747 www.thisisleaf.co.uk

This unusual cafe serves as a combination tea shop, live music venue, book club meeting spot, craft exhibition center, and creative writing center (plus, there's a bike store attached). Hidden in the brick walls of an old industrial area, the tea shop has a casual aura that is aided by the presence of some of Liverpool's mellowest altenative types. Try a soup and sandwich deal *(£5.49)*, and if you're still hungry, the dessert menu with flapjacks and sponge cakes *(£2.05)* looks delectable.

i Menu changes daily. Credit card surcharge 5%. Food served noon-7pm. Free Wi-Fi. ⓢ Sandwiches £3.35. Entrees £4.45-6. Beer £2.70-3.15. ⏰ Open M-Th 8am-midnight, F-Sa 9am-2am, Su 8am-midnight.

TRIBECA BAR AND PIZZERIA — ITALIAN, BAR ❷

15-19 Berry St. ☎0151 707 2528 www.tribeca-liverpool.co.uk

With flourescent green walls, a killer speaker system and over 12 varieties of pizza *(£5-6)*, this is a solid place to start off the night. The chef cooks pizzas in an oven that opens onto the rest of the restaurant, and the restaurant's two-story floor plan is spacious, with comfortable booths, funky fake fireplaces, Rolling Stones posters, and a clear roof window that lets the night sky peek in. A cocktail and New York-style homemade pizza—what better combo is there?

ⓢ Pizzas £5-6. Shots £2. ⏰ Open M-Th noon-1am, F-Sa noon-3am, Su noon-1am.

MAHARAJA — INDIAN ❷

34-36 London Rd. ☎0151 709 2006 www.maharajaliverpool.co.uk

The first southern Indian restuarant in the northwest of England sticks true to its Keralan roots, mixing delicious spices like cinnamon, ginger, and cloves with curry leaves, black pepper, and garlic to create an appealing taste and distinct flavor. The owners claim that Christopher Columbus sought India in avid pursuit of the spices from Kerala—we don't doubt it.

 # 2min. walk from Lime Street station. i Vegetarian options available. ⓢ Business lunch £7 (2 or 3 curries, vegetable side dish, rice, and dessert). Entrees £7-14.50. ⏰ Business lunch noon-2pm.

TOKYOU NOODLE BAR — PAN-ASIAN ❷

7 Berry St. ☎0151 445 1023

Simple but reliably tasty, this small Berry St. locale dishes out a wide variety of pan-Asian dishes at reasonable prices. Most of the cuisine is Cantonese, but the menu includes a mix of Japanese and Malaysian. Get your meal with either chopsticks or a fork at one of their communal wooden tables. We won't judge.

ⓢ Entrees £3.80-6.20. ⏰ Open daily 12:30pm-11:30pm.

DELIFONSECA — DELI, RESTAURANT ❷

12 Stanley St. ☎0151 255 0808 www.delifonseca.co.u

A bustling local favorite situated atop a deli, Delifonseca features local specialites of cheeses, hummus, spices, meats, and plenty of vegetarian options, displayed on a blackboard. No matter what's in season, you're going to get an excellent sandwich.

 # Down the street from Met and Cavern Quarters, between Victoria St. and Dale St. Granite building, bright green sign. ⓢ Entrees £12 and under. Soups £5. ⏰ Deli open M-Sa 8am-9pm. Dining area open M-Sa noon-late.

BISTRO PIERRE — FRENCH ❸

14 Button St. ☎0151 227 2577 www.bistropierre.com

Tastefully traditional, Bistro Pierre isn't ashamed of clichés (in line with the attitude of its Cavern Club neighbor). It embraces its French heritage with wine, candles, and red tablecloths. The food is authentic and carefully created.

 # Cavern Quarter (near Mathew St.). i Early-bird special M-Th 4:30-7pm, F-Sa 4:30-6:30pm. ⓢ Entrees from £7.90. Early-bird 3-course menu £10.95. ⏰ Open M-Sa 4:30-10pm.

THE BEER HOUSE PUB GRUB ❸

41-51 Greenland St. ☎0151 708 3575 www.contemporaryurbancentre.org

This huge pub has a lively atmosphere, large tables for groups, a good selection of beers, and specialty curry nights. Traditional English options are supplemeted by all-day breakfasts, pastas, and main-course salads. Quaint wooden tables and chairs lend the place a Victorian feel, and SkySports blasts in the background, displaying your sporting event of choice.

Contemporary Urban Centre. Entry off Jamaica St. i Open mic night Su. Entrees under £10. Open daily 11am-11pm. Kitchen open 11am-9pm.

CAFE LATINO CAFE, ITALIAN ❷

28a Bold St. ☎0151 709 4217

Looking out on the frenzy of shoppers and artists of busy Bold St., this upstairs cafe presents simple but affordable meals. The authentic Italian owners offer 10 kinds of pasta and nine types of pizza *(£4)*.

Look for the sign hanging from the second story. Up 3 flights stairs. Pizzas and pastas £4-5. Open Tu-Sa 9am-5pm.

THE HOPE AND ANCHOR PUB GRUB ❷

Maryland St. ☎0151 702 7911

For cheap eats, set your anchor down here. Solid deals like burger and a beer with chips *(£4)* from 3pm onwards (or you can substitute curry). Located right next to the campus of the University of Liverpool, this is a student hotspot, equipped with pool tables and a beer garden. Try the puddings *(£2.85-£3.50)* and, if you're feeling funky, pop a coin in the jukebox.

Off of Hope St., near intersection with Hardman St. i Karaoke night on W. Free Wi-Fi. Entrees £4-7.50. Open M-W 11:30am-midnight, Th 11:30am-2am, F 11:30am-midnight, Sa-Su 10am-midnight.

NIGHTLIFE

Liverpool nightlife has changed dramatically since the days when Lennon and McCartney roamed these streets. With ever-increasing influxes of students (the student population of Liverpool currently stands at about 70,000), the post-dinner party scene has expanded drastically. Luckily for travelers, the pubs and bars here try to tailor their music and prices with the scant student budget in mind. Less felicitously, the newer arrivals lack a distinctive Liverpudlian feel. Chain clubs, Australian bars, joints with Beyoncé blasting just don't have that Fab Four charm.

Still, the students bring with them many perks. Keep an eye out for special mid-week promotion nights, when clubs offer cheap drinks and no covers. Also, unlike London, Liverpool has many bars and pubs that remain open until 4am to cater to their very young night-owl patrons. **Concert Square,** centrally located in the heart of the **Ropewalks,** is the center of the clubbing scene on weekends and is a popular site for Stags and Hens partiers, while **Matthew Street** features Beatles-centric nightlife. Liverpool's musical legacy has left an indelible stamp on the nightlife scene across the whole city however; this is one of the top cities in Great Britain for live music—clubs, pubs, and bars in all parts of town showcase both new local talent and major international acts. The bars and clubs on **Seel Street** are at the heart of Liverpool's indie scene.

THE PHILHARMONIC PUB

36 Hope St. ☎0151 707 2837

With the Philharmonic's beautiful woodwork, exquisite mosaic floors, ornate tiling, copper panels, and an excellent bar that serves quality local cask ale, it's no wonder that John Lennon once complained that one of the worst things about being famous was "not being able to go to the Phil for a pint." What is surprising, however, is that this clasically elegant bar has still remained a student haunt at heart, frequented by young people, older locals, and tourists alike. Make sure you check out the unique tiling of the mens' washrooms. (If you're of the female persuasion, ask at the bar for permission to avoid interrupting some poor guy.) Sadly, the women's bathrooms aren't up to the same standards because, when this place opened its doors at the turn of the 20th century, Liverpudlian women didn't probe the pub scene the way they do now.

Across from Philharmonic Concert Hall. Draughts from £2. Open daily 10am-midnight.

THE PEACOCK — BAR

49-51 Seel St. ☎0151 709 2146

Classier and with more character than many of the generic Ropewalks haunts. This bar has brick walls, chandeliers, outside patio areas, and a roof terrace. Drinks are reasonably priced and a good rock music selection blasts downstairs, while the upstairs tends to dance music and frenzied partiers.

Ropewalks. St. Peter's Sq. and Seel St. Open M-F noon-2am, Sa noon-3am, Su noon-2am.

THE CAVERN CLUB — CLUB, MUSIC VENUE

10 Mathew St. ☎0151 236 1965 www.cavernclub.org

This world-famous cellar venue is best known as the site the Beatles' early gigs: the stage under these famed arches is where the city of Liverpool first fell in love with John, Paul, George and...Pete Best (sorry, Ringo!). The Beatles played over 300 shows here, the last being a farewell in August 1963. Other acts weren't bad, either—The Rolling Stones, the Kinks, Elton John, and Queen, among others, have played here (check out the "Wall of Fame" tiles outside to see if your favorite artists have graced the stage). Today, owners try hard to recreate the original vibe. There are two rooms for live music—from newly-signed acts to tribute bands to famous names. One big difference is that today there's a bar where you can grab a pint *(£3)*. Back in the day, the Beatles had to cross the street to the Grapes Pub to have a beer because the Cavern was alcohol-free. Come prepared for elated Beatles tourists who, after 40 years, still haven't managed to master the true grace of "The Twist."

Cavern Quarter. Cover depends on the act. £2.50 for Th Beatle Tribute Night. Open from 11am daily.

HANNAH'S BAR — BAR, RESTAURANT, LIVE MUSIC VENUE

2 Leece St. ☎0151 708 5959 www.barhannah.co.uk

While this bar's recent renovation has given it a more posh vibe, it's a student place in essence. Many local musicians of the present-day Liverpool music scene played their first gigs here. Perks include two stories of seating, cozy couches off to the side, a neat skylight roof, and an upstairs outdoor area where you can sit with your drink and enjoy nighttime views of the old church.

Right next to St. Luke's Church. Open M-F 11am-2am, Sa 10am-2am, Su 10am-12:30am.

MELLO MELLO — BAR, LIVE MUSIC VENUE

40-42 Slater St. ☎0151 707 0898 www.mellomello.co.uk

They call it Mello Mello (quite rightly). This raggedly stylish alternative bar feels kind of like a homey living room and music practice room. There are old typewriters propped up on tables, burlap bags lining the walls in back of the bar, and a large collection of board games waiting to be played. A diverse indie crowd frequents this favorite hideout to listen to jazz groups and experimental bands, laugh at bi-weekly "Comedy Knight," enjoy art displays, and relish a mellow drink. In accordance with the vibe, all of the alcohol is organic.

Corner of Slater and Parr St. Open M-Sa 1pm-late.

BAR CA VA — BAR

4a Wood St. ☎0151 709 9300

This trendy bar tempts the Liverpool youth with its cheap drinks, funky decor, and excellent alternative DJs. Liquor lovers will be smitten: tequila is dirt cheap

(£1 per shot) and comes in loads of crazy flavors. If the conversation begins to tire, let your eyes wander to the old movie posters, magazine articles, concert fliers, and record covers that plaster the walls from ceiling to floor.

i Free Wi-Fi. Open daily 1pm-late (1-2am depending on the crowd and the bouncer's discretion).

MODO BAR, CLUB

1 Concert Sq. ☎0151 709 8832 www.modoliverpool.co.uk

Busy, young, well-established, and trendy, with a huge outdoor beer-garden area is super-popular in the summer and sometimes even gets full mid-week. Beware large crowds and slow service on warm weekend days. If you decide to brave it, bring friends and try a 4-pint cocktail pitcher *(£10)*.

Concert Sq. is between Wood St. and Fleet St. Lots of drink deals: 2-4-1 house cocktails £3 (except F and Sa after 8pm), £4.95 cocktails, £8 for pitcher of cocktails or lager pitchers or bottle of wine (except F and Sa after 8pm) £1 chasers, £2.50 double vodka and NRG (except F and Sa after 8pm). Open M-Th noon-2am, F-Sa noon-3am, Su noon-2am.

BUMPER CLUB

14-18 Hardman St. ☎0151 707 9902 www.bumperliverpool.co.uk

On three floors of '70s-style fun, "Bumplings" (Liverpool's nocturnal night animals) enjoy Grolsch beer *(£1.50)*, bottle and shot deals *(£2)*, and Jagerbombs *(£2.20)* until 4am, every day. Loud music and lots of wild dancing on weekends to indie-pop. Check listings for local bands and DJs.

Hardman St, by the Fly and the Loaf and the intersection with S. Hunter St. No cover. Open daily 5pm-4am.

KRAZY HOUSE CLUB

16 Wood St. ☎0151 708 5016 www.thekrazyhouse.co.uk

With three floors and three bars, this large former warehouse blasts out tunes to the masses. There's a little something for goths, hippies and punks. Krazy House is one of the best-known rock clubs in the area. Each floor has its own themed DJs (including heavy metal and indie). Check out the website for theme nights.

Cover free (early in the night)-£5. Open Th 10pm-4am, F 9pm-4am, Sa 10pm-4am.

BAA BAR WINE BAR

43-45 Fleet St. ☎0151 708 8673 www.baabar.co.uk

Shots, shots, shots! Only £1 each! Spin the wheel of misfortune to determine your fate. This is a major pregame spot for partiers heading out to the clubs: groups come in masses and order tray-fulls of yummy flavored shooters like Tutti Frutti and Bar Berry. The upstairs floor, however, is a clubby area, with blasting DJs and, better yet, no cover.

Beer bottles from £3. Wine bottles from £12.95. Open daily until 4am.

THE ZANZIBAR CLUB CLUB

43 Seel St. ☎0151 707 0633 www.thezanzibarclub.com

Students flock to hear live music at Zanzibar Club, which features eclectic acts, club nights, and good drink offers. An exotic feel keeps the venue in touch with its chosen name.

Corner of Slater St. and Seel St. Open W-Sa 7:30pm-1am.

THE FONT BAR, PUB

Unit 3 Arrad St. ☎0151 706 0345 www.thefontbar.wordpress.com

In the heart of the University of Liverpool neighborhood is this relaxed and popular student pub. Soak in the colorful artwork while you eat a chili burrito *(£5.25)* and down cheap cocktails. Thursday quiz nights offer the possibility of winning a crate of beer.

i Free Wi-Fi. Mixed drinks from £2. Open M-F 11am-11pm, Su noon-10:30pm. Kitchen open M-Sa 11:30am-7:30pm, Su noon-6pm.

JACARANDA BAR

21-23 Slater St. ☎0151 708 9424

With its eclectic mix of posters, murals, and Beatles memoribilia, the "Jac" stays true to Beatles lore (the original quartet played here several items). Previously owned by the first Beatles manager, Alan Williams (a.ka. The Man Who Let the Beatles Get Away) the bar is still hopping, crowded with young locals and tourists alike, both on weekends and during the week.

Slater St. Beer bottles from £2. Open M-Sa noon-2am, Su noon-10:30pm.

SLATERS BAR BAR

26 Slater St. ☎0151 708 6990

"The College of Knowledge" is a student favorite. Tucked away on Slater Street, the bar offers cheap beer and your favorite tunes on the juke box. Crowds get larger as the day gets later—watch out for lines on weekends.

Pints from £1.30 Open daily noon-1am.

THE PILGRIM PUB

34 Pilgrim St. ☎0151 709 2302

With a relaxed atmosphere and cheap drinks, this is another favored student hangout. Live music plays on weekends, and drafts start low *(£1.10 per bottle)*. In nice weather, groups of friends gather outside in the beer garden.

Open daily 10am-11pm.

JUPITERS BAR

10 Hackins Hey ☎0151 227 5265

Karaoke is the specialty of this GLBT bar at the edge of Liverpool's gay district. Jupiters boasts reasonably priced drinks, large TVs for sporting events, and pool tables. Popular nights are "Thursgays" and "Sungays."

Serves food. Free Wi-Fi. Open M-Th noon-11:30pm.

G BAR CLUB

1-3 Eberle St. ☎0151 236 4416 www.g-bar.com

Well-liked by both students and drag queens, this gay-friendly spot is a popular late-night post-clubbing venue. The commercial dance music keeps pumping all night long, and the three floors include a cozy "Love Lounge" for canoodling upstairs.

Off of Dale St., by Moorfields Rail. Cover £2-7. Cocktails £3-5. Open Th 10pm-4am, F 10pm-5am, Sa 10pm-8am, Su 10pm-3am.

ARTS AND CULTURE

Liverpool was the European Capital of Culture in 2008, and it doesn't let anyone forget it. The city prides itself on its art and music offerings, ranging from Beatles reincarnations to a thriving indie scene to world-class orchestras and theaters.

PHILHARMONIC HALL CLASSICAL MUSIC

Hope St. ☎0151 709 3789 www.liverpoolphil.com

This famed Art Deco concert hall stands in the place of the building that burned down in a fire in 1933. While mostly associated with classical music, it also has put on contemporary concerts, film screenings, and comedy shows and has hosted Frank Sinatra and the Beatles. There's a plaque dating from the 1912 commemorating the famed Orchestra who perished on the R.M.S. Titanic, because they were contracted for the voyage by music agents from Liverpool.

Between Myrtle St. and Caledonia St. (and between the two Cathedrals). i 3hr. tours available £15 per person. Must be booked in advance. Box office open M-Sa 10am-5:30pm.

EVERYMAN THEATRE THEATRE

5-9 Hope St. ☎0151 709 4776 www.everymanplayhouse.com

The Everyman has basically been Everything, from a chapel to a cinema to a boxing arena to a theater space. It was here, for example, that sculptor Arthur Dooley, an ex-boxer, was rumored to engage in a fight with art lecturer Arthur Ballard, also a former boxer. Today, though, the theater puts on its own productions and promotes native Liverpool playwrights, as well as welcoming outside shows from Britain and the world.

Corner of Hope St. and Oxford St/Mt.Pleasant, across from Metropolitan Cathedral. i Student discounts available. Tickets £5-50. Standbys (day of) for under 26s £5. Box office open performance days M-Sa 11:15am-7:30pm, non-performance days M-F 10am-6pm.

LIVERPOOL PLAYHOUSE THEATRE

Williamson Sq. 0151 709 4776 www.everymanplayhouse.com

The counterpart to the Everyman, the Playhouse focuses on traditional theater. Three times a year it produces its own shows. The building itself dates back to 1866 and is the only Victorian theater still in active use in Merseyside.

Tickets £5-40, concessions £1-36. Standbys (day of) for under 26s £5. Box office open performance days M-Sa 10am-7:30pm, non-performance days M-Sa 10am-6pm.

ECHO ARENA ARENA

Arena and Convention Centre Liverpool 0844 8000 400 www.echoarena.com

Opening in honor of Liverpool's christening as the European Capital of Culture in 2008, this award-winning building located next to Albert Dock has been host to a wide range of events like the MTV Europe Music Awards, Cirque du Soleil, concerts by Bob Dylan, Beyonce, and Elton John, and the third Cabinet meeting to ever take place outside of London.

Kings Dock, Liverpool Waterfront. Tickets are about £15-40, but vary by performance. Generally no concessions.

LIVERPOOL EMPIRE THEATRE CINEMA

Lime St. 0844 847 2525 www.LiverpoolEmpire.org.uk

Focuses primarily on mainstream touring musicals from outside cities. Comedies and music shows are popular too. Book in advance.

Right near train station. Tickets £43 and under. Most shows offer concessions prices, but check beforehand. Box office open performance days Mo-Sa noon-8pm, Su 2hr. before curtain; non-performance days M-Sa noon-6pm.

UNITY THEATRE THEATRE

1 Hope Pl. 0151 709 4988 www.unitytheatreliverpool.co.uk

In the 1930s, this was a politically active, subversive theater. Today, it stays true to its independent roots, showing the works of local and little-known playwrights.

Off of Hardman St is Hope St. Hope Pl. is left off Hope St. Tickets £2.50-12.50. Concessions available, vary depending on the show. Ticket office open M 1pm-6pm, Tu-Sa 10:30am-6pm, closes at 8:30pm on performance nights.

BEATLE WEEK FESTIVAL

0151 236 9091

Beatlemania hits Liverpool every August. The festival features live entertainment all day long, along with a convention, art exhibitions, flea markets, and tours. Over two hundred bands. Check with the TIC for details and listings for the current year. Cavern Club offers tours and packages.

Aug.

INTERNATIONAL STREET THEATRE FESTIVAL FESTIVAL

0151 709 3334 www.brouhaha.uk.com

Liverpool's largest and most popular festival features dancers, musicians, acrobats, street theater performers, stilt-walkers, and carnival artists, among others. The celebrations involve both the performers and the audience, and thousands crowd the streets to take part in the festivities. Kicks off annually with a carnival.

July-Aug.

ESSENTIALS

Practicalities

- **TOURIST OFFICES:** *(08 Place, Whitechapel and Anchor Courtyard, and at Albert Dock. ☎0151 233 2008 www.visitliverpool.com* *i* Pick up a free copy of **Liverpool Events Guide,** or **Days Out.** Internet use £1 per 15min. Books accommdations for free via accommodation hotline *☎0844 870 0123* or in person. *Open M-Sa 10am-5pm, Su 11am-4pm.)*
- **TOURS: Mendips and 20 Forthlin Road.** Mendips was the childhood home of Lennon, Forthlin Rd. was the family home of Paul McCartney right through early Beatles Years. Book in advance. *(☎0151 427 7231. www.nationaltrust.org.uk/beatles. £16.80).* Hop-on, hop-off tours are offered at **Lime Street Station.** *(☎0151 203 3920 www.city-sightseeing.com £8, concessions £6.)* **Magical Mystery Tours** offers 2hr. tour of Beatles sites like Strawberry Field and Penny Ln. *(☎0151 236 9091 £14.95.)* If you'd rather explore the sights yourself, pick up a free "How to get to the Beatles Attractions in Merseyside" brochure from the TIC. For the price of a Saveaway day-ticket *(£3.30)* you can take the bus around town to all of the major Beatles sights.
- **BEYOND TOURISM: JobCentre Plus.** *(20 Williamson Sq. ☎0151 801 5700 www.jobcentreplus.gov.uk. Open M-F 9am-5pm.)* **The Volunteer Centre.** *(151 Dale Street. ☎0151 237 3975. www.volunteercentreliverpool.org.uk. Open M-F 9am-5pm.)*
- **BANKS:** Located throughout the shopping district. **HSBC.** *(99-100 Cord. St. Open M 9am-5pm, Tu 9:30am-5pm, W 9am-5pm, Th 9am-7pm. F, Sa 9am-5pm.)*
- **LUGGAGE STORAGE: Lime St. Station.** *(£3 per bag for 0-3 hr., £5 for 3-6hr., £7 for up to 24hr.)*
- **LAUNDROMATS: Associated Liver Launderettes Ltd.** *(98 North Hill St. ☎0151 280 7091. Open daily 8am-6:30pm. Last load 6pm.)*
- **INTERNET ACCESS: Central Library.** *(William Brown St. ☎0151 233 5845. Open M-Th 9am-7:30pm, Su noon-5pm.)* Free Wi-Fi with food or drink purchase at many cafes around town, including Tabac, and the Piazza at Metropolitan Cathedral. Liverpool City Council has placed kiosks around downtown that allow you to send free emails (with 5min. time limit) and look at electronic maps.
- **POST OFFICE:** *(35-37 Leece St. ☎08457 223 344. Open M-F 8:45am-5:30pm, Sa 8:45am-12:30pm)* and **Liverpool One** *(inside of WHSmith, 1-3 S. John St. Open M-Sa 9am-5:30pm.)*

Emergency!

- **HOSPITAL: Royal University Liverpool Hospital.** *(Prescot St. ☎0151 706 2000.)* For non-emergencies, **NHS Walk-In Centre.** *(Great Charlotte St. ☎0845 46 47 Open M-F 7am-10pm, Sa-Su 9am-10pm.)*

Getting There

By Plane

Liverpool John Lennon Airport, just 7mi. from the city center, has flights from across Europe such as Barcelona, Madrid, Paris, and Dublin. 86 or 86A bus will drop you right near Lime St. station. The 500 and 80A also run to the city center *(www.liverpoolairport.com).*

By Train

Liverpool Lime St. Station is located in the heart of the city center, and offers trains *(☎08457 48 49 50 www.nationalrail.co.uk)* to **Manchester Piccadilly** *(§ £9.80. 45min., 3 per hr.)* and **Birmingham** *(§ £24.60. 1¾hr., 2 per hr.)*. **Virgin Trains** *(☎08719 774 222 www.virgintrains.co.uk)* runs Express service to **London Euston** *(§ £65.20 2hr., 1 per hr.)*.

By Bus

Norton Street Station operates **National Express** buses *(☎0845 600 7245)* to **Birmingham** *(§ £13. 3hr., 4 per day)*, **London** *(§ £28 5½hr., 4-5 per day)*, and **Manchester** *(§ £7. 1hr., 1 per hr.)*.

By Ferry

Ferries arrive at and depart from Pier Head, north of Albert Dock. **The Isle of Man Steam Packet Company** *(www.steam-packet.com)* runs ferries from **St. Nicholas Place, Princes Parade** *(2½hr.)* to the **Isle of Man,** during the summer. **P &O Irish Ferries** *(☎0871 66 44 777 www.poirishsea.com)* runs ferries from **Dublin** to Liverpool *(8hr.)* from Liverpool Freeport Bootle. **Norfolk Line** *(☎0844 499 0007 www.norfolkline.com)* has trips to and from Liverpool to **Belfast** and **Dublin,** Tuesday through Saturday, starting from £20 and leaving from 12 Quays Terminal, Tower Rd., Birkenhead.

Getting Around

By Train

Merseyrail Trains *(☎0151 227 5181 www.merseytravel.gov.uk)* run from three major stops in the city (Moorfields, James St., and Central) on three outbound lines to the surrounding town and out to Southport, to Preston, and to the coast.

By Bus

Local buses *(☎0870 608 2608)*, operated by **Arriva** and **Stagecoach** are based out of Queen's Square Bus Station, Pardise St. Station, and Liverpool One. Each company sells DayRiders for unlimited day travel *(£3)*. **Merseyside Saveaway** are good for one-day travel on buses, trains, and ferries in the area after 9:30am weekdays and all day Saturday and Sunday. Tickets are available for purchase at Central Train Station *(☎0151 236 6056 www.merseytravel.gov.uk § £3.30 for the main city area, and £4.50 for the surrounding Merseyside areas)*.

By Taxis

For a **taxi,** call **Mersey Cabs** *(☎0151 207 2222)* or **Liver Cabs** *(☎0151 708 7080)*. Like London, Liverpool's cabs are black.

manchester ☎0161

The **Industrial Revolution** transformed the sleepy village of Manchester into Britain's urban powerhouse. More than that, it transformed Manchester from a quintessentially English town into a city that's anything but conventional—a city of mavericks, rebels, and trendsetters, people who were perpetually challenging the status quo and relentlessly pushing for their rights. This is the home of the Co-Operative Movement and Free Trade, the place where Suffragettes began their campaigns, even the place that inspired Engels to help create the Communist Manifesto. Long after the industry that built this city had come and gone, that industrious spirit has remained, coloring the art, music, culture, and attitudes of the city with a revolutionary tint. Mancunians are proud of their heritage and their city; they walk around with a certain swagger to the bars, the clubs, the music venues, even the legendary football venue: it's the people that give this urban center its character, and they won't let you forget it. "Manchester...the belly and guts of the Nation," wrote George Orwell. Indeed.

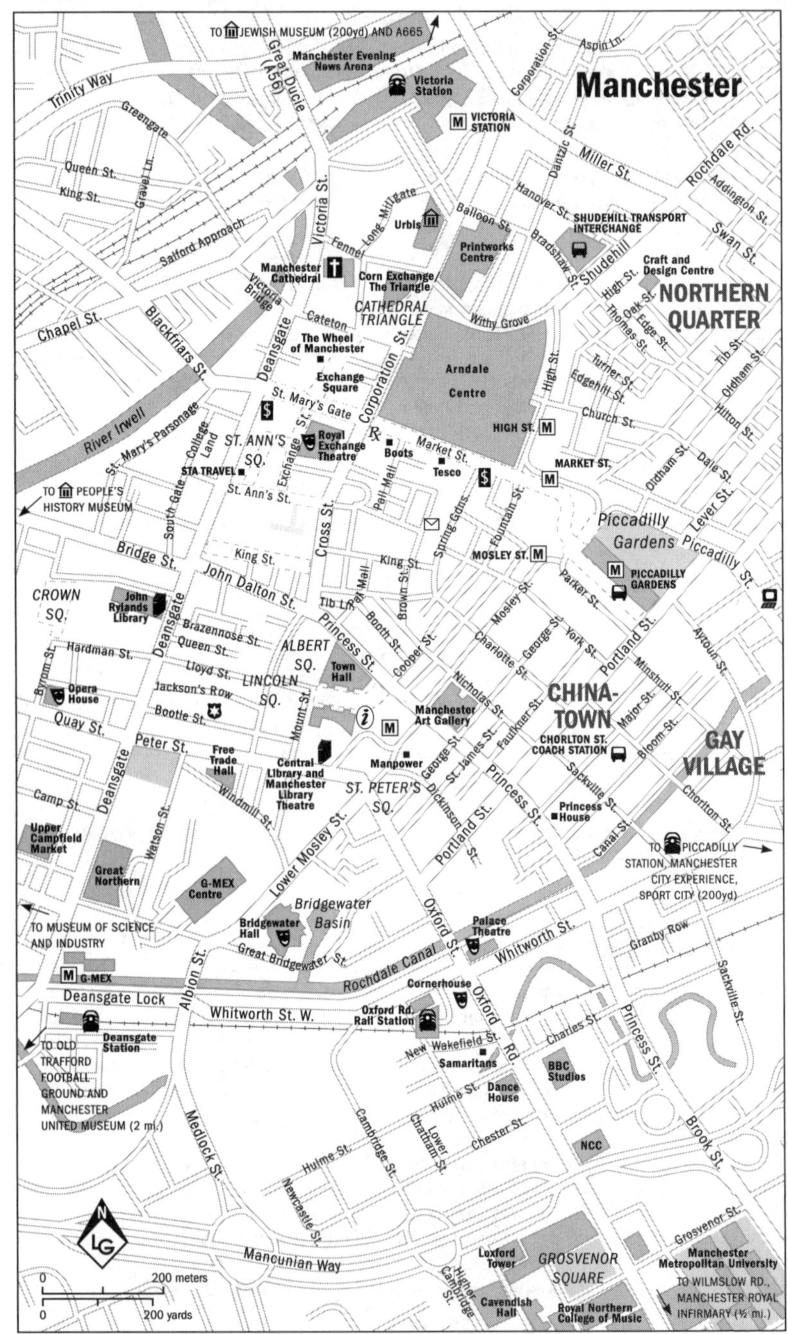
Manchester
TO JEWISH MUSEUM (200yd) AND A665
Manchester Evening News Arena
Victoria Station
VICTORIA STATION
Great Ducie (A56)
Trinity Way
Greengate
Corporation St.
Aspin Ln.
Dantzic St.
Miller St.
Rochdale Rd.
Addington St.
Queen St.
King St.
Gravel Ln.
Victoria St.
Long Millgate
Urbis
Balloon St.
Hanover St.
SHUDEHILL TRANSPORT INTERCHANGE
Swan St.
Salford Approach
Fennel
Printworks Centre
Bradshaw St.
Shudehill
Craft and Design Centre
Manchester Cathedral
Corn Exchange/ The Triangle
High St.
NORTHERN QUARTER
Victoria Bridge
CATHEDRAL TRIANGLE
Thomas St.
Oak St.
Edge St.
Chapel St.
Blackfriars St.
Cateton
Withy Grove
The Wheel of Manchester
Arndale Centre
High St.
Tib St.
Oldham St.
Deansgate
Exchange Square
Turner St.
Edgehill St.
Corporation St.
St. Mary's Gate
Church St.
Hilton St.
River Irwell
St. Mary's Parsonage
College Land
ST. ANN'S SQ.
Royal Exchange Theatre
Boots
HIGH ST.
Exchange St.
Market St.
STA TRAVEL
Tesco
MARKET ST.
Oldham St.
Dale St.
St. Ann's St.
TO PEOPLE'S HISTORY MUSEUM
South Gate
Pall Mall
Fountain St.
Lever St.
Cross St.
Spring Gdns.
Piccadilly Gardens
Piccadilly St.
Bridge St.
King St.
King St.
MOSLEY ST.
PICCADILLY GARDENS
John Dalton St.
Brown St.
Parker St.
CROWN SQ.
John Rylands Library
Tib Ln.
Fat Mall
Mosley St.
Brazennose St.
Booth St.
Princess St.
Cooper St.
Charlotte St.
George St.
York St.
Portland St.
Aytoun St.
Queen St.
ALBERT SQ.
Byrom St.
Hardman St.
Town Hall
Lloyd St.
LINCOLN SQ.
Opera House
Jackson's Row
Nicholas St.
Minshull St.
Bootle St.
Manchester Art Gallery
CHINA-TOWN
Faulkner St.
Major St.
Quay St.
Mount St.
Peter St.
Free Trade Hall
Central Library and Manchester Library Theatre
Manpower
George St.
St. James St.
CHORLTON ST. COACH STATION
Bloom St.
GAY VILLAGE
Deansgate
ST. PETER'S SQ.
Sackville St.
Camp St.
Watson St.
Windmill St.
Lower Mosley St.
Dickinson St.
Princess St.
Princess House
Chorlton St.
Upper Campfield Market
Portland St.
Canal St.
TO PICCADILLY STATION, MANCHESTER CITY EXPERIENCE, SPORT CITY (200yd)
Great Northern
G-MEX Centre
Bridgewater Basin
Oxford St.
Palace Theatre
Whitworth St.
Granby Row
TO MUSEUM OF SCIENCE AND INDUSTRY
Bridgewater Hall
Great Bridgewater St.
Albion St.
Rochdale Canal
Sackville St.
G-MEX
Cornerhouse
Oxford Rd.
Deansgate Lock
Whitworth St. W.
Oxford Rd. Rail Station
Charles St.
Princess St.
Deansgate Station
New Wakefield St.
TO OLD TRAFFORD FOOTBALL GROUND AND MANCHESTER UNITED MUSEUM (2 mi.)
Samaritans
BBC Studios
Hulme St.
Dance House
Medlock St.
Cambridge St.
Lower Chatham St.
Chester St.
Hulme St.
NCC
Brook St.
Newcastle St.
Grosvenor St.
Mancunian Way
Loxford Tower
GROSVENOR SQUARE
Manchester Metropolitan University
Higher Cambridge St.
TO WILMSLOW RD., MANCHESTER ROYAL INFIRMARY (½ mi.)
Cavendish Hall
Royal Northern College of Music
0
200 meters
0
200 yards
LG
N

ORIENTATION

The city center is a strangely-shaped polygon formed by Victoria Station to the north, Piccadilly Station to the east, the canals to the south, and the River Irwell to the west. **Piccadilly Gardens** serves as a city center of sorts and is a popular meeting spot; thousands of Mancunians make their way across this plaza during the average workday. The **Northern Quarter,** home to the indie scene, is located, logically, in the north of the city, a few blocks away from the Gardens. **St. Ann's Square** and **King Street** to the west are homes to much of the city's shopping, while **Market Street** borders on **Arndale Centre,** Manchester's large inner-city shopping mall. **Deansgate** runs down the northwest side of the city center, and hosts many bars, pubs, and entertainment. Oxford Rd., running from north to south, is probably the busiest street in town, and it will take you out to the university area.

ACCOMMODATIONS

HILTON CHAMBERS — HOSTEL ❷

15 Hilton St. ☎0161 236 4414 www.hattersgroup.com

Run by the Hatters group, this place has all the key features of a good hostel (central location, friendly staff, clean facilities), plus a modern, posh atmosphere. All dorms have ensuite bathrooms. This hostel is right in the middle of Manchester's bohemian Northern Quarter.

From the train station, follow signs to Piccadily Gardens. Then go straight on Oldham Rd. and make a right on Hilton St. White building on your left. i Wi-Fi £12 per week. Internet £1 per 30min., £2 per hr. Free luggage storage. 24hr. light breakfast included. Laundry downstairs. Ⓢ Dorms £15-30; doubles from £45. Reception 24hr.

THE HATTERS HOSTEL — HOSTEL ❷

50 Newton St. ☎0161 236 9500 www.hattersgroup.com

The Hilton might have some posh spice, but Hatters Hostel is where the party's at. Inside a renovated hat factory, you'll find a clean, inexpensive hostel with great common spaces and a social atmosphere. Be sure to ask about the weekly pub crawl. It's easily accesible by train or bus. Come prepared for the sounds of joyful partiers on weekends.

5min. from bus station. Take Newton St. off of Portland St. from Piccadilly Gardens. i Free luggage storage. Self-catering kitchen. Wi-Fi £5 per day. Free light breakfast included and available all day. Ⓢ Dorms from £14.50-£24.50. Doubles from £25, singles from £27. Reception 24hr.

YHA MANCHESTER — HOSTEL ❷

Potato Wharf, Castlefield ☎0845 371 9647 www.yha.org.uk

With pleasant waterfront views and large rooms, this sleek hostel is a 15min. walk from the bus and train stations. If it's raining, fear not—you can always pick up a UK flag umbrella from the reception for only £3.50.

Metrolink to Deansgate and follow signs to Youth Hostel. i Full breakfast £5. Laundry facilities and self-catering kitchen. Internet £1 per 15min.; Wi-Fi £8 per day. Ⓢ Single-sex 4-person dorms £16-24.50 per night, depending on time of week and availability. £3 charge for non-YHA members.

UNIVERSITY OF MANCHESTER — DORM ❷

www.accommodation.manchester.ac.uk

If you're looking for a straightforward campus dorm feel, the University offers summer accommodations in many of its campus areas: **City Central** *(☎0161 306 3198),* right next to swimming facilities; **City North** *(☎0161 306 3131),* close to the libraries and academic buildings; **City South** *(☎0161 273 2926),* near major art and culture venues; **Victoria Park** *(☎0161 306 9840),* a leafy park area about 10min. bus ride from city center; and **Fallowfield** *(☎0161 306 9900),* a student suburb known for its social scene.

i Bedding not included. Ethernet cables available in some dorms. Laundry facilities. Most have self-catering kitchens. ⑤ Standard singles from £14.10 per night, £99.75 per week; ensuite singles from £17.92/125. Discounts for students attending UK universities.

NEW UNION HOTEL
HOTEL ❸

111 Princess St. ☎0161 228 1492 www.newunionhotel.com/hotel

Located right in the heart of Gay Village and atop a bar/showroom, this small hotel features large, recently redesigned rooms with ensuite bathrooms and small HDTVs. Be warned that this area is abuzz with people at night. It's no wonder their advertisement claims that this is "where the weekend never ends." Breakfast in bed for £3.

Corner of Princess St. and Canal St. From the train station, take Whitworth St. and make a right onto Princess St. ℹ Free Wi-Fi. £20 key deposit required. ⑤ Doubles M-Th £40, F £50, Sa £55, Su £40. Twins M-Th £50, F £60, Sa £65, Su £50.

THE MILLSTONE HOTEL
HOTEL ❷

67 Thomas St. ☎0161 839 0213

Conveniently located in the bohemian Northern Quarter, Millstone Hotel has small but adequate ensuite rooms. You'll get a very warm welcome upon arrival from the colorful bar regulars at the pub downstairs.

Take Lever St. from Piccadilly Gardens, then make a left onto Thomas St. By the intersection with Tib St. ⑤ Singles from £25; doubles from £40.

SIGHTS

MUSEUM OF SCIENCE AND INDUSTRY
♿ MUSEUM

Liverpool Rd. ☎0161 606 0177 www.mosi.org.uk

This massive complex is the site of the world's oldest surviving passenger railway, but you'll find much more inside: airplanes, steam engines, railcars, and many other remnants of the old industrial Manchester. Power Hall (where Matthew Boulton claimed to sell "what all the world deserves—power") shows the evolution of energy over time. Live demonstrations are often offered for free by museum staff; check schedule upon arrival.

Metrolink to G-Mex and follow brown signs. Bus 33 from Piccadilly Gardens also stops outside, as do the free No. 2 and No. 3 Metroshuttle buses. ⑤ Free. Open daily 10am-5pm.

MANCHESTER ART GALLERY
♿ MUSEUM

Mosley St. ☎0161 235 8888 www.manchestergalleries.org

Manchester's largest gallery covers many periods, but is most famous for its Pre-Raphaelite paintings. Check out the exhibit on Manchester for an introduction to the city's rich artistic history. Ask for a free collections highlights leaflet in the entrance hall or at the information desk.

Between Princess St. and Nicholas St. Metrolink to St. Peter's Sq. ⑤ Free. Open Tu-Su 10am-5pm. Free tours Sa-Su 2-3pm.

PEOPLE'S HISTORY MUSEUM
♿ MUSEUM

Spinningfields ☎0161 838 9190 www.phm.org.uk

Reopened in 2010 and newly doubled in size, the People's History Museum will teach you about working people in Britain in a city that has been at the forefont of industry. Its archives unveil the progression of a city whose strides and advances toward democracy have circulated around the world. Their collection of 18th- and 19th-century political cartoons is particularly impressive, as are the photos of the English Suffragettes, many of whom were forcibly carted off and carried away.

Left Bank, Spinningfields. Corner of Left Bank and Quay St. Right near Salford Rail Station. ⑤ Free. Open daily 10am-5pm.

JOHN RYLANDS LIBRARY
♿ LIBRARY

150 Deansgate ☎0161 306 0555 www.library.manchester.ac.uk

With a picturesque interior that dates back to the 1890s, this gorgeous building's got one of the UK's most impressive collections of printed books and manuscripts. Perhaps the most famous piece is the St. John's Fragment, the earliest known piece of the New Testament in existence.

Accessible via free Metro-Shuttle buses. City center, corner Wood St. of Deansgate. Free. Open daily 10am-5pm.

THE WHEEL OF MANCHESTER AMUSEMENT

Exchange Sq. ☎0161 831 9918 www.worldtouristattractions.co.uk

This 60 mi. ride in the sky is a must for any visitor who wants to see all of Manchester. With spectacular views over one of Europe's fastest changing urban landscapes. The 42 capsules each seat up to eight people, but those who like to stay classy can ride in a VIP capsule, complete with DVD, glass floors and champagne.

Next to Manchester Arndale. i A/C. £6.50, £5 concessions. 10% discount if you book online. Open M-Th 10am-9pm, F-Sa 10am-midnight, Su 10am-7pm.

FOOTBALL

MANCHESTER UNITED SPORTS STADIUM

Old Trafford, Sir Matt Busby Way ☎0161 868 8000 wwww.manutd.com

Manchester United calls itself the most popular football club on earth and greatest football story every told. With a record 18 league titles and record 11 FA Cups (English football championships), Manchester United, like the New York Yankees, is revered, hated, and respected for its greatness. Known as the Red Devils to fans and foes alike, Manchester United is also the richest football club in the world, with a $1.5 billion value according to Forbes Magazine. The Manchester United Museum and Tour Centre (at the Old Trafford football stadium) display memoribilia dating from the club's inception in 1878 to its recent successes. Once you emerge from the tunnel at this "Theatre of Dreams" you can imagine you have 80,000 fans cheering for you.

Take the Metrolink to Old Trafford, then follow signs. i Tours not available on match days and are subject to change at short notice. On the day before a Champions League home game, tours end at 3pm. Prebooking encouraged. Musuem £9, museum and tour £12.50. Concessions £8.50. The Museum and Tour Centre open M-F 9:30am-5pm, with the exception of match days. Tours operate up to every 10min. from 9:40am-4.30pm.

FOOD

A hostel owner put it best when asked for a recommendation for a good place to eat in Manchester. "Well, what do you want to eat?" "I don't know, something English," said the guest. "Ah, well that's a different question. You can either have something good or something English." Cheap kebab and curry places are sprinkled throughout the city, and its legendary Chinatown has a wide variety of cheaper specials, offered by most of the restaurants during lunch hours in the form of a multi-course "Businessman's Lunch." When the sun goes down and evening rolls around, many of Manchester's young hip types like to wine and dine at the stylish cafe-bars that line the Northern Quarter and Deansgate. **Manchester Markets** (*www.manchestermarkets.com*) runs an open-air market located on King St., Exchange Sq., and St. Ann's Sq., for weeks-long stints during the spring and summer. The markets are full of delicious but cheap street vendors food and live music. Inquire at the TIC about dates. For the ambitious cooking types, there is a **Tesco** supermarket at 58-66 Market St., right across from Arndale Centre. (*Open M 7am-midnight, Tu-F 6am-midnight, Sa 6am-10pm, Su 11am-5pm.*)

SOUP KITCHEN SOUP, SANDWICH ❶

31-33 Spear St. ☎0161 236 5100 www.soup-kitchen.co.uk

No, we're not suggesting that being on a budget means you're homeless. These

long communal wooden tables are the site for some delicious deals: soup and sandwich *(£5; noon-5pm)*, or better yet, soup or sandwich with a pint *(£5; 5-8pm)*. Evenings transform the cafe into a live music venue. Check website for listings.
Stevenson Sq. Sandwiches £3. Soup £3. Open M-Sa 9am-11pm, Su 9am-4pm.

TAMPOPO NOODLE HOUSE ASIAN ❷
16 Albert Sq. ☎0161 819 1966 www.tampopo.co.uk
This popular shop feels like home to many fans of pan-Asian cuisine, it offers street food from Singapore, the Philippines, Vietnam, Indonesia, Japan, and Malaysia. Don't be fooled, though; you're still in Manchester. Try the stir-fried specials, made fresh in their hot wok *(from £6.50)*.
Across from Town Hall. i Other locations: The Orient (Trafford Centre) and Triangle Shopping Center (Exchange Sq.). Entrees £6.50-9.50. 2 courses for £6.95 from noon-7pm. Open M-Sa noon-11pm, Su noon-10pm.

BARBURITTOS TEX-MEX ❶
1 Piccadilly Gardens ☎0161 747 6165 www.barbritto.co.uk
Centrally located right in Piccadily Gardens, Barburitto's is fast, cheap, and tasty, selling tacos, nachos, burrito bowls, and, of course, regular old burritos *(£4.25-5.25)*. The menu offers the following definition of a burrito: "a little donkey; diminutive of burro (we don't sell these)." There's a 20% discount if you flash that handy student ID of yours.
Right on the square in Piccadilly Gardens. i Other locations: 134 The Orient (Trafford Centre). Burritos £4.25-5.25. Open M-W 11am-9pm, Th-Sa 11am-1am, Su noon-7pm.

TEACUP CAFE ❶
53-55 Thomas St. ☎0161 834 2004
Stylish and trendy yet unpretentious, this cute vegetarian cafe and coffee shop features polka-dot tablecloths, quality coffee, yummy sandwiches *(£3.75)* and fruity smoothies named for musicians *(£3.65)*. Don't leave without trying one of their homemade to-die-for pastries.
Hilton St. turns into Thomas St. Open M 8:30am-5pm, Tu-F 8:30am-6pm, Sa 10am-7pm.

THE OX PUB PUB GRUB ❸
71 Liverpool Rd. ☎0161 839 7760 www.theox.co.uk
This excellent gastro-pub has a pricey but high-quality wine list and a comfortable atmosphere. The small beer garden outside by the canal is a great place to have a drink in the nice weather, and the food has won multiple awards for its quality.
Castlefield. Opposite Museum of Science and Industry. Corner of Stone St. and Liverpool Rd. Open M-Th 11:30am-midnight, F-Sa 11:30am-1am, Su 11:30am-midnight.

CIAO BELLA ITALIAN ❸
42 Portland St. ☎0161 236 6631 www.ciaobella-restaurant.com
This underground Italian restaurant provides an authentic atmosphere and features romantic candles to complement its tasty pasta. Don't pass up the garlic bread.
i Takeout available. 2-course lunch menu £9. Open M-Th noon-3pm and 5pm-midnight, F-Su noon-late.

NIGHTLIFE

Nightlife is such an important part of the Mancunian life that many "daytime" establishments are really just masquerading as such; when the sun goes down, their true selves come out. As Manchester fancies itself England's cultural capital, it's only fitting that its nightlife is hip and trendy. Centered on Oldham St., the Northern Quarter is home to some of Manchester's best live music and its alternative vibe is perfect for the young, artsy folk. If you're feeling unsafe crossing from Piccaddilly to Swan

St. or Great Ancoats St., use Oldham St., where the neon-lit clubs (and their massive bouncers) lend reassurance. For less indie, more standard American dance tunes, the hotspot in town is Deansgate Locks, which has four bars and a comedy club right next to each other in an old railway station. The Gay Village runs along Canal Street, once a run-down part of the city, and has since become one of the best places to go out in Manchester when the weather behaves itself: many Gay Village establishments have outdoor seating right on the water.

DRY BAR — BAR, CONCERT VENUE

28-30 Oldham St. ☎0161 236 9840

A good sound system, great location, occasional live acts, and wide selection of beers make this popular Northern Quarter hangout the perfect place to start off your night. It's also popular during the day, when Manchester hipsters grab a beer and people-watch the passer-by on Oldham St.

Oldham St. is right off of Piccadilly Gardens. Open M-Th 11am-1am, F-Sa 11am-3am, Su noon-2am.

TROF — BAR, CAFE, RESTAURANT

6 Thomas St. ☎0161 833 3197 www.trof.co.uk

This three-story bohemian cafe and bar and restaurant is multi-functional—a great place for scrambled eggs on toast *(£3.75)* and Wi-Fi in the morning; bangers and mash *(£5.95)* in the afternoon; and more than 40 international beers at night, when the party really gets started. The blackbird next to items on the menu marks the "Cheep Cheep Menu" *(under £5)*.

Northern Quarter, continue on Thomas St. away from Hilton St. i All local meats. Open M-Th 10am-1am, F-Sa 10am-3am, Su 10am-midnight.

SIMPLE BAR — BAR, RESTAURANT.

8 Dorsey St. ☎0161 832 9494 ww.cordbar.co.uk

This chic joint is packed even during the week and is a premier place for a meal (like the delicious mac and cheese) and a drink. Happy hour runs through 8pm on weeknights, so chase down your dessert with a bottle of wine *(£6.95)* and sit back to the relaxing tunes.

NIGHT AND DAY — BAR, CLUB, CONCERT VENUE

26 Oldham St. ☎0161 236 1822 www.nightnday.org

At the heart of the Northern Quarter, Night and Day Cafe is a well-known institution in the Manchester music scene. Top acts play nighttime gigs at this dark venue during the week and weekends, while a great food menu is offered during the day. Sweet sound system, but no draught beer.

Oldham St. is right off Piccadilly Gardens. Cover ranges from free to £20. Hours vary depending on the act.

THE THIRSTY SCHOLAR — BAR, VENUE

50 New Wakefield St. ☎0161 236 6071 www.thirstyscholar.co.uk

There's live music every night and a juke box during the day, so rock out as long as you'd like. The heated outdoor seating area is good for a midday drink or veggie pub grub. The pub claims to be Manchester's only vegetarian and vegan city center pub.

Free. Open M-Th noon-1am, F-Sa noon-2am, Su noon-1am.

BLUU — BAR

85 High St. ☎0161 839 7195 www.bluu.co.uk

This hip bar in the Northern district has a sophisticated feel and terrific cocktails. Beware of lines outside on Friday and Saturday nights.

Corner of Thomas and High St. Northern Quarter. Open M-Tu noon-midnight, W noon-1am, Th noon-1 or 2am, F 1pm-2am, Sa 11am-2am, Su noon-midnight.

CORD

BAR

8 Dorsey St. ☎0161 832 9494 ww.cordbar.co.uk

Corduroy meets style at this cozy home to bohemian intellectual. Hidden away off of the main drag, this cozy bar serves good drinks at great prices, from cocktails *(£5)* to beer on draught *(£3.10).*

Left off of Tib St. Open M-Th noon-11pm, F-Sa noon-1am, Su 3-10:30pm.

QUEER

BAR, CLUB

4 Canal St. ☎0161 228 1360 www.queer-manchester.com

Huge booths, red leather sofas, flatscreen TVs, and bumpin' music provide the perfect atmosphere for this classy gay bar. Trannyoke *(Tu 9pm)* is a fan favorite, but not quite as popular as Morning Glory *(£7 at the door, £5 in advance),* a weekly celebration featuring bouncy house music, held every Sunday from 4am-10am. What better way to start your day?

In the middle of Canal St. No cover except for Morning Glory. Open M-Th 11am-late, F 11am-2am, Sa 11am-2:30am, Su 4am-10am and 11am-late. Kitchen open 11am-8pm.

BAA BAR

CLUB

27 Sackville St. ☎0161 247 7997 www.baabar.co.uk

This friendly joint welcomes a diverse crowd to a funky '70s theme played out under its retro orange lamps. Tastefully tacky here means super-cheap shots and fun music. All the walls are giant mirrors, which makes the club feel twice as big. But be careful, that cute person making eye contact from across the room might just be you.

Gay Village. Open M-Sa 5pm-2am, Su 5pm-1am.

ARTS AND CULTURE

ROYAL EXCHANGE THEATER

ST. ANN'S SQUARE

St. Ann's Sq. ☎0161 833 9833 www.royalexchange.co.uk

At the site of the former Manchester Cotton Exchange now sits one of the grandest modern theaters in England. The theater itself is a seven-sided, glass-walled capsule, literally suspended from huge marble pillars inside the former **Great Hall of the Exchange.** Every one of the 700 seats in the theater is less than 9m from the circular stage, so you're guaranteed a great view for your money.

*Public entrances on St. Anna's Square and on Cross St. Across from Boots. Metrolink: Market St. **i** Check website or call for show listings. Tickets £8.50-29.60. Concessions £6.50. Student standbys ½-price on the day of the performance only (except Sa night); M anyone aged under 26 can get the best available seats for £4. Visit royalexchange.co.uk/guestlist for information on "A Night Less Ordinary," the Arts Council initiative that distributes at the Royal Exchange. Ticket office open M-F 9:30am-7:30pm, Sa 9:30am-8pm.*

BRIDGEWATER HALL

QUAYS

Lower Mosley St. ☎0161 907 9000 www.bridgewater-hall.co.uk

Home to the **Hallé Orchestra**, the **Hallé Choir** and the **Manchester Boys Choir,** Bridgewater Hall is also a regular venue for the **BBC Philharmonic** and **Manchester Camerata.** The hall is named for the third Duke of Bridgewater, who commissioned the canal that runs across Manchester.

Guided Tours £5. Tickets £6-75. Concessions are available for some shows. Call or inquire at box office. Box office open on performance days M-Sa 10am-8pm, Su noon-8pm; on non-performance days M-Sa 10am-6pm.

THE CORNERHOUSE

ST. PETER'S SQUARE

70 Oxford St. ☎0161 228 7621 www.cornerhouse.org

Cornerhouse is Manchester's **International Centre for Contemporary Visual Arts and Film.** It hosts frequent artsy-type events during the week, including screenings of indie films and gallery showings of artwork and photography. The downstairs cafe is always hopping. Get a "Reel Deal" *(£11.20)* on Monday—you get a ticket to the film, a pizza, and a pint.

Metrolink: St. Peter's Sq. Art galleries free. Films: Matinee £5, concessions £3.50; evenings (from 5pm) £7/5. Box office open M-Su noon-8pm. Cornerhouse and bar open M-Th 9:30am-11pm, F-Sa 9:30am-midnight, Su 11:30am-10:30pm. Galleries open Tu-Sa noon-8pm, Su noon-6pm. Bookshop open daily noon-8pm.

MANCHESTER CRAFT AND DESIGN CENTRE NORTHERN QUARTER

17 Oak St. 0161 832 4274 www.craftanddesign.com

Once a Victorian fish market, this glass-roofed atrium now displays crafts, from specialty stationary to handmade jewelry. A good stop if you're looking for artsy souvenirs or a gift for Mother's Day.

Near Shudehill bus and train station. Oak St., Cathedral Gardens, between Victoria Station and Exchange Sq. Open M-Sa 10am-5:30pm.

PALACE THEATRE OXFORD RD.

Oxford Rd. 0844 847 2277

This theater has been proudly serving Manchester since 1891, featuring a variety of classical productions in opera, ballet, and dramas.

Take Whitworth St. from Piccadilly Gardens and make a right on Oxford St. Near Oxford Rd. Rail Station. i Student concessions available for some shows. Tickets from £10. Ticket office open M-Sa 10am-6pm and 2hr. before performances.

QUEER UP NORTH GAY VILLAGE

0843 208 1840 www.queerupnorth.com

Since 1992, Queer Up North has been one of the best GLBT festivals in Manchester. During late May, the latest trends in queer culture (theater, cabaret, music, art, ideas) come to Manchester for a festival.

Buy tickets in person or in advance, prices vary depending on the event. Concessions available. Late May.

MANCHESTER PRIDE GAY VILLAGE

0161 236 7474 www.manchesterpride.com

Traditionally held on the August bank holiday weekend, this is the biggest gay festival in Manchester, featuring live entertainment (from sporting events to art to parades) throughout the Gay Village.

£17.50 for 4 days; Early bird tickets £12.50. From £10 for individual day tickets.

ESSENTIALS

Practicalities

- **TOURIST INFORMATION CENTER: Manchester Visitor Centre,** at the corner of Portland St. and Piccadilly, books accommodations for free and distributes the *Manchester Pocket Map, Where to Stay,* and *All About Manchester. (0871 222 8233 www.visitmanchester.com Open M-Sa 10am-5:30pm, Su 10:30am-5:30pm.)*
- **TOURS:** Guided Walks and private tours available from the TIC. **Manchester Guided Walks and Tours** pamphlets are available at the TIC that have full listings of tour times and themes, which change daily. *(£6, concessions £5.)* **Manchester Ghost Walk** runs from outside the Tourist Information Centre every M and Tu at 7pm. See website for additonal times. *(07775 313 208 www.manchesterghostwalk.co.uk £6, concessions £5.)*
- **STUDENT TRAVEL: STA Travel.** *(14A Oxford Road, across from BBC Studios. Open M-Sa 10am-6pm.)*
- **BANKS: Barclays** branches are located throughout the city center. *(86-88 Market St. 0845 755 5555 Open M-W 9am-6pm, Th 10am-7pm, F 9am-6pm, Sa 10am-4pm, Su 11am-3pm.)*

- **POST OFFICE:** *(Brown St. and Marriots Court with Bureau de Change. ⏰ Open M 9am-6pm, Tu 9:30am-6pm, W-Sa 9am-6pm.)*

Emergency!

- **PHARMACY: Boots.** *(32 Market St., Piccadilly ⏰ Open M-F 7:30am-6:30pm, Sa 8:30am-5:30pm, Su noon-5:30pm.)*
- **HOSPITAL: Manchester Royal Infirmary.** *(Oxford Rd. ☎0161 276 1234.)* For non-emergencies, **Manchester Piccadilly NHS Walk-In Centre.** *(1st Floor Gateway House, Station Approach. ☎0161 233 2525 ⏰ Open M-F 7am-7pm.)*

Getting There

By Plane

Manchester International Airport in the south of the city is the largest airport in the UK outside of London. Serves most major cities in Europe and North America, South America, Africa, and Asia. Direct trains run from the airport to Piccadilly and Oxford Road stations every 20min. *(£3).*

By Train

Manchester Piccadilly is the main station. It is connected to **Manchester Victoria,** which also offers inter-city trips, by the Metrolink, serve Manchester. Additional service to local areas is available at the Deansgate and Oxford Road stations. Ticket prices are higher for travel during peak hours *(⏰ Daily 7-9:30am and 4-7pm).* **Manchester Piccadilly Station.** *(London Rd. ⏰ Station reception open 4:30am-10:30pm, Su 7am-10:30pm.)* Trains to many cities including **Birmingham** *(£22.50 ⏰ 1½hr., 2 every hr.)*; **Edinburgh** *(£51.50 ⏰ 3½hr., 1 per hr.)*; **London Euston** *(£54 ⏰ 2-3hr., every 20min.)*; **Liverpool** *(£8 ⏰ 1hr., 3 per hr.)*; **Leeds** *(£15.50 ⏰ 1hr., every 15min.)* and **York** *(£21.70 ⏰ 1½hr., every 20min.).* **Manchester Victoria** *(Victoria St. ℹ Serves trains mostly from the north. ⏰ Ticket office open M-Sa 6:30am-10pm, Su 8am-10pm.)* has less frequent service than Manchester Piccadilly.

By Bus

Chorlton St. Coach Station is located between Chinatown and the Gay Village. *(⏰ Ticket office open daily 7am-7pm.)* **National Express** *(☎0817 818 181)* and **Stagecoach Megabus** *(☎0871 266 3333)* run to **Birmingham** *(£14-16 ⏰ 1½hr., every 2-3hr.),* **Leeds** *(£8.70 ⏰ 1hr. 10min., every hr.),* **Liverpool** *(£6.50 ⏰ 1hr., every hr.),* **London** *(£27.60 ⏰ 5½hr, every hr.),* and **Sheffield** *(£8 ⏰ 1½hr., 3 per day.).*

Getting Around

By Bus

Piccadilly Gardens is home to about 50 bus stops with lines headed mainly to the south, and the new **Shudehill** station to the north runs buses to the North and West. Get a free route map from the TIC. A FirstDay allows for unlimited bus travel for £4. **Metroshuttle** *(☎0161 817 8985)* bus service runs free buses on three lines from the city center to the main rail stations, attractions, and shopping areas throughout the city. Buses run every 5-10min., M-Sa 7am-7pm, Su 10am-6pm, though the purple line doesn't run on Sundays. Beware, however, that traffic in the city center can make trips slow.

By Tram

Metrolink trams *(☎0161 205 2000 www.metrolink.co.uk)* connect eight stops in the city center with **Altrincham** in the southwest, **Bury** in the northeast, and **Eccles** in the west *(tickets £0.80-4, runs every 12min.).* **DaySaver** is a Travelcard accepted by most bus, train, and tram companies in the city and allows you to transfer *(www.systemonetravelcards.co.uk).*

By Taxi

Like London, taxis in Manchester are black cabs. Hail in front of town hall or at Piccadilly Gardens. **Mantax** cabs *(☎0161 230 3333)* are hail-able, while **Radio Cars** *(☎0161 236 8033)* only takes reservations in advance.

leeds ☎0113

While often overshadowed by its more glamorous counterparts, Leeds, the fastest-growing city in the UK, is a city just waiting to say "Hey you, look at me." Whether it's caught up to its cohorts yet is debatable, but it's undeniable that Leeds is not without its own accolades: this was the site of Britain's first permanent traffic lights, first shopping mall, and the home of Mel B. (a.k.a. **Scary Spice**). It's not surprising, then, that Leeds is a modern, sleek, and diverse city with large business districts, great shopping, lots of traffic, and a strong music scene. Leeds is also one of the largest "college towns" in the UK, with three universities, the largest being the **University of Leeds** (32,000 students and former employer of **Professor JRR Tolkien**), and 200,000 students in total. Leeds has the second most public parks of any city in England after London, and it's the only city outside London with its own ballet and opera companies. Loiners, as Leedsfolk are known, take care of their city.

ORIENTATION

Most of Leeds's city center is contained within the Leeds **Inner Ring Road,** a loop that runs around the northern parts of the city. **Briggate,** the main street, runs north-south, and doubles as a pedestrianized shopping area. Nearby **Queen Victoria Street** (part of the **Victoria Quarter**) is encircled by a glass roof. **Millennium Square,** to the North,

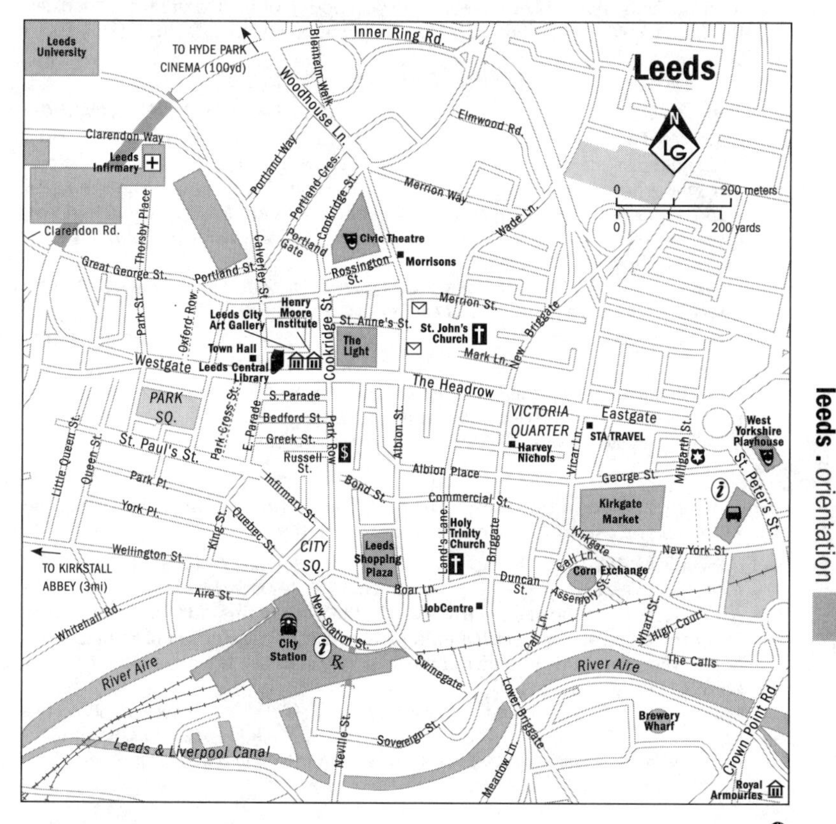

is a recently redeveloped area and, with its large open public space, is a common reference point. The area right near Leeds Railway Station is known as **City Square** (even thought it's actually more of a triangle), and this part borders on the **Financial and Legal Quarter** which centers around **Park Row,** the main financial street. To the northeast sits the university area: think College Park, Happy Valley, Ann Arbor—your American college town of choice—with slightly run-down row houses, nondescript apartments, and beer cans in the street. Ah, what charm.

ACCOMMODATIONS

Leeds has no hostels and few budget accommodations within the city center. Some budget travelers choose to book standard rooms at the budget chain hotels (Holiday Inn Express, Etap Hotel) near the formerly industrialized waterfront area of Clarence Dock, by the Armouries. There are some good deals to be had, especially during the week. Woodsley Road, in the college area around Leeds University and about 1½ mi. outside of the main downtown, has a series of four bed and breakfasts within the span of one block. To get there, take the **Free Bus** from the city center to the corner of Clarendon and Hyde Terr. (Leeds Dental Institute), or its a 25min. walk from the train station. Head east on Great George St., which becomes Clarendon Rd., and turn left on Woodsley Rd.

AVALON GUEST HOUSE
BED AND BREAKFAST ❸

132 Woodsley Road ☎0113 243 2545 www.avalonguesthouseleeds.co.uk

Near the University of Leeds, this is the best option of the B and Bs on Woodsley Rd. Large, clean rooms, all with blue walls and many ensuite, professional service, and a solid breakfast.

i Breakfast included. Parking facilites. $ Singles from £28; doubles from £40.

OAK VILLA HOTEL
BED AND BREAKFAST ❸

57 Cardigan Rd. ☎0113 275 8439 www.oakvillahotel.co.uk

Located in the suburb of Headingley, best-known for its cricket stadium, a picturesque wooded area. There is a small commercial district within a few minutes walking district with a supemarket, deli, and launderette. Very clean and tidy rooms boast large windows. About a 20min. bus ride from the city center, it includes a beautiful garden area.

Take the 18, 18A, 74 or 75 buses from City Square or the 56 from Quarry Hill. Get off at the Victoria Road junction stop. $ Singles from £30; doubles from £50.

THE GLENGARTH
BED AND BREAKFAST ❸

162 Woodsley Rd. ☎0113 245 7940 www.theglengarth.co.uk

The Glengarth has all the basic features of a decent B and B. Most of the bedrooms are ensuite, and deals are available for longer stays.

i Parking facilities available. $ Singles from £30; doubles from £45.

SIGHTS

Leeds offers many free attractions; some of the best ones are a bit of hike from the city center, so don't shy away from public transportation.

KIRKSTALL ABBEY
MUSEUM, GARDEN, RUINS

Abbey Walk, Kirkstall ☎0113 230 5492 www.leeds.co.uk/abbeyhouse

About 15min. outside of downtown Leeds, the ruins of this old Cistercian monastery provide a gorgeous setting for a picnic. The Abbey House museum directly across the street will give you a glimpse of Victorian Leeds with recreated shops, streets, and residences.

Take the 33 or 33a bus from the bus station to Kirkstall. $ Park free. Museum £3.60, concessions £2.60. Park open daily dawn-dusk. Ruins open Apr-Sept Tu-F 10am-5pm, Sa-Su 10am-6pm; Oct-Mar Tu-Th 10am-4pm, Sa-Su 10am-4pm. Museum open Tu-F 10am-5pm, Sa noon-5pm, Su 10am-5pm. Last entry 1hr. before close.

ROYAL ARMOURIES MUSEUM

Armouries Dr. ☎08700 344 344 www.royalarmouries.org

Opened by the Queen herself in 1996 to store weapons and such that used to be stored in the Tower of London. Themed galleries highlight the history of war, hunting, and self-defense. Live demonstrations of jousting from April to October, Saturday and Sunday at 2pm. A convenient layout and intense battle re-enactments.

From the bus station, head south on Church Lane, bear right at Kirkgate, then follow the Crown Point Bridge across the river, and make a right onto Armouries Way. Follow signs. Pedestrian maps available for download on the website. Free. Open daily 10am-5pm.

LEEDS CITY ART GALLERY AND HENRY MOORE INSTITUTE MUSEUM

74 The Headrow ☎0113 247 8256 www.leeds.gov.uk/artgallery

The City Art Gallery features prints, watercolors, paintings, sculpture, photography, and contemporary art; the beautiful Tiled Hall cafe is adjacent. The neighboring institute, named for the first sculpture student at the Leeds College of Art, is a museum featuring the abstract works of Henry Moore.

The buildings are right next to each other in the city center, on the Headrow, in between The Light and Leeds Town Hall. Both free. Leeds Art Gallery open M-Sa 10am-5pm, Su 1-5pm. Henry Moore Institue open Tu 10am-5:30pm, W 10am-9pm, Th 10am-5:30pm.

FOOD

Park Row downtown has many restaurants featuring international cuisine. The university area has its own share of ethnic food, for cheaper prices. Leeds' **Kirkgate Market** *(Open M-W 8am-5:30pm, Th-Sa 7:30am-5:30pm)* is the largest indoor market in all of Europe and, along with its spectacular exterior architecture, is host to tons of cheap eats, from snacks like nuts, fruit, and ice cream to full meals.

PICKLES AND POTTER DELI TAKEOUT, DELI ❷

22 Queens Arcade ☎0113 242 7702

This small but comfortable deli is home to the best cheap eats in the Briggate shopping district. The friendly staff serves sandwiches *(£3.90-£4.75)* and "fab" cakes. Everything is cheaper if you get it takeaway.

Victoria Quarter, Queens Arcade is in between Lands Ln. and Briggate. Open M-Sa 9am-5pm, Su 10:30am-5pm.

ART'S CAFE BAR CAFE ❸

42 Call Ln. ☎0113 243 8243 www.artscafebar.co.uk

With simple decor and artwork from local artists on the bright yellow walls, this is an ideally charming atmosphere for a casual meal. Try the lunch menu of salads and sandwiches *(noon-6pm)* if you're short on pounds *(£4.50-6.50).*

*1 block south of Corn Exchange. **i** Lunch Menu available noon-6pm. Early bird special M-F, Su noon-7pm, 2 courses £12.50, 3 courses £15. Entrees £9.95-14.50. Salads and sandwiches £4.50-£6.50. Open M-F noon-11pm, Sa noon-11pm, Su 10:30am-11pm.*

MOORISH INTERNATIONAL, TAKEOUT ❷

225 Hyde Park Rd. ☎0113 225 3862 www.moorishcatering.co.uk

The unique menu at this hole-in-the-wall encompasses all of the culinary influences of the Moors—Arabic, Spanish, French, North African, and Mediterranean cuisine. The couches, music, lighting, and authentic decor might have you convinced you're in a hookah bar. Deals for lunch include hummus, olives, and pita *(£2.50)* and delicious regional smoothie drinks *(£3).*

Right across from Woodhouse Moors. Lunch menu £3.50-6. Entrees £6-9.90. Open M-F 3pm-midnight, Sa-Su noon-midnight.

PRIMO'S GOURMET HOT DOGS CAFE, AMERICAN ❶

Unit 12 A/B, Leeds Corn Exchange ☎0113 345 8901 www.primosgourmethodogs.co.uk

Sit in comfortable seats outdoors at this shop in the Leeds Corn Exchange, built in 1861, and enjoy a delicious specialized hot dog, with nine styles of high-quality sausage, fresh bread from a local bakery, and 35 different toppings *(£3.85)* or a New-York Style deli bagel *(£3.45)* with a cup of gourmet freshly-ground coffee *(£2)*. Cheap, tasty dishes, with good dill pickles on the side.

Unit 12 A/B, The Corn Exchange. Entrees £3.45-3.85. Ice cream from £1.85. Open daily 9am-5pm.

NIGHTLIFE

Leeds thinks of itself as the clubbing capital of the north—the club Oceana is, after all, home to the largest illumninated dance floor in Europe—but that doesn't mean that straight-up clubbing is the only option. Leeds has a solid collection of vibrant, lived-in, indie bars with good music and some of the best live music venues in the North. Most of the hottest bars and clubs are centered around **Call Lane,** near the Corn Exchange. Don't be fooled by its Victorian style or by the former Temperance Hotel on Boar Lane—this area is always hopping on weekends. However, the crowd here is young and professional, so prices can be steep. For some cheaper options, check out the area around the intersection of Vicar Ln. and New Briggate. You'll find six or seven solid bars right near each other.

SANDINISTA — RESTAURANT, BAR

5 Cross Belgrave St. ☎0113 305 0372 www.sandinistaleeds.co.uk

This cantina bar is lively and charmingly battered, with postcards from across the world (look for Nicaragua) lining its fading walls. Enjoy Sangria and tapas with your friends until you're shouting, "*Viva la revolution!*"

Corner of Belgrave and Merrion Pl. Open M-W 3pm-3am, Th-Su noon-3am.

JAKE'S BAR AND GRILL — BAR, GRILL

29 Call Ln. ☎0113 243 1110 www.jakesbar.co.uk

Jake's is a friendly, relaxed bar with quality service and drinks, but as the night goes on, the music gets louder and the crowd gets rowdier. Lots of space to bring your whole posse and add to the noise.

"Pigout for a fiver" special until 7:30pm. Beer from £3. Cocktails £6-8. Burgers £5-6. Open M-F 5pm-2am, Sa 12:30pm-3am, Su 5pm-2am.

HIFI CLUB — CLUB, PERFORMANCE VENUE

2 Central Rd. ☎0113 242 7353 www.thehificlub.co.uk

On the smaller side, this spirited club is the best spot in town for getting your groove back. Funk, Motown, jazz, and soul groups perform as the club turns into one massive dance floor. Check out the popular Funk Soul Nation every Friday night *(10:30pm-3am; £5 cover)*.

Central Rd. is off of Duncan St. (Boar Rd. becomes Duncan St.) Cover ranges from free to £12. Hours vary depending on the night and the event, so call ahead.

BLAYD'S BAR — BAR

3-7 Blayds Yard ☎0113 244 5590

This small but lively bar attracts a mixed crowd of all ages and a staff that regularly breaks into song and dance. The atmosphere is relaxed and the clientele friendly. Take advantage of the daily happy hour *(4-6pm)* with discounts on most draught beers and spirits. Quiz night is on Wednesdays.

Up the alley, off Lower Briggate just above the Golden Lion Hotel. Open M-Th 2-11pm, F-Sa 2pm-1am, Su 1-10:30pm.

QUEEN'S COURT — BAR, CLUB

167-168 Lower Briggate ☎0113 245 9449 www.queenscourtleeds.com

Queens Court claims to be Leeds's only 100% gay bar and nightclub. The young, trendy crowd floods the upstairs "Loft Area" complete with dance podiums and poles. Open until 4am (or 6am for one Saturday a month), this is definitely one of Leeds's top options for nightlife. Monday nights feature the "Pink Pounder" from 8pm to 4am—all drinks are only £1.

From the train station turn right and go along Boar Ln. Turn right at Briggate. To Gain entrace to both Queens Ct. and The Loft from Lower Briggate, enter the Courtyard through the passageway between Queens Ct. and Bar Fibre. i Taxi ranks outside every night. Open M-Th noon-4am, Sa noon-5am, Su noon-1am.

LEEDS UNIVERSITY UNION, BAR, CLUB, PERFORMANCE VENUE

Lifton Place ☎0113 380 1332

In 2009, Leeds University Union was named the number one students' union in Britain at the National Union of Students (NUS) Awards. Leeds University Union (LUU) is home to Stylus, a nightclub located at the base of the student union building. It hosts both live acts, like the Kooks, and club nights. Fruity Fridays are a popular themed club night; for dates and details check out www.fruityfridays.com. The legendary Refec is where **The Who** recorded their 1970 album "Live at Leeds." **Led Zeppelin, Bob Marley, The Rolling Stones, The Jam, Elton John, Pink Floyd,** and **Jimi Hendrix** have played here. More recently, **The Strokes, The Kaiser Chiefs,** and **Arctic Monkeys** graced the stage at the Refec. The Union also has its own bars, including **Old Bar,** the original campus pub.

The 1, 95, 96 and X84 buses from Leeds bus station will take you to the University. Follow signs to Student Union building. i All Refectory gigs and most club nights are open to non-students as well as students. Concert tickets start at £10.

ARTS AND CULTURE

HYDE PARK PICTURE HOUSE BURLEY PARK

Brudenell Rd. ☎0113 275 2045 www.hydeparkpicturehouse.co.uk

Converted to a cinema in 1914, this is the second oldest continually operating cinema in the UK. Today, it shows a diverse, eccentric mix of indie films, arthouse pictures, classic black and white and foreign films as well as the occasional mainstream movie. There are at least two screenings per evening—true to its origins, this is a single-screen cinema—check out the website for current listings. Fun facts: this place has an organ and is the only remaining theater in the UK to use gas lighting.

Corner of Brudenell Rd. and Queens Rd. Take the #56 bus from the city center, stops right outside the cinema. £5.80. Concesssions £4.50. Sa matinees £3.50. Online booking available. Ticket office open daily 6-10pm and 30min. before screenings.

THE COCKPIT SWINEGATE

Swinegate ☎0113 244 1573 www.thecockpit.co.uk

This independent live music and club venue was constructed beneath a series of three railway arches, giving it a unique feel. Since 1994 the likes of **Coldplay, The White Stripes, Amy Winehouse, The Flaming Lips, Panic at the Disco!, The Killers, Fall Out Boy,** and **Bloc Party** have taken the stage—well, the *three* stages—at the Cockpit. You can watch gigs most nights of the week, from local bands to more pricey national acts. The Cockpit also features "emo" club nights, unique to Leeds. Call ahead or check out the website for listings.

At the intersection of Sovereign St., New Station St., and The Calls. Tickets £4-30.

CARRIAGEWORKS MILLENIUM SQ.

The Electric Press, Millennium Sq. ☎0113 224 3801 www.carriageworkstheatre.org.uk

Carriageworks showcases a mix of film, dance, theater, community events and workshops, with a special emphasis on local groups. The building overlooks the glass-roofed and heated courtyard which in early Victorian times was home to the "West Riding Carriage Manufactory"—hence, the name Carriageworks.

Millenium Sq. i Those under 26 should check out the website for "A Night Less Ordinary," a

program which gives out free tickets for theatrical performances. Tickets starting at £1. Concessions can't be claimed online, so you need to bring proof to box office. Box office open M-Sa 10am-8pm, Su 30min. before scheduled performances.

SHOPPING

Leeds is home to some of the best shopping in England. As the "Knightsbridge of the North" it features over 1000 stores, 4.3 million sq. ft. of retail space, and thousands of accomplished bargain shoppers.

The **Briggate Shopping District** was one of the first shopping districts in all of England to go pedestrian. On nice days, thousands of Loiners will pack the streets on the look out for good deals. **The Victoria Quarter** is located inside architecturally beautiful old arcades and showcases luxury stores like **Harvey Nichols** and **Vivienne Westwood.** The **Merrion Centre** dates back to the 1960s and was at one time the largest shopping center in Europe. Meanwhile, brand new complexes like **The Light** have given shopping a more modern feel.

While Leeds shopping may seem too classy for your pocketbook, there are some more affordable options. A farmers' market is held at Leeds Kirkgate open market, George St. (next to the bus station) on every first and third Sunday of the month *(9am-2pm)*. **St. John's Shopping Centre** has many American brands at affordable prices. Meanwhile, **Lifton Place** (Leeds University Student Union) is host to the Affordable Vintage Fashion Fair *(www.vintagefair.co.uk)* every few months, with stacks of clothes selling at bargain prices.

ESSENTIALS

Practicalities

- **TOURIST OFFICES: Leeds Visitor Center** right in the train station. Gives out free maps and free copies of *Inside Out*, a helpful guide with accommodation, entertainment, and food listings. *(☎0113 242 524 Open M 10am-5:30pm, Tu-Sa 9am-5:30pm, Su 10am-4pm.)*
- **BUDGET TRAVEL: STA Travel.** *(88 Vicar Lane ☎0871 702 9827 Open M-W 9am-6pm, Th 9am-8pm, F 9am-6pm, Sa 10am-6pm, Su 11am-5pm.)* and 182 Woodhouse Ln. *(☎0871 702 9828 Open M-Th 10am-6pm; F 10:30am-6pm.)*
- **TOURS: City Sightseeing** offers a 12-stop, hop-on, hop-off bus tour through the downtown area. *(☎01423 566061 www.city-sightseeing.com £7.50, concessions £5.50 Runs May-Sept daily 9:30am-5pm; Oct-May Sa-Su 9:30am-5pm.)* **Leeds City Cruisers** has 1hr. hop-on, hop-off boat tours on weekends May 22-Sept 26 and daily in Aug, leaving on the hour from 11am-3pm from Clarence Dock. *(☎0845 388 4901 £3, concessions £2.)* The TIC has free handouts for a self-guided walking tour around the city center.
- **BANKS:** Many line Park Row, including **Lloyd's TSB** (6-7 Park Row).
- **BEYOND TOURISM: JobCentre Plus.** *(12-14 Briggate ☎0113 215 5000 Open M-W 10am-4pm, Th-F 9am-4pm.)*
- **LUGGAGE STORAGE:** At train station. *(£3 for up to 3hr., £5 for 3-5 hr., £7 for up to 24hr.)*
- **INTERNET ACCESS:** Free Wi-Fi in **Starbucks** and **Wetherspoons** in the railway station as well as in various coffee shops around town, like **Caffè Nero.** Free Internet use in **Leeds Central Library.** *(Headrow between Calverly and Cookbridge St., right next to Leeds Art Gallery. Free internet (ID required). Least crowded in the morning. Open M-W 9am-8pm, Th-F 9am-5pm, Sa 10am-5pm, Su 1-5pm.)*
- **POST OFFICE:** *(116 Albion St. ☎0845 722 3344 Open M-Sa 9am-5:30pm.)*

- **POSTAL CODE:** LS2 8LP.

Emergency!

- **POLICE:** Millgarth St., directly north of bus station. *(☎0845 606 0606.)*
- **PHARMACY: Boots** in Leeds City Station. *(☎08457 484950 ⏰ Open M-F 6am-midnight, Sa 8am-midnight, Su 9am-midnight.)*
- **HOSPITAL: Leeds General Infirmary,** Great George St. *(☎0113 243 2799.)* For non-emergencies, **NHS Walk-in Center.** *(The Headrow, in the Light Shopping Centre on Headrow. ☎0870 818 0003 ⏰ Open M-F 7am-7pm.)*

Getting There

The A1 and M1 connect Leeds to the north and south, and the M62 to the east and west.

By Train

Leeds Station, City Sq. *(New Station St. ⏰ Ticket Office open 24hr. Information Centre open M-Sa 6:45am-8:15pm, Su 10am-5:45pm.)* Trains *(☎0845 748 4950 www.nationalrail.co.uk)* run from Leeds to most major cities, including **London King's Cross** *(⏰ 2½hr., 2 per hr. ⓢ £82.70)*, **Manchester** *(ⓢ £15.60. ⏰ 1hr., 4 per hr.)*, and **York** *(ⓢ £10.50. ⏰ 30min., 5 per hr.).*

By Bus

City Bus Station. *(York St. next to Kirkgate Market. ⏰ Ticket Office open M 8:30am-5:30pm, Tu 9am-5:30pm, W-F 8:30am-5:30pm, Sa 9am-4:30pm.)* **National Express** *(☎0871 81 81 78)* operates from Leeds to most major cities, including **Birmingham** *(ⓢ £27.30. ⏰ 3½hr, 1 per hr.)*; **Edinburgh** *(ⓢ £46.40. ⏰ 7hr., 2 per day)*; **Glasgow** *(ⓢ £46.50. ⏰ 6hr., 1 per day)*; **Liverpool** *(ⓢ £11.30. ⏰ 2¼hr., 1 per hr.)*; **London** *(ⓢ £21.30. ⏰ 4½hr., 1-2 per hr.)*; **Manchester** *(ⓢ £8.40. ⏰ 1hr., 1 per hr.)*; and **York** *(ⓢ £5.70. ⏰ 45min., 3 per day.).*

By Plane

Leeds Bradford International Airport is a half hour from the city center by bus and has flights to and from other UK cities like **Belfast, Edinburgh,** and **London,** along with international flights to France, Turkey, Italy, Spain, and many other European countries.

Getting Around

By Bus

City Bus Station has buses that run throughout the city and to its outskirts. Many buses also stop in front of the train station and at stops on Infirmary St. Bus fares vary with distance traveled, but generally hover around £2 for a one-way ticket. All-day passes are available for purchase on **First** buses *(☎0845 604 5460 www.firstgroup.com)* for within the Leeds metropolitan boundaries *(ⓢ £3.20. ⏰ After 9:30am)* and for all of West Yorkshire *(ⓢ £4).*

The city also runs a free bus service that makes a loop around the downtown area, stopping at the train station, bus station, and most of the major shopping areas *(runs M-Sa 6:30am-7:30pm).* Free maps at the TIC or at the bus station.

By Taxi

City Cabs *(☎0113 246 9999).* **Streamline Telecabs** *(☎0113 263 7777).* **New Yellow Cars** *(☎0113 234 5666).*

The trials and tribulations of the Romans, the Anglo-Saxons, the Vikings, the Normans, and finally, the York City football club are written into the streets of ancient York. Home to the famed "snickelways," tight, narrow alleyways that weave in and out of the city streets, and to some of England's most notorious ghost stories and scandals, York is kooky in its own medieval way. The well-named Shambles, York's most famous antiquated street is a mess of narrow, creaky old buildings that look like they're about to fall over as they hover clumsily over the street. Whip-Ma-Whop-Ma Gate wins the prize for York's shortest street with the longest name, the meaning of which remains disputed. Some claim this was the place where dogs, or people were publicly whipped, while others argue that the expression was a medieval saying for "You call this a street?!"

ORIENTATION

The best introduction to York is a walk along its medieval walls (2½ mi.), especially the northeast section and behind the cathedral. The walls are accessible up stairways by the four main bars (here, "bar" means "gate," not "pub," although there are plenty of those around, too). Beware the tourist stampede, which only subsides in early morning and just before the walls close at dusk. All roads in York seem to lead to **St. Helen's Square,** a convenient meeting spot with its access to the **Minster,** museum gardens, shops, and food establishments. The towering Minster is a helpful compass; look up and you can figure out which direction to follow.

ACCOMMODATIONS

FOSS BANK GUEST HOUSE — BED AND BREAKFAST ❸

16 Huntington Rd. ☎01904 635548 www.fossbank.co.uk

Within a 5min. walk of the city center, the Foss Bank Guest House has spacious and sunny rooms, big windows, delicious breakfasts with fresh local ingredients, and a cozy common area boasting couches and a TV. This is a deal that can't be beat! Every room even has its own shower—literally right in the room.

Take the 12 bus toward Haxby to first stop on Huntington Rd. ℹ Free Wi-Fi. Min. stay 2 nights when it includes F or Sa. Special rates available for weekly bookings. Ⓢ Singles £33; doubles with shower £58, ensuite £70.

YHA YORK INTERNATIONAL — HOSTEL ❷

42 Water End ☎0845 371 9051

An otherwise scenic 20min. stroll from the train station along the "Dame Judi Dench" river path (named for the famed Yorkie actress) becomes quite the schlep with a heavy pack on your back. However, this handsome Victorian house's wooded area with plentiful outdoor seating, garden, and nearby bike paths make the hike worthwhile. School groups frequent the area, so be prepared for hoards of children. Self-catering kitchen. Lockers in dorms for personal storage.

Take Dame Judi Dench path from Lendal bridge and follow signs for hostel. ℹ Breakfast £5. Laundry facilities. Internet. Ⓢ Dorms £16-22. Reception open 7am-10:30pm; 24hr. access.

RIVERSIDE CARAVAN AND CAMPING PARK — CAMPING PARK ❶

Ferry Ln. ☎01904 705 812

Three miles south of York off the A64, this small, secluded site is right on the edge of the River Ouse. Note that it's a popular place for campers during the summer.

Take Bus #11 to Bishopthorpe from railway station. Get off on Main St. or ask the driver to let you off at the campground. ℹ Cash only. Ⓢ Prices starting at £10 per night, depending on size of your tent. Open Easter-Oct.

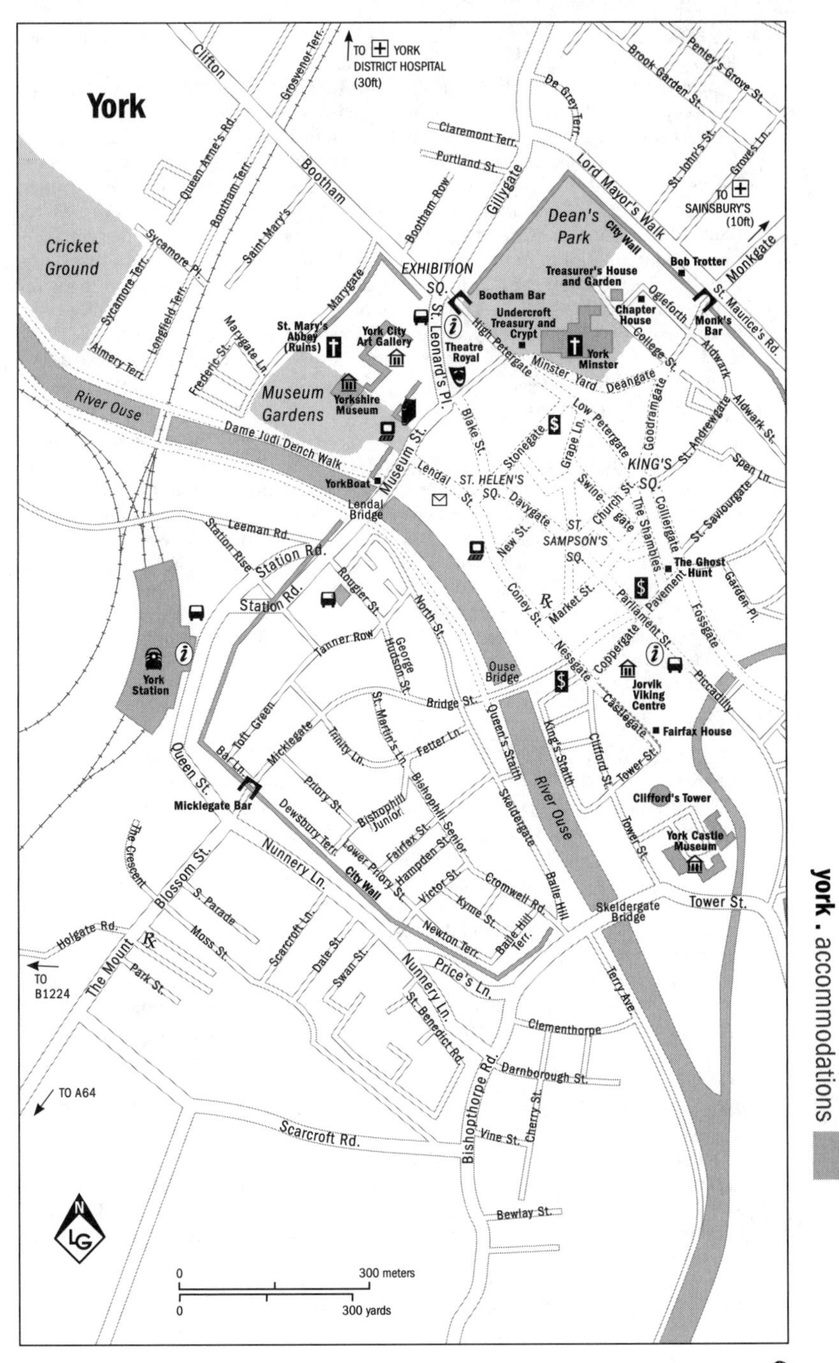
York
TO YORK DISTRICT HOSPITAL (30ft)
TO SAINSBURY'S (10ft)
Cricket Ground
Museum Gardens
Dean's Park
City Wall
River Ouse
Bob Trotter
Treasurer's House and Garden
Bootham Bar
Undercroft Treasury and Crypt
Chapter House
Monk's Bar
St. Mary's Abbey (Ruins)
York City Art Gallery
Theatre Royal
York Minster
Yorkshire Museum
YorkBoat
Lendal Bridge
The Ghost Hunt
York Station
Ouse Bridge
Jorvik Viking Centre
Fairfax House
Clifford's Tower
York Castle Museum
Micklegate Bar
Skeldergate Bridge
TO B1224
TO A64
EXHIBITION SQ.
ST. HELEN'S SQ.
KING'S SQ.
ST. SAMPSON'S SQ.
0
300 meters
300 yards

ACE HOTEL HOTEL ❷

88-90 Mickelgate ☎01904 627 720 www.acehotelyork.co.uk

Formerly known as York Backpackers, this hotel has recently undergone a two-million-pound refurbishment, and now boasts a grand sweeping staircase, game room, TV, internet lounges, and a bar. Housed in a 1752 Georgian style building, Ace Hotel embraces its historic past: placards on doors introduce each room's former functions and myths (e.g., "This 18th century room housed the butler 'Addison' who took advantage of many of the girl servants and was known as 'Wicked Addison'" or "One of the cook and kitchen staff, Caroline, hung herself on this landing due to contracting syphilis"). Each dorm room has a tiny bathroom, storage lockers, and individual reading lights. It's convenient to the train station and the bus station. The ghost stories may keep you up at night, but at least there's no need to worry about catching syphilis here any more!

i Continental breakfast included. Air conditioning. Free Wi-Fi. Ⓢ Dorms £19.50-25.50; private twins £60. Reception 24hr.

BAR CONVENT GUEST HOUSE BED& BREAKFAST ❸

17 Blossom St. ☎01904 464 902 www.bar-convent.org.uk

The "oldest living convent in England," the Bar Convent Guest House was founded in 1686. Its earliest residents lived when Catholic worship was forbidden by law and the penalty for celebrating Catholic ceremonies or keeping a Catholic school was imprisonment or worse. (The community ended up calling in York-born architect Thomas Atkinson to design a hidden chapel so that they could still get their Catholic worship on.) Not to worry, though; the guest house now has modern amenities, like a TV room and kitchen on every floor.

 # Right outside Micklegate, a 5min. walk from the city center. i Laundry facilities. Continental breakfast included; full English breakfast available for purchase. Free Wi-Fi. Ⓢ Singles from £33, doubles from £64. Sa night £10 more.

SIGHTS

YORK CASTLE MUSEUM MUSEUM

Eye of York ☎01904 687687 www.yorkcastlemuseum.org.uk

This museum focuses on the details of daily life, from shillings to shit. Explore, for instance, the city of Kirkgate, a remnant of Victorian Britain: the year is 1870, Vicky is on the throne, factories have brought tremendous wealth and proverty, some men have the vote, women do not, children leave school to work at age 12, and the British Empire encompasses a quarter of the world. The exhibit on "keeping clean" charts the evolution of household hygiene over time, through objects like vacuum cleaners, privies, and chamber pots. Downstairs in the Prison at York Castle, those with English roots can hunt down the black sheep of their family's past; archives trace you back to any of your debt-holding, thieving, or revolutionary forebears who might have spent time imprisoned in York Castle during the 1700s.

 # Between Tower and Piccadilly St. i Only the downstairs is wheelchair-accessible. Ⓢ £8, concessions £7. Open daily 9:30am-5pm.

YORKSHIRE MUSEUM AND GARDENS MUSEUM, GARDEN

Museum Gardens ☎01904 687 687 www.yorkshiremuseum.org.uk

The beautiful, recently restored Yorkshire Museum is hidden within 10 acres of greenery and the medieval ruins of St. Mary's Abbey. The public-minded Yorkshire Philosophical Society built this Georgian museum in the heart of the city back in 1840. It chronicles the long story of their beloved York, from the Ice Age through World War II.

 # Next to Lendal Bridge; entrances on Museum St. and Marygate. Ⓢ Museum £5, concessions £4. Gardens free. Museum open daily 10am-5pm. Museum gardens open daily in summer 7am-8pm; in winter 7am-6pm.

JORVIK VIKING CENTRE — MUSEUM

Coppergate ☎01904 615 505 www.jorvik-viking-centre.co.uk

All aboard "time capsules" that take you on a journey though the sights (and smells) the Viking city of Jorvik. Explore remains of 1000-year-old houses, and learn stories of battles and bone-rotting diseases. Luckily, a narrator translates the Old English and Old Norse for you.

A few blocks north of Clifford's Tower. i Call ahead to book. Only one wheelchair allowed in the center at a time. £8.95, concessions £7. Open daily Apr-Oct 10am-5pm; Nov-Mar 10am-4pm.

CLIFFORD'S TOWER — HISTORICAL SITE

Tower St. ☎01904 646 940 www.english-heritage.org.uk/yorkshire

Clifford's Tower is the only remaining medieval section of York Castle. Despite its prominent position, it represents one of the lowest points of York's history. In 1190, about 150 York Jews took refuge in the tower after being attacked by a local mob. Rather than renounce their faith or be murdered, most of them took their own lives in desperation. Today, the tower is open to visitors and boasts panoramic views of the city.

Center of "Castle Area." £3.50, concessions £3. Open daily Apr-Sept 10am-6pm; Oct 10am-5pm; Nov-Mar 10am-4pm. Last entry 15min. before close.

TREASURER'S HOUSE AND GARDEN — GARDEN

Minster Yard ☎01904 624 247

With 13 historic interiors and over 400 years of period design, the Treasurer's House displays the collections of Frank Green, the wealthy Yorkshireman who owned the building from 1897. Green designed the building with rooms fit for royalty, beautiful gardens, and a view overlooking the minster. He donated the house to the National Trust in 1930 but cared so fiercely about the work he'd done that he threatened to haunt the house if any of his furniture was moved. Meanwhile, in 1953, heating engineer Harry Martindale claimed to see the ghosts of Roman soldiers marching in the cellar of Treasurer's House. Today, ghost tours of the haunted region downstairs are available.

Entrance just behind York Minster. i £6, ghost cellar only £3. Audio tours and Braille guides available. Open M-Th and Sa-Su Apr-Oct 11am-4:30pm; Nov-Mar 11am-3pm.

YORK ART GALLERY — ART GALLERY

Exhibition Square ☎01904 687 687 www.yorkartgallery.org.uk

Displays over six centuries of British and European art, including ceramics, glassware, studio pottery, and paintings. Hosts an impressive collection of 19th-century William Etty paintings. Etty is York's most famous artist, largely known as the first British painter to make it big by painting men in the nude, despite of protest from the public and the press of the time.

On Bootham St., between Bootham Rd. and Gillygate. Free. Open daily 10am-5pm.

YORK MINSTER — CATHEDRAL

Deangate ☎0844 939 0011 www.yorkminster.org

In 1736, Francis Drake called it, "not only a single monument to the city and these northern parts, but to the whole kingdom." The seat of the Archbishop of York and the largest Gothic church in Northern Europe, the Norman-built minster is York's crowning achievement and treasure, and it towers over York's shops and crooked streets today just as it did six centuries ago, displaying an estimated half of all the medieval stained glass in England. The Minster's arches began a new trend with Gothic arches that pointed toward heaven, letting in the light from above. The 15th-century Great East Window, which depicts the beginning and end of the world in more than 100 small scenes, is the world's largest medieval stained glass window. The main chamber of the church is almost always overrun with throngs of picture-snapping tourists, but the tombs and stonework are less crowded and equally impressive. Look for the statue of Archbishop Lamplugh toward the East Window; he has two right feet.

i Free daily tours 10am-3pm. Ⓢ £8, including admission to undercroft, treasury, and crypt, concessions £7; short guide £2; illustrated guide £5. Ⓞ Open Apr-Oct M-Sa 9am-5:30pm, Su noon-3:45pm; Nov-Mar M-Sa 9:30am-5pm, Su noon-3:45pm.

UNDERCROFT TREASURY AND CRYPT — TREASURY

Traveling underground takes you back in time, from the site of an Old Roman fortress to a structure built by the Normans who wanted to evoke images of the Romans' military might. The treasury displays Yorkshire silver, pewter, rare stones, chalices, and treasures of old archbishops.

Ⓞ Open M-Sa 9:30am-5:30pm.

CHAPTER HOUSE — HISTORICAL SITE

The chapter house was where day-to-day affairs of the minster were run, and is still used as a meeting place by the dean and chapter today. Each wall contains six seats to emphasize the equality of all canons and to make it impossible for the Dean (a senior Anglican priest who runs the day-to-day functions of the minster) to sit at the head of the meeting. With all the distractions of its unique, octagonal shape, beautiful ceilings, and walls with exquisite medieval carvings, dating from 1270-80, make sure you don't miss the gargoyles that sit atop the stalls; their facial expressions display all ranges of emotion, from jocularity to the agony of a soul in torture.

ⓄOpen M-Sa 9am-5pm, Su noon-3:45pm.

TOWER — LANDMARK

The prize for climbing the 275 steps is spectactular views of York's and Minster's medieval pinnacles and gargoyles. If that's not reward enough, you can buy a handy badge at the end to boast of your accomplishment.

Ⓢ £5, concessions £4. Ⓞ Open M-Sa 9:45am-4:45pm, Su 12:45-3:45pm. Open later during peak times. Last entry Nov-Mar 30min. before dusk.

FOOD

Affordable cafes, coffee shops, and delis line York's quaint cobblestone streets. For those with a sweet tooth, York has loads of fudge stores, ice cream carts, and even milkshake shops, with the cheapest in Newgate Market alongside crafts and specialty vendors. The main market day is on Saturday.

OSCAR'S WINE BAR AND BISTRO — BAR, BISTRO ❸

27 Swinegate ☎01904 652 002 www.oscarswinebar.com

Considering the big portions, good burgers *(£8-13)* and lively atmosphere, it's no wonder this local favorite is packed all week. Try the lasagna *(£8)* in either its vegetarian or meat form, and if you're feeling classy, a champagne cocktail *(£7)* to top it off. Make reservations for the weekend.

i Happy hour M 4pm-close, Tu-F 4-7pm, Su 4pm-close. Ⓢ Entrees from £8. Ⓞ Open M-Th 11:30am-midnight, F-Sa 11:30am-1am, Su 11am-midnight.

EL PIANO — VEGAN ❷

15-17 Grape Ln. ☎01904 610 676 www.el-piano.com

No eggs, milk, or cheese... and surprisingly delicious, even for the dairy-lovers among us. This 100% vegan restaurant offers delicious tapas-style meals with Thai, Indian, Mexican, and African dishes, among others, and everything is organic and locally-grown. The bright walls and funky decor create a warm, inviting atmosphere.

Ⓢ Tapas £4-5. Ⓞ Open M-Sa 10am-midnight.

EVIL EYE LOUNGE
THAI ❷

42 Stonegate ☎01904 464 002 www.evileyelounge.com

This three-story establishment is what locals consider a cool place to take your friends when they come visit York. From crazy-colored walls to comfy beds to delicious Thai dishes, this place will take you out of your element. Over 40 countries are represented in spirits, and the menu discriminates against "common" beers. Don't be deceived by the liquor shop out front; look out for the big blue eye as you walk down the street.

i Internet £2 per hr. Entrees £6-10. Open M-Th 10am-midnight, F-Sa 10am-1am, Su 11am-midnight.

KING'S ARMS
PUB ❶

3 King's Staith ☎01904 659 435

On nice days, the riverside seating area of this historic pub floods with locals and tourists who take their cheap Sam Smith's ales outside and sit barefoot, feet dangling over the river. If you're the nervous type, check the display inside that charts the water levels of past deluges that have ravaged the pub.

Pints from £2. Open M-Sa 11am-11pm, Su noon-10:30pm.

MR. SANDWICH
SANDWICHES ❶

37 The Shambles ☎01904 643 500 www.mrsandwich.co.uk

Pick one of 42 types of sandwiches—combinations of chicken, roast pork, cheddar cheese, and fig among others. And here's the best part: they're only £1! Really. If the choice gets too difficult, shell out an extra £0.50 for the "Greedy Pig"—all of the items that the masterful Mr. Sandwich (or, shall we say, £andwich) can fit in between two bulging slices of bread.

i Takeaway only. Open M-Sa 8am-5pm.

VICTOR J'S ART BAR
CAFE ❷

1A Finkle St. ☎01904 541 771 www.vjsartbar.co.uk

What exactly is an "art bar," you ask? This cafe displays paintings and drawings of local artists on its walls, and all of the pieces are available for purchase. Large, tasty ciabattas and wraps *(£6)* and burgers *(£6)* make for a satisfying lunch, while cocktails and illuminated Art Deco decor heat this place up at night.

Hidden off an alley off Stonegate. i Free Wi-Fi. Entrees £5-11. Open M-W 10am-12am, Th-Sa 10am-1am, Su 11am-6pm.

THE FUDGE KITCHEN
SWEETS ❶

58 Low Petergate ☎01904 645 596 www.fudgekitchen.co.uk

Sticky, smooth, creamy—a full sensory experience. We're talking about fudge. The masters of fudge at this candy kitchen, dressed in straw hats and elf-like aprons, hand out free samples and give fudge-making demonstrations with sparkling commentary at no charge. The delicious strawberry fudge is just one of 16 flavors you can try or take home in gift boxes.

Fudge slices from £3.80. Open M-Sa 10am-6pm, Su 10am-5:30pm.

ARTS AND CULTURE

THEATRE ROYAL
THEATER

St. Leonard's Pl. ☎01904 623 568 www.yorktheatreroyal.co.uk

The theater building, constructed in 1744, is a show in and of itself. Around Christmastime, pantomimes are the most popoular event here; you must book months in advance to attend. Visitors rave about the York cycle of mystery plays. The local tradition takes place every four years, when 200 residents of York work with the theater staff to present a community spectacle. While watching the performers on stage, look out for the wisps of gray mist, known as the ghost of the Gray Lady. She is believed to be a sign of good fortune; the last time she appeared was in 1995 during a dress rehearsal for Moll Flanders—which proceeded to win a national award.

From £1.50. Student discounts available for some shows. Box office open on performance days M-Sa 10am-8pm, on non-performance days M 10am-6pm, Tu-Sa 10am-8pm.

YORK EARLY MUSIC FESTIVAL FESTIVAL

01904 658 338 http://www.ncem.co.uk/

Each July, York hosts Britain's largest festival of traditional music. A variety of acts (primarily classical) perform at historic sites around the city, ranging from minster to guildhalls. The event has a special theme each year.

From £12 per performance, students £5. July.

VOLABLOT VIKING FESTIVAL FESTIVAL

1904 615 505

Every February, hundreds of Viking wannabes swarm the city of York (on Jorvik) in honor of the city's Viking heritage. Lectures, crafts, cultural events, and storytelling are accompanied by full-scale battle reenactments as Yorkshiremen embrace their inner seafaring conquerors.

Tickets from £10. Feb.

YORKSHIRE RACES HORSERACING

York Racecourse 01904 620 911 www.yorkracecourse.co.uk

Horseracing in York dates back to the reign of Emperor Severus during Roman rule. York's historic track was recently named Flat Racecourse of the Year, and Pope John Paul visited here in 1982. The most important races take place in August, when spectators show up in their finest attire to bellow from the stands, rooting for their picks.

From £30. May-Oct.

ESSENTIALS

Practicalities

- **TOURIST INFORMATION CENTER:** Books rooms for £4 plus 10% deposit. The center distributes a free mini-guide with a detailed map, and sells *Snickelways of York* (£6), a handwritten booklet of walks through York's alleyways. Also sells the Yorkshire Pass, which includes package admission to over 70 sights in the region *(1-day £28, 2-day £38, 3-day £44). (1 Museum St. Open M-Sa 9am-6pm; Su 10am-5pm.)*
- **TOURS:** Themed City walking tours are available with **YorkWalk Guided Walks,** which offers 1½-2hr. tours that leave from the Museum Gardens Gate on Museum St. *(01904 622 303 www.yorkwalk.co.uk Tours given daily Feb-Nov 10:30 and 2:15pm. W June-Aug additional 6pm walking tour. Sa and Su only Dec-Jan.).* **City Sightseeing** *(01904 655585 www.yorkbus.co.uk)* operates a 16-stop, hop-on, hop-off bus tour around the city *(£10, concessions £7).* **York Pullman Tours** *(01904 662 922 www.yorkpullmanbus.co.uk)* also offers hop-on/hop-off service *(£7.50, concessions £6).* **YorkBoat** (01904 628324 www.yorkboat.co.uk) runs daily tours on the River Ouse from Lendal Bridge Landing, approximately every 30min. starting at 10:30am *(£7.50, concessions £6.50).* Ghost Tours run rampant in York. For a more historical approach, try the oldest one, the **Original Ghost Walk of York** *(01759 373090)* which meets nightly at the King's Arms Pub (Ouse Bridge) at 8pm. For more theatrical renditions, the **Ghost Walk of York** *(07757 706752)* leaves nighly from oustide The Evil Eye (Stonegate) at 7:30pm *(£5).*
- **LUGGAGE STORAGE:** At York Station. £5 per item.
- **BANKS: Barclays.** *(1-3 Parliament St. 01904 772 299.)* Others are located

throughout the city center; many around Parliament St. and Coney St.

- **INTERNET:** Free at **York Central Library.** Free with purchase at some coffee shops and pubs around town. Available for purchase at Evil Eye Cafe.
- **POST OFFICE:** *(22 Lendal ☎ 0845 722 3344 ⏰ Open M-Sa 9am-5:30pm.)*
- **POSTCODE:** YO1 8BP.

Emergency!

- **PHARMACY: Boots.** *(48 Coney St. ☎ 01904 653 657.)*
- **HOSPITAL: York District Hospital.** *(Wiggington Rd. ☎01904 631 313.)* For non-emergencies, **NHS Walk-In Clinic.** *(31 Monkgate St. ☎01904 674 557 ⏰ Open daily 8am-6pm.)*

Getting There

By Train

York Station on Station Rd. run trains to **Edinburgh** *(Ⓢ £70. ⏰ 2hr. 30min., 2 per hr.);* **London King's Cross** *(Ⓢ £85. ⏰ 2 hr., 2-3 per hr.);* **Newcastle** *(Ⓢ £26.40. ⏰ 1hr., approx. every 20min.);* and Scarborough *(Ⓢ £13. ⏰ 50min., every hr.).* Tickets are cheaper when purchased in advance. Trains run sporadically outside of peak hours.

By Bus

Stations at 20 Rougier St., Exhibition Sq., the train station, and on Piccadilly. Most inter-city buses leave from outside of the train station. **National Express** coaches *(☎08717-818-178)* to **Edinburgh** *(Ⓢ £13. ⏰ 6hr. 30min., 2 per day);* **London** *(Ⓢ £26. ⏰ 5hr. 30min., 14 per day);* **Leeds** *(Ⓢ £5.20. ⏰ 1hr., every 20min.);* and **Manchester** *(Ⓢ £14. ⏰ 3hr., 17 per day).*

Getting Around

By Bus

The city center is completly walkable. To access many of York's out-of-town attractions and the coast use the local **Coastliner** bus service *(www.coastliner.co.uk)* which runs regularly to **Leeds, Malton, Pickering, Scarborough, Filey** and **Whitby.** For regular services around York, **FirstYork** *(☎0871 200 22 33)* sells day passes *(Ⓢ £3.70)* that cover all rides on their line for the full day. Bus stations are located at 20 Rougier St., Exhibition Sq., Picadillly, the Stonebow, and at York Station.

By Taxi

To book a taxi in York, call **Station Taxis** *(☎01904 623 332).*

By Bicycle

Rent a bicycle at **Bob Trotter.** *(13-15 Lord Mayor's Walk. ☎01904 622 868 Ⓢ £15 per day, £13 after 1pm. £50 deposit required. ⏰ Open M-Sa 9am-5:30pm.)*

newcastle-upon-tyne ☎0191

Once upon a time on the little island of Britain, a city called Newcastle-upon-Tyne was building 25% of the world's ships. Today, the city produces the world's wildest parties. Bottoms-up!

In fact, Newcastle-upon-Tyne is newly reinvigorated in more ways than one. The birthplace of the electric lightbulb, the gas turbine, and the steam locomotive, the city maintains its enterprising spirit, with its forays into the world of modern art, and public works projects, from a trendy waterfront area to concert halls and science museums.

The town's residents are known as Geordies. You can detect a true Geordie by

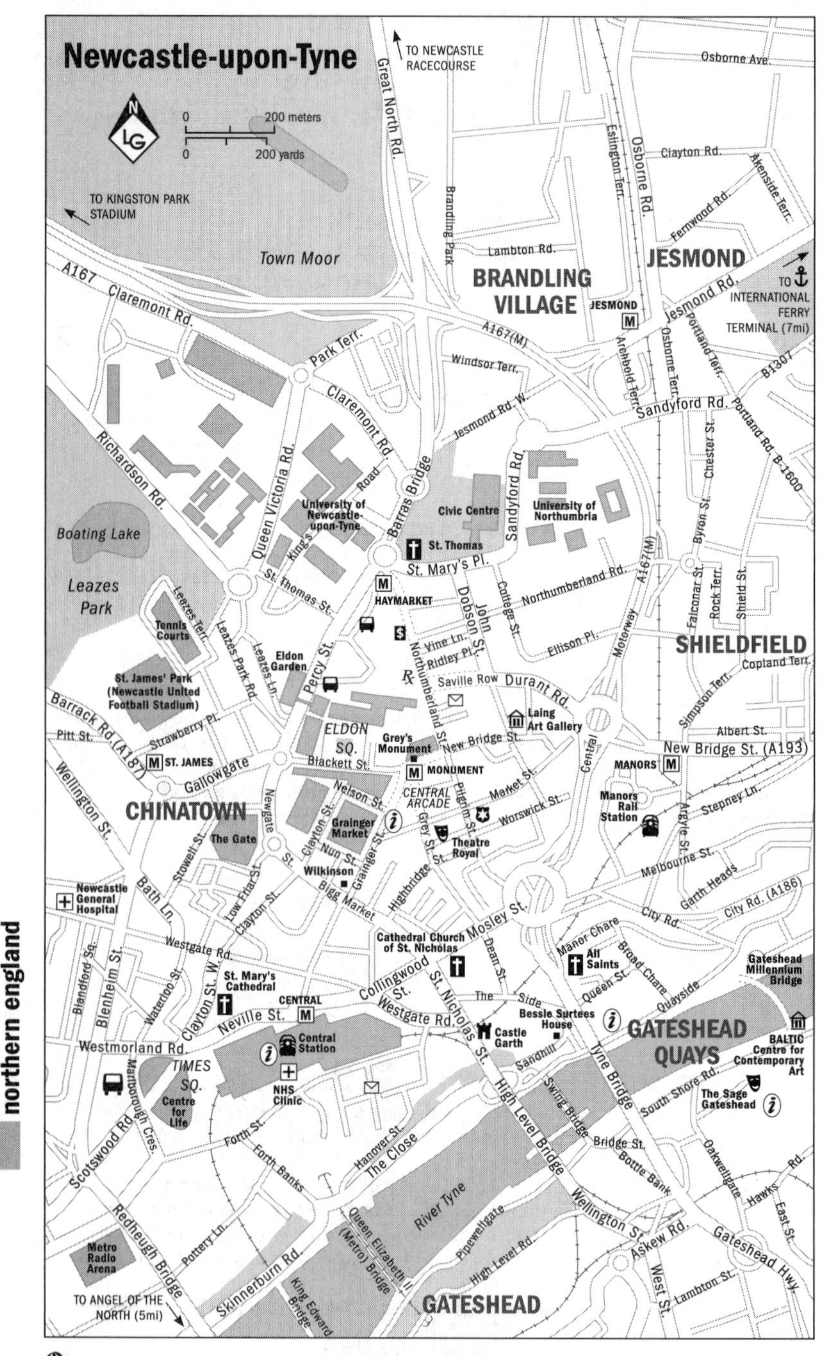

northern england

his thick accent and his ability to go with the flow—both of the situation and of the Brown ale, for which locals have a particular affinity. You may also be able to spot a Geordie by his black and white clothing. In the early days, the Blackfriar monks within the city walls wore white tunics and black cloaks. Now, however, black and white vestments mark a Magpie, a member of Toon Army—or, in more comprehensible terms, a fan of the Newcastle United Football Club.

ORIENTATION

Grey's Monument is the center of **Grainger Town,** the historic heart of Newcastle; most of the main streets of this charming 19th-century Georgian neighborhood and the major shopping areas connect directly at the monument. The Newcastle Quayside is a trendy area around the river banks, about a 10min. walk from Grainger Town. Here, Newcastle is connected to neighboring **Gateshead** by a series of stylish bridges. Jesmond is a Victorian suburb just to the northeast of the city center. Keep an eye out for the blue tourist markers handily placed around town, as street signs here are notoriously sparse.

ACCOMMODATIONS

ALBATROSS BACKPACKERS — HOSTEL ❷

51 Grainger St. ☎0191 233 1330 www.albatrossnewcastle.com

The location of this urban hostel can't be beat—two blocks from the train station, right next to a major shopping area, in the middle of the elegant surroundings of Grainger Town, and close to major nightlife spots. The "chill-out cellar" feels like a Rathskeller-style beer hall, with dark wood tables, stone walls, and people of all ages jabbering in many languages.

2min. walk from Central Train Station; take Grainger St. 2 blocks up. i Checkout is strictly 11am (late fee enforced). Satellite TV and a 24hr. kitchen with free coffee, tea, and toast. Free Wi-Fi. Internet Cafe £1 per 30min. Free house safe and storage. £5 key deposit required. Ⓢ Dorms £16.50-22.50. Reception 24hr. No curfew.

YHA NEWCASTLE — HOSTEL ❷

107 Jesmond Rd. ☎0191 281 2570 www.yha.org.uk

An attractive, refurbished old house in a residential neighborhood. Single-sex dorm rooms, each with big windows and a basin sink. Includes a full English breakfast. Make reservations in advance.

ⓂJesmond. i Internet computer use £3 per hr. Wi-Fi £5 per day, £12 per 3 days. Ⓢ Dorms £18; doubles £45. Additional £3 charge for non-YHA members. Reception daily 7am-11pm.

HANSEN HOTEL — HOTEL ❷

131 Sandyford Rd. ☎0191 281 0289

Ensuite baths are included in these modest but pleasant rooms, along with tea and coffee machines and towels. Mostly single beds at the Hansen (whew, no bunks).

ⓂJesmond. i Free Wi-Fi. Full English Breakfast included. Book in advance as rooms fill quickly, especially in summer. Ⓢ Singles £30; doubles £40-50; £20 per person for 3, 4, 5, or 6 people.

UNIVERSITY OF NORTHUMBRIA — DORMS ❷

Sandyford Rd. ☎0191 227 4717 www.northumbria.ac.uk/conferences

University dormitories are available for rent during summer months. Rooms in Claude Gibb Hall, complete with TVs and tea- and coffee makers, include full English breakfast. Students with a university ID can take a room in Laingdon Hall, a basic small dorm room on a hall shared with Northumbria students. All rooms have shared bath.

ⓂHaymarket. Near intersection with A167(M). Reception located in Claude Gibb Hall. Ⓢ Claude Gibb M-Th £28.80, F-Sa £36.50, Su £28.80. Laingdon Hall rooms £15. Halls open at various times throughout the year, so call ahead for exact dates. Reception M-Th 8am-10pm, F-Sa 24hr., Su 8am-10pm.

BRANDLING GUEST HOUSE — GUESTHOUSE ❸

4 Brandling Park ☎0191 281 3175 www.brandlingguesthouse.co.uk

Tidy, comfortable rooms with privacy (thanks to thick walls and individual keys). Complete with sofa-filled lounge. Across the street from a leafy park.

Ⓜ Jesmond. A 5min. walk from Jesmond metro station and a 15min. walk from the city center. i Ensuite rooms available. Ⓢ Singles from £33; doubles from £58.

SIGHTS

The Newcastle city center has an impressive collection of sights, but a visit to Newcastle isn't complete without a trip to the Geordies' pride, the **Angel of the North** (Bus #21 or #22 from Eldon Square). This work of public modern art stands at 65 ft. tall (the height of four double decker buses), has a wingspan of 175 ft. (wider than a Boeing 757), and is perhaps the most recognizable piece of public modern art in all of Britain (viewed by 33 million people every year).

BALTIC CENTRE FOR CONTEMPORARY ART — MUSEUM

South Shore Rd., Gateshead Quays. ☎0191 478 1922 www.balticmill.com

The BALTIC has become a symbol of the revitalized English northeast; its transformation from an old flour mill into a cultural center reflects the reenergization of the old industrial, city. The designer's vision was to make an "art factory," a place where art could be made as well as exhibited—hence, not a "museum" in its title. Take the super speedy elevator up to the fifth floor for great views of the river and of Newcastle's cityscape.

Take the Gatehead Millenium Bridge right across the Tyne. Ⓢ Free. M 10am-6pm, Tu 10:30am-6pm, Su 10am-6pm. Free guided tours at 11:00am and 4:00pm, except Th at 11am).

CASTLE GARTH — CASTLE

St. Nicholas St. ☎0191 232 7938 www.castlekeep-newcastle.org.uk

The new castle upon the Tyne, the city's namesake, was founded in 1080 by Robert Curthose, the eldest and "bastard" son of William the Conqueror. (William himself was an illegitimate child.) Robert eventually went and fathered two illegitimate children himself, proving that bastardy runs in the family. The structure that actually stands today was built by Henry II between 1168-1178. Displays inside the castle explain the strategic importance of its geographic spot. Ascend the dizzying spiral staircase for stunning views of the city and river.

Walk three blocks east from Central Station. Ⓢ £4, concessions £2.50. M-Sa 10am-5pm, Su noon-5pm. Last entry 4:15pm.

QUAYSIDE — WATERFRONT

On a temperate day, the waterfront area is packed with tourists and residents alike. You haven't seen Newcastle if you haven't seen the Tyne Bridge (1928), a decades-old reminder of the city's prominence in shipping. Aussies might notice a resemblance to the Sydney Harbour Bridge. Take a walk across one of Newcastle's famed pedestrian-friendly bridges, like **Gateshead Millenium Bridge,** the **High Level Bridge,** or **Swing Bridge,** which swivels once or twice a day, allowing ships to pass, and grab yourself some gelato at **Risis Ices,** which has sold ice cream since 1898. Just keep your eyes on the path for oncoming cyclists.

CATHEDRAL CHURCH OF ST. NICHOLAS — CHURCH

Mosley St. ☎0191 232 1939 www.stnicholascathedral.co.uk

Newcastle's most storied church is seeping with history. During a nine-week siege of Newcastle in 1644, Scottish invaders threatened to bomb and destroy the Cathedral's famed lantern tower with a cannon, but their plan was averted when Newcastle mayor Sir John Marley put his Scottish prisoners in the tower, saving the building. The bells that ring daily for services date back to the 15th century.

Walk three blocks east from Central Station. Ⓢ Free. Open for viewing M-F 7:30am-6pm, Sa 8am-4pm, Su 7:30am-noon and 4-7pm.

BESSIE SURTEES HOUSE HISTORIC HOUSE

The Close, 41-44 Sandhill ☎0191 269 1200

These two five-story 16th- and 17th-century merchant's homes are rare remnants of Jacobean domestic architecture. More fun, though, are the saucy stories of scandals past that took place here. Bessie Surtees pissed off her loaded Newcastle banker father, Aubone Surtees, by falling head over heels with a poor pauper, John Scott. She escaped through the back window and ran off to elope in Scotland. All's well that ends well, as the man that was "unfit" for his daughter's hand wound up becoming Lord Chancellor of England, and the family happily reconciled. In 2009, graffiti artists vandalized this house, creating a brand-new scandal in Newcastle.

Quayside. Free. Partial wheelchair accessibility. Open M-F 10am-4pm.

CENTRE FOR LIFE ENTERTAINMENT CENTER

Times Sq. ☎0191 243 8210 www.life.org.uk

This modern complex stands in stark contrast with its classic architectural neighbor, the Central Train Station. The flagship institution of the recently constructed Times Square area is not yet as hopping as Times Square in New York City. However, with a planetarium theater, motion ride, ice skating rink, and 3D movies, it's a veritable paradise to any child... or child at heart. Make sure you save time to help Professor Pukestopper zap bacteria in the "Cell Wars" section.

Times Sq., on Scotswood Rd. by the train station. Bring your Metro pass and get £1.50 off of admission. £10, concessions £8. Open M-Sa 10am-6pm, Su 11am-6pm.

LAING ART GALLERY GALLERY

Higham Pl. ☎0191 232 7734 www.twmuseums.org.uk/laing/

A more traditional counterpart to the modern art of the BALTIC, the Laing Art Gallery displays a permanent collection of Pre-Raphaelite paintings and many works of John Martin, son of Newcastle. Although the gallery never used to show modern art, that's beginning to change.

Free. Open M-Sa 10am-8pm, Su 10am-6pm.

SAINT JAMES' PARK PARK

Strawberry Pl. ☎0844 372 1892 www.nufc.co.uk

Saint James Park is home to Newcastle United. Faithful fans are known as the "Toon Army," and while other fans jokingly call them Looney (haha), their devotion is nothing to scoff at. Games can be a hot ticket in town, so book at least two weeks in advance. The team is moving up to a higher league soon, so check back for this season's latest ticket prices.

ⓂSt. James Park. Tours £10, £7 concessions. Matchday tours add £3. Box office open M-F 9am-5pm, Sa 9am-3pm. Call ahead on game days. Tickets go fast, book at least 2 weeks in advance.

KINGSTON PARK STADIUM STADIUM

Brunton Rd. ☎ 0871 226 60 60 www.newcastle-falcons.co.uk

Home to the Newcastle falcons rugby team, the biggest and most succesful club in Northern England. Sit in the south stand for the loudest singing fans.

ⓂKingston Park. From £10. Ticket office open M-F 10am-5pm, Sa 10am-6pm, Su 11am-5pm.

NEWCASTLE RACECOURSE RACETRACK

High Gosforth Park ☎0191 236 2020 www.newcastle-racecourse.co.uk

Located 3 miles north of the city center and set in the 812 acre High Gosforth Park Estate, the Racecourse hosts about 30 race meetings each year. A highlight of the season is the popular Beeswing Ladies Day in July, named for the most famous horse never to have captured the Plate. Beeswing won 46 of her 51 races (an impressive winning percentage of .902!) and bore many children and grandchildren, nine of whom continued on to win the Derby.

 # ⓂRegent Centre. Free bus shuttle service runs to the Racecourse from the station on race-days. Ⓢ Prices range, tickets usually come in package deals starting at £15.

FOOD

Newcastle's buffets, bistros, brasseries, and barbeques offer a variety of cuisines, ranging in nationality, price, and, of course, the kind of beer sold at the bar. Keep an eye out for the curry, burger, and coffee shops that line Grainger Town with signs for happy hour deals. In the heart of the city center, the historic **Grainger Market** (*# Grainger St., by the monument. Open M 9am-5pm, Tu 9am-5:30pm, W 9am-5pm, Th-Sa 9am-5:30pm.*) hosts suppliers of many a cheap eat—deli meats, fruits and vegetables, fish, and baked goods—all alongside the world's smallest Marks and Spencer store. Newcastle also boasts its own modest **Chinatown** (Stowell St.). Stop by in the late afternoon for affordable all-you-can-eat and buffet specials *(£5-£8).*

PANI'S CAFE — CAFE ❷

61-65 High Bridge St. ☎0191 232 4366 www.paniscafe.com

There's nothing like the smell of freshly cooked pasta to make you feel right at home. The ravioli and wait staff with rich Italian accents will make gals and some guys question why they decided to visit Britain instead of Italy. Casual atmosphere and dress.

 # Vegetarian options available. Ⓢ Entrees £6-13. Open M-Sa 10am-10pm.

BLAKE'S COFFEE HOUSE — CAFE ❶

53 Grey St. ☎0191 261 5463

A quirky local favorite, cozy, intimate Blake's has wooden tables and stone walls. Tasty, fresh sandwiches *(£3-£5)* and coffee make for a cheap but filling lunch or breakfast.

i Free Wi-Fi. Cash only. Open M-F 7am-6pm, Sa 7:30am-5:30pm, Su 10am-4pm.

VALLEY JUNCTION 397 — INDIAN ❸

Archbold Terr. ☎0191 281 6397 www.valleyrestaurants.co.uk

Take a gastronomic journey from Britain to India! Out of an old train car originally used as a saloon for travelling wealthy families comes some tasty chicken biryani, flavored rice, mild spices, and sultanas in ghee *(£10.95).* The restaurant is a convenient distance from Newcastle and Northumbria University.

 # ⓂJesmond. Open Tu-Sa noon-2pm and 6-11:30pm, Su 6-11:30pm.

BARN ASIA — ASIAN ❸

Waterloo Sq., St. James Blvd. ☎0191 221 1000 www.barnasia.com

Chow down on delicious Pan-Asian cuisine amidst funky, bright decorations (from the owner's latest trip to Vietnam) adding a hip touch on Newcastle's interpretation of "Asia." Wash down your Whole Thai drunken seabass *(£16)* with a glass of wine *(£3-6).*

Ⓢ Entrees £10-£17. Early bird special Tu-F 6-7pm is 2 courses for £13 or 3 courses for £15. Open Tu-Th 6-9:45pm, F noon-2pm and 6-9:45pm, Sa 6-9:45pm.

THE HANCOCK — BURGERS ❶

2A Hancock St. ☎0191 281 5653 www.screampubs.co.uk/thehancocknewcastleupontyne

Bare bones but super cheap, and therefore ideal for skint students. On summer days, the lively outdoor beer garden is flooded with university students hoping to catch some rays, win a few games of pool, and get plastered, all in the middle of the afternoon.

i Beer and burger deal after 3pm for £4. Th student night, drinks from £1.25. Open M-W 11:30am-11pm, Th-Sa 11:30am-1am, Su noon-10:30pm.

BLACKFRIARS RESTAURANT GOURMET 4

Friar St. ☎0191 232 5533 www.blackfriarsrestaurant.co.uk

Blackfriars is the oldest dining room in the UK and proud of it. Before it served gourmet delicacies to upscale Geordies, it served the residents of the Blackfriar monastery. Adventurous eaters might try local specialties like braised County Durham pork belly with sage and apple gnocchi *(£16)*. For those looking to enjoy the atmosphere without completely emptying their wallets, the summer brings alfresco dining on the patio with the more affordable Terrace Menu *(drinks £4-£6; traditional English sandwiches £4)*.

Early set menu 6-7pm is 2 entrees for £12.50, 3 for £15. Open Apr-Sept M-Sa 11am-5pm and 6pm-late, Su 11am-4pm; Oct-Mar M-Sa noon-2:30pm and 6pm-late, Su noon-4pm.

NIGHTLIFE

Social drinking is nothing new in Newcastle. The culture of intoxication has been around since the days when beer was safer to drink than water. Yet while (in)famous for its crazy party scene, Newcastle's rockin' clubs and chilled-out pubs, can fit every type of personality. **The Gate** *(www.thegatenewcastle.co.uk)* is a new comer to the Newcastle nightlife scene, that's an all-in-one cinema, bar, restaurant, club, and casino that's a boon to its younger crowd. This complex and the area surrounding it attract large hordes of students during the year; much of their traffic comes by way of nearby Northumbria and Newcastle Universities. Geordies are notoriously immune to weather, so girls will be decked out in mini-dresses and impossible heels no matter the weather outside at clubs. Rumor has it that a local can spot a tourist by how much clothing she is wearing. For guys, the dressing game is a little easier—and a whole lot less chill-inducing.

The **Central Station** area is renowned for its great live music, while **Bigg Market** is truly the part of the city that established Newcastle as a prime partying destination, with over 20 pubs in its boundaries alone making it a popular site for Stags and Hens (bachelor and bachelorette) parties. Meanwhile, the **Quayside** is home to some of the posher waterfront bars that suit a slightly older demographic. Although the Haymarket area is one of the quieter parts of town, it boasts fine selections of quality beer and really heats up on game day. The **"Pink Triangle "** along Westmorland Rd., St. James Blvd. and Marlborough Crescent hosts an active gay night scene. Check out www.newcastlegayscene.co.uk for hot events and openings in this neighborhood.

THE CLUNY CLUB

36 Lime St. ☎0191 230 4474

This excellent music club is the beating, thumping heart of Newcastle's burgeoning music scene. Both local and national bands in a range of genres play live every night, while happy customers sit back comfortably in the adjacent bar with a draught lager of choice in hand. Make sure you keep track of that LP *(£4)* you pick up at the merch table—the band you see here tonight will be big tomorrow.

Head down to the Quayside, then follow the blue signs to the Cluny or Ouseburn (about a 20-min. walk). Cover £10-20. Beer from £3, wine from £7.45. Shows usually start at 8pm. Open M-W 11:30am-11pm, Th 11:30-12am, F-Sa 11:30am-1am, Su noon-10:30pm.

REVOLUTION BAR

Collingwood St. ☎0191 261 5774

The British are coming. It's time for a Revolution—but not the American, tea-drinking kind. This revolution is about vodka, but you'll want to treat yourself to the specialty raspberry mojito *(£6)*. Flashing lights and hipster music, aren't really revolutionary, yet it's still trendy without trying too hard.

Open M-Th 11:30am-1am, F-Sa 10am-2am. Food served until 8pm.

TIGER TIGER BAR, RESTAURANT

The Gate, Newgate Street ☎0191 235 7065 www.tigertiger-newcastle.co.uk

If one bar is not enough to bring out your inner animal, try six bars in one. Roarrr. Each bar boast its own theme—'90s, Groovy '70s, etc. Posh VIP room for special people (you have to call in advance). House mixed drinks *(£4)* are worth the wait at the bar. Phone ahead or go on the website to be added to the guest list for Fridays and Saturdays and skip over the often lengthy lines.

Cover £5-11. Open M-Th noon-2am, F-Sa noon-3am, Su noon-12:30am.

POPOLO BAR

82 Pilgrim St. ☎0191 232 8923 wwww.popolo.co.uk

This classy bar adorned with modern art and lit with modish red lighting, is pricey, but their specialty mojitos *(from £6)* are worth the pricetag. Better yet, stop by for Mojito Wednesdays *(mojitos £4 starting 6pm)*. Sip on one of over 60 drinks and enjoy the Americana diner decor. For an hour or two, you'll think you're across the pond.

Open M-Tu 11am-midnight, W-Sa 11am-1am, Su 11am-midnight.

DIGITAL CLUB

Times Sq. ☎0191 261 9755 www.yourfutureisdigital.com

This future-themed club embraces forward-thinking scenery. A great sound system combined with mega-sized plasma TV screens mirroring the DJ's moves creates an alternate technological universe. Friday nights are always hopping, so avoid being fashionably late if you want to beat the queues!

Cover from £5-18. Student discounts available. Hours change weekly; call ahead to check. Earliest opening is 10pm, latest closing is 4am.

THE YARD CLUB

2 Scotswood ☎0191 232 2037

The relaxed downstairs bar area is a good spot for a late afternon drink at this GLBT-friendly pub. Upstairs is where the music blasts and people get their respective grooves on. The place becomes much more clubby on Friday and Saturday nights.

Open M-Th 3pm-2am, F-Sa 2pm-2am, Su 3pm-2am.

THE HEAD OF STEAM PUB

2 Neville St. ☎0191 230 4326 www.headofsteam.com

If you're coming in just for the night, hop off the train and roll in for live music and a beer. Head down the stairs to an intimate venue with a sound system that's a little too excellent. Bring your earplugs if you can't handle the noise! Live music plays nightly downstairs, but you can also sit at a darkly lit bar upstairs.

Right across the from the railway station. Open M-Th noon-2am, F-Sa noon-3am, Su noon-2am.

THE POWERHOUSE CLUB

Westmorland Rd. ☎0191 261 6824

Night fever, night fever! A labyrinth of stairs and doors open to a bouncing, vibrant wave of dancing. The first floor plays booming dance music while leather booths stood at the ready to give your tired feet a quick break. If you don't know how to boogie, there's an outdoor smoking terrace for warm summer nights, complete with a bar in the center.

Cover £1-10. Bring student ID for discounts. Open M 11pm-4am, F 11pm-4am, Sa 11pm-5am, Su 11:30pm-3:30am. Sstays open until 6am the 1st and last Sa of every month.

SAM JACKS  BAR

The Gate, Newgate St. ☎0191 261 8982 www.samjacks.com

This is a favorite of the students of Northumbria University, so it plays host to mostly a young crowd. There's a rodeo bull free for riding, a dentist chair atop

the bar for lap dances, and shot-pouring, scantily-clad dancers who perform on elevated stages, plus big TVs to witness all the failures of Newcastle F.C.
No cover. Mixed drinks £2-4. Open daily 4pm-1am.

MOOD BAR
The Gate, Newgate St. 0191 230 6360 www.moodbars.com
Men on stilts and lively DJs distinguish this bar from its otherwise standard features. Buzzing young crowds and reasonably priced drinks.
Open M-Tu 11am-2am, W 11am-3am, Th-Su 11am-2am.

FLORITA'S MIAMI BAR AND TROPICAL GARDEN BAR
28-32 Collingwood St. 0191 230 4114 www.floritasbar.com
Sip on tropical drinks and enjoy the outdoor garden with barbeque. Drink out of a watermelon with friends, or if you're less adventurous, try a Frozen Passion Fruit Daiquiri.
Drinks £4.75-20. Open M-Th 5pm-2am, F-Sa noon-3pm, Su 5pm-2am. Happy hour M-F 5-7pm.

ARTS AND CULTURE

THEATRE ROYAL CITY CENTER
100 Grey St. 08448 11 21 21 www.theatreroyal.co.uk
Theatre Royal, built in 1837, is one of the oldest and most historic theaters in the UK. BBC calls it "Newcastle Cultural Temple." Most of Britain's popular traveling shows make a stop here, and the theater itself is home to the National Theatre, Opera North, the Rambert Dance Company, and the Grey Lady, the theater's resident ghost. In 1899, right after a showing of Shakespeare's *Macbeth*, a fire broke out and destroyed the whole building. Geordies, however, recouped and rebuilt. Today, The Royal Shakespeare Company makes an annual stopover here for a month and considers the theater its northern base.
Ⓜ Monument. Follow signs to theater. i ½-price tickets available from 9am on the day of the performance. Students can get tickets for £10 on first nights (with a few exceptions, check with Box Office for details). Box office open M-Tu 9am-8pm, W 10am-8pm, Th-Sa 9am-8pm.

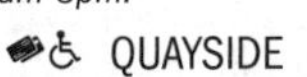

SAGE GATESHEAD CONCERT HALL QUAYSIDE
St. Mary's Sq., Gateshead Quays. 0191 443 4661 www.thesagegateshead.org
This award-winning waterfront building contains 3500 sq. m of glass on the roof in 280 panels (equivalent to 8.3 basketball courts) and over 18 million liters of concrete (equivalent to 31,675,572 pints of Newcastle Brown Ale). The Concert Hall is the home base for the **Northern Sinfonia,** the region's chamber orchestra, and **Folkworks,** an agency aimed toward promoting traditional forms of music and dance (think harps and recorders, not the Rolling Stones). Check ahead for performance listings and prices.
Gateshead Quayside. Concerts from £3.50 and up. Building open to visitors 9am-9pm. Box office open daily 10am-8pm.

ESSENTIALS

Practicalities

- **TOURIST INFORMATION CENTER:** Accommodations bookings available at TIC. Helpful maps and brochures, including free copies of Crack magazine that has monthly listings of music, comedy, cinema, and theater in the area. Free 15min. internet use. *(8-9 Central Arcade, The Guildhall, Quayside 0191 277 8000 www.newcastle.gov.uk/core.nsf/a/touristinfocentres Open M-F 9:30am-5:30pm and Sa 9am-5:30pm. Guildhall location open M-F 10am-5pm, Sa 9am-5pm, Su 9am-4pm.)*
- **TOURS:** The tourist information center gives walking tours starting from Market St. *(£3 per person June-Sept 11am).* **City Sightseeing** *(0191 228 8900*

www.city-sightseeing.com) offers Open Top bus tours that leave from Central Train Station *(£8, concessions £6).*

- **BANKS: Barclays,** 120 Grainger St. (near Grey's Monument) with several locations in the city center.
- **LUGGAGE STORAGE:** At Central Train Station. (*£5 per 24hr. Open M-Sa 8am-8pm, Su 9am-8pm.)*
- **INTERNET ACCESS:** Free 15min. access at the tourist information centers. Many coffee shops offer free Wi-Fi. The newly reopened **Newcastle City Library** *(33 New Bridge St. ☎0191 277 4100 www.newcastle.gov.uk/libraries Open M-Th 8:30am-5:30pm, F-Sa 8:30am-5:30pm, Su 11am-5pm)* offers beautiful facilities for studying or leisure and has free Wi-Fi for guests and members.
- **POST OFFICE:** Inside **WHSmith** building, 2nd floor. Many others located throughout town. *(36 Northumberland St. ☎0845 722 3344 Open M-Sa 9am-5:30pm.)*
- **POSTCODE:** NE1 7DE.

Emergency!

- **POLICE: Pilgrim St. Station** at the corner of Pilgrim St. and Market St. *(☎0345 604 3043 for non-emergencies).*
- **HOSPITAL:** For emergencies, **Newcastle General Hospital.** *(Westgate Rd. ☎0191 233 6161).* For non-emergencies, **NHS Walk-In Centre.** *(The Bar Unit 5, St. James Gate ☎0191 233 3760 www.newcastlecentralwalkincentre.co.uk M-F 8am-8pm.)*

Getting There

Newcastle lies 1hr. 45min. north of York on the A19 and 1hr. east of Carlisle on the A69. Edinburgh is 2hr. 30min. north of Newcastle on the A1, which follows the North Sea coast, or on the A68, which cuts inland.

By Air

Newcastle International Airport *(☎0870 122 1488 www.newcastleairport.com)* has flights from other cities in the UK, Europe, and around the world. About 20-25min. from Newcastle city center by metro.

By Train

Newcastle Central Station *(Neville St. ☎08457 484 950 M-Sa 4:30am-9:20pm, Su 7:10am-10pm. Advance tickets sold M-F 7am-8pm, Sa 7am-7pm, Su 8:40am-8pm)* runs trains to **Carlisle** *(£12.90. 1hr. 3min., every hr.)*; **Durham** *(£5.40. 15min., 4 per hr.)*; **London King's Cross** *(£133 3hr., 3 per hr.)*; **Edinburgh** *(£42. 1hr. 3min., 3 per hr.)*; and **York** *(£26.40. 1hr., 4 per hr.).*

By Bus

Newcastle has 3 main bus stations. Newcastle Coach station at St. James Blvd. National Express *(☎8717 818 178)* buses to **Edinburgh** *(£17.50. 3 hr., 3 per day),* **Glasgow** *(£34. 4 hr., 2 per day)* and **London** *(£27. 7hr., 5 per day).* **Haymarket Station,** by the metro stop, and adjunct **Eldon Square Station,** Percy St., are the gateways for local and regional service by **Arriva** *(☎0871 200 22 33 www.arrivabus.co.uk),* **Stagecoach** *(☎0191 276 1411),* and **Go Northeast** *(☎0845 606 0260 www.simplygo.com).*

By Ferry

International Ferry Terminal, Royal Quays, 7 mi. east of Newcastle. **DFDS Seaways** *(☎0871 522 9955 www.dfdsseaways.co.uk)* offers ferry service to **Amsterdam** *(from £139).* DFDS offers a special bus to the ferry terminal from Newcastle Central Station before each sailing *(£3.50. 20min.)* or take the metro to Percy Main; from the station, it's a 20min. walk.

Getting Around

For a large city, Newcastle is fairly compact, which makes traveling within its perimeter pretty hassle-free. Streets are pedestrian-friendly, and most of the popular neighborhoods are within walking distance of each other.

By Bus and Train

For tired feet after a long day of walking, there is the **Tyne and Wear Metro,** a light rail system connecting all major destinations in the region (not just for the city). There are three main stops in the city center: **Haymarket, Monument,** and **Saint James.** Metro trains run daily from 5:30am to midnight, every 5-10 minutes during the day and every 10-20 minutes during the evenings. Tickets can be purchased from machines at all metro stations. If you're planning to make a few journeys, buy a Metro DaySaver *(£3.90)* and you'll be all set for a day's unlimited travel. The Green Line will take you to the airport *(20min.),* while the Yellow Line takes you to the coast. Tickets are £3.90 for weekends and weekdays after 9am, £4.80 before 9am. A **DayRover,** available at metro and bus stations (and also on the bus) covers unlimited travel by bus or train within Tyne and Wear *(£6.10).* An **Explorer** ticket *(☎0871 200 22 33)* covers buses, trains, and ferries throughout all of Northumbria and can be purchased on the bus *(£8, concessions £7).*

By Taxi

While one should always be aware of surroundings, especially when going out to explore nightlife, Newcastle has a safe reputation. There are plenty of people out and about, and conveniently, it doesn't get dark in the summertime until about 10pm. However, if you are ever feeling uncomfortable walking late at night, there are taxi ranks marshalled by police officers at The Gate *(F-Sa),* The Bigg Market *(F-Sa),* and Times Square *(Sa)* from 10pm to 4am to ensure you get back safely. For taxis at any time of day, call **Noda Taxi** *(☎0191 222 1888)* or **A.B.C Taxis** *(☎0191 406 3438).*

durham ☎0191

Bounded by cobbled streets, dominated by the Norman cathedral that looms overhead, and surrounded by picturesque rivers, travel writer Bill Bryson called it "a perfect little city," and many agree. (Durham itself was so flattered by this kind description that they crowned Bryson as Chancellor of their beloved University.) Durham is a proud city: proud of its heritage as the seat of the semi-autonomous land of the Prince Bishops, proud of its mantle as the ancient "Cradle of Christianity," even of former resident Joseph Borruwlawski, a Polish dwarf better known as "The Little Count." Durham is so proud, in fact, that Burruwlaski's portrait hangs in City Hall.

Durham began as a home to the cult following of the great Cuthbert (eventually St. Cuthbert). A monk renowned for his miracle-making, fairness, and athletic prowess, he died an early, tragic death. But when Cuthbert's body was uncovered having resisted decay years after his death, people declared it a miracle, and consequently, eager travelers arrived in hoards to his monastery. Thus the city of Durham was born, destined to be a tourist attraction. Unfortunately, this immense popularity meant it invited some undesirable visitors, too—like the Vikings.

ORIENTATION

Durham is small, condensed, and easily traveled by foot, though travelers with backpacks may curse the steep hills of its cobblestone streets. Durham Cathedral dominates the city skyline and serves as a good orientation point. On both sides, ancient and modern footbridges connect the shores of the **River Wear,** while quaint walking paths along the water provide pedestrians with a peaceful place to introduce oneself to the town. Durham's medieval streetfare, however, wasn't designed for massive traffic jams of the 20th century, and after many an accident, Durham became the first city in England to have a congestion charge (£2 pounds when you leave the city center during daytime hours). **Saddler Street** is Durham's main downtown shopping and restaurant thoroughfare. Note the theater references (read: Shakespeare's Pub), as the city's main theater used to be located here. Also look out for a plaque marking the home of **Mrs. Clements,** the first person to grind mustard seeds and the founder of Durham mustard (apparently, King George II was quite a fan of this locally-produced condiment).

ACCOMMODATIONS

Many of the members of Durham University's college system offer up their dorms for summer housing for tourists. Call **Event Durham** *(☎0191 334 3800)* for information on accommodations at the other colleges.

UNIVERSITY COLLEGE — DORMS ❸

Durham Castle ☎0191 334 4106 www.durhamcastle.com

Live like royalty in the hallowed halls of Durham Castle. These may just be the sweetest digs you'll ever sleep in; this place was made for MTV Cribs. If you're feeling especially luxurious, book the Bishop's Suite, a massive two-room affair with 17th-century tapestries on the walls and magnificent views of the river. Includes breakfast in the Great Hall. Reserve in advance for weekends, as there are many weddings here and rooms fill up fast.

Across from the Cathedral. Singles from £28.50; doubles from £51; Bishop's Suite £180. Open July-Sept.

MRS. M.T. KOLTAI'S — GUEST HOUSE ❸

10 Gilesgate ☎0191 386 2026

Clean, quiet, and easily accessible from the city center *(about a 10 minute walk).* Come for the best deal in town during the months of the university term.

Follow signs from train station to the TIC; 10 Gilesgate is past Claypath, up a hill, on the left. i Breakfast closes at 8:30am. Singles £25; doubles £45.

ST. CHAD'S COLLEGE — DORMS ❸

18 North Bailey ☎0191 334 2887 www.durhamcastle.com

One of Durham's most traditional and esteemed colleges offers summer housing in its facilities, with discounts for YHA members. Prices include breakfast in the college's stately dining hall.

Behind Durham Cathedral. i Parking available. Singles £22.50, non-YHA members £26.50, ensuite £36.50; doubles £48, ensuite £68. Open July-Sept. Reception open 9am-11pm.

SIGHTS

Durham University reigns supreme over the city's cultural life, as it owns many of the city's major sites. **Durham University Botanic Garden** *(☎0191 334 5521 www.durham.ac.uk/botanic.garden £4)* features 22 acres of exotic trees from the Himalayas, and that far-off place called America. The **University's Museum of Archeology** *(☎0191 334 5521 www.duham.ac.uk/fulling.mill £1, students free)* helps visitors get in touch with the area's Anglo-Saxon roots. But the city's most famed sights by far are the magnificent 11th-century cathedral and castle, also owned by—you guessed it—Durham University.

DURHAM CATHEDRAL — CHURCH

☎0191 386 4266 www.durhamcathedral.co.uk

Built between 1093 and 1133, this magnificent Norman cathedral is a World Heritage Site and the shrine of Durham's beloved St. Cuthbert. It is hailed as the finest Norman cathedral in the world. The information desk sells short pocket guides *(£1)* and illustrated guides *(£5)* to help direct your visit. The north door and the sanctuary knocker on the outside are notable because during the Middle

Ages, people could come seek sanctuary in the cathedral. By simply grasping the knocker, the felon was granted 37 days of safety, called "peculiar sanctuary," that applied to all crimes, even as high as treason. To the left of the information desk is the simple tomb of the Venerable Bede, the 8th-century author of the very first history of England. The stunning nave was the first in England to incorporate pointed arches. Behind the choir is the tomb of the revered **Saint Cuthbert,** whose followers were inspired to build what would later become Durham Cathedral after a vivid vision from God. Check out the clock; it dates from 1632, but if it looks a little funny to you, that's because the Victorians disliked its old-fashioned style and in 1845 removed its case and mounted the face right on the wall. It was restored in 1938. The bishop's throne, next to the choir, has been controversial since its construction in the 14th century; it stands nearly 3 in. higher than the pope's throne at the Vatican. Meanwhile, a dizzying trip up the 325 steps of the central tower *(£5)* yields spectacular views of Durham from 218 ft. up in the air. The Monks' Dormitory *(£1)* harbors rare stones and casts of crosses under a massive ceiling that's lasted six centuries. The Treasures of St. Cuthbert *(£2.50, concessions £2),* off the cloister, holds ancient holy manuscrips dating back 1300 years as well as the rings and seals of the bishops.

i No photos allowed, no flip-flops allowed on tower. Ⓢ Entrance is free, donation recommended. ⏰ Open Sept-June daily 9:30am-6pm; July-Aug M-Sa 9:30am-8pm, Su 12:30-8pm.

DURHAM CASTLE CASTLE

☎0191 334 3800 wwww.durham.ac.uk/university.college/tours

Dating from 1072, the Castle was the seat of Durham's prince bishops, the political and nominally-religious ruling powers of the area, until 1837. It now houses University College, the foundation college of Durham University. Its Great Hall was built in 1284 and now serves the students of University College as a dining hall, while the extensive kitchen area dates from 1499. The oldest feature of the castle is its unusual Norman chapel. At graduation time, University College students are robed in the Great Hall of the Castle and then proceed on to the ceremony in the cathedral.

Across the Green from Durham Cathedral. i Accessible by guided tour only, about 50min. Call ahead of time to inquire about tour times; they are subject to change. Ⓢ £5, concessions £3.50. ⏰ Term-time tours 2, 3, 4pm. During breaks 10, 11am, noon.

ARTS AND CULTURE

The last Durham pit closed in 1994, but this laboring legacy continues with the Miners' Gala, held on the second Saturday of every July. Miners hold banners, march in a parade, and tout the proud heritage of North East England.

GALA THEATRE AND CINEMA CITY CENTER

1 Millenium Sq. ☎0191 332 4040 www.galadurham.co.uk

500-seat theater with a rooftop studio. The Summer Festival is no longer around, but the in-house productions, comedy, ballets pantomine, plays, and musicals cycle through this modern building all year long.

Next to Tourist Information. Ⓢ Tickets £16-26. ⏰ Box Office open M-Sa 10am-8:30pm; Su 2:30pm-8:30pm.

DURHAM FESTIVAL AND REGATTA RIVER TYNE

River Tyne www.durham-regatta.org.uk

The second oldest regatta in England dates back to 1834. Widely considered the premier race in the North of England, Durham residents and tourists alike flood the riverbanks to watch the races and enjoy live music, food, and other vendor tents.

Follow signs for the Cathedral and Castle, and the Regatta is signposted from North Road. Ⓢ £2.50, concessions free. ⏰ June.

ESSENTIALS

Practicalities

- **TOURIST INFORMATION CENTER:** The TIC is on the eastern side of the Millburnsgate Bridge. The office will book accommodations for £3. Pick up free copies of *What's On* and *Week Ahead*for listings of arts and cuture events. *(2 Millenium Pl. ☎0191 384 3720 Open M-Sa 9:30am-5:30pm, Su 11am-4pm.)*
- **TOURS:** The TIC offers guided walks of the city *(May-Sept Sa-Su 2pm £4)*, as well as Ghost and Grisly Death Walks *(July-Sept M 7:30pm £5)*.
- **STA TRAVEL:** *(☎0871 702 9817 Open M-F 10am-6pm; Sa 10am-5pm.)*
- **BANKS:** **Barclays,** Market Pl., and others around it.
- **POLICE: NEW ELVET** *(☎0345 60 60 365)*.
- **INTERNET:** Free at the library and for customers at Varsity *(46 Saddler St.)*, Waterhouse *(65 North Rd.)*, Bishops Mill *(Walkergate Complex)*, Esquires Cafe *(22 Silver St.)*, Hide Bar and Grill *(39 Sadddler St.)*, and Freeman's Quay Gym *(Freeman's Place)*.
- **POST OFFICE:** *(33 Silver St. ☎0845 722 3344 Open M -F 9am-5:30pm; Sa 9am-4pm.)*
- **POSTCODE:** DH1 3RE.

Getting There

The train station *(Ticket office open M-F 6am-8pm, Sa 6am-7pm, Su 8am-8pm)* is up a hill to the west of town. **Trains** *(☎08457 48 49 50)* run frequently to **Edinburgh** *(£35.50. 2hr., 2 per hr.)*, **London King's Cross** *(£133. 3hr., 2 per hr.)*, **Newcastle** *(£5.90. 2hr., 2 per hr.)*, and **York** *(£21.90. 45min., 4 per hr.)*.

National Express **buses** *(☎08705 808 080)* depart from the bus station at North Rd., across Framwellgate Bridge to **Newcastle** *(£3.30. 30min., 3 per day)*, **Edinburgh** *(£27.30. 4hr., 2 per day)*, **Leeds** *(£16.10. 2½hr., 4 per day)*, and **London** *(£32.70. 7hr., 5 per day)*. **Arriva** *(www.arrivabus.co.uk)* buses X2 and X41 run to Eldon Sq. station in nearby Newcastle *(£6. 1½hr., 2 per hr.)*.

Getting Around

Drivers should know that Durham's small narrow streets are a recipe for traffic disaster; driving should be easy to avoid as the major areas are all adjacent to each other. Durham Cathedral Bus *(daily every 20min.)* links the cathedral, rail station, car and coach parks, and the bus station (boarding point on North Rd.). There are plenty of **taxi** companies in town, including **Mac's** *(☎0191 384 1329)* and **Paddy's** *(☎0191 386 6662)*.

SCOTLAND

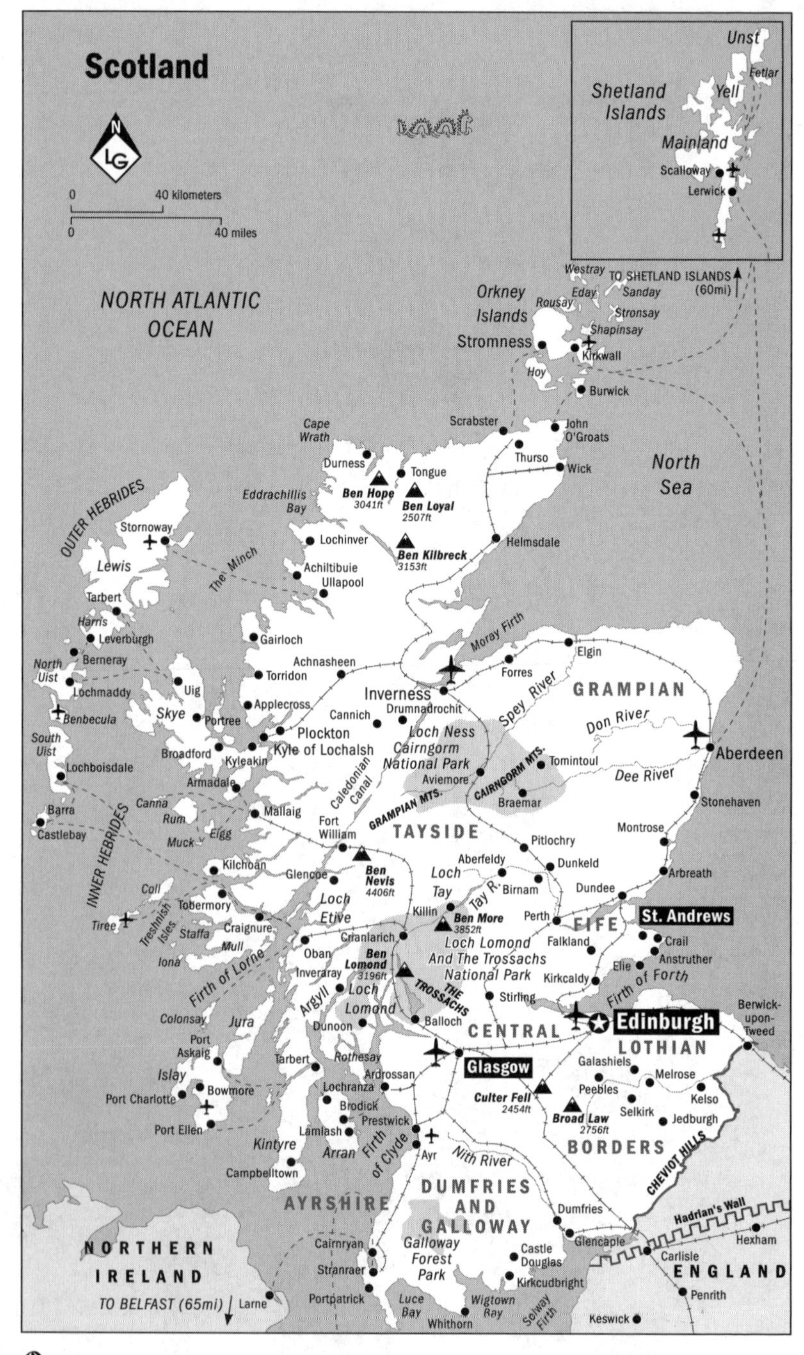
Scotland
40 kilometers
40 miles
NORTH ATLANTIC OCEAN
North Sea
Shetland Islands
Unst
Fetlar
Yell
Mainland
Scalloway
Lerwick
TO SHETLAND ISLANDS (60mi)
Orkney Islands
Westray
Eday
Sanday
Rousay
Stronsay
Shapinsay
Stromness
Kirkwall
Hoy
Burwick
Scrabster
John O'Groats
Thurso
Wick
Cape Wrath
Durness
Tongue
Ben Hope 3041ft
Ben Loyal 2507ft
Eddrachillis Bay
Lochinver
Ben Kilbreck 3153ft
Helmsdale
Achiltibuie
Ullapool
OUTER HEBRIDES
Stornoway
Lewis
The Minch
Tarbert
Harris
Leverburgh
Berneray
North Uist
Lochmaddy
Benbecula
South Uist
Lochboisdale
Barra
Castlebay
Uig
Skye
Portree
Gairloch
Achnasheen
Torridon
Applecross
Moray Firth
Forres
Elgin
Inverness
Drumnadrochit
Cannich
Spey River
GRAMPIAN
Don River
Aberdeen
Plockton
Kyle of Lochalsh
Kyleakin
Broadford
Loch Ness
Cairngorm National Park
Tomintoul
CAIRNGORM MTS.
Dee River
Aviemore
Braemar
Stonehaven
Armadale
Canna
Rum
Eigg
Muck
Mallaig
Caledonian Canal
GRAMPIAN MTS.
Fort William
TAYSIDE
Montrose
Pitlochry
Aberfeldy
Dunkeld
Arbreath
INNER HEBRIDES
Kilchoan
Glencoe
Ben Nevis 4406ft
Loch Tay
Tay R.
Birnam
Dundee
Coll
Tobermory
Loch Etive
Killin
Ben More 3852ft
Perth
FIFE
St. Andrews
Tiree
Treshnish Isles
Staffa
Craignure
Mull
Crianlarich
Loch Lomond And The Trossachs National Park
Falkland
Crail
Anstruther
Iona
Oban
Ben Lomond 3196ft
Elie
Firth of Forth
Firth of Lorne
Inveraray
THE TROSSACHS
Kirkcaldy
Stirling
Argyll
Loch Lomond
Colonsay
Jura
Dunoon
Balloch
CENTRAL
Edinburgh
Berwick-upon-Tweed
Port Askaig
LOTHIAN
Tarbert
Rothesay
Glasgow
Galashiels
Islay
Ardrossan
Melrose
Bowmore
Port Charlotte
Lochranza
Culter Fell 2454ft
Peebles
Kelso
Brodick
Selkirk
Broad Law 2756ft
Jedburgh
Port Ellen
Prestwick
Lamlash
Kintyre
Arran
Firth of Clyde
Ayr
BORDERS
Nith River
CHEVIOT HILLS
Campbelltown
DUMFRIES AND GALLOWAY
AYRSHIRE
Dumfries
Hadrian's Wall
NORTHERN IRELAND
Cairnryan
Galloway Forest Park
Glencaple
Hexham
Castle Douglas
Carlisle
ENGLAND
Stranraer
Kirkcudbright
Penrith
TO BELFAST (65mi)
Larne
Portpatrick
Luce Bay
Wigtown Bay
Solway Firth
Whithorn
Keswick

EDINBURGH

It's a city that moves. Visitors from Vikings to Vikings fans have been streaming to Scotland's ancient capital for years, and the population of the city swells by roughly one million during the month of August. Festival season, or **"Fest"** is a time when free entertainment is so thick in the streets that walking down to the pub might take half an hour. Even when Edinburgh isn't party central, it's packed with locals with an intense pride for their city. Coax some of it out of them over a **"pint and a blether"** (Scottish-speak for drink and a chat). A majestic city, it's one of those places where you watch the sun go down from the top of a hill and wonder just how you managed to end up here, a rebuttal in stone and whiskey to the idea that you can't have an awesome time at a latitude north of Moscow. However you got here, keep doing what you're doing: Edinburgh was made for you.

greatest hits

- **RIDES AND LIQUOR.** Take a carnival ride in a keg at the Scotch Whisky Experience (p. 289).
- **FAR-OUT PASTRY.** Try the delectable macaroons at Madeleine (p. 296), the most futuristic cafe in town.
- **THE GORY STORY.** Feel a little bit like Dr. Frankenstein with a pit-stop at The Surgeon's Hall Museum (p. 306).
- **ONLY A QUID.** Enjoy the student scene and £1 drinks on Octopussy Club night at HMV Picture House (p. 307).

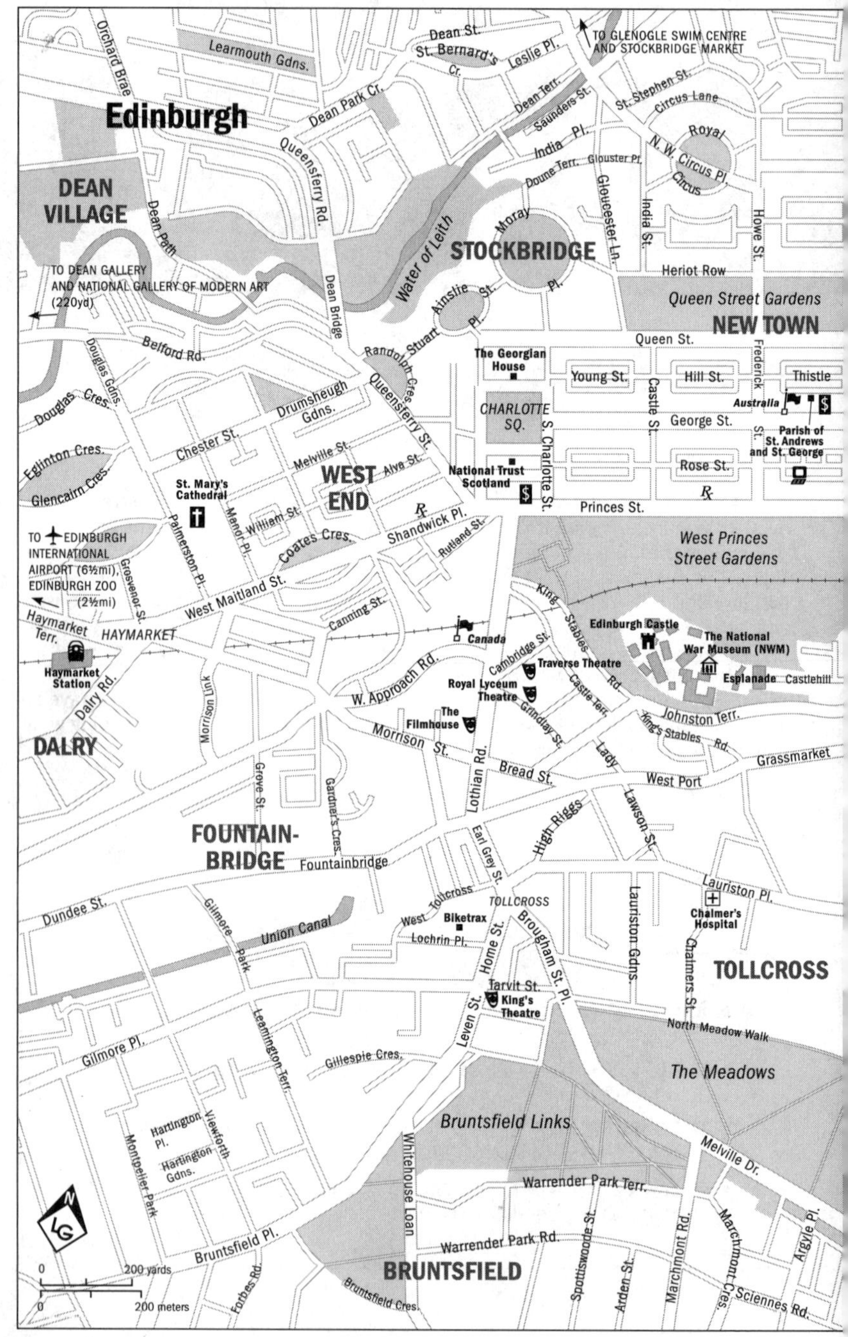
Edinburgh
DEAN VILLAGE
STOCKBRIDGE
NEW TOWN
WEST END
DALRY
FOUNTAIN-BRIDGE
TOLLCROSS
BRUNTSFIELD
HAYMARKET
TO GLENOGLE SWIM CENTRE AND STOCKBRIDGE MARKET
TO DEAN GALLERY AND NATIONAL GALLERY OF MODERN ART (220yd)
TO EDINBURGH INTERNATIONAL AIRPORT (6½mi), EDINBURGH ZOO (2½mi)
Queen Street Gardens
West Princes Street Gardens
The Meadows
Bruntsfield Links
Water of Leith
Union Canal
The Georgian House
CHARLOTTE SQ.
National Trust Scotland
St. Mary's Cathedral
Australia
Thistle
Parish of St. Andrews and St. George
Canada
Edinburgh Castle
The National War Museum (NWM)
Esplanade
Castlehill
Traverse Theatre
Royal Lyceum Theatre
The Filmhouse
Haymarket Station
Biketrax
King's Theatre
Chalmer's Hospital
Learmouth Gdns.
Orchard Brae
Dean St.
St. Bernard's Cr.
Leslie Pl.
Dean Park Cr.
Queensferry Rd.
Dean Terr.
Saunders St.
St. Stephen St.
Circus Lane
Royal Circus
N. W. Circus Pl.
India Pl.
Glouster Pl.
Doune Terr.
Gloucester Ln.
India St.
Howe St.
Moray Pl.
Dean Path
Dean Bridge
Heriot Row
Ainslie Pl.
Stuart St.
Belford Rd.
Queen St.
Randolph Cres.
Queensferry St.
Douglas Gdns.
Douglas Cres.
Drumsheugh Gdns.
Young St.
Castle St.
Hill St.
Frederick St.
George St.
Chester St.
Melville St.
Alva St.
S. Charlotte St.
Rose St.
Eglinton Cres.
Glencairn Cres.
Palmerston Pl.
Manor Pl.
William St.
Shandwick Pl.
Princes St.
Coates Cres.
Rutland St.
Grosvenor St.
West Maitland St.
King Stables Rd.
Haymarket Terr.
Canning St.
Cambridge St.
Castle Terr.
Dalry Rd.
W. Approach Rd.
Grindlay St.
Johnston Terr.
Morrison Link
King's Stables Rd.
Morrison St.
Lothian Rd.
Bread St.
Lady Lawson St.
West Port
Grassmarket
Grove St.
Gardner's Cres.
High Riggs
Earl Grey St.
Fountainbridge
Lauriston Pl.
Dundee St.
Gilmore Park
West Tollcross
TOLLCROSS
Lochrin Pl.
Home St.
Brougham St.
Lauriston Gdns.
Chalmers St.
Tarvit St.
Leven St.
Brougham Pl.
North Meadow Walk
Gilmore Pl.
Leamington Terr.
Gillespie Cres.
Hartington Pl.
Viewforth
Hartington Gdns.
Montpelier Park
Whitehouse Loan
Melville Dr.
Warrender Park Terr.
Warrender Park Rd.
Spottiswoode St.
Marchmont Rd.
Marchmont Cres.
Argyle Pl.
Bruntsfield Pl.
Forbes Rd.
Bruntsfield Cres.
Arden St.
Sciennes Rd.
0
200 yards
200 meters

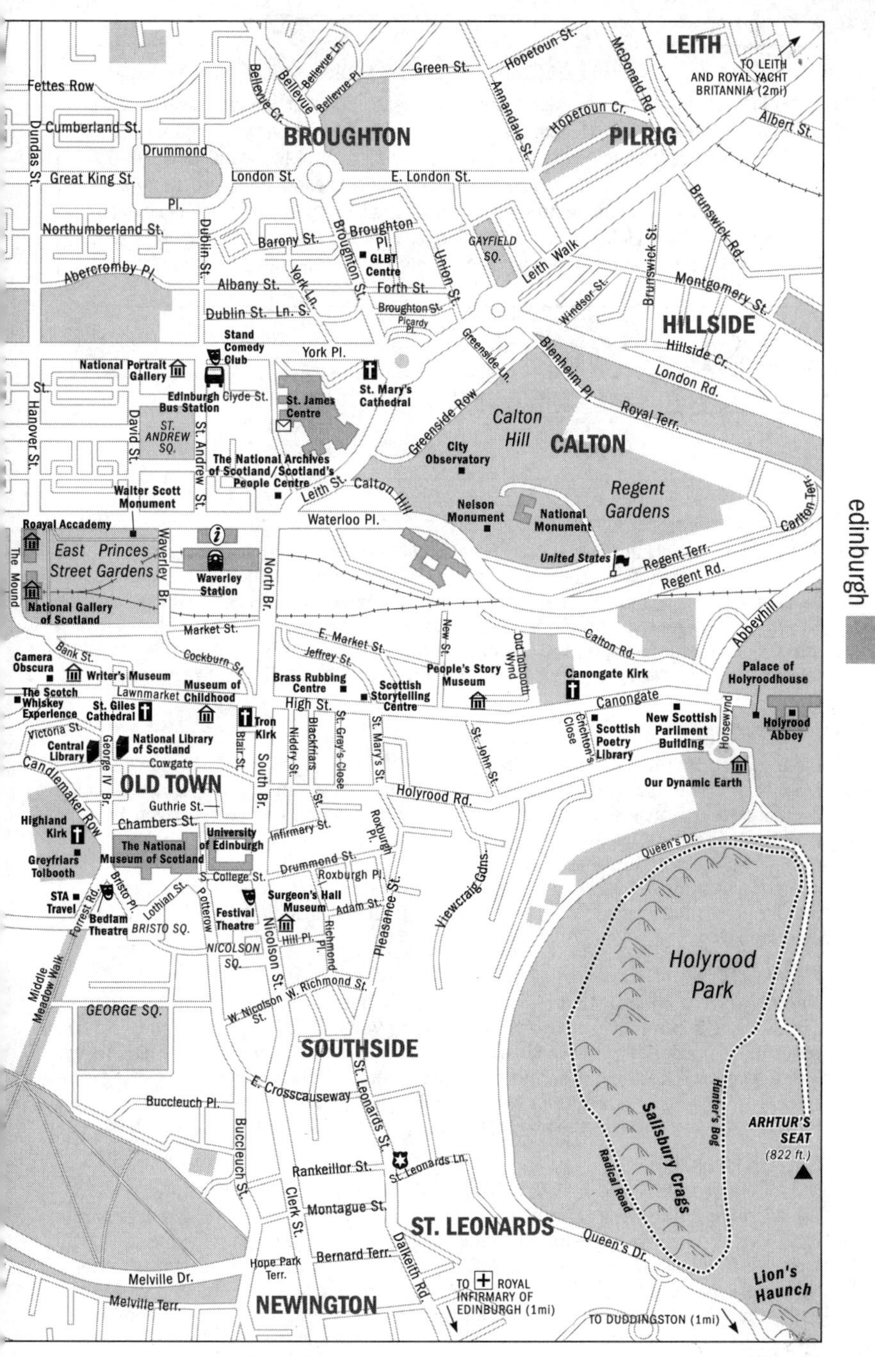
LEITH
TO LEITH AND ROYAL YACHT BRITANNIA (2mi)
BROUGHTON
PILRIG
HILLSIDE
CALTON
OLD TOWN
SOUTHSIDE
ST. LEONARDS
NEWINGTON
Calton Hill
Regent Gardens
East Princes Street Gardens
Holyrood Park
Salisbury Crags
ARHTUR'S SEAT (822 ft.)
Lion's Haunch
Hunter's Bog
Radical Road
GLBT Centre
Stand Comedy Club
National Portrait Gallery
Edinburgh Bus Station
St. James Centre
St. Mary's Cathedral
City Observatory
The National Archives of Scotland/Scotland's People Centre
Walter Scott Monument
Nelson Monument
National Monument
United States
Roayal Accademy
Waverley Station
National Gallery of Scotland
Camera Obscura
Writer's Museum
Museum of Childhood
The Scotch Whiskey Experience
St. Giles Cathedral
Tron Kirk
Brass Rubbing Centre
Scottish Storytelling Centre
People's Story Museum
Canongate Kirk
Palace of Holyroodhouse
Holyrood Abbey
Scottish Poetry Library
New Scottish Parliment Building
Our Dynamic Earth
Central Library
National Library of Scotland
Highland Kirk
Greyfriars Tolbooth
The National Museum of Scotland
University of Edinburgh
STA Travel
Bedlam Theatre
Festival Theatre
Surgeon's Hall Museum
TO ROYAL INFIRMARY OF EDINBURGH (1mi)
TO DUDDINGSTON (1mi)
GAYFIELD SQ.
ST. ANDREW SQ.
BRISTO SQ.
NICOLSON SQ.
GEORGE SQ.
Fettes Row
Cumberland St.
Dundas St.
Drummond Pl.
Great King St.
Northumberland St.
Abercromby Pl.
Dublin St.
Albany St.
Dublin St. Ln. S.
London St.
E. London St.
Barony St.
Broughton Pl.
Broughton St.
York Ln.
Forth St.
Broughton St. Ln.
Picardy Pl.
York Pl.
Union St.
Leith Walk
Green St.
Hopetoun St.
Hopetoun Cr.
McDonald Rd.
Annandale St.
Albert St.
Brunswick Rd.
Brunswick St.
Montgomery St.
Windsor St.
Hillside Cr.
London Rd.
Royal Terr.
Blenheim Pl.
Greenside Ln.
Greenside Row
Bellevue
Bellevue Cr.
Bellevue Ln.
Bellevue Pl.
Hanover St.
David St.
St. Andrew St.
Clyde St.
Leith St.
Calton Hill
Waterloo Pl.
Regent Terr.
Regent Rd.
Carlton Terr.
Waverley Br.
The Mound
North Br.
Market St.
E. Market St.
Jeffrey St.
New St.
Old Tolbooth Wynd
Calton Rd.
Abbeyhill
Bank St.
Cockburn St.
Lawnmarket
High St.
Canongate
Horsewynd
Crichton's Close
St. John St.
Victoria St.
George IV Br.
Cowgate
Blair St.
South Br.
Niddry St.
Blackfriars St.
St. Gray's Close
St. Mary's St.
Holyrood Rd.
Candlemaker Row
Guthrie St.
Chambers St.
Infirmary St.
Roxburgh Pl.
Drummond St.
S. College St.
Roxburgh Pl.
Adam St.
Pleasance St.
Viewcraig Gdns.
Queen's Dr.
Bristo Pl.
Forrest Rd.
Lothian St.
Potterow
Nicolson St.
Hill Pl.
Richmond Pl.
W. Richmond St.
W. Nicolson St.
Middle Meadow Walk
E. Crosscauseway
St. Leonards St.
Buccleuch Pl.
Buccleuch St.
St. Leonards Ln.
Rankeillor St.
Clerk St.
Montague St.
Dalkeith Rd.
Bernard Terr.
Hope Park Terr.
Melville Dr.
Melville Terr.

edinburgh

student life

Edinburgh may not have Glasgow's club scene, but that doesn't mean it isn't Scotland's capital for student life. **The University of Edinburgh** is home to over 24,000 students who, live, study, and drink just south of the **Royal Mile.** Yet the forward-thinking city also has some of Britain's most talented artists, so it's no wonder Edinburgh hosts the world's largest arts festival. Every August, mobs of students from around the globe arrive for **The Fringe,** where you too can hear great music, watch great theater, and make some new best friends. Why settle for a pub?

orientation

call me

The phone code for Edinburgh is ☎131.

Edinburgh's most famous neighborhoods **(Old Town, New Town)** are easily divisible, as they are separated by a large gully which houses **Waverley Station** and **Princes's Street Gardens.** This ravine is bisected by three bridges: **Waverley Bridge, North Bridge,** and **The Mound.** Stockbridge is to the north of **New Town** (walk as if you were heading to Leith and the sea) and **Haymarket** and **Dalry** are in the area west of New Town. **The Meadows, Tolcross,** and the **West End** are all over the hill from Old Town, off toward the south end of town.

OLD TOWN

It's heralded by the giant castle that sits atop the rocky crags that divide Old Town from New Town. It's winding streets are surrounded by four-and-five-story Georgian buildings that house everything from storytelling centers to party-driven hostels. Old Town is where it's at. Its where you'll take the most pictures, it's where you'll drink, sleep, shop, and eat. You'll be hard pressed to find another neighborhood some days—there's just so much to do. However, everyone else knows this too, so make sure to hit up Old Town when you're feeling particularly ready for a tourist onslaught.

NEW TOWN

New Town isn't actually that new. It would have been new when it was designed by James Craig in the 1760s, but by this point it's down pat. Following a simple, grid-like pattern, it's bordered by **Queen Street** to the north and **Prince Street** to the south. **George Street,** a central thoroughfare, runs through the middle. The various intersecting thoroughfare have branches of their own, usually smaller streets with housing or shops. **Rose Street,** which houses the majority of the pubs in New Town, is one of these.

STOCKBRIDGE

Put on your best polo, becase we're heading to the Edinburgh Country Club—Stockbridge. Full of the top tier of upper crust of society, it's a bit like a separate city, with its own restaurants, drinking, and way of life. Forgot your monocle? No worries: find one among the posh leftovers sold in the Stockbridge charity shops. As we always say, if you can't beat 'em, join 'em; if you can't join 'em, wear their cast-offs. When you're not scrounging through the thrift stores, you can meander through the streets, pop into a cafe, stop off at a nice restaurant. or just wander on down through the **Water of Leith.**

HAYMARKET AND DALRY

Haymarket and Dalry are not that pretty, at least compared to the rest of Edinburgh. This may be why it is home to some of the city's cheaper housing. A few good food stops are to be found, and those looking for a night out in this area will find cheap drinks. Be warned, there are some Old Guard pubs here that aren't the friendliest.

TOLLCROSS AND WEST END

Owned and dominated by the huge expanse of green that is the meadows, the West End is nevertheless right in the middle of the city, but you'll be seeing far fewer tourists out this way, except during festival time, when it's impossible to open your eyes without seeing a tourist. **Lothian Road** is home to several great pubs, and continuing up to **Home Street** will take you to the local cinema, **The Cameo.** The **University of Edinburgh** is isolated enough from the city that none of the pubs or bars in the area are student-dominated, but you'll find several full of a distinctly younger crowd. If you fancy it, take a putter and a chipping iron and head out to the **Bruntsfield Links,** where you can play on a 30+ chipping course. Get out to Tollcross and the West End. You'll feel better with less tourists around, and the locals will be more kindly disposed to you for the very same reason.

accommodations

Possibly more so than any other city in the UK, Edinburgh's accommodations options are defined by its neighborhoods. In New Town, you're looking at guesthouses and lodges on the upper end of the price range. Stockbridge has virtually no accommodations to speak of. Old Town is home to the majority of the hostels in town, all of which are right in the center of the action and, for those who wish to keep their distance from the Grassmarket, hostels and hotels fill Haymarket and Dalry, and Tolcross and the West End.

OLD TOWN

ART ROCH HOSTEL — HOSTEL ❶

2 Westport, Grassmarket ☎0131 228 9981 www.artrochhostel.com

The new kid on the block, the Art Roch is already showing everybody else how it's done. With cool, airy dorms featuring sturdy wooden bunks (instead of squeaking metal), this will be a comfortable palce to hit the sack. However, you'll be *really* comfortable when you're hanging out, as the lounge-and-kitchen area is the size of a small airport and fits a kitchen, ping-pong table, TV, chairs and couches, and even a teepee, all with plenty of room to spare.

i Wi-Fi available. $ High-season dorms £12, £80 per week; low-season dorms £9 per night; singles £20. Reception 24hr.

SMART CITY HOSTELS — HOSTEL ❸

50 Blackfriars St. ☎0131 524 1989 www.smartcityhostels.com

Smart City is clean, white, and efficient. Unfortunately, so is a hospital. Catering to families and those looking to "stay at a hostel" without any of the backpackers, the SCH is large, modern and spotless, with an elevator up to every floor and a massive cafe and bar on the ground floor, often with kids chasing each other round the pool table.

Turn onto Blackriars St. from High St. i Breakfast £4.50. Kitchen available. $ 10- to 12-bed dorm £17-30; 4-bed dorm £21-32. Add £2 on weekends. Reception 24hr.

BUDGET BACKPACKERS

HOSTEL ❷

37-39 Cowgate St. ☎0131 226 6351 www.budgetbackpackers.com

A surf-green hostel just a few drunken steps from the pub-filled Grassmarket, Budget Backpackers is a vibrant place that's bound to be packed during the summer with young travelers searching for the next party. If you are staying in (we're not going to say you'll be the only one, but...) there's a DVD and movie rental at the lobby.

i Breakfast £2. Wi-Fi £1 per week. Internet £1 per 30min. Book well ahead of July-Aug for summer reservations. Ⓢ High-season dorms £20-40; low-season dorms £10-20. Reception 24hr.

EDINBURGH BACKPACKERS

HOSTEL ❶

65 Cockburn St. ☎0131 220 1717 www.hoppo.com

You'll get those quads in shape hiking up and down the many **stairs** of this tower. Dorms in EB are basic, but with new people coming in all the time, you're certainly not going to be lacking excursion partners. The hostel's kitchen has cupboards with dry erase markers so you can write down which foods are yours (threat level depends on how hungry the bro in the other room is). The lounge shows *Braveheart* (a *lot*) and stag parties have been known to frequent the place, so be ready for a fun, if raucous, time.

Cockburn St. winds off of High St. i Wi-Fi free. Internet £1 per 30min. Ⓢ Dorms M-F £10, Sa-Su £13-16; singles £25. Reception 24hr.

COWGATE HOSTEL

HOSTEL ❷

96 Cowgate ☎0131 226 2153 www.cowgatehostel.com

Apartment-style hosteling—now *this* is different. In this series of individual little flats, you'll be bunking with a smaller group of people than at a normal hostel. You'll share the same kitchen, bath, and lounge area as a group. For those traveling solo, this will either be a chance to make some good friends or a really quick way of finding out that the people you're staying with are jerks. Regardless, the place is nice. Head to the blue and orange lobby for internet and tourist information.

i Wi-Fi free. Coffee and tea free. Ⓢ Dorms Aug £22, Sept-July £10 per person. Reception 8am-11pm.

HIGH STREET HOSTEL

HOSTEL ❷

8-18 Blackfriars St. ☎0131 557 3984 www.highstreethostel.com

With suits of armor sitting in the windows of the lobby and a spiraling staircase leading down to murals of paradise scenes, the High Street Hostel, dating back to 1985, is the "original backpackers hostel" of Edinburgh. They still have their character-based feel, with pool games on Tuesday nights and burger nights on Friday. Hang out with your hostel-mates at the tables down in the lounge, it's pretty likely somebody's got a **drinking game** going.

i Wi-Fi in lobby. Laundry service £2.50. Ⓢ 15-bed dorms £14-15; 4-bed dorms £15-18; twins and doubles £45-55.

CASTLE ROCK HOSTEL

HOSTEL ❷

15 Johnston Terr. ☎0131 225 9666 www.castlerockedinburgh.com

Actually much closer to the castle than most of the hostels on the Royal Mile, the Castle Rock benefits from its location on the smaller sidestreet Johnston Terráce—it makes for much less tourist traffic. Castle Rock offers nice wooden bunks, a sweet lounge area, and—it's rumored—the option to work off your next night's stay. However, this all depends on whether or not there's work to be had. Make sure to ask before you show up broke.

South of West Princes St. Gardens. i Movie night daily 8pm. Ⓢ Dorms £13-15. Reception 24hr.

NEW TOWN

Accommodations in New Town, with the exception of Caledonian Backpackers, are usually far out of the budget traveler's pocket. However, should you have a little extra cash to spend, there are some fantastic guest houses in the area. No matter where you stay, you'll be near all the action.

CALEDONIAN BACKPACKERS — HOSTEL ❶

3 Queensferry St. ☎0131 226 2939 www.caledonianbackpackers.com

By far the best budget option in New Town, and not just because it's the only one, this 250-bed monster is comfortable and crazy all at the same time. With free Wi-Fi, internet, and kitchen use, as well as a fully stocked bar, it's not cheap fun, it's cheap *and* fun. Check out the beanbag-filled theater, where you can watch free movies anytime on a projector screen. The murals on the walls depict everything from rock stars to penguins, and the hostel has about as wide a range of people stop in.

West End of the city center, across from the Caledonian Hotel. Breakfast 6am-noon. Laundry: wash £1; dry £1. 18+ only. Female-only dorms available. Wi-Fi, Internet, and kitchen free. Dorms £13-20. Reception 24hr.

BALLANTRAE HOTEL — HOTEL ❹

8 York Pl. ☎0131 478 4748

The first thing to greet anyone walking in the door of this hostel is the winding staircase, complete with decorated wooden handrails. The rooms, all with high Victorian ceilings, are very nicely furnished. Big beds are a major plus. Some of the rooms even have fireplaces, though using them will get you in trouble.

Walk west along Queen St., which becomes York Pl. Full breakfast included. Singles £50-75; doubles £70-140; triples £80-160. Prices vary with season.

FREDERICK HOUSE HOTEL — HOTEL ❹

42 Frederick St. ☎0131 226 1999 www.townhousehotels.co.uk

Classy Frederick House has the furniture and the long hallway to prove its status. With nicely furnished rooms (and some really oddly-shaped bathrooms), it's a good choice if you can catch it when it's cheap: prices seem designed to prove just how much they can shift over the course of a year.

Wi-Fi available. Singles £30-160; doubles £50-180. Reception 24hr.

OSBOURNE HOTEL — HOTEL ❹

51-59 York Pl. ☎0131 556 5577 ww.osbournehotel.co.uk

An option that's feasible in the off-season, the Osbourne Hotel offers bare but comfortable rooms in an older building in Edinburgh's New Town. Occasionally you'll find a room that gets great natural light.

Walk west along Queen St., becomes York Pl. Apr-Sept singles £50; doubles £65; triples £78; quads £90. Aug singles £65; doubles £80; triples £90; quads £100. Oct-Mar singles £35; doubles £50; triples £66; quads £78.

QUEEN'S GUESTHOUSE — GUESTHOUSE ❹

45 Queen St. ☎0131 226 2000 www.queensgh.com

This place is wicked expensive, but if you win the lotto and can afford it for a night, it's amazing. It's the only lodging in town the offers the five-star hotel atmosphere and comforts along with the amazingly friendly hospitality of a guesthouse. The managers will make sure that you're comfortable here, which isn't hard considering that your room (no matter which one it is) is gorgeous.

Along the south edge of Queen Street Gardens. Full breakfast included. Singles £60-120; doubles £170-300; family suite £145-199; executive suit £190-275.

ELDER YORK GUESTHOUSE — GUESTHOUSE ❸

38 Elder St. ☎0131 556 1926 www.elderyork.co.uk

Providing relatively constant prices throughout the year, the Elder York Guesthouse benefits from three distinct things: a prime location a few yards away from the bus station, a beautiful and shining breakfast area, and large, airy rooms. And then there's the wonderful hospitality of new owners Harry and his wife, who are doing a fine job of running the place.

Right off of York Pl. and St. James Pl. Cancellations in July-Aug should give 1 week notice. Aug £60 per person; Sept-Jul £40 per person.

HAYMARKET AND DALRY

THE HOSTEL — HOSTEL ❷

3 Clifton Terr. ☎0131 313 1031 www.edinburghcitycentrehostels.co.uk

Haymarket and Dalry's hostel, "The Hostel" (this is going to get confusing, isn't it?) is spotlessly clean. Having just undergone a massive renovation and refurbishment, its carefully color-coordinated lounge space has pool tables and a large flatscreen TV as well as free tea and coffee. Bear in mind, though, that The Hostel is intent on maintaining its stellar appearance, as evidenced by the long list of rules on the wall.

Right in Haymarket. Continental breakfast £1. Towel rental £1, £5 deposit. 16-bed dorms £7-12; 5-bed dorms £12-14; 3-bed dorms £14-20. Reception 24hr. Lounge open 8am-11pm.

PIRIES HOTEL — HOTEL ❹

4-8 Coates Garden ☎0131 337 1108 www.pirieshotel.com

A nice, Georgian hotel located among a string of other similar ones, Piries has a small bar in the lobby and those paper rings that hold the pillows in place. It's the little things that count, right?

Right in Haymarket. Wi-Fi available for a fee. Doubles in summer £80; in winter £60.

TOLLCROSS AND WEST END

ARGYLE BACKPACKERS — HOSTEL ❷

14 Argyle Pl. ☎0131 667 9991 www.argyle-backpackers.co.uk

Argyle is a great place for those who like to keep the party time outside and the cool, lounging-around time in the hostel. A beautiful red kitchen connects to a covered skylight area that in turn links to an outdoor seating area. The lounge space has two computers for guest use as well as a big-screen TV and wood-burning fireplace.

In Aug, prices generally increase £5 and min. 3-night stay. M-F 10-bed dorm £13.50; 6-bed dorm £15; 4-bed dorm £16.50; doubles £48. Weekend 10-bed dorm £15.50; 6-bed dorm £17; 4-bed dorm £18.50; doubles £52. Reception 9am-10pm; call ahead to arrange a late check-in.

CRUACHAN GUESTHOUSE — GUESTHOUSE ❹

53 Gilmore Pl. ☎0131 229 6219 www.cruachanguesthouse.co.uk

Another nice Guesthouse on Gilmore Place, the Cruachan has high-ceilinged, comfortable rooms. It may not be decorated with an eye for contemporary style, but the owner is nice. Plus, that floral pattern on your bed won't show up when you turn out the light.

Breakfast included. Rooms £60-80.

KINGSVIEW GUESTHOUSE — GUESTHOUSE ❸

28 Gilmore Pl. ☎0131 229 8004 www.kingsviewguesthouse.com

You can look for hummingbirds buzzing about the entryway garden as you eat breakfast in the front room of this quaint little Victorian guesthouse. The rooms are quaint but comfortable, with tiny desktop flatscreens.

Dog-friendly. High-season £40; low-season £27.50.

OLD TOWN

THE SCOTCH WHISKY EXPERIENCE

TOUR

354 Castlehill, the Royal Mile ☎0131 220 0441 www.scotchwhiskyexperience.co.uk

Beginning with a carnival ride in giant barrels (it's a good thing that this happens before the drinking), you'll be explained the process of distilling single-malt whiskey by a ghostly apparition with a serious penchant for the elixir. Then after a short look at the barrel-making process, you'll be ushered into the tasting room, where an informed guide will offer you smells representative of each whiskey-making region in Scotland. At the end of that segment of the tour, you'll select the whiskey you want to taste and head to the display room, which houses the Diageo Claive Vidiz Collection of whiskeys, almost 3500 of them. There you'll learn how to properly enjoy your whiskey and have the opportunity to purchase a bottle from the store, should you find one that you really enjoy. Good luck walking home!

By the bottom of West Princes St. Gardens. Silver tour (basic) £11.50, students and seniors £20, children £6, family £27. Gold tour (advanced) £20, student and senior £17.45. The Collection Tour £20. Open daily 10am-6:30pm. Last tour daily 5pm.

NATIONAL LIBRARY OF SCOTLAND

LIBRARY

57 George IV Bridge ☎0131 623 3700 www.nls.uk

Yes, it's a working research library and you can get a borrower's card (free with valid ID), but who wants to do that on holiday? Instead, make a stop to check out the exhibit space in the library's large entryway. Each focusing on a different author or theme, the different displays are put up in a large, attractive space that makes it a bit like a museum instead of a library.

There's a cafe open in the library as well. Library open M-F 9:30am-8:30pm, Sa 9:30am-1pm. Cafe open M-F 9:30am-8:30pm, Sa 9:30am-1pm, Su 2-5pm.

BRASS RUBBING CENTRE

ARTS CENTER

Trinity Apse, Chalmers Close, 42 High St. ☎0131 556 4364

Located in what seems like a one-room cathedral complete with sky-high echoey ceilings and stone gargoyles, is this oddball activity. Pick out a brass plates of Pictish designs *(prices vary according to size)* and the center will supply you with all the materials you need to do a rubbing and create your own take-home artwork. Work on anything from a plate as big as your hand *(£1)*, to a life-size Pictish knight *(£20)*.

Cash only. Open M-Sa 10am-noon and 1-5pm. Last rubbings at 4:15pm. During festival open M-Sa 10am-noon and 1-5pm and Su noon-5pm.

ST. GILES CATHEDRAL

CATHEDRAL

St. Giles Cathedral, High St. ☎0131 225 9442

The stonework on the outside is finer than your granny's lace doily, and the inside's just as beautiful. With glowing stained-glass windows that cast enormous rainbows onto the walls in the late morning and a massive wooden organ near the center of the building, St. Giles is so photo-worthy that you'll find yourself looking like the ultimate tourist and trying to get a shot of everything. However, you won't be the only one, and the constant flow of tourist traffic means that St. Giles is hard-pressed for that calming atmosphere associated with cathedrals. Still, get someone to take your picture in front of a jewel-like window and you'll be more colorful than Captain Planet at Chuck E. Cheese's.

Tours available, inquire inside. Free. Open May-Sept M-F 9am-7pm, Sa 9am-5pm, Su 1-5pm; Oct-Apr M-Sa 9am-5pm, Su 1-5pm and for services.

SCOTTISH STORYTELLING CENTRE
CULTURAL EXPERIENCE

43-45 High St. ☎0131 556 9579 www.scottishstorytellingcentre.co.uk

Possibly one of a kind, the Scottish Storytelling Centre is just that: a place where people tell tall tales. Featuring Scotsmen and women from all over as well as professional storytellers from Canada, Japan, Africa and beyond, the center also runs storytelling workshops in case you'd like to make sure you have something to say about your trip other than, "Yeah, Scotland. It was cool."

£4-10. Open Jul-Aug M-Sa 10am-6pm, Su noon-6pm; Sept-June M-Sa 10am-6pm. Open later when events are on.

THE WRITER'S MUSEUM
MUSEUM

Ladystairs House, Ladystairs Close, The Royal Mile ☎0131 529 4901

Housed in the majestic Ladystairs mansion is a sanctuary of the works and personal belongings of three of Scotland's greatest authors: **Sir Walter Scott, Robert Burns,** and **Robert Louis Stevenson.** From mannequined displays to locks of hair and writing desks, it's great for a quiet wander whether you've read the collected works of all three or are simply interested in discovering why *Treasure Island* was so damn good.

Half-hidden in one of the small, tunnelled "close" passages off of the Royal Mile. Free. Open M-Sa 10am-5pm. During the festival, M-Sa 10am-5pm, Su noon-5pm.

THE NATIONAL WAR MUSEUM (NWM)
MUSEUM

Hospital Square, Castle Hill ☎0131 247 0413 www.edinburghcastle.gov.uk

Located inside the Castle grounds, the NWM is "free," but only after you've shelled out the cash for a ticket to the castle. Still, it's definitely worth a stop, whether your tastes run to old decorative swords or old, decorative admiral's pistols. It turns out that the evolution of the Scottish soldier and his weaponry is a smorgasbord of the instruments of death.

Free. Open in summer 9:45am-5:45pm; in winter 9:45am-4:45pm.

CAMERA OBSCURA AND THE WORLD OF ILLUSIONS
VISUAL ATTRACTION

Camera Obscura, Castlehill, The Royal Mile ☎0131 226 3709 www.camera-obscura.co.uk

Just across the street from the Scottish Whisky Experience is this slightly more kid-friendly option. The actual "camera obscura," a combination of reflecting lenses and mirrors, presents a live-action, birds-eye view of the city. However, if it's overcast, your picture will be dimmer (heads-up: you're in Scotland), and if you're not on the bottom level of seating, chances are high that some little kid's noggin is going to be eagerly "obscuring" yours. The rest of the exhibition is a series of floors full of holograms, illusions, and distortions. They even have a maze of mirrors. This sight scores high on the "kids-take-ability" scale but might be a bit boring for the single traveler.

i Ask the desk for the next Camera Obscura showtime upon arrival. £9.25, students and seniors £7.25, ages 5-15 £6.25. Open daily first 2 weeks of June 9:30am-6pm, second 2 weeks of June 9:30am-7pm; July-Aug 9:30am-7:30pm; Nov-Mar 10am-5pm; Mar-May 9:30am-6pm.

THE NATIONAL MUSEUM OF SCOTLAND
MUSEUM

NMOS, Chambers St. ☎0131 247 4422 www.nms.ac.uk

Housed in an enormous modern "castle" complete with winding staircases and enormous open spaces, this museum features nine floors to check out. Here's the crazy part: that's with half it closed for a massive, £46,000,000 renovation that is going to take it "into the 21st century." The exhibits here are as wide ranging as you would expect, from "The Kingdom of the Scots," featuring powder horns and ancient Pictish stonework, to "Scotland: A Changing Nation," showing Scotland in places you'd never expect—inventors, innovators, and even Ewan McGregor. (Seriously, who knew he was Scottish?) As a final stop, hit up the rooftop terrace for some awesome castle photo ops. But beware: you'll be fair

game for the Camera Obscura tours up there. They're watching.
3 daily tours at 11:30am, 1;30, 3:30pm. Free. Open daily 10am-5pm.

EDINBURGH CASTLE — CASTLE

Edinburgh Castle, Castle Hill ☎0131 225 9846 www.edinburghcastle.gov.uk

It's the first thing you see on the skyline in Edinburgh and one of the most arresting structures on the planet: the Edinburgh Castle just can't be beat. From the top you'll get all sorts of brilliant photo ops, and there are several different places where you can snap that perfect pic. However, everyone else in town has the exact same idea, so don't be surprised if you find yourself jockeying for frame space. The **"Honours of the Kingdom"** (or the Scottish Royal Jewels) exhibit funnels you along a winding display of murals and mannequins before finally reaching the jewels. If the place is busy, this can take up to 40min., so be warned. Stop by at the top of the hour to see the changing of the guard at the front entrance.
Within West Princes Street Gardens. Wheelchair access patrons should phone in advance to set up a tour. £14, seniors £11.20, children £7.50. Open in in summer 9:30am-6pm, winter 9:30am-5pm. Last entry 45min. before close.

NEW TOWN

NATIONAL GALLERY OF SCOTLAND — MUSEUM

The Mound, just across Princes St. ☎0131 624 6200 www.nationalgalleries.org

At the National Gallery, even the rooms in which the artwork is hung seem designed to make you take your time. The place is octagonally designed and painted a royal red. You'll not want to rush your way through this collection of pre-1900 works, including some fantastic pieces by Raphael and El Greco.
Free. Special exhibits £5-10. Open M-W 10am-5pm, Th 10am-7pm, F-Su 10am-5pm.

NATIONAL TRUST SCOTLAND — NATIONAL TRUST, GALLERY

28 Charlotte St. ☎0844 493 2100 www.nts.org.uk

The group in charge of conserving cultural sites, artifacts, and buildings in Scotland, National Trust Scotland keeps its head office here, where it also maintains a small gallery full of works by 20th-century Scottish artists, a bookshop, a restaurant, and a cafe.
Gallery open M-F 9am-4:30pm. Cafe, bookshop, and restaurant open M-Sa 9:30am-5pm.

ST. ANDREWS SQUARE — PARK

At the end of George St.

It's not the most "interactive" of sights, but it is a perfectly enjoyable park with long benches, lots of grass and even a little coffee hut right there in the square. Check out the giant pillar (the **Melville Monument**) in the center. It was the first edifice erected with an iron balance crane for all the crane enthusiasts reading.
Open daily 8am-8pm.

PARISH OF ST. ANDREW AND ST. GEORGE — CHURCH

13 George St. ☎0131 225 3847 www.standrewsandstgeorges.org.uk

Whether you're coming to pray, visit the stained glass, or simply escape the sounds of traffic, the Parish of St. Andrew and St. George offers a beautiful, calming atmosphere. An ampitheater-style church, it's got several rows of seating on the lower levels and a wrap-around balcony above.
Free. Open M-F 10am-3pm.

ST. MARY'S CATHEDRAL — CATHEDRAL

York Pl.

If nothing else, come to "St. Mary's" to see the beautiful kings with angel wings, and perhaps some of the biggest organ pipes we've ever seen.
Free. Open daily 8am-7pm.

THE NATIONAL ARCHIVES OF SCOTLAND — NATIONAL ASSEMBLY

17a Charlotte Sq. ☎0131 535 1400 www.nas.gov.uk

A small collection about dusty old documents inhabits the much larger National Archives. Luckily, feather quills and old ink blotters are cooler than you would think. Look for the facsimile reproductions of government documents ascertaining the existence of the Loch Ness monster on the display boards.

i Water cooler available. Free. Open M-F 9am-4:30pm.

SCOTLAND'S PEOPLE CENTRE — HERITAGE SITE

2 Prince's St. ☎0131 314 4300 www.gro-scotland.gov.uk

Do you have a kilt hiding in the underwear drawer for "special occasions?" Come find out for sure if you have some Scottish blood running through your veins at Scotland's People Centre, where you can access their electronic birth, death, and marriage records to try and trace your family back to its roots.

i Records run 1855-2008. Geneology services £10. Open M-F 9am-4:30pm.

THE GEORGIAN HOUSE — MUSEUM

7 Charlotte Sq. ☎0844 493 2100 www.nts.org.uk

Essentially the perfect replica of a Victorian household, the Georgian House tour starts in the basement, where you can see a 16min. introductory video that's as informative as it is boring. Move on to the kitchen and cellar to see old sugar and booze respectively. Moving up the stairs and floors you'll see drawing and dining rooms as well as a bedroom with so much floral print that the guys from the "Home and Design Network" would have a cardiac arrest.

£5.50, concessions £4.50, family £15, members free. Open daily 10am-6pm. Last entry 30min. before close.

THE WALTER SCOTT MONUMENT — SCALABLE MONUMENT

West Princes St. ☎0131 529 4068

The tower dedicated to Scotland's most famous author sticks up out of the ground and extends—well, a really long way up. You can make the climb to the top of this famous Edinburgh landmark, though it's worth bearing in mind that there are 287 steps to the top, and it's a squeeze as you near the summit. You also may have to wait for a while to get down from the top: there's only room for around six people on the stairs and no way to get down if people are coming up.

STOCKBRIDGE

GLENOGLE SWIM CENTRE — SWIMMING

Glenogle Rd., Stockbridge ☎0131 343 6376 www.edinburghleisure.co.uk

Having just undergone an £18,000,000 renovation, the Glenogle Swim Centre is totally state of the art, with a 25m pool, a sauna, and a steamroom. The best part? It's all available for public use. The best best part? It's all available for public use, for cheap. They also have a gym and fitness classes. Makes you re-consider your wild idea to go down and swim in the freezing Atlantic, doesn't it?

Swim costs £4. Sauna and steamroom £.60. Open M-F 7am-10pm, Sa-Su 8am-6pm.

STOCKBRIDGE MARKET — MARKET ARCHWAY

At the junction of St. Stephens Pl. and St. Stephens St., Stockbridge

Before you go grab your all-hemp, recycled grocery bag and head off to get your fix of farmers' market veggies, it's worth knowing that the Stockbridge *Market* no longer exists—it's been replaced by houses. However, the **old archway,** with its engraved lettering and protruding lamp is still there, and it makes for quite a picturesque scene. Grab the camera, snap a few quick shots and stroll down through the pathway, now covered by trees. Or just head off to the art gallery next to the entrance.

WATER OF LEITH NATURE WALK

A beautiful way to spend an afternoon or a date is to take a walk along the paved paths that line this small river, flowing through New Town and Stockbridge. Green trees and foliage hang over the path, providing some shade for when you want to sit down on one of the many benches that line the water. If you follow it long enough, you'll come up underneath the massive, arched underbelly of the Dean Bridge.

THE ROYAL BOTANIC GARDENS BOTANIC GARDENS

20a Inverleith Row ☎0131 552 7171 www.rbge.org.uk

A center for plant research and conservation, this place is nuts (seeds and spores too) for plants. The entrance and visitors centre is beautifully impressive, with a glass facade and white, spinning windmill in front. Entrance to the gardens themselves is free, but to get in to the Glasshouses for the real, misty green experience, you'll have to pay.

Glasshosues £4, concessions £3, children £1, family £8. Open daily Apr-Sept 10am-6pm, Mar-Oct 10am-5pm.

TOLLCROSS AND WEST END

THE MEADOWS PUBLIC PARK

Located on the southwestern end of town, the Meadows are a beautiful, welcome respite from the honking cars and blabbing people inside the city. With wide-open, grass-covered fields intersected by paths covered by the shade of trees, it's no wonder that during the festival the Meadows become a hotspot for people to gather and throw frisbees, barbecue, and generally just have a great time. There are also 16 tennis courts and a playground on one end.

i If you want to make sure of your spot on a tennis court during the summer months, call ahead to reserve at ☎0131 444 1969. Courts open Apr-June M-F 4-9pm, Sa-Su 10am-6pm; July-Aug M-F 9am-9pm, Sa-Su 10am-7:30pm; Sept M-F 4-9pm, Sa-Su 10am-6pm.

food

Edinburgh, like any heavily touristed city, has just about any kind of cuisine you might be hankering for. So if you haven't quite gotten up the gumption to try haggis yet, try some fantastical veggie creations over at **David Bann's** or a huge plate of beef curry over at the **Mosque Kitchen.** You can do a wine and cheese night at the hostel if you stock up at **I. J. Mellis** in Stockbridge. In short, the possibilities are endless.

OLD TOWN

DAVID BANN VEGETARIAN ❸

56-58 St. Mary's St. ☎0131 556 5888 www.davidbann.com

At this all-vegetarian restaurant, you're not going be suffering through your salad. How's a watercress, beetroot, and goat cheese salad sound? Good? We thought so. Enjoy your meal and maybe one of the excellently spicy **Bloody Marys** in the attractive, modern interior.

Entrees £15-20. Open M-Th 11am-10pm, F 11am-10:30pm, Sa 10am-10:30pm, Su 10am-10pm.

LE CAFÉ ROYALE CAFE ❷

274 Cannongate St. ☎0131 652 3534

A people watcher's paradise, the entire front of this café swings open in good weather, leaving you with a covered fresh-air view of the street outside. A few quaint round tables, local artwork on the walls and a central support beam that looks like it was ripped out of the Titanic complete the ensemble. Grab a

coffee—it's strong and fresh. Let the watch begin.
All coffee under £2. Open daily 8am-around 8pm.

ELEPHANT CAFÉ CAFE, BAR ❸
21 George IV Bridge ☎0131 220 5355 www.elephanthouse.biz
Harry Potter and company were birthed here on scribbled napkins. The cafe serves both coffee and booze, making you wonder which one **J.K. Rowling** was drinking when she had her "inspiration." Choose yours. They also have a selection of pastries and pies.
£5 min. Coffee £1.50-2.75. Beer £3 per bottle. Open M-F 8am-11pm, Sa-Su 9am-11pm.

RISTORANTE GENNARO ITALIAN ❸
64 Grassmarket St. ☎0131 226 3706
The best way to pick out an Italian restaurant is obvious—look for the one that's full. The second method requires a quick peek at the menu—is it in Italian? **Ristorante Gennaro** fulfills both of these requirements, seeing its tables fill every night and a menu that has English translations. Dim lighting and a deep red color scheme accentuate the fancy feel, but students as well as a pre-theater crowd are known to turn up.
Appetizers £1.50-9. Pizza £8-12. Fish entrees £12-14, meat entrees £14-19.50. Open daily noon-11pm.

CAFÉ TRUVA CAFE ❷
231-253 Cannongate St. ☎0131 556 9524 www.cafetruva.com
Cafes on the Royal Mile are many, but there may not be any that can rival Café Truva in terms of great outdoor seating. With small tables set out underneath the stone arches of the entryway, the cafe boasts a view that overlooks the Royal Mile along a row of picturesque houses. The food is Turkish and Mediterranean, but they also have a great selection of truffles and chocolates.
Coffee £1.50-2.10. Open M-Th 8am-9pm, F-Su 8am-10 or 11pm.

THE LITTLE INN SANDWICHES ❶
1 Johnston Terr. ☎0775 661 4407
One of the smallest places on the Royal Mile (the only seating is a little bench outside the shop), it's probably so small because it's selling sandwiches at cheap prices on some prime real estate. Grab a soup and a baguette *(£1.90)* or a tasty milkshake for next to nothing *(£2.40).*
Breakfast rolls £1.40-2.70. Open daily 6:30am-3pm. Open late during festival.

MAXIE'S BISTRO RESTAURANT ❸
5b Johnston Terr. ☎0131 226 7770 www.maxies.co.uk
To get to Maxie's you'll have to descend two sets of stairs flanked by paintings of old cigarette ads and one remarkably square-jawed woman (Maxie?) to the basement of the builiding. You can sit inside there, but if you're smart you'll immediately walk up another set of stairs to the terrace. Overlooking the city 50 feet above the ground, it's the perfect place to enjoy your well-cooked meal.
Starters £3.50-7. Entrees £7.95-16.95. Open daily 11am-11pm.

THE BOTHY SANDWICHES ❶
37 Grassmarket ☎0131 225 2322 www.thebothydeli.co.uk
Don't pass on the great toasted sandwiches *(£1-3)*—and they're big, guys—and amazing lemon-lime slushies *(£1-2)* from this small, easily passable place on Grassmarket. The owner is unduly kind to her customers, and you're sure to feel more than welcome from the time you arrive to the time you leave satisfied.
i 10% student discount with ID. American milkshakes £1.30. Coffee £1.25-1.75. Open daily 7am-5pm, with later hours during the summer.

NEW TOWN

THE UNDERGROUND CAFÉ (TUC) — CAFE ❶

34 Eden St. ☎0131 624 7161

A surprisingly great local dive—you'll literally be going down some steep stairs to get to it—located just a few steps away from the Edinburgh bus station, TUC has a charming interior and delicious food. Check out the local artwork on the walls or browse through the festival information resting conveniently on top of an old piano in the entrance.

Soup with bread £1.75-2.75. Open M-F 7:30am-4pm, Sa 8:30am-4pm.

WOLFITS — RESTAURANT, DELI ❶

200 Rose St. ☎0131 225 5096

We have no idea why this restaurant is called "Wolfits." What we do know is that this small establishment sells good food cheap. Soups and buttered baguettes go for under £3. There's not *really* an atmosphere, but you can watch music videos on the television while you wolf it down.

Open daily 7:30am-4pm.

INDIAN THALI RESTAURANT — RESTAURANT ❸

1-3 York Pl. ☎0131 557 9899

With a deep, royal red interior filled with flower vases, this isn't your typical stop-off for a quick bite. The Bollywood music's playing, but if that doesn't drag you in, you can grab some takeaway—it comes with free rice.

Entrees £8-11. Breakfast sandwiches £1-3. Open M 5:30-11pm, Tu-Sa noon-2:30pm and. Open daily 5:30-11pm.

THE CONAN DOYLE — PUB GRUB ❷

71-73 York Pl. ☎0131 557 9539

In the neighborhood where **Sir Arthur Conan Doyle** himself used to live, there's memorabilia—Sherlock Holmes and otherwise—galore in this resto pub. A good value for a full cooked breakfast (veggie or not). Come by on the weekends when it's more of a pub and receive the same kind of value on drinks. Also, enjoy the comfy armchairs galore.

Breakfast from £5. Open M-Th 9am-11:45pm, F-Sa 9am-1am, Su 12:30pm-midnight.

BROWN SUGAR — CAFE ❶

39 Queen St. ☎0131 623 7770

There aren't really any attention-grabbing words like "arresting" or "insane" to describe Brown Sugar. And that's what makes it great. Located on a corner just across the street from the park-like Queen's gardens, it's a spot where you can grab a nice coffee, sit back, munch on some homemade **banana bread** and watch the world go by. How's that for arresting?

Americano £1.90. Cadbury's hot chocolate £1.60. Open M-F 7am-3:30pm, Sa 10am-4pm.

MIRÓ CANTINA MEXICANA — MEXICAN ❸

184 Rose St. ☎0131 225 4376

It's a *fiesta* in here! Or at least, that's what the paint job would have you believe. Bright yellows and wild patterns cover the inside (and outside) of this eatery. A little more "Mexican" than "Taco Bell," this place offers a big plate of nachos with beans, jalapeños, melted cheese, salsa, sour cream, and guacamole *(£5)*. Even the outdoor seating has a festive paint job.

Selection of Mexican beers £3.10-3.25. Open daily in summer noon-10:30pm; in winter noon-2:30pm and 5:30-10pm.

JUICE ALMIGHTY — COFFEE, JUICE BAR ❸

7a Castle St. ☎0131 220 6879 www.juicealmighty.com

The bright, neon interior of this smoothie shop is matched by the equally bubbly staff. If the healthy fruit smoothies aren't fortifying enough for you, buy a large and receive a shot of wheatgrass *(£1)*. They also serve hot foods, such as soups and baked potatoes.

Coffee only £1 until noon. Open M-F 7:30am-7pm, Sa 8am-1am, Su 10:30am-6pm.

FINNEGAN'S SANDWICH SHOP SANDWICHES ❶

28 Queensferry St. ☎0131 226 5005

A great stop for a quick bite if you're hungry, you can get your food in one of two ways: quick or quicker. The quick way: order from the counter and have your food made on the spot. The quicker way: grab a freshly-made sandwich from off the shelf and take it to go.

Sandwiches £2-2.40. Homemade soups £1.50. Open M-F 7am-3pm.

MUSSEL INN SEAFOOD ❸

61-65 Rose St. ☎0131 225 5979 www.mussel-inn.com

Serving mussels brought in from the west lochs of Scotland and the Shetland Isles, the Inn only dishes out food that's fresh and savory. As if the natural taste wasn't enough, they serve pots with Moroccan, shallot, and bleu cheese flavors as well. It's a crowded place, so you may have to "mussell your way inn" on the weekends. Or book ahead.

0.5kilo pot of mussels £4.80-5.80, 1kg. pot of mussels £9.60-11.60. Open M-Th noon-3pm and 5:30-10pm, F-Sa noon-10pm, Su 12:30-10pm.

HENDERSON'S WINE BAR ❸

94 Hanover St. ☎0131 225 2131 www.hendersonsofedinburgh.co.uk

What began in 1962 as a way for the Henderson family to sell off the surplus produce at their farm and earn a little cash has continued—and then some. Now featuring a deli, bistro, wine bar, and art gallery, Henderson's is a full-blown industry. However, they still maintain their organic, high quality standard.

i Check out their alternative location at John's Church at the end of Prince's St. Lunch specials £9-10. 2 side salads £2.40. Organic lager £3.10. Open M-Sa 8am-10:30pm.

STOCKBRIDGE

BELLS DINER DINER ❸

7 St. Stephen St. ☎0131 225 4673

We at **Let's Go** are not picky about burgers. For us, as long as it's hot, has a bun, and isn't from a franchise with a "drive-thru," we're pretty happy. However, there are occasions in one's life where one is exposed to burger greatness, and Bells Diner is one of those experiences. The burgers cost a bit more than you'd usually pay *(£8-10)* but are well worth the expenditure. Also, they come with a full plate of chips (fries) and a selection of six different dipping sauces..

i Reservations for weekend evenings recommended. Open M-F 6-10pm, Sa noon-10pm, Su 6-10pm.

MADELEINE CAFE ❷

27b Raeburn Pl. ☎0131 332 8455

An intensely modern, intensely chic cafe with the most futuristic bathrooms you've ever seen (seriously, it's like NASA designed the loo...), Madeleine earns the thumbpick for the macaroons. These light wafery cookied sandwiches are sweet but tart, in flavors like vanilla, chocolate, raspberry, and mango *(all for £.80 each)*. You can't stop eating them. Seriously, we tried. You can't (mumble crunch yum!) stop...

Cakes and coffees £1.40-5. Open T-Sa 10am-5:30pm, Su 11am-5:30pm.

GREEN GROCER'S GROCERY ❶

11 Deanhaugh St. ☎0131 332 7384

Get your fresh apples, nectarines, carrots, and any other type of fresh munch-

able you may be interested in here. Head inside the store for the more sinful foodstuffs, such as chocolates and soft drinks.
Open daily 6:30am-9pm.

SAN MARCO ITALIAN ❹
10-11 Mary's Pl. ☎0131 332 1569
An Italian bistro, San Marco's offers all your Italian staples, such as an *insalata caprese* with sliced mozzarella and tomato with fresh basil and olive oil *(£4.95)* and pizzas *(£10)*. The meat dishes will run you a bit more *(£15-25)*. This is a bank-buster, but you're sure to leave with a belly full of soul-satisfying pasta.
Open M-F 5:30-11pm, Sa noon-2pm and 5:30-11pm, Su 12:30pm-midnight.

PIZZA EXPRESS PIZZA ❷
1 Deanhaugh St. ☎0131 332 7229 www.pizzaexpress.com
A pro in the art of family dining, Pizza Express always has children in high chairs with happy, pizza-filled faces. A large, airy blue and white establishment, this Pizza Express may have some of the best outdoor seating in Stockbridge, right along the water of Leith. Get out there to escape the constant calls of, "No, junior, we keep our napkins in our laps."
Pizza £6.50-10. Open M-Th and Su 11:30am-10:30pm.

I. J. MELLIS DELI ❸
6 Bakers Pl. ☎0131 225 6566 www.mellischeese.co.uk
Yeah, you may be paying the same for some cheese and cured meat as you would for a big plate of fish and chips, but where else are you going to find *Pyrenees Chevre* goat cheese? Not at the chippies you aren't.
Open M-F 9am-6:30pm, Sa 9am-6pm, Su 10am-5pm.

PECKHAM'S DELI ❷
48 Raeburn Pl. ☎0131 332 8844 www.peckhams.co.uk
Half cafe with sit-down coffees and an outdoor terrace and half specialty food and booze store, Peckham's attractive warm interior is matched by the friendliness of the staff and the surprising affordability of its merchandise. Get a freshly-baked loaf of bread *(from £1)*, and then supplement it with any number of cheeses, salamis, or quiches.
Open M-Sa 8am-11pm, Su 9am-10pm.

CAFÉ PLUM CAFE ❶
96 Raeburn Pl. ☎0795 781 1703
Plum is a tiny, purple and white cafe down on Raeburn with one hell of a coffee and tea selection. In a country that plays cricket, a game in which taking a break for afternoon tea is actually part of the procedure, you'd think you'd usually be able to find a little variety; Café Plum provides this variety, with 12 different teas and coffee that are brought in weekly, ensuring their freshness.
House salad £2.75. Coffee £1.30-2.50. Full breakfast £5.50. Open M-W 8am-5pm, Th-F 8am-6pm, Sa 9am-5pm, Su 10:30am-5pm.

HAYMARKET AND DALRY

GOOD SEED BISTRO BISTRO ❸
100-102 Dalry Rd. ☎0131 337 3803 www.goodseedbistro.com
The new kid on the block, the Good Seed Bistro is doing everything right: classy interior, a relaxed vibe. They serve weekday lunch specials *(2 courses, £7.95)*. Interested in coming during the mornings? Coffee and cakes are cheap, too *(£4.50)*.
i Wi-Fi available. Open M-Th noon-10pm, F-Sa noon-11pm, Su noon-4pm.

CLIFTON FISH BAR FISH AND CHIPS ❶
10 Clifton Terr. ☎0131 346 8723 www.clifton-fish-bar.justeat.co.uk
A tiny fish 'n chips joint with two slap-happy fry cooks who are more than ready

to play on the job, the Clifton Fish Bar sells cheap pizzas, calzones, and chips. Order the "munchy box," with chicken pakora, vegetable pakora, donner meat, chips and a can of soda *(just £8.99).*

10 in. calzone £4.-5.50. 7 in. pizza £3. Open M-Th 4:30pm-1am, F-Sa 4:30pm-2am, Su 4:30pm-1am.

XIANGBALA HOTPOT — RESTAURANT 3

63 Dalry Rd. ☎0131 313 4408

A slightly different take on restaurant culture, the Xiangbala Hotpot *(£15 per person)* is all you can eat for 2hr. With a silver boiling pot in the middle of the smooth black tables, meats, seafood, and veggies are introduced into boiling broths and then eaten.

Open daily 3-11pm.

SCOOBY'S — SANDWICHES 2

95 Morisson St. ☎0131 221 1877

A DIY (do-it-yourself) sandwich shop with a BWU (banter with us) attitude. Scooby's does a mean spicy tuna mayo or spicy meatball soup. Or if none of the stuff on the board strikes your fancy, just take a look at the ingredients and go nuts.

Soup and sandwiches from £2.50. Open M-F 6:30am-3pm.

PG'S SANDWICH BAR — SANDWICHES 1

127 Morrison St. ☎0131 228 8763

Another small shop that's seriously lacking in decor, but damn if it ain't cheap and delicious! Get a sausage and haggis roll or a sandwich. They also do mac and cheese should you begin feeling nostalgic...

Sausage and haggis rolls £.85, sandwiches £3.50. Open M-F 7am-2pm.

MORRISSON BAKERY — BAKERY 1

147 Morisson St. ☎0131 229 6471

You'll be able to know you're getting close to Morrisson Bakery by the smell. However, unlike when you know you're getting close to someone who's had too much to drink, this smell is delicious. With fresh cakes and donuts as well as meat pies, it's an excellent stop at any time of the day or night (considering they're open for most of both, being a bakery and all).

All pastries under £1. Pies £1-2.

THE SIZZLING SCOT — SCOTTISH 3

103-105 Dalry Rd. ☎0131 337 7744 www.sizzlingscot.co.uk

A good local spot that fills with the smells of good food and the hum of conversation as the night goes on, this restaurant uses the best in Scottish ingredients—McSween's haggis, Aberdeen Angus, and Orkney Island ice cream. Try it with some toffee or hot fudge.

Soups £3. Burgers £9.50. Entrees £7.95-11.50. Open M 5-10pm, Tu-Sa noon-2pm and 5-10pm, Su 5-10pm.

TOLLCROSS AND WEST END

THE MOSQUE KITCHEN — CURRY 1

19a West Nicholson St.

The guys at the Mosque Kitchen don't mess around. There's not "atmosphere" to speak of—just some covered outdoor cafeteria seating—but you don't need it, as you'll be too busy staring at your giant plate of delicious rice and curry to care.

Veggie curry plate £3.50, meat £4.50, chicken £3. Open daily noon-8pm; closed F 1-1:45pm for prayers.

VICTOR HUGO CONTINENTAL DELICATESSEN — DELI 2

26-27 Melville Terr. ☎0131 667 1827 victorhugodeli.com

A true combination of deli and cafe, Victor Hugo's has little booths along the walls perfect for snuggling up with a coffee. The inside is a great place to wonder when the pissing rain is going to stop. Or if you've got a slightly more benevolent attitude towards the weather, you can sit outside and enjoy the rain—from underneath the awnings of course. With locals who've been coming back since 1940 as well as students who come for the belly-filling mac in cheese, it's everybody's favorite. Try the award-winning Ramsay of Carluke bacon roll *(£2.85)*.

Teas £1.60. Open M-F 8am-10pm; Sa-Su 8am-8pm. During festival, open daily 8am-11pm.

BRAZILIAN SENSATION BRAZILIAN ❶

117-119 Buccleuch St. ☎0131 667 0400 www.braziliansensation.co.uk

Brazilian Sensation is a smallish but elaborately decorated restaurant that can't get enough of its South American namesake. Even the mannequin in the window is decked out in Brazilian gear. Serving rolls and sandwiches as well as a large variety of tropical fruit smoothies *(£3.50)*.

Baguettes £2.75. Open M-Sa noon-4pm; during the festival open daily noon-4pm.

PETER'S YARD CAFE ❸

27 Simpson Ln. ☎0131 229 5876 www.petersyard.com

Peter's Yard, a Swedish style cafe housed right in the heart of the University of Edinburgh, serves hot cinnamon buns as well as *Kladdkaka* (a Swedish chocolate cake). The cafe is housed in a clear glass box, so those sitting outside on the balcony may **spy** on those sitting inside and vice versa. Unfortunately, it seems that most of the people coming to Peter's Yard aren't interesting enough to spy on.

Kladdkaka £2.70. Coffee £1.75-2.95. Open M-F 7am-6pm, Sa-Su 9am-6pm.

TEA TREE TEA CAFE ❷

13 Bread St. ☎0131 228 3100 www.teatreetea.com

Ordering at Tea Tree Tea is a bit like seeing your grandmother for the first time in a long time: you'll be bombarded with questions about how you're doing. Except that the baristas here have fewer wrinkles and won't pinch your cheeks. Order yourself a fantastic chai latté, and sit down among the green walls while you try and remember what your grades were last semester so you can tell your new friend behind the counter.

A pot of tea, sandwich, and cake under £7. Open M-F 7am-7pm, Sa-Su 9am-7pm.

MADE IN FRANCE FRENCH CAFE ❷

5 Lochrin Pl. ☎0131 221 1184

"A cute little French place on the west end..." See? It even sounds adorable. With French posters and framed Monet prints, it's a nice place to enjoy the tiny quiches and tarts. You can also pick up some wine or preserves from their shelves and take them home. *La vie...c'est tres belle.*

Baguettes from £2.60. Open M-F 8am-4pm, Sa 10am-4pm.

MONSTER MASH CAFÉ BRITISH ❷

20 Forest Row ☎0131 225 7069

This one's a belly-buster. Seriously. The fare here's typical British staples—sausages and mash but cooked to perfection and served with one of several gravies. The big thing though is just that: the huge plates. Come by at dinnnertime and skip breakfast the next day.

1 sausage and mash £7, 2 sausages and mash £9. Open daily 9am-10pm; during festival open 9am-11pm.

THE TREEHOUSE CAFÉ CAFE ❷

44 Leven St. ☎0131 656 0513

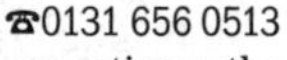

At this great local hangout for students, couples, and locals, sometimes the owner even comes by to sing a few tunes. It's no surprise then, that there are records and musical scores hung on the walls. More unexpectedly, there's great coffee and delectable cakes to be had with all that folky goodness. Come by on

Sundays to hear live folk music *(from 3-4:30pm).*
Coffee from £1.50-1.75. Open M-Sa 8am-5pm, Su 9am-5pm.

THE NEW LEAF ORGANIC GROCERIES 3
23 Argyle Pl. ☎0131 228 8840
Featuring a selection of organic, natural, and fair-trade items ranging from juice blenders to granola bars, The New Leaf offers a 5% discount for students and even has a little play area in front. The latter's probably not for you though...
i Gluten- or dairy-free items available. Prices vary. Open M-Sa 9:30am-6pm.

nightlife

Edinburgh, despite being the "prettier little sister" to Glasgow, has nowhere near the same club scene. This town full of **pubs and bars,** however, buzzes happily on the weekends and skyrockets in intensity during the festivals in August. Each specific neighborhood will have its own variations on the classic pub, from the tourist-heavy areas along the Royal Mile, to the strange collection of odd and local watering holes on **Rose Street** in New Town, to the posh, hip new bars in Stockbridge.

Drinking in Scotland, and in Edinburgh especially, isn't about "going on the piss" (though that is a part of it), but about finding the right place for yourself, your group, your night, and your state of mind—no matter how much that last one may be altered throughout the night.

OLD TOWN

BANNERMAN'S BAR, MUSIC VENUE
212 Cowgate ☎0131 556 3254 www.myspace.com/bannermanslive
With a subterranean, half-barrel auditorium for the live acts, the soundproofing in Bannerman's is so good, if you want to sit in the bar and have a friendly chat, you can...while a rock show goes on next door. A wide selection of beers and cask ales are available, but if you want to try the house special, go for the **"Jager U-boat."** What is a Jager U-boat, you ask? Just place your fingers in your ears, grab a small bottle of Jager with your teeth, tilt your head back and—*Whoosh!* hear the bubbles of the ocean as you decend...into a drunken stupor. Nah, you'll be fine, and Bannerman's is a kick-ass place to hang out.
i Live shows £4-8 cover. Jager U-boat £2. Pints £3.40-3.65. Open daily Sept-July noon-1am; Aug noon-3am.

WHITE HART INN PUB
34 Grassmarket ☎0131 226 2806
The Grassmarket's oldest pub (est. 1516), the White Hart Inn retains its olden feel, with faded photographs on the walls, beer steins hanging from the ceilings, and one slightly creepy bust of William Burke by the door. Famous patrons of the pub include Scotland's favorite poet, **Robert Burns.** Grab a pint and see if your poetical stylings are loosed.
Pints £2.85-4. Spirits £2.95-12.49. Open M-Th 11am-midnight, F-Sa 11am-1am, Su 11am-midnight.

GREYFRIARS BOBBY'S BAR PUB
30-34 Candlemaker Row ☎0131 225 8328
Named after one of Edinburgh's local legends—Greyfriars Bobby, a terrier so faithful that slept at his owner's grave for the next 14 years until his own death. The citizens here buried him next to his beloved owner and the loyal pooch entered annals of local legend. There's a statue of Bobby outside this pub, and it's a popular photo spot for tourists of all nationalities. The pub itself is a pretty

standard alehouse, but if you want to contemplate Bobby's loyalty from across the street you can sit outside and have a beer.

Ales £2.80-3. Spirits £3. Open M-Sa 11am-midnight, Su 11:30am-midnight.

BLACK BULL PUB

12 Grassmarket St. ☎0131 225 6636

The floors, the walls, and the ceiling, the place look like the inside of an oak tree. A really big oak tree. The Black Bull is enormous, with ample room for you and a party of any size to find seats in one of the warmly lit booths or on a plush leather sofa. Serving real cask ales, it's more a hang-out than a dance bar, but there are DJs on the weekends.

i Folk session M. Live bands play most Th. Spirits £2-2.60. Pints £2.60-3.45. Open M-F 11am-1am, Sa-Su 10am-1am.

THE BANSHEE LABYRINTH CLUB

29-35 Niddry St. ☎0131 558 8209 www.thebansheelabyrinth.com

Built into the side of a hill and just above Edinburgh's famous "haunted vaults" (the Auld Reekie tours actually end here), the Banshee Labyrinth is a maze of stairs and tunnels, low-ceilinged cave-like rooms and Addams Family inspired bars. There are three bars and seven rooms, a pool hall and a cinema, plus a pole-dancing area. Note the sign that absolves the bar from any injuries you may sustain from your "sexy dancing."

Spirits with mixer £2.50. Pints £2.70-3.40. Open daily 12:30pm-3am.

SIN CLUB

207 Cowgate ☎0131 220 6176 www.club-sin.com

A recently-remade club and one of the Cowgate's newest nightlife options, Sin lives up to its name, getting crazy during the week, on the weekends, whenever. With more fog and spinning lights than that alien spaceship in *Men In Black* and a massive downstairs dance floor, you can head up to the mezzanine level if you—ahem—have just one sip too many and need to find your friends again.

Cowgate. Bottles £2. Pints £2.49. Open daily 10pm-3am; during festival 1pm-5am.

WHISTLE BINKIES 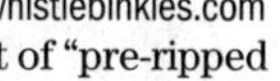 BAR, LIVE MUSIC

46 Southbridge ☎0131 557 5114 www.whistlebinkies.com

A popular place to see smaller live acts, Whistle Binkies has a sort of "pre-ripped jeans" feel—there are lots of old barrels and comfortable ratty stools, but the holes in the wall with brick underneath are definitely stylized. Framed photos of famous musicians are carefully hung and illuminated, though notably not behind the stage, where things might get messy.

i Live music M-F, Su nights. DJ Sa nights. Pints £3.40-3.60. Spirits £1.60-3.30. Open M-Th 5pm-3am, F-Su 1pm-3am.

THE CITY CAFÉ BAR, MUSIC

19 Blair St. ☎0131 220 0125

A hotspot for students and young Edinburgers to party at before heading out to the clubs. Styled like a '50s soda fountain, it's got retro red countertops and a second bar downstairs if you just can't wait to really get your groove on.

i Coffee and food available during the day. Wi-Fi available. Pints £3-4. Open daily 11am-1am. During the festival, open daily 11am-3am. DJs play W-Sa.

CABARET VOLTAIRE CLUB

36-38 Blair St. ☎0131 220 6176 www.thecabaretvoltaire.com

One of Edinburgh's most popular nightlife spots, Cabaret Voltaire has a line that begins leading out the door of the Cab Volt as soon as the club opens up around 11:30pm. The queue grows longer throughout the night. Located just above the "haunted vaults" used by the Ghost tours, the actual club has much of that low-ceilinged, brick, domed feel. Lots of red neon keeps things a little naughty without being strip-club worthy.

Cover up to £12. Open daily 7pm-3am.

NEW TOWN

CITIZEN SMITH

BAR

168 Rose St. ☎0131 225 5979

The only independently owned and run bar on Rose Street, Citizen Smith is a haven for all things folk, blues, rock, alt rock, and indie. There's live music every night on the somewhat improvised stage, but try to show up in August for their own, private "Woodstock," where 50 bands play over the span of three days. Come in, sit down, and admire the giant cardboard arachnid on the ceiling.

Pints £3.30. Open daily in summer 4pm-1am; in winter 2pm-1am; during festival 1pm-3am.

ROSE AND CROWN

PUB

170 Rose St. ☎0131 225 4039

In this decent bar with molded ceilings live music is on three nights a week here. Other than that and the occasional DJ, however, it's a pretty chill place, simply a nice place to get a cider and sit out in the sun.

Pints £3-3.30. Spirits £3.15-4. Open daily 11am-1am.

JEYKLL AND HYDE BAR

BAR

112 Hanover St. ☎0131 224 2002 www.eeriepubs.co.uk

A dark and foreboding—who are we kidding, this place is meant to look creepy on purpose. It's called the Jeykll and Hyde Bar! Still, with iron chandeliers and high-backed "creeeeepy" chairs, they do an okay job. Dracula could have lived here, but he would have been drunk on Bloody Marys the whole time.

i Bring your passport, the license isn't going to work here. Pints £1.50-3. Mixed drinks £5. Open M-Sa noon-1am, Su 12:30pm-10pm.

QUEEN'S ARMS

PUB

49 Frederick St. ☎0131 225 1045

Having recently undergone a massive refurbishment, the Queen's Arms is classier than ever. It's still got that traditional feel, with a padded bar, bookshelf full of classics and wiry chandeliers, but it's all got that new-pub smell. Take it all in over one of their hand-pulled ales. Can we say anymore about its classy classic-ness?

i The Queen's Arms is the 1st pub in Scotland to have Blue Moon on draft. Pints £3-3.50. Spirits £2.75 and up. Open M-Sa 11am-1am, Su 12:30pm-1am.

BLACK ROSE TAVERN

BAR

49 Rose St. ☎0131 220 0414 www.blackrosetavern.com

If you've ever grown a beard to impress the guys in Pantera or ever bought a guitar with more sharp ends than your Swiss Army knife, you'll enjoy the Black Rose. With "rock karaoke" on Wednesdays and a major skeleton obsession and various tattoos among the staff, the Black Rose is great for rockers of all types. **Jagermeister** is the self-proclaimed house wine. What more do you want?

i Open mic night on T. Quiz on W just before the karaoke. Pints £2.80-3.65. Spirits from £1.20-1.60. Open M-Sa 11am-1am, Su 12:30pm-1am.

EL BARRIO

BAR, CLUB

47 Hanover St. ☎0131 220 6818 www.elbarrio.co.uk

New Town's only club is rowdy enough on its own. Open until 3am everyday, this basement of brightly colored walls and Latin music becomes packed with people on the weekends, as the photos on the walls will attest. Laugh at the most intoxicated people you see on the walls and then come back next week to make sure you haven't joined their ranks.

Spirits and mixer £3-3.80. Pints £3.50. Open daily noon-3am.

ROSE STREET BREWERY
PUB

55-57 Rose St. ☎0131 220 1227

A local's pub, the Rose Street Brewery actually used to be a brewery, but has since been promoted to a place where you can drink it rather than make it. The restaurant upstairs is a popular spot for tourists and serves a mean steak. A plain but comfortable interior, a wooden entry space will take you down a pair of step onto a strangely kilt-like carpet.

i 4 ales available; 2 constant, 2 rotating. Pints £2.70-3.40. Spirits £2.55. Bar open M-Th 11am-11pm, F-Sa 11am-1am, Su 11am-11pm. Restaurant open daily noon-10pm.

LORD BODO'S BAR
BAR

3 Dublin St. ☎0131 477 2563

You could walk by Lord Bodo's bar and say to yourself, "Why, that doesn't look like much of a bar." The exterior's not much to look at, it's true, but the inside is seriously classy, with brown suede chairs and stained wood all around. Grab a martini and get out the tux Bond fans.

Pints £2.70-3. Mixed drinks £3.50-4. Open M-Th 11am-11:30pm, F-Sa 11am-1:30am, Su 11am-11:30pm.

DIRTY DICK'S
PUB

159 Rose St. ☎0131 260 9920 dirtydicksedinburgh@gmail.com

I spy, among the bric-a-brac housed in Dirty Dick's: a sea of upside-down golf clubs, a picture of **Alfred Hitchcock,** somewhat creepy teddy bears, a full pint of beer stuck upside down on the ceiling, and an accordion.

Pints £3.30. Spirits £2.60. Open M-Sa 11am-1am, Su noon-1am.

STOCKBRIDGE

THE ANTIQUARIAN
PUB

68-72 St. Stephens St. ☎0131 225 2858 www.theantiquarybar.co.uk

Its entrance may be hidden at the bottom of a small stairwell in Stockbridge, but this bar let's its people and atmosphere do the talking. A great local crowd with a jovial attitude hang out here, and if you come by on Tuesday night around 8pm you can get in on one hell of a poker game. You probably won't win (some of these guys are legit), but you will have a lot of fun at this bar.

Spirits £2.10-3.50. Pints £3-3.55. Open M noon-11pm, T-W noon-midnight, Th-Sa noon-1am, Su noon-12:30am.

AVOCA BAR
BAR

4-6 Dean St. ☎0131 315 3311 www.avocabarandgrill.co.uk

A regulars' watering hole, Avoca is your typical food and booze stop. The building is quite nice, with more of those Victorian moldings we've seen so much of, but the bar itself is fairly spare on decoration. A nice place to come in and have a private chat.

Pints £3-4.15. Spirits £2.70. Open M-Th 11am-midnight, F-Sa 11am-1am, Su 11am-midnight.

HAMILTON'S
BAR

16-18 Hamilton Pl. ☎0131 225 8513 www.hamiltonsedinburgh.co.uk

With lots of posh, leather couches and very "in" '60s pop art on the back wall, it's no surprise to see that everyone in Hamilton's is well-dressed, mild-mannered and sipping on glasses of wine. Should you like to go and join them, you'd be wise, though it's certainly not necessary, to spiff yourself up a bit. Look at you, you need to wash behind those ears before you go out drinking!

Pints £3.30-4.50. Spirits £3.10. Open daily Aug 9am=3am; Sept-Nov 9am-1am; Dec 9am-3am; Jan-July 9am-1am.

ST. VINCENT BAR
BAR

11 St. Vincent St. ☎0131 225 7447 www.stvincentbar.com

From the outside the St. Vincent Bar looks like a normal pub...and actually, it looks pretty normal from the inside as well. However, it's a *Let's Go* favorite in terms of pub quirks: St. Vincent's allows you to purchase two pints of your favorite ale "to go." That's right. Tell 'em you feel like drinking at home, and they'll give you a lovely carton of beer. Now that's brilliant.

Pints £3.04-3.85. Open M-Sa 11am-1am, Su 12:30pm-1am. During festival open until 3am.

HECTOR'S
BAR

47-49 Deanhaugh St. ☎0131 343 1735 www.hectorsstockbridge.co.uk

A hip, trendy bar in the heart of Stockbridge, Hector's burns the candles all night long, until the wax falls on the tables. It's got a classy yet laid-back feel, thanks to wraparound couches complete with funky pillows and a dark purple interior that enhance the aura. A heavily local patronage keeps things from getting too fancy-schmancy. Hector's stocks a wide selection of wines, ales, and beers as well as an organic cider.

Pints £3-3.50. Organic cider £3.10. Open M-W noon-midnight, Th-F noon-1am, Sa 11am-1am, Su 11am-midnight.

THE STOCKBRIDGE TAP
PUB

2-6 Raeburn Pl. ☎0131 343 3000

A great local place right next to Hector's, the Stockbridge Tap sees everyone from old men to young girls come in to enjoy the hefty ale selection. If you've got the time and the liver for it, try to drink the spectrum.

Spirits £2.40. Pints £3-3.30. Open M-Th noon-midnight, F-Sa noon-1am, Su 12:30pm-midnight.

HAYMARKET AND DALRY

CARTER'S
BAR

185 Morrison St. ☎0131 228 9149

Unlike the concept pubs of Haymarket and Dalry, Carter's has an artsy feel accentuated by the candle wax dripping down the stairs and the mismatched couches and chairs in the loft. A place for live music, they set up small shows in the downstairs space. Come on Wednesday for Bluegrass. As the sign painted on the wall says, "Are you gonna piss about all day?—Or are you coming in?" Do the latter.

i Music begins 9-9:30pm. Spirits £2.30-3.30. Pints £2.90-3.20. Open M-Sa noon-1am, Su 12:30pm-1am.

THE MERCAT BAR
PUB

28 West Maitland St. ☎0131 225 8716 www.mercatbar.com

A pub that's renowned locally for it's grub, the Mercat Bar has owners that'll swear it's a bar before a restaurant. Still, with classy tables illuminated under an orange glow and only the lights from the taps to signal out the bar, that'll be up to you to decide.

i Be on the lookout for daily specials. Spirits from £2.20. Pints £3.20-3.70. Entrees £9-12. Open daily 9am-1am; during the festival daily 7:30am-1am.

DIANE'S POOL HALL
PUB, POOL HALL

242 Morrison St. ☎0131 228 1156

"Diane's" is a bit of a strange name for this pub, considering it's mostly men who frequent it. However, Haymarket could just be lacking in female pool sharks. With nine tables all for £.20 a game, it's a good place to get snookered.

Pints £2.10-2.60. Spirits around £1.55. Cash only. Open daily 8am-midnight.

RYRIE'S PUB

1a Haymarket Terr.

A traditional, old-fashioned bar, Ryrie's lays out its whiskeys in a long line in a glass case above the bar, making your choice even more difficult. If you're not in for booze, they serve pub grub until 7pm. People-watching's not really an option, as the windows are old stained glass.

Pints £2-3.35. Spirits £3.25. Open M-Sa 9am-1am, Su 12:30pm-1am. Kitchen open until 7pm.

HAYMARKET BAR PUB

11-15a West Maitland St. ☎0131 228 2537

A strange combination of sports bar and tasteful gastropub, the Haymarket bar has pictures of muddy rugby players about to smash each others' faces hung next to tasteful pastel paintings of bucolic country scenes. Come by for a quiz on Sunday or for any sporting event on television. If you get there early enough you might be able to score one of the little booths by the windows or the small upstairs loft.

Pints £2-3. Spirits £2.09-3.09. Open M-Sa 9am-midnight or 1am, Su 12:30pm-midnight.

TOLLCROSS AND WEST END

THE LINKS BAR SPORTS BAR

2-4 Alvanley Terr. ☎0131 229 3854

A sports bar with all the typical trimmings—pool tables *(£1 per game)*, pictures of sports greats, cases full of old sporting memorabilia such as ancient golf clubs and stinky old shoes (thank God they're in a case), and a name like The Links Bar (what more do you need?). For those who really don't care what Jack Nicklaus's handicap was during the 1982 British Open, the other half of the bar is an ultra-modern, wooden tube with blue lighting.

Pints £2.95-3.75. Spirits £2-2.50. Open daily 9am-1am.

HENDRICKS BAR

1a Barclay Pl. ☎0131 229 2442

A classy young-professionals bar with a decor that could be put up in an interior design catalogue. Thistle wallpaper and little black lamps above the bar illuminate the LBDs that show up on the weekends. No live music or quiz over here though guys. This place is fancy.

Pints £3.15-4.50. Mixed drinks 2-for-1 M-Th £5.49. Open M-Th 11am-11pm, F-Sa 11am-1am, Su 11am-11pm.

CUCKOO'S NEXT BAR

69 Home St. ☎0131 228 1078

A smaller, student bar with a tiki feel, the booths are lined by a row of bamboo pieces and the mirrors on the walls are framed by what looks to be a bird's nest gatherings. Unless you're really going nuts here though, it looks like the only thing making the name pertinent is the empty bird cage at the back of the bar. There are quizzes on Mondays, musical bingo on Thursdays and an open mic night the second Wednesday of every month.

Pints £2.50-3.50. Mixed drinks from £3.50. Open daily noon-midnight or 1am.

THE EARL OF MARCHMOUNT BAR

22 Marchmount St. ☎0131 662 1877

A talker's bar, the Earl of Marchmount fills up with students around 9pm during the year. There's also a really great outdoor covered seating area. We said talker's bar, but that must be when they're not playing music: jazz on Sundays at 3:30pm, Celtic music every other Monday, Bluegass on the odd Tuesday, and DJs on Saturday. Maybe you'll just shut up and listen to the music.

Pints £3. Thistle Cross (strong cider) £4.25. Open M-Sa 11am-1am, Su 11am-midnight.

THE BLUE BLAZER PUB

2 Spittal St. ☎0131 229 5030

A heavily local place, the Blue Blazer refuses to let rules cramp their sense of humor. As the sign above the door says, "We at the Blue Blazer take our drinking very seriously. Anyone who appears to be having fun will be asked to leave." We think they're kidding. When we were there, people laughed and talked in front of the wood fireplace.

Pints £3.10-3.40. Open Sept-July M-Sa 11am-1am, Su 12:30pm-1am; Aug M-Sa 11am-3am, Su 12:30pm-3am.

THE ILLICIT STILL BAR, PUB

2 Broughton St. ☎0131 228 2633 www.theillicitstill.com

Badass names accompany badass bars. Don't let the purple exterior fool you; the Illicit Still keeps its empty malt whiskey boxes on display like trophies of war. A small entrance opens up into a large bar with long red benches so you'll to lean against during the comedy show every Tuesday night at 8pm.

i Quiz Su 8pm. Bottled beer from £1.80. Spirits £2.50-3.50. Open daily 4pm-1am; during festival 4pm-3am.

BENNET'S BAR PUB

8 Leven St. ☎0131 229 5143

A great local haunt right next to the **King's Theatre** (currently under renovation), Bennet's has seen actors act out pantomines over pints (in preparation for an upcoming show) or nip in for a quick one during intermission (apparently the beer-laden rehearsals didn't turn out well). A beautiful older pub, it's separated from the busy street by a pair of double doors with flowered stained glass. A giant wooden gantry houses the booze behind the bar.

Spirits £1.70-2.20. Pints £2.80-3.20. Open M-Sa 11am-1am, Su 5pm-11pm or midnight.

arts and culture

Edinburgh becomes the world capital for arts and culture every August during the city's **Fringe Festival.** The Fringe publishes its own program of activities, available in hard copy from the Fringe office and online. A world-famous orgy of the performing arts, the Fringe Festival encompasses shows in theater, dance, comedy, opera, and more. The festival was begun in 1947 when eight rebellious theater groups not invited to perform at the International Festival decided that "the show must go on." The organization was formalized, and thus, the world's largest arts festival was born. *(180 High Street. ☎131 226 0026. www.edfringe.com.)* For all listings and local events during the rest of the year, check out *The List* (*www.list.co.uk £2.25*) available at newsstands.

MUSEUMS AND GALLERIES

SURGEON'S HALL MUSEUM OLD TOWN

Surgeon's Hall, Nicholson St. ☎0131 527 1649 www.rcact.ac.uk

Full of some of the nastiest body parts perfectly preserved in formaldhyde and the wickedest-looking tools you've ever seen, this museum showcases every little bit of the history of surgery, and some stuff that must just be there to shock. The exhibit detailing the gruesome story of **Burke** and **Hare,** who murdered innocent citizens in order to receive the cash for supplying early doctors with bodies, actually has a pocketbook made from Burke's very **human skin.** Before we had photography we had painting, and there are several *technically* beautiful oils of festering wounds. What can we say? It's great. Just don't come on a full stomach.

Disabled visitors will want to call in advance to arrange a visit. £5, concession £3, family (2 adults, 3 children) £15. Open Sept-July M-F; Aug M-F 10am-4pm, Sa-Su noon-4pm.

HENDERSON GALLERY — NEW TOWN

4 Thistle St. Ln. ☎0131 225 7464 www.hendersongallery.com

With around nine full rotating exhibitions a year, this isn't just some gallery set up by a sandwich shop, come check out the attractive loft space where paintings from all sorts of artists, from graffitti to fine art.

Out the back door of Henderson's. Ask a member of the staff. Open Sept-July M-Sa 11am-6pm; Aug Tu-Sa 11am-6pm.

ALPHA ART — NEW TOWN

52 Hamilton Pl. ☎0131 226 3066 www.alpha-art.co.uk

With a collection of original and limited-edition prints from artists that are local, UK-based and international, Alpha Art has a huge range of stuff. Great oils, silk-screens, and sculptures abound.

Open T-F 10am-6pm, Sa 10am-5pm, Su noon-5pm.

SCOTLANDART.COM — NEW TOWN

1 St. Stephen Pl. ☎0131 225 6257 www.scotlandart.com

With over 1000 original pieces between their Glasgow and Edinburgh branches, as well an extensive online selection (they've got computers right there in the gallery if you want to check it out) the guys at www.scotlandart.com are there to make sure you find what you're looking for. For those of us on a traveler's budget, however, it may suffice simply to browse around.

Browsing free. Artwork expensive. Open T-F 10:30am-5:30pm, Sa 10am-5:30pm, Su noon-5pm.

RM ART — NEW TOWN

51 St. Stephens St. ☎0797 357 4175 www.rosiemackenzieart.com

The most affordable of the art galleries in Stockbridge, Rosie Mackenzie Art has a nice selection of unique, handmade jewelry as well as sculptures and paintings from various local artists. That T-Rex with the Gibson Les Paul necklace that we picked up was fantastic.

Prices vary. Open W-Sa noon-5pm, Su 1-4pm.

MUSEUM OF CHILDHOOD — OLD TOWN

42 High St. ☎0131 529 4142

This museum showcases a collection of old childrens' toys including building blocks and bassinets, plus onecreepy "Kids Forever" sculpture. The kids in the Museum of Childhood, however, seem less interested in the exhibits and more interested in the toys at the gift shop. Go figure.

Free. Open M-Sa 10am-5pm, Su noon-5pm. Last entry 30min. before close.

MUSIC

HMV PICTURE HOUSE — WEST END

31 Lothian Road ☎0131 221 2280 www.edinburgh-picturehouse.co.uk

A beautiful place to watch things get messy, the HMV Picture House sees the likes of Imogen Heap and Less Than Jake, plus other big names, on the reg. On Thursday nights they do the intense, "Octopussy Club night," popular with students because of its £1 drinks. Who would have guessed?

Box Office M-F 12pm-2pm, Sa-Su 12pm-4pm.

THE BONGO CLUB — CANONGATE

37 Holyrood Road ☎0131 558 8844 www.thebongoclub.co.uk

Half club, half live music venue, half arts space...wait, how many halves is that?

Bongo does it all, throwing raging parties on the weekends in their jungle-esque main room, with a stage for bands and live DJ set-up. Head upstairs during the day to check out the revolving art exhibitions in the café.

Prices vary. Cover entrance F-Sa £3-12 depending on the act. Café open 1pm-7pm. Club open 11pm-3am. Open 7pm-10pm when music gigs are on.

THE JAZZ BAR OLD TOWN

1A Chambers St. ☎0131 220 4298 www.thejazzbar.co.uk

This is a perfect venue to hear blues, hip-hop, funk, and all that jazz. The Jazz Bar hosts not one, but three shows most nights: "Tea Time" *(Tu-Sa 6-8:30pm)* is acoustic, "The Early Gig" *(daily 8:30-11:30pm)* is jazzy and "Late N' Live" *(daily 11:30pm-3am)* is funky and electric.

Off of South Bridge St. Cover cash only. Cover after Tea Time £1-5. No cover during Tea Time. Open M-F 5pm-3am, Sa 2:30pm-3am, Su 7:30pm-3am; during Fringe Festival until 5am.

DANCE

GHILLIE DHU WEST END ❸

2-4 Rutland Pl. ☎0131 222 9930 ghillie-dhu.co.uk

A heavily-touristed bar in what used to be a church building, the room upstairs (with an organ, high columned ceilings and 3 awesome chandeliers) still does wedddings. More importantly, however, it's the space used for the **traditional Scottish jigs** and dancing that are put on. Head on over if you feel like getting down to some serious bagpipe music.

Pints £2.95-3.60. Spirits £2.75. Whiskeys £2.75-17.50. Open M-F 8am-3am, Sa 10am-3am, Su noon-3am.

THEATER

THE BEDLAM THEATRE OLD TOWN ❶

116 Bristol Pl. ☎0131 225 9893 www.bedlamtheatre.co.uk

The oldest student-run theater in Great Britain, the Bedlam (named after a nearby mental institution) is full of fun and crazy performances, several by the **Edinburgh University Theatre Company (EUTC).** The "Improverts," the University Improv group, who play every Friday at 10:30pm and every night at 12:30am during the festival, shouldn't be missed.

Those requiring disabled access should provide advance notice. Tickets £3.50-5, students usually receive a £1 discount. Aug-May, just knock and someone will be there to greet you.

EDINBURGH PLAYHOUSE OLD TOWN

18-22 Greenside Pl. ☎0844 847 1660 www.edinburghplayhouse.org.uk

Originally built to be a cinema, which it remained for 40 years, the Edinburgh Playhouse underwent a massive renovation in 1993 and now revels in its status as one of the most popular theaters in the city.

Ticket prices vary. Box office open performance M-Sa noon-8pm; non-performance days M-Sa noon-6pm.

USHER HALL WEST END

Usher Hall, Lothian Rd. ☎0131 228 1155 www.usherhall.co.uk

The massive, white and royal-red concert hall has seen everyone from **Ella Fitzgerald** to Beck. Book online or visit their premises in person to inquire about upcoming shows.

Ticket prices vary. Box office open M-Sa 10am-5:30pm. Su shows open 1pm-1hr. before the event.

FESTIVAL THEATRE OLD TOWN

13-29 Nicholson St. ☎0131 529 6000 www.eft.co.uk

Holding shows throughout the year, the Festival Theatre really gets going around festival season in August. With 1927 seats and the largest stage in Scotland, it's huge and a great deal for students who are able to score standby tickets for just £10. Call after noon the day of the show to inquire.

Average show tickets £20. Box office open performance days M-Sa 10am-8pm; non-performance days M-Sa 10am-6pm.

FILM

THE CAMEO

WEST END ❷

38 Home St. ☎0871 902 5723 www.picturehouses.co.uk

Scotland's second oldest cinema and one of the last to show independent, foreign, and cult flicks, the Cameo is a great place to see something other than the next steaming pile of whatever James Cameron has whipped up. Check the calender to see when the monthly showing of the "so-bad-its-good" cult classic, "The Room" is playing, then head off to the bar after the movie gets out.

£6.80, matinee £5.80, student concession £4.50-5.20. Open M-Th 11am-midnight, F-Sa 11am-1am, Su 11am-midnight.

shopping

CLOTHING

W.M. ARMSTONG AND SONS VINTAGE EMPORIUM

OLD TOWN

83 Grassmarket ☎0131 220 5557 www.armstrongsvintage.co.uk

The largest vintage store in Britain has three physical shops and an online store. Still, if you're shopping online, you're likely to miss the giant papier-mâché trapeze artist dangling upside down in one of the Grassmarket location's crowded display rooms. You'll probably also miss out on the £1 box, full of all sorts of fun odds and ends. And you miss out on the sunglasses, boots, dresses—hell, just go to the store already.

Student discounts available. Open M-Th 10am-5:30pm, F-Sa 10am-6pm, Su noon-6pm.

W.M. ARMSTONG AND SONS VINTAGE EMPORIUM

STOCKBRIDGE

64-66 Clark St. ☎0131 667 3056 www.armstongsvintage.co.uk

Hey! You guys already did this one! Guess again: Armstong's is so good they've got multiple stores, and their Clark street location is just as excellent as their Grassmarket spot. This one's got WWI military helmets next to tiny pairs of leiderhosen, elevator shoes, and pimpwear—you know the drill. Awesome.

Prices vary. Open M-W 10am-5:30pm, Th 10am-7pm, F-Su 10am-6pm.

ELAIN'E VINTAGE CLOTHING

STOCKBRIDGE

55 St. Stephens St. ☎0131 225 5783

A well-known and fun establishment down in Stockbridge, Elaine's got herself a collection of vintage stuff ranging from the 1920's onward. A great selection of dresses and high-heels (we're not saying they're always there, but **Prada** shoes have been known to frequent this establishment) and a nice collection of men's shirts and jackets.

Prices vary. Open T-Sa 1pm-6pm.

ROHAN

NEW TOWN

86 George St. ☎0131 225 4876 www.rohan.co.uk

A store that totally, completely, entirely devotes its time to crafting clothing for travelers. Now, before you think "camping gear," think again—this is normal clothing (they've even got sport coats) that has been amped up for the rigors of intense travel. It's light, breathable, packable, and full of secret pockets so you can transport your passport and—cough!—other materials safely across the border.

Good travel gear doesn't come cheap. T-shirts run up to £30. Open M-Sa 9:30am-5:30pm.

STATE OF MIND BOUTIQUE (SMB) — CANONGATE

20 St. Mary's St. ☎0131 556 0215 www.stateofmindboutique.co.uk

Showcasing the hipstery-est and baggiest specialty clothing from NYC, LA, Tokyo and Scotland, SMB sells button-ups and T-shirts as well as a large selection of Vans and Converse. Ask about brands that can't be found outside of Edinburgh or Scotland.

i 10% Student discount available. Open daily 11am-6pm everyday.

BOOKS

THE OLD TOWN BOOKSHOP — OLD TOWN

8 Victoria St. ☎0131 225 9237 www.oldtownbookshop.com

Walking into the Old Town Bookshop, a wonderful little bookstore in the middle of Victoria St., is like walking into an well-tended study. A small space with books rising up to the ceiling, this shop carries an impressive collection of rare and vintage books as well as old paperback books you always wanted to read but never did *(£1)*. Antique prints and maps are also available.

Prices vary. Open M-Sa 10:30am-5:45pm.

BLACKWELL BOOKS — OLD TOWN

53-62 South Bridge ☎0131 622 8222 www.blackwell.co.uk

A retail chain selling lots of titles at retail prices, there's not a lot of character but you're likely to find that book you couldn't locate in the smaller local shops. Small sale section available.

Prices vary. Open M-F 9am-8pm, Sa 9am-6pm, Su noon-6pm.

ST. JOHN CHARITY BOOKS PLUS — STOCKBRIDGE

20 Deanhaugh St. ☎0131 332 4911 www.stjohnbookshop.co.uk

A secondhand bookshop with the best of both worlds, St. John's has a collection of old penguin paperbacks *(£1-2)* or a large collection of antiquarian books for those looking to pick up that rare first edition of **Henry James** that you're sure is worth millions but have never actually finished.

Open M-Sa 10am-5pm, Su noon-4pm.

TRANS-REAL FICTION — OLD TOWN

7 Cowgatehead ☎0131 226 2822 www.transreal.co.uk

Surrounded by the ancient castles of Edinburgh and Scotland, who wouldn't be craving a good sci-fi or fantasy novel? Trans-Real Fiction's got your fix, as well as a selection of **stuffed animals.** Have at you! Taste my sword!

Just at the end of Grassmarket. Open M-F 11am-6pm, Sa 10am-6pm, Su noon-5pm.

OXFAM BOOKS — STOCKBRIDGE

25 Raeburn Pl. ☎0131 332 9632

A charity shop for secondhand books, they do everything from popular fiction to classics. It's for charity people! Buy yourself some reading material!

Prices vary. Open M-F 9:30am-5:30pm, Sa 10am-5:30pm.

THE BOOK SHOP — SOUTHSIDE

45 Clerk St. ☎0131 668 3142

This small shop offers mostly secondhand books at discount prices. What new stock they have immediately receives a 60% markdown. How's that for a sale? Used vinyl and antique book sections available as well.

Discounted prices. Open M-Sa 10am-6pm, Su noon-4pm.

THE WORKS
OLD TOWN

63 Princes St. ☎0131 539 0007 www.theworks.co.uk

Housing a selection of books both popular fiction and classic, The Works sells them at factory outlet prices. If you see more than one you like, why not take two or three? *(3 for £5; £1.95 each).*

Open daily 8:30am-9pm.

OUTDOOR MARKETS

EDINBURGH FARMER'S MARKET
OLD TOWN

Castle Terr. www.edinburghfarmersmarket.co.uk

With over 65 separate providers, the Edinburgh Farmers Market is a great place for face painting (for kiddies or you, if you're so inclined), slow cooking demonstrations *(first Sa of every month),* and, of course, the freshest foodstuffs you can imagine.

Castle Terr. is just off Lothian Rd. at the end of Princes St. Open Sa 9am-2pm.

LIQUOR STORES

THE WHISKY STORE
OLD TOWN

28 Victoria St. ☎0131 225 4666 www.whiskyshop.com

The end-all for whiskey drinkers (besides a hangover) the guys at the Whisky Store really know their stuff. So much so that they'll take you on a "tutored tasting," *(introductory £12.50, specialized £25)* to help you find the perfect bottle. They also have live casks, right there, and you can fill up your own bottle with stuff that's guaranteed to be unique not just to Scotland, but to that very shop.

i Call ahead to set up tutored tastings. Prices vary. Open Sept-June M-Sa 10am-6pm, Su 11am-6pm; in daily Jul 10am-7pm; in daily Aug 10am-8pm.

ROBERT GRAHAM WHISKY AND CIGARS
NEW TOWN

194a Rose St. ☎0131 226 1874 www.robertgraham1874.com

It's a whiskey shop on the pub-filled Rose St.—whodathunkit? From the tiny bottles *(£4-20)* to the full-size models, the items sold at this shop vary in quality and price—but all have whiskey in them. Robert Graham also sells cigars, pipes, and all the accoutrements you could ever need to sit in your study and act like James Bond.

Whiskey prices vary between £20-500. Open M-W 10:30am-6pm, Th-F 10:30am-7pm, Sa 10:30am-7:30pm.

ELECTRONICS

LAPTOP REPAIR CENTRE
OLD TOWN

6 Greyfriars Pl.

A brand-new option for those seeking salvation for their slow or non-functioning computer, PC or Mac. they'll add ram, clean out junk space, or reset your hard drive if necessary. If you're in the market, they also usually have a few second-hand laptops for sale.

All repairs under £69. Open M-Sa 9am-6pm.

FURNITURE

HABITAT
OLD TOWN

32 Shandwick Pl. ☎0844 499 1114 habitat.co.uk

A classy but reasonably priced option, Habitat has everything from couches and chairs to wall decorations and **kitsch.** Think of it as IKEA, but not.

Open M-W 10am-6pm, Th 10am-7pm, F 10am-6pm, Sa 9:30am-6pm, Su 11am-6pm.

INHOUSE LIMITED
NEW TOWN

28 Howe St. ☎0131 225 2888 www.inhouse-uk.com

With a selection of the most Modern of the Modern in furniture pieces, you could

make your flat look like a **Samuel Beckett** play—minimalist. It'll cost you though.
Prices vary, but lean towards the high end. Open T-Sa 9am-5:30pm.

OMNI FURNISHING
NEW TOWN

6-10 Earl Grey St. ☎0131 221 1200 www.omnifurnishings.co.uk

Specializing in wooden pieces (and, from the lovely smell of fresh cut wood inside the display rooms, newly-made pieces at that), OMNI has a wide selection of tables, chairs, and other furnishings.

Prices vary. Open M-F 10am-6pm, Sa 9:30am-5pm, Su noon-5pm.

ANTIQUES

UNICORN ANTIQUES
NEW TOWN

65 Dundas St. ☎0131 556 7176

Run by a few little old ladies on the far end of New Town, you may have to paw your way through a few doorknobs, but it'll be worth it when you find that awesome one of a kind souvenir you've been looking for. Bear in mind that this is a hodge-podge collection, so you're not going to find any signs pointing out where "cool 19th-century photographs" are. The best antique stores are all like this.

From Queen St., turn onto Dundas St. and follow for 3 blocks. Open M-Sa 10:30am-6:30pm.

CAVANAGH ANTIQUES
OLD TOWN

49 Cockburn St. ☎0131 226 3391

Specializing in metal knick-knacks and everything shiny, this shop has a large selection of coins, medals, and both costume and upper-end jewelry.

Cockburn St., off of High St. on Royal Mile.

HARLEQUIN ANTIQUES
OLD TOWN

30 Bruntsfield Pl. ☎0131 228 9446

A **clocks** and watches specialist, Harlequin has lots of beautiful old wrist and pocket watches, as well as that gorgeous grandfather clock you've always wanted. The only question is how to get it home. They also do repairs.

Bruntsfield Pl., on the West edge of Meadow Park. Prices vary. Open M-Sa 10am-5pm.

DEPARTMENT STORES

ST. JAMES SHOPPING CENTRE
OLD TOWN

1 Leith St. ☎0131 557 0050 www.stjamesshopping.com

Get yer shop on at St. James's, with over 60 different shops of every genre, as well as department stores, a food court, and an internet cafe.

Off of Waterloo Pl., a 5min. walk from Waverley Station. Internet cafe first floor. Open M-W 9am-6pm, Th 9am-8pm, F-Sa 9am-6pm, Su 10am-6pm.

PRINCES MALL
NEW TOWN

Princes Plaza, Princes St. ☎0131 557 9179 www.princesmall-edinburgh.co.uk

An underground mall that gets its natural light from the plaza above, it's got escalators connecting the floors, a food court, and more retail than you can shake a stick, or a pound sterling, at.

On the South Side of Princes St. at the east end. Side by side with Waverley Train Station. Open M-W 8:30am-6:30pm, Th 8:30am-7:30pm, F-Sa 8:30am-6:30pm, Su 10:30am-5:30pm.

PRACTICALITIES

- **TOURIST OFFICE: Visit Scotland Information Centre** is the largest tourist information centre in Scotland. The friendly representatives from this Edinburgh branch will help you book accommodations, city tours, and coach and bus tours. The office also houses a souvenir shop and Internet center. *(3 Princes St. Across from Waverley Station. ☎08452 255 121. www.visitscotland.com. Credit cards accepted. Open Sept-June M-Sa 9am-5pm, Su 10am-5pm; Jul-Aug M-Sa 9am-7pm, Su 10am-7pm.)*
- **POST OFFICE: Newington Branch.** *(41 S. Clark St. ☎0131 667 1154. Open M-Sa 9am-5:30pm, Su 9am-12:30pm.)* **Forest Row Post Office** *(32 Forest Row. ☎0131 225 3957. Open M-F 8:30am-6pm, Sa 8:30am-5pm.)* **Saint Mary's Street Post Office** *(46 St. Mary's St. ☎0131 556 6351. Open M-F 9am-5:30pm, Sa 9am-12:30pm.)*
- **POST OFFICE: Frederick St. Post Office.** *(40 Frederick St. ☎08457 740 740. Open M-F 9am-5:30pm except T open at 9:30am, Sa 9am-12:30pm.)*
- **INTERNET CAFE: E-Corner Internet.** *(54 Blackfriars St. ☎0131 558 7858. info@e-corner.co.uk Internet £.50 per 10min., £1.80 per 1 hr. Printing £.29 per page. International calls £.10 per min. to landlines. Open M-F 9am-10pm, Sa-Su 10am-9pm.)* **PC Emergency Internet.** *(13 Frederick St. ☎0754 363 3242. info@e-corner.co.uk. Internet £2 per hr. Day pass 9am-9pm £6. Printing £.50 per page for first 5 pages, £.25 per page after that. Open M-F 9am-10pm, Sa-Su 10am-9pm.)*
- **PHARMACY: Boots.** *(32 West Maitlin St. ☎0131 225 7436. Credit cards accepted. Open M-F 8am-6pm, Sa 9am-6pm.)* **Royal Mile Pharmacy** *(67 High St. ☎0131 556 1971. royalmilepharmacy@hotmail.com. Credit cards accepted. Open M-F 9am-6pm, Sa 9am-5pm.)*
- **BANK: Barclays.** *(1 St. Andrews Sq. ☎0845 755 5555. www.barclays.co.uk. Credit cards accepted. Open M-F 9am-5pm, Sa 10am-2pm.)*
- **ATM: Barclays** has 24hr. ATM out front. *(72 George St. ☎0131 470 6000. www.barclays.co.uk. Open M-F 9am-5pm, Sa 10am-2pm.)*

GETTING THERE

By Train

Waverley Train Station *(between Princes St., Market St. and Waverley Bridge. ☎08457 484 950. www.networkrail.co.uk. Open M-Sa 12:45am-4am, Su 12:45am-6am.)* has trains to **Aberdeen** *(£33.20. 2½hr.; M-Sa every hr., Su 8 per day.)*; **Glasgow** *(£9.70. 1hr., 4 per hr.)*; **Inverness** *(£32. 3½hr., every 2hr.)*; **London King's Cross** *(£103. 4¾hr., every hr.)*; **Stirling** *(£6.10. 50min., 2 per hr.)*. **Haymarket Train Station** is smaller, but has service to destinations throughout Scotland *(Haymarket Terrace. www.scotrail.com. Open M-Sa 5:10am-12:30am, Su 7:45am-12:45am. Ticket office open daily 7:45am-9:30pm.)*.

GETTING AROUND

Buses

Getting around in Edinburgh is always easiest on **foot,** so unless you've just completed your trip through the Himalayas, you shouldn't find you're too sore at the end of the day. However, for those who really dislike hoofin' it, **Lothian Buses** have routes zig-zagging all over the city. *To make your way around Edinburgh, use Lothian buses (Lothian*

Buses Plc., Annandale St. ☎0131 555 6363 wwww.lothianbuses.com Ⓢ Daytime singles £1.20, child £.70; day pass £3/2.40; city singles (detachable day passes) 20 for £24. All-night ticket available for night buses £3.)

The first thing you should note about the bus system in Edinburgh is that most bus stops will have both an electronic screen alerting you to which lines are in service and the ETA of their arrival at the stop. The second is that there is a ticket machine at the stop, so buying your ticket in advance will save the bus driver a lot of chagrin (and perhaps save you from a telling off). Major lines for Lothian buses include the **24, 29,** and **42 buses**, running from Stockbridge, through city center all the way to Newington St. on the South End. The 24 Line heads off toward Mixto St. and Arthur's Seat, the 42 bends west to end at Portobello by Dynamic Earth, and the 29 ends at the Royal Infirmary. The **12, 26 and 31 buses** all come in from the Northwest and the Haymarket/Dalry area, the 12 bending off to the Northeast after passing through city center, the 26 heading south toward Newington and Mixto St. and the 31 pulling the same route but diverging to head Southwest into Liberton and Gracemount.

Taxis

Call **Central Taxis** *(8 St Peter's Buildings, Gilmore Pl. ☎0131 229 2468 www.taxis-edinburgh.co.uk Open 24hr.)* to get a cab in Edinburgh. With over 400 cabs and a 24/7 booking policy, Central cabs are by far the best taxi company to call when you need a lift. Book online if you're lacking in the phone department, and they'll arrive within 5-10min.

GLASGOW AND ST. ANDREWS

Admit it, fearless backpacking Anglophiles. You've always wanted to try on a kilt, and bagpipes really do make you emotional. If you think Scotland is all sentimentality, though, strap yourself in: visit thumping **Glasgow,** the industrial heart of a Scotland with tons of delicious food, crowds of students, and more Gothic architecture than you can shake a buttress at. And natives are called Glaswegians. How awesome is that? The birthplace of golf, **St. Andrews** is another popular destination in Scotland, and not only for your portly uncle. Even if putting isn't your thing, you're bound to spot a hottie in plaid pants.

greatest hits

- **GLASWEGIAN GHOULS.** Head to Glasgow's spooky Necropolis (p. 319), just across the water from the cathedral.
- **TIPSY-ISH.** Does "Uisge Beatha" look like a mouthful? The whiskies are. Stop by the "Ish" for a proper education in Scots drinking (p. 324).
- **PRESERVE US!** When you think of Glasgow do you think of preserved bodies and death masks? Check out the Hunterian Museum (p. 319).
- **NORTH SEA CATCH.** If you think you've had fish and chips in England, think again. At Tailend Restaurant (p. 331), the batter really is better.

student life

Glasgow is the place where the magic happens for youth from Scotland around the world: powerhouses include the **University of Glasgow,** one of the oldest and largest in the UK, and the **Glasgow School of Art,** a mecca for international students farther east in Garnethill, a neighborhood dense with art galleries. Students are movers and shakers in the eating scene; check out **Naked Soup** in Glasgow, a eatery popular with young folks. In St. Andrews, students from the University of St. Andrews and other young people can be found at local dives like the **Whey Pat Tavern.**

glasgow ☎0141

There's a running joke among residents of Glasgow and Edinburgh, that the only good thing about the other is the sign on the highway announcing your departure. A heavy rivalry exists between the two, and Glaswegians often face heavy criticism from their fashionable and trendy neighbor. Glasgow isn't the prettiest city in the world, though it is certainly no longer the predictable industrial giant it used to be. The city teems with students and a fantastic party scene as well as enough different restaurants to make your taste buds sore from overuse. The West End by the University is almost its own city, feeling much more communal and local than the Gothic city center.

ORIENTATION

Glasgow can essentially be divided into two distinct areas: the **city center,** with the shopping center, **Queen St., Central Station,** and **George Square** all located within walking distance of one another; and the **West End,** home to the **University of Glasgow, Kelvingrove Park and Gallery,** and the majority of Glasgow's hostels. The main pedestrian and shopping thoroughfares include the east end of **Sauchiehall St.,** which takes a right turn to become **Buchanan St.,** passing in front of **Nelson Mandela Place.** To get from the city center to the West End, walk from Buchanan onto **Sauchihall St.** and continue until the pedestrian access ends. From there, walk up the hill to **Renfrew St.** (which will take you past a large group of guesthouses and hotels as well as the Glasgow School of Art) and continue onward. At the end of Renfrew St., you will be led over a busy merging of streets by a footbridge. After crossing over you should walk right to get to **Woodlands Rd.,** which will take you to **Great Western Rd.** and the West End.

ACCOMMODATIONS

Backpackers who like to hop off the train and directly into a hostel will be disappointed—the majority of Glasgow's budget options require a hike to the West End. The walk from the station is only about 20min., but with that pack on—well, a cab's cheap *(around £5).* For those looking for something a little higher up the hostel-hotel food chain, Renfrew St. above Sauchiehall St. has a long row of guesthouses and hotels. Expect seasonal rate fluctuations.

WEST END BACKPACKERS HOSTEL ❶

3 Bank St. ☎0141 337 7000 www.glasgowwestendbackpackers.co.uk

West End Backpackers is a laid-back, chill hostel with clean dorms (the sheets smell so lovely) and a great lounge area. Guests receive free computer and kitchen use *and* breakfast. Choose between the larger, sunnier rooms upstairs or the more private basement dorms.

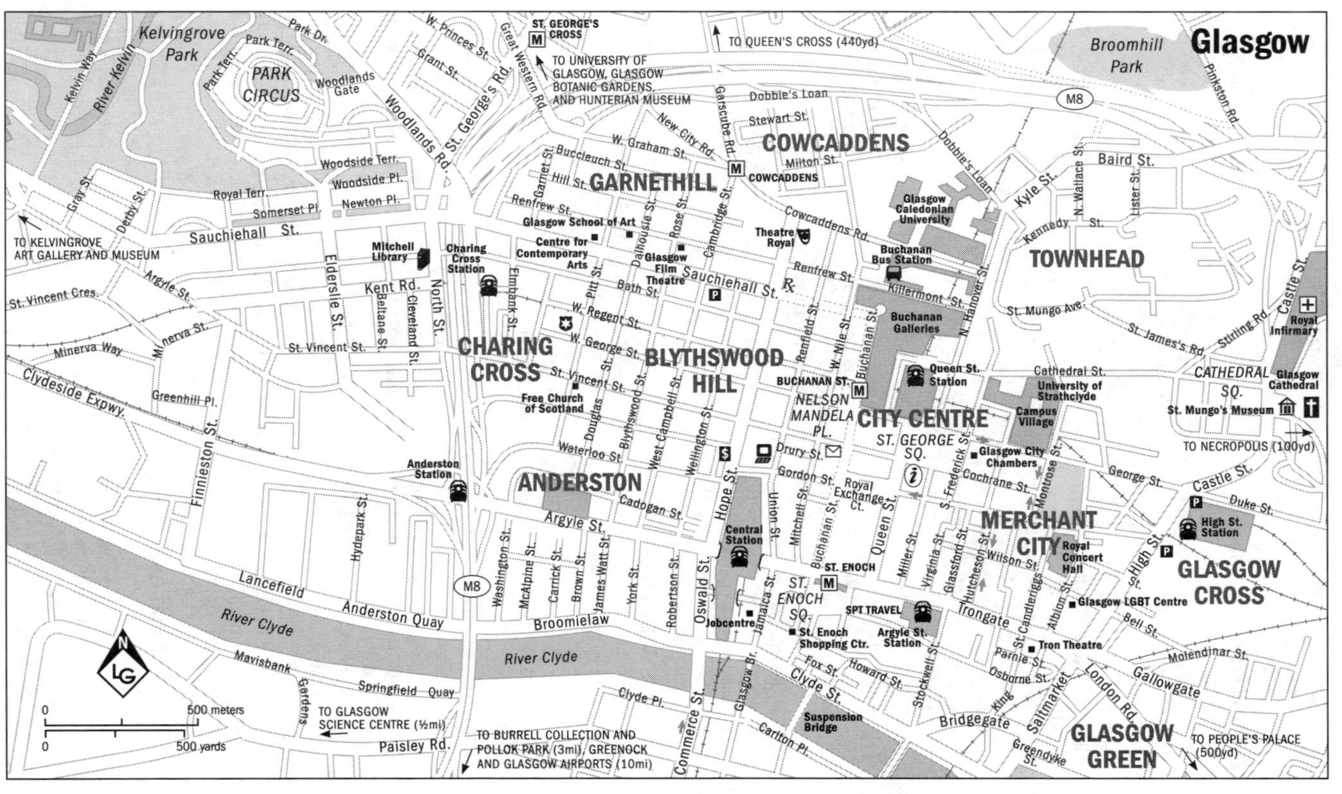
Glasgow
Broomhill Park
Pinkston Rd.
M8
TO QUEEN'S CROSS (440yd)
ST. GEORGE'S CROSS
TO UNIVERSITY OF GLASGOW, GLASGOW BOTANIC GARDENS, AND HUNTERIAN MUSEUM
Kelvingrove Park
River Kelvin
Kelvin Way
PARK CIRCUS
Park Dr.
Park Terr.
Woodlands Gate
Woodlands Rd.
St. George's Rd.
W. Princes St.
Grant St.
Great Western Rd.
Dobbie's Loan
Garscube Rd.
Stewart St.
New City Rd.
COWCADDENS
Milton St.
W. Graham St.
Buccleuch St.
Hill St.
Garnet St.
GARNETHILL
Renfrew St.
Glasgow School of Art
Dalhousie St.
Rose St.
Cambridge St.
Cowcaddens Rd.
Theatre Royal
Glasgow Caledonian University
Kyle St.
N. Wallace St.
Baird St.
Lister St.
Kennedy St.
TOWNHEAD
Castle St.
Royal Infirmary
St. Mungo Ave.
St. James's Rd.
Stirling Rd.
CATHEDRAL SQ.
Glasgow Cathedral
St. Mungo's Museum
TO NECROPOLIS (100yd)
Woodside Terr.
Woodside Pl.
Newton Pl.
Royal Terr.
Somerset Pl.
Gray St.
Derby St.
TO KELVINGROVE ART GALLERY AND MUSEUM
Sauchiehall St.
Mitchell Library
Charing Cross Station
Centre for Contemporary Arts
Glasgow Film Theatre
Bath St.
Buchanan Bus Station
Renfrew St.
Killermont St.
N. Hanover St.
Buchanan Galleries
Argyle St.
St. Vincent Cres.
Eldersile St.
Kent Rd.
Beltane St.
Cleveland St.
North St.
Elmbank St.
Pitt St.
W. Regent St.
Minerva St.
Minerva Way
St. Vincent St.
CHARING CROSS
W. George St.
BLYTHSWOOD HILL
Renfield St.
W. Nile St.
Buchanan St.
Queen St. Station
Cathedral St.
University of Strathclyde
Clydeside Expwy.
Greenhill Pl.
Free Church of Scotland
Douglas St.
Blythswood St.
West Campbell St.
Wellington St.
BUCHANAN ST.
NELSON MANDELA PL.
CITY CENTRE
Campus Village
ST. GEORGE SQ.
Glasgow City Chambers
Waterloo St.
Drury St.
Finnieston St.
Anderston Station
ANDERSTON
Cadogan St.
Hope St.
Gordon St.
Royal Exchange Ct.
S. Frederick St.
Cochrane St.
Montrose St.
George St.
Castle St.
Duke St.
High St. Station
Hydepark St.
Argyle St.
Central Station
Union St.
Mitchell St.
Buchanan St.
Queen St.
Miller St.
Virginia St.
Glassford St.
Hutcheson St.
Wilson St.
MERCHANT CITY
Royal Concert Hall
High St.
GLASGOW CROSS
Washington St.
McAlpine St.
Carrick St.
Brown St.
James Watt St.
York St.
Robertson St.
Oswald St.
ST. ENOCH
ST. ENOCH SQ.
SPT TRAVEL
Candleriggs
Albion St.
Glasgow LGBT Centre
Lancefield
Anderston Quay
Broomielaw
Jobcentre
Jamaica St.
St. Enoch Shopping Ctr.
Argyle St. Station
Trongate
Bell St.
River Clyde
Tron Theatre
Parnie St.
Osborne St.
Molendinar St.
Gallowgate
London Rd.
Mavisbank Gardens
Springfield Quay
Clyde Pl.
Glasgow Br.
Fox St.
Howard St.
Clyde St.
Stockwell St.
Bridgegate
King St.
Saltmarket
Suspension Bridge
500 meters
500 yards
0
TO GLASGOW SCIENCE CENTRE (½mi)
Paisley Rd.
TO BURRELL COLLECTION AND POLLOK PARK (3mi), GREENOCK AND GLASGOW AIRPORTS (10mi)
Commerce St.
Carlton Pl.
Greendyke St.
GLASGOW GREEN
TO PEOPLE'S PALACE (500yd)
N
LG

Just off Great Western Rd. 4 blocks from University of Glasgow campus. i Linen and towels included. 10-bed dorms £14, 6-bed £15, 4-bed £16. Reception closes at midnight. Breakfast 8-10am.

THE WILLOW GUESTHOUSE 
GUESTHOUSE ❸

228 Renfrew St. ☎0141 332 2332

This is probably the best deal among the guesthouses in terms of quality for money. The rooms in the Willow are tastefully decorated and spacious. Come down in the morning for breakfast, which has been jovially described as "a scorcher."

i Large TVs in the rooms. Singles £35; doubles £50.

MCLAY'S GUESTHOUSE GUESTHOUSE ❸

264-276 Renfrew St. ☎0141 332 4796 www.mclays.com

A good, closer-to-budget guesthouse, McLays has a full Scottish breakfast included in the price of the room. There are several standard rooms which, though lacking baths, do have sinks and mirrors. Relax out on the patio under the umbrellas in rain or shine.

Singles £28; doubles £48; family £70. Reception 24hr.

SYHA HOSTEL ❷

7-8 Park Terr. ☎0141 332 3004 www.syha.org.uk

Like any hostel that is part of a chain, this hostel is full on beds (around 140) and short on character. It's good if you need to book something at the last minute. They do have their own cafe downstairs where you can get coffee or beer and use the internet or book exchange.

From St. George's Rd., turn onto Woodlands Rd. and then left onto Duff St. Follow on Lynedoch St. and turn left and then right onto Woodlands Terr. until it becomes Park Terr. Follow around the circle. i Kitchen and lounge use available. Non-members pay approx. £2 more. 6-8 bed dorms £20-25.

THE HERITAGE HOTEL 
HOTEL ❹

4 Alfred Terr. ☎0141 339 6955 www.theheritagehotel.net

Heritage has a "Best Western" feel and rooms with all the accoutrements—table, chairs, TV, tea and biscuits, soap and shampoos, the whole nine yards—so you can already anticipate the somewhat higher prices.

Off Great Western Rd. i Full Scottish breakfast included. Singles £40; doubles and twins £60.

THE BOTANIC HOTEL HOTEL ❸

1 Alfred Terr. ☎0141 337 7007 www.botanichotel.co.uk

A comfortable and well-decorated (framed photos of palm trees, anyone?) hotel just off Great Western road, the Botanic features large suits, all with windows and TVs.

Off Great Western Rd. Singles £30-35; doubles £55; family £75.

ALBA LODGE GUESTHOUSE ❷

232 Renfrew St. ☎0141 332 2588 albalodge.co.uk

If you enjoy long, hot showers, take a room at the Alba lodge. Ensuite rooms have enormous bathrooms. A family-run place, this guesthouse benefits from a helpful and friendly staff. Look for the flowers on the front stoop.

i Discounts for extended stays. Singles £35; doubles £45-60.

HAMPTON COURT GUESTHOUSE GUESTHOUSE ❷

230 Renfrew St. ☎0141 332 6623 www.haptoncourtguesthouse.co.uk

All the rooms are pink. Pink. Still, this guesthouse with a funky red-patterned carpet and winding staircase has nicely-sized and comfortable rooms. Tourist information is available downstairs.

Singles £28, with bath £33; doubles £52.

VICTORIAN HOUSE HOTEL

HOTEL ❸

212 Renfrew St. ☎0141 332 0129 www.thevictorian.co.uk

With 59 clean but somewhat bland rooms, the Victorian hotel has ensuite baths, Wi-Fi, 24hr. reception, and plenty of closet space.

Renfrew St. i Breakfast included. Singles £32, with bath £35; double £55-60. Reception 24hr.

THE RENNIE MACINTOSH HOTEL

HOTEL❷

218-220 Renfrew St. ☎0141 333 9992 www.rmghotels.com

The lobby of this hotel has been modeled after the interior design of Charles Rennie Macintosh. The rooms are small but carefully furnished, with glossy furniture and desks in the rooms. Wi-Fi available in the lobby.

i 10% discount for stays of 3 nights or more. July-Aug singles £35; doubles £55. Sept-May singles £30; doubles £48.

BUNKUM BACKPACKERS

HOSTEL❶

26 Hillhead St. ☎0141 581 4481 bunkumglasgow@hotmail.com

The hostel is located next to a nursery. But that's okay, because you'll be out during the day, right? The dorms in this high-ceiling establishment win the prize for largest rooms and fewest beds, which means you can really spread out and get comfy.

Traveling west on Great Western Rd., turn onto Hillhead St. and walk down 2 blocks. July-Aug dorms £14; doubles £36. Sept-Jun dorms £12; doubles £16 per person.

SIGHTS

KELVINGROVE ART GALLERY AND MUSEUM

♿ MUSEUM

Argyle St. ☎0141 276 9599 www.glasgowmuseums.com

Built to be a museum and opened in 1901, the gallery is a beautiful red brick structure that looks more like a cathedral than a museum. In fact, if you come around at 1pm, you can hear the giant organ above the main space being played. Oh, and the stuff inside the building is cool too—works by Cézanne, Monet, Gauguin, Van Gogh, and "Christ of St. John of the Cross" by Salvador Dalí.

5min. walk from Kelvinhall subway station and 10min. walk from Kelvinbridge subway station. i Dalí's Christ of St. John of the Cross on loan until Feb. 2011. £1 suggested donation. Open M-Th 10am-5pm, F 11am-5pm, Sa 10am-5pm, Su 11am-5pm.

HUNTERIAN MUSEUM

MUSEUM

Gilbert Scott Building ☎0141 330 4221 www.hunterian.gla.ac.uk

Founded in 1807 to display the collections of William Hunter, prominent physician and Scotland's foremost collector of weird crap, the museum exhibits everything from human organs in formaldehyde, the death mask of Sir Isaac Newton, and the side-by-side comparison of the penis bones of a walrus and weasel. (Gents, one of these will boost confidence; the other will not.)

Glasgow University. i The main display room for the Hunterian Museum will be closed for roof construction until approx. Apr 2011. Free. Open M-F 9:30am-5pm.

GLASGOW CATHEDRAL AND NECROPOLIS

Castle St. ☎0141 552 6891 www.historic-scotland.gob.uk

A Glasgow must-see, the cathedral is just as stony, gothic and impressive as the castles from your adventure books growing up. Head into its bowels to view the tomb of the city's patron saint, St. Mungo. The Necropolis, across the bridge from the Cathedral, is even better and spookier. A climb to the peak of the cemetery will give you some of the best views in Glasgow.

From High St. Rail, follow High St. north until it becomes Castle St. i Volunteer guides give

tours of the cathedral during opening hours in the summer. Cathedral open Apr-Sept 9:30am-5pm, Su 1-5pm; Oct-Mar M-Sa 9:30am-4pm, Su 1-4pm.

ST. MUNGO'S MUSEUM MUSEUM

2 Castle St. ☎0141 276 1625 glasgowmuseums.com

St. Mungo's offers a small exhibit of religious artifacts from all over the world, including Catholic stained glass, Greek pottery, statues of Buddha, and religious artifacts from Scotland. Note that the top floor is also the kids "discovery centre," so you may be stepping over construction paper scraps up there.

Souvenir shop downstairs accepts credit cards. Open M-Th 10am-5pm, F 11am-5pm, Sa 10am-5pm, Su 11am-5pm.

GLASGOW GALLERY OF MODERN ART MUSEUM

Royal Exchange Sq. ☎0141 287 3050 www.glasgowmuseums.com

The GOMA, four stories of rotating exhibitions of the most modern (and often the most confusing) works from both Glaswegian and international artists, is so funky inside they've even got the windows painted with a swirling blue. Keep an eye out for the room with the flashing sign that shouts out fun facts like, "the soldier eats your stomach!" We can't tell if they're kidding.

From Glasgow Central Low Level Rail Station, walk east on Gordon St. Turn right onto Buchanan St. and then make a left onto Exchange Pl. Free. Open M-W 10am-5pm, Th 10am-8pm, F-Sa 10am-5pm, Su 11am-5pm.

ST. GEORGE'S SQUARE PLAZA

City Center

An enormous, red-paved, statue-filled plaza in the center of town, St. George's Square is lined with wooden benches where you can sit and enjoy the sunshine. Carefully consider your plan to feed the pigeons, as those birds have become drunk with power and think nothing of flying just inches past your head. Those statues of Scotland's greats didn't get their white hair from getting older.

Take subway to St. George's Cross.

GLASGOW CITY CHAMBERS CITY HALL

82 George Sq. ☎0141 287 4018 www.glasgow.co.uk

Opened in 1888, the Glasgow City Chambers beats out St. Peter's in Vatican City for largest marble staircase by one flight. Other than that, it's got a giant banquet hall with three different murals depicting different aspects of Scotland's culture. In the portraits hall, look for the depiction of Lord Provost Pat Lally who, judging from the portrait, must have been Glasgow's first resident supervillain.

From Glasgow Queen St. Rail Station, walk west on George St. Free. Tours 30min., M-F 10:30am and 2:30pm.

GLASGOW BOTANIC GARDENS PUBLIC PARK

West End www.glasgow.gov.uk/en/residents/parks_outdoors

With lots of lawn space for laying out, if and when it's ever sunny, and public greenhouses where you can examine all sort of flora, the Glasgow Botanic Gardens is a relaxing place to spend an afternoon. Keep an eye out for an ice cream truck at the entrance, which scoops out delicious cones *(£1)*.

At the intersection of Byers and Great Western Rd. Botanic Gardens visitor's center open daily 11am-4pm.

UNIVERSITY OF GLASGOW UNIVERSITY

Glasgow University, University Ave., Gilbert Scott building ☎0141 330 5511 www.gla.ac.uk

You'll see the heavily Gothic hollowed spire from a distance, but head to University Drive and the visitor's center to pick up a brochure for a self-guided tour. Voted by *Times Higher Education* as having the best campus in Scotland, the U of G is full of cathedral archways and great photo opportunites.

Located in the West End of Glasgow, 3 mi. from the city center. Self-guided tour pamphlet £3. Visitor's center open M-Sa 9:30am-5pm.

GLASGOW SCHOOL OF ART — ART SCHOOL

167 Renfrew St. ☎0141 353 4530 www.gsa.ac.uk

The masterwork of famous Scottish architect Charles Rennie Macintosh, the GSA is a labyrthine edifice of concrete, sculpture, and steel. Explore the place from top to bottom while led by excitable tour guides recruited from the school. Get ready to hear all about the incredible amount of symbolism and imagery that has been incorporated into the building. Still a working institution, Glasgow School of Art is home to plaster casts of famous Greek sculptures, several of which became eunuchs during the censorship-happy Victorian era. Tours last approximately 1hr.

Enter at 11 Dalhouse St. for tour entrances. Tours Apr-Sept daily 10, 11am, noon, 1, 2, 3, 4, and 5pm. Tours Oct-Mar daily 11am and 3pm. Visitors in wheelchairs will want to call ahead and book for the 11am tour. £8.75, students £7, family £23.50. Open daily Apr-Sept 9:30am-6:30pm; Oct-Mar daily 10am-5pm.

FOOD

Glasgow may look like a big, gritty city (who are we kidding, it *is* a big gritty city), but you will eat like royalty here. The dining options are endless, and cover about as wide a range of tastes as you can imagine. From chippies to bistros and everything in between, you'll be able to take your significant other out for a fancy dinner and then satisfy your drunken 3am craving all on the same block.

MANCINI'S — ITALIAN ❸

315-321 Great Western Rd. ☎0141 339 5544 www.mancini-restaurant.co.uk

Two round chandeliers sit above high wooden tables at this Italian *ristorante*. With generous portions of pasta *(£3.50-7.50)* and soup and sandwich options for just a fiver, you're not going to have to bust your bank to get great food here. However, if you're not hungry, you can simply stop in to grab a glass of champagne or a cocktail.

Between St. Mary's Cathedral and Napiershall St. All wines sold by the glass. Open M-Th 8am-1am, F-Sa 10am-1am, Su 8am-1am. Restaurant open until 10:30pm.

NAKED SOUP — SOUP ❶

6 Kersland St. ☎0141 334 8999

Offering a big cup of great soup, a huge chunk of fresh buttered bread, and your choice of fruit *(£3)*, this place is delicious *and* cheap. It's so good you'll want to keep a Naked Soup menu along with your dirty magazines.

Just off Great Western Rd. Open M-Th 9am-8pm, F 9am-6pm, Sa 10am-6pm, Su 11am-5pm.

BIBLOCAFÉ — CAFE ❷

262 Woodlands Rd. ☎0141 339 7645 www.biblocafe.co.uk

To put it bluntly, this place is the bomb. A cozy, sit-down coffeeshop and secondhand bookstore, Biblocafé is made really special by the people who frequent it. Lou Munday and her crew of coffee "minions" are some of the most instantly likeable people on the planet. If you enjoy sarcastic humor and witty banter, step in and get hooked.

Ⓜ Kelvinbridge. Take S. Woodlands Rd. toward St. George's Rd. Coffee from £2. Flavored mochas and lattés from £3. Open M-F 8:30am-8:30pm, Sa-Su 9:30am-8:30pm, holidays 10am-6pm.

BEANSCENE CAFE ❷

40-42 Woodlands Rd. ☎0141 352 9800 beanscene.co.uk

Nobody coming to Beanscene plans to take their coffee on the go—the plentiful couches and welcoming creaky wood floor make it hard to tear yourself away. You'll see people studying, chatting, or even sleeping (didn't get to the coffee quick enough) at this cafe. Smoothies are also available.

ⓂKelvinbridge. Take S. Woodlands Rd. toward St. George's Rd. i Live music once a month, but inquire within. Coffee £1.50-3. Open M-Sa 8am-10:30pm, Su 9am-10:30pm.

O'NEILL'S IRISH ❸

453 Sauchiehall St. ☎0141 353 4371 oneills.co.uk

O'Neill's is a self-proclaimed Irish restaurant in Scotland, and the schtick feels a bit forced (those Guinness signs are just too clean!). Still, the food is hot and hearty and you can score some Guinness-battered fish and chips *(£6).*

ⓂCowcaddens. i Vegetarian options available. Open M-W noon-midnight, Th noon-2am, F-Sa noon-3am, Su noon-2am.

WILLOW TEA ROOMS 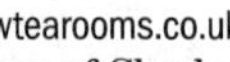 CAFE ❸

97 Buchanan St. ☎0141 204 5242 www.willowtearooms.co.uk

With the high-backed chairs based on the original, influential designs of Charles Rennie Macintosh, the Willow Tea Rooms create a dainty, scone-filled paradise for the passing wanderer. Sit by the windows upstairs and enjoy one classy tea experience.

ⓂBuchanan. Cakes £12.25. Open M-Sa 9am-5pm, Su 11am-5pm. Last orders 30min. before close.

BRADFORD'S BAKERY AND CAFÉ CAFE ❷

245 Sauchiehall St. ☎0141 332 1008 hrbradfords.co.uk

The downstairs of this cafe has two rows of pastry shelves in a rainbow of colors. The upstairs, with tables and window views of Sauchiehall St. below, offers full meals as well as coffee and sweets.

ⓂCowcaddens. i Wheelchair accessibility limited to downstairs pastry shop. Entrees £5-10. Desserts up to £4. Open M-Sa 8am-5pm.

WAITROSE GROCERY GROCERY STORE ❸

373 Byers Rd. ☎0141 337 3314 www.waitrose.com

Waitrose is an upper end grocery store with hints of Whole Foods and a strong finish reminiscent of Trader Joe's.

ⓂHillhead. Open M-F 8:30am-9pm, Sa 8:30am-8pm, Su 9am-8pm.

GRASSROOTS ORGANIC ORGANIC GROCERY STORE ❸

20 Woodlands Rd. ☎0141 353 3278 www.grassrootsorganic.com

A 90% organic grocery store, pastry and sandwich bar, and wineseller, there's nothing Grassroots can't do. They even have free tofu samples.

ⓂKelvinbridge. Take S. Woodlands Rd. toward St. George's Rd. Open M-W 8:30am-6pm, Th-F 8:30am-7pm, Sa 9am-6pm, Su 11am-5pm.

MARIO'S PLACE FISH AND CHIPS ❷

285 Byers Rd. ☎0141 334 6561

At this fish and chips joint that doesn't skimp on the portions or the deep-frying, you can get a well-priced cod supper *(£6).* Sit-down or takeaway, it doesn't matter to these guys. They'll make it quick and tasty.

ⓂHillhead. Walk north on Byers St. Open M-Th 9am-midnight, F-Sa 9am-1am, Su 9am-midnight.

THE LEFT BANK MEDITERRANEAN ❸

33-35 Gibson St. ☎0141 339 5659 www.theleftbank.co.uk

One of Glasgow's most varied eateries, you can get everything from chips and salsa to cayenne-dusted squid with homemade lime mayo here. Come during the week for the *prix-fixe* menu if you want to save a little dough.

Ⓜ Kelvinbridge. Walk south to Gibson St. Ⓢ 2 courses £11, 3 courses £13. i Vegetarian and vegan options available. Open M-F 10am-midnight, Sa-Su 10am-midnight.

BIER HALL REPUBLIC AND PIZZA BAR PIZZA ❷

9 Gordon St. ☎0141 204 0706

Bier Hall offers a two-for-one pizza deal every day noon-10pm, when you can score two big pizzas for an incredibly cheap price *(£7-11)*. They do have an extensive international beer selection, though, so you'll be paying back all the money you just saved.

1 block from Glasgow Central Low Level Station. i Vegetarian and vegan options available. Ⓢ Pizza £8-11. Kitchen open M-Sa noon-10pm, Su 12:30-10pm. Bar open M-Sa noon-midnight, Su 12:30pm-midnight.

PARADISE RESTAURANT PERSIAN ❷

411-413 Great Western Rd. ☎0141 339 2170 www.persianparadise.co.uk

In Paradise, water streams down the windows into pools with goldfish below and ornamental decorations are everywhere. Now if only the food were as exciting as the decor. Student lunch deal provides a decent two-course meal *(£6)*.

i Vegetarian options available. Open daily noon-10:30pm.

STRAVAIGIN GLOBAL ❹

28 Gibson St. ☎0141 334 2665 www.stravaigin.com

Signs that a restaurant must be expensive: they have a cheese section on their menu. Signs that a restaurant must be great: it's packed with people. Stravaigin exhibits both and is so unique that they offer their own recipe of haggis. They even manage to do a vegetarian haggis, though no one's quite sure how.

From Great Western Rd., turn onto Bank St. for 3 blocks, then turn left onto Gibson St. and follow 2 blocks. Ⓢ Appetizers £3.65-12. Entrees up to £23. Open daily 11am-midnight.

LITTLE ITALY ITALIAN ❷

205 Byers Rd. ☎0141 339 5627 littleitalyglasgow.com

Little Italy looks like a cross between a diner and sit-down restaurant, but you'll cease to care what it is once you get ahold of one of their giant, 16 in. pizzas. The pies are great to eat in groups, but they're aren't alone on the menu—pastas, lasagnas, and salads abound.

Ⓜ Hillhead. 1 block south on Byers Rd. Ⓢ Pizzas from £8.20. Open M-Th 8am-10pm, F-Sa 8am-1am, Su 10am-10pm.

GARDEN FRESH EXOTICS GROCERIES ❶

28-30 Park Rd. ☎334 4200

In this small produce market, these guys bring in goods every day, so what you're getting is guaranteed to be fresh.

Ⓜ Kelvinbridge. Open daily 9am-8pm.

NANAKUSA JAPANESE ❸

441 Sauchiehall St. ☎0741 331 6303 www.nanakusa.co.uk

Nanakusa offers sushi and Japanese grill options in an atmosphere that leaves modern completely behind in favor of the weirdly futuristic. The long, low tables in front of color-changing window panes make you feel like you're in an extremely relaxed disco while you eat. The staff is courteous and prompt.

Ⓜ Cowcaddens. Take Rose St. south and turn right onto Sauchiehall St. Ⓢ Saki singles for £4. Entrees £3-7. Open M-Th noon-2:30pm and 5-11pm, F-Sa noon-2am, Su 5-11pm.

TINDERBOX CAFE ❷

114 Ingram St. ☎0141 552 6907

Finding strong coffee in Great Britain can be difficult. Fortunately for those of us who need java with a kick, Glasgow's got Tinderbox. Serving dark, bold coffees and lunch meals, it's a good place to get a boost.

Ⓜ Buchanan St. Follow W. George St. east to Montrose St. Coffee £1-3. Lunch £3-7. Open daily 7:15am-10pm.

NIGHTLIFE

Glasgow plus nightlife equals great parties. That's almost 'nuff said, but we'll go on. Whether you want to sit down and belt out some karaoke or get dolled up to find some classy clubs, Glasgow's got a great scene. There are several good clubs on Bath St. in the city center as well as in the West End. Friday and Saturday nights draw the biggest and sloppiest crowds, but **Sauchiehall Street** has it going on every night of the week.

STEREO BAR, RESTAURANT, LIVE MUSIC

20-28 Renfield Ln. ☎0141 222 2254

Much like a vegan, the upstairs restaurant area is thin and green (kidding, kidding). Serving organic ales *(£4.05)* as well as normal brews, the music space downstairs is a concrete box, where a great sound system helps make up for the not-so-great acoustics. Tapas are available until midnight in case you get peckish after all that unadulterated ale.

1 block north of Glasgow Central Low Level Rail Station. Entrees £7-7.50. Open M-Tu noon-midnight, W-Su noon-3am.

BUFF CLUB CLUB

142 Bath Ln. ☎0141 221 7711 www.buffclub.com

One of the most popular clubs in Glasgow, the Buff Club is like a '20s speakeasy, with a gold and red interior reminiscent of a classy hotel lobby and a two-floored dance area upstairs reminiscent of awesome. Funk and soul can be heard all night long.

Turn left off of Bath St. at Blytheswood St. and then turn left again. i Electronica night on Tu. Look for weekly vodka+mixer promos. ATM available. Pints £3. Open daily 11pm-3am.

UISGE BEATHA PUB

232-246 Woodlands Rd. ☎0141 332 1622

All right, before you go into the Uisge Beatha, repeat after us: "Ish-kah Vay-ha." Get it right or risk looking like a helpless newbie. With a bar staff guaranteed to know everyone by name (including you, if you give them 5min.) and a wide range of whiskeys and beers, the "Ish" is a must. Stop by on Sundays for a trad band that occasionally swells to two dozen musicians.

Ⓜ Kelvinbridge. Follow Woodlands Rd. i Quiz night on W. Pints £2.70-3.45. Spirits £2.80-3. Open M-Sa noon-midnight, Su 12:30pm-midnight.

LAKOTA BAR

110-114 West George St. ☎0141 332 9724 www.lakotabars.co.uk

Lakota is a cocktail bar with plaid-shirted bartenders and deer heads above the bar. This place has a lot of room to roam, with chill booths on one end and a disco ball on the other. Upstairs you'll find the '80s bar Reflex.

Ⓜ Buchanan St. Lakota open M-Sa 9am-midnight, Su 10am-midnight. Reflex open F-Sa 8pm-midnight.

THE HORSESHOE BAR BAR

17-19 Drury St. ☎0141 248 6368 www.facebook.com/thehorseshoebar

A huge, wraparound bar lined with standing old men greets you in the downstairs segment of this double-sided pub. Yes, the bottom floor is a bit quiet, but head upstairs to the karaoke bar to see tables full of people making conversation over the sweet sounds of the next "star" of the stage. Come in from noon to 3pm and get a three-course lunch any day *(£4).*

1 block west of Glasgow Central Low Level Rail Station. Wheelchair accessibility limited to downstairs. Pints £2.25-2.70. Wine from £6. Open M-Sa 10am-midnight, Su 12:30pm-midnight.

DRUM AND MONKEY PUB

93 Vincent St. 0141 221 6636

An ex-bank that now stores whiskey instead of cash, the Drum and Monkey is an old man's bar for sure, but it's also a good drinks bar, with friendly bartenders and a snazzy atmosphere.

Buchanan St. Open M-Th 11am-11pm, F-Sa 11am-midnight, Su 11am-10pm.

HILLHEAD BOOKCLUB BAR

17 Vinicombe St. 0141 576 1700 www.hillheadbookclub.co.uk

One of the new bars on the block, the Bookclub is in an old cinema, so you're not going to be jockeying for space unless things get really busy. Two floors of booths line an open floor area in this hipster-esque bar. Try their special "Hillhead Strawberry Mojito," which is way more taste and booze than you'd normally be getting for that price *(£3).* If you see Andrew the barman, tell him we say hi.

Hillhead. Follow Byers Rd. north to Vinicombe St. Open daily 11am-midnight.

THE BOX CLUB

431 Sauchihall St. www.box-glasgow.co.uk

In comparison to the Nice n' Sleazy a few doors down, the Box trades beards and flannel for leather bracelets and hard rock. Live music plays from 9pm to midnight, and then DJs take over from midnight-3am...every night. The party certainly never stops here, but what's with all the weird bondage images on the walls? Ignore the posters, please, and listen to the music.

Buchanan. Walk down Rose St. to Sauchihall St. Pints £2-4. Open M-Th 5pm-3am, F-Su 4pm-3am.

PIVO PIVO BAR, LIVE MUSIC

15 Waterloo St. 0141 564 8100 www.myspace.com/pivopivo

Pivo Pivo is the best place to hear all of the unsigned and unknown Glaswegian music acts. There's a band on every night at this bunker-like former Czech hall. With good acoustics and a nice stage area. You could be feet away from the next Franz Ferdinand or Belle and Sebastian. Jazz happens on Saturday afternoons.

1 block west of Glasgow Central Low Level Rail. Large variety of beers. Beer £3-4. Mixed drinks £3. Covers for bands £3-5. Open M-Sa noon-midnight.

THE BELLE PUB

617 Great Western Rd. 0141 339 9229

With a stone hearth and wood-burning fireplace. The Belle is busiest during the winter months when it may just be the warmest place in the West End...that serves alcohol. With large international selection of bottled beers *(£2-4)* and one weird stag's head with red antlers, this place is definitely worth a closer look.

Kelvinbridge. Walk west on Great Western Rd. The red-antlered stag rejects the term "Demon deer." Cash only. Open daily noon-midnight.

THE GARAGE CLUB

490 Sauchiehall St. 0141 332 1120 www.garageglasgow.co.uk

The giant truck coming out of the wall above the door says it all—this place is either going to be a traffic jam or an accident. Screaming students dance and drink to the music in one of several bars to be found at the end of the club's many staircases. Wise locals says it's good to go in large groups—heed their advice.

Cowcaddens. Walk down Rose St. to Sauchihall St. Cover M-Th £5, students £3; F-Sa £7/5; Su £5/3. Free before 11pm. Cash only. Open daily 11pm-3am.

HUMMINGBIRD

CLUB

186 Bath St. ☎0845 166 6039

An enormous, four-floor, and heavily stylized establishment, the Hummingbird features three private karaoke rooms (each seating 10-15 crooners) as well as a mezzanine bar and a downstairs club space. You may see people wandering around with cocktails larger than their heads—those are the "fishbowls," a house specialty. A late 20s crowd slowly stop acting their age as the night wears on.

Ⓜ Cowcaddens. Walk down Rose St. and turn right onto Bath St. Open M-F 5pm-1am, Sa-Su noon-3am.

NICE N' SLEAZY

BAR, LIVE MUSIC

421 Sauchiehall St. ☎0141 333 0900 www.nicensleazy.com

A musician's bar, this is the place where you'll see the bartender and the customer in a heated argument—about which Jeff Beck album was the greatest, *Blow by Blow* or *Live with the Jan Hammer Group* (the answer is the latter). With paintings of snakes chasing flowers and hipster mustaches, Nice n' Sleazy's is a great bar where you can come in and immediately start talking music with the barstaff.

Ⓜ Cowcaddens. Walk down Rose St. to Sauchihall St. i "Nice n' Sleazy" T-shirts £20. Ⓢ Black and White Russians £2. Pints £2.70-3.30. Open M-Sa noon-3am, Su 1:30pm-3am.

KING TUT'S

BAR, LIVE MUSIC

272 St. Vincent St. ☎0141 221 5279 www.kingtuts.co.uk

The names of bands that have played here, and then gone to hit it big, like The Verve, Radiohead, and Florence and the Machine, have been printed on the stairs leading from the bar to the stage area. They're so big that they've even got their own lager, King Tut's *(£3 per pint)*. Got a band? Drop off your demo in the mailbox inside and hope to be heard.

Ⓜ Buchanan St. i 10min. concerts daily. Ⓢ Lager £3. Open M-Sa noon-1am, Su 6pm-midnight.

ARTS AND CULTURE

GLASGOW ROYAL CONCERT HALL (GRCH)

CITY CENTER

2 Sauchiehall St. ☎0141 353 8000 www.glasgowconcerthalls.com

A music performance space with a capacity of 2000, the GRCH regularly hosts acts of the Elvis Costello/Robert Cray caliber. Shows at this venue offer any sweet sounds you could be yearning for—from jazz to classical to Celtic.

Ⓜ Buchanan. On the corner of Sauchiehall and Buchanan St. Open M-Sa 10am-6pm.

ESSENTIALS

Practicalities

- **TOURIST OFFICE: Visit Scotland,** the tourist information office, books hotels and B and B's (though, strangely, not hostels), in addition to providing free maps, information, and visitors' guides. Of course, there's also a souvenir shop. *(Open July-Aug M-W 9am-8pm, Th 9:30am-8pm, F-Sa 9am-8pm, Su 10am-6pm. Sept-June shop closes around 5 or 6pm.)*
- **CURRENCY EXCHANGE: Bank of Scotland.** *(54 Sauchiehall St. ☎0845 780 1801 www.bankofscotland.co.uk Open M-Tu 9am-5pm, W 9:30am-5pm, Th-Sa 9am-5pm.)*
- **POST OFFICES: Sauchiehall St.** has a *bureau de change* in addition to regular postal services. *(177 Sauchiehall St. ☎08457740740 www.postoffice.co.uk Open M-Sa 9am-5:30pm.)* Glasgow General Post Office is the big daddy of post offices

in Glasgow and also has a bureau de change. *(47 St. Vincent St. ☎0141 204 4400 postoffice.co.uk Open M-Sa 9am-5:30pm.)*

Emergency!

- **LATE-NIGHT PHARMACIES: Park Road Pharmacy.** *(405 Great Western Rd. ☎0141 339 5979 www.postoffice.co.uk i Credit cards accepted. Open M-F 9am-6pm, Sa 9am-5pm.)* **Boots.** *(200 Sauchiehall St. i Credit cards accepted. Open M-W 8am-6pm, Th 8am-8pm, F 8am-6pm, Sa 8am-6pm, Su 10am-6pm.)*

Getting There

Edinburgh Bus Station is the main hub for Edinburgh. Buses come in from Scotland, England, and beyond. *(#9 Elder St. ☎0131 652 5920 www.citylink.co.uk Luggage storage £2.50-3.50 per 3hr.; £5-7 per 24 hr. Lost token £6. Toilets £.30; exact change necessary. Ticket office open daily 9am-8pm.)* Several different bus companies run routes to and from Edinburgh, including **National Express** *(☎08705 80 80 80 www.nationalexpress.com)* linking England and Scotland, **Scottish Citlink** *(☎08705 50 50 50 www.citylink.co.uk)* which connects towns within Scotland, and **Stagecoach** *(☎0870 608 2 608 www.stagecoachbus.com).*

Getting Around

The **subway** or **Underground** in Glasgow (called **"Clockwork Orange"**) is operated by the Strathclyde Partnership for Transport. There are 15 subway stops in Glasgow that lie on one circle. The Glasgow subway operates every 4-8min. Mondays to Saturdays between 6:30am and 11:30pm. On Sundays service is restricted to 11am-6pm, with trains every 8min. Trains take approximately 24min. for an entire circle. *(Single journey £1.20. 10 trips £10. "Discovery Ticket" for 1 day unlimited travel after 9:30am or all day Su £3.50.)*

st. andrews ☎01334

The town of St. Andrews, besides being a mecca for every tourist to ever get turned on by Jack Nicklaus' putting prowess or Tiger Woods's "long drive," is a beautiful seaside university town. Quite possibly one of the most cosmopolitan towns in Europe, St. Andrews swells in population during term time as thousands of students, many of them international, attend the **University of St. Andrews,** Scotland's oldest university. It's perhaps thanks to the students that a few good bars and affordable restaurants have kept the fancy plaid pants "golfers" establishments at bay. Still, **golf** reigns supreme here (the Scots *did* invent the thing) and, pro shops, putting greens, whirring golf carts, hotels, restaurants, and bars all cater to those out to improve their swing. Just keep them away from the fine china.

ORIENTATION

Figuring out where you are in **St. Andrews** is never hard, partly because it's not very big, partly because the street system is easily navegable, and partly because you're awesome with directions. It helps to have self-confidence, right? The city's layout of the city can essentiallly be divided into the **east end** by the Cathedral and the St. Andrews Castle and the **west end** near the Royal and Ancient Golf Club. The three main arteries that traverse the city are **North St.,** closest to the ocean, **Market St.,** the main thoroughfare, and **South St.,** which ends on the eastern end with an arch from the ancient walled city. Getting off at the bus station, exit and turn left at the roundabout to find yourself at the eastern end of Market St. From there, the world is your oyster. Seriously, you could go find some, the ocean's right there.

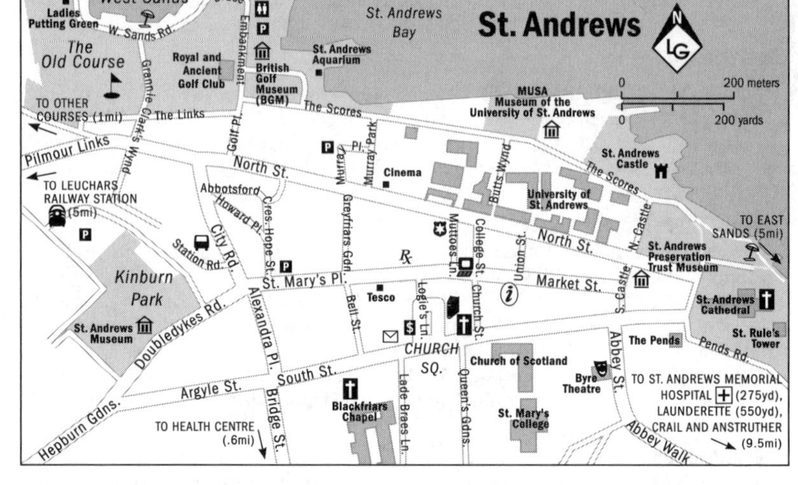

ACCOMMODATIONS

Accommodations in St. Andrews are, unfortunately, seriously lacking for the budgeter. There's only one year-round hostel, and the B and Bs, even in the off season, are fairly costly. The one upshot is that, for such a small town, there is a lot of variety. Book ahead to make sure you've got a place before taking the train or bus and bear in mind that prices rise significantly during the high season *(especially July-Aug)* and become ungodly expensive the week before, during and after the British Open *(late June, alternate years).*

ST. ANDREWS TOURIST HOSTEL

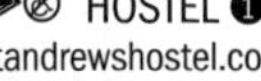
HOSTEL ❶

Inchcape House, St. Mary's Pl. ☎01334 474 306 www.standrewshostel.com

This place isn't going to win any awards in the "original name" department, but it's comfortable, centrally located and cheap, which is really about all you should hope for. Check out the "What's on in St. Andrews" board or rent some clubs and hit the links *(£6).*

i Kitchen and lounge use available. Ⓢ M-F dorms from £12; Sa-Su up to £30. Reception open daily 8am-3pm and 6-10pm.

THE DUNVEGAN HOTEL

HOTEL ❹

7 Pilmour Pl., North St. ☎01334 473 105 www.dunveganhotel.com

As their business card claims, the hotel is "only a 9-iron from the Old Course." Still, the chances that you can afford to play on the Old Course are basically nil, and the chance that you'll be able to stay in the Dunvegan aren't much better. Still, you should stop by the bar to have a drink and check out all the famous celebrities (Clint Eastwood? Hello?) that have visited the hotel.

i Breakfast included. Doubles only. Ⓢ In summer £160; in winter £100.

ARDGOWAN HOTEL

HOTEL ❹

2 Playfair Terr. ☎01334 472 970 www.ardgowanhotel.co.uk

Yeah, it's expensive, but it's actually not that much pricier than some of the B and Bs or guesthouses in the area, and it'll make you feel like you're living the high life. With huge rooms including flatscreens, tables and desks, chairs and ottomans, snacks and coffee and tea supplies, this place has got the works. Listen for the seagulls cawing through the open skylight as you climb the stairs.

Ⓢ High-season rooms approx. £100; low-season £60.

CRAIGMORE GUESTHOUSE GUESTHOUSE ❹
#3 Murray Park ☎01334 472 142 www.standrewscraigmore.com
This place was *made* for golfing tourists. The little gnome-like statue of a golfer at the bottom of the stairs says it all. If, for some reason, it doesn't, the comfortable rooms with patterned wallpaper provide a compelling addendum.
i Full Scottish breakfast included. Ⓢ Shared occupancy rooms £45; singles £65.

ARRAN HOUSE GUESTHOUSE ❸
5 Murray Pk. ☎01334 474 724 www.arranhousestandrews.co.uk
The rooms in Arran House have the kind of plush, fluffy comforters you usually associate with five-star hotels. There's also that one really sweet blankie you had when you were little. With a friendly owner, amazing bathrooms (showers with power heads), and lots of natural light in the upstairs rooms, this is a great option in the guesthouse department.
i Full breakfast included. Free Wi-Fi. Ⓢ In summer £40; in winter £35.

SIGHTS

Great Scot! There are things to see in St. Andrews that aren't golf-related? We were as surprised as you were; the best are listed below.

ST. ANDREWS CASTLE CASTLE
The Scores ☎01334 477 196 www.historic-scotland.gov.uk
There's a lot of history that goes along with St. Andrews Castle, but what got our attention was the chance to climb down a sweet tunnel! Beseiged in 1546-47, the castle has a mine, constructed by those doing the beseiging, and a counter-mine, constructed frantically by the beseiged to keep their enemies from getting in. You can climb down into both of them. This isn't your kiddie fair ride either—these tunnels are cramped and damp, and it takes a bit of finesse to manuever in them. You game? Oh yeah, the outside of the castle is cool, too.
Ⓢ £5.20, concessions £4.20, children £3.10. Open daily Apr-Sept 9:30am-5:30pm, Oct-Mar 9:30am-4:30pm.

BRITISH GOLF MUSEUM (BGM) MUSEUM
Bruce Embankment ☎01334 460 046 www.britishgolfmuseum.co.uk
We threw in one sight that deals with golf—there was just no way to escape it! (For more on the sport, see the aptly titled **Golf** section, p. 330). The BGM is an attractive and well laid-out museum with more golf clubs than a Florida retiree's garage. It also has holy relics from the world of golf, such as **Tiger Woods's** sweatstained cap. A long and detailed history of the sport is here, too. However, the best part might be the interactive bit at the end where you can "putt-er" around with old as well as new clubs on a small green at the end of the museum
Ⓢ £6, concessions £5, under 15 £3, under 5 free. Open Apr-Oct M-Sa 9:30am-5pm, daily Nov-Dec 10am-4pm, daily Jan-Mar 10am-4pm.

ST. ANDREWS AQUARIUM AQUARIUM
The Scores ☎475 985 www.standrewsaquarium.co.uk
Unless you're really into fish (aren't we all) this may be a little below your age-level. With lots of information tablets of the pop-up variety and, some piranhas, rays, and poisonous frogs, the aquarium is full of one other (land) species: small children.
i Only one half of the aquarium is wheelchair-accessible, but access is free to that half. Ⓢ £6.90, students £6.10, children £5.20, family (2 adults + 2 children) £22.20, teachers £4.10. Open daily in summer 10am-5pm; in winter 10am-4pm.

MUSA: MUSEUM OF THE UNIVERSITY OF ST. ANDREWS MUSEUM

7a The Scores ☎461 660 museuminquiries@st-andrews.ac.uk

Showcasing highlights from the University's collection of the old, revered and bizarre (an old lobster kept in formaldhyde because it has a deformed claw?), the MUSA is definitely worth a look. The exhibit describing the "Silver Arrow" competition, which was held to find the school's best archer, has a really funny interactive game display. Among the gold and silver maces and 17th-century paintings, there's tons to see—you can even laugh at golfers' bad shots from afar with the free telescope on the terrace.

Free. Open Apr-Oct M-Sa 10am-5pm; Su noon-4pm; Nov-Mar Th-Su noon-4pm.

THE WEST SANDS BEACH

Just west of the beginning of the Old Course

When the tide's out, there are over 200 yd. of fine, gorgeous sand for you to meander upon at this beautiful stretch of beach. People come here to build sandcastles, play a little bit of beach soccer, or just generally enjoy themselves. Check out the tide pools to maybe see a couple of crabs that haven't been devoured by the many seagulls. Watch out for jellyfish, though.

ST. ANDREWS CATHEDRAL RUINS

Bottom of Market and South St. ☎472 563 www.historic-scotland.gov.uk

It's not that you "can't miss" seeing the ruins of what, when it was finished in 1318, was Scotland's largest building—it's just that, quite literally, you can't miss it. It's huge. This huge building dominates the eastern end of town. Wandering around the grassy fields that used to hold choirs is quite the experience. Get to the visitors' center to visit the museum that houses some of the intricate, stonework artifacts that have been recovered. The museum also contains the sarcophagus of St. Andrew himself.

£4.20, seniors £3.40, ages 5-15 £2.50. Open daily Apr-Sept 9:30am-5:30pm, Oct-May 9:30am-4pm.

glasgow and st. andrews

GOLF

Welcome to the sport that's an excuse to drink whiskey while pretending to exercise (and indeed, the first golf matches were accompanied by a mandatory meal and drink). That thing your dad did every Father's Day, Labor day, Sunday... well, any day really. The long and short of it is, golf was invented here in St. Andrews, and people know it. This is probably the only town where, on certain blocks, pro shops actually outnumber residential housing. 2010 marked the 150th anniversary of the **British Open,** which was held on the **Old Course,** the town's most famous course of Scottish style "links." Nine holes out. Turn around. Nine holes in. Repeat.

DAVID JOY HISTORIAN

The Grange ☎01334 475 133 www.golfhistorian.co.uk

A native St. Andrean, David Joy has spent his life loving, living, and appreciating golf. He's now created a one-man show in which he portrays the inventor of the sport of golf himself, Tom Morris. This act has taken Joy to golf course inaugurations across the globe. If you're around during the British Open, he can be seen nightly at the **Byre Theatre.** Alternatively, if you'd like to chat directly with Mr. Joy about local culture and history, give him a call.

LADIES PUTTING GREEN PUTTING GREENS

Ladies Putting Club, West Sands ☎01334 475 196

A good option for the uninitiated, the Ladies Putting Club offers a "Himalayas" course (think miniature golf course without all the windmills) of rolling greens and 18 holes, right next to the Old Course.

i Prices per 18 holes. £2, seniors £1, under age 16 £1. Open Apr-Sept M-F 10:30am-6:30pm. Members-only M-Tu 4:45-5:30pm, W noon-4pm, Th 10-11am, F 4:45-5:30pm.

FOOD

Food in St. Andrews comes in one of two varieties—the expensive and the cheap. Strangely enough, sometimes these don't coordinate in a manner consistent with the usual "cost for quality" mentality. Get your chips, sammies, and frozen pizzas at **Tesco.** There are also two 24hr. ATMs outside. *(138-140 Market St. www.tesco.com Open M-Sa 6am-midnight, Su 9am-midnight.)*

THE TAILEND RESTAURANT — RESTAURANT ❷

130 Market St. ☎01334 474 070 www.tailsendrestaurant.co.uk

Y'know, anyone can make a fish and chips (I mean c'mon. Ingredients? Fish. Chips.), but there are very few places that can *make* fish 'n chips, and the Tailend Restaurant is one of those few. It's the batter. There's a seating area in the back of the restaurant, but these types of meals are at their best when you get them out of the little cardboard box and eat while sitting on a park bench. Maybe you could even walk over and get a view of the sea. That is, if you can stave off temptation that long.

Fish and chips supper £5.80, ½-supper £3.20. Open daily 11:30am-10:30pm.

ZEST — CAFE, SMOOTHIES ❷

95 South St. ☎01334 471 451

Look for the bright green plastic chairs outside on the sidewalk terrace and you've found this coffee and smoothie destination. Scan the menu for those selections with a green apple logo—they're options created with an eye toward healthy living. By the time you smell those scones, though, you won't care if they're healthy or not.

i Free Wi-Fi. Coffee £1.30-2.70. Smoothies £3-4.25. Open M-Sa 8am-6:30pm, Su 9am-6:30pm.

FLIP! — RESTAURANT ❷

171 South St. ☎01334 470 470 www.flipfun.co.uk

One of the new shops on the block, Flip! works to practice "eco-friendly fast food." With a menu comprised of brown, white, or gluten-free breads, and fair-trade coffee, they're well on their way. Try your sandwich "floppy" (naan bread), "flip" (a wrap), or "flipini" (panini style).

i Takeaway or sit-in available. Sandwiches around £3.50. Open daily 11am-8pm.

MAISHA — RESTAURANT ❸

5 College St. ☎01334 476 666 www.maisharestaurant.co.uk

The food's nice and the ambience relaxing...but what's with the music? That sitar belongs in a Spongebob Squarepants cartoon, not in a place where people desire to have a meal! If you have the power to block out music from your mind, Maisha is worth it for excellent curries and other Indian fare. Try the 3-course lunch (their first course: papdoms).

Cross street between Market and North St. 3-course lunch special £5.95. Open daily 11am-3pm and 5-11pm.

THE GRILL HOUSE RESTAURANT — RESTAURANT ❸

Inchcape House, St. Mary's Pl. ☎01334 470 500 www.houserestaurants.com

A local favorite, this place does Americanized fare—complete with the over-sized plates. The interior comes straight out of a Cancún tourist cantina, with colorfully painted walls and Corona ads on the walls.

Entrees £7-16. Open daily noon-10:30pm.

THE SEAFOOD RESTAURANT RESTAURANT ❺

The Scores (next to the Aquarium) ☎01334 479 475 www.theseafoodrestaurant.com

A little glass box down by the ocean holds one of St. Andrews's finest restaurants. Fresh catch is brought in everyday and prepared in the kitchen in the middle of the dining area, so you can see your meal being prepared as well as the ocean from where you're sitting. There's no (official) dress code, though you should do your best to look smart. No kids under 12 allowed during dinner.

2-course lunch £22, 3-course lunch £26. 3-course dinner 3 £45. Open M-Su noon-2:30pm and 6:30-10pm.

TASTE CAFE ❶

77-79 Market St. ☎01334 277 959

The local student coffeeshop, Taste is small, and couches surround a wood burning stove make it feel like a cabin. If you're in during term time, you might get wrapped up in an intense philosophy debate.

On North St., near the West End. i Coffee is organic and fair-trade. Americano £1.20. Latté £1.70. Open in summer 8am-8pm; term time 8am-10pm.

NIGHTLIFE

If you're looking for a late night out with dancing and boozing and possibly some stripping, go somewhere else. Nightlife in St. Andrews revolves around pub culture, and some of the most original, most local, and most unchanged places can be found here. The **Central** and **Keys** bars are the obvious spots, but the **Whey Pat** (down past the arch on South St.) is a must-hit, and the **Rule** is worth a look as well. (Read: students. Lots of them.) Not bad for a sleepy little golf town, eh?

WHEY PAT TAVERN PUB ❷

1 Bridge St. ☎01334 477 740 whey.standrews@belhavenpubs.net

A real ale hall, the Whey Pat has four ales on tap (this mean hand-pulled—none of that "cold-brewed" crap). Of those four, three are in month-long rotation. Add on 40+ malt whiskeys to try, and one raucously fun dominos night *(W)* and you've got a great place to get silly. The University of St. Andrews also voted their nachos the best in town.

At the western end of South St., just through the arch. i Folk music session Tu nights. Pints £2.40-3.55. Open M-W 11am-midnight, Th-Sa 11am-1am, Su 11am-midnight.

NPH CINEMA CINEMA ❸

117 North St. ☎01334 474 902 www.nphcinema.co.uk

Showing a selection of new releases, the New Picture House has three theaters and, these days shows some 3D movies.

i 3D films £1.50 extra. £6, children £4.30, seniors £5. Open 5:30-around 11pm. Matinees Sa-Su 2pm.

THE RULE BAR ❷

130 Market St. ☎01334 473 473 mccleesemcplace.com

It's the largest bar in St. Andrews, and the students come in droves. Even during the summer months, more young people hit this nightlife spot than anywere else. With two floors for seating and a large open space downstairs for dancing, it'll make you think that maybe the party scene in St. Andrews isn't so small at all.

Open M-Th 9am-midnight, F-Sa 9am-1am, Su 9am-11pm.

THE WEST PORT BAR ❷

170 South St. ☎01334 473 186 www.maclay.com

A classy, golden bar (no seriously, the light is golden) on the end of South St., the West Port has a HUGE beer garden which should be taken advantage of during the warm summer months. Even in the winter months, the umbrellas keep things dry and the heat lamps keep things warm, so, really, don't limit yourself. If you do choose to sit inside, check out the booths with TVs built right into the wall.

Pints £3-4. Mixed drinks £5. Open daily 9am-midnight.

THE KEYS BAR BAR ❷

87 Market St. ☎01334 472 414

The Keys works like this: you walk into the bar, everyone in the bar looks up to see if they know you and they either say hello if they do or return to their drinks if they don't. It's up to you to find out how many visits it takes to become a "regular." The interior is no frills, but what did you expect?

Spirits £1.40. Pints £2.85. Open M-Th 11am-midnight, F-Sa 11am-1am, Su 11am-midnight.

THE CENTRAL BAR PUB ❸

77-79 Market St. ☎01334 478 296

It's the biggest and most noticeable bar on Market St., and more than likely, the first place you'll stop. Good thing The Central Bar, one of the oldest pubs in St. Andrews, has retained its image and atmosphere, and supplies you with the largest collection of real ales in town (8 different kinds).

Spirits £2.35-5. Pints from £2.75-3.10. Open M-Th 11am-midnight, F-Sa 11am-12:15am, Su 11am-midnight.

ESSENTIALS

Practicalities

- **TOURIST OFFICE:** At **Visit Scotland Visitor Information Centre,** the information, maps, and brochures are all free, as is the booking service. They also book tickets for tours. *(70 Market St. ☎01334 474609 www.visitscotland.com Open Sept-June M-Sa 9:15am-5pm; July-Aug M-Sa 9:15am-7pm, Su 10am-7pm.)*
- **BANKS: Santander Bank** has one 24hr. ATM with free withdrawals. *(145 Market St. ☎04857 654321 www.santander.co.uk Open M-F 9am-5pm, Sa 9am-12:30pm.)*

Emergency!

- **PHARMACY: Boots.** *(119 Market St. ☎01334 474 306 Open M-Sa 8:30am-5:30pm, Su noon-5:30pm.)*
- **POLICE:** *(100 North St. ☎switchboard 08456 005 702, emergencies ☎999 Open 24hr.)*

Getting There

By Bus

St. Andrews Bus Station *(City Rd. ☎01334 474238 www.stagecoachbus.com. i Luggage lockers £1. Toilets £.20. Ticket office open M-F 9am-1pm and 2-5pm, Sa 9am-noon)*, in addition to being your bus arrival/departure point, is also a place where you can book your train tickets. Popular bus destinations include: **#23 Stirling** *(every 2hr. M-Sa 9:30am-7:30pm)*; **#96 Leuchars/Dundee**: Luechars *(5 buses from 6am-10am, then hourly until 4:50pm; 5 buses from 5-11pm)*; **Dundee** *(6 buses 6:30-10:15am, then hourly until 5:15pm; 5 buses from 5-11pm).*

By Train

Queen Street Station has service all over Scotland and England. Book online if you can't get into the ticket office. *(George Sq. and N. Hanover St. ☎0845 748 4950 www.scotrail.co.uk i Luggage storage is available M-Sa 7am-10:30pm, Su 9am-10:30pm. £5 per day for small, £6 per day for medium, £7 per day for large. Ticket office open 7am-10pm. Station open 6am-last train, around 11:30pm.)* Popular destinations include **Edinburgh** *(£11.60. 50min, 4* *every hr. 6am-11:30pm.)*, **Aberdeen** *(£40.30. 2hr., 2 every hr. from 7:15am-10:50pm.)*, and **Fort William** *(£23. 4hr., 10+ trains per day).*

Getting Around

There are practically no taxis in St. Andrews because everybody can walk everywhere. Hope you're not lazy!

NORTHERN IRELAND

Northern Ireland
SCOTLAND
Rathlin Island
North Channel
Ballintoy
Carrick-a-Rede Rope Bridge
Giant's Causeway
Cushendun
Cairnryan
Bushmills
Bally-castle
Kirkcolm
Malin Head
Portrush
Cushendall
Portstewart
Glenariff (Waterfoot)
Stranraer
INISHOWEN PENINSULA
Coleraine
Ballymoney
Glenariff Forest Park
Carnloug
Glenarm
Portpatrick
Lough Foyle
Antrim Mts.
Ballygalley
Limavady
Larne
Islandmagee
Derryveagh Mts.
Derry/Londonderry
COUNTY ANTRIM
Carrick-fergus
Dungiven
Maghera
Bangor
Letterkenny
COUNTY DERRY
Antrim
Newtown-Abbey
Newtownards
Belfast
Greyabbey
Strabane
Strangford Lough
ARDS PENINSULA
COUNTY DONEGAL
NORTHERN IRELAND
Lough Neagh
Lisburn
Ballynahinch
Portaferry
COUNTY TYRONE
Craigavon
LECALE PENINSULA
Castlederg
Omagh
Dungannon
COUNTY DOWN
Portadown
Downpatrick
Kesh
Donegal
Castlewellan
Dundrum Bay
Lower Lough Erne
Aughnacloy
Armagh
Newcastle
COUNTY ARMAGH
Mourne Mts.
Newry
Belleek
COUNTY FERMANAGH
Monaghan
Warrenpoint
Enniskillen
Kilkeel
Irish Sea
Linaskea
Carlingford
Belcoo
Upper Lough Erne
COUNTY MONAGHAN
COOLEY PENINSULA
Dundalk
Sligo
COUNTY SLIGO
Lough Allen
COUNTY CAVAN
IRELAND
A2
A26
A37
A8
A6
A5
A4
A3
N16
N1
N2
N3
0
20 kilometers
20 miles

BELFAST

Finally able to breathe after years of conflict, Belfast is coming into its own as a burgeoning metropolis. Its various shopping centers sell everything from strawberries to luxury watchwear. The city's people are kind and friendly, even though you don't have to go far to find someone who not only remembers "the Troubles," but can also recall a time when a policeman frisked you before you entered the city center. But far from having resentment and a "hush-hush" attitude, the people of Belfast enagage with their history; black cab tours of West Belfast, the area of hottest conflict, have become a popular tourist attraction. Think of Belfast as Dublin's badass older brother who plays in a band: he's cool, gritty, and gets tons of groupies. Head to Belfast to become one yourself.

greatest hits

- **BELFAST RAGER.** Party on the three floors of Belfast's epic club Lavery's (p. 347)...if you can handle it.
- **MUSE ON.** Museums like the Ulster Museum (p. 342) also come in a different flavor in Belfast. Don't let the dinosaur eat that Dutch Master!
- **SPANISH ARMADA.** Conquer the night at The Spaniard (p. 348), Belfast's extraordinary, exclusive bar.
- **THE SANDWICHING HOUR.** Fight through the masses to the excellent sandwiches at Sarnie's (p. 346), Belfast's top deli.

student life

Belfast is home to a vibrant student scene, anchored by universities including **Queen's University.** Cheap eats soon follow, and you can get in on the action at restaurants like the excellent **Molly's Yard,** where eating fine cuisine in a lot just north of campus is just a part of everyday life. And **Belfast** may just give the Edinburgh scene a run for its money. The city has a club called **Filthy McNasty's.** Come on now. The list goes on from there, including the fast-paced, debauched **Rain,** as well as the **Duke of York,** an incredible bar (not to mention the launching pad for Snow Patrol).

orientation

call me

The phone code for Belfast is ☎028.

What's with all the Donegalls? Okay, get this: **Donegall Square** surrounds the city hall, **Donegall Road** runs from the west, crossing through town at **Shaftesbury Square** and becoming **Donegall Pass,** and finally, there's **Donegall Street** that runs right through the heart of the cathedral district. Lesson to be learned? If someone gives you directions via a "Donegall" anything, make sure you get a second opinion. Belfast is a slim city, running mostly north to south, with the previously conflicted **Fall** and **Shankill Roads** in West Belfast usually just being visited by tourists in a cab. **Queen's University** lies south of the city center along **University Road** (follow Bedford St. and Dublin Rd. from City Hall) and houses most of the student life and nearly all of the budget accommodations in Belfast. What was called the "Golden Mile" in past years—the triangle of Dublin Rd., Great Victoria, and Bruce St.—is now pretty much dead. A few fast-food joints and the odd pub can be found there, but the new hotspot for nightlife is the **Cathedral Quarter,** the area above City Hall near the **River Lagan.**

THE UNIVERSITY DISTRICT

The University District centers on Queen's University but extends into the residental neighborhoods to the west and south. The **Student Union, The Botanic,** and **Eglantine Inn** are all popular student bars, and there are several hostels and bed and breakfasts on **Eglantine** and **Fitzwilliam Streets. Lisburn Road** provides the other, far-side north-south channel, and also has several good restaurants and cafes. If you ever get disoriented, ask for either Lisburn or University Rd. and you'll be able to point yourself back toward the city center.

THE CATHEDRAL QUARTER

Boasting the hottest nightclubs and several bars, the Cathedral Quarter is experiencing an upsurge in both popularity and establishments—this is where you'll find the new pub on the block. **High Street** provides a neat "bottom" to the neighborhood, which extends up to the **University of Ulster** and east over to **North Street.** Full of smaller streets, Waring street has some good bars and luxury hotels, and then there's that Donegall street again.

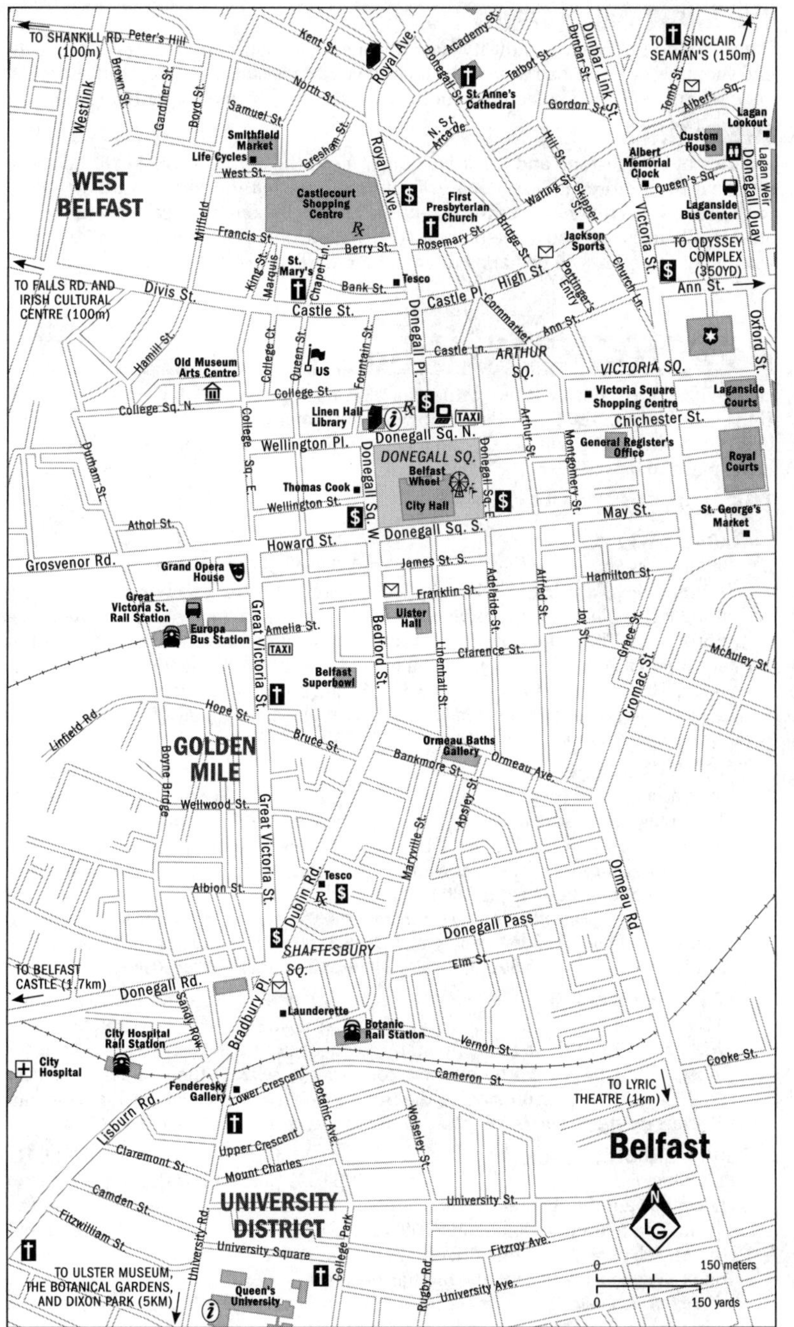
Belfast
WEST BELFAST
GOLDEN MILE
UNIVERSITY DISTRICT
TO SHANKILL RD. (100m)
TO SINCLAIR SEAMAN'S (150m)
TO FALLS RD. AND IRISH CULTURAL CENTRE (100m)
TO ODYSSEY COMPLEX (350YD)
TO BELFAST CASTLE (1.7km)
TO LYRIC THEATRE (1km)
TO ULSTER MUSEUM, THE BOTANICAL GARDENS, AND DIXON PARK (5KM)
Smithfield Market
Life Cycles
Castlecourt Shopping Centre
St. Anne's Cathedral
First Presbyterian Church
St. Mary's
Tesco
Jackson Sports
Custom House
Albert Memorial Clock
Lagan Lookout
Laganside Bus Center
Old Museum Arts Centre
US
Linen Hall Library
Victoria Square Shopping Centre
Laganside Courts
General Register's Office
Royal Courts
Thomas Cook
Belfast Wheel
City Hall
St. George's Market
Grand Opera House
Great Victoria St. Rail Station
Europa Bus Station
Ulster Hall
Belfast Superbowl
Ormeau Baths Gallery
Launderette
Botanic Rail Station
City Hospital Rail Station
City Hospital
Fenderesky Gallery
Queen's University
DONEGALL SQ.
ARTHUR SQ.
VICTORIA SQ.
SHAFTESBURY SQ.
TAXI
0 150 meters
0 150 yards
LG

THE SHOPPING DISTRICT

Right next to the Entries and City Hall, the shopping district houses the more high-end shopping of Belfast as well as the massive **Victoria Square** and **Castlecourt** shopping centers. Shoppers will be happy to note that Belfast is much cheaper than Dublin.

THE ENTRIES

A series of cobblestone and brick walking streets, the entries provide all the shopping that the Victoria and Castlecourt centers can't. The term "entry" actually refers to tiny alleyways that have "covered" entrances in between shops on the wider open streets. Chances are you'll see them as you walk around, but if you need help, just ask someone and they'll be happy to point you to the nearest one.

accommodations

Belfast has a great hostel scene, with several promising options lying close to Queen's University. Most of the B and Bs are down along that area as well. In fact, aside from luxury hotels and the odd hostel down in the city center area, the university district is the place to be.

THE UNIVERSITY DISTRICT

VAGABONDS — HOSTEL ❷

#9 University Rd. ☎028 9543 8772 www.vagabondsbelfast.com

A brand-new, "for backpackers by backpackers" hostel, Vagabonds does everything right. Clean dorms, great common spaces, and a fantastic staff are all the norm here. The manager and his motley crew of employees are guaranteed to show you a good time. So good you might have to stay home for a night and just relax. That's OK, though—Monday movie night means free popcorn. Enjoy.

From Donegall Sq., follow Bedford St. onto Dublin Rd. and University Rd. i Tourist information available. Ⓢ Rates vary. Dorms £13-16.

PADDY'S PALACE — HOSTEL ❷

68 Lisburn Rd. ☎028 9033 3367 www.paddyspalace.com

The rules list is sort of long when you walk in the door (no disruption, food and drink only in the kitchen—but Paddy's Palace is pretty nice. The carpets are a different color in every room just to change it up. You can score a free continental breakfast from 7:30 to 9:30am.

Across the street from Arnie's, on the corner of Fitzwilliam and Lisburn. i Continental breakfast included. Ⓢ 12-bed dorm M-F £9.50, Sa-Su £10; 8-bed M-F £13, Sa-Su £14; 6-bed M-F £14, Sa-Su £15; 4-bed M-F £16, Sa-Su £17; doubles £40-45. Breakfast 7:30-9:30am.

THE GEORGE B AND B — BED AND BREAKFAST ❸

9 Eglantine Ave. ☎028 9043 9619 the-george@hotmail.co.uk

With the help of their fantastic staff, the George provides a budget option for those willing to pay a little bit more for privacy. Relax in the wonderfully decorated sitting room or outside on the front bench in the (occasional) Belfast sun.

Across the street from Marine House. Ⓢ Singles £30; doubles £50. Breakfast 7-9am.

LAGAN'S HOSTEL — HOSTEL ❷

121 Fitzroy Ave. ☎0754 041 8246 www.laganbackpackers.com

Lagan's is another hostel that has built its reputation entirely on its service. The dorms are plain but clean and you'll enjoy the benefit of free Wi-Fi throughout the hostel, as well as a free full breakfast. Check out the comments in the sign-in book to see just how high the bar has been set.

i Kitchen use available. Ⓢ 8-bed dorms M-F £12, Sa-Su £13; 6-bed M-F £13, Sa-Su £14; 4-bed

M-F £14 Sa-Su £15; 3-bed M-F £15, Sa-Su £16. Singles M-F £25, Sa-Su £28, doubles M-F £18, Sa-Su £20. Reception 24hr.

ARNIE'S BACKPACKERS
HOSTEL 1

63 Fitzwilliam St. ☎028 9024 2867 www.arniesbackpackers.co.uk

Yet another excellent hostel in Belfast, Arnie's has the local vibe going on. Play with Arnie's two dogs in the backyard seating area or sit down in the lounge; the tiny 13 in. TV will help you keep your focus on meeting new friends.

On Fitzwilliam St., on the Lisburn Rd. side. i The #1 bunk in the 4-bed dorm is lofted and offers more privacy than the rest. Computer £1 per 30min.; proceeds donated to charity. Kitchen available. 8-bed dorm £10 per person; 4-bed £12 per person.

MARINE HOUSE
GUESTHOUSE 3

30 Eglantine Ave. ☎028 9066 2828 www.marinehouse3star.com

The amazing rooms in an enormous, classic Victorian home make beautiful Marine House the best B and B on the block. However, the real gem of the establishment is the owner Nat, who is incredibly kind to all of his guests, helping them find attractions and offering advice.

On Eglantine Ave. near Lisburn Rd. i Full Irish breakfast included. Singles £45; doubles £60.

THE GOLDEN MILE

PREMIER INN
HOTEL 4

2-6 Waring St. ☎028 9072 7130 www.premierinn.com

A hotel by any other name would smell...pretty much the same, as it turns out. One of a UK-based chain of hotels, Premier Inn is clean and comfortable but essentially the same as every other chain hotel you've ever stayed in. Except for the purple decor, that is.

5min. walk northwest of Donegall Sq. Rooms £60. Reception 24hr.

THE MERCHANT HOTEL
HOTEL 5

35-39 Waring St. ☎028 9023 4888 www.themerchanthotel.com

We're only really including this because it's so absurdly, over-the-top nice. With rooms that will make you think you've died and gone to hotel heaven, these bad boys run for three digits a night *(£220-450)*. Out of your price range? Yeah, ours too. Still, check out the cocktail bar where sculpted angels will look down on you as you drink.

Doubles £220; junior suites £300; suites £450. Reception 24hr.

THE SHOPPING DISTRICT

BELFAST INTERNATIONAL HOSTEL
HOSTEL 2

22-32 Donegall Rd. ☎028 9031 5435 info@hini.org.uk

BIH is like a McDonalds—you only get it really late at night and you don't really want it. Housed in a corporate office space, it has over 200 rooms and less than a pint's worth of character. Still, if you can't find a room in Belfast, head here and you're guaranteed a clean place to stay for the night.

Just off Shaftesbury Sq. i Presentation of passport or other valid ID necessary for check-in. Dorms M-F £11, Sa-Su £12; standard singles M-F £21, Sa-Su £22.

EUROPA HOTEL
HOTEL 5

Great Victoria St. www.hastingshotels.com

The Europa hotel holds the dubious record of being the most bombed building in Belfast, with over 30 attempts and three explosions. They've put in some explosion-proof glass at this point, and fortunately, nobody's woken up in a rubble heap. Rooms here are actually quite luxurious.

From Donegall Sq. S., walk west on Howard St. and turn. i Wi-Fi £6 per 90min. Doubles from £100. Reception 24hr.

sights

From the **Saint Anne's Cathedral** with its elegant and pointy architecture, to the **W5 Children Activities Center** (think giant Tinkertoys), Belfast has a multitude of things to see. To recommend just a few, the **city hall** tour is worth either a history lesson or a laugh, depending on how you choose to experience it; **Queen's University** is elegant or overpriced depending on how you choose to look at it; and the **Crown Bar** is either memorable or not, depending on how much you choose to drink.

THE UNIVERSITY DISTRICT

ULSTER MUSEUM — MUSEUM

Botanic Ave. ☎028 9042 8428 www.nmni.com

Operating on five floors, and covering art, history, and natural history, this museum has a hell of a lot of exhibits. Even better, all of them are very good. See everything from famous Italian art pieces to **T-rex** heads. By the time you finish, you'll have gotten your tourist fix for the entire month.

Just inside the Botanic Gardens South of Queen's University, on the right. Free. Open Tu-Sa 10am-5pm.

THE BOTANICAL GARDENS — PARK

Belfast Gardens Park

Not to be confused with "The Botanic Inn" sports bar across the street (serving relaxation of a different genre), the Botanical Gardens are an excellent spot to check out some scenery, watch people walk their dogs, or examine one of the old-fashioned greenhouses. Bets are still off as to why there's a pine tree in a cage in the middle of the park though.

Just south of Queen's University on University Rd. Free.

QUEEN'S UNIVERSITY — UNIVERSITY

Queen's University Belfast, University Rd. ☎028 9097 5252 www.qub.ac.uk

Looking more like the cathedrals of Rome than the inside of your third grade classroom, this school should definitely be passed through and admired. If you pick up the "Walkabout Queen's" pamphlet, you'll take a similar route to the guided tours, with no need to tip the brochure when you're done! (Unless, of course, you thought the brochure was cute, and then you could maybe ask it to dinner and then, well...). The nine stops will take you at least an hour to get through.

To get to the visitor's center, just walk through the main entrance. Call ahead to arrange a guided tour. Free. Visitors' center open M-Sa 9:30am-4:30pm, Su 10am-1am.

THE GOLDEN MILE

ST. ANNE'S CATHEDRAL — CATHEDRAL

Donegall St.

Possibly the only time that Gothic and modern architecture have been mixed to positive results, the cavernous interior of the gaudy St. Anne's Cathedral is broken up by the "Spire of Hope," a giant space needle (we're not kidding) jutting through the center of the ceiling and extending into the sky above. Dedicated in 2007, this addition proclaims hope to a city that had none for such a long time.

On the corner of Donegall and Talbot St. 1 block south of the University of Ulster. Free. Donations encouraged. Open M-F 10am-4pm.

ST. GEORGE'S MARKET — MARKET

Waterfront

First opened in 1890, some things about the St. George's market haven't changed—you'll still get a strong smell of raw fish and meat as you walk in the entrance. Still, the market has changed with time, and now find everything from handmade jewelry to spices to antiques. Check it out Saturday mornings and listen to the live music that goes on right in the middle of everything. A short history of the market can be found on placards inside the east entrance.

On the corner of Oxford and May St. Prices vary. Haggle. Open F 6am-2pm, Sa 10am-2pm, Su 8am-2pm.

THE SHOPPING DISTRICT

BELFAST CITY HALL AND TOUR — CITY TOUR

City Hall ☎028 9027 0456

The free, approximately 1hr. tour of Belfast City Hall offers you the opportunity to do several things: admire giant silver scepters and funny old robes, sit in the seats of all the big-wig politicos that are using that funny clothing, and touch furniture that was supposed to go on the Titanic but never made it inside. It's also informative and historical—we almost forgot that those are important too.

Donegall Sq. Sign up in the foyer of the building, through the front entrance. Free. Tours M-F 11am, 2, and 3pm. Sa 2 and 3pm.

ORMEAU BATHS GALLERY — GALLERY

18a Oremeau Ave. ☎028 9032 1402 www.ormeaubaths.co.uk

Housed in an old Victorian bathhouse—you'll see a few hopefully-empty tubs as you walk in the door, the Ormeau Baths gallery rotates between eight and ten exhibits of all sorts throughout the year. It's a perfect space for a gallery. Quiet, spacious and full of strange echoes, you can almost hear splashing Victorians commenting on the paintings.

3 blocks south of Donegall Sq. on Linenhall St. i Occasionally offers workshops for kids. Free. Open Tu-Sa 10am-5:30pm.

GRAND OPERA HOUSE — OPERA

Great Victoria St. ☎028 9024 1919 www.goh.co.uk

There are few opera houses you'd expect to see elephants in, but of the few, this one might be the best. Inspired by England's former Indian territories, the decor for the Grand Opera House in Belfast incorporates Hindu gods, wooden elephant heads, and pineapple carvings. If you don't get in to see a show (which can be done on the cheap if you call in for standby tickets), at least try and get in to see the theater space. An elephant would never forget it.

Across from the Spires Mall. Prices vary, but usually expect to pay £8-30.

THE ENTRIES

CUSTOM HOUSE — HISTORICAL SITE

Custom House Sq.

The Custom House isn't the most interactive of things to visit. In fact, all you can really do here is walk around and admire Charles Lanyon's architectural work. The Custom House was completed in 1857 to help with Belfast's emerging status as a commercial trading giant. Fun factoid: novelist **Anthony Trollope** worked in the Post Office here for several years.

With your back to city hall, walk right on Chichester St., turn left on Victoria St. and it'll be on your left. Viewing Gallery open M 10am-6pm, Tu-F 10am-9pm, Sa 10am-6pm, Su 1-6pm.

VICTORIA SQUARE SHOPPING CENTRE — MALL

Victoria Sq.

This mall is just a mall (albeit a really, really big one), but it is worth it to scale five plus floors to get a view of Belfast from the clear dome at the top. Get dizzy climbing the stairs or be lazy and take the elevator—it's your choice.

With your back to city hall, walk right on Chichester St., turn left on Victoria St. It'll be on your left. Open M-Tu 9:30am-6pm, W-F 9:30am-9pm, Sa 9am-6pm, Su 1-6pm.

ODYSSEY COMPLEX ENTERTAINMENT COMPLEX

2 Queen's Quay ☎028 9076 6000 www.odysseyarena.com

Not a mall, but if it's not that, then no one's really quite sure what it is. Housing a movie theater—a W5 complex that's essentially Chuck E. Cheese's with a dash of "science" thrown in to make it fieldtrip-accessible—and the Odyssey Arena, which hosts major music acts such as Pearl Jam.

Right off of the Botanic Gardens. Box office open M-F 10am-6pm, Sa 10am-5pm, Su and holidays closed except on event days.

food

Thank God for whose a city whose food options are drunk-friendly. The number of kebab, burger, chip, and Chinese places open late at night here is astounding. They're everywhere, but especially near **Shaftesbury Square** and the university. When you've woken up and had enough water to feel normal again, however, there are also some places that have especially tasty treats. We've listed some of the best below.

THE UNIVERSITY DISTRICT

MOLLY'S YARD RESTAURANT RESTAURANT ❷

1 College Green Mews, Botanic Ave. ☎028 9032 2600 www.mollysyard.co.uk

Come into the weird, garage-like "yard" of Molly's Yard and take a seat at one of the wooden tables outside or one of the candle-graced tables inside. It's your choice—either way you're going to get great eats. Best of all, it's cheap *(dinner £6.95-9.50)*. For this caliber of food, that's amazing. Try the Asian marinated beef skewer with mooli and mango salad with toasted almonds and soy dipping sauce *(£9)*.

1 block south of University St., above the school campus. Dinner entrees £7-9.50. Open M-Th noon-9pm, F-Sa noon-6pm. Evening menu available M-Th 6-9pm, F-Sa 6-9:30pm.

KOOKY'S CAFÉ CAFE ❷

112 Lisburn Rd. ☎029 068 7338

Kooky's Café isn't so much "kooky" as it is a good place to get your morning coffee fix. There are some pieces of modern art on the walls, and yes, those mirrors are wavy instead of square, but the overall feel is much chiller than its name suggests. Grab a "Veggie Works" breakfast with a free-range egg and pull down the morning's paper from the rack.

South of city center. From Donegall Sq., follow Bedford St. straight onto Dublin Rd. and finally Lisburn Rd. Lunch sandwiches £3.25-4. Open M-F 9am-4pm, Sa-Su 10am-3pm.

THE BARKING DOG RESTAURANT ❸

31-32 Malone Rd. ☎028 9066 1885 thebarkingdogoffice@gmail.com

Try the homemade linguini with crab meat, chilli, and lemon and herb butter *(small £6.50, large £11.50)* at this modern chic restaurant with doggie prints on the fence. The candles on your table are real, and they illuminate the older couples that will be dining all around you.

Next to the Botanic Inn on Malone Rd. Entrees £10-20. Open M-Th noon-3:30pm and 5:30-10pm; F-Sa noon-3pm and 5:30-11pm; Su 1-9pm.

THE GOLDEN MILE

NICK'S WAREHOUSE BISTRO ❸

35-39 Hill St. ☎028 9043 9690 www.nickswarehouse.co.uk

Expressionist paintings sit next to home photos at this bistro-esque restaurant. With an enormous wine selection *(£3-5 per glass)* and a comfortable brick interior, Nick's Warehouse gives you all the frills of a high-end restaurant with none of the pretense.

5min. walk Northwest of Donegall Sq. Wine £3-5. Open Tu-Th noon-3pm and 6-9:30pm, F-Sa noon-3pm and 6-10pm.

THE CHIPPIE FAST FOOD ❶

29 Lower North St. ☎028 9043 9619

Absolutely the cheapest option around, everything at the Chippie goes for under £3.30. Several chip variations (that's "fries" to you Amur'can folk) including "gravy chip," "garlic chip," and "curry chip," are here to tempt. If that doesn't whet your palate then go for a quarter poind. Try the Hawaiian burger *(£2.85)*.

3min. walk north of Donegall Sq. Fish £3.30. Everything else £3. Open M-W 10:30am-6pm, Th 10:30am-9pm, F-Sa-6pm.

PRINTER'S CAFÉ RESTAURANT, CAFE ❷

33 Lower Donegall St. ☎028 9031 3406

Down the street from the Duke of York is this BBQ paradise. Get chargrilled Thai beef patties with Asian salad, warm pita bread, satay sauce and sweet chilli sauce *(£8.25)*. Or, if you're just into getting some food in you before heading off to drink at the DOY, grab a sandwich from their takeaway counter at the front of the building.

i Vegetarian options available. Lunch £4-10. Open M-Sa lunch 11:30am-3pm. Dinner F-Sa 5:30-9:30pm.

21 SOCIAL RESTAURANT, BAR ❹

1 Hill St. ☎028 9024 1415 www.21social.co.uk

The newest of the new, chic places on the block, 21 social has three floors—the restaurant downstairs, the well-healed bar upstairs and the VIP bar "Cigarette Girl," which you won't see the inside of unless you've got a big wad of cash in your pocket. Head back to reality and try the risotto of forest mushrooms and cashel blue cheese topped with truffle foam *(£9)*.

Across the street from the Merchant Hotel. £8-14.50. Open M-Tu 11:30am-11pm, W til 12am, Th-Sa til 1am, Su til 9pm.

2TAPS TAPAS BAR ❸

42 Waring St. ☎028 9031 1414 www.2tapswinebar.com

Why they didn't just call it "2Tapas" is a mystery to us as well. This Spanish-influenced tapas bar serves a "Creme Catalan" (orange-infused brulee) and sangria by the jug *(£12)*. The interior is full of wood paneling and wrap-around booths. If you want to head outside, however, the samba music will follow.

5min. walk northwest of Donegall Sq. Lunch plates £7. Tapas £3.50-5. Entrees £12-15. Open in summer daily noon-8pm; fall-spring Tu-Sa noon-8pm.

THE SHOPPING DISTRICT

MADE IN BELFAST IRISH ❸

Units 1 and 2, Wellington St. ☎028 9024 6712 www.madeinbelfastni.com

The welcome mat inside the door declares "Shake your arse for a hip Belfast!" and you best obey, or you're not going to fit in, with the smatterings of wallpaper scraps, mirrors, and spraypaint on the walls set up leopard couches and furry pillows. Even if you're afraid of having a color-induced seizure, you should still come in and eat. The food is all fresh and wholesome and comes in large quantities.

1 block west of Donegall Sq. i Wine and cocktail menu available. Meals £5-10. Open M-W noon-3pm and 5:30-10pm, Th-Sa noon-3pm and 5:30-11pm. Su 12:30-4pm and 6-9pm.

AM:PM RESTAURANT ❸

42 Upper Arthur St. ☎028 9024 9009

Wow, the candelabras here actually get some use. Atmosphere's the thing here, with flowers, mirrors, and tiny lamps that hold candles on your table. It's up to you to decide if the quality matches the jump in price.

1 block east of Donegall Sq. Lunch dishes £5-10. Pints £3.40. Open M-Th 10am-midnight, F-Sa 10am-1am, Su noon-midnight.

FOUNTAIN COFFEE — CAFE ❷

27-29 Fountain St. ☎028 9024 6655

These homemade pastries go the extra mile, thanks to the expert chef. Take one out onto the large terrace area in front of the big bay windows. Student discount 10% with ID.

North of Donegall Sq. i Vegetarian options available. Sandwiches £5-7. Entrees £6.50-7. Coffee £1.30-2.25. Open M-W 7am-6pm, Th 7am-8pm, F-Sa 7am-6pm, Su 11am-5pm.

THE LITTLE CUPCAKE CAFÉ — CUPCAKES ❶

8 Bedford St. ☎028 9024 1751 www.thelittlecupcake.co.uk

Hiding just a minute's walk away from Belfast City Hall, in the middle of the business district, is a tiny little cafe that looks like your grandmother's house. Flowered wallpaper and plaid-embroidered couches don't mean your Grannie can bake like this, though—unless your Grannie actually does make ultra decadent cupcakes of all kinds *(£1.70 each)*. Raspberry white chocolate? Latté? Cookies and cream? Yes, yes, yes, please.

Directly off Donegall Sq. S. Milkshakes £2.20. Cupcakes £1.70 each. Coffee £1-2. Open M-F 8am-6pm, Sa 10:30am-6pm, Su 1-6pm.

THE ENTRIES

SARNIE'S — DELI ❶

35 Rosemary St.

This is a real-deal deli. Squeeze yourself into the tiny interior, wait your turn, order your food (make sure you know what you want beforehand), and wham! Take your foot-long sub outside though, or you'll be trying to get your sandwich to your mouth around somebody else's elbow.

North of Donegall Sq. i Outdoor seating area available. Sandwiches £3.50. Soups £2. Open M-F 6am-3pm.

belfast

CLEMENT'S COFFEE

37-39 Rosemary St. ☎028 9032 2293

Clement's motto is "we're religious about coffee." You'd think that, in a city with Belfast's history, such a remark might spark some ire. Well, everybody's too busy enjoying the coffee to care. Possibly the best latté in town can be found here *(£2)*. Sandwiches and panini available as well. Sit outside or crash in the leather couches by the big bay windows.

North of Donnegal Sq., next to Sarnie's. i Vegetarian options available. Coffee £2-3. Sandwiches and wraps £2-3. Panini £5. Open M-F 8am-5:30pm, Sa 9am-5:30pm, Su noon-5pm.

DOORSTEPS — RESTAURANT ❶

64 Ann St. ☎028 9024 5544 www.doorsteps.com

A good place to head for hearty sandwiches quick on the spot. Grab and go with any of the cold cuts and either sit outside or take it away. The decor of the restaurant won't intrigue your appetite nearly as much as the food.

2 blocks west of Queen's Bridge. i Vegetarian options available. Coffee £1.20-1.65. Sandwiches £3-3.50. Open daily 7am-5:30pm.

nightlife

Belfast's nightlife thrives in the university district and the Cathedral Quarter. On the weekends it'll seem like everyone in town is out, and toward one or two in the morning, you'll find it harder to get into clubs—and even harder to move once you get in. Drinks abound, and Belfast at 3am sees a lot of singing, staggering, and general merriment. Taxi drivers seem to get a little bit picky in the early hours as well, so try and sober up (or at least look it) when attempting to hail a cab.

THE UNIVERSITY DISTRICT

LAVERY'S — PUB, CLUB

12-16 Bradbury Pl. ☎028 9087 1106 www.laverysbelfast.com

Everybody's heard of it, and if they haven't been there themselves it's only because they haven't gotten off the binky yet. Lavery's is huge, with three floors (a bar, music venue, and club), all of which feel spacious—until the weekends, when the crowd spills out the door. Happy hours Monday through Thursday mean all drinks are £2.85. During the week, the third floor is an awesome pool hall.

At the bottom of Shaftsbury Sq. i Outdoor seating available. Pints £3.20. Open M-Sa 11:30am-1am, Su 12:30pm-midnight.

KATY DALY'S, THE SPRING AND AIRBRAKE, LIMELIGHT — CLUB

17 Ormeau Ave. ☎028 9032 7007 www.cdleisure.co.uk

Three spots in one! (Well, you still have to pay for each of them, but they're all right together.) Bar-hop without ever leaving the block: start at Katy Daly's bar and check out how many piercings the person next to you has, then move over to the S and A for some live music, and end at Limelight, where all drinks are £2 on Fridays.

4 blocks south of Donegall Sq. Katy Daly's open M-Sa noon-1am, Su 6pm-midnight. Spring and Airbrake open Tu 9pm-2am; other nights vary. Limelight open Tu 9pm-2am, Th 9pm-2am, F-Sa 10pm-2am.

THE BOTANIC INN — BAR, CLUB

23-27 Malone Rd. ☎028 9058 9740 www.botanicinnlimited.com

Belfast's sports bar, "the Bot" gets packed on the weekends and during sporting events. Check out signed rugby jerseys, boxing gloves and a trophy case. Show up on Sunday for the carvery menu *(£6)*, and wash it down with some local Belfast Ale. Framed photos of burly men in short-shorts abound.

Follow University St. to the south until it becomes Malone Rd. i Nightclub upstairs open on the weekends from 10pm. Pints £3.10-3.60. Open M-Sa 11:30am-1am, Su noon-midnight.

THE STIFF KITTEN — CLUB

1 Bankmore Sq. ☎028 9023 8700 www.thestiffkitten.com

That is some LOUD techno music. The Stiff Kitten on a Saturday compares with Berlin or Amsterdam in terms of pulse-pounding tracks and streaming lights. When you get tired of dancing, head over to the Blue Bar where you can sit down, or head next door to the SK bar, where all age groups mingle in a much more relaxed environment. Who needs perfect hearing anyway?

Walk south from Donegall Sq. on Bedford St. i Come on Th and F for £1.50 and £2 drinks respectively. Open M noon-1am, Tu noon-2am, W noon-1am, Th noon-2:30am, F noon-2:30am, Sa noon-3am.

THE EGLANTINE INN — BAR

32-40 Malone Rd. ☎028 9038 1994

Across the street from "the Bot" is "the Eg," and this heavily student-patronized bar's got black leather couches *and* a foosball table. The kind of students you see playing or sitting depend on the night, but check out Tuesday for quiz night and compete in the hopes of winning some free wine.

Across the street from The Botanic Inn. Most pints £3. Open M 11:30am-11pm, Tu 11:30am-midnight, W-Sa 11:30am-1am, Su noon-midnight.

THE GOLDEN MILE

THE SPANIARD — BAR

3 Skipper St. ☎028 9023 2448 www.thespaniardbar.com

If you can get in over the steep 25+ age requirement, this is the place to be. A hugely popular bar, it's filled with pictures of Salvador Dalí (you get the feeling all of the bartenders wish they had his mustache) and old vinyl. Try the "Extraordinary," with Havana Cuba rum, squeezed lime, and ginger beer.

Walk west on Donegall Sq. N., down Chichester St. 3 blocks. Make a left onto Victoria St. and follow until you make a left onto High St. Walk 1 block and turn right onto Skipper St. Pints £3.30. 25+. Open M-Sa noon-1am, Su noon-midnight.

RAIN — CLUB

10-14 Tomb St. ☎078 1051 8625 www.inforainclub.co.uk

The most excellent late night club spot for Belfastians, Rain is a two-story club powerhouse complete with sunken dance floors, a packed beer garden, and a line out the door that gets longer throughout the night. Arrive early if you want to pay a smaller cover.

Near the river Lagan in the Cathedral quarter. M-Th and Su £2 drinks all night. Open daily 9pm-3am.

THE FRONT PAGE — PUB, CLUB

11 Donegall St. ☎028 9024 6369 www.thefrontpagebar.co.uk

Downstairs, you'll find quiet beer drinkers watching their horses at the track. At the club upstairs, a younger crowd grooves everynight at 7pm, with live music and DJs in the place of track condition discussions.

Near the intersection of Donegall and Academy St. Wheelchair accessibility limited to downstairs. Pints £3. Open M-Sa 11:30am-1am, Su 11:30am-11:30pm.

RONNIE DREW'S — PUB, BAR

78-83 May St. ☎028 9024 2046 www.ronniedrews.com

Right next door to St. George's market, RD's is a bit out of the way, but the booths are comfy, and, more importantly, the drinks are cheap. Come on Thursday or Friday nights to listen to some trad before heading out to the more expensive spots.

From Donegall Sq. S., walk down May St. for 3½ blocks. Dinner deal includes any entree and 2 drinks. Pints £2.75. Lunch meals £6. Dinner deal £10. Open M-Th 9am-11pm, F-Sa 9am-1am, Su 9am-midnight.

THE JOHN HEWITT — PUB

51 Donegall St. ☎028 9023 3768 www.thejohnhewitt.com

Housed in an old newspaper building and run by the neighboring unemployment office, all the money you spend at the Hewitt goes back into the community (just don't spend yourself into the line next door). With 14 different beers on tap, including drafts from all four of the local microbreweries, you'll have a hard time trying every one in a night. Good thing there's live music six nights a week then—you can just come back tomorrow.

Near the intersection of Donegall and Academy St. Live music 6 nights per week. W night "charity night." Pints from £3.20. Open M-F 11:30am-1am, Sa noon-1am, Su 7pm-midnight.

THE SHOPPING DISTRICT

FILTHY MCNASTY'S — PUB

45 Dublin Rd.

Mannequins in body suits and tutus guard the entrance to this trendy club. FM's is scheduled to open up a big, open-air venue to handle their live-music schedule, so look for that. An alternative crowd hangs out here, and if you wanna get really McNasty, shots are cheap *(£3).*

i Weekly specials on the board. Pints £3.30. Open daily noon-1am.

THE APARTMENT — BAR

2-4 Donegall Sq. W. ☎028 9050 9777 www.apartmentbelfast.com

On the top floor of the Apartment all that separates you from the night air below are big glass panes. And while the exterior of City Hall below is Victorian, the interior of this bar could have come straight out of 1972. Long, flat furniture and funky '70s soul make it a hotspot for an older, slightly more cash-heavy crowd.

i Su £0.50 off all cocktails. Open M-F 7:30am-1am, Sa 9am-1am, Su 10am-midnight.

CROWN BAR — BAR

46 Great Victoria St. ☎028 9024 3187 www.crownbar.com

One of the most famous bars in Belfast, there are ornaments on the Crown's ornaments. A Victorian era bar with 10 famous "snugs," or enclosed wooden booths, you'll want to call ahead if you're with a group or want to get a snug at peak hours. Take pictures next to the impressive wood and tile work or simply get your snuggie on.

Lunch menu £3-9. Pints £3.50-4. Open M-Sa noon-3pm. Bar open M-Sa noon-10:30pm, Su 12:30-9pm.

THE ENTRIES

THE DUKE OF YORK — PUB

2-10 Commercial Ct. ☎028 9024 1062

There's so many bar mirrors inside, you'll think you had "Jameson" tattooed on your forehead—the Duke of York takes bric-a-brac to a whole new level. See live music on Friday and Saturday, and maybe you'll catch the next Snow Patrol (they got their start here).

Just off of Donegall St. i Outdoor seating available. Pints £3.10. Open M-Sa 11:30am-1am, Su 2pm-midnight.

THE MORNING STAR — PUB

17 Pottinger's Entry ☎028 9023 5986 www.morningstar.com

While the party here's not exactly a bumptastic grindfest, Morning Star's an excellent place to have a few afternoon beers or, alternatively, get a massive plate from the ample buffet *(£5).* If you're feeling like you could eat a horse, go for cow instead and order the 24 oz. rumpsteak. The old men betting on the **horses** will be pissed were you to eat their entertainment.

Walk up Donegall Pl. and turn right onto Castle St. Follow to the intersection of High St. and Pottingers Entry. Pints £2.50-3.10. Open M-Th 10:30am-11pm, F-Su 10:30am-1am (but you have until 1:30am to finish your drinks).

MCCRACKEN'S — PUB

4 Joy's Entry ☎028 9032 6711 www.mccrackenscafebar.co.uk

A newer, trendier version of the traditional Irish pub, McCracken's has substituted the boring bar stools for funky, green-seated ones and installed some portraits of famous Irish writers, but a la Andy Warhol. The crowd is trendier as well, tending to offer more for the well-dressed young professional crowd than the older Irish regulars or crazy high school kids.

5min. walk Northwest of Donegall Sq. i Su jazz night 6:30-8:30pm. Pints £3.15-3.25. Open M-W 11:30am-9:30pm, Th 11:30am-11pm, F 11:30am-1am, Sa 11:30am-3am, Su 1-9pm.

arts and culture

BELFAST COMMUNITY CIRCUS SCHOOL — CIRCUS TRAINING

Gordon St. ☎028 9023 6007 www.belfastcircus.org

You're traveling, why not run away to the circus? Adult classes every Wednesday night focus on a different circus skill and include a warm up and cool down.

Belfast Cathedral Quarter. i Open to all skill levels. 18+. Lessons £5. Lessons W 7:30-9:30pm.

FESTIVAL OF FOOLS — FESTIVAL

Gordon St. *www.foolsfestival.com*

The Festival of Fools is North Ireland's only street festival, run by the Belfast Community Circus School. The event is reputedly "the very best of international street theatre."

Apr. 29-May 30, 2010.

ULSTER HALL — THEATER

Bedford St. ☎028 9033 4400 www.ulsterhall.co.uk

A famous music venue that has seen the likes of both **Van Morrison** and Rory Gallagher, Ulster Hall also has a close affinity with a different supergroup: the BBC orchestra. Come in June and look for the "lunchtime concerts" *(£5)*. Or come to watch people getting rough during the boxing and wrestling matches.

4 blocks south of Donegall Sq. on Bedford St. Tickets £20-30. Open M-F 9am-5pm, Sa 10am-5pm. Open before and during shows.

essentials

PRACTICALITIES

- **TOURIST OFFICES: Belfast Welcome Centre** is one of the only tourism offices (and by far the biggest) in Belfast and is also the only place to go for luggage storage *(£3 for up to 4 hr., £4.50 for over 4hrs)*. Aside from taking in your bags and bothering to be open everyday except Christmas, the BWC provides all the tourism info you could ever want, assistance booking tours, a gift shop, currency exchange and internet café. They must be listening to a lot of Vanilla Ice over there, because their mantra seems to be, "You got a problem? Yo, I'll solve it." *(47 Donegall Pl. Just up the main road extending away from city hall on the left. ☎028 9024 6609 www.gotobelfast.com i Touchscreen information kiosk available. Two 24hr. ATMs located outside Belfast Welcome Centre. Open Oct-May M-Sa 9am-5:30pm, Su 11am-4pm; June-Sept M-Sa 9am-7pm, Su 11am-4pm.)*
- **TOURS:** Operating since 1992, **McComb's Tours** has the longest running Giant's causeway tour, and their guides are friendly and knowledgable. However, just because they've been around since 1992 doesn't mean they're behind the times, all of their buses are less than two years old. Take the causeway tour *(£20 full day, £18 express)* or the City Tour *(£12)*. 20% discount available for patrons of the International Youth Hostel, in which McComb's has their office. *(22-32 Donegall Rd. ☎028 9031 5333 www.mccombstravel.com; info@mccombstravel.com Open daily 8am-10pm.)* The **Titanic Walking Tour** is a 2½hr. tour that takes you on a leisurely, 1 mi. walk through Queen's island, and outlining the achievements of the designers and builders of the Titanic (every one except building a boat that floats). Purchase tickets at the start of the tour, at Belfast Welcome Centre, or online. *(Meet outside the Odyssey Complex. ☎0790 435 0339 www.titanicwalk.com Tours 11am and 2pm.)* The **Original Tour** offers taxi tours through the Falls and Shankhill neighborhoods, with

a local guide to tell the history of "the troubles." The Original Tour can be cheap if you get together a group. *(☎077 5156 5359 Ⓢ £8 per person. Min. £25.)*

- **BANKS: Bank of Ireland.** *(28 University Rd. ℹ Two 24hr. ATMs. ⏰ Open M-Tu 9:30am-4:30pm, W 10am-4:30pm, Th-F 9:30am-4:30pm.)* **First Trust Bank.** *(Across the street from the front of city hall. ℹ 2 24hr. ATMs. ⏰ Open M-Tu 9:30am-4:30pm, W 10am-4:30pm, Th-F 9:30am-4:30pm.)* **Belfast GPO** has currency exchange *(12-16 Bridge St. ☎ 9032 0337 🖳postoffice.co.uk ⏰ Open M-Sa 9am-5:30pm).*
- **INTERNET ACCESS: Revelations** gives a discount to students and hostelers, if your hostel doesn't have internet already. *(27 Shaftesbury Sq. ☎028 9032 0337 🖳www.revelations.co.uk; admin@revelations.co.uk Ⓢ £1.10 per 15min., per 20min. for students and hostelers. ⏰ Open M-F 8am-10pm, Sa 10am-6pm, Su 11am-7pm.)*
- **POST OFFICES: Belfast GPO** can tend to all of your postal service needs. *(12-16 Bridge St. ☎028 9032 0337 🖳postoffice.co.uk ⏰ Open M-Sa 9am-5:30pm.)* You can also head to the **Bedford Street** branch of the post office. *(16-22 Bedford St. ☎028 9032 2293 ⏰ Open M-F 9am-5:30pm.)*

EMERGENCY!

- **POLICE STATION:** *(Ann St. ☎0845 600 8000 for switchboard, ☎999 for emergencies. 🖳www.psni.co.uk ⏰ 24hr. assistance.)*
- **PHARMACIES:** At **Boots** wade through an enormous make-up section and head upstairs to get to the pharmacy. *(⇟ 35-47 Donegall St. ☎9024 2332 🖳www.belfasttrust.hscni.net ⏰ Open M-F 8am-9pm, Sa 8am-7pm, Su 1-6pm.)*
- **HOSPITALS: Belfast City Hospital.** *(Lisburn Rd. ☎9032 9241 for switchboard, ☎999 for emergencies. 🖳www.belfasttrust.hscni.net ⏰ Open 24hr.)*

GETTING THERE

By Plane

Belfast International Airport *(Belfast BT29 4AB ☎028 9448 4848 🖳www.belfastairport.com; info.desk@bfs.aero ℹ Passengers who require additional mobility assistance should call +44 (0) 28 9448 4957.)* has flights all over Europe, the US, and beyond, and features the following airlines: **Air Lingus** (*☎0871 7185 000 🖳www.aerlingus.com*) with flights to and from Barcelona, Faro, Lanzarote (Arrecife), London Heathrow, Malaga, Munich, Rome Leonardo Da Vinci, Tenerife; **Continental** (*☎0845 607 6760 (UK) or 1 890 925 252 (ROI) 🖳www.continental.com/uk*) with flights to and from New York; **easyJet** (*☎0905 821 0905 🖳www.easyJet.com*), with flights to and from Alicante, Amsterdam, Barcelona, Bristol, Edinburgh, Faro, Geneva, Glasgow, Ibiza, Krakow, Liverpool, London Gatwick, London Stansted, Malaga, Newcastle, Nice, Palma Majorca, Paris Charles de Gaulle; **Jet2.com** (*☎0871 226 1 737 🖳www.jet2.com*), with flights to Blackpool, Chambery, Dubrovnik, Ibiza, Jersey, Leeds Bradford, Mahon, Murcia, Newquay, Palma Majorca, Pisa, Toulouse, Tenerife; **Manx2.com** *(☎0871 200 0440 🖳www.manx2.com*) with flights to and from the Isle of Man, Galway, Cork; **Thomas Cook** *(☎0871 895 0055 🖳www.thomascook.com*), with flights to and from Lanzarote, Alicante, Antalya, Bodrum, Corfu, Cancun, Dalaman, Faro, Fuerteventura, Heraklion, Ibiza, Larnaca, Las Palmas, Mahon, Monastir, Palma, Puerto Plata, Reus, Rhodes, Sanford Orlando, Sharm el Sheikh, Tenerife, Toulouse, Veronal; **Thompson Airways** *(☎0871 895 0055 🖳www.thomson.co.uk*), with flights to and from Lanzarote, Malaga, Bodrum, Bourgas, Dalaman, Grenoble, Lapland, Las Palmas, Naples, Palma, Reus, Tenerife.

By Train

Belfast Central Train Station runs all over Northern Ireland and down to the Republic as well. Major destinations include Dublin *(2hr.)*, Londonderry *(2¼hr.)* and Neary *(50min.)*. Check the website for times and prices, as both are subject to frequent change. *(Central Station, E. Bridge St. ☎209 066 6630 www.translink.co.uk Open M-Sa 6:20am-8:10pm, Su 10am-7:30pm.)*

GETTING AROUND

Transportation cards and tickets are available at the **pink kiosks** in Donegall Sq. W. *(Open M-F 8am-6pm, Sa 9am-5:20pm)* and around the city.

By Bus

Belfast has 2 bus services. Many local bus routes connect through **Laganside Bus Station, Queens Sq. Metro** bus service *(☎9066 6630 www.translink.co.uk)* operates from Donegall Sq. Twelve main routes cover Belfast. **Ulsterbus** "blue buses" cover the suburbs. *(Day passes £3. Travel within the city center £1 (£2.30 beyond), under 16 £0.50.)* **Nightlink** buses travel from Donegall Sq. W. to towns outside Belfast *(£3.50. Sa 1 and 2am)*.

By Taxi

Metered taxis run through the city 24hr. Look for the following companies: **Value Cabs** *(☎9080 9080)*; **City Cab** *(☎9024 2000)*; **Fon a Cab** *(☎9033 3333)*.

By Bicycle

For bike rental, head to **McConvey Cycles.** *(183 Ormeau Rd. ☎9033 0322 www.mcconvey.com Locks supplied. Prices per day: M £20, Tu-Th £10, F-Su £20. £40 per week. Open M-W 9am-6pm, Th 9am-8pm, F-Sa 9am-6pm.)*

THE REPUBLIC OF IRELAND

DUBLIN

Pull up a pint of **Guinness,** sit down, and listen up. If you're reading this, chances are you've recently arrived in Dublin, capital of the Republic of Ireland. Now that you're here, however, what's to be done? You can('t) very well sit around drinking Guinness the *whole* time you're there. Fortunately, Dublin has something for every type of traveler. You can get wasted in **Temple Bar** with a motley crew of tourists, visit museums of everything from natural history to modern art, tour both the Guinness Storehouse *and* the Jameson Distillery, wile away the day poking your head into luxury clothing stores on Grafton Street, see live music and hit the impressive club scene around Camden, Wexford, and Harcourt Streets...we could continue all day long. The important thing to remember, though, is that Dublin is a fantastic city, with incredibly friendly inhabitants and a vibrancy that never seems to dim. See as much of it as you can—don't constrain yourself to specific areas because you're sure that things just couldn't get any better. They can, and they will.

greatest hits

- **SICK FLICKS.** Hit up the DVD collection at the Irish Film Institute (p. 364), then catch a movie or two.
- **REJOYCE.** At the James Joyce Centre (p. 367), you can pay homage to one of the forefathers of literary Modernism.
- **SHAMROCK AND ROLL.** Whelan's bar (p. 374) features predominantly alternative music, with not one but *two* stages.
- **CLUBLIN.** Head to Tripod (p. 372) on Grafton St. for top-shelf live music.

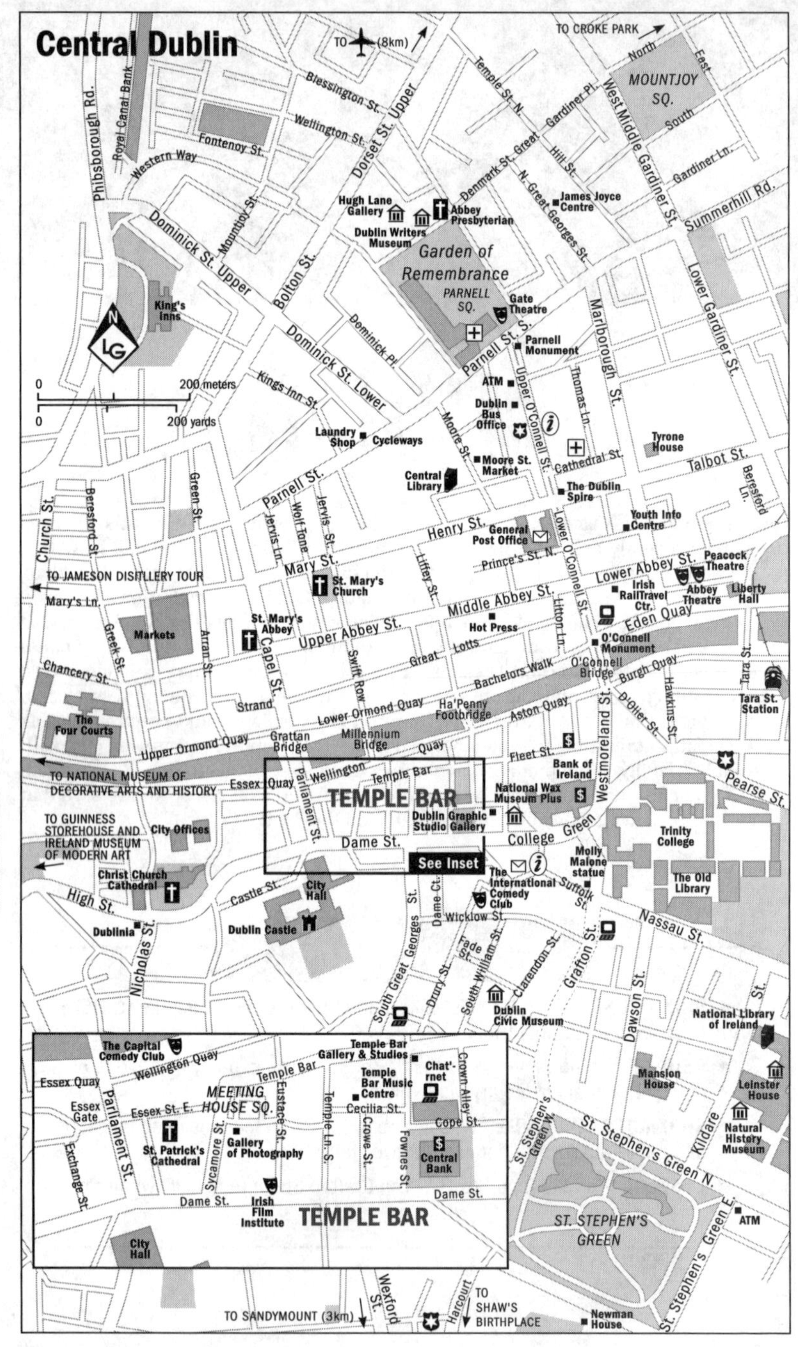
Central Dublin
TO (8km)
TO CROKE PARK
MOUNTJOY SQ.
Hugh Lane Gallery
Dublin Writers Museum
Abbey Presbyterian
James Joyce Centre
Garden of Remembrance
PARNELL SQ.
Gate Theatre
Parnell Monument
King's Inns
ATM
Dublin Bus Office
Laundry Shop
Cycleways
Moore St. Market
Central Library
The Dublin Spire
Tyrone House
Youth Info Centre
General Post Office
St. Mary's Church
Peacock Theatre
Abbey Theatre
Irish RailTravel Ctr.
Liberty Hall
TO JAMESON DISITLLERY TOUR
St. Mary's Abbey
Markets
Hot Press
O'Connell Monument
O'Connell Bridge
Tara St. Station
The Four Courts
Ha'Penny Footbridge
Grattan Bridge
Millennium Bridge
TO NATIONAL MUSEUM OF DECORATIVE ARTS AND HISTORY
Bank of Ireland
National Wax Museum Plus
TEMPLE BAR
Dublin Graphic Studio Gallery
TO GUINNESS STOREHOUSE AND IRELAND MUSEUM OF MODERN ART
City Offices
Trinity College
See Inset
Molly Malone statue
The International Comedy Club
Christ Church Cathedral
City Hall
The Old Library
Dublinia
Dublin Castle
Dublin Civic Museum
National Library of Ireland
Mansion House
Leinster House
Natural History Museum
ST. STEPHEN'S GREEN
ATM
TO SANDYMOUNT (3km)
TO SHAW'S BIRTHPLACE
Newman House
The Capital Comedy Club
Temple Bar Gallery & Studios
Chat'rnet
Temple Bar Music Centre
MEETING HOUSE SQ.
Essex Gate
St. Patrick's Cathedral
Gallery of Photography
Central Bank
Irish Film Institute
City Hall
200 meters
200 yards
Phibsborough Rd.
Royal Canal Bank
Blessington St.
Wellington St.
Fontenoy St.
Western Way
Dorset St. Upper
Temple St. N.
Gardiner Pl.
West Middle Gardiner St.
Gardiner Ln.
Summerhill Rd.
Denmark St. Great
N. Great Georges St.
Hill St.
Dominick St. Upper
Dominick St. Lower
Dominick Pl.
Mountjoy St.
Bolton St.
Kings Inn St.
Parnell St.
Lower Gardiner St.
Marlborough St.
Thomas Ln.
Upper O'Connell St.
Moore St.
Cathedral St.
Talbot St.
Beresford Ln.
Church St.
Beresford St.
Green St.
Jervis Ln.
Wolf Tone
Jervis St.
Henry St.
Mary St.
Liffey St.
Prince's St. N.
Lower O'Connell St.
Lower Abbey St.
Middle Abbey St.
Mary's Ln.
Greek St.
Arran St.
Capel St.
Upper Abbey St.
Swift Row
Great Strand
Lotts
Litton Ln.
Eden Quay
Chancery St.
Bachelors Walk
Burgh Quay
Strand
Lower Ormond Quay
Aston Quay
Westmoreland St.
D'Olier St.
Hawkins St.
Tara St.
Upper Ormond Quay
Quay
Fleet St.
Pearse St.
Essex Quay
Wellington
Temple Bar
Parliament St.
Dame St.
College Green
High St.
Castle St.
Nicholas St.
South Great Georges St.
Dame Ct.
Wicklow St.
Suffolk St.
Nassau St.
Fade St.
Drury St.
South William St.
Clarendon St.
Grafton St.
Dawson St.
Kildare St.
St. Stephen's Green W.
St. Stephen's Green N.
St. Stephen's Green E.
St. Stephen's Green S.
Wexford St.
Harcourt
Wellington Quay
Essex St. E.
Exchange St.
Sycamore St.
Eustace St.
Temple Ln. S.
Crowe St.
Fownes St.
Cecilia St.
Crown Alley
Cope St.

student life

For students traveling to Dublin, a trip to the **Guinness Storehouse** is a no-brainer. Not only do you receive free samples during a how-to-drink-a-pint tutorial, but you also get a free pint at the top of the building. After ascending countless flights of stairs to reach the top of the building (which is, appropriately, pint-shaped), you'll probably be ready to throw one back anyway.

orientation

Dublin's an easy city to get around, despite its size. The **River Liffey** draws a natural divide between the north and south sides of the city. The south side is known for its swankier, more ritzy areas, but the north is in no way short on gems. Dividing the two halves further are the different neighborhoods of Dublin. They range from the smallish, touristy area known as **Temple Bar** to the **Grafton Street** region to the South Georgian area, to the Viking and medieval section, including Christchurch Cathedral.

Large north-south dividing streets include the major artery on the north side, **O'Connell Street** (which has pedestrian **Henry** and **Talbot Streets** flanking it on either side) and **Parliament Street,** which provides another street-bridge-street thoroughfare farther inland.

TEMPLE BAR AND THE QUAYS

It's a bit silly to put an "Orientation" section in for Temple Bar because chances are if you're in Temple Bar on a weekend, you'll be so drunk that just making it to the end of the block will seem like a challenge. However, maybe the next morning (or afternoon), when you feel like walking around, take the main east-west street (**Temple Bar Street,** go figure) and diverge on any of the multiple lanes that run north-south from there. Heading north will take you up towards the River Liffey and the Quays while heading south will take you towards **Dame St., Dublin Castle,** and **Trinity College.**

The Quays (pronounced "Keys") are even more straightforward to navigate. You'll walk either on the north side (**Ormond Quay** and **Bachelors Walk**) or on the south side (**Wellington** and **Merchant's Quay**). Head west to go inland towards the Guinness Storehouse and the Irish Rail Heuston Station, and east towards the ferry terminal and port.

GRAFTON STREET

Ah Grafton Street, pedestrian highway of purchase pleasure. Taking off from the meeting of **Suffolk** and **Nassau Streets,** Grafton Street climbs on a slight incline (*Let's Go* listings will refer to Grafton directions as being either "up" or "down") up from **Trinity College** to **St. Stephen's Green.** Small, pedestrian walkways branch off on either side of the street and lead to more shops and, more importantly, several excellent pubs.

Shopping on Grafton Street is not for the faint of heart—or of cash. Several top tier brands have outlets here, and Dublin's not exactly a pennypincher's paradise. However, there are some gems that won't rob you of all the money you saved to get from Dublin to Prague. Check out the clothing listings for more detail there.

Even if you're not buying, Grafton Street is a place you don't want to miss. Window shopping here is made more enjoyable by the presence of a hodge-podge collection of street performers, who busk from dawn until (yes, we said it), dusk. Visit during the weekend to catch some great acts.

on hearing irish for the first time

For those that don't know, Ireland's official language is English, but equal status is given to Gaelic, or Irish. All signs appear in both languages, the Irish appearing first, and then English underneath it. Taking this into account, I was surprised to find that, after I'd been in Ireland a few days, I still hadn't heard any Gaelic being spoken.

I was sitting down in a pub (I have a feeling I'm going to be writing that a lot) and just sort of gazing off into space at a table on the terrace, when I heard two middle-aged guys come out and sit down at the table next to me. They were deep in conversation, and gesticulating wildly. One would reach over the table to push the other on the shoulder, as if to admonish him for some unknown offense. The other would respond in kind by speaking even louder, and continuing on long after I would have assumed a normal human breath could be sustained.

At last! I was hearing Gaelic. It had to be. I'd been sitting there doing nothing but trying to pick up a few words of what was being said (yes, I know, I was eavesdropping, but it's not like I had anybody to talk to) and I hadn't gotten a thing. I leaned in a little closer, just to be sure. The guy sitting closest to me turned and said something to me, and pointed at my notebook on the table.

"What?" I said.

He followed with another completely unintelligible phrase.

"I'm sorry I don't understand." I told him.

He rolled his eyes, and, as if he were talking to a 3-year-old having the "no hitting" rule explained to him for the first time, said (and I'm approximating), "Whazschatyerrdoiinderr?"

Oh. They're speaking...English. Maybe those Irish accents are a little thicker than I thought.

Asa Bush

GARDINER STREET AND CUSTOMS HOUSE

Dublin City Council might as well just get it over with and rename Gardiner Street "Hostel Row." The place is littered with them. The street runs north to south parallel to O'Connell Street, and the easiest way to get there is to take the pedestrian **North Earl Street** from **O'Connell** (you'll know you're going in the right direction if you pass by the **statue of James Joyce**) and follow it as it turns into **Talbot Street,** which is only partially a pedestrian street. After **Marlborough Street,** the next cross street will be Gardiner. Turn left or right, you won't escape the endless stream of signs offering you free Wi-Fi, full Irish breakfasts, and clean sheets. That last one's a priority, so make sure to ask.

WEST OF TEMPLE BAR

When you've had enough of Temple Bar's late night shenanigans and Grafton street's lost it's charm (read: when your credit card maxes out), head west. Like the cowboys of old, strike out for gold and adventure. Follow the northern side of the Liffey west and along the quays until you reach **Bow Street** on the **Arran Quay.** Turn right and walk a few blocks up—Eureka! Gold! Liquid gold Jameson whiskey at the distillery tour! Now that you're rich, take **Lord Edward Street** west through nearly all of its changes—**High Street, Cornmarket,** and **Thomas Streets,** but it's worth it to turn left on to **Crane Street,** enter the **Guinness Storehouse,** scale the stairs (or take the elevator if you find yourself exceptionally parched) to the **Gravity Bar,** where you may survey the long, dusty trail you blazed. Accept your pint of Guinness gladly, and feel the rich rewards that accompany the neighborhoods west of Temple Bar.

All banter aside, the area west of Temple Bar constitutes a huge portion of Dublin. Phoenix park sits on its inland edge, and a walk there from the city center would take up a significant portion of your day. However, there are several great things to see along the way. On the south side, **Christchurch Cathedral, Dublinia,** and the **Irish Museum of Modern Art;** on the left, in contrast, is the impressive architecture of the **Four Courts** and the **National Museum of Decorative Arts and Military History,** housed at Collins Barracks. Don't be afeared o' heading out into the sunset and making a day out of enjoying a part of Dublin that all your lazy friends will never get to.

NORTH OF O'CONNELL STREET

Past the **O'Connell Monument,** with it's bullet-riddled Victory, past the spire, that unequivocal proof that absurdly phallic sculpture is not dead, and finally, past the **Parnell Monument,** which, uh, well...so we can't think of a joke for that one. It's there anyway and you're past it. Past all of these things you'll find a neighborhood caught in a strange limbo—somewhere between being too close to the city center to really be residential, but not far enough away to escape all of downtown Dublin's hustle-and-bustle. The result is an area with smaller and more local shops, and a much smaller percentage of tourists on the sidewalk. There are things to see up here—the **Gardens of Remembrance** are worth a look, and the **Hugh Lane Gallery** might just beat out the Irish Museum of Modern Art in terms of scale and presentation. And of course, for all the Joyceans in the audience, the **James Joyce Centre** is just up the road on **North Great George's Street.**

DORSET STREET AND DRUMCONDRA

Okay, things to know about Dorset Street. It's dodgy. Like, not a place you want to take Fluffy for a walk after dark. Located far past the **Parnell Monument** and running east to west, it has a few hostels and restaurants, but there's really nothing to see. If you're thinking about trying to find a place away from the city proper, a much better place is **Upper Drumcondra Road.** The top of this street, near **Griffith Avenue,** is a very safe residential area, and the B and Bs in that part of town bring none of the hassle of the city center and have the added benefit of a real neighborhood feel.

accommodations

Dublin is expensive, no two ways about it. Expect to pay at least €15 per night for a hostel dorm room, and often times more. Banking on the heavy party traffic, hostels, guesthouses and hotels in Dublin have all adopted a "week" and "weekend" rate, with the latter usually being around a one-quarter increase from the weekday price, so bear that in mind if you're planning a weekend trip.

TEMPLE BAR AND THE QUAYS

Temple Bar accommodations are usually filled with younger travelers—backpackers especially—who are interested in going out and having a good time. Note that any hostel in the Temple Bar area is bound to be noisy at night, and that you might have to deal with people coming into the dorm room at late hours.

BARNACLES TEMPLE BAR HOUSE — HOSTEL ❶

19 Temple Ln. ☎01 671 6277 barnacles.ie

Have a great time and meet fellow travelers at this Temple Bar funhouse. The exterior looks small but hides several different dorms and private rooms, a large common room, and a kitchen, the latter of which serves a free light breakfast. The modern decorating will appeal to hipsters traveling through Dublin, while the friendly staff is always happy to help GLBT guests find gay-friendly nightlife in the area.

Down towards the Liffey from Dame St. Laundry €7 per bag. Towel and lock rental €1.50 plus €5 returnable deposit. Dorms €10-33; private rooms €30-44. No curfew; present hostel-issued security pass after 11pm.

FOUR COURTS HOSTEL — HOSTEL 2

15-17 Merchants Quay — ☎01 672 5839 www.fourcourtshostel.com

Unless you're *really* lazy and don't want to walk the two blocks down to Temple Bar from the Quay, this might just be the best hostel in Dublin. "Staff Drink fund: We need beer!" reads the tip jar, and the staff are determined to keep things lighthearted. Tons of complimentary services (DVD, Wii or guitar rental) are all available with a presentation of ID. The dorms themselves are comfortable with lofty ceilings that serve as stuffiness reducer or snore amplifiers, depending on your perspective.

Riverside, Merchant's Quay. Credit card min. €15, 24hr. cancellation policy. Dorms €15 per week, €19 per weekend. No curfew; present hostel-issued security pass.

LITTON LANE HOSTEL — HOSTEL 2

Litton Ln. — ☎01 872 8389 www.irish-hostel.com

If you ever looked at Freddie Mercury's sweaty pantsuit in a Hard Rock Café and didn't gag, you'll love this hostel. Housed in what used to be a recording studio for the likes of U2, Van Morrison, and The Cranberries, it's now been completely remodeled. The rock vibe remains, however, as painted murals of artists and lyrics follow you down the hallways of each floor.

On Bachelor's Walk, north side of the Liffey. Bathrooms shared. Group discounts available. 10 bed dorm weekday €12, weekend €14; 8 bed dorm €13/15; 6 bed dorm €14/16; private twins €45; doubles €50; 3-bed apartment €75 per night. No curfew; present hostel-issued security pass.

RIVERHOUSE HOTEL — HOTEL 4

23-24 Eustace St. — ☎01 670 7655 www.riverhousehotel.com

For those who are able to spend a bit more but still want to stay in the Temple Bar area, the Riverhouse Hotel is the place to go. A local feel carries throughout, despite its heavily touristed neighborhood.

Temple Bar; look for a deep-red front with gilded lettering. Discounts for extended stays. High season €50-110; low season €45-90.

GRAFTON STREET

AVALON HOUSE — HOSTEL 2

25 Aungier St. — ☎01 475 0001 www.avalonhouse.ie

A hugely popular hostel on the south end of town, Avalon house boasts free Wi-Fi, computers for guest use, a movie projector and DVD rental, ping-pong, pool table, and book exchange. And those are just the perks. Also available are laundry machines and an ISA 10% student discount for the first night. Chill out downstairs with a good flick, or head upstairs to the cafe to chat up your fellow travelers.

Follow South Great George's St. until it turns in Aungier St. Rates change daily, so check website for more information. Reception 24hr.

CENTRAL HOTEL — HOTEL 5

1-5 Exchequer St. — ☎01 679 7302 www.centralhotel.com

Plush green carpets, huge framed mirrors, Victorian paintings of stockings and petticoats, and that's just in the lobby! This posh hotel's rates change daily, so check the website for booking info. However, expect to pay double on the weekends. Continental *(€5)* and full Irish *(€10)* breakfasts available.

Tourist kiosk available in lobby. Reception 24hr.

KELLY'S HOTEL

HOTEL ❸

36 South Great George's St. ☎01 648 0010 www.kellysdublin.com

If you're into white walls and minimalist furniture you'll be quite at home in this ultra-chic, ultra-modern hotel. The rooms are comfortable, with big beds and modern bathrooms. The doubles are a little on the small side, however. Free breakfast available at Le Gueulenton next door. Both Kelly's hotel and Grafton Guesthouse get noisy at night from the bars below, so make sure to request a quiet room.

Turn right off of Grafton St. and continue until you reach South Great George's St. Rates change daily. Check website for more information. Reception 24hr.

GRAFTON GUESTHOUSE

HOTEL ❸

26-27 South Great George's St. ☎01 648 0010 www.kellysdublin.com

A more traditional version of what is to be found over at Kelly's Hotel, the Grafton Guesthouse offers comfortable, not-white ensuite rooms. The creaking wooden stairs and high ceilings of the hotel will only serve to remind you that you're residing in one of the oldest parts of Dublin.

Just down the street from Kelly's Hotel. i Reception in Kelly's Hotel. Prices change daily, so check the website for more information. Reception in Kelly's hotel, 24hr.

ALBANY HOUSE

BED AND BREAKFAST ❹

84 Harcourt St. ☎01 475 1092 www.albanyhousedublin.com

Okay, this one's a bit on the steep-side, pricewise, but it's worth it. The Albany House is located in a wonderful Georgian home, with more elaborate molding than month-old bread. Rooms are large with very modern bathrooms. All rooms ensuite.

From the top of Grafton St. continue straight the length of St. Stephen's Green and continue on to Harcourt St. It will be on the left. i Continental breakfast included. Wi-Fi available in lobby. Check website for rates.

GARDINER STREET AND CUSTOMS HOUSE

Gardiner Street might as well be called Hostel Row. There are tons of hostels, hotels, guesthouses, lodges, and B and Bs all the way down the street. If it's a place where people stay, chances are it's located here. It's a quick walk down to the city center and Temple Bar, though if you're coming back late from a night out you'll want to be careful. A taxi might be the best bet.

HOLYHEAD B AND B

BED AND BREAKFAST ❷

42 Lower Gardiner St. ☎01 873 5889

A bed and breakfast with a real, classic feel to it, Holyhead has winding stairways take you up to beautitul window landings where you can sit and enjoy the morning sun. The rooms themselves are nice (although some of them sport a paint job that is radically different than the classic decor of the interior).

i Breakfast and Wi-Fi available. Rooms range from €30-60 during the week, with an increase on the weekends.

GLOBETROTTERS HOSTEL

HOSTEL ❸

47-48 Lower Gardiner St. ☎01 873 5893 www.globetrottersdublin.com

There's a reason "Hostelworld" has ranked Globetrotters as one of the best more than once—it lives up to its self-styled high standards. With comfortable dorms and incredibly swanky singles and doubles, all the rooms here are ensuite and come with a full Irish breakfast. Hidden perk: if you're staying in single or double rooms, dial 0 on your phone to order a drink from the bar to be delivered up to your room.

i Kitchen and Wi-Fi available. Dorms M-F €18, Sa-Su €20. Singles ensuite €60-70; doubles €40-45 per person.

ABBOTT LODGE

HOTEL ❸

87-88 Lower Gardiner St. ☎01 836 5548 www.abbottlodge.com

A beautiful lodge, where, if you book at the right time, you can get a room at a decent price. Book in advance to secure the best rates. Breakfast is included—full Irish from 8:30-10am, with continental available before that.

i Breakfast included. Ⓢ Singles from around €30; doubles €50.

ABRAHAM HOUSE

HOSTEL ❶

82-83 Lower Gardiner St. ☎01 855 0600 www.abraham-house.ie

One of the good bargain options on Lower Gardiner St. There are no lockers—just a luggage storage room, so bring along your own lock or pay for one. The dorm rooms are small but clean. Meet other travelers over breakfast.

i Breakfast included. Sheets included. Safety deposit boxes are €1 per night+€10 deposit. Free Wi-Fi in the lobby, as well as a TV and DVD rental in the sitting room. All rooms ensuite. Ⓢ Beds from €9. Expect a raise in prices for weekend and holiday stays. Reception 24hr.

HAZEL BROOK GUEST HOUSE

BED AND BREAKFAST❷

85-86 Lower Gardiner St. ☎01 836 5003 www.hazelbrookhouse.ie

A well-furnished and comfortable Gardiner St. option, Hazel Brook offers free Wi-Fi in all rooms, as well as a full Irish or contitnental breakfast from 8-10am. Another high-ceilinged Georgian option, this one differs from the others in that you won't have bunk beds or lockers in the rooms.

i Breakfast and Wi-Fi available. Coffee and TV available in all rooms. Ⓢ €40-100+ depending on the day, so check the website for rates.

DORSET STREET AND DRUMCONDRA

Dorset Street and Drumcondra both lie on the outskirts of Dublin city center, so you're looking at a long walk or bus ride into town. That being said, it can be a nice escape. However, you should always be careful about how you find your way home late at night. Walking is not a good idea, and the buses stop running at 11:30pm, so if you plan on staying out later than that, make sure to set aside some of your cash for a taxi.

ASHLING HOUSE/AZALEA LODGE

BED AND BREAKFAST❹

168 Upper Drumcondra Rd./67 Upper Drumcondra Rd. ☎01 837 5432/01 837 0300

Owned by the same couple, these two B and Bs might just be the greatest thing since sliced bread. Or, perhaps, scones, which you'll receive upon entering the door of the Azalea Lodge. Breakfast at the Ashling is continental, and the prices slightly cheaper because of it. But if you're willing to splurge, everything in the full Irish at Azalea is fresh and cooked to order. Amazing.

i All rooms ensuite. Ⓢ Rooms €70-80 per night.

THE DUBLIN CENTRAL HOSTEL

HOSTEL ❶

5 Blessington St., Dublin 7 ☎01 086 385 3832

Having just been recently renovated, this hostel is spotless but unfortunately lacks flavor. Hopefully things pick up with time, but meanwhile you can enjoy kitchen use, a pool table, and free TV inside its freshly painted walls.

From the top of Parnell Sq., cross Dorset St. and on to Blesington. i Lockers free for those staying under 1 week. All rooms ensuite. Credit cards will be accepted soon. Ⓢ 4-bed dorm M-F €12, Sa-Su €16; 8-bed €10/14; private room €40/50.

TINODE HOUSE

GUESTHOUSE ❷

170 Upper Drumcondra Rd. ☎01 837 2277 tinodehouse.com; info@tinodehouse.com

A spotless, cozy option up drumcondra, this B and B features a glass covered sitting area (complete with board games!) as well as a outside patio. The dining room will make you feel like you're back at home.

i All rooms with cable TV. Ⓢ €40-45 per person.

bloomin'

The other day was June 16th, 2010.

This is significant in Ireland and Dublin as it marks the 106th "Bloomsday," a celebration of James Joyce's epic Modernist novel, which takes place over an 18 hour span on this day in Dublin.

Needless to say, the literary geeks were out in full force (myself included).

People get into it here, I'm not joking. I saw so many people dressed up in early 20th century garb that I felt like I was walking through a Charles Dickens novel. There are public readings and memorized recitations done in the streets and some of the pubs sell at 1904 prices (this last bit was a highlight).

On this day, I went out to the Martello Tower in Sandycove, leaving on the DART train at 7:23am. The gunrest of the tower, overlooking the ocean and Dublin Bay, is where the novel begins at 8am sharp, and I didn't want to miss it. Unfortunately, my timing was just slightly off, and I got off the train at around 7:50 in the morning. I had ten minutes to get from the station to the tower. I found my way down to the beach. I could just see the tower on the edge of town. Ah crap, that's way farther away than the guy I asked for directions said! I started jogging. I started jogging towards the tower in hiking boots and jeans with a backpack. I had one moment, as I was beginning to sweat, where I thought about just how silly all of this was, how I was running myself out of breath because I wanted to be somewhere where something had happened (fictionally happened!) over 100 years ago.

I made it, wheezing, to the tower, paid my entry (it's now a Joyce museum), and climbed the winding staircase to the open air at the top and...

It was great.

I made it at 8:02 (knew I should have sprung for those track shoes), and missed only the first few sentences. There were only a few people there, around 8 or 10, and the reading of the first chapter was shared. There were those who read as if they were acting, full of inflections and dialects, and others who slowly meandered over each word and phrase. But people would look up every now and again, and look out at the ocean, and then back down at the book in their hands.

I'll say it again, it was great.

Asa Bush

TEMPLE BAR AND THE QUAYS

The good thing about sightseeing in Temple Bar is that everything's so close together. And the Quays? Hit the river and run in either direction.

JAMESON DISTILLERY TOUR

WHISKEY DISTILLERY TOUR

Bow St., Smithfield Dublin 7

☎01 807 2355 jamesonwhiskey.com

Hooray! Another tour that rewards you by offering free drinks! It's common knowledge now, but if you volunteer at the end of a short video that introduces the tour, you'll get to participate in a whiskey tasting at the end of the walk through Jameson Distillery. If your hand isn't called upon, you'll still get that complimentary whiskey at the end, but those who are chosen will receive a certificate denoting them as Jameson "official whiskey tasters." Whatever that means. The tour lasts around 1hr. 15min. and showcases the process of whiskey distillation from start to finish. Restaurant and gift shop in the lobby.

Walk on the north side of the Liffey down to Arran quay, turn right and follow the signs to the Jameson distillery. Tour: €13.50, student €11, senior €10, child €8, family (2-4) €30. Open M-Sa 9am-5:15pm, Su 10am-5:15pm (last tour 5:15pm).

IRISH FILM INSTITUTE — CINEMA

#6 Eustace St. ☎01 679 5744 irishfilm.ie

Walking down a long hallway paved in movie reels and plastered with classic movie posters, this refurbished Quaker building is a movie junkie's dream-come-true. Skylights let the natural light filter in as you can enjoy a drink in the bars, a bite to eat from the restaurant, or check out the in-house DVD store. Then hit up the cinema, checking out indie and Irish flicks. Look for the monthly director's retrospectives; if the director's Irish, you might just get to attend a Q and A session.

Movie tickets €7.75 until 6pm, afterwards €9.20. Film institute open M-F 10am-6pm; cinema open M-F 10am-9:30pm.

NATIONAL WAX MUSEUM PLUS — MUSEUM

Foster Pl., Dublin 2 ☎01 671 8873 www.waxmuseumplus.ie; hello@waxmuseumplue.ie

This is how wax museums should be: get your educational quota done early (you start with the "Writers' Room" and "History Vaults") and then move on into the fun stuff (Hannibal horror rooms and waxen celebrities). Get closer to Pierce Brosnan's ruggedly strong chin than you ever thought possible.

Across from the Trinity College entrance near Grafton street. i Parental advisory for 16 and under for Horror room. €10, students and seniors €9, children €7, family €30. Open daily 10am-7pm.

DUBLIN GRAPHIC STUDIO GALLERY — ART GALLERY

"Through the arch" off Cope St. ☎01 679 8021 gallery@graphicstudiodublin.com

An artist-owned gallery where 99% percent of the works on display are up for sale, any purchase you make will help fund artist workshops and give awards to local art students. But even if you're not buying, the gallery is a great stop.

Prices vary. Open M-F 10am-5:30pm, Sa 11am-5pm.

GALLERY OF PHOTOGRAPHY — PHOTOGRAPHY GALLERY

Meeting House Sq., Temple bar ☎01 671 4654 www.galleryofphotography.ie

A photo gallery that showcases both graduate student and professional work two stories of winding exhibit space makes for a wonderful—and free, free is always good—wander. Check out their large selection of photography books and pick up a postcard in the lobby.

At the back of the square. Free. Open Tu-Sa 11am-6pm, Su 1-6pm.

GRAFTON STREET

TRINITY COLLEGE — UNIVERSITY TOUR

Trinity College, College Green www.tcd.ie

Tours given by Trinity students describe a history of the college that is full of fun and quirky historical facts. Ghosts, deadly student feuds and more await you, stories told with all the college sarcasm money can buy. The climax of the tour is at the **Old Library,** where participants are led into the room that showcases the famous **Book of Kells.** The book itself is housed in a dark and crowded room, so you have to squint and jostle to get a good look. More easily enjoyed is the **Long Room,** a wonderful, wood-paneled room that stretches the length of the building and houses (in shelves upon shelves) some of the university's oldest and rarest books. A rotating themed exhibition of some of them is available for perusal in the glass display cases that run the length of the room.

Crossing O'Connell Brige onto Westmoreland St., walk 5min. It will be on your left. Tour plus

admission to the Old Library and Book of Kells €10, tour without admission to library €5. Admission to library without tour €9. Tours M-Sa 10:15, 10:40, 11:05am, 11:35am, 12:10, 12:45, 2:15, 3, 3:40pm.

NATIONAL LIBRARY OF IRELAND LIBRARY

7 Kildare street ☎01 603 0200 www.nli.ie

The main show, so to speak, is the exhibition detailing the life and works of **William Butler Yeats.** A circular space with a bench allows you to listen to recordings of Yeats's poetry accompanied by associative images projected on the screens. Several items from Yeats's life are on display as well, including his ring, collections of his poetry, and even a lock of his hair.

Follow Nassau St. along Trinity College, and turn right on Kildare. Free. Open M-W 9:30am-9pm, Th-F 9:30am-5pm, Sa 9:30am-1pm. Guided tours led through the exhibit daily at 3:30pm.

NATURAL HISTORY MUSEUM MUSEUM

Merrion St., Dublin 2 ☎01 677 7444 ext 361 www.museum.ie

The ground floor of this museum houses fauna from all over the island, including skeletons of the Ancient Irish Elk (it's like Bambi from hell), as well as tons of other birds and bugs and fish. When you've finished with that, head upstairs to the world exhibit, where you can get your fix for rhinos, hippos and giraffes.

Follow Nassau St. (it turns into Clare St.) and then turn Merrion Sq. west. Free. Open T-Sa 10am-5pm, Su 2pm-5pm.

DUBLIN CASTLE CASTLE/GOVERNMENT BUILDING❷

Dublin Castle, State Apartments, Dame St. ☎01 677 7129 www.dublincastle.ie

Built by the English in the 13th century, the original "Dublin Castle" burned down in an accidental fire. Whoops. The castle was rebuilt in the 18th century, and was the headquarters of British rule in Ireland until the Irish revolution in 1920. Now it's a series of governmental buildings. The tour will take you through several impressive state rooms, including the blue carpeted "ballroom," where the President of Ireland is now inaugurated. The tour ends in the bowels of one of the castle's original towers. You can see the darkly colored waters that once formed a pool in the castle gardens, giving the city its name—the Irish "*Dubh* " (black), and "*Linn* " (pool).

Walk over the O'Connell Bridge past Temple Bar and turn right onto Dame St. Follow Dame St. for 10min. and Dublin Castle will be on the left. €4.50, seniors and students €3.50, under 12 €2. Open M-F 10am-4:45pm, Sa-Su and public holidays 2pm-4:45pm.

WEST OF TEMPLE BAR

Okay, so some of the places out here require a bit of a hike, but you're up for it, right? No? Don't feel like walking for 45min. during your vacation? Not a problem. Take the Dublin sightseeing bus tours—part of their circuit involves stops at all of the places listed below.

GUINNESS STOREHOUSE BEER TOUR

St. James' Gate ☎01 471 4668 www.guinness_storehouse.com

The Guinness storehouse is a 5-story exhibit centered entirely around...just kidding. How's this? It's a tour of an old beer factory. At the Guinness storehouse you get to spend time examining old Guinness ads, learning how to properly drink a pint (free samples!), and, at the top of the building, have a free pint of Guinness at the Gravity Bar, a circular glass bar that looks out over all of Dublin. Here's what you need to know: great tour, great views, free beer. Sound good? You bet.

*Follow Dame street as it turns into: High, Cornmarket, and Thomas St., and then turn left on Crane St. The Dublin hop-on, hop-off tour buses are also a good way to go. **i** Tour brochures available in mulitple languages. Huge selection of Guinness merchandise for sale. €15, seniors* *and students €11, students under 18 €9, children 6-12 €5. Open daily Sept-June 9:30am-5pm; July-Aug 9:30am-7pm.*

NATIONAL MUSEUM OF DECORATIVE ARTS AND HISTORY — MUSEUM

Collins Barracks, Benburb St. ☎01 677 7444

Fitting: that an old military barracks should now house a military history museum. Not so fitting: that the same barracks should house a decorative arts museum. Admittedly, it's a weird combination—exhibits of Ireland's tumultuous history side by side with cabinets housing oriental plates, but it's something you shouldn't miss. Check out the interactive features of the "barracks life" exhibit in particular.

Walk inland on the north side of the Liffey for approx. 30min. i No photos of the exhibits allowed. Free. Open T-Sa 10am-5pm, Su 2pm-5pm.

IRELAND MUSEUM OF MODERN ART (IMMA) — MUSEUM

Royal Hospital, Military road, Kilmainham ☎01 612 9900 www.imma.ie

Located in an old military hospital, the rooms here are so white and blank you'll have trouble figuring out whether they're part of the exhibition or not. Usually housing three or four separate exhibits, the long halls and quiet atmosphere of the IMMA are perfect for contemplating whether the artist you're seeing was actually influenced by Jackson Pollock, or just spilled some extra paint on the canvas.

i Guided tours are given for free every W, F, and Su at 2:30pm. Free. Open T 10am-5:30pm, W 10:30am-5:30pm, Th-Sa 10am-5:30pm, Su 12pm-5:30pm.

NORTH OF O'CONNELL STREET

For the Hugh Lane Gallery and the Gardens of Remembrance, you'll want to head behind the Parnell monument and to the top of Parnell Sq. Leaving the Hugh Lane Gallery, turn left to get to the Writers Museum, and the James Joyce Centre is just a few blocks down in the same direction.

DUBLIN WRITERS MUSEUM — MUSEUM

18 Parnell Sq. ☎01 872 2077 www.writersmuseum.com

James Joyce may have his own digs just up the road, but Ireland's other greats are also being remembered in style. The DWM showcases old manuscripts, first editions, and tons of memorabilia (read: old pipes and typewriters up the ying yang). Head upstairs to see the one thing the James Joyce Centre doesn't have—his piano—and then come back down and admire both the artistry on the wall and the beautiful home itself. If you really like the house, thank the father of Irish whiskey, John Jameson, who lived in it from 1891 to 1914 and is responsible for much of the renovation.

Continue walking along Parnell St. north with the Hugh Lane Gallery on your left; the museum is at the end of the block. i Cafe and gift shop. €7.50, seniors and students €6.30, children €4.70, family (2+2) €18.70. Open M-Sa 10am-5pm, Su 11am-5pm. Last entry 45min. before close.

THE HUGH LANE GALLERY — ART GALLERY

166 Parnell Sq. ☎01 222 5564 www.hughlane.ie

A modern art gallery that's so modern, it doesn't even have to show you just art: the works of the famous painter Francis Bacon are here, but so is his studio. Literally. An exact replica of one of his studios has been brought in and assembled right in the gallery, so now you can see just how much disorder it takes to create art. Upstairs and downstairs collections are interesting and slightly less messy, at least the art there is restricted to the canvas.

At the top of Parnell Sq., across the street from the Gardens of Remembrance. i Cafe and bookstore downstairs. Free. Suggested donation €2. Open Tu-Th 10am-6pm, F-Sa 10am-5pm, Su 11am-5pm.

JAMES JOYCE CENTRE MUSEUM

35 North Great George's St. ☎01 878 8547 www.jamesjoyce.ie

A Georgian house on North Great George's St. now houses the James Joyce Centre. Part museum, part headquarters for Joyce fanatics of Dublin, it's also a mecca for Joyce fanatics from the rest of the world. And trust us, there are plenty. Pieces of note include a copy of Joyce's deathmask, a table at which part of "Ulysses" was written, and the door to 7 Eccles St., the fictional residence of Leopold Bloom.

Walk up O'Connell St. to the Parnell Statue, turn right onto Parnell St. and then left onto North Great George's St. *i* *Group discounts available.* *€5, students and seniors €4.* *Open Tu-Sa 10am-5pm, Su noon-5pm.*

DORSET STREET AND DRUMCONDRA

Croke Park is a little bit, okay, a lotta bit, out of the way. However, it's also roughly the size of an aircraft carrier, so it's hard to miss. Take a taxi, or walk your way up along Drumcondra.

CROKE PARK SPORTS STADIUM

Croke Park, Jones Rd. ☎01 819 2323 www.crokepark.ie

Taking you for a run-around the magnificent Croke Park Stadium, home of Gaelic football and hurling, this tour covers the stadium from top to bottom, literally. You'll hit the locker room, players lounge, and corporate top boxes. Holding 82,300 occupants when full, Croke Park is the 4th largest stadium in Europe—pretty impressive when you consider that all Gaelic sports are amateur sports. Those burly players? Yeah, they all have day jobs. The museum is informative for those interested in picking up the history, but for those who've really been wondering what it's like to play Gaelic sports can try them out on the second floor, where you can try your luck with a hurling bat or test your foot accuracy kicking a Gaelic football. Of course, the truest way to experience Croke Park is to see a game, so ask about tickets while you're there.

Buses that pass by Croke Park are the 3, 11, 11a, 16, 16a, 46a and 123. *Tour and museum €11, museum only €6; students and seniors €8.50/4.50; under 12 €7.50/4; under 5 free/free; family €30/16.* *Open Sept-June M-F 9:30am-5pm, Su noon-5pm; July-Aug M-F 9:30am-6pm, Su noon-6pm. Last tour at 3pm.*

GARDENS OF REMEMBRANCE PUBLIC PARK

Up past the Parnell Monument, just below Dorset St.

A nice place to escape and rest your legs or get out of the hustle-and-bustle of the city around you, the Gardens of Remembrance are defined by a giant, cross-shaped pool at the bottom, and a large statue of falling men and women and rising geese at the end. Mind you don't sit on the grass, though—they've got signs there to tell you it's a no-no.

Free to the public.

food

Dublin's food is, contrary to popular belief, very good. Sure, there are a lot of boiled and fried foods liberally doused in salt, but time and practice have honed those dishes down to their delicious cores. More exotic flavors have come to Dublin thanks to the **Celtic Tiger,** and a huge variety of ethnic restaurants can be found all over the city. Unfortunately, there are also a slew of bad fast food chains. Here's the traveler's rule of thumb: if it smells the same back home as it does in Dublin, shy away.

TEMPLE BAR AND THE QUAYS

If there's a place to escape Ireland's infamy as a country with "bad" or "dull" food options (though these are words that are thrown around by other people, and *Let's Go* has always held Irish cuisine in high regard), that place is Temple Bar. It's got traditional Irish fare, rest assured, but it's also become quite the cosmopolitan neighborhood. You also won't have far to go to find several international options.

PANEM — CAFE 1

21 Lower Ormond Quay, Dub 1 — ☎01 872 8510

Run by a Sicilian man and his Irish wife, Panem has got your coffee and pastry fix covered. With imported Italian coffee *(€2.50-3)* and the mind-meltingly delicious Sicilian almond biscuits for just *(€1)* each, Panem will become your morning, or afternoon, or evening, ritual.

Over the Millenium Bridge from Temple Bar. €.90-6.50. Cash only. Open M-Sa 9am-5pm.

TANTE ZOE'S — CREOLE 4

1 Crow St., Temple Bar — ☎01 679 4407 tantezoes.com

The food's all Creole, all the time (jambalayas and gumbos are the *plat du jour, toujours*), but the ambience is divided. Sit upstairs for the feel of a French bistro or head downstairs for a close-quartered jazz club. Come Saturday nights to hear the singing waitress.

1 block west of Central Bank Plaza, head north on Crow St. €7-30. Open M-Th noon-10pm, F-Sa noon-11pm, Su noon-10pm.

BOTTICELLI'S — ICE CREAM 1

No. 3 Temple Bar St. — ☎01 672 7289 www.botticelli.ie

Providing Temple Bar's ice cream fix, Botticelli's serves Italian gelato in cups or cones from €2.50-5. Flavors include banana, tiramisu, and Italian *cioccolato*. Coffee is served as well.

Temple Bar St., across from The Temple Bar. Cash only. Open 11am-midnight everyday.

GERTRUDE'S CAFE AND RESTAURANT — CAFE 2

3-4 Bedford Row, Temple Bar — ☎01 677 9043

A comfortable cafe both in view of the Quays and Temple Bar street, Gertrude's is a good place to grab your morning coffee and watch the passers-by. Gertrude's offers coffee varieties *(€2.50-3.25)* as well as sandwiches *(€7-9)* and pizzas *(€9-14)*. Servers are affable, but you can push the doorbell outside on the terrace if you don't see anyone.

Just north of Gogarty's, Temple Bar. €2.50-14. Open daily 8am-6pm.

ISKANDERS — LATE NIGHT 1

30 Dame St. — ☎01 670 4013

After a long night of drinking, you'll swear it's the greatest thing you've ever eaten. Oh, and it's good sober, too. Iskander's is a Dublin institution and its massive shawarma with fries and a coke *(€10)* should not be missed.

Cash only. Open daily 11am-5am.

STAGE DOOR CAFÉ — CAFE 1

10b-11 East Essex St., Temple Bar — ☎01 677 6297

Though the sign from its old namesake, the "Lemon Jelly Café" is still on, this cafe has undergone a serious renovation to make the atmosphere as fun and eclectic as the food and drink are tasty. A full Irish breakfast is available all day, or you can select from fresh pastries, cakes, and quiches. There's also a "create your own" sandwich or wrap option available *(€6.95.)* Take your meal out on the terrace to allow the sun's rays curative powers to work on your hangover.

i Wi-Fi coming soon. Coffee €2-6. Food €3-9. Open M-F 8am-9 or 10pm, Sa-Su 9am-10:30pm.

GALLAGHER'S BOXTY HOUSE IRISH ❸

20-21 Temple Bar st., Temple Bar ☎01 677 2762 www.boxtyhouse.ie

Nearly all of the pubs in the Temple Bar area serve some kind of Irish food, but Gallagher's takes it a step further with an interior most reminiscent of a 19th-century Irish household. It features "Boxty," a dish of potato pancakes with meat and veggie fillings, that'll fill you up, even if it doesn't exactly shock your taste buds. You might find it hard to choose a drink at this joint's full bar.

On Temple Bar St., just off Anglesea St. Appetizers €4-11. Entrees €19-23. Open M-Th 10am-11pm, F-Sa 10am-11:30pm, Su 10am-11pm.

MILANO ITALIAN ❷

19 East Essex St., Temple Bar ☎01 670 3384 www.milano.ie

Serves fresh, made-in-front-of-you pizzas in either a "classic" or "romana" style, a thinner, crispier crust. The modern interior, with sweeping lines and tiny table lamps, ensures a nice evening out, even in the screaming Temple Bar.

€7-15. Open M-Sa noon-10:30pm, Su noon-10pm.

GRAFTON STREET

CORNUCOPIA VEGETARIAN ❷

19-20 Wicklow St. ☎01 677 7583 www.cornucopia.ie

Prepare to get your health on. Cornucopia serves meals that are vegan, gluten-free, wheat-free, yeast-free, dairy-free, egg-free, and (of course) low-fat. Despite their alarming lack of harmful ingredients, the food is delicious and comes served up hearty buffet style. You can even try some organic wine *(€5.35 per glass, €21.50 per bottle).*

Just down Wicklow St. from the tourist information office. i Upcoming bands post flyers for shows in the entrance. Open M-W noon-9pm, Th-Sa noon-10:30pm, Su noon-8:30pm.

BUTLER'S CHOCOLATE CAFÉ CAFE ❷

Wicklow St. ☎01 671 0591 www.butlerschocolates.com

The Butler's advertising is very, very good. First, you walk in and delicious looking chocolate is shown being made on the TV. "No," you tell yourself, and you approach the counter but...gasp! They have all of their delicious truffles on display under a glass counter at the register!

Wicklow St. across the street from Munchies Cafe. Coffee €2-3.50. Boxes of take-away chocolate €2-50. Open M-F 7:45am-7pm, Sa 9am-7pm, Su 10:30am-7pm.

CAPTAIN AMERICA'S STEAKHOUSE ❹

44 Grafton St. ☎01 671 5266 www.captainamericas.com

Believe it or not, Captain America's is an Ireland-themed rock memorabilia restaurant that's heavy on the U2. Plates here are pricey, but if you're willing to swing it, head down towards the seats by the window. That way, you'll have a window to distract you from Sinead O'Connor's portrait.

At the top of Grafton street on the left. Plates run from €10-17, steaks more. Open M-W noon-10:30pm, Th-Su noon-9 or 10pm-ish.

HANLEY'S CORNISH PASTIES PASTIES ❶

Dawson St., across from the Mayor's residence www.hanleyspasties.com

Serving up hot and fresh Cornish pasties, croissants filled with cheese, meats and veggies, grab one of these for just a few euro and continue moving—they just beg to be eaten on the go.

i Coffee available as well. Pastries generally under €5. Veggie and cheese €3.95, cheese, leek and bacon €4.95.

CEDAR TREE LEBANESE RESTAURANT LEBANESE ❷

11 St. Andrew's St. ☎01 677 2121

Offering cheap but delicious lunchtime options such as *kafta harra*, *kibbe say-*

neih and falafel, this is a good lunchtime spot, with excellent mosaic work on the tables and walls. Complement your meal with Almaza, the Lebanese beer.
Turn off of Suffolk street onto St. Andrews street. Wraps €5.50. Entrees €7.75. Open M-Sa 11:30am-11pm, Su 2pm-10:30pm.

BEWLEY'S ORIENTAL CAFÉ — CAFE 3
78-79 Grafton St. ☎01 672 7720 www.bewleys.com
A Grafton Street institution, Bewley's is something to see in itself. Beautiful stained glass windows by Dublin artist Harry Clark line the downstairs walls, making the place look more cathedral than cafe. If you're looking for a "cafe's cafe" then head upstairs, where you can sit out on the tiny balcony overlooking the street. Oh, and did we forget to mention the amazing coffee and extensive dessert section of the menu?
About midway up Grafton St. on the right hand side. Coffee €2-4.50. Lunch €6-16. Open M-Th 7:30am-10pm, F-Sa 7:30am-11pm, Su 7:30am-10pm.

NORTH OF O'CONNELL STREET

TESCO — SUPERMARKET 2
Moland House, Talbot St. ☎01 887 0980
Don't feel like going out to eat? Pick up some goods to go at Tesco. There's also a 24hr. ATM outside that accepts just about any credit card.
Across from the Irish Life shopping mall. Open M-Sa 7am-11pm, Su 8am-10pm.

DORSET STREET AND DRUMCONDRA

THE LOVIN' SPOON — RESTAURANT/CAFE 1
13 N. Frederick St.
A small, local place that serves good food fresh, the Lovin' Spoon isn't into putting up pretense. Go in, grab your food and keep rolling seems to be the overall attitude here. Sandwiches come in several varieties *(€3.60-6)*, while coffee and juice are also available *(€2.20)*.
Between Parnell Sq. and Dorset St. Open M-F 7am-6pm, Sa 9am-4pm.

TESCO — GROCERY 2
22 Upper Drumcondra Rd. ☎01 837 7632
For those staying way out in Drumcondra's boonies, this Tesco is available for your grocery shopping.
Open M-Sa 8am-10pm, Su 10am-10pm.

THE TASTY HUT — RESTAURANT 2
61 Upper Dorset St. ☎01 8733756
Okay, so the place looks like a dump. Don't be fooled. Offering cheap late-night grub (both burgers and Indian food), it tastes great. So great you might actually stay to eat it in the restaurant.
Burgers €3.50-5. Indian plates up to €13.50. Open daily noon-4am. Delivery Tu-Su 5pm-midnight, F-Sa 5pm-1am.

nightlife

Holy crap. Dublin knows how to party. Temple Bar sees crazy parties every night, and on the weekends the locals come out and things really get goin'. The best cluster of real, honest-to-goodness house-pumpin', beat layin' clubs can be found on **Harcourt Street** and **Harcourt Road**, up by **St. Stephen's Green.** An area with several excellent clubs, **Camden** and **Wexford Streets** (referred to as the **"Village"**) is nearby. **South William Street** has some great bars and pub options as well.

TEMPLE BAR AND THE QUAYS

There's one neighborhood in Dublin where you're nearly guaranteed all of the following: public drunkenness, public vomiting, public nudity, a stag party, a hen party, women in high heels and halter tops, men in high heels and halter tops, beer, beer, and more beer. If you're staying at a hostel here, chances are you're not planning on making the most of their foosball table. On any given night, Temple Bar's streets fill with tourists walking about in various stages of inebriation. It might not be the thing you want to do every night, but it's certainly something you can't miss.

PANTI BAR — BAR, CLUB

7-8 Capel St. ☎01 874 0710 www.pantibar.com

Panti Bar gives the Dragon a run for its money at its across-the-river location that fills up quickly on the weekends. Go early to grab a table or show up whenever to mingle. There's a dance floor downstairs. Just follow the breasted Absolut bottle running down the "Absolut Panti" sign.

From Parliament St. and Temple Bar, take the Grattan bridge over the Liffey to Capel St. The bar will be on your right. Drinks half price on Sunday.

PEADAR KEARNEY'S — PUB

64 Dame St. ☎01 707 9701

Named for the composer of the Irish National Anthem who grew up upstairs, it's only fitting that this pub has great live music, seven nights a week. Come in early and score a cheap drink *(€3.50)*, or wait until the band starts up at 9pm. Brian Brody is a one-man musical powerhouse on Saturday nights. Don't miss it.

On Dame St. on the south side of Temple Bar. ***i*** *No cover. When daily specials end, look for drinks to be approx. €5. Cash only. Open noon-1am everyday. Happy hour M-F noon-7pm, Sa-Su noon-5pm.*

ALCHEMY — CLUB

Fleet St., Temple Bar ☎01 612 9390 alchemydublin.ie

While the design of the building may be poor (two flights of stairs to get down to the club?), especially poor for drunks, the interior of the club could have been taken straight from NYC. Top 40 hits blare all night long, and upturned liquor bottles behind the bar get constant use. Students should come on Wednesday, when there are discounted drinks or on Sunday when admission is free.

Cover F-Sa €9. Guinness and lager €5. Open W-Su 10:30pm-3am.

GOGARTY'S — BAR

58 Fleet St. ☎01 671 1822 www.gogartys.ie

Okay, it's basically a tourist trap, and you'll be hard-pressed to find a local here, but it's a pretty cool tourist trap, with three floors, two bars, a beer garden and a very posh a la carte restaurant on the top. Live music from 1:30pm, moving upstairs at 8pm, and continuing all night long.

On the easter edge of Temple Bar. Bar food approx. €5-15, upstairs expect a price jump. AE/MC/V. Open M-Sa 10:30am-2:30am, Su 12pm-1am.

TEMPLE BAR — BAR

47-48 Temple Bar St. ☎01 672 5287 templebarpubdublin.com

With possibly the best "beer garden" in the area, *the* Temple Bar (not the neighborhood, we're trying to be specific here) is a pun-merited hotspot on a sunny day. Expect to pay the TB standard €5 for a pint and slightly more for a mixed drink. Music starts with Traditional Irish songs at 2pm and moves onto U2 at night.

On Temple Bar street, in Temple Bar. If you can't find it there's nothing we can do for you.) ***i*** *No cover. Guinness €4.95, lager €5.50. Open M-W 10:30am-12:30am, Th 10:30am-2am, F-Sa 10:30am-2:30am and Su noon-1am.*

FITZSIMON'S BAR AND CLUB
BAR, CLUB

21-22 Wellington Quay ☎01 677 9315 www.fitzsimonshotel.com

A tourist-heavy bar, but with good reason. Located in the heart of Temple Bar, Fitzsimon's has five different floors, including a nightclub, cocktail bar and open-air rooftop terrace. Hugely popular on the weekends, this emporium of nightlife entertainment is open until 2:30am daily. Be forewarned, there's no AC in the club downstairs, so it can turn into a sweatbox.

*On the corner of Eustace and East Essex St. **i** Fitzsimon's also has a hotel and restaurant. A €6 vodka and coke and a €5.50 gin and tonic are both available until 11pm. Stout €4.85, lager €5.35. Open daily noon-2:30am.*

THE BRAZEN HEAD
PUB

20 Lower Bridge St., Merchant's Quay ☎01 679 5186

The oldest pub in Ireland, The Brazen Head was opened in 1198. That's 561 years before the invention of Guinness and 737 years before the founding of AA. This place knows what being a pub is all about. In fact, it still looks pretty Medieval: walls are covered with pictures of an Irish past, benches are well-worn, and the outdoor courtyard is reminiscent of something you'd find in the Middle Ages. In celebration of the 250th anniversary of Guinness, and its founder, Arthur Guinness, in 2009, Tom Jones came to sing at the Pub. How cool is that?

*A few blocks west down the Quay from Temple Bar, turn south on Lower Bridge St. **i** No cover. Pints around €5, food €5-20. Open M-Th 10:30am-midnight, F-Sa 10:30am-12:30am, Su 10:30am-midnight.*

THE PORTERHOUSE
BAR, PUB

16-18 Parliment St. ☎01 679 8847 porterhousebrewco.com

Imagine it: a three story bar, with live music every night, the wall lined with beers of amber and gold. Sounds like heaven, right? Well, it exists. The Porterhouse is the largest independent Irish brewing company, putting out nine of their own beers year-round and several seasonals. Try the "daily beer promotion," which allows you to pick up a different brew from around the world every day *(€4)*. Musical acts perform on a stage in between floors, so you can look up from the groundfloor, or down from the third floor balcony.

*1 block up Parliment from the Quay. **i** Food available until 9:30pm. Pints run around €4.30-5. Open M-W 11:30am-midnight, Th 11:30am-1:30am, F-Sa 11:30am-2:30am, Su 12:30pm-11pm.*

THE MEZZ
BAR, CLUB

23-24 Eustace St., Temple Bar ☎01 670 7655 www.mezz.ie

Your hard rock option in Temple Bar, the Mezz is actually two different venues: the upstairs bar, where the decor is a magazine and poster collage straight out of your "angsty" phase and the downstairs, which is even louder and more raucous with walls painted by a professional graffiti artist. Don't be fooled if you can't hear the music from the outside. The Mezz spent loads of money in the 2009 to completely soundproof the place. Just hop inside and get your jam on.

*Head south from the Milennium Bridge up Eustace street and the Mezz will be on your left. **i** No cover Pints around €5. Open daily 5pm-2:30am.*

GRAFTON STREET

TRIPOD
CLUB

37 Harcourt St. ☎01 475 9750 www.podconcerts.ie

Some stone towers hide dragons, this one hides great live music and dance venue. The main hall houses international DJs and other forms of dance music. Early in the morning on a Friday or Saturday night, this place is packed with sweaty dancers. Heading over the Pod around the base of the tower will put you in—well, a pod—that's running a different beat, with house music and a

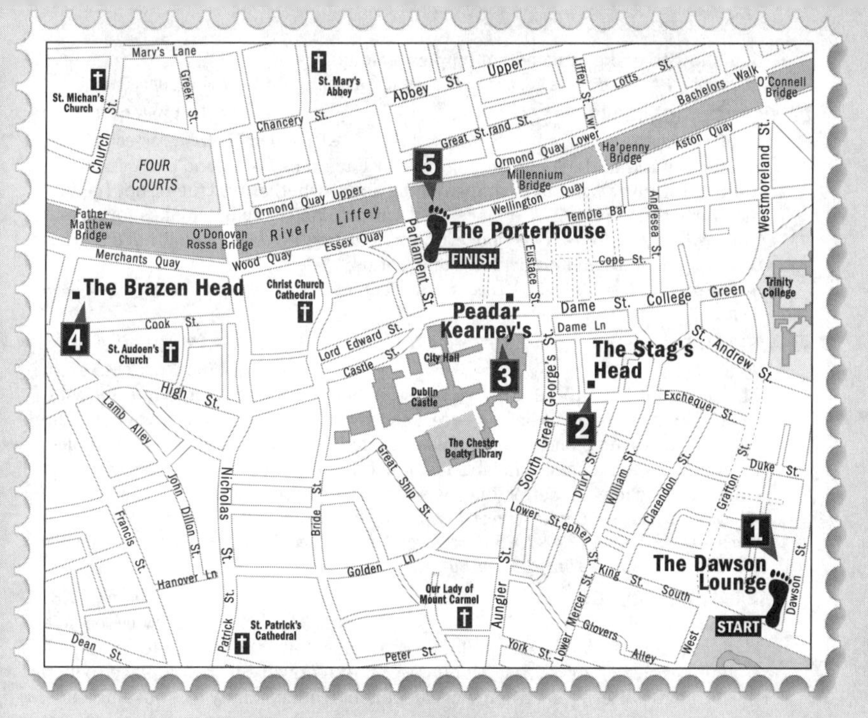

publin walking tour

The capital of Ireland is known for a few things: James Joyce, brogues, and, of course, brew. For those steadfast enough to tackle a true pub crawl, we've consolidated some of the city's best pubs below. Pace yourself, though.

1. THE DAWSON LOUNGE. Start your pub tour at the Dawson Lounge at 25 Dawson St. This pleasantly traditional pub is the smallest pub in Ireland. What it lacks in size, it makes up for with its robust brews.

2. THE STAG'S HEAD. Next on the itinerary, head to the Stag's Head at 1 Dame Ct. To get here from Dawson Lounge, head northeast all the way down Grafton St.; take a left onto Wicklow St. and a left onto Exchequer St; take a right onto Dame Ct., and you're there. Everything's very Victorian here; and, of course, there's taxidermy on the wall.

3. PEADAR KEARNEY'S. Once you've re-hydrated, soldier onto Peadar Kearney's, just a couple of blocks from the Stag's Head. This joint is named for the composer of the Irish National Anthem, and before the night is over, you, too, will be belting that tune.

4. THE BRAZEN HEAD. When you walk out of Peadar's, take a left and continue west for a few blocks; you'll stumble upon the Brazen Head at 20 Lower Bridge St., Merchant's Quay. This establishment, my friends, is Dublin's oldest bar.

5. THE PORTERHOUSE. It'll be a bit of a trek, but once you've sufficiently shot the breeze (and the shots) with the old chaps at the Brazen Head, head on over to The Porterhouse at 16-18 Parliment St. This place boasts three stouts, three ales, and three lagers. Try some, but not all of them. By this point in the evening, we're not sure how you'll be holiding up.

WALKING TOUR

Let's Go

www.letsgo.com

lightshow to make drugged-out hippies jealous.

Beamish €4. Mixed drinks €5. Mid-week deals for students. Open T-Sa 4:30pm-3am.

COPPER FACE JACKS CLUB

29-30 Harcourt St. 01 475 8777 www.jackson-court.ie

Rumor has it that the longstanding Copper Face Jacks is a good place for those looking for love. Without saying anything about whether it's true or not (gentlemen never kiss and tell), Copper's, as it's affectionately called, makes for a great time. With two floors, two dance floors, and two big bars, you'll have a great time. Say hello to an intoxicated Cupid for us.

i 20+ only. Guinness €4.50. Lager €4.80. Cover €5+. Ages 20+ only. Open daily 4pm-3am.

WHELAN'S BAR, MUSIC VENUE

25 Wexford St. 01 478 0766 whelanslive.com

The place for Dublin's alternative music, Whelan's boasts a large interior, with several bars, a excellent balcony area, and two stages. The main stage hosts the biggest names in up-and-coming music, while the smaller stage upstairs handles local and acoustic acts. Whelan's is a must. (Note that the view from the main stage balcony may be better, but the sound will not be. Choose carefully.)

Follow South Great George's street 15min. away from the river. Whelan's is on the right. Guinness €4.40. Lagers €4.90. €5-10 cover for the club after 10:30pm on weekends. Open M-F 2:30pm-2:30am, Sa 5pm-2:30am, Su 5pm-1:30am.

THE DAWSON LOUNGE PUB

25 Dawson street 01 671 0311 www.dawsonslounge.ie

Protect yourself from nuclear fallout by climbing down the stairs into "the smallest pub on earth" (or at least, Dublin). A bit of a novelty, it's a fun place to stop by during the afternoons when you can benefit from its dimly lit, cool ambience. Let it get crowded, however, and you'll uncomfortably realize that it's really just a walk-in closet with a Guinness tap.

From the top of Grafton St., walk 1 block left. Turn left again, the pub will be on your left. i Tiny packages of peanuts also available for purchase. Open M-Th 12:30pm-11:30pm, F-Sa 12:30pm-12:30am, Su 3pm-11pm.

GRAFTON LOUNGE CLUB

Unit 2, Royal Hibernian Way, Dawson St. 01 679 6260 www.thegraftonlounge.ie

With weird, funky furniture, a pool table downstairs, and so many people wearing white you might actually need to put on your sunglasses at night: the Grafton Lounge is a place for beautiful people to be seen. Don't think of showing up looking scruffy. DJs pump out the tunes from Th-Su.

Guinness €5. Mixed drinks from €10. Open M-W 11am-11:30pm, Th-Sa 11am-2:30am, Su 4:30pm-1:30am.

DAVY BRYNE'S PUB

21 Duke St. 01 677 5217 www.davybrynes.com

Getting a famous mention in James Joyce's "Ulysses," this literary pub fills up on Bloomsday with patrons looking for gorgonzola sandwiches and glasses of "burgundy" (the same meal consumed by the novel's main character). On days that *don't* celebrate major Irish writers, the pub is also a pretty great place to get a pint and hang out.

Heading on Grafton St. towards St. Stephen's Green. Turn left on Duke St. Food runs between €5-17. Extensive wine selection €5-7.50 per glass. Open M-Th 11am-11:30pm, F-Sa 11am-12:30am, Su 11am-11pm.

D TWO CLUB

60 Harcourt St. 01 476 4600 www.dtwonightclub.com

This is where George of the Dublin jungle comes to get his pint. A popular club,

its enormous jungle themed beer gardens is packed on the weekends, especially during the summer. Come in before 8pm and all drinks are €3.50.
Lagers €5. Guinness €4.90 after 11pm.

CAPITOL LOUNGE CLUB, COCKTAIL LOUNGE
1-2 Aungier St. ☎01 475 7166 www.capitol.ie
Cocktails are the thing at the Capitol lounge—€5, all day, everyday. With over 100 different variations on the menu, you're going to have watch yourself to make sure you don't get sloppy. Head upstairs where the music's slightly softer to chat with friends or wade through the crowd downstairs as the DJs put out that house music pulse.
i 21+ only. No cover. Open daily 3pm-3am.

PYGMALION BAR, CLUB
Powerscourt Centre, South William St. ☎01 633 4479 pygmaliondublin@gmail.com
An attractive bar with attractive people, the biggest pull for Pygmalion is their half-price drinks on Sundays. Look for it to really fill up then. Drinks at their normal prices are reasonable, and there's an extensive cocktail menu from €8.50-10. Guinness after church, anyone?
i Outside seating available. Guinness €4.70. Lagers €4.90.

DICEY'S GARDEN CLUB
21-25 Harcourt St. ☎01 478 4066 www.russellcourthotel.ie
Another club that looks like somebody threw some lights in the hotel lobby—and then you hit the beer garden, or two levels of wrap-around balconies and a dance floor below.
i 21+ only. Cover: T €2, W €3.50, Th €3, F €4, Sa €5. Open daily noon-2:30am.

THE "NO NAME BAR" BAR
#3 Fade St. (Next to Hogan's Bar on South Great George's St.)
Looking like a sweet Manhattan flat from the early 1960s, this place could have been a sweet beat hangout. The brick walls and sparse furniture in this bar gives the 20-something crowd a chance to mingle. And mingle they do, over much-craved mojitos and homemade Bloody Marys. Get your groove on weeknights as the DJs take over from 8pm til close.
Follow South Great George's St. until you see Hogan's Bar; turn left. Guinness €4.50. Lager €5. Barfood on weekdays €10 or less. Open M-W 1pm-11:30pm, Th 1pm-1am, F-Sa 1pm-2:30am, Su 1pm-1am.

THE DRAGON BAR, CLUB
64-65 South Great George's St. ☎01 478 1590 thedragon@capitalbars.com
A heady combination of Paris chic, neon Vegas, and the Addams family, the Dragon is a gay bar popular with a younger crowd than the Georges, and it really gets hopping around midnight. Check out the extremely entertaining drag/dance shows on Monday, Saturday or Thursday and join in under the light of the spinning disco ball.
From Dame St., follow South Great George's St. up a few blocks. i Mezzanine and second dance floor upstairs. Pints €3-6. Open M 8pm-3am, Tu 8-11:30pm, W-Sa 8pm-3am, Su 8-11:30pm.

THE CAMDEN PALACE CLUB
84-87 Lower Camden St. ☎01 478 0808 www.camden-deluxe.com
Dear. God. Somebody let out the crazy. The Camden Palace takes everything over-the-top and then throws it overboard. In a huge ampitheater of a club, people get freaky on the light-up go-go platforms (and with each other). Can't seem to find it? Look for the guys swinging fire-tipped chains outside the entrance on a weekend night.
Follow Great St. George's street as it turns into Aungier, and then into Camden. The club will be

on your right. ***i*** *IDs are a must.* *Guinness €4.70. Lagers €5. Mixed drinks €8. Cover €10 on weekends.* *Pool hall and bar open daily noon-3am. Nightclub only open Th-Sa.*

THE STAG'S HEAD PUB

1 Dame Ct. ☎01 679 3687 thestagshead@fitzgeraldgroup.ie

Established in 1895, the Stag's Head is the everyman pub of Dublin. Everybody drinks here. Businessmen drinking next to soccer hooligans drinking next to punk rockers. Oh yeah, and there actually is a giant stag's head in there.

Dame Court has a small entrance on Dame St. Ask around. *Guinness €4.55. Lager €4.90.*

arts and culture

THEATER

THE GAIETY THEATRE THEATRE

South King St. ☎01 677 1717 www.gaietytheatre.ie

A beautiful old house theater with three levels of red velvet seating. Student discounts are offered up to 15%, but another good money saving tip (regular prices run anywhere from €25-55) is to go for the "restricted view" seats. Rumor has it that the large drop in price is only coupled with a small loss of stage visibility. Check the website for a complete show schedule. Riverdance comes for two months every summer—Riverdance!

Walk to the top of Grafton St. and turn right. ***i*** *No exchanges or refunds. Doors close promptly when the show begins. Concessions available.* *Tickets prices vary.* *Box office open M-Sa 10am-7pm.*

BEWLEY'S CAFÉ THEATRE THEATRE

78-79 Grafton St. ☎01 086 878 4001 www.bewleys.com

A good place for lunchtime entertainment as well as jazz or cabaret in the evenings.

About halfway up Grafton St. on the right. ***i*** *Call or email the office for booking about.* *Tickets range €10-20.*

PROJECT ARTS CENTRE THEATRE

39 East Essex St. ☎01 881 9613 www.projectartscentre.ie

A big, hard-to-miss blue building sitting in the middle of Temple Bar, the Project Arts Centre has upstairs and downstairs theaters, as well as a gallery space. Stop in to check out upcoming shows and take advantage of some free coffee and W-Fi. Check the website for show schedules.

Tickets €20-25. *Box office open M-Sa 11am-7pm. Gallery open M-Sa 11am-8pm.*

ABBEY THEATRE THEATRE

26-27 Lower Abbey St. ☎01 878 7222 www.abbeytheatre.ie

First opened in 1904 through the efforts of a certain Mr. William Butler Yeats, the Abbey Theatre has burned down, been moved away, moved back, and rebuilt on its original location, and is supposed to move again in 2012. Apparently the physical space is doing its best to mimic the creative atmosphere, which has been promoting an ever-changing landscape of new Irish writers.

From O'Connell St., turn right.

DANCE

These two shows make up for their touristy atmospheres with all the dancin' and jiggin' you could ever want.

ARLINGTON HOTEL TEMPLE BAR IRISH DANCE

16-18 Lord Edward St. ☎01 670 8777 www.arlingtonhotel.ie

With a raised stage in contrast to the Blarney Inn, where the dancing is done right on the pub floor, the Arlington hotel knows they've got quite a show. Spring for the three course dinner plus a show *(€30)*, and you'll get set up at a table front and center. If you don't feel like eating, however, you're still welcome to enjoy the performance. Just make sure you grab a drink from the bar.

i "Pour your own pint" tables available as well. Shows daily 8:30-11pm.

BLARNEY INN PUB IRISH DANCE

1-2 Nassau St. ☎01 679 4388 www.blarneyinn.com

Irish dancing from Thursday to Saturday. The show begins at 8pm, but the dancers don't usually come on until 9pm. Performers are either co-ed or all-female, depending on the day.

From Trinity college, follow Nassau St. with the College on your left. The Blarney Inn Pub will be on your right on the corner of Kildare St. Entrees €15. Open M-F 10:30am-11pm or midnight, Sa-Su 9am-11pm or midnight.

FESTIVALS

STREET PERFORMANCE WORLD CHAMPIONSHIPS FESTIVAL

Merrion Sq. www.spwc.ie

The best street performers in the world come to compete for honor, glory, and that €2-coin you've got rolling around in your pocket (but admission is free). A must-see.

From Trinity College follow Nassau St. east, along Clare Street to Merrion Sq. Free. Donations encouraged. June.

TRINITY COLLEGE DUBLIN SHAKESPEARE FESTIVAL FESTIVAL

Trinity College, College Green Dublin 2 ☎01 896 2242 www.dublinshakespeare.com

Running during the first or second week of June, this festival is put on by Trinity College's drama club, the Dublin University Players, and offers main event shows on campus, as well as free shows in parks across Dublin throughout the week. You can buy tickets inside Trinity College, or just ask the nearest person you see strumming a lute.

From O'Connell Bridge, follow Westmoreland St. to Trinity College on the left. €18, seniors and children €12.50, students €10.

shopping

CLOTHING

THE HARLEQUIN TEMPLE BAR AND THE QUAYS

13 Castle Market ☎01 671 0202 susannaharlequin@hotmail.com

The Harlequin is a great little vintage shop where you'll have trouble finding something that *doesn't* totally match your new retro ensemble. With three floors, costume jewelry, and the sexiest collection of men's velvet jackets this side of the Channel, it's a must-hit for any clothing shopper.

i Upstairs and downstairs not wheelchair-accessible. M-W 10am-6pm, Th 10am-8pm, F 10am-6pm, Th 10am-8pm, Sa 9:30am-6pm, Su 12:30-5:30pm.

GENIUS WEST OF TEMPLE BAR

Powerscourt Centre, Clarendon St. ☎01 679 7851 www.genius.ie

A store whose merchandise seems designed to make you feel stupid in whatever *you're* wearing, Genius offers a classy assortment of name brand jackets and men's accessories, as well as a large selection of stylish leather boots. It's up to you to decide if throwing down €100+ for boots is a smart move or not.

i Annual sales in June and Jan. Open M-W 10am-6pm, Th 10am-8pm, F-Su 10am-6pm.

AVOCA TEMPLE BAR AND THE QUAYS

11-13 Suffolk St. ☎01 677 4215 www.avoca.ie

This home of Irish-made items has it all. Women's clothing, throws and scarves, a cafe upstairs, and a pantry full of their own homemade scones, jams and other sweet things.

Down the street from Dublin Tourism on Suffolk St. Open M-W 10am-6pm, Th 10am-7pm, F-Sa 10am-6pm, Su 11am-6pm.

INDIGO AND CLOTH WEST OF TEMPLE BAR

Basement 27, South William St. ☎01 670 6403 www.indigoandcloth.com

Down in a little basement shop on South Williams St. lies God's own collection of trendy clothing. Carrying alternating top tier brands, this little shop makes sure you get your bang for your buck. Unfortunately, a lot of bang means a lot of buck, and simple tops or T-shirts here can run up to €60, and jackets or dresses up to €350. If you can spring, you'll be one impeccably dressed individual walking the streets of Dublin.

Open M-W noon-6pm, Th noon-7pm, F noon-6pm, Sa 10am-6pm, Su 1pm-5pm.

FLIP TEMPLE BAR AND THE QUAYS

4 Fownes St. Upper ☎01 671 4299 www.flipclothing.com

Open since the mid-'80s when Temple Bar had none of its present day veneer, Flip clothing is a combination of vintage and not, with leather and military jackets, funky Hawaiian prints, and a liberal price negotiation policy. You're getting a great deal might just depend on how willing you are to beg.

T-shirts from €15. Jeans from €20. Open M-W 10am-6pm, Th 11am-7pm, F-Sa 10am-6pm, Su 1-6pm.

GREAT OUTDOORS GRAFTON ST.

Chatham St. ☎01 679 4293 www.greatoutdoors.ie

If you need bugspray, tents, sleeping bags, or a waterproof anything, head to Great Outdoors to find it. A wide range of outdoor equipment, it'll help you survive your trek through the mountains...or just stay dry under Ireland's never ending rain.

Turn right on Chatham St. just before you get to the top of Grafton street. i Some outdoor clubs' discounts honored. Open M-W 10am-6pm, Th 10am-8pm, F 10am-6pm, Sa 9:30am-6pm, Su 12:30-5:30pm.

THE EAGER BEAVER TEMPLE BAR AND THE QUAYS

17 Crown Alley ☎01 677 3342

The longest operating vintage shop in Temple Bar lives up to its name, you won't be able to wait before getting in here to check out their selection of new and vintage wear. An extensive collection brought in from Germany, UK, and Holland. Check out the downstairs collection of tweeds or ask the owner Robert for a good place to get a beer. He'll pint you in the right direction. Ha.

Levis from €20-30. Tweed jackets from €35-40. Open M-Sa 10am-7pm, Su noon-6pm.

FAT FACE TEMPLE BAR AND THE QUAYS

31 Exchequer St. ☎01 677 2415 www.fatface.com

Okay, so the name doesn't exactly scream style, but that's all advertising...we think. An England-based company begun when a couple of "ski bums" (again, their words, not ours), Fat Face offers surfer chic reminiscent of Quiksilver, but with a much funnier name.

PATAGONIA TEMPLE BAR AND THE QUAYS

24-26 Exchequer St. ☎01 670 5748/49 www.patagonia.com

A European outlet store, this Patagonia sells discontinued stock at reduced prices. If you're looking for durable but attractive travel wear, this is a good bet.

Open M-Th 10am-6pm, W 10am-8pm, F 10am-6pm, Sa 9:30am-6pm, Su 1pm-5pm.

BOOKS

BARGAIN BOOKS — GRAFTON ST.

37 Grafton St.

Damn. You've just finished that new Dan Brown novel and the hostel's book exchange is looking a little weak. Head over to Bargain Books, where factory outlet prices are the thing. Copies of *Ulysses* run just €3. Do you dare?

Almost to the top of Grafton St. on your left. Cash only. M-Tu 9am-7pm, W 9am-8pm, Th-F 9am-8:30pm, Sa-Su 9am-7pm.

TEMPLE BAR BOOK MARKET — TEMPLE BAR AND THE QUAYS

Temple Bar Sq. www.templebar.ie

Every Saturday and Sunday local booksellers set up tents and deal new, used, and antique books here at good prices.

Just through Merchant's Arch on Temple Bar St. Books from €3. Sa-Su 11am-6pm.

DUBRAY'S BOOKS — GRAFTON ST.

36 Grafton St. ☎01 677 5568 www.dubraybooks.ie

A multi-level bookstore offering new titles. Check out either the sale section or the staff recommends, available in a handy pamphlet available at the counter.

Almost to the top of Grafton street on the left. Open M-F 9am-9pm, Sa 9am-7pm, Su 9am-6pm.

CENTRAL LIBRARY — EAST OF O'CONNELL ST.

Ilac Shopping Centre, 12 Earl St. N. ☎01 873 4333 centrallibrary@dublincity.ie

In Dublin for a while and low on cash? Looking to read something other than the *Let's Go* in your hands? Take out a free library card at this convienent location. Just bring along an ID and proof of address.

From O'Connell St., turn left onto Henry street. The iLac Centre is on your right. Free. Open M-Th 10am-8pm, F-Sa 10am-5pm.

BOOKWORMS — WEST OF O'CONNELL ST.

75 Middle Abbey St. ☎01 873 5772 booba@eircom.net

A long-standing discount and secondhand bookstore, the emphasis here is on prices. Cheap prices. Very few of the titles here are sold retail. With books upon shelves, boxes and other strange forms of display, it's a chaotic yet organized book-lovers paradise.

From O'Connell St., turn left on to Middle Abbey St. i Children and young readers sections. Open M-F 9:30am-7:30pm, Sa 9:30am-7pm, Su 1-6pm.

THE SECRET BOOK AND RECORD STORE — WEST OF GRAFTON ST.

15a Wicklow St. ☎01 679 7272

It's hard to find, but worth finding. The SBARS has extensive used and new sections, including a classics section *(€3 each)*. Combine that with a charming staff and mellow mood music from Freebird records and you've got one hell of a music/literary combo.

Look for a little door with a small sign, and follow the hallway. Open daily M-W 11am-6:30pm, Th 11am-7:30pm, F-Su 11am-6:30pm.

BOOKS UPSTAIRS — TEMPLE BAR AND THE QUAYS

36 College Green ☎01 679 6687 info@booksirish.com

A fun bookstore divided into many different subjects, including fiction, philosophy, religion, gay, and many others. Articles and book reviews tacked to the bulletin board alert you to what's hot off the press.

Across the street from Trinity College at the bottom of Grafton St. Open M-F 10am-7pm, Sa 10am-6pm, Su 2-6pm.

THE WINDING STAIR BOOKSTORE TEMPLE BAR AND THE QUAYS
40 Lower Ormond Quay ☎01 872 6576 bookshop@winding-stair.com
A fun, local bookstore that gives a 10% discount to students. Come in to find a hefty selection of new and used titles.
Across the Milennium Bridge from Temple Bar. Open M-W 10am-7pm, Th-Sa 10am-8pm, Su noon-7pm.

OUTDOOR MARKETS

SOUTH CITY MARKET OR ST. GEORGE'S ARCADE NORTH OF O'CONNELL ST.
South Great George's St.
This open-air market is a good place to find vintage wear, old LPs, used CDs and DVDs, weird Asian goods ("Hello Kitty" bra, anyone?), coffee, flowers, jewelry, used books and more.
Walking up Grafton St., turn right onto Johnson's St. and follow it to the South City Market. Open M-F 10:30am-6:30pm, Sa 10:30am-6:30pm, Su noon-6pm.

LIQUOR STORES

Ah, the fine art of boozin'. The establishments below have been chosen for their selection and for the personable, welcoming nature of their staff. If you're interested in become a professional whiskey drinker, or at least maintaining the claim when you're sober, head to either of these bottle shops. If you're just interested in finding a cheap bottle of wine to take to the party, there are liquor stores located all over Dublin, handily marked with the vaguely black-market sounding "off license." Cheers.

CELTIC WHISKEY SHOP SOUTH OF GRAFTON ST.
24 Dawson St. ☎01 675 9744 www.celticwhiskeyshop.com
Whether you're looking to get a bunch of those tiny bottles that you find in hotel minibars, or paying €3000 for a single bottle, you can find what you're looking for here. Wine, whiskey, and microbrews available. Daily whiskey tastings make even the shopping experience smooth.
Walk to the top of Grafton St. and turn left, and then left again on Dawson St. Prices vary.

JAMES FOX GRAFTON ST.
119 Grafton St. ☎01 677 0533 www.jamesfox.ie
Besides having an extensive selection of Irish and Scotch whiskeys from all prices ranges, James Fox specializes in cigars. If you've been thinking about grabbing that Cohiba, now's the time to do it.
At the bottom of Grafton street. i Cigar accessories available as well. Open M-Sa 9:30am-6pm, Su 12:30-5:30pm.

ELECTRONICS

COMPUB AND MAC EXCHANGE GRAFTON ST.
11 Grafton St. ☎01 507 9107 www.compub.com
Apple users, you didn't think we were going to leave you out in the cold, did you? Compub offers a wide selection of Mac products, including iPods and Macbooks. They also have a tech support group, and, if you've got a warranty they'll gladly accept it. If not, however, it's €75 for a diagnostic test plus the cost of your repair.
Just Down Grafton St. from the Molly Malone statue. Open M-W 9am-7pm, Th 9am-9pm, F-Sa 9am-7pm, Su 11am-6pm.

PHILLIPS TEMPLE BAR AND THE QUAYS
19-22 Dame St. ☎01 474 0788 www.phillipsshop.ie
Phillips on Dame St. has adapters for your gear, though bear in mind they don't have converters. No cameras either. They do have a large selection of headphones (including the noise-cancelling ones) though.
Open M-W 10am-6pm, Th 10am-7pm, F-Sa 10am-6pm, Su 1-5pm.

SONY CENTRE LOWER O'CONNELL ST.

17 Lower O'Connell St. ☎01 873 1512 www.sonycentres.co.uk

This store offers cameras and memory cards, as well as laptop cases and other travel accessories. The boys at Sony Centre will help you with troubleshooting problems, but they don't have a certified tech center.

When heading up O'Connell St., it will be on the right. Open M-W 10am-6pm, Th 10am-7pm, F-Sa 10am-6pm, Su 1-5pm.

FURNITURE

NOONE FURNITURE NORTH OF THE QUAYS

36 Talbot St. ☎01 855 6731 www.noonefurniture@eircom.net

Offers a large selection of all types of furniture, but if you don't see what you're looking for, just inform the staff and they'll order it for you from the catalogue. Free assembly and delivery with purchase. It doesn't get much better than that.

On Talbot St., down near Connolly Station. Prices vary, but single beds from €300. Open M-Sa 9:30am-5pm.

BEDROOM ELEGANCE UPPER DORSET ST.

55-56 Upper Dorset St. ☎01 872 8210 bedroomelegance.ie

Offering made-to-measure furniture, this stuff is custom, so go in with an idea of what you want. That wrap-around couch with the 10 cupholders can be done, they just need to know about it.

Open M-F 9:20am-5:30pm, Sa 9:30am-4pm.

ANTIQUES

THE CARBOOT SHOP THE QUAYS

Eden Quay www.thecarbootshop.com

Right on the river, the Carboot hop is your best bet for antiques north of the Liffey. Bric-a-brac and curio are in abundance. If things look busy, stay away: you may be charged a €1 entrance fee. However, if the shop is empty, enter with the hope of getting a great deal.

Across the brige to the north side, turn right and walk a few blocks. Prices vary. Open M-Sa 11am-6pm.

JOHNSON'S COURT VINTAGE EMPORIUM SOUTHWEST OF GRAFTON ST.

12A Johnson's Ct. ☎01 670 6825

A store full of so many knick-knacks and interesting pieces you'll wonder how you're ever going to leave. The owner has a large selection of items from Ireland as well as a significant collection brought in from the rest of Europe.

From Grafton St., follow Johnson St. Open M-Sa 10:30am-5:30pm.

COURTVILLE ANTIQUES WEST OF TEMPLE BAR

Powerscourt Townhouse, South William St. ☎01 679 4042 www.courtvilleantiques.com

Sick of people telling you that their 1999, oversized Aerosmith concert T-shirt is an "antique?" Come to Courtville Antiques, where almost all of the items are certified as being *at least* 100 years old. A fine selection of women's jewelry, old paintings, and some beautiful glassware from County Cork.

Open T-F 11am-5:30pm, Sa 10am-5:30pm.

DEPARTMENT STORES

PENNYS DEPARTMENT STORE O'CONNELL ST.

O'Connell St. ☎01 656 6666 www.pennys.ie

Imagine if Wal-mart were Irish. Now imagine that it's good, and even cheaper. Now you've got Pennys. This department store chain is beloved in Ireland, and with T-shirts or sneakers from €5, the love is well-deserved. Traveling long? Get yourself some new undies stat *(€2-3)*.

On O'Connell St., just below the GPO. Cheap. Open M-W 8:30am-8pm, Th-F 8:30am-9pm, Sa 8:30am-7pm, Su 11am-7pm.

POWERSCOURT CENTRE WEST OF GRAFTON ST.

59 South William St. www.powerscourtcentre.com

The "artsy" shopping center, the Powerscourt is the place to go for antiques (there's a whole wing dedicated to them), as well as painting and photography galleries. Sit down in the café on the ground floor and enjoy the sunshine filtering down through the massive skylight installed over the courtyard.

Take Johnson's St. right from Grafton and walk 1 block. Open M-F 10am-6pm, Th 10am-8pm, Sa 9am-6pm, Su noon-6pm.

ST. STEPHEN'S GREEN SHOPPING CENTRE GRAFTON ST.

At the top of Grafton St. ☎01 478 0888 www.stephensgreen.com

A mall offering your usual collection of retail chains (Quiksilver, GameStop, etc.), there's no real reason to go in here if you're not shopping, except maybe to observe the incredibly large clock that hangs from the ceiling.

At the top of Grafton St., across from St. Stephen's Green. i Toilet use €.20. Open M-W 9am-7pm, Th 9am-9pm, F-Sa 9am-7pm, Su 11am-6pm.

CLERYS DEPARTMENT STORE O'CONNELL ST.

18-27 O'Connell St. ☎01 878 6000 www.clerys.com

Much more your Mom's store, Clerys doesn't really hold much appeal for the student traveler. Still, if you're looking for an easy way to browse for a few hours it has 4 floors of shopping, including a restaurant on the top floor.

Across the street from Pennys. i Customer service desk located on the 2nd floor. Open M-W 10am-6:30pm, Th 10am-9pm, F 10am-6:30pm, Sa 9am-7pm.

essentials

PRACTICALITIES

- **TOURIST OFFICES: College Green Tourism Office,** Dublin's only independent tourist agency, will help you get a jump on any tour you have in mind. From booking tickets to the Guinness storehouse to reserving your stay for the night, they do it all. However, it's worth stating that they are a booking service, and while they can answer most of your questions, if you're looking for information in general you should head over to Dublin Tourism on Suffolk street. *(37 College Green, Dublin 2. ☎01 410 0700 info@daytours.ie Open daily 8:30am-9pm.)* To get to **Dublin Tourism (O'Connell St. branch),** from the river, walk up O'Connell street. It's on the right. An off-shoot of the Dublin Tourism head offices in the converted St. Andrew's cathedral, this office offers many of the same services (tour bookings, room reservations and general tourist information), just in slightly more boring building. Tourist gift shop available. *(14 O'Connell St. ☎01 874 6064 visitdublin.com* Open M-Sa 9am-5pm.) To get to the **Northern Ireland Tourist Board,** from college green, walk up Suffolk St. Dublin Tourism will be on your right. The Dublin place to go for information on Belfast and Northern Ireland, they're also a booking service, and will make you any reservations you require, free of charge. *(Inside Dublin Tourism. ☎ 01 605 7732 www.discovernorthernireland.com Open Sept-June M-Sa 9am-5:30pm, Su 10:30am-3pm; July-Aug M-Sa 9am-7pm.)* Finally, to get to **Dublin Tourism,** from the college green, walk up Suffolk St. Dublin Tourism will be on your right. Located in a converted church with beautiful arched ceilings and stained glass windows, this may be the only tourist office that's a sight in itself. The staff are knowledgeable and friendly. Head to the general information desk with broad questions, or head over to one of the many tour companies that have desks in the office. *(The former St. Andrew's church, Suffolk St. ☎01 605 7700 www.visitdublin.com Open M-Sa 9:30am-5pm, Su 10:30am-3pm.)*

- **LUGGAGE STORAGE:** To get to **Global Internet Café** head over the bridge and on to O'Connell St.; it will be on the right. A nice internet café (and they actually do serve coffee), possibly the best thing about this place is their luggage storage rates. A lot of hassle averted for a little money. *(8 Lower O'Connell St. ☎01 873 9100 www.globalhq.ie Internet: first 20min. €1.45, student €1.30; 20-40min €2.25/2; 40-60min. €2.95/2.65. Luggage storage: 1st day €3.95, each additional day €1.95. Open M-F 8am-10pm, Sa 9am-9pm, Su 10am-9pm.)*
- **ATMS:** A 24hr. ATM can be found at the bottom of Grafton Street, across Nassau Street from the Molly Malone statue. There are two 24hr. ATMs at the **Ulster Bank** on Dame street across from the Wax Museum Plus.
- **CURRENCY EXCHANGE:** Does paper exchanges as well as card withdrawls. €6000 limit. *(1 Westmoreland St. ☎01 670 6724 Open M-Th 9am-6pm, F-Sa 9am-8pm, Su 10am-6pm.)*
- **POST OFFICES:** To get to **Dublin General Post Office,** walk up O'Connell St. from the river for 5min., the post office is on the left hand side. At the time of this book's printing, a museum detailing the 1916 Easter uprising (which took place in front of the Post Office) was scheduled to be opened. Oh, and they send mail too. *(O'Connell St., Dublin 1 ☎01 705 7000 www.anpost.ie Open M-Sa 8:30am-6pm.)*
- **POSTAL CODE:** Dublin 1 (General Post Office). Even-numbered codes are for areas south of the Liffey, while odd-numbered codes are for the north.

EMERGENCY!

- **PHARMACIES: Hickey's Pharmacy** is up Grafton St. on the left. *(21 Grafton St. ☎ 679 0467 Open M-Th 8:30am- 8:30pm, F 8:30am-8pm, Sa-Su 10:30am-6pm.)*
- **HICKEY'SPHARMACY:** Hickey's is on O'Connell St., right after the bridge. It's the same company as the Grafton St. branch—this one's just open a little later. *(55 Lower O'Connell St. ☎01 873 0427 www.hickeyspharmacy.ie Prices vary. Open M-F 7:30am-10pm, Sa 8am-10pm, Su 10am-10pm.)*
- **TEMPLE BAR PHARMACY:** *(21 Essex St. ☎670 9751 Open M-W 9:30am-7pm, Th-Sa 9:30am-8pm, Su 1pm-5pm.)*
- **WOMEN'S ASSISTANCE: Dublin Rape Crisis Center** provides a 24 hr. hotline, free counseling, advocacy and legal advice for victims of recent rape or sexual abuse. *(70 Lower Leeson St. ☎24hr. toll-free national hotline 1800 77 8888; office number 661 4911 www.drcc.ie Services are offered free of charge. Open M-F 8am-7pm, Sa 9am-4pm.*

GETTING THERE

By Air

Flights go through **Dublin International Airport** (*www.dublinairport.com; information.queries@daa.ie*). The DIA houses desks for several different flight companies, some of which do flight bookings at the desk.

- **RYANAIR:** Available for last minute changes to your tix, no phone or booking done here. Do that on ryanair.com.
- **LUFTHANSA:** German based airline has both a reservations number and the weirdest hours ever. *(☎01 855 4455 Open daily 5am-7am, 8:15am-12:30pm, 3:30pm-5:30pm.)*

- **AERARANN:** For domestic flights in Ireland. Book online or reserve at the desk. *(☎0818210210 www.aerarann.com Open daily 5:30am-10pm.)*
- **AERLINGUS:** Book flights, change flights, collect excess baggage *(i There's a 20kilo weight limit)*. Rebooking. *(www.aerlingus.com.)*
- **U.S. AIRWAYS:** Rebookings, delayed flights and customer service. *(☎8090925065 www.usairways.com Open daily 7:30am-noon.)*
- **CONTINENTAL AIRLINES:** *(☎189 092 5252 www.continental.com).*
- **AIRFRANCE:** *(☎ 01 605 0383 www.airfrance.ie Open M-F 4am-7:50pm, Sa 4am-5:45pm, Su 4am-7:50pm.)*
- **DELTA:** *(☎1850 088 2031 www.delta.com Open 6am-1pm. May change according to day's flight schedule.)*

By Car

- **BUDGET:** *(☎01 844 5150 www.budget.ie Open daily 5am-1am.)*
- **HERTZ:** *(☎01 844 5466 www.hertz.ie Open daily 5am-1am.)*
- **EUROPCAR:** *(☎01 844 4199 www.europcar.com Open daily 6am-11pm.)*
- **SIXT RENT-A-CAR:** *(☎01 018 1204 www.sixt.ie Open daily 6am-midnight.)*
- **AVIS:** *(☎01 605 7563 www.avis.ie Open M-F 5am-11:30pm, Sa 5am-11pm, Su 5am-11:30pm.)*

GETTING AROUND

By Bus

The price of your bus fare in Dublin depends on how far you're traveling (listed in stages) and run 1-3 €1.15, 4-7 €1.60, 8-13 €1.80 and over 13 stages €2.20. The "Rambler Pass" allows you to travel on any bus for a set amount of time, is pretty steep, so only buy it if you're sure to be moving around quite a bit (1 day pass €6, 3 day €13.30, 5 day €20). The buses themselves run all over Dublin. Times vary, but buses can usually be caught every 8-20min. from 6am-8am and every 30min. from 8pm-midnight. *(59 O'Connell St. ☎01 973 4222 www.dublinbus.ie.)*

By Taxi

Taxis in Dublin are, much like everything else, expensive. Expect to pay anywhere from €7-10 to get from one destination to another, and more if you're heading across town. Obey the general rules of foreign taxi travel—ask ahead to find the shortest route to your destination, and then make sure the cabbie follows it. Blue Cabs is the predominant taxi company in Dublin. They offer wheelchair-accessible cabs. Call ahead of time to book. *(66/67 Butterly Business Park, Kilmore Rd., Dublin 5 ☎01 802 2222 bluecabs.ie; info@bluecabs.ie.)*

There are groups of taxi cabs (called "ranks") in four neighborhoods in Dublin. In **Temple Bar,** the ranks can be found on the Aston Quay and on the college green in front of the Wax Museum and Bank of Ireland. In the **Grafton Street area,** find taxis near the intersection of Dawson and Duke St. (on Harry St., off the top of Grafton St. and to the right). Next, in the **Viking/Medieval area** of town, pick up taxis on Christchurch Pl. across the street from the Christchurch Cathedral. Finally, a rank can be found **north of O'Connell Street** on Eden Quay just to the right of the O'Connell Monument, in the median of O'Connell St. just south of the Parnell Monument, and on Sackville Pl., (walk ¼ of the way up O'Connell St. and turn right).

ESSENTIALS

You don't have to be a rocket scientist to plan a good trip. (It might help, but it's not required.) You do, however, need to be well prepared, and that's what we can do for you. Essentials is the chapter that gives you all the nitty-gritty you need to know for your trip: the hard information gleaned from 50 years of collective wisdom (and that phone call to Britain the other day that put us on hold for an hour). Planning your trip? Check. Staying safe and healthy? Check. The dirt on transportation? Check. We've also thrown in communications info and meteorological charts, just for good measure. Plus, for overall trip-planning advice from what to pack (as much money and as little underwear as possible) to how to take a good passport photo (it's physically impossible; consider airbrushing), you can also check out the Essentials section of www.letsgo.com.

We're not going to lie—this chapter is tough for us to write, and you might not find it as fun of a read as 101 or Discover. But please, for the love of all that is good, read it! It's super helpful, and, most importantly, it means we didn't compile all this technical info and put it in one place for you (yes YOU) for nothing.

greatest hits

- **GET A VISA.** Put it on your spring-cleaning list, since you'll need to apply six to eight weeks in advance (p. 386).
- **JUST THE TIP.** Service is sometimes included on restaurant bills. Double check your receipt to make sure you tip your waiter (p. 388).
- **USE A WEB-BASED EMAIL ACCOUNT.** Using an online service like Gmail will save you lots of time in internet cafes (p. 395).
- **NEVER PASS ON A BUS PASS.** Did someone say unlimited rides for $20 a month (p. 392)?
- **FERRY TALES DO COME TRUE.** Check out ferry prices. Some destinations in Britain and Ireland are inaccessible except by boat (p. 394).
- **A PINT AIN'T SO PINT SIZED.** The Imperial Pint is 20 oz., as opposed to the traditional 16 oz. American pint. Chug accordingly.

planning your trip

entrance requirements

- **PASSPORT:** Required for citizens of Australia, Canada, New Zealand and the US.
- **VISA:** Required for citizens of Australia, Canada, New Zealand, and the US only for stays of longer than 90 days.
- **WORK PERMIT:** Required for all foreigners planning to work in the UK.

DOCUMENTS AND FORMALITIES

You've got your visa, your invitation, and your work permit, just like *Let's Go* told you to, and then you realize you've forgotten the most important thing: your passport. Well, we're not going to let that happen. **Don't forget your passport!**

Visas

EU citizens do not need a visa to globetrot through Britain and Ireland. Citizens of Australia, Canada, New Zealand, and the US do not need a visa for stays of up to 90 days, but this three-month period begins upon entry into any of the countries that belong to the EU's **freedom of movement** zone. Those staying longer than 90 days may purchase a visa at British consulates. A visa costs £65 and allows the holder to spend six months in the UK.

Double-check entrance requirements at the nearest embassy or consulate of Britain for up-to-date information before departure. US citizens can also consult http://travel.state.gov.

A long-term multiple-entry visa usually costs £205 and allows visitors to spend a year or more in Britain. If you plan to work or study in Britain, these policy changes may affect your plans. Under the new visa policy, all visa applicants are divided into five tiers, with priority given to skilled workers. Introduced in February of 2008, the new visa system will be implemented on a staggered basis. Consult the UK Visa Bureau website (*www.visabureau.com/uk*) to determine your visa eligibility.

Entering Britain to study requires a special visa. For more information, see the **Beyond Tourism** chapter (p. 411).

Work Permits

Entry to the UK as a traveler does not include the right to work, which is authorized only with a work permit. For more information, see **Beyond Tourism.**

TIME DIFFERENCES

Great Britain and Ireland are on Greenwich Mean Time (GMT) and observes Daylight Saving Time. This means that it is 5hr. ahead of New York City, 8hr. ahead of Los Angeles, 10hr. behind Sydney, and 11hr. behind New Zealand (note that Australia observes Daylight Savings Time from October to March, the opposite of the Northern Hemispheres—therefore, it is 9hr. ahead of Britain from March to October and 11hr. ahead from October to March, for an average of 10hr.).

embassies and consulates

For addresses of British embassies in countries not listed here, consult the Foreign and Commonwealth Office (☎020 7008 1500; wwww.fco.gov.uk). Some cities have a British consulate that handle most of the same functions as an embassy.

UK CONSULAR SERVICES ABROAD

- **AUSTRALIA:** *Commonwealth Ave., Yarralumla, ACT 2600 (☎61 026 270 6666 http://ukinaustralia.fco.gov.uk). Consular section (UK passports and visas), Piccadilly House, 39 Brindabella Circuit, Brindabella Business Park, Canberra Airport, Canberra ACT 2609 (☎61 1902 941 555). Consulates-general in Brisband, Melbourne, Perth, and Sydney; Consulate in Adelaide.*
- **CANADA:** *80 Elgrin St., Ottowa, ON K19P 5K7 (☎613 237 1530 www.britainincanada.org). Consulate-General, 777 Bay St., Ste. 2800, Toronto, ON M5G 2G2 (☎416-593-1290). Other consulates-general in Montreal and Vancouver; Honorary Consuls in Quebec City, St. John's, and Winnipeg.*
- **IRELAND:** *29 Merrion Rd., Ballsbridge, Dublin 4 (☎353 01 205 3700 www.britishembassy.ie).*
- **NEW ZEALAND:** *44 Hill St., Thorndon, Wellington 6011 (☎64 04 924 2888 www.britain.org.nz); mail to P.O. Box 1812, Wellington 6140. Consulate-General: 151 Queen St., Auckland (☎64 09 303 2973); mail to Private Bag 92014, Auckland.*
- **US:** *3100 MAssachusetts Ave. NW , Washington, D.C. 20008 (☎202 588 7800 www.britainusa.com). Consulate-general: 845 Third Ave., New York, NY 10022 (☎212 745 0200). Other offices in Atlanta, Boston, Chicago, Houston, Los Angeles, and San Francisco. Consulates in Dallas, Denver, Miami and Seattle.*

IRISH CONSULAR SERVICES ABROAD

- **AUSTRALIA:** *20 Arkana St., Yarralumla, Canberra ACT 2600 (☎61 02 6273 3022).*
- **CANADA:** *130 Albert St., Ste. 1105, Ottowa, K1P 5G4, Ontario (☎613 233 6281).*
- **NEW ZEALAND:** *Honorary Consul General, Citibank Building, 23 Customs Street East, Level 7, Auckland (☎64 09 977 2252).*
- **UK:** *17 Grosvenor Pl., London SW1X 7HR (☎020 7235 2171). Consulates: 16 Randolph Crescent, Edinburgh EH3 7TT (☎0131 226 7711); Brunel House, 2 Fitzalan Rd., Cardiff CF24 OEB (☎029 2066 2000).*
- **US:** *2234 Massachusetts Ave. NW, Washington D.C. 2008 (☎202-462-3939 www.ireland-emb.org). Consulate-general: 345 Park Ave., 17th fl., New York, NY 10154-0037 (☎212-319-2555). Other consulates-general in Boston, Chicago, and San Francisco.*

atms and pins

To use a debit or credit card to withdraw money from a cash machine (ATM) in Europe, you must have a four-digit Personal Identification Number (PIN). If your PIN is longer than four digits, ask your bank whether you can just use the first four or whether you'll need a new one. Credit cards don't usually come with PINs, so if you intend to hit up ATMs in Europe with a credit card to get cash advances, call your credit card company before leaving to request one.

Travelers with alphabetic rather than numeric PINs may also be thrown off by the absence of letters on European cash machines. Here are the corresponding numbers to use: 1 = QZ; 2 = ABC; 3 = DEF; 4 = GHI; 5 = JKL; 6 = MNO; 7 = PRS; 8 = TUV; 9 = WXY. Note that if you mistakenly punch the wrong code into the machine multiple (often three) times, it can swallow (gulp!) your card for good.

GETTING MONEY FROM HOME

Stuff happens. When stuff happens, you might need some money. When you need some money, the easiest and cheapest solution is to have someone back home make a deposit to your bank account. Otherwise, consider one of the following options.

Wiring Money

Arranging a **bank money transfer** means asking a bank back home to wire money to a bank in Britain. This is the cheapest way to transfer cash, but it's also the slowest and most agonizing, usually taking several days or more. Note that some banks may only release your funds in local currency, potentially sticking you with a poor exchange rate; inquire about this in advance. Money transfer services like **Western Union** are faster and more convenient than bank transfers—but also much pricier. Western Union has many locations worldwide. To find one, visit www.westernunion.com or call the appropriate number: in Australia ☎1800 173 833, in Canada and the US ☎800-325-6000, in the UK ☎0800 735 1815, or in Ireland, ☎353 66 979 1843. To wire money using a credit card in Canada and the US, call ☎800-CALL-CASH; in the UK, ☎0800 731 1815. Money transfer services are also available to **American Express** cardholders and at selected **Thomas Cook** offices.

US State Department (US Citizens only)

In serious emergencies only, the US State Department will forward money within hours to the nearest consular office, which will then disburse it according to instructions for a US$30 fee. If you wish to use this service, you must contact the Overseas Citizens Services division of the US State Department *(☎1 202 501 4444, from US ☎888 407 4747).*

TIPPING AND BARGAINING

Tips in restaurants are often included in the bill (sometimes as a "service charge"). If gratuity is not included, you should tip your server about 12.5%. Taxi drivers should receive a 10% tip, and bellhops and chambermaids usually expect£1-3. To the great relief of many budget travelers, tipping is not expected at pubs and bars in Britain and Ireland. Bargaining is generally unheard of in UK shops.

TAXES

The UK has a 17.5% value added tax (VAT), a sales tax applied to everything but food, books, medicine, and children's clothing. The tax is included in the amount indicated on the price tag. The prices stated in *Let's Go* include VAT. Upon exiting Britain, non-EU citizens can reclaim VAT (minus an administrative fee) through the Retail Export Scheme, although the complex procedure is probably only worthwhile for large purchases. You can obtain refunds only for goods you take out of the country (not for accommodations or meals). Participating shops display a "Tax-Free Shopping" sign and may have a minimum purchase of £50-100 before they offer refunds. To claim a refund, fill out the form you are given in the shop, and present it with the goods and receipts at customs upon departure (look for the Tax-Free Refund desk at the airport). At peak times, this process can take up to an hour. You must leave the country within three months of your purchase in order to claim a refund, and you must apply before leaving the UK.

safety and health

GENERAL ADVICE

In any type of crisis, the most important thing to do is **stay calm.** Your country's embassy abroad (p. 387) is usually your best resource in an emergency; registering with that embassy upon arrival in the country is a good idea. The government offices listed in the **Travel Advisories** feature at the end of this section can provide information on the services they offer their citizens in case of emergencies abroad.

Local Laws And Police

Police presence in cities is prevalent, and most small towns have police stations. There are two types of police officers in Britain: regular officers with full police powers and police community support officers (PCSO) who have limited police power and focus on community maintenance and safety. The national emergency numbers are ☎999 and ☎112. Numbers for local police stations are listed under each individual city or town.

Drugs And Alcohol

Remember that you are subject to the laws of the country in which you travel. If you carry insulin, syringes, or prescription drugs while you travel, it is vital to have a copy of the prescriptions and a note from your doctor. The Brits love to drink while the Irish live to drink, so the presence of alcohol is unavoidable. In trying to keep up with the locals, remember that the Imperial pint is 20 oz., as opposed to the 16oz. US pint. The drinking age in the UK is 18 (14 to enter, 16 for beer and wine with food). Smoking is banned in enclosed public spaces in Britain and Ireland, including pubs and restaurants.

SPECIFIC CONCERNS

Northern Ireland

Border checkpoints in the UK have been removed, and armed soldiers and vehicles are less visible in Belfast and Derry. Do not take photographs of soldiers, military installations, or vehicles; the film will be confiscated and you may be detained for questioning. Taking pictures of political murals is not a crime, although many people feel uncomfortable doing so in residential neighborhoods.

Terrorism

The bombings of July 7, 2005 in the London Underground revealed the vulnerability of large European cities to terrorist attacks and resulted in the enforcement of stringent safety measures at airports and major tourist sights throughout British cities.

Allow extra time for airport security and do not pack sharp objects in your carry-on luggage—they will be confiscated. Unattended luggage is always considered suspicious and is also liable to confiscation. Check your home country's foreign affairs office for travel information and advisories, and be sure to follow the local news while in the UK.

Pre-Departure Health

Matching a prescription to a foreign equivalent is not always easy, safe, or possible, so if you take **prescription drugs,** carry up-to-date prescriptions or a statement from your doctor stating the medications' trade names, manufacturers, chemical names, and dosages. Be sure to keep all medication with you in your carry-on luggage.

Immunizations And Precautions

Travelers over two years old should make sure that the following vaccines are up to date: MMR (for measles, mumps, and rubella); DTaP or Td (for diphtheria, tetanus, and pertussis); IPV (for polio); Hib (for *Haemophilus influenzae* B); and HepB (for Hepatitis B). For recommendations on immunizations and prophylaxis, check with a doctor and consult the **Centers for Disease Control and Prevention (CDC)** in the US or the equivalent in your home country. *(☎1 800 CDC INFO/232 4636 www.cdc.gov/travel)*

STAYING HEALTHY

Diseases And Environmental Hazards

Common sense is the simplest prescription for good health while you travel. Drink lots of fluids to prevent dehydration and constipation, and wear sturdy, broken-in shoes and clean socks. The British Isles are in the gulf stream, so temperatures are mild: around 40°F in winter and 65°F in summer. In the Scottish highlands and mountains temperatures reach greater extremes. When in areas of high altitude, be sure to dress in layers that can be peeled off as needed. Allow your body a couple of days to adjust to decreased oxygen levels before exerting yourself. Note that alcohol is more potent and UV rays are stronger at high elevations.

Many diseases are transmitted by insects—mainly mosquitoes, fleas, ticks, and lice. Be aware of insects in wet or forested areas, especially while hiking and camping. Wear long pants and long sleeves, tuck your pants into your socks, and use a mosquito net. Use insect repellents such as DEET and soak or spray your gear with permethrin (licensed in the US only for use on clothing). Mosquitoes—responsible for malaria, dengue fever, and yellow fever—can be particularly abundant in wet, swampy, or wooded areas. Ticks—which can carry Lyme and other diseases—can be particularly dangerous in rural and forested regions of Britain.

getting around

For information on how to get to Britain and save a bundle while doing so, check out the Essentials section of **www.letsgo.com.** (In case you can't tell, we think our website's the bomb.)

BY PLANE

When it comes to airfare, a little effort can save you a lot of cash. If your plans are flexible enough to deal with the restrictions, courier fares are the cheapest. Tickets bought from consolidators and for standby seating are also good deals, but last-minute specials, airfare wars, and charter flights often beat these fares. The key is to hunt around, to be flexible, and to ask persistently about discounts. Students, seniors, and those under 26 should never pay full price for a ticket. Beware of the extremely exorbitant fees often tacked on to your ticket price. They can sometimes be equal to the cost of the ticket.

travel advisories

The following government offices provide travel information and advisories by telephone, by fax, or via the web:

- **AUSTRALIA: Department of Foreign Affairs and Trade.** *(☎61 2 6261 1111 www.dfat.gov.au)*
- **CANADA: Department of Foreign Affairs and International Trade (DFAIT).** Call or visit the website for the free booklet *Bon Voyage...But. (☎1 800 267 8376 www.dfait-maeci.gc.ca)*
- **NEW ZEALAND: Ministry of Foreign Affairs.** *(☎64 4 439 8000 www.mfat.govt.nz)*
- **UK: Foreign and Commonwealth Office.** *(☎44 20 7008 1500 www.fco.gov.uk)*
- **US: Department of State.** *(☎888 407 4747 from the US, 1 202 501 4444 elsewhere http://travel.state.gov)*

Commercial Airlines

For small-scale travel on the continent, *Let's Go* suggests **budget airlines** for budget travelers, but more traditional carriers have made efforts to keep up with the revolution. The **Star Alliance Europe Airpass** offers low economy-class fares for travel within Europe to 220 destinations in 45 countries. The pass is available to non-European passengers on Star Alliance carriers, including United and Continental Airlines *(www.staralliance.com)*. **EuropebyAir's** snazzy FlightPass also allows you to hop between hundreds of cities in Europe and North Africa. *(☎1 888 321 4737 www.europebyair.com Ⓢ Most flights US$99.)*

budget airlines

The recent emergence of no-frills airlines has made hopscotching around Europe by air increasingly affordable. Though these flights often feature inconvenient hours or serve less popular regional airports, with ticket prices often dipping into single digits, it's never been faster or easier to jet across the continent. The following resources will be useful not only for criss-crossing Britain but also for those ever-popular weekend trips to nearby international destinations.

- **BMIBABY:** *☎0871 224 0224 for the UK, 44 870 126 6726 elsewhere www.bmibaby.com.*
- **EASYJET:** *☎44 871 244 2366, 10p per min. www.easyjet.com Ⓢ UK£50-150.*
- **RYANAIR:** *☎0818 30 30 30 for Ireland, 0871 246 0000 for the UK www.ryanair.com.*
- **STERLING:** *☎70 10 84 84 for Denmark, 0870 787 8038 for the UK www.sterling.dk.*
- **TRANSAVIA:** *☎020 7365 4997 for the UK www.transavia.com Ⓢ From €49 one-way.*
- **WIZZ AIR:** *☎0904 475 9500 for the UK, 65p per min. www.wizzair.com.*

In addition, a number of European airlines offer discount coupon packets. Most are only available as tack-ons for transatlantic passengers, but some are stand-alone offers. Most must be purchased before departure, so research in advance. For example, **oneworld,** a coalition of 10 major international airlines, offers deals and cheap connections all over the world, including within Europe. *(www.oneworld.com)*

BY TRAIN

Trains in Britain are generally comfortable, convenient, and reasonably swift, crisscrossing the length and breadth of the island. Second-class compartments, which seat from two to six, are great places to meet fellow travelers. Make sure you are on the correct car, as trains sometimes split at crossroads. Towns listed in parentheses on European train schedules require a train switch at the town listed immediately before the parentheses. In cities with more than one train station, the city name is given first, followed by the station name (for example, "Manchester Piccadilly" and "Manchester Victoria" are Manchester's two major stations).

In general, traveling by train costs more than by bus. You can either buy a **railpass,** which allows you unlimited travel within a particular region for a given period of time, or rely on buying individual **point-to-point** tickets as you go. Almost all countries give students or youths (under 26, usually) direct discounts on regular domestic rail tickets, and many also sell a student or youth card that provides 20-50% off all fares for up to a year.

rail resources

- **WWW.RAILEUROPE.COM:** Info on rail travel and railpasses.
- **POINT-TO-POINT FARES AND SCHEDULES:** www.raileurope.com/us/rail/fares_schedules/index.htm allows you to calculate whether buying a railpass would save you money.
- **WWW.RAILSAVER.COM:** Uses your itinerary to calculate the best railpass for your trip.
- **WWW.RAILFANEUROPE.NET:** Links to rail servers throughout Europe.
- **WWW.LETSGO.COM:** Check out the Essentials section for more details.

BY BUS

The British distinuish between buses (short local routes) and coaches (long distances). *Let's Go* uses the term "buses" for both. Regional passes offer unlimited travel within a given area for a certain number of days; these are often called Rovers, Ramblers, or Explorers, and they usually offer cost-effective travel. Plan ahead and book tickets online in order to take advantage of discounts.

Though European trains and railpasses are extremely popular, in some cases buses prove a better option. In Britain, long-distance travel is extensive and cheap. Often cheaper than railpasses, **international bus passes** allow unlimited travel on a hop-on, hop-off basis between major European cities. **Busabout,** for instance, offers three interconnecting bus circuits covering 29 of Europe's best bus hubs. *(☎+44 8450 267 514 www.busabout.com 1 circuit in high season starts at US$579, students US$549.)* **Eurolines,** meanwhile, is the largest operator of Europe-wide coach services. We get misty-eyed just thinking about their unlimited 15- and 30-day passes to 41 major European cities. *(☎08717 818 181 www.eurolines.com High season 15-day pass €345, 30-day pass €455; under 26 €290/375. Mid-season €240/330; under 26 €205/270. Low season €205/310; under 26 €175/240.)* **National Express** *(☎08705 808 080; www.nationalexpress.com)* is the principal

operator of long-distance bus services in Britain, although **Scottish Citylink** (☎08705 505 050 💻www.citylink.co.uk) has extensive coverage in Scotland with discounts available for seniors (over 50), students, and young persons (16-25). The Brit Xplorer passes offer unlimited travel for a set number of days (7 days £79, 14 days £139, 28 days £219; www.nationalexpress.com). For those who plan far ahead, the best option is National Express's Fun Fares, only available online, which offer a limited number of seats on buses from London starting at, amazingly, £1. Tourist Information Centres carry timetables for regional buses and will help befuddled travelers decipher them.

Ulsterbus (☎028 9066 6630 💻www.ulsterbus.co.uk) runs extensive and reliable routes throughout Northern Ireland. Pick up a free regional timetable at any station. The Emerald Card, designed for travel in the Republic of Ireland as well as Northern Ireland, offers unlimited travel on Ulsterbus. The card works for eight days out of 15 (£115, under 16 £58) or 15 out of 30 consecutive days (£200/50).

BY BOAT

Most European ferries are quite comfortable; the cheapest ticket typically still includes a reclining chair or couchette. Fares jump sharply in July and August. Ask for discounts; ISIC and Eurail Pass holders get many reductions and free trips. You'll occasionally have to pay a port tax (under US$10).

Many of Britain's northern and western islands are inaccessible except by ferry. Ticket fares vary but almost always increase for automobiles. Be sure to board at least 15min. prior to departure. A directory of UK ferries can be found at 💻www.seaview.co.uk/ferries.html.

ferries

- **CALEDONIAN MACBRAYNE.** *The Ferry Terminal, Gourock PA19 1QP To call from Australia, dial ☎01475 650 100 💻www.calmac.co.uk).* The MacDaddy of Scottish ferries, with routes in the Hebrides and along the wetst coast of Scotland. Sells various combo packages for convenient cost-effective island-hopping in the Scottish Islands.
- **NORFOLKLINE.** *Norfolk House, Eastern Docks, Dover CT16 1JA (☎0870 870 1020 💻www.norfolkline-ferries.com).* Between Liverpool, Dublin and Belfast.
- **P&O FERRIE.** *Channel House, Channel View Rd., Dover CT17 9TJ (☎08716 645 645 💻www.poferries.com).* Operates ferries between Britain, Ireland and the continent.
- **STENA LINE.** *Stena House (☎08705 707 070 💻www.stenaline.co.uk).* Offers ferries from Stranraer to Belfast.

BY BICYCLE

Much of the British countryside is well-suited for cycling. Consult tourist offices for local touring routes and always bring along the appropriate Ordinance Survey maps. Some youth hostels rent bicycles for low prices, and in Britain train stations rent bikes and often allow you to drop them off elsewhere. Keep safety in mind—even well-traveled routes cover uneven terrain, which might prove difficult to you easy riders. In addition to **panniers** (US$40-150) to hold your luggage, you'll need a good **helmet** (US$10-40), and a sturdy **lock** (from US$30). For more country-specific books on biking through the UK, try **Mountaineers Books.** *(1001 SW Klickitat Way, Ste. 201, Seattle, WA 98134, USA ☎1 206 223 6303 💻www.mountaineersbooks.org)*

keeping in touch

BY EMAIL AND INTERNET

Hello and welcome to the 21st century, where you can check your email in most major European cities, though sometimes you'll have to pay a few bucks or buy a drink for internet access. Although in some places it's possible to forge a remote link with your home server, in most cases this is a much slower (and thus more expensive) option than taking advantage of free **web-based email accounts** (e.g., **www.gmail.com**). **Internet cafes** and the occasional free internet terminal at a public library or university are listed in the **Practicalities** sections of cities that we cover. For lists of additional cybercafes in Britain, check out www.cybercaptive.com.

Wireless hot spots make internet access possible in public and remote places. Unfortunately, they also pose security risks. Hot spots are public, open networks that use unencrypted, unsecured connections. They are susceptible to hacks and "packet sniffing"—the theft of passwords and other private information. To prevent problems, disable "ad hoc" mode, turn off file sharing and network discovery, encrypt your email, turn on your firewall, beware of phony networks, and watch for over-the-shoulder creeps.

BY TELEPHONE

Calling Home From Britain

Prepaid phone cards are a common and relatively inexpensive means of calling abroad. Each one comes with a Personal Identification Number (PIN) and a toll-free access number. You call the access number and then follow the directions for dialing your PIN. To purchase prepaid phone cards, check online for the best rates; www.callingcards.com is a good place to start. Online providers generally send your access number and PIN via email, with no actual "card" involved. You can also call home with prepaid phone cards purchased in Britain.

If you have internet access, your best—i.e., cheapest, most convenient, and most tech-savvy—bet is probably our good friend **Skype.** *(www.skype.com)* You can even videochat if you have one of those new-fangled webcams. Calls to other Skype us-

international calls

To call Britain or Ireland from home or to call home from Britain or Ireland, dial:

- **1. THE INTERNATIONAL DIALING PREFIX.** To call from Australia, dial ☎0011; Canada or the US, ☎011; Ireland, New Zealand, or the UK, ☎00.
- **2. THE COUNTRY CODE OF THE COUNTRY YOU WANT TO CALL.** To call Australia, dial ☎61; Canada or the US, ☎1; Ireland, ☎353; New Zealand, ☎64; the UK, ☎44.
- **3. THE CITY/AREA CODE.** *Let's Go* lists the city/area codes for cities and towns in Britain opposite the city or town name, next to a ☎, as well as in every phone number. If the first digit is a zero (e.g., ☎020 for London), **omit the zero** when calling from abroad (e.g., dial ☎20 from Canada to call London).
- **4. THE LOCAL NUMBER.**
- **5. EXAMPLES:** To call the US embassy in London from New York, dial ☎011 44 20 7499 9000. To call the British embassy in Washington from London, dial ☎00 1 202 588 7800. To call the US embassy in London from London, dial ☎020 7499 9000.

ers are free; calls to landlines and mobiles worldwide start at US$0.021 per minute, depending on where you're calling.

Another option is a **calling card,** linked to a major national telecommunications service in your home country. Calls are billed collect or to your account. Cards generally come with instructions for dialing both domestically and internationally.

Placing a collect call through an international operator can be expensive but may be necessary in case of an emergency. You can frequently call collect without even possessing a company's calling card just by calling its access number and following the instructions.

Cellular Phones

Cell phones are everywhere in the UK, although the Brits call them "mobile phones." Competitive, low prices and the variety of calling plans make them accessible even for short-term, low-budget travelers. Also, Britain has developed a text-messaging culture. For most visitors to the UK, a pay-as-you-go plan is the most attractive option. Pick up an eligible mobile (from £25) and recharge, or top up, with a card purchased at a grocery store, online, or by phone. Incoming calls and incoming text messages are always free. **Vodaphone** (*www.vodaphone.co.uk*) and **T-Mobile** (*www.t-mobile.co.uk*) are among the biggest providers.

The international standard for cell phones is **Global System for Mobile Communication (GSM).** To make and receive calls in Britain,you will need a GSM-compatible phone and a **SIM (Subscriber Identity Module) card,** a country-specific, thumbnail-size chip that gives you a local phone number and plugs you into the local network. Many SIM cards are prepaid, and incoming calls are frequently free. You can buy additional cards or vouchers (usually available at convenience stores) to "top up" your phone. For more information on GSM phones, check out www.telestial.com. Companies like **Cellular Abroad** *(www.cellularabroad.com)* and **OneSimCard** *(www.onesimcard.com)* rent cell phones and SIM cards that work in a variety of destinations around the world.

BY SNAIL MAIL

Sending Mail Home From Britain

Airmail is the best way to send mail home fromBritain or Ireland. **Aerogrammes,** printed sheets that fold into envelopes and travel via airmail, are available at post offices. Write "airmail" or "*par avion*" on the front. Most post offices will charge exorbitant fees or simply refuse to send aerogrammes with enclosures. Surface mail is by far the cheapest and slowest way to send mail. It takes one to two months to cross the Atlantic and one to three to cross the Pacific—good for heavy items you won't need for a while, like souvenirs that you've acquired along the way.

Sending Mail To Britain

In addition to the standard postage system whose rates are listed below, **Federal Express** handles express mail services from most countries to Britain. *(☎1 800 463 3339 www.fedex.com)* Sending a postcard within Britain costs £.24, while sending letters (up to 100g) domestically requires £.27.

There are several ways to arrange pickup of letters sent to you while you are abroad. Mail can be sent via **Poste Restante** (General Delivery) to almost any city or town in Britain with a post office.Address Poste Restanteletters like so:

William SHAKESPEARE
Poste Restante
2/3 Henley St.
Stratford-upon-Avon CV37 6PU
United Kingdom

The mail will go to a special desk in the central post office, unless you specify a post office by street address or postal code. It's best to use the largest post office, since mail may be sent there regardless. It is usually safer and quicker, though more expensive, to send mail express or registered. Bring your passport (or other photo ID) for pickup; if the clerks insist that there is nothing for you, ask them to check under your first name as well. *Let's Go* lists post offices in the **Practicalities** section for each city and most towns.

American Express has travel offices throughout the world that offer a free **Client Letter Service** (mail held up to 30 days and forwarded upon request) for cardholders who contact them in advance. Some offices provide these services to non-cardholders (especially AmEx Travelers Cheque holders), but call ahead to make sure. For a complete list of AmEx locations, call ☎1 800 528 4800 or visit www.americanexpress.com/travel.

climate

We'd love to tell you that everything you've heard about British weather is false... but we're not here to lie to you. Britain is traditionally cool and precipitation is considerably higher than other European destinations. Don't let the weather keep you from traveling to this wonderful country, but be prepared for some damp, chilly days during your stay.

AVG. TEMP. (LOW/ HIGH), PRECIP.	JANUARY			APRIL			JULY			OCTOBER		
	°C	°F	mm	°C	°F	mm	°C	°F	mm	°C	°F	mm
London	2/6	36/43	54	6/13	43/55	37	14/22	57/72	57	8/14	46/57	57
Edinburgh	1/6	34/43	57	4/11	39/52	39	11/18	52/64	83	7/12	45/54	65
Dublin	1/8	34/46	67	4/13	39/55	45	11/20	52/68	70	6/14	43/57	70
Belfast	2/6	36/43	80	4/12	39/54	48	11/18	52/64	94	7/13	45/55	83

To convert from degrees Fahrenheit to degrees Celsius, subtract 32 and multiply by 5/9. To convert from Celsius to Fahrenheit, multiply by 9/5 and add 32.

°CELSIUS	-5	0	5	10	15	20	25	30	35	40
°FAHRENHEIT	23	32	41	50	59	68	77	86	95	104

measurements

Like the rest of the rational world, Britain uses the metric system. The basic unit of length is the meter (m), which is divided into 100 centimeters (cm) or 1000 millimeters (mm). One thousand meters make up one kilometer (km). Fluids are measured in liters (L), each divided into 1000 milliliters (mL). A liter of pure water weighs one kilogram (kg), the unit of mass that is divided into 1000 grams (g). One metric ton is 1000kg. Gallons in the US and those in Britain are not identical: one US gallon equals 0.83 Imperial gallons.

MEASUREMENT CONVERSIONS	
1 inch (in.) = 25.4mm	1 millimeter (mm) = 0.039 in.
1 foot (ft.) = 0.305m	1 meter (m) = 3.28 ft.
1 yard (yd.) = 0.914m	1 meter (m) = 1.094 yd.
1 mile (mi.) = 1.609km	1 kilometer (km) = 0.621 mi.

1 ounce (oz.) = 28.35g	1 gram (g) = 0.035 oz.
1 pound (lb.) = 0.454kg	1 kilogram (kg) = 2.205 lb.
1 fluid ounce (fl. oz.) = 29.57mL	1 milliliter (mL) = 0.034 fl. oz.
1 gallon (gal.) = 3.785L	1 liter (L) = 0.264 gal.

let's go online

Plan your next trip on our spiffy website, www.letsgo.com. It features full book content, the latest travel info on your favorite destinations, and tons of interactive features: make your own itinerary, read blogs from our trusty Researcher-Writers, browse our photo library, watch exclusive videos, check out our newsletter, find travel deals, follow us on Facebook, and buy new guides. Plus, if this Essentials wasn't enough for you, we've got even more online. We're always updating and adding new features, so check back often!

GREAT BRITAIN 101

During your time in Britain, you're probably going to want to walk the walk and talk the talk of the locals—whether you're volunteering at the **Fringe** in Edinburgh, studying for a semester at Oxford or Cambridge, or gallavanting through the posh shops of London. You're just dying to know about the everyday happenings—what sports teams to root for, what to read, what to eat. Well, here's the skinny—though you won't stay that way if you spend too much time around British cuisine.

facts and figures

- **TIME WILLIAM THE CONQUEROR ORDERED ALL HIS CITIZENS TO GO TO BED:** 8:00pm.
- **PERSON HER MAJESTY THE QUEEN MUST GAIN PERMISSION FROM BEFORE ENTERING THE CITY OF LONDON:** The Lord Mayor
- **CUPS OF TEA CONSUMED IN BRITAIN ANNUALLY:** 60.2 billion
- **NUMBER OF JOHN SMITHS IN LONDON:** 30,000
- **NUMBER OF MINUTES BIG BEN WAS SLOWED DOWN WHEN A FLOCK OF BIRDS LANDED ON THE MINUTE HAND IN 1945:** 5

history

WHEN IN ROME

We might think of it as the Sceptered Isle; but, despite the water water everywhere, invasion has happened to the British elite quite a few times. Prehistorically, the islands were occupied by the Celts, builders of Stonehenge and wearers of blue facepaint *(woad)*.

Caesar tested the waters in 55 BC, but the Romans moved in to stay in 43 AD. (This followed Caligula's poorly planned assaults, which mostly involved collecting seashells on the coast of Normandy.) Castle Hill in Cambridge was a key post, allowing the Romans to keep an eye out over the River Cam. Along both sides of the River Thames, they established the city of Londinium (sound familiar?). Sadly for them, the settlement was soon burned by the Iceni tribe and their warrior queen, Bouticca. Roman trade began to flourish at the River Fleet—the largest subterranean river in modern-day London—until the Vikings blew up their spot with a series of assaults.

THE SAXON AND VIKING ERA

The Saxons invaded from what is now Germany, bringing their language (which would eventually become the basis for English as we know it). According to myth, King Arthur and his knights can be credited with holding off the invading Germans for the duration of his reign. The four main groups of invaders formed four kingdoms—Essex, Sussex, Wessex and Middlesex, which still exist today as four of the larger English counties. In reaction to the Vikings raiding and pillaging their way south from their Scottish landing points, the Saxon lords unified their territories (along with a few other large counties) into a single English kingdom. In 886, Anglo-Saxon King Alfred the Great negotiated peace with Guthrum, king of the Vikings, ushering in Anglo-Saxon supremacy.

THE MIDDLE AGES

The Normans were a different kind of invader, shaping England to fit the mold of continental European civilization. The powerful Norman nobility spoke a dialect of French, while the Saxon peasantry stuck to their Germanic-based Old English. The Norman-Saxon tension led straight to the creation of one of the earliest Rebels With A Cause—Robin Hood. Still, the Saxons hung on, and sometime during the course of the Hundred Years' War the distinction between Norman and Saxon was trumped by the tension between French and English. Norman adventurers also set up shop in Ireland, but embraced the good life there so fast they were said to be "more Irish than the Irish."

In 1290, **King Edward I** expelled all Jews from England. The population of London continued to dwindle until the horrors of the **Bubonic Plague**.

No sooner had the Hundred Years' War been taken care of than the War of the Roses was underway. (In case you're keeping score, rose-wise, York is white and Lancaster is red.) Lancaster started off in power, then about halfway through, York took over and hung on until their most famous member, Richard III was killed at Bosworth. The Lancastrian favorite at the time, Henry, quickly declared himself king (the VII), married Richard's niece, invented a symbol that combined both the red and the white roses, naming it after his own Tudor family.

As awesome as ending a giant war is, Henry VII is probably less famous than his son. Who, after all, has had more game than Henry VIII? He married a nice Spanish princess, Catherine of Aragon (his elder brother's widow, incidentally). But then he met a young lady named Anne Boleyn. He became infatuated with her and decided to ditch wife #1 (poor Cat), but the pope wouldn't annul the existing marriage. Anne refused to become his mistress, so Henry decided to ditch the Catholic Church and start his own church. And thus the Church of England was born. Henry went on to have four more wives and (finally) a son and heir with the third wife, Jane Seymour, who died just a few days after giving birth.

ELIZABETHAN ERA

After brief reigns by her brother and sister, Henry's daughter Elizabeth took the throne and ushered in more than forty years of military domination beating Phillip II all the way back to Spain, proliferation of the arts, not to mention the proliferation of William Shakespeare, and exploration of the New World (Virginia? Named for virginal Queen Bess). Since she never married or had children, the crown went to her Scottish cousin James upon her death.

Meanwhile, English colonies were popping up all over the world. There were permanent English settlements in Massachusetts, Virginia, and several Caribbean islands by the mid-seventeenth century. The growth of mercantilism spawned the **British East India Company,** expanding British trade with Asia.

THE COMMONWEALTH AND ITS AFTERMATH

While the Stuart Kings were second to none at expanding the empire, their teamwork with Parliament could use work, and James's son Charles sparked a war that lead to his decapitation. Consequently, Oliver Cromwell was installed as "Lord Protector" to run the country. Cromwell was dead set against fun of all types, and went so far as to outlaw Christmas. After Cromwell's death, the Commonwealth collapsed under the lackluster leadership of Cromwell's son Richard, but the subsequent **Restoration** of **Charles II,** son of the beheaded king, did not end the turmoil. Debate raged in Parliament over the succession of Charles's Catholic brother **James II.** Amid the politicking, the two parties that would dominate English politics for the next two centuries emerged: the **Whigs** opposed the kings and supported reform; the **Tories** supported hereditary succession.

CONVERSION AND ENLIGHTENMENT

James II took the throne in 1685 but was deposed three years later by his son-in-law **William of Orange.** In the **"Glorious Revolution"** of 1688, the Dutch Protestant William and his wife Mary forced James to France and implemented a **Bill of Rights,** ensuring the Protestantism of future monarchs. Supporters of James II (called **Jacobites**) remained a serious threat until 1745, when James II's grandson Charles, commonly known as **Bonnie Prince Charlie,** failed in his attempt to recapture the throne. In 1707, England and Scotland were formally united under the same crown.

By the end of the **Seven Years' War** (1756-63), Britain controlled Canada, 13 unruly colonies to the west, and much of the Caribbean. Parliament prospered thanks to the ineffectual leadership of the Hanoverian kings, **George I, II,** and **III,** and the position of prime minister eclipsed the monarchy at the seat of power. Britain's uppity transatlantic colony declared, fought for, and won its independence between 1776 and 1783, but the crown's overseas empire continued to grow elsewhere. Meanwhile, **Sir Isaac Newton** theorized the laws of gravity and invented calculus on the side, and Enlightenment figures **Thomas Hobbes, John Locke,** and **Jeremy Bentham** made significant contributions to political and philosophical thought. Religious fervor occasionally returned, with Bible-thumping **Methodists** preaching to outdoor crowds in the middle of the century.

THE VICTORIAN ERA

The Victorian era, from 1837-1901, was the height of the British Empire. After William IV died, his niece **Victoria** became the crown monarch in 1837, ruling for almost seventy years. With colonies including Canada, India, Australia, and New Zealand, as well as an empire in Africa founded by British adventurers like Cecil Rhodes, the sun literally never set on the Empire. (Bonus: It was always cocktail hour somewhere.) The **Great London Exhibition** of 1851, held at Paxton's 1800-foot Crystal Palace in Hyde Park introduced daguerreotypes, the world's biggest diamond, and other anomalies of the 19th century, showing the rest of the world who was still boss. Great victories were accompanied by troubles like the Great Famine in Ireland and the industrial pains of laboring pains.

TURN OF THE 20TH CENTURY

When Queen Victoria died in 1909, her son Edward oversaw an era of ostentatious wealth at the heigh of British imperial power. This renewed optimism and luxury, commemorated by such writers as P.G. Wodehouse and Hector Hugh Munro, petered out in merely five years, as the Edwardian Era was rudely ended by World War I.

THE WORLD WARS

Thirteen years after her death, Victoria's grandchildren went to war against each other—Germany (led by Wilhelm II) declared war against Britain (George V) and Russia (Nicholas II, the husband of Vic's granddaughter Alexandra). The Great War lasted four years and nearly a million British soldiers died. Following the Great War, the UK was plunged into a depression, with thousands out of work and starving. Labor unions fomented strikes, while Irish militants declared their independence. Twenty years later, after a nervous interwar period, fighting broke out with Germany again.

The Second World War brought the fighting even closer to home for the British. Hitler didn't hesitate to send his bombers over London to force the surrender of the last free power of Europe. Thousands died in the air raids known as the "Blitz," and thousands more died on the battlefield. By 1945, nearly half a million Brits had lost their lines in the war. The two World Wars spelled the last for the British Empire; the Commonwealth nations of Canada, Australia, and New Zealand took independence, and India and British Africa followed.

lay of the land

The British Isles consist of two large and many small islands, located off the Northwestern coast of continental Europe. They are separated from the European mainland by the North Sea and the English Channel, and from one another by the Irish Sea. The larger island—the eastern one—contains the countries of England (south and east), Scotland (north) and Wales (west). The smaller of the two large islands is Ireland. Several small islands, such as Shetland, Jersey, the Hebrides, and the Isle of Mann are scattered throughout the surrounding area. Terrain is generally low and rolling in England and mountainous in Scotland and Wales. Much of Great Britain consists of the rolling moors that are often exploited in BBC serials. To the north, the moors are dwarfed by the Pennine mountain chain.

British flora and fauna aren'ts exotic, but they are memorable. Whether it's a partridge or (hush-hush) fox hunt, a chance meeting with Mr. Toad or Peter Rabbit, the characters of Britain are as animal as human. Don't go looking for wolves or bears, as both are extinct in Britain—Paddington Bear, though naturalized, is a Peruvian immigrant.

people and customs

MOTHER TONGUES

"Native" Brits come in four basic flavors–English, Irish, Scottish, and Welsh, and the corresponding languages are all still spoken, although English is the dominant tongue in all four countries. Wales has preserved their native tongue the best, with Welsh translations on every sign and official document and a reasonable percentage of fluent speakers. Irish Gaelic is being aggressively preserved by the Irish government, with classes taught in primary schools. Scottish Gaelic is not as widely taught, and lingers mainly in the outer islands.

JUST DUCKING AROUND

When it comes to slang, you might think the British just make it up on the spot. Poultry inspires affectionate names for girls, which include "bird" and "duck." Derogatory language is particularly entertaining. Let's be honest: if you're called a "big girl's blouse" or "namby pamby" (translation for both: wimp) will you be able to keep a straight face?

food and drink

LET'S GO PUBBIN'

Bars constitute a huge part of culture all over Great Britain, especially tourist-filled London. Pub-goers won't have to tip, but that's only because there's no table service, so sidle up to the bartender for some shots. Ordering at the bar usually proves an exciting way to meet a fellow Carlsberg connoisseur. England predominantly brews ales, a variety of which can be found in any pub with a feisty crowd looking to down some premium bitter pale ale.

KNOW YOUR MEATS

Fish and chips (to be eaten with malt vinegar rather than ketchup) continue as the go-to "experience" of eating in England. Order "bangers and mash" if you're craving some sausage slathered in onion gravy and mashed potatoes. For the pork lovers, a pork pie cooked from lard pastry with chopped pork bits topped off with pork jelly should satisfy your porker. The more carniverous traveler may also enjoy shepherd's pie, a lamb casserole dish covered with a layer of mashed potatoes.

ARE THEY PUDDING US ON?

Bread and butter, sticky toffee, spotted dick suet—just a few of the pudding varieties on the menu in Brtain. The Brits hold pudding in a special place (and it's not their hearts). Mind you, English pudding is not swimply sweet and jiggly. In Britain, the term refers to any rich, dairy-based dessert. Other non-sweet savory dishes also take the name, like Yorkshire pudding, black pudding, and blood pudding.

TEA FOR TWO

Avoid stuffing yourself too much during lunch time when in London in order to make room for afternoon tea, the light English meal eaten a few hours before dinner. Originating in the 17th century when Catherine of Braganza brought the custom over from Portugal, it is now make it an essential part of the day. Loose tea served with milk and sugar accompanies cucumber and cress sandwiches, scones, and other jam pastries. Some Brits prefer High Tea to replace afternoon tea and dinner. This informal meal usually consists of cold meats, sandwiches, and small desserts; don't think it's an elaborate, high-class tea party. It originated when the family was too lazy to cook anything substantial. Oops.

GASTRONOMIC MULTICULTURALISM

London's Chinatown, located just beyond Leicester Square, houses various supermarkets, as well as cheap restaurants for a meal with a little bit of (Kung) Pao. Indian food is readily accessible on Brick Lane in East London. Lined with cafés and shops, the area's potent smell of spices and curry is impossible to avoid. Middle Eastern fare is represented by the many eateries.

sports and recreation

FOOTBALL

Football is by far the most popular sport in Britain, and by "football" we mean soccer—you know, that game you actually play with your feet. Britain's most famous (and sexiest) player is, of course, David Beckham, but close runners-up are Wayne Rooney, Ashley Cole, and John Terry. Play is divided into FIFA/World Cup and Premiere League categories, with many Premiere Leaguers playing for their countries in the Cup. Well-known British Premiere League clubs include Arsenal, Celtic, Chelsea, Liverpool, Manchester United, and West Ham. Club preference is usually regional, although there will occasionally be the odd Arsenal fan in Chelsea neighborhoods. Devotion to clubs is often passionate and occasionally violent; the term "soccer hooligan" is a reference to the post-game behavior of some rowdy fans.

RUGBY

Rugby was allegedly created in 1823 by William Webb Ellis, a then-student at the Rugby School. Although the sport has now spread to France, Russia, and beyond, it remains most popular in the United Kingdom. The Rugby Football League oversees all professional competitions in England, dealing with all major competitions in the country, such as the Anglo-Welsh EDF Energy Cup and the English Guinness Premiership. The London Wasps regularly compete in these along with other major European championships, including the Heineken Cup, which they won in the 2006-07 season. We'll drink to that.

CRICKET

Thousands of English play this summer time sport, though professional teams usually play in the Oval in Kennington in south London and Lord's in the St. John's Wood area. Each team consists of eleven players with around six specializing batsmen and the others as bowlers, as well as a wicket-keeper. The bowler runs up to the pitch to toss the ball; the batsman can only score after hitting the ball and running to the other side of the oval cricket pitch, getting past the crease. Like baseball, the runner can be taken out via fielders; unlike baseball, you have to wear clownish hockey padding. True MVPs of the game, called all-rounders, pop up in a game every now and then to show off their mastery at the game, making all the other mere batters hate them. The London Cricket Club, formed in 1722 by members of what was known as a "Gentlemen's Club," still hosts games at the Artillery Club against international competitors. It's unclear whether the pompousness of the "Noblemen"—their other moniker of said social organization—has ceased.

TENNIS

Held in the London suburb of the same name, Wimbledon remains the oldest tennis tournament in the world, and attracts hoards of Andre Agassi groupies annually. The championship begins in late June and runs into July with five events held in competition. Besides a strict dress code of all white for tournament players, more bizarre customs during Wimbledon include eating strawberries and cream and drinking Pimms spritzers, a type of gin-based summer cocktail.

HURLING

Hurling, an almost solely Irish game, can best be described as an extremely violent cross between American football, lacrosse, golf, and field hockey. A stick (the hurley) is used to propel the ball toward a goal. The ball may be picked up, however, and carried in the hand for several steps, after which point it can be bounced off the ground or the hurley and then carried again. Tackling is encouraged.

HORSEMANSHIP

With over 60 racecourses in Great Britain alone, the equestrian-obsessed Brits never seemed to have gotten over their pony phase. The National Hunt, in which horses jump over fences and hurdles, along with flat racing mark the two major forms of racing in the country. The Ascot Racecourse in the Berkshire suburb of London remains one of the most popular venues for gamblers. Along with racing, horse showing recently picked up in equestrian recreational activities with the London International Horse Show at the Olympia Grand and National Halls. Pony fanatics enter their steeds in agility tests and dressage competitions for the hopes of glory at this annual competition.

TABLOIDS

London remains notorious for its psychotic paparazzi. *The Sun*, one of the most read gossip publications, regularly reports (read: stalks) on the activities of international celebrities in London. Their friendliness toward the famous has gotten them into legal snafus more than once—Ewan McGregor took them to court and won nearly £48000 in damages when they published vacation photos of him and his family. The *Daily Mirror*, another publication specializing in scandals, had to shy away from the public eye itself when the rag mag published doctored photos of British soldiers harassing Iraqi soldiers. Causing then-editor Piers Morgan—who was also ironically a competitor on Donald Trump's "The Apprentice"—to step down from his position, the hoax dramatically tarnished what little reputation remained of the paper.

Of course, if you're looking for some serious reading, you've got plenty to chose from—though we can't promise you"ll steer clear of celebrity gossip. London's major newspapers are the *Times*, the *Guardian*, and the *Telegraph*, while the *Monitor*, *Edinbugh Evening News*, and the *Scotsman* are among the leading papers in Scotland.

FILM AND TELEVISION

Lights in London

Besides serving as the setting for multiple international blockbusters like *Love Actually* and *Notting Hill*, London's various neighborhoods almost act as their own characters in various movies throughout film history. The image of "Swinging London" began the huge cinematic boom in the 1960s, as foreign filmmakers began to capitalize on its appeal, churning out quirky classics like *Alfie* **(Michael Caine)** and *Bedazzled* **(Raquel Welch)**. With its rich history of royal melodrama and Shakespearean men in tights, London offers itself as a historical place for period projects, its old monuments acting as the real deal in BBC miniseries that usually end up going straight to DVD. Perhaps competing for Paris for the sappiest city prize, the city also promulgates its romantic charm in films, featured as a posh place to fall in love, usually with the help of a lofty, fetishized accent. Most recently, comedies have found success after wrapping up shooting in London, such as *Bend It Like Beckham* **(Keira Knightley)** and *About A Boy* **(Hugh Grant).**

British film has recently become synonymous with subtle, well-acted period pieces (and they are incredibly good at period pieces), but film made in Britain by Brits can be as silly as Monty Python, as action-packed as James Bond, or as classic as the Royal Shakespeare Company's filmed theatrical productions.

The Other Tube

Television is an interesting blend of original, uniquely British shows (full of inside jokes about the NHS and council housing) and imports from America. The typical British televison season consists of either six or 13 episodes, much shorter than the full American television season of 21 or 22 episodes. While a number of originally British shows have been brought to America and remade, translation between the two cultures is hit or miss, with the misses (*Life on Mars*, *Coupling*, *Red Dwarf*) vastly outnumbering the hits (*The Office*, *Pop Idol/American Idol*, *Antiques Roadshow*). The evening soap-opera has remained popular in Britain, with *Coronation Street*, *Eastenders*, *Neighbours* and *Hollyoaks* holding on to respectable viewerships even after decades on the air.

fine arts

ART AND ARCHITECTURE

London's Gothicism

Westminster Abbey in London still stands as one of the most ornate—and borderline garish—examples of medieval Gothic architecture in Britain, with exquisitely refined stained glass and structural columns running vertically. The **Tower of London**, built in the late 11th century, also exemplifies the Medieval English style of concentric interiors, serving as a castle, fortress, and prison during the last millennium.

Elizabethan Vernacular

Beginning in 1599, the construction of the **Globe Theater,** home of Shakespeare and his acting troupe, the Lord Chamberlain's Men, marked the start of early Renaissance style architecture. You'll know the building by its octagonal shape and a timber frame, Tudor wings, symmetrical towers, and a gratuitous number of mullioned windows.

The Georgian Era

During the 18th century, London expanded to include several villages nearby, taking in much Georgian architecture along with it. Rectangular sash windows decorate brick houses, setting Georgian houses apart from Victorian ones that donned arched or pointed windows. Parapets also make Georgian houses within inner London easy to spot.

History Painting

As the most definable movement of Great Britain, representations of momentous historical events trumps all other genres in English art history. Prominent artists of the 1700s include **Sir James Thornhill** and **William Hogarth**. Thornhill, influenced by Italian baroque artists, served as court painter for George I and later rose to become a member of parliament. Revered for his astute inclusion of English habits and temperaments of the time, Hogarth constructed his image as a legitimate portrait artist, a story painter, and a political cartoonist who poked fun at the arranged marriages of the British upper class in a series called *Marriage à-la-mode*. Depicting suicides and murders committed by unhappy wives, Hogarth shows how things, even in posh British society, can get too real.

The Gothic Revival

Beginning in the 1740s, Victorian Gothic aesthetics grew in popularity as the English sought to revive old medieval styles, and **A.W.N. Pugin,** who headed the construction of the House of Parliament, that Gothic style acted as a symbol of a purer society. Also known as **Westminster Palace,** this city landmark gives the architectural aficionado a titillating experience, including **Big Ben** and **Victoria Tower**.

University of Cambridge

The university's long history has given way to a mixture of various architectural styles, mixing and often clashing both ancient and modern characteristics. **King's College** steals the thunder from most other buildings on campus as a model of Gothic architecture from the 15th century. Inside, vaults, stained glass, and woodcarvings spanning several hundred years combine to create a unique and historical atmosphere. The Bridge of Sighs, designed by **Henry Hutchison** in 1831, occupies a romantic span across the **River Cam** in St. John's College. The imposing University Library, designed by Sir Giles Gilbert Scott in the 1930s who also built the Tate Modern, presides over the grounds like an overbearing foreman; it's most notable for Scott's signature industrial style.

Get Cultured

Art and history zealots usually find it difficult to break away from the museum scene of London, even for happy hour at a pub in Kensington. With free admissions into some of the world's most well curated galleries, London provides a lot of culture for not even a tuppence. Located in Bloomsbury on the northeastern edge of the city, the **British Museum** houses an astonishing collection of anthropological and cultural artifacts. Established through the will of physician Sir Hans Sloane, the museum's original "collection of curiosities" has expanded into far-reaching exhibits of Greek, Roman, and Egyptian objects. The **Tate Modern,** a part of the Tate museum group in Britain, owns some of the most rare Rothko and Matisse works on the planet, which are perhaps trumped by the building itself. Designed by Herzog and de Meuron—the same firm who led the construction of the Bird's Nest for the Beijing Olympics—the Tate was formerly a power station. The industrial capacity of the building's former life proved appropriate for its current use, as the Turbine Hall, once a storage area for electricity generators, now houses new sprawling exhibitions by contemporary artists. Most classical art historians prefer to trek over to Trafalgar Square to the **National Gallery.** With paintings dating back as early as the 13th century, the museum has faced severe opposition to its overzealous restoration techniques; prestigious art historians such as Ernst Gombrich have implored the museum to keep it natural.

literature

Let's face it: British writers left America—their much younger, Anglophone cousin—with some huge literary shoes to fill. *Beowulf* and the *Canterbury Tales* laid the foundation for a literary tradition that has shaken the world—just ask Shakespeare. Britain's department of the Republic of Letters has always been well-staffed: from Milton, Austen, and Dickens to Joyce, Eliot, and Waugh, it'll be all you can do to not feel guilty about finishing your reading in those British classes.

holidays and festivals

BOXING DAY

December 26th is now just a practical post-Christmas day off to be spent lazing in pyjamas or traveling home from holiday trips. Originally it was celebrated by the servant classes that were required to work on Christmas Day; the "boxing" part of the name refers to the practice of rich families boxing up their unwanted clothes or gifts and sending them home with the servants. The origin of regifting!

THE QUEEN'S BIRTHDAY

Her Majesty's day of birth is celebrated on varying Saturdays in June. The current Queen's actual date of birth is April 21st, but the holiday is celebrated in the summertime in the hopes that the weather will cooperate with the agenda of parades, picnics, and announcement of the Birthday Honours or, "who's getting knighted."

BANK HOLIDAYS

These are public holidays declared each year by the Queen. Bank Holidays occur each year in May and August, as well as several other statutory days, depending on region. St Patrick's Day, for example, is a Bank Holiday in Northern Ireland, but not in England, Scotland, or Wales.

GUY FAKWES' DAY

"Remember, remember the fifth of November, the gunpowder, treason and plot." This day commemorates Guy Fawkes' failed attempts to blow up the Houses of Parliament. Lots of bonfires, lots of fireworks, lots of burning in effigy.

CAMBRIDGE FOLK FESTIVAL

Held in Cherry Hinton Hall in one of Cambridge's suburban villages, the annual music gathering brings together a widespread variety of folk musicians. Broadcast live on BBC Radio, the festival's two main stages serve as host to burgeoning figures in the British music industry. With previous performers including Paul Simon and Joan Baez, the venue acts as somewhat of a career launcher. Folk lovers usually grab umbrellas and lounge chairs to shelter themselves from weather and relax during the long three-day weekend in late July. Since gaining popularity from its inception in 1964, tickets have sold out immediately in most recent years.

LORD MAYOR'S SHOW

When King John granted a charter for the citizens of London to elect their own Lord Mayor in 1215, he may not have imagined the pageantry that would follow Londoners into the modern era, where flamboyant floats and garish costumes decorate the streets each year on the second Saturday in November. Historically, the proceedings took place via horseback or barges on the River Thames—the parade term "floats" was actually derived from the Lord Mayor's traditional romp through the city by boat. In 1710, a drunken flower girl uprooted then-Lord Mayer Sir Gilbert Heathcote from his horse, initiating a change to a state coach procession known for its six-horse coach (only to be outdone by the Queen, who has eight steeds during formal public outings). At 11pm, the parade takes off after swinging by the Mansion House, the Lord Mayor's official residence, to pick the old chap up, stopping by St. Paul's Cathedral to receive the Dean's blessing. The showy ordeal, including the Twelve Great Livery Companies (Merchant Taylors, Haberdashers, Ironmongers and more), usually ends more than three hours later after the procession winds down along the river, followed by an evening spectacle of fireworks.

government and politics

The United Kingdom is a bicameral parliamentary constitutional monarchy. Try saying that ten times fast. Although the Queen (or king) is the nominal executive, that power is exercised only by and on the advice of a cabinet of ministers, all of whom are drawn from the houses of Parliament.

Much like the American system, the Parliament consists of two separate bodies; the House of Commons far outshowing the House of Lords. For each parliamentary session, the Speaker of the House and the Lord Speaker respectively chairs the proceedings.

The Commons consists of a group of democratically-elected representatives from across the country. The Prime Minister is chosen by the Queen (on the recommendation of her advisors) as the person most likely to be able to lead a cohesive majority within the Commons. Occassionally, as was the case at the 2010 election that unseated the Labour Party, a coalition among several parties is required to reach the majority. Elections are held at least every five years, although they can be called more frequently at the Prime Minister's discretion. The House of Lords was traditionally comprised of hereditary peerages handed down over generations, but a series of reforms in the 1990s and early 2000s substantially decreased the trend, and now most of the peers are "lifetime peers," or people who have accomplished something extraordinary in their lives and have thus been rewarded with a peerage. Originally, the House of Lords held almost all the parliamentary power, but a combination of legislation and practice has seriously curtailed their influence.

There are two major parties in the British government: the Conservative Party and the Labour Party, with positions you might expect. The third group is the Liberal Democrat party, while other nationalist parties fill out the palette.

BEYOND TOURISM

If you are reading this, then you are a member of an elite group—and we don't mean the literate. You're a student preparing for a semester abroad. You're a 20-something taking a gap year to save the trees, the whales, or the dates. You're an 80-year-old woman who has devoted her life to egg-laying platypuses and whatever the heck is up with that. In short, you're a traveler, not a tourist; like any good spy, you don't observe your surroundings—you become an active part of them.

Your mission, should you choose to accept it, is to study, volunteer, or work abroad as laid out in the dossier—er, chapter—below. We leave the rest (when to go, whom to bring, and how many changes of underwear to pack) in your hands. This message will **self-destruct** in five seconds. Good luck.

greatest hits

- **BE A SHAKESPEARE NERD.** Participate in a workshop at Shakespeare's Globe Theatre through King's College London and learn all the methods to all the madness (p. 414).
- **SUPPLY AND DEMAND.** Become an economist extraordinaire at London School of Economics (p. 414).
- **TEACH THE TOTS.** With the right qualifications, you may be able to snag a teaching gig in England, Scotland, or Wales (p. 419).
- **READING, WRITING, ROWING.** Study at Cambridge or Oxford, where your classes are one-on-one tutorials—and stay for The Race (p. 414).

what's in a name?

Great Britain technically refers to the largest European island, which includes England, Scotland, and Wales. It is often used, however, as a synonym for the United Kingdom of Great Britain and Northern Ireland, or the UK. Think it couldn't get any more confusing? Britain sans the "Great" refers to just England and Wales; the term dates back to Roman times when modern Scotland was not part of the conquered territory (and the English were still in Germany).

studying

Not surprisingly, English-language countries are among the most popular destinations for American travelers, with the United Kingdom alone attracting tens of thousands of study abroad students each year. If you're looking for a true cultural immersion experience but that high-school Spanish is beyond rusty, don't despair. Great Britain beckons. You get the adorable foreign accents without needing to awkwardly stumble through phrasebooks.

Whether you're lusting after Prince William (sorry, ladies, he already graduated) or looking to experience the famed Oxbridge tutorial system, English universities offer something for everyone. Before you jet off, do your research to figure out what program best fits your needs and your budget. **The British Council** is an excellent resource for choosing the right institution and preparing to study in the UK. *(www.educationuk.org)* Devoted to international student mobility to and from the UK, the Council for International Student Affairs is another important resource for the practical aspects of living abroad. *(9-17 St. Albans Pl., London N1 ONX ☎020 7288 4330 www.ukcisa.org.uk)*

UNIVERSITIES

England is the only country in the world that attracts more international students than the United States, and it's no surprise when you consider that University of Cambridge, University of Oxford, University College London, and Imperial College London all ranked in the top ten world universities in 2009, according to the *Times Higher Education*. (Ok, so the *Times Higher Education* is a British publication, but they have reason to toot their own horn...) England isn't the only bastion of academia, however. The University of Edinburgh, the University of St. Andrew's, and the University of Glasgow, all located in Scotland, boast excellent programs for international students. For those looking to enroll directly in a British university, the **Universities and Colleges Admissions Service (UCAS)** offers listings geared toward international applicants, and can be searched by subject area. *(www.ucas.com)* If you're already a college student and planning to study abroad, visit your study abroad office or check out www.studyabroad.com. Be sure to apply early, as larger institutions fill up fast.

International Programs

AMERICAN INSTITUTE FOR FOREIGN STUDY (AIFS)

River Plaza, 9 West Broad Street Stamford, CT 06902 ☎800-727-2437 www.aifs.com

With programs in 17 different countries and over 50,000 participants each year, AIFS is one of the oldest and largest cultural exchange organizations out there. Offers semester, year-long, and summer programs in London, as well as internship opportunities.

Semester $14,495-15,995; 3- to 12-week summer programs $5,495-10,995.

visa information

If you're planning to stay for more than a short trip, chances are you need a visa. Find out online at www.ukvisas.gov.uk. As of March 31, 2009, foreigners planning to study abroad in the UK are required to apply for a visa under Tier 4: (General) Student and (Child) Student of the new points-based immigration system. Immigration officials will request a letter of acceptance from your UK university and proof of funding for your first year of study, as well as a valid passport, from all people wishing to study in the UK. Student visas cost £199, and application forms can be obtained online at the website above.

INSTITUTE FOR STUDY ABROAD BUTLER UNIVERSITY (IFSA)

1100 W. 42nd Street, Ste. 305, Indianapolis, IN 46208 ☎800-858-0229 www.ifsa-butler.org
IFSA organizes semester and full year programs; students directly enroll at their choice of dozens of universities throughout England, Scotland, and Wales.
i Some programs have required minimum GPAs. $ Semester up to $23,275.

ARCADIA UNIVERSITY

450 S. Easton Rd., Glenside, PA 19038 ☎866-927-2234 www.arcadia.edu/abroad
Arcadia offers dozens of semester and full year programs in England, Scotland, and Wales. Summer programs, internship opportunities, and even graduate summer programs in literature and creative writing.
$ Semester, excluding meals, up to $22,450.

INSTITUTE FOR THE INTERNATIONAL EDUCATION OF STUDENTS

33 N. LaSalle St., 15th fl. Chicago, IL 60602 ☎800-995-1750 www.iesabroad.org
IES offers summer, semester, and year-long programs in London and term-time programs at St. Catherine's College at Oxford. In London, students can either take IES courses or enroll in one of seven London universities, including the Courtauld Institute of Art and the Mountview Academy of Theater Arts.
$ Semester $13,885-$21,320; 7- to 9-week summer program $6,995-7,340.

CULTURAL EXPERIENCES ABROAD (CEA)

2005 W. 14th St., Suite 113, Tempe, AZ 85281 ☎800-266-4441 www.gowithcea.com
CEA offers summer, semester, or academic year programs in London affiliated with Goldsmiths College, University of Westminster, and the Foundation for International Education. Students live in residence halls at their university.
$ Semester $14,495 to $16,595; 3-week summer program $4,295.

CCIS STUDY ABROAD

2000 P Street, NW, Suite 503 Washington, DC 20036 ☎800-453-6956 www.ccisabroad.org
The College Consortium for International Studies (CCIS) is a partnership of colleges and universities that sponsors study abroad programs around the world. In England, students can choose between summer and term-time programs in London and Lancashire.
$ Semester, excluding meals, up to $13,500.

AHA INTERNATIONAL

70 NW Couch St. Ste. 242 Portland, OR 97209 ☎800-654-2051 www.ahastudyabroad.org
Participate in summer, quarter-, and semester-long study abroad programs in London. Students live in homestays or residence halls and take courses in literature, politics, theater, history, and art history at AHA's London Centre.
$ Semester $14,300.

COUNCIL ON INTERNATIONAL EDUCATIONAL EXCHANGE

300 Fore Street, Portland, ME 04101 ☎800-407-8839 www.ciee.org

CIEE has 4 different semester- or year-long programs in London oriented towards a range of interests, from Asian and African studies to media, arts, and design.

Semester $17,100-$18,500.

SCHOOL FOR INTERNATIONAL TRAINING (SIT)

PO Box 676, 1 Kipling Road, Brattleboro, VT 05302 USA ☎888-272-7881 www.sit.edu/studyabroad

Priding itself on its field-based approach, SIT's unique programs in the Republic of Ireland and Northern Ireland are devoted to the study of sectarian and ethnic conflict and the reconstruction of Irish identity. The program is based in Dublin, where students meet with academics, government officials, and social activists, and take a field study seminar to prepare for individual research.

Semester $20,905.

GREAT BRITAIN PROGRAMS

The universities listed below are only a few of the many UK institutions that open their gates to foreign students for summer, single term, or year-long study. Prices listed are an estimate of fees for non-EU citizens. In most cases, room and board are not included. Almost all of these universities offer summer programs as well; check online for more details.

LONDON SCHOOL OF ECONOMICS (LSE)

Houghton Street, London, WC2A 2AE ☎20 7405 7686 www.lse.ac.uk

LSE accepts international students who have completed at least two years of undergraduate study for a year-long general course, running from October to July.

i Minimum GPA requirements vary by department. Tuition £14,426

KING'S COLLEGE LONDON

Strand, London WC2R 2LS ☎020 7836 5454 www.kcl.ac.uk

Main campus on the Strand; Guy's and Waterloo campuses located across Thames. World-renowned War Studies Department. In conjunction with the Globe Education Practitioners and Courses Faculty, the English Department at KCL offers a 2-week course at Shakespeare's Globe Theatre to international students only.

Fall semester £5,700-8,374; spring semester £7,100-10,238; full year £12,800-16,700.

UNIVERSITY OF CAMBRIDGE

The Old Schools, Trinity Lane, Cambridge CB2 1TN ☎12 23 33 3308 www.cam.ac.uk

Unlike your typical American university, Cambridge comprises 29 undergraduate colleges. Your college is where you eat, sleep, and have your "supervision"—Cambridge-speak for one-on-one or small group lessons with a professor. Lectures are optional, so you can sleep in and not even feel guilty about it.

Full year £15,000-19,000.

UNIVERSITY OF OXFORD

University Offices, Wellington Square, Oxford, OX1 2JD ☎18 65 27 0000 www.ox.ac.uk

Like Cambridge, Oxford operates on the tutorial system and has 38 independent, self-governing colleges. (Sorry—Gryffindor isn't one of them, but the Great Hall in Harry Potter was based on Christ Church, one of the Oxford colleges.) Check individual college and departmental websites for more information.

Full year up to £19,700.

UNIVERSITY OF EDINBURGH

Old College, South Bridge Edinburgh EH8 9YL ☎13 16 50 4296 www.ed.ac.uk

Edinburgh offers a number of opportunities for American students wishing to study abroad, including a year-long program for high school graduates and a parliamentary program in which you study with MSPs in the Scottish Parliament. Admissions requirements vary by degree program; check online for more details.

Full year £11,100-11,600.

UNIVERSITY OF ST. ANDREWS

University of St Andrews, St Andrews, Fife KY16 9AJ, Scotland ☎13 34 47 6161 www.st-andrews.ac.uk

Worried about being the only non-kilt-wearer at Scotland's oldest university? Never fear; approximately 20% of the student body at St. Andrews is international. St. Andrews also offers a month-long Scottish Studies Summer Program geared toward high school students and an International Summer Programme for college students who have completed at least 2 years of college.

Full year £12,600; summer program £2900.

UNIVERSITY OF GLASGOW

University Avenue, Glasgow, Lanarkshire G12 ☎14 13 30 6062 www.gla.ac.uk

Scotland's largest city, Glasgow was voted "politest city in the UK." Can you think of a happier place to hit the books? The university has 9 faculties, including arts, education, engineering, medicine, and veterinary medicine.

Full year tuition and living costs £18,540.

UNIVERSITY OF LEEDS

University of Leeds, Leeds LS2 9JT ☎11 33 43 4023 www.leeds.ac.uk

With over 33,000 full-time students, Leeds is the second largest university in the UK and among the best for science, engineering, and medical studies.

Full year £10,200-14,200.

UNIVERSITY COLLEGE LONDON

Gower Street, London WC1E ☎13 34 47 6161 www.ucl.ac.uk

Located in the center of London, UCL hosts students from nearly 140 different countries.

Full year £12,770-16,725.

COOKING SCHOOLS

We know the old adage: "Heaven is where the police are British, the chefs are Italian, the mechanics are German, the lovers are French, and the organizers are Swiss. Hell is where the police are German, the chefs are British, the mechanics are French, the lovers are Swiss, and the organizers are Italian." But British food has improved over the years, and so have the opportunities for studying British and ethnic cuisine.

COOKERY SCHOOL

15B Little Portland Street London W1W 8BW ☎20 76 31 4590 www.cookeryschool.co.uk

Courses at the Cookery School cater to all experience levels. Day-long classes ranging from "Seasonal English" to "Thai All Day."

Classes£90-130.

EAT DRINK TALK

Unit 102, 190 St John St, London ☎20 76 89 6693 www.eatdrinktalk.co.uk

Reputedly offers "the best cooking classes in London." Unlike some of its traditional counterparts, this culinary school emphasizes modern, stylish cooking.

Day-long classes £85-115.

TEASMITH

6 Lamb St, London E1 6EA ☎20 72 47 1333 www.teasmith.co.uk

Learn the art of tea, perfected long ago by the British, and enjoy perfectly matched tea cakes at a tea master class, Th 7-9:30pm.

Classes £35 per person.

volunteering

Just because you're traveling in a first-world country, home to high tea and posh accents, don't think there isn't service work to be done. If you're looking to volunteer, start by searching online for charities that match your interests and schedule. **CharitiesDirect.com** offers extensive listings on hundreds of Britain-based charities, while **Volunteer Now** *(www.volunteernow.co.uk)* features listings of volunteer opportunities in England, specifically for volunteers ages 16-25. The **Volunteer Development Agency in Northern Ireland** *(☎28 90 23 6100 www.volunteering-ni.org)* offers training and assistance for volunteers. International websites like **www.idealist.org**, **www.volunteerabroad.com**, and **www.servenet.org** are all excellent resources. The **Council on International Educational Exchange** *(☎20 75 53 7600 www.ciee.org)* allows you to search volunteer opportunities by region and project type. Lastly, the parent organization **Volunteers for Peace** *(www.vfp.org)* can facilitate your search, offering placements in International Voluntary Service projects across Britain.

PEACE PROCESS

Tensions in Ireland have eased since the Good Friday Agreement was signed in 1998, but reconciliation is an ongoing project. Volunteering with the organizations listed below serves as a good opportunity for foreigners looking to advance political and social change in Northern Ireland.

- **KILCRANNY HOUSE:** A residential center that provides a safe space for Protestants and Catholics to explore nonviolence and conflict resolution. *(☎28 70 32 1816 www.kilcrannyhouse.org)*
- **CORRYMEELA COMMUNITY:** A residential Christian community designed to bring Protestants and Catholics together to work for peace. Over 6,000 people participate in Corrymeela programs each year. Meals and accommodation provided for volunteers. *(☎28 70 32 1816 www.corrymeela.org)*

CONSERVATION AND ARCHAEOLOGY

What better way to see the British countryside than to do conservation work and pretend you live in a Victorian estate? The largest organization in Britain for environmental conservation is the **British Trust for Conservation Volunteers** (BTCV) *(☎28 90 64 5169 www.cvni.org)*. Many national parks have volunteer programs; the **Association of National Park Authorities** can contact individual park offices. Below is a list of other conservation agencies.

- **EARTHWATCH EUROPE:** Think summer camp meets service work, with volunteer opportunities like excavating a Roman military and civilian settlement at the UNESCO Hadrian's Wall World Heritage Site and conducting wildlife research in the coastal waters of Southwest Scotland. *(☎18 65 31 8838 www.earthwatch.org/europe i Programs range from 3-14 days. $ Up to £1195.)*
- **GROUNDWORK:** One of the biggest environmental organizations in the UK, Groundwork has dozens of branches scattered throughout the country. Contact a local branch for more information. *(☎12 12 36 8565 www.groundwork.org.uk)*
- **WORLD-WIDE OPPORTUNITIES ON ORGANIC FARMS (WWOOF):** "WWOOF-ing," which takes its name from World Wide Opportunities on Organic Farms (WWOOF), involves an international network devoted to helping people create more sustainable lifestyles, has become increasingly popular in recent years for budget travelers. Volunteers work on a farm in exchange for free food, accommodation, and opportunities to learn first-hand about sustainable agriculture and organic farming techniques. *(www.wwoof.org.uk)*

- **THE NATIONAL TRUST:** When you think of National Trust volunteers, you probably think of batty old ladies with a peculiar passion for the decorative arts. False. The Trust now offers opportunities specifically for young people and is one of the best ways to discover British history in the flesh. *(☎87 04 58 4000 www.nationaltrust.org.uk/volunteering)*
- **THE WILDLIFE TRUSTS:** For those more drawn to nature reserves than manor houses, the Wildlife Trusts has 47 local branches. Volunteers work on projects ranging from community gardening to species surveying. *(☎87 00 36 7711 www.wildlifetrusts.org)*
- **VINDOLANDA TRUST:** Volunteers excavate a Roman fort dating back to 85 AD. *(☎14 34 34 4277 www.vindolanda.com* ***i*** Site open Apr to mid-Sept. 1-week min. stay. *£50 excavation fee for up to 2 wks., £20 per additional week.)*

YOUTH AND THE COMMUNITY

Youth and community-based volunteer work will probably be one of the most rewarding and challenging experiences you have abroad. Most of the listings below involve working directly with low-income families, at-risk youth, or inmates.

- **PRISON ADVICE& CARE TRUST (PACT):** PACT recruits volunteers for a wide range of projects including advising visiting families, playing with children and serving refreshments at the visitors' center, lending support to prisoners during their first night in prison, and helping ex-prisoners transition back into the community. *(☎20 77 35 9535 www.prisonadvice.org.uk)*
- **BARNARDO'S:** Volunteers can work either directly with abused and underprivileged children or in one of Barnardo's retail outlets. Also offers a 12-week summer volunteer program. International volunteers only accepted with support of government agency in your home country. *(☎20 85 50 8822 www.barnardos.co.uk)*
- **CITIZENS ADVICE BUREAU:** The Citizens Advice Bureau started out as an emergency war service when World War II broke out. Today, trained volunteers at the 438 bureaus across the country give free advice on legal, financial, and other issues. *(☎20 78 33 2181 www.citizensadvice.org.uk)*
- **COMMUNITY SERVICE VOLUNTEERS:** Over 150,000 people volunteer each year with CSV on issues such as child protection services and adult education. Full-time volunteers spend 4 months to a year volunteering and are provided with meals, accommodation, and a weekly stipend. *(☎20 72 78 6601 www.csv.org.uk)*

REFUGEE AND IMMIGRANT ISSUES

Immigration is as much a hot-button issue in Britain as it is in the United States, particularly since the creation of the European Union. Net migration has risen from just a few tens of thousands per year in the early 90s to over 200,000 in recent years. The issue is particularly affecting cities: nearly 50% of all births in London in 2008 were to foreign-born mothers. The British immigration minister has promised a clampdown on the number of immigrants and asylum-seekers, while human-rights organizations like Amnesty International have fought against detention centers and raids on undocumented workers. The **Association of Visitors to Immigrant Detainees(AVID)** is the national umbrella organization for charities working to assist immigration detainees. The organizations listed below also provide information, legal assistance, and material aid to immigrants and refugees. Note that because of the nature of the work, most of these volunteer opportunities require a long-term commitment.

- **ASYLUM WELCOME:** Volunteers provide advice on social, legal, and health services, help run summer sports and activities for young refugees, and work to raise awareness of the issues faced by asylum seekers and immigration detainees. *(☎18 65 72 2082 www.asylum-welcome.org)*

- **HASLAR VISITORS GROUP:** Trained volunteers commit to weekly afternoon visits to immigration detainees at the Haslar Immigration Removal Centre, operated by the prison service. Volunteers offer warmth, conversation and, occasionally, help finding solicitors and people to put up bail. *(☎23 92 83 9222 www.haslarvisitors.org.uk)*
- **LONDON DETAINEE SUPPORT GROUP:** LDSG offers support and mentorship to detainees in London. Volunteers work at detention centers in Colnbrook and Harmondsworth and are required to make a 6-month commitment. *(☎20 72 26 3114 www.ldsg.org.uk)*
- **REFUGEE ACTION:** Volunteers take on specific roles, including interpreting, mentoring refugees, and providing employment or career advice. Contact a local Refugee Action office for more information on volunteer opportunities. *(☎20 76 54 7700 www.refugee-action.org.uk)*

LONDON 2012 OLYMPIC GAMES

The Olympic Games themselves last less than three weeks, but preparations and planning take years. London 2012 will need up to 70,000 volunteers and many are already signing on to get involved.

- **OLYMPIC DELIVERY AUTHORITY (ODA):** Volunteers at the games will assist with a range of tasks, from spectator services to language translation and medical care. In the meantime, Trailblazer volunteers work 1 day a week in the Organizing Committee offices, carrying out various administrative duties. *(☎20 02 01 2000 www.london-2012.co.uk)*

working

In 2008, the UK Border Agency switched from a work-based system to a points-based immigration system. In other words, the good news is you don't need a job offer when you apply to enter or stay in the UK. The bad news is you need to pass a points-based assessment. Points are allotted based on your personal background (age, qualifications, previous earnings, and experience in the UK), English fluency, and whether you have funds available. Foreign students with a valid student visa can work up to 20 hours per week, except during official school or university vacations. Recent grads looking to work in the UK should check out the information provided by the UK Council for International Student Affairs. *(www.ukcisa.org.uk/student/working_after.php)* Of course, those lucky souls who are citizens of most countries in the European Economic Area or Switzerland are free to live and work in the UK.

LONG-TERM WORK

If you're planning to work long enough in Britain to start spewing "righty-o" and "jolly good!" (read: more than 3 months), we recommend that you start your search well in advance. International placement agencies are often the easiest way to find employment abroad, especially for those interested in teaching. Although they are often only available to college students, internships are a good way to ease into working abroad. Be wary of advertisements for companies claiming to be able get you a job abroad for a fee—often the same listings are available online or in newspapers. Some reputable organizations are listed below.

- **INTERNATIONAL ASSOCIATION FOR THE EXCHANGE OF STUDENTS FOR TECHNICAL EXPERIENCE (IAESTE):** Positions available for students currently enrolled full-time in a Bachelor's or Master's degree program in scientific disiplines, engineering and technology, agriculture, and applied arts. Most placements for 8-12 wks. during the summer, but some longer-term placements are also available. Apply through your home country's IAESTE branch. *(☎20 73 89 4771 www.iaeste.org)*

- **INTERNATIONAL COOPERATIVE EDUCATION:** Geared specifically toward American students looking for summer or term-time employment throughout the globe. Opportunities in England and Scotland include working at the Mini Cooper plant in Oxford, a medical software company in Edinburgh, or the commerce department of the US Embassy in London. *(☎1-650-323-4944 www.icemenlo.com Ⓢ Costs include a $250 application fee and a $900 placement fee.)*
- **HANSARD SCHOLAR PROGRAMME:** A non-partisan political research charity devoted to promoting public involvement in politics, the Hansard Society runs a summer program for international students that combines classes at the London School of Economics with internships in British government. *(☎20 74 38 1223 www.hansard-society.org.uk Ⓢ Summer program £7630.)*

Teaching

No one ever went into teaching to strike it rich, and teaching in Britain is no exception. There are three types of British schools. State schools are government-funded and correspond to what we would call public schools in the States, while public schools are, confusingly, privately funded independent schools. International schools can be either state or public and cater largely to children of ex-pats. The academic year is divided into autumn (September to Christmas), spring (early January to Easter), and summer (Easter to late July) terms. Applications to teach at state schools must pass through local governments, while public and international schools must be applied to individually.

Foreigners looking for a permanent teaching position at a state school in England or Wales must have **Qualified Teacher Status(QTS),** which involves postgraduate teacher training or a teaching assessment for those with extensive experience outside of the UK. For more information on the **Initial Teacher Training (ITT),** see www.tda.gov.uk. The **General Teaching Council for Scotland** *(www.gtcs.org.uk)* regulates the teaching profession in Scotland and requires different qualifications for primary- and secondary-school certification. The **Scottish Education Department** has more information on teaching opportunities and certification requirements for internationals at www.teachinginscotland.com. The **British Council** *(www.britishcouncil.org)* has extensive information for prospective teachers in the UK generally. Placement agencies or university fellowship programs are the best resources for finding teaching jobs. The alternative is to contact schools directly or to try your luck once you arrive in Britain. In the latter case, the best time to look is several weeks before the start of the academic year. The following organizations are extremely helpful in placing teachers in Britain.

- **COUNCIL FOR INTERNATIONAL EXCHANGE OF SCHOLARS:** An American organization that administers the Fulbright program for faculty and professionals. *(☎1-202-686-4000 www.cies.org)*
- **ETEACH:** UK-based online recruitment service for teachers that allows you to search by the subject you want to teach. *(☎84 54 56 4384 www.eteach.com)*
- **EUROPEAN COUNCIL OF INTERNATIONAL SCHOOLS (ECIS):** Runs recruitment services for international schools in the UK and elsewhere. Check their website for more information on obtaining an International Teacher Certificate (ITC). *(☎17 30 26 8244 www.ecis.org)*
- **INTERNATIONAL SCHOOLS SERVICES (ISS):** A New Jersey-based organization, ISS hires teachers for more than 200 overseas schools, including some in Britain.

Candidates should have teaching experience and a bachelor's degree. (☎*1-609-452-0990* 🖳*www.iss.edu* Ⓢ $185 application fee)

Au Pair Work

Au pairs are typically women (although sometimes men) aged 18-27 who work as live-in nannies, caring for children and doing light housework in foreign countries in exchange for room, board, and a small spending allowance or stipend. One perk of the job is that it allows you to get to know Britain without the high expenses of traveling. Drawbacks, however, can include mediocre pay and long hours. In the UK, the recommended salary for an au pair is approximately £50 per week for 25 hours. Some families will also defray travel expenses to and from Britain. Much of the au pair experience depends on the family with which you are placed. Au pairs from outside the European Economic Area need a letter of invitation from their host family to obtain a visa. The agencies below are a good starting point for looking for employment as an au pair. EU nationals can work as an au pair in the UK without any formalities, but the Youth Mobility Scheme, which has replaced the au pair visa program, is only open to citizens of Australia, New Zealand, Canada, and Japan.

- **AU PAIR UK:** Connects host families with prospective au pairs. (☎*20 85 37 3253* 🖳*www.aupair.uk.com*)
- **ALMONDBURY AU PAIR AGENCY:** Lists job openings in the UK and Ireland. (☎*18 03 38 0795* 🖳*www.aupair-agency.com*)
- **CHILDCARE INTERNATIONAL:** British employment agency that pairs au pairs with host families. (☎*20 89 06 3116* 🖳*www.childint.co.uk*)

more visa info

Swiss and European Economic Area (EEA) nationals (excluding Bulgarians and Romanians) do not need a visa to work in the UK. If you live in a Commonwealth country (including Australia, Canada, and New Zealand) and if your parents or grandparents were born in the UK, you can apply for UK Ancestry Employment and work without a visa (make sure you have all the relevant birth certificates that can prove your connection to the UK). Tier 5 youth mobility and temporary worker visas allow citizens of Australia, New Zealand, Canada or Japan aged 18 to 30 to work in the United Kingdom for a limited period to satisfy primarily non-economic objectives.

SHORT-TERM WORK

Don't be discouraged by the difficulty of obtaining a short-term work permit. Many travelers work odd jobs for a few weeks at a time to help cover the next leg of their journey, while others work a few hours a day at a hostel in exchange for free or discounted room and/or board. Most often, these short-term jobs are found by word of mouth or by expressing interest to the owner of a hostel or restaurant. Due to high turnover in the tourism industry, many places are eager for help, even if it is only temporary.

- **BRITISH UNIVERSITIES NORTH AMERICA CLUB (BUNAC):** Lists establishments that have hired short-term workers in the past. (☎*20 72 51 3472* 🖳*www.bunac.org*)
- **YOUTH HOSTEL ASSOCIATION:** Lists job openings on website and hires short-term workers from a pool of globetrotters. Ask at individual hostels as well. (🖳*www.yha.org.uk, in Scotland* 🖳*www.syha.org.uk*)

Other Opportunities By Region

England

Most English cities and larger towns have job spaces to fill, especially during the high season, mainly in pubs or restaurants. Brighton is especially accommodating to people looking for temporary work. Job hunting may be harder in the northern cities, where unemployment is higher. Check newspapers for listings or get in touch with a job placement organization like **AgencyCentral** (*www.agencycentral.co.uk*).

Wales

Many areas of Wales suffer from chronically high unemployment rates, so short-term work can be hard to come by. If you're determined to find a job in Wales, try looking in Cardiff, where temporary gigs may be available, especially during rugby season (Sept-May).

Scotland

The **Edinburgh Fringe Festival** in August is the world's largest arts festival and provides many job opportunities. Glasgow is also lively during the summer and temporary domestic and food service jobs may be available. Thousands of employment opportunities in Scotland can be searched online at www.s1jobs.com.

tell the world

If your friends are tired of hearing about that time you saved a baby orangutan in Indonesia, there's clearly only one thing to do: get new friends. Find them at our website, www.letsgo.com, where you can post your study-, volunteer-, or work-abroad stories for other, more appreciative community members to read.

INDEX

d

e

f

g

h

i

j

k

l

m

n

o

p

q

r

s

t

u

v

w

y

MAP INDEX

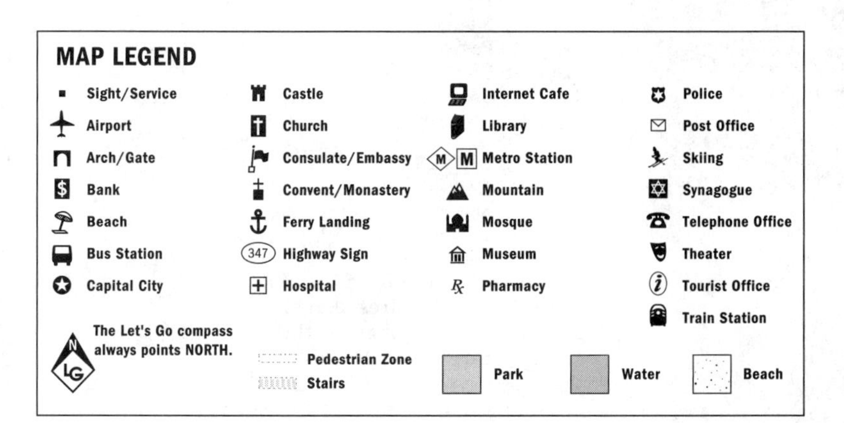

MAP LEGEND
Sight/Service
Airport
Arch/Gate
Bank
Beach
Bus Station
Capital City
Castle
Church
Consulate/Embassy
Convent/Monastery
Ferry Landing
347
Highway Sign
Hospital
Internet Cafe
Library
M
M
Metro Station
Mountain
Mosque
Museum
Pharmacy
Police
Post Office
Skiing
Synagogue
Telephone Office
Theater
Tourist Office
Train Station
N
LG
The Let's Go compass always points NORTH.
Pedestrian Zone
Stairs
Park
Water
Beach

ACKNOWLEDGMENTS

MEAGAN THANKS: Meagan thanks: Matt for his unwavering dedication and fresh-to-deathness, even when *Rocky* ate my life; you're the best RM an Ed could ask for. Our RWs for their tireless work and adventurous spirits. DBarbs for MEdits and chop-busting. Marykate for calming my crazy. Sara and DChoi, who kept me rollin' on the RIVER. Joe for his marketing prowess, but mostly his smiles. Nathaniel for flawless editorial *and* ticket management. Ashley for teaching Meags how to make moves in the roughest times. I'm not really tryna forget Colleenie Bear and Sarah for making Fun Pod the best. Joey G. for hugs and *Glee*. Thanks to Betty White, Leslie Uggams, Cher, Meryl, Marge, and all the other deeves. HRST 2010 for Tater Tots and fishnet therapy. Matt and Chris for being so sweet when Maj had to edit. Here's to Billy Shakes, Ginny Woolf, and Jude Law. Thank you to Mrs. O'Brien and Nicole. Finally, thank you, mom, for your constant support.

MATT THANKS: Our RWs, for their terrific work on the road. Meg, for being a friend, a grandma, a wordsmith and an Anglophile. Daniel, for his multilingual motivational speaking. Marykate, for answering my XV hourly questions. Colleen, for being the best. Colleen, for being not the worst. Sarah, for sharing my favorite corner of 67 Mt. Auburn. Ashley, for helping me lock it up by day and rip it up by night. Nathaniel and Sara, for all the late-night help and snack foods. Joe Molimock, for making marketing moves. DChoi, for his technological wizardry. Joe Gaspard, for assisting my caffeine addiction. Bronwen, for putting the number one in P1. Hasty Pudding Theatricals. Not floods. Anybody who brought me from homeless to Harvard. Elisandre, for starting the week off right. Drake. Snuggies. Bolt Bus. Mom, dad, Rachel, Edna, and the rest of my family. And of course, Fun Pod: make big love, not war.

LET'S GO masthead

DIRECTOR OF PUBLISHING Ashley R. Laporte
EXECUTIVE EDITOR Nathaniel Rakich
PRODUCTION AND DESIGN DIRECTOR Sara Plana
PUBLICITY AND MARKETING DIRECTOR Joseph Molimock
MANAGING EDITORS Charlotte Alter, Daniel C. Barbero, Marykate Jasper, Iya Megre
TECHNOLOGY PROJECT MANAGERS Daniel J. Choi, C. Alexander Tremblay
PRODUCTION ASSOCIATES Rebecca Cooper, Melissa Niu
FINANCIAL ASSOCIATE Louis Caputo

DIRECTOR OF IT Yasha Iravantchi
PRESIDENT Meagan Hill
GENERAL MANAGER Jim McKellar

ABOUT LET'S GO

THE STUDENT TRAVEL GUIDE

Let's Go publishes the world's favorite student travel guides, written entirely by Harvard students. Armed with pens, notebooks, and a few changes of clothes stuffed into their backpacks, our student researchers go across continents, through time zones, and above expectations to seek out invaluable travel experiences for our readers. Because we are a completely student-run company, we have a unique perspective on how students travel, where they want to go, and what they're looking to do when they get there. If your dream is to grab a machete and forge through the jungles of Costa Rica, we can take you there. If you'd rather bask in the Riviera sun at a beachside cafe, we'll set you a table. In short, we write for readers who know that there's more to travel than tour buses. To keep up, visit our website, www.letsgo.com, where you can sign up to blog, post photos from your trips, and connect with the Let's Go community.

TRAVELING BEYOND TOURISM

We're on a mission to provide our readers with sharp, fresh coverage packed with socially responsible opportunities to go beyond tourism. Each guide's Beyond Tourism chapter shares ideas about responsible travel, study abroad, and how to give back to the places you visit while on the road. To help you gain a deeper connection with the places you travel, our fearless researchers scour the globe to give you the heads-up on both world-renowned and off-the-beaten-track opportunities. We've also opened our pages to respected writers and scholars to hear their takes on the countries and regions we cover, and asked travelers who have worked, studied, or volunteered abroad to contribute first-person accounts of their experiences.

FIFTY-ONE YEARS OF WISDOM

Let's Go has been on the road for 51 years and counting. We've grown a lot since publishing our first 20-page pamphlet to Europe in 1960, but five decades and 60 titles later, our witty, candid guides are still researched and written entirely by students on shoestring budgets who know that train strikes, stolen luggage, food poisoning, and marriage proposals are all part of a day's work. Meanwhile, we're still bringing readers fresh new features, such as a student-life section with advice on how and where to meet students from around the world; a revamped, user-friendly layout for our listings; and greater emphasis on the experiences that make travel abroad a rite of passage for readers of all ages. And, of course, this year's 16 titles—including five brand-new guides—are still brimming with editorial honesty, a commitment to students, and our irreverent style.

THE LET'S GO COMMUNITY

More than just a travel guide company, Let's Go is a community that reaches from our headquarters in Cambridge, MA, all across the globe. Our small staff of dedicated student editors, writers, and tech nerds comes together because of our shared passion for travel and our desire to help other travelers get the most out of their experience. We love it when our readers become part of the Let's Go community as well—when you travel, drop us a postcard (67 Mt. Auburn St., Cambridge, MA 02138, USA), send us an email (feedback@letsgo.com), or sign up on our website (www.letsgo.com) to tell us about your adventures and discoveries.

For more information, updated travel coverage, and news from our researcher team, visit us online at www.letsgo.com.

THANKS TO OUR SPONSORS

- **SMART HYDE PARK INN.** 48-49 Inverness Terrace, London, W2 3JA. ☎44 (0)20 7229 0000.
- **SMART HYDE PARK VIEW.** 16 Leinster Terrace, London, W2 3EU. ☎44 (0)20 7402 4101.
- **SMART HYDE PARK HOSTEL.** 2-6 Inverness Terrace, London, W2 3HU; ☎44 (0)20 3355 1441.
- **SMART CAMDEN INN.** 55-57 Bayham Street, London, NW1 0AA; ☎44 (0)20 7388 8900.
- **SMART RUSSELL SQUARE.** 70-72 Guilford Street, London, WC1N 1DF; ☎44 (0)20 7833 8818.
- **SMART ROYAL BAYSWATER HOSTEL.** 121 Bayswater Road, London, W2 3JH; ☎44 (0)20 7229 8888. www.smartbackpackers.com.
- **DELHI BRASSERIE.** 134 Cromwell Road, Kensington SW7 4HA. ☎44 (0)20 7370 7617. Theatreland Branch, 44 Frith Street, Soho London, W1D 4SB. ☎44 (0)20 7437 8261. www.delhibrasserie.com.

notes

HELPING LET'S GO. If you want to share your discoveries, suggestions, or corrections, please drop us a line. We appreciate every piece of correspondence, whether a postcard, a 10-page email, or a coconut. Visit Let's Go at **www.letsgo.com** or send an email to:

feedback@letsgo.com, subject: "Let's Go Great Britain with Belfast and Dublin"

Address mail to:

Let's Go Great Britain with Belfast and Dublin, 67 Mount Auburn St., Cambridge, MA 02138, USA

In addition to the invaluable travel advice our readers share with us, many are kind enough to offer their services as researchers or editors. Unfortunately, our charter enables us to employ only currently enrolled Harvard students.

Maps © Let's Go and Avalon Travel
Design Support by Jane Musser, Sarah Juckniess, Tim McGrath
Distributed by Publishers Group West.
Printed in Canada by Friesens Corp.

ISBN-13: 978-1-59880-704-2

Thirty-third edition
10 9 8 7 6 5 4 3 2 1

Let's Go Great Britain with Belfast and Dublin is written by Let's Go Publications, 67 Mt. Auburn St., Cambridge, MA 02138, USA.

LEGAL DISCLAIMER. For 50 years, Let's Go has published the world's favorite budget travel guides, written entirely by students and updated periodically based on the personal anecdotes and travel experiences of our student writers. Although every effort was made to ensure that the information was correct at the time of going to press, the author and publisher do not assume and hereby disclaim any liability to any party for any loss or damage caused by errors, omissions, or any potential travel disruption due to labor or financial difficulty, whether such errors or omissions result from negligence, accident, or any other cause.

ADVERTISING DISCLAIMER. All advertisements appearing in Let's Go publications are sold by an independent agency not affiliated with the editorial production of the guides. Advertisers are never given preferential treatment, and the guides are researched, written, and published independent of advertising. Advertisements do not imply endorsement of products or services by Let's Go, and Let's Go does not vouch for the accuracy of information provided in advertisements.
If you are interested in purchasing advertising space in a Let's Go publication, contact Edman & Company at ☎1-203-656-1000.

quick reference

YOUR GUIDE TO LET'S GO ICONS

☎ Phone numbers	Not wheelchair-accessible	Has A/C
Websites	Has internet access	Directions
Takes credit cards	Has outdoor seating	*i* Other hard info
Cash only	▼ Is GLBT or GLBT-friendly	Prices
Wheelchair-accessible	Serves alcohol	Hours

PRICE RANGES

Let's Go includes price ranges, marked by icons ❶ through ❺, in accommodations and food listings. For an expanded explanation, see the chart in How To Use This Book.

BRITAIN	❶	❷	❸	❹	❺
ACCOMMODATIONS	under £20	£20-28	£28-35	£35-42	over £42
FOOD	under £6	£6-12	£12-18	£18-24	over £24

DUBLIN	❶	❷	❸	❹	❺
ACCOMMODATIONS	under €25	€25-39	€39-57	€57-73	over €73
FOOD	under €7	€7-13	€13-18	€18-26	over €26

IMPORTANT PHONE NUMBERS

EMERGENCY: ☎999			
ISOS Alarm Center	☎(+44) 20 8762 8008	ISIC Hotline	☎(+44) 20 8762 8110
Domestic Operator in UK	☎100	International Operator in UK	☎155
Operator in Ireland	☎114	Directory Inquiries in UK	☎118 118
Directory Inquiries in Ireland	☎11 850	US State Department	☎888 877 8339
U.S. Consulate in London	☎020 7499 9000	U.S. Consulate in Edinburgh	☎[+44] 0131 556 8315
U.S. Welsh Affairs Office	☎[44] 029 2078 6633	U.S. Embassy in Dublin	☎01 668 8777
Western Union in UK	☎0800 735 1815	Western in Ireland	☎353 66 979 1843

CURRENCY CONVERSIONS

AUS$1 = UK£0.57	UK£1 = AUS$1.71	NZ$1 = UK£0.48	UK£1 = NZ$2.10
CDN$1 = UK£0.63	UK£1 = CDN$1.58	UK£1 = UK£1	UK£1 = UK£1
EUR€1 = UK£0.85	UK£1 = EUR€1.18	US$1 = UK£0.65	UK£1 = US$1.53

TEMPERATURE CONVERSIONS

°CELSIUS	-5	0	5	10	15	20	25	30	35	40
°FAHRENHEIT	23	32	41	50	59	68	77	86	95	104

MEASUREMENT CONVERSIONS

1 inch (in.) = 25.4mm	1 millimeter (mm) = 0.039 in.
1 foot (ft.) = 0.305m	1 meter (m) = 3.28 ft.
1 mile (mi.) = 1.609km	1 kilometer (km) = 0.621 mi.
1 pound (lb.) = 0.454kg	1 kilogram (kg) = 2.205 lb.
1 gallon (gal.) = 3.785L	1 liter (L) = 0.264 gal.